PRO
TOOLS® 7
POWER!

THE COMPREHENSIVE GUIDE

Colin MacQueen

with Steve Albanese

THOMSON

COURSE TECHNOLOGY

Professional ■ Technical ■ Reference

ISBN: 1-59863-006-7

Library of Congress Catalog Card Number: 2005931878

Printed in the United States of America.

06 07 08 09 10 PH 10 9 8 7 6 5 4 3

Professional ■ Technical ■ Reference

Thomson Course Technology PTR, a division of Thomson Course Technology
25 Thomson Place
Boston, MA 02210
http://www.courseptr.com

Publisher and General Manager:
Stacy L. Hiquet

Associate Director of Marketing:
Sarah O'Donnell

Manager of Editorial Services:
Heather Talbot

Marketing Manager:
Mark Hughes

Senior Acquisitions Editor:
Todd Jensen

Marketing Coordinator:
Jordan Casey

Project Editor:
Kate Shoup Welsh

Technical Reviewer:
Nikki Smith

PTR Editorial Services Coordinator:
Elizabeth Furbish

Copy Editor:
Carla Spoon

Interior Layout Tech:
Digital Publishing Services

Cover Designers:
Mike Tanamachi and Nancy Goulet

CD-ROM Producer:
Steve Albanese

CD-ROM Authors:
Colin MacQueen, Steve Thomas, and John Hughes

Indexer:
Sharon Shock

Proofreader:
Gene Redding

} Acknowledgments

Colin MacQueen Wishes to Thank:

My wife Jenny, my mother, and the rest of my family; George, Gracie, Lola, and Buddy for canine moral support and comic relief; Neil MacQueen (Sunday Software), Brian Alexander (SOS Productions), Jenn Agnew (Circa Music), Eric Farnbauch (Upbeat Recordings), Steve Thomas, Adam Castillo, Greg Robles, Digidesign, Todd Jensen, Kate Shoup Welsh, Nikki Smith, Carla Spoon, Michael Tanamachi, Mark Garvey, Robert Guérin, Pep Agulló, Andy Hagerman, Jon Stevens, Jim Kilgore, Marc Ankerman, Luigi Bezzera (thanks for inventing espresso, dude), Camilo Rodriguez (y su salsa combo), Bodegas Muga (viva La Rioja), Steve Albanese, and the jam side up.

Steve Albanese Wishes to Thank:

Digidesign, Ed Grey, Claudio Curcio, Benny Sanchez, Mike Freitas, Andy Cook, Scott Wilson, John Whitcore, Dave Froker, Andrew Harris, Chris Hammond, Tom Graham, Dino Virella, Gil Gowing, Jon Ondo, Bobby Lombardi, Mitch Thomas, Paul Bundschuh, Jim Cooper, Larry Berger, Colin McDowell, Chris Borgia, Andy Hildebrand, Marco Albert, Matt Ward, Alan Jewitt, Joe Hunt, Joe Schmigaluchi, Lipps Elliot, Dyrk Ashton, Jeff Ciampa, Chris Leatherman, Matt Cooke, Tom Boyer, Chris Fidler, Kris Schultz, Corey Tomasso, Brian Caviness, Dave Egan, Bob Albanese, Steve Thomas, Andy Shafran, Todd Jensen, Mark Garvey, Johnson Brothers, Brian Stritenberger, Colin MacQueen, Mom, Dad, my understanding wife Lisa, Luke, Isabella, and the man upstairs.

} About the Authors

Colin MacQueen

Colin MacQueen is the author of the *Digital Audio Dictionary* (Prompt Publications) with Steve Albanese; *Pro Tools 6 Power!* (Thomson Course Technology), covering 6.xx versions of Pro Tools; and *Pro Tools Power!* (Muska & Lipman/Thomson Course Technology), covering 5.xx versions. He wrote and created the movie tutorials for various interactive CD-ROMs about audio and MIDI topics, including *Pro Tools 7 CSi Starter* and *Pro Tools 6 CSi Starter*, *Cubase SX2 CSi Starter*, and *Cubase SX CSi Master*; collaborated with Robert Guérin on *Cubase SX3 CSi Starter*; assisted Dave Egan as co-author of *Garage-Band CSi Starter*; and contributed several movie tutorials to *Audio Plug-Ins CSi Master*. A musician, composer, technical writer, sound designer, and virtual audio engineer, he has been involved for years with the music- and video-production industries and live performance, as well as in the distribution of Digidesign products in the USA and Spain. As an educator regarding digital audio–related topics, he has taught at broadcast school and university programs. Colin also created or edited much of the text in the original *Cool School Interactus*, the Cool Breeze CD-ROM series about Pro Tools, general digital audio, and MIDI sequencing topics, as well as serving as technical editor on various recent CSi volumes. Other recent credits include spoken-word projects in numerous languages, as well as original music production and interactive sound design for 13 original CD-ROM titles by Sunday Software. In addition to sound design and audio production, Colin plays a mean guitar, doubles on bass, sings like a bird (albeit some yet unknown species), and quantizes the heck out of a keyboard performance.

Steve Albanese

Steve Albanese is an interactive media developer, audio engineer, media systems consultant, and founder of the Cool Breeze Systems, Inc. and Cool School Interactus training environments. Steve continued the development of CSi and new learning products at Thomson Course Technology in Boston, Massachusetts. His years of educational and development experience include his role as Media Production Supervisor at the Recording Workshop, Chief Instructor Pro School Midwest, and President of Cool Breeze Systems. Steve has also worked for years as an audio professional, recording, mixing, and mastering many music projects; posting videos and films; and providing sound for television commercials, radio spots, and interactive media. Steve co-authored the *Digital Audio Dictionary, Pro Tools 6 Power!* and *Pro Tools Power!, CSi vol. 1—Pro Tools Basics, CSi vol. 2—Pro Tools Tips and Plug-ins,* and *CSi vol. 3—Desktop Audio,* with Colin MacQueen; and has written and edited the "Cool Tip" monthly column for *Electronic Musician* magazine.

TABLE OF $\mathcal{J}$ Contents

CHAPTER 15 Sound Design for Interactive Media **445**

CHAPTER 16 Bouncing to Disk, Other File Formats **463**

Introduction

We've been using Pro Tools since it arrived on the scene, and before that, Sound Tools II, Sound Tools, and the original Sound Designer program. Digidesign has consistently set the standard for reliable, logical systems that respond to real-world needs for audio production. Hats off to 'em!

Pro Tools has basically been an industry standard since it was introduced, and it is used in a variety of industries and applications: multimedia, post and music production, journalism, and broadcast, among others. There are many excellent learning resources for Pro Tools users, including books, support and educational material on the Digidesign Web site, Digidesign/Avid certified training centers, university and recording school programs, plus our own (ahem!) interactive CD-ROM series.

In this book, we've tried to pull together a comprehensive overview of Pro Tools operation, the currently available configurations, the major areas where Pro Tools is commonly used, and the essential technical background necessary to get your Pro Tools rig interacting with the world around it. Our intention is to:

* Jump-start new Pro Tools users, both those with a solid audio background and people who are more or less new to hands-on audio production.

* Get more-experienced users much deeper into the program, and into areas that may be more unfamiliar.

✳ Drop some interesting or thought-provoking tips on the experienced Pro Tools user.

For this reason, we make an effort to communicate on several levels simultaneously: general concepts, step-by-step instructions, technical detail where it helps to clarify concepts, plus suggestions for peripherals and techniques that will save you time. First, we review the currently available Pro Tools configurations (which we revisit in more detail in Chapter 3, "Your System Configuration"), then walk through basic concepts, reviewing the essential functions in the main Pro Tools windows and menus (but not *all* of them—that's what the PDF documentation is for!). Our objective is help you become productive in Pro Tools in the least possible amount of time. For that reason, we will always try to ground any theoretical aside or description of a Pro Tools function with real-world examples.

How to Use This Book

You can read this book from start to finish, jump directly to certain chapters if you prefer, or graze throughout. We try to use the plainest language possible, but in some of the technical asides, the single simplest way to accurately describe a concept may still be a little dense. (It's the nature of the subject matter!) In these cases, don't sweat technical details upon your first reading. Get the big picture first; you can always review later for further depth.

All users should take a moment to review the basic information in Chapter 2, "Pro Tools Terms and Concepts." These establish bedrock concepts and vocabulary, and are essential for understanding how Pro Tools works. If you're new to *all* of this, including audio and MIDI in general, begin with Chapter 1, "About Pro Tools"—we'll give you a jump start.

Who Can Benefit

Aside from covering LE, M-Powered, and HD versions on Mac and Windows, we've challenged ourselves to ensure that this book provides useful information for the following:

✳ New users of Pro Tools

✳ Experienced users seeking to broaden their knowledge, or to branch into other areas of production

❉ Veteran users (we've been using Pro Tools since it came out, and still found out some interesting tips while researching and writing this book!)

Quick Start for You Impatient Types

Blah, blah, blah... You just cranked up Pro Tools, and you're not even sure where to start. Well, the *Pro Tools Reference Guide* (a PDF document included with the program) is definitely worth your time. You might print out some major sections (also a good idea with the Keyboard Shortcuts guide) and lug it around with you for the next few weeks; take it to lunch, for instance. Respect where it's due: Digidesign does a good job on its manuals!

If you're a first-timer and anxious to get started with Pro Tools (and have already successfully installed the software and configured the hardware), you might go straight to Chapter 4, "Creating Your First Pro Tools Session." We walk you through creating a session, creating audio tracks and Auxiliary Inputs, recording and editing some audio, inserting effects plug-ins, and performing simple mix automation.

Once you've gotten that out of your system, you can push ahead through the chapters about the Transport, Edit, and Mix windows. Even better, check out Chapter 2 first. We lay down the basic elements and lingo you absolutely must understand to work sensibly with Pro Tools.

Conventions Used in This Book

Besides covering LE, M-Powered, and HD versions of Pro Tools for music, post, and multimedia users at all levels, everything in this book is equally applicable to Windows and Macintosh versions unless noted otherwise.

Keyboard Shortcuts (Macintosh/Windows)

Rather than focusing exclusively on Macintosh or Windows keyboard shortcuts (and making you consult a legend somewhere in the back of the book to find the equivalent for your computer), we've opted to always include both: first the Mac key command (since the majority of Pro Tools systems are Mac-based, although not to an overwhelming degree), followed by the Windows equivalent in parentheses.

With several exceptions, for the most part the following Mac/Win key equivalents apply in Pro Tools:

* The Mac Command key is usually the Ctrl key in Windows.
* The Mac Option key is usually the Alt key in Windows.
* The Mac Control key is often the Start key in Windows.

Be aware, though, that these key equivalents don't necessarily apply to other programs!

Pro Tools Versions

This book is directed toward users of Pro Tools 7, in its LE, M-Powered, and HD versions. The predecessor to this book, *Pro Tools 6 Power!* (ISBN 1-59200-505-5), covers 6.xx versions of Pro Tools (and will be an appropriate choice for 24|Mix and Digi 001 users, for example).

Digidesign is doing a great job of steadily evolving the Pro Tools platform. It was introduced in 1991 as a four-in, four-out system with a handful of built-in effects (no plug-ins or TDM yet, but with a killer sound and an interface that blew everybody else away!). Pro Tools was (and remains) *the* product in the hard-disk recording category that literally revolutionized the recording industry. Since then, top-end configurations have progressed to literally scores of potential I/O channels, a potential depth of signal routing and plug-in processing that's downright scary, and 24-bit audio at sample rates up to 192 kHz. Pro Tools systems are used around the world for every conceivable audio application: music, film, television, spoken-word, research, forensics, restoration, sound design, and so on.

There are currently three versions of the Pro Tools 7 software (as detailed in Chapter 3, "Your System Configuration," and elsewhere). Each supports specific audio hardware: Pro Tools LE (Mbox 2, Digi 002/002 Rack, and the now-discontinued original Mbox), Pro Tools M-Powered (purchased separately for use with one of various supported M-Audio interfaces), and Pro Tools HD (Pro Tools|HD hardware).

(The now-discontinued Pro Tools 24|Mix, Pro Tools|24, and Pro Tools III systems were based on a TDM plug-in architecture similar to the current-generation Pro Tools|HD hardware. Likewise, Digi 001 and ToolBox systems used previous LE versions of Pro Tools. However, none of these systems are compatible with Pro Tools version 7.)

Where appropriate, we will point out features that are only available in HD systems—or are not available in M-Powered, for example. For the most part, the HD version of Pro Tools includes all software features of the LE and M-Powered versions. Where there are restrictions or changes (for example, recommendations about how to order RTAS and TDM plug-ins in your tracks, or the more full-featured version of Beat Detective in the HD version of Pro Tools), we will let you know.

(In addition to the preceding, Pro Tools Free 5.01—a limited-feature version for Mac OS9 and Windows 98 *only*—is available as a free download from Digidesign's Web site.)

What's NOT in This Book

Every effort has been made to make *Pro Tools 7 Power!* the most comprehensive and multilevel book possible. That said, it should be noted that the Pro Tools program is so powerful, so ubiquitous, that one could go on forever exploring its applications in one specialized field after another. At the same time, we have to assume that the reader has a certain basic level of preparation, that it's understood that space doesn't permit references to all the previous generations of the hardware and software, and that the reader understands that the basic concepts explained here will continue to be valid even as Digidesign continues to release new versions.

Computer Fundamentals

We obviously can't dedicate space here to cover basic computer concepts. If you don't know how to empty your Trash or Recycle Bin, open a menu, or open a Control Panel, or you don't know the difference between a folder and a file, you should go to one of the many excellent resources out there to learn about this. Nonetheless, you really *do* need to understand how your computer works, as well as how to maintain your operating system, disks and files, and so on, in order to get the most out of your Pro Tools system—there's just no getting around it. Your computer, as the platform for Pro Tools, is now one of the tools of your craft. Just as you have to change the strings on your own instrument, replace the batteries in stompboxes, clean the heads on your tape recorders (until you've gotten rid of them all!), and pick up coffee mugs when clients leave for the day, you have to be able to navigate your computer system; it goes with the territory.

In Chapter 3, "Your System Configuration," we review computer and hard-drive requirements for Pro Tools specifically, and the basic peripherals most users need (like MIDI and SMPTE interfaces, mixers and microphone preamps, and a good system for monitoring audio playback).

Older "Legacy" Versions of Pro Tools

Hey, we have a hard enough time keeping up with the *new* versions! Many *discontinued* Pro Tools systems are just as functional today as when they were new—*very* functional. For example, even though Digi 001 and Mix | 24 models were discontinued in early 2004, they deliver excellent performance on an adequate system, and will probably continue in production at many facilities for quite some time (with 6.4/6.4.1 versions of Pro Tools software—they don't work with Pro Tools 6.7 or higher, let alone Pro Tools 7).

As mentioned previously, the predecessor to this book, *Pro Tools 6 Power!* (ISBN 1-59200-505-5), covers 6.xx versions of Pro Tools, and will be ideal for users of these systems. In addition to discussing 6.7 enhancements, that book also distinguishes features that are different in the 6.4.x and earlier software versions for 24 | Mix, Digi 001, and ToolBox systems.

Older-generation Pro Tools III hardware configurations were also TDM systems (with Pro Tools software 5.01 in Mac OS9 only—this hardware does *not* support any higher versions). However, if you are using any of these older systems, be *very* cautious about upgrading your computer hardware or operating system. By no means should you assume that a newer operating system, even if it *is* compatible with your older computer, is best for your version of Pro Tools. For example, no 5.xx version of Pro Tools works under Macintosh OS X, even in Classic mode, and no version prior to 6.9.2 works under the Macintosh 10.4.x "Tiger" operating system. Go to the Support section of Digidesign's Web site for compatibility information on these legacy systems!

Lastly, if your system is limited to one of the 5.xx versions of the Pro Tools software (including Pro Tools Free 5.01), consider taking a look at *Pro Tools Power!* (ISBN 1-929685-57-2), which specifically covers that generation of the Pro Tools software and hardware.

Future Versions of Pro Tools, TBA Next Week/ Month/Year...

We've made a concerted effort to create content that will continue to be meaningful, even as new releases of Pro Tools appear. As of this writing, our descriptions are based on currently shipping Pro Tools version 7. Minor upgrades are always coming out, usually for bug fixes or to support new hardware options; and farther down the road, more significant upgrades will undoubtedly introduce additional features.

Most likely, the actual operational changes will be minor; but compared to these hypothetical future versions, you may note discrepancies in a few of our screenshots. Again, we expect the basic concepts explained in this book to remain valid well into future versions of Pro Tools.

Computer and digital audio technologies move forward very quickly. As a general rule, if you're using current Pro Tools hardware, you will want the fastest computer out there (although not *necessarily* the very latest operating system), as long as you see that model in the Compatibility listings on Digidesign's Web site. We're always bemused when people berate Digidesign and other digital audio workstation manufacturers for not supporting the latest all-important new operating system from Apple or Microsoft within weeks. (It's as if you suddenly become a square overnight, just because you don't rush out to get this season's clever haircut, or dumb-looking shoes!) Understand that Pro Tools is a demanding, real-time application. It pushes the capabilities of a computer and its operating system, and it takes *time* to make this program as (relatively) bulletproof as it is!

Again, this book aims to be useful for Pro Tools LE (Mbox 2/Mbox, Digi 002/002 Rack) and M-Powered (various M-Audio interfaces), as well as for Pro Tools HD (for Pro Tools|HD systems). So, if you've got an LE or M-Powered system, for example, please bear with us if we devote time to a number of HD-specific features—at least it will give you an idea what you have to look forward to when all those royalty checks come in!

Other Programs

We do discuss some stereo editing programs for checking, tweaking, or converting bounced files, plus common CD-burning software. But we can't dedicate pages to walking you through step-by-step operations in these audio programs, or standard system utilities. There's just not space! However, we will tell you that we find Norton SystemWorks (Norton Utilities) extremely useful for maintaining a Pro Tools rig (especially Disk Doctor and Speed Disk, which we use often—although we *don't* recommend enabling the File Saver feature on Pro Tools systems). Some Macintosh users prefer the Tech Tool or DiskWarrior programs, which also do a great job of keeping your hard disks free of errors that can interfere with Pro Tools' performance.

Also, features comparisons with other multitrack audio/MIDI programs don't fit given our space constraints. Logic Pro, Cubase SX, Nuendo, Digital Performer, SONAR, Reason, ACID, Ableton Live, and others are all fine programs—each, like Pro Tools, with its strengths and weaknesses. Several of them cohabitate with Pro Tools on our own computers! Obviously, many of their features overlap with Pro Tools'—recording and editing audio and MIDI, applying effects, automation, and bouncing mixes. But we can't tell you which is right for your needs; it really depends on your working style and personal preference. Furthermore, sometimes one program is more suited to certain projects than others. But Pro Tools is a powerful production environment; you can do just about anything with it, and the fact that you're holding this book in your hands says a lot already. So, we promise not to go off onto any of those tangents, you know, where we say "one of the things we really like about Pro Audio Munch XXL that we wish Pro Tools had is..." Let's leave that to the online forums!

Thank You!

If you're a new Pro Tools user, you're in for a treat. We can tell you from personal experience that the hands-on, non-linear audio experience you are undertaking will completely transform your creative process, and for that matter, change your perception of audio in general. If you *already* know your way around the program, we promise to take you much deeper into this powerful production environment. Even if you are already a veteran user, we've made an effort to provide tips and applications that will get you thinking in new directions.

But before all that, let us take the opportunity to say thank you for purchasing this book! We sincerely appreciate your confidence, and hope its content serves to energize your learning experience and enrich your creative process.

Notes, Tips, and Cautions

You'll notice a lot of shaded text boxes throughout the book that provide additional information related to the surrounding text. In order to make this material more accessible as you browse though the pages, it has been organized into four basic categories:

Notes

Notes provide additional material, interesting tidbits, or further in-depth information related to the current topic. We've tried to set this book up so that you can either read chapter text, consulting the notes for auxiliary information, or graze through the notes themselves while you're at lunch or commuting, for example—or seated away from your computer!

Tips

Tips point out features of Pro Tools that many users seem to overlook, make specific recommendations based on our experience, or suggest workarounds for common problems. Again, we've made an effort to provide both beginner's tips and more sophisticated suggestions, so that users of any level can browse this book for useful ideas.

Cautions

If an operation might cause you to lose data, wreck your stuff, or look like a bonehead in front of your client, it will generally appear as a *caution*.

CSi Examples

The CD-ROM in the back of this book contains sample movie tutorials from Pro Tools–related volumes in the *CSi* (*Cool School Interactus*) interactive learning environment, published by Thomson Course Technology. Whenever one of these movies touches upon a concept under discussion, a note with this icon appears within the chapter. Sometimes simply seeing a feature in operation makes everything much clearer—that's the whole mission of the CSi series. Check it out!

1 } About Pro Tools

If you're just starting in the digital audio production world, this chapter and the next will help you get a grasp on basic concepts. They introduce Pro Tools, providing a very basic overview of the digital-recording process, digital audio file formats, and MIDI.

If you're experienced with audio production but completely new to Pro Tools and computer-based recording, prepare yourself for a revelatory experience. In *linear* methods of working with music and audio (like digital and analog tape recorders, for instance), everything has to be assembled and mixed in real time. You can't change the order of recorded events without creating a new copy or, worse yet, *destructively* cutting up the tape in order to switch things around! Digital audio workstations like Pro Tools, on the other hand, allow you to alter the order of audio events on any track, at any time—while still laying down takes, or even during the final phases of mixdown. Pro Tools provides microscopic editing precision (down to the sample level—44,100 or 48,000 time slices per second, or even more with Digi 002 and Pro Tools|HD systems), so you can easily create seamless edits almost anywhere within the recorded audio. (And trust us, we've spent enough time meticulously eliminating breaths, lip smacks, chair squeaks, and other noises to assure you that the editing power of Pro Tools is limited only by your perseverance!)

Likewise, audio mixing with Pro Tools will completely transform your outlook. Traditionally, mixing down from multiple source tracks to a stereo master was essentially a live performance, which often required more than one set of hands. Audio engineers would repeat the same song or scene literally dozens of times, each time attempting to repeat and improve upon mixing moves from the previous pass. With Pro Tools, often as not, you will start to build your mix even while still recording tracks. And of course, every aspect of the Pro Tools mix can be automated, down to this same microscopic level of precision, so your creative ambitions will increase correspondingly.

Lastly, Pro Tools offers a vast amount of control for shaping and processing your sound. Not only is high-quality signal processing (effects) included with all versions of Pro Tools, but its open architecture accommodates *plug-in* software from third parties—everything from "vintage" compressors and reverbs to amp and tape simulators, and much more. Because

I

✻ ✻ ✻

the entire virtual signal-processing environment is in the digital domain, the chronic noise floor problems associated with numerous audio devices and cables in a traditional studio are a thing of the past. Again, how far you take your audio-effects processing in Pro Tools depends not as much on your system's capabilities (which, budget permitting, can always be upgraded) as on how maniacal, ambitious, or just plain creative *you* want to be!

What Is Pro Tools?

In a nutshell, Pro Tools is computer software for Macintosh and Windows computers used to create audio projects through recording, editing, and automated mixing of hard disk–based digital audio and MIDI. Current Pro Tools configurations are based on the LE, M-Powered, or HD version of the software. They include dedicated audio hardware from Digidesign—cards and/or external audio interfaces. In contrast, the legacy Pro Tools Free 5.01 version (still available as a free download) relies exclusively on the audio inputs/outputs used by the host computer's operating system.

Digidesign develops the Pro Tools software and manufactures cards, external audio interfaces, and other peripheral equipment for your system. Most of Digidesign's Pro Tools hardware configurations start from a core system, including both software and hardware. However, the M-Powered version of Pro Tools consists solely of the software (plus the USB-based iLok copy protection device; more about this later), to which you must add your choice of one of the supported audio interfaces from M-Audio. To this core system, you can add peripherals—MIDI or synchronization interfaces, mixers for monitoring or routing multiple sources, and so on. On HD systems, you can expand the Pro Tools configuration itself to add more processing power or additional input/output channels.

Here is a brief overview of current hardware configurations and Pro Tools software versions. (In Chapter 3, "Your System Configuration," we discuss each of these Pro Tools system configurations in greater detail. We also review some "legacy" hardware, like the original Mbox (which, although discontinued, *is* compatible with Pro Tools 7), and also some discontinued systems that aren't compatible with Pro Tools 7, such as the Digi 001, 24 | Mix, ToolBox (based on the Audiomedia III card), and others. Chapter 17, "Pro Tools Power: The Next Step," also provides more information about expansion options for the various Pro Tools hardware configurations.)

❋ **Mbox 2.** The successor to the original Mbox, the Mbox 2 was introduced by Digidesign in fall 2005. This external, desktop audio interface includes Pro Tools LE software and is connected to the computer's USB port. In addition to two analog I/O channels—each of which has separate input jacks for microphone, line (¼-inch balanced TRS), and instrument levels—the Mbox 2 supports using the S/PDIF digital I/O (with RCA connectors) simultaneously, allowing up to 4×4 operation with Pro Tools. It also features one MIDI input and one MIDI output. The microphone preamps, designed by Digidesign, offer superior specs compared to the original Mbox. Currently, it is shipping with the Pro Tools Ignition Pack plug-in bundle.

❋ **Mbox.** This configuration consists of Pro Tools LE software, plus an external Mbox audio interface connected to the computer's USB port that features two total channels of audio I/O (input/output) switchable between analog (with ¼-inch balanced TRS connectors and also analog audio inserts) and S/PDIF digital I/O (with RCA connectors). Like its Mbox 2 successor and all the other current Digidesign hardware, the Mbox is capable of 24- or 16-bit operation. While it does support Pro Tools 7 software, the Mbox is now discontinued, having been replaced by the more powerful Mbox 2.

❋ **Digi 002.** This configuration consists of Pro Tools LE software, plus a single external, multichannel audio interface/control surface connected to the computer's FireWire port (a.k.a. IEE 1394). The interface supports up to 18 channels of audio input/output (16- or 24-bit recording at sample rates up to 96 kHz) between its eight analog, stereo S/PDIF, and eight-channel ADAT Lightpipe digital I/O. Four high-quality XLR microphone preamp inputs with phantom power and individual trim controls are also included on the first four input channels. The Digi 002 interface provides one MIDI in, two MIDI outs, headphone output, dedicated monitor output, and an Alternate Source input (for tape/CD players, for example). A desktop unit, the Digi 002 is not only an interface for audio I/O but also a control surface for Pro Tools, including Transport buttons, motorized faders, Solo/Mute buttons, assignable rotary encoders, LED *scribble strip* displays, and other dedicated buttons for Pro Tools functions. It can also operate as a standalone digital mixer, with a fixed selection of onboard effects.

❋ **Digi 002 Rack.** Same as the Digi 002, but in a rackmountable format without the control surface.

❋ **M-Powered systems.** These configurations consist of Pro Tools M-Powered software, plus one of various supported audio hardware options from M-Audio. Some of the M-Audio hardware options are PCI cards with either breakout cables or external interfaces; others are external interfaces connected to the computer's FireWire port (a.k.a. IEE 1394). The number and type of audio, MIDI, and word clock inputs/outputs varies according to the model. The Pro Tools M-Powered software is purchased separately from the M-Audio interface and includes an iLok USB Smart Key that contains an authorization for the program. This iLok (like the one that many users purchase separately for other versions of Pro Tools) can also be used for authorizing additional plug-ins and programs. (For those who are keeping score, the first version of Pro Tools M-Powered was 6.8, and there was no 6.8 version for either Pro Tools LE or HD. For Pro Tools 7, the HD, LE, and M-Powered versions were introduced simultaneously.) In Chapter 3 we discuss the M-Audio hardware options for Pro Tools M-Powered in more detail. While there *are* some key differences regarding support of external control surfaces and several optional software packages for Pro Tools (DV Toolkit and DigiTranslator), the feature sets of the M-Powered and LE versions of Pro Tools are nearly identical.

❋ **Pro Tools|HD.** These systems consist of the Pro Tools HD software, plus a variety of external audio interfaces connected to one or more PCI cards in the computer—or an external expansion chassis in larger systems. These cards incorporate specialized DSP processors to support the TDM plug-in and signal-routing architecture. You can add additional cards to these systems to expand their DSP and I/O capabilities and to support a larger number of audio interfaces. While each audio hardware option for the previously-listed LE and M-Powered systems supports a fixed number of input/output channels, these expandable HD system configurations can potentially support a much larger number of audio connections. Pro Tools|HD systems consist of the Pro Tools HD software (known as the TDM version prior to Pro Tools 7), plus one or more external audio interface(s) connected to the HD Core PCI card. HD|2 and HD|3 configurations from Digidesign add one or two HD Accel cards, respectively. (The Accel card replaced the Process card used on the first generation of HD systems.) These PCI cards in HD systems incorporate powerful DSP processors to support the TDM II architecture introduced with Pro Tools|HD systems in 2002, allowing 16- or 24-bit recording and playback at sample rates of up to 192 kHz. Additional HD Accel cards can be added to any of these configurations; accordingly, you may hear users talking about "HD|4" or "HD|5" systems, to describe how many PCI cards are in their HD configuration. The expandable Pro Tools|HD system configurations support many more channels of I/O— up to 32 channels of audio I/O per card—than previous TDM-based systems such as 24| Mix (now discontinued, and not supported with any Pro Tools version higher than 6.4.1).

Users often add other hardware devices (from Digidesign and third parties) to complete these configurations. (Figure 1.1 shows one example of a large Pro Tools configuration.) These may include MIDI interfaces, synchronization peripherals for SMPTE time code or video sync, external MIDI controllers, keyboards and modules, digital audio routers and mixers, microphone pre-amps, external control surfaces (such as the one shown in Figure 1.1), and interfaces for multitrack digital audio recorders from Alesis, Tascam, and others. Some of these are discussed in Chapter 3.

❋ **Note: Three Generations of Pro Tools (7, 6, and 5)**

Interesting as it is, we won't recount the entire Pro Tools history back to 1991, when version 1 hit the street. However, it's useful to understand the general characteristics of the last three major versions of Pro Tools—including version 7, the focus of this book—because they're still being used today in both professional and project studio settings.

❋ **Pro Tools version 7.** Introduced in fall of 2005. In addition to a long-overdue reorganization of the menu structure, key new features include region looping, region grouping (even on multiple tracks), real-time (non-destructive) properties for MIDI tracks, sends doubled to 10 per track, enhancements to Separate Region and Strip Silence functions, REX/Acid file support, Instrument tracks, use of RTAS plug-ins on any track type in HD versions, support for multiprocessor computers and multicore processors, plus drag and drop enhancements from the Region List and the Workspace window.

❋ **Pro Tools version 6.** Introduced at the end of 2002. A major upgrade from previous generations of Pro Tools and the first version for Macintosh OS X or Windows XP. The Project and Workspace browsers were new, as were DigiGrooves, Groove Quantize, many features in the MIDI Operations window, the Click plug-in, iLok support, and use of core MIDI services on Mac OS X (instead of OMS, used in previous Macintosh versions).

❋ **Pro Tools version 5.** Introduced in 2000, this was the first generation of Pro Tools to offer an LE version (host-based plug-in processing, not requiring TDM hardware). All 5.xx versions of Pro Tools require Macintosh OS 9 (although 8.6 was technically supported in some earlier versions, including Pro Tools Free 5.01), Windows 98/ME, or Windows 2000. The Digi 001 audio interface (now discontinued) was introduced simultaneously with version 5 as the first hardware option for the LE version of Pro Tools. The DigiTranslator program for OMF transfers between Pro Tools and Avid video editing systems (among others) was also introduced with this generation of the Pro Tools software. This was the version that introduced recording and editing of MIDI events within Pro Tools, with all the associated features in MIDI tracks. Multiple ruler formats and markers in the Edit window timeline were also new features, as were Marker memory locations and the time compression/expansion mode of the Trimmer tool.

Figure 1.1   This Pro Tools rig features Pro Tools|HD hardware, a D-Control worksurface, and surround monitors. (Photo courtesy of Digidesign.)

How It Works

Pro Tools records both digital audio and MIDI data and provides software tools for editing both. Let's be very clear about the difference between the two...

Digital Audio Is Data Representing Audio Waveforms

In digital audio recording, an input signal from an analog source (a varying voltage from a microphone or other device) arrives at an analog-to-digital (A/D) converter (often abbreviated as ADC). This converter periodically measures the level (*amplitude*) of the incoming audio signal, and this series of numerical values (*samples*) is stored into a file or encoded onto a tape. This is the *digitizing* process, where a continuous, real-world phenomenon is converted into a series of numbers at a fixed rate. As when you capture an image with your computer's scanner, when audio is recorded digitally, the continuous variations of a natural phenomenon are captured at a fixed resolution, converted into a series of numbers, and then saved within a file.

The goal is to measure these constant voltage fluctuations within the original incoming audio signal often enough (at a high enough *sample rate*) and precisely enough (at a sufficient *bit-depth*) so that when the measurements are played back (converted back into a series of voltage changes on an analog audio output by the digital-to-analog converter, DAC), they resemble the original source fairly closely. Figure 1.2 provides a signal-flow diagram for the hard disk recording process.

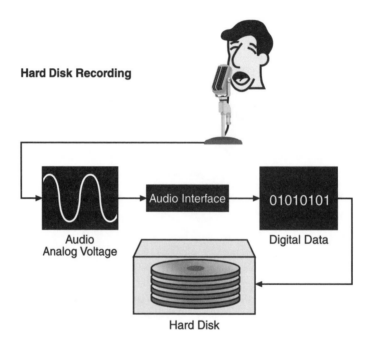

Figure 1.2   Hard disk recording: signal flow.

MIDI Is Data Representing Performance Events and Controller Data

MIDI is a data format and communications protocol, originally developed for transmitting and receiving (and later recording or playing back) performance events: when a note was triggered and at what velocity; the movement of pedals, sliders, and knobs; and so on. MIDI keyboards, controllers, and sound modules thus speak a common "language," so that they can be connected, or so that a performance originally created on one device can be played back on another.

Although Pro Tools also offers many features as a MIDI sequencer and allows MIDI-compatible musical instruments and effects to be incorporated into the same recording/editing environment as audio, MIDI is *not* audio. Sometimes, an external MIDI module is selected as the destination for events sent from each MIDI track, and that's what actually produces sound—in response to the MIDI event messages received. When using external MIDI devices, their audio outputs must be routed back into the Pro Tools audio interface in order for their audio signal to be incorporated into your Pro Tools mix. Typically, this might be done through an Aux Input track that monitors the physical audio input where they are connected, as shown in Figure 1.3—more about this later.

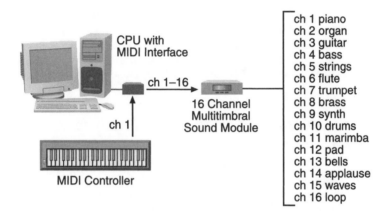

Figure 1.3 A basic MIDI configuration, with an external MIDI keyboard controller and sound module.

On the other hand, many users prefer *software*-based instruments—either separate programs or plug-ins that are enabled ("instantiated") on Pro Tools tracks. In this case, the virtual instrument is chosen as the destination from one or more MIDI tracks, in much the same way as an external module. Version 7 introduced a new track type, Instrument tracks, which combines aspects of an Aux In track (as seen in the Mix window) containing an instrument plug-in and a single MIDI track (as seen in the Edit window). Instrument tracks save screen space as well as offering other conveniences and are covered in more detail in Chapter 6, "The Edit Window," and Chapter 7, "The Mix Window."

❋ **Note: More About MIDI**

The MIDI (short for *Musical Instrument Digital Interface*) standard was developed in the early 1980s by audio and musical-instrument manufacturers to allow synthesizers, drum machines, and similar devices to be interconnected. MIDI is both a serial communications protocol and a standardized set of messages to describe the events that these devices generate (or receive). For example, a MIDI message might specify which key was pressed and how quickly, how far the pitch bender or modulation wheel was moved, when the sustain pedal was pressed and released, and so on. MIDI does *not* record or transmit sound; it transmits performance *events* as data!

Very soon after MIDI-compatible synthesizers appeared on the market, dedicated computer programs for recording and reproducing MIDI data became available, known as *MIDI sequencers*. Like Pro Tools, these programs capture MIDI events (with the appropriate time references) from an external MIDI keyboard or other controller via a *MIDI interface* that converts the MIDI protocol into a data format the computer can understand and provide software editing tools to modify and play back MIDI events.

❋ **Note: Where Audio and MIDI Data Are Stored in Pro Tools**

The basic Pro Tools document is called a *session* file. It contains the mix configuration, references to external audio files and region definitions, automation, track names, and other parameters. The session file also contains all MIDI data you record or create in that session (this includes all the MIDI regions you see in the Region List, some of which may be currently placed into tracks). In contrast, the audio regions you deal with in Pro Tools are actually *pointers* (references) to separate audio files on the hard disk.

Multitrack Recording, Mixdown, and Mastering: An Overview

In most audio recordings, numerous channels are separately recorded—from multiple microphones, electric instruments, synthesizers, and other sources. These might be recorded onto separate tracks of a tape in a traditional studio or, in the case of Pro Tools, into separate audio files, which you can view within tracks in the Edit window. Having each sound source available on a separately recorded track allows for subsequent manipulation of the sounds, such as changing their relative volumes and apparent locations, plus correcting any mistakes. You can record additional tracks as you listen to previously recorded material; this process is known as *overdubbing*.

Mixdown (often called *remix* in the United Kingdom) is the final stage in the recording process, where multiple sources of audio are combined into a standard playback format—one mono channel, a stereo channel pair, or even more channels in surround mixing. This might be done in real time, as when a stereo mix is recorded to a DAT or other mastering recorder. In the case of Pro Tools, however, often as not the mix is *bounced* to disk as a new file. During mixdown, the audio engineer (that's you!) balances volume levels, establishes the apparent spatial placement of each sound source, and applies equalization, dynamics processing, and other types of signal processing to alter sounds. Additionally, sounds can be routed to other locations (either external or internal, in the case of Pro Tools), where additional effects processing (such as delay or reverb) might be applied. Obviously, as a performer, Pro Tools offers you unprecedented control over your finished mix. As anyone who has followed commercial music over the past years has observed, creative mixing techniques are often as much a part of the artistic process as the initial performances. For that matter, many musically interesting pieces are being created with Pro Tools that don't directly involve any live performers at all, further obliterating the distinction between performer and engineer.

Mastering is the processing and transfer of finished audio mixes to a medium suitable for duplication. This ranges from simple sequencing of songs and trimming beginnings/endings to application of signal processing in order to improve uniformity of the material (especially when recorded at different times and places) and sophisticated effects processing (dynamics processing and equalization in particular) that compensates for the characteristics of the final playback medium.

Many of the onscreen objects in Pro Tools resemble traditional elements in this process—the Mix window and the Transport buttons, for example. But although it is convenient to think of Pro Tools as a *virtual* studio, and certainly many of the metaphors from traditional audio production do apply, working in this environment does require adjusting to a new mindset—many things simply have no counterpart in a "normal" studio. The reader with old-school audio experience will find all this very refreshing and inspiring! The segmentation of functions and project phases, the linearity, and the relative lack of editing precision that typify tape-based recording (whether analog or digital) disappear with Pro Tools.

Back when digital audio workstation technology was still relatively new, we always found ourselves making parallels to traditional recording technology in order to explain the Pro Tools work process (effects racks and patchbays, source/tape switches on mixer channels, gain stages, sync mode, two-track mastering recorders, and so on). As time goes by, though, we meet more users who have never heard of all this stuff! *All they've ever known* is digital audio, and computer-based implementations at that. The stock metaphors from traditional studios that Pro Tools supposedly emulates are "virtually" losing their meaning for this new generation of audio gearheads—they wouldn't know a splicing block from a wood planer! So if you *are* an audio-production veteran, and this is your first experience with a nonlinear audio production system, be prepared for some pleasant surprises and a new mental geometry for your work process.

Digital Audio Basics

This section summarizes in a few paragraphs a major subject that typically fills entire books! Obviously, the intent here is simply to set up the context in which Pro Tools exists, not to get you up to speed on the ins and outs of digital audio at large. If all this is brand new for you, we urge you to check out one of any number of excellent resources for learning more about sound recording and digital audio. We mention a few in Appendix A, "Further Study and Resources on the Web."

Introduction: Analog Recording

Electronic audio recording consists of three basic phases: First, there is a sound out there—a disturbance of the air (or other medium) that is an actual mechanical (acoustical) phenomenon. Second, a *transducer* converts this acoustical energy to an electrical signal—a microphone, for instance. And lastly, you somehow need to *store* these voltage variations produced by the transducer over time, so that you can reproduce them afterward.

On traditional (analog) tape recorders, an electromagnet realigns magnetic particles (or domains) on the surface of a moving tape, varying the intensity of its magnetic field in response to variations in the incoming voltage. This is a fairly continuous process, at least as far as the density of the magnetic coating and the speed of the tape permit. When the magnetically stored level variations on the tape are converted back into voltages through an amplifier and speakers, the result is fairly comparable, or analogous, to the original signal. This is *analog* recording. A real-time chain of physical components directly converts energy from acoustic (mechanical) to electrical to magnetic form and then back again.

Sampling Theory Overview

Digital audio recording proceeds a little differently. Through *sampling* (capturing a series of data through measurements of the input audio signal at fixed time intervals), each value captured for the incoming audio voltage (called a *sample*) is converted into a digital word (a binary number with a fixed number of digits) by a logical circuit. This series of numbers is then stored in RAM, on tape, or onto a computer disk. In the case of conventional audio CDs, the *sample rate* is 44,100 times per second (44.1 kHz, or kilohertz) in stereo. For conventional tape-based video applications, 48,000 times per second (48 kHz) is the norm for the digital audio tracks incorporated in video tape formats such as BetaCam, D1, D2, and DVcam (as well as camcorders in Mini DV format); 96 kHz is the standard for DVD-Audio discs.

Most Pro Tools configurations enable you to choose between several different sample rates and bit-depths, both as the recording format for your session and also for any mixdown files you eventually save to disk. Both options affect audio quality in very different ways, and your best choice for a given situation depends on many factors; you don't *always* want to burden your system's processing capacity or waste disk space by simply choosing the highest possible resolution for each parameter. For now, though, just keep these two basic principles in mind:

* The more times per second an incoming audio signal is measured, the more high-frequency information you can accurately capture. (*Higher Sample Rate = Higher Frequency Range.*) See Figure 1.4.

* The more binary digits (bits) in the digital word representing each sample (that is, the bigger the number used to represent the sample's relative amplitude), the more intermediate levels of voltage you can accurately capture before each value gets rounded off to the nearest number. Like using graph paper with a more closely spaced grid, being able to capture finer gradations in signal level gives you a more accurate representation of the original waveform. (*Higher Bit Depth = Lower Quantization Error, a kind of distortion.*) See Figure 1.5.

Hard-disk recording systems like Pro Tools record digital audio and store the sample data onto hard disk as audio files. Although one might think it would be great to have an insanely high sample rate and a huge number of bits per audio sample, the resultant audio files would also be proportionately larger. This makes more demands on the host computer, requires more disk space, and so on—so there are always practical limits. (Many also argue that, given the inherent limitations of human hearing, 24-bit resolution is sufficient for initial audio recording and the final playback medium. Per this view, improvements in audio quality will center

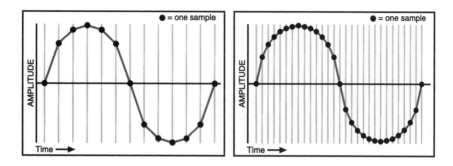

Figure 1.4 Higher sample rates produce more accurate recordings, capturing higher frequencies.

Bit-Resolution

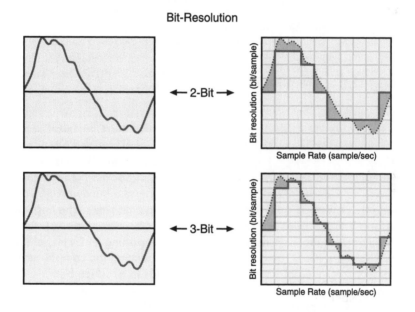

Figure 1.5 Recording at higher bit-depths means less "rounding" and a better signal/error ratio.

on how digital signals are combined and processed in the software environment and the characteristics of ADC and DAC hardware that will always color the sound to some degree.) One of the reasons the audio CD standard was established at 44.1 kHz (44,100 cycles per second, or Hertz) was that this sampling rate easily allowed maximum fundamental frequencies of up to 20 kHz to be captured, roughly corresponding to the upper limit of adult human hearing. At 16 bits per stereo sample, reasonably good-sounding streams of audio data could be reliably played back on the CD drive mechanisms that could be economically manufactured back when the audio CD format was developed. For initial *recording* of audio tracks, however, 24-bit audio is currently the norm—regardless of the final resolution of the delivery medium.

❄ **Note: Higher Sample Rate = Higher Frequency Range**

The *Nyquist Frequency* (ideally, the highest frequency you can accurately record) corresponds to half the current sample rate. The *Nyquist Theorem* (named after a mathematician) describes how the sample rate (number of digital measurements per second) must be at least twice that of the highest-frequency sound you want to record (so that both negative and positive excursions of a periodic waveform can be captured). If only a portion of a high-frequency waveform were captured, digital artifacts called *aliasing* would be created. Aliasing consists of spurious frequencies present when a digital audio recording is played back, due to partial and erroneous capture of incoming high-frequency information while recording. (In practice, we're talking here about the higher-frequency harmonics of more complex waveforms, not their fundamental pitch.) Therefore, to eliminate the possibility of any incoming frequencies higher than the Nyquist limit hitting the analog-digital audio converters, digital audio devices incorporate some sort of low-pass filter. In practice, this actually eliminates frequencies substantially *below* exactly half the sample rate, as much due to cost considerations as physical limitations on filter design. That's why the audio CD standard, with a 44.1 kHz sampling rate, reaches frequencies only up to 20,000 rather than the theoretical 22,050 Hz Nyquist limit (half the sample rate).

Until not too long ago, 44.1 kHz and 48 kHz were the most common sample rates for professional audio applications, with bit-depths (the number of binary digits per sample, which determines sample accuracy) of 16, 20, 24, and occasionally 32 bits. The high-end Pro Tools|HD systems pushed the envelope a little further, supporting 24-bit audio at sample rates of 88.2, 96, 176.4, or 192 kHz (according to the audio hardware in your Pro Tools|HD configuration), as well as 44.1 kHz and 48 kHz sample rates. The Digi 002 and 002 Rack also support sample rates up to 96 kHz and 24-bit resolution, as do many of the M-Powered hardware configurations (with some also supporting 192 kHz, although not with the M-Powered software itself). Since downsampling (reducing the sample rate, either via a software process or an external hardware device) tends to produce better-sounding results when the source and target sample rates represent an even multiple, many users will record at 88.2 or 176.4 kHz on projects destined for audio CDs at 44.1 kHz and 96 or 192 kHz for video projects going to 48 kHz.

❄ **Note: Digital Audio File Formats**

Numerous file formats are used for storing data representing digital audio waveforms. Here are some of the more common ones that will be relevant to your work in Pro Tools:

❄ **WAV (pronounced "wave").** Native to the Microsoft Windows environment and also supported by many Macintosh programs, including Pro Tools, the WAV format is similar to the AIF format, described next. Some Windows multimedia programs *only* support audio files in WAV format. Pro Tools can always import and convert WAV files, or bounce to disk in WAV format, even while using AIF (or SDII on Mac versions) as the session's recording file format.

Broadcast WAV format (BWF). This is a backward-compatible extension of the WAV format that you can select in Pro Tools as a new session's recording format. For recording at any sample rate higher than 48 kHz, all versions of Pro Tools *require* this format, even on Macintosh computers. Broadcast WAV allows ownership information to be embedded in the audio files. More importantly, Broadcast WAV files support embedded time code information, which can be useful for correctly spotting files to their original location—even in other programs that also support this format, such as video editors or other digital audio workstations. Especially when compatibility between Windows and Macintosh versions of Pro Tools is a potential concern, this audio file format is often the best choice. Using Broadcast WAV may also improve compatibility, or at the very least eliminate a conversion step, when sharing audio or OMF files with video-editing systems across platforms. In fact, Broadcast WAV is the audio file format that the AES recommends for submission and long-term archiving of music projects.

❊ **AIF or AIFF (Audio Interchange File Format).** A mono/stereo file format originally developed by Apple, AIF has been extensively supported in interactive and electronic media applications for both Macintosh and Windows platforms. However, as with the audio industry, many interactive content developers are also migrating toward Broadcast WAV as the norm for long-term compatibility; be sure to check before starting the project! The AIF format also supports loop points for samplers or sample playback programs (although you have to create these loop points in some program other than Pro Tools). Loop points within an AIF file are also recognized by Macromedia Director and some other interactive applications. When providing audio files for CD or Internet developers, video editors, or similar applications, this format can be one of your safest bets. Note: Director and Flash developers may use *markers*, or *cue points*, to tag specific locations within an AIF (or WAV) audio file. Like loop markers, you can't create these directly in Pro Tools but may be asked to do so using other programs such as Peak (Mac), WaveLab (Windows), or Sound Forge (Windows). AIF format is supported in Pro Tools for 48 kHz and 44.1 KHz sessions only—for all higher sampling rates, Broadcast WAV format must be used instead.

❊ **SDII, or SD2.** Earlier Macintosh versions of Pro Tools recorded audio to disk exclusively in Sound Designer II format. Sound Designer was Digidesign's groundbreaking Macintosh audio-editing program, introduced in the 1980s. From its beginnings as a simple mono editing program for samplers (transmitting sample data—slowly—via MIDI!), it evolved into a robust stereo hard-disk recording and editing environment based on Digidesign's Sound Tools II hardware, the precursor to Pro Tools that quickly became the industry standard for editing and mastering stereo audio. SDII files can be mono or stereo, with bit-depths of 16, 20, or 24 bits. They include loop points (for samplers) and region definitions (more about this in Chapter 2, "Pro Tools Terms and Concepts"). With current versions of Pro Tools, most users should use AIF or Broadcast WAV format as the record file format for their sessions because, among other things, these are more widely supported by other audio programs, especially on Windows. However, if compatibility with older legacy Pro Tools systems or Pro Tools Free 5.01 for Macintosh is a concern, there may still be specific situations where Mac users will choose this format. SDII files don't support sample rates higher than 48 kHz and cannot be used as the audio recording format for *any* Windows XP version of Pro Tools.

❊ **QuickTime.** This digital video file format developed by Apple is common under both Mac and Windows and is available as a free download that includes the QuickTime Player application. Audio-only Quick-Times are essentially AIFF files with resources designating QuickTime playback and will sometimes be requested by interactive developers. The audio tracks within QuickTime video movies are also often AIF format. You can import QuickTime movies into Pro Tools sessions as your video master for post-production and then *bounce* Pro Tools audio mixes directly back out into a new copy of that QuickTime movie file.

❊ **MP3 (MPEG Audio, Layer 3).** This compressed audio format uses a *lossy* compression method in which some amount of the original information is permanently lost in the process. The lower the *bit rate* (how much data per second, measured in kilobits, is required to play back the audio file), the more noticeable the compromise of audio quality will be. The amount of size reduction in MP3 encoding before drastic degradation is impressive, however—on the order of 5:1 or greater. As the reader is surely aware, the MP3 format is enormously popular for exchanging music files on the Internet. It is also increasingly common in audio files for interactive media because MP3 compression yields much better-sounding results than the older method of decreasing file size by reducing sample rate, let alone the drastic measure of converting down to 8-bit resolution. Pro Tools users involved with interactive developers (or bands trying to promote themselves on the Internet) may be asked by these clients to save out mixes as MP3 files.

* **MPEG-4.** Though formalized in 1998, this format did not become an official International Standard until 2000. This compression standard builds upon digital television technology. Apple's QuickTime file format was adapted as the basis for the MPEG-4 file format, and Apple has played an active role in its development. The more advanced audio encoding used in MPEG-4 produces smaller files/better audio quality than MP3.

* **AAC (Advanced Audio Coding).** AAC is implemented in a variant of MPEG-4 that has been popularized by Apple for online purchasing and download of audio files at its iTunes Music Store. It is much more efficient at audio data compression than MP3, producing comparable results at file sizes as much as 30% smaller.

* **RealAudio.** Developed by Real Networks, this streaming, compressed audio file format is often used on the Internet. Because RealPlayer is available to any user as a free download (and also supports streaming video files), some companies and media organizations use this technology to deliver audio and video content over the Web, which means you may occasionally be asked to deliver mixes in RealAudio format. Audio can be reduced to various throughputs (with audible compression artifacts at more extreme compression levels), according to requirements. *SureStream* technology allows several different versions of the audio to be incorporated into a single RealAudio file link, with the appropriate density being selected for playback according to the bandwidth available for each user's Internet connection. Note, however, that many users resist installing RealPlayer on their systems because of the invasive nature of this company's software (changing preferences for media file types, near-impossibility of a complete uninstall on Windows systems, and so on), which can be a major inconvenience—especially for audio and other media production professionals.

* **ReCycle (REX).** This audio format is optimized for time-sliced loops—that is, audio files that have been analyzed and broken down into their rhythmic components. The format was developed for the ReCycle program by Propellerheads, and the current iteration of the file format is actually called REX2. Many loop-oriented programs, such as Reason and Cubase SX, support using REX2 files in their editing/ mixing environment. Loops can then be played at any tempo without pitch changes. Also, having individual rhythmic components automatically sliced up makes it much easier to rearrange them into new rhythmic patterns. You can import REX files into Pro Tools by dragging them from the Workspace browser window or desktop directly into the Region List. The time slices within these source REX files subsequently appear in the Region List as "auto-created" regions.

* **ACID.** Yet another format optimized for time-sliced loops and allowing for transformation to new tempos and keys—named for the ACID program by Sony (originally developed by Sonic Foundry). Like REX files, you can bring ACID files into Pro Tools by dragging into the Region List from the Workspace browser window or desktop, and additional regions are automatically created for any time slices they contain.

MIDI Basics

As stated earlier, MIDI stands for *Musical Instrument Digital Interface*. First, let's reiterate what MIDI is: a communications protocol (with a standard data structure, cabling, DIN-5 connectors, and interfaces) for transmitting, receiving, and storing performance events. *MIDI events* are control (and timing) messages—they are *not* audio! The reception of a MIDI event may cause devices to emit audio, such as when a Note On event is transmitted from a Pro Tools MIDI track to a synth module (connected to your computer's MIDI interface) or to a software instrument plug-in. Of course, MIDI also has many other applications. It's used, for example, to change parameters on external effects, to edit internal patches in sound modules, to control lighting, and to automate mixing boards.

When you arm a MIDI (or Instrument) track for recording in Pro Tools, it looks for incoming MIDI event data from the selected MIDI interface/port for that track. When you press a key on your synth keyboard, for example, a Note On message is transmitted to Pro Tools. This Note On event includes two parameters: the number of the note you pressed and the velocity with which the key was struck, as shown in Figure 1.6. Likewise, when you release each key, a Note Off event is sent, specifying the note number and its release velocity. The pitch bend, modulation, aftertouch (channel pressure), and other interpretive moves you perform on the MIDI controller are transmitted in a similar fashion. (Other "interpretive moves" like hair-flipping, pouting, and your Serious Artist expression are completely lost on Pro Tools. Sorry!)

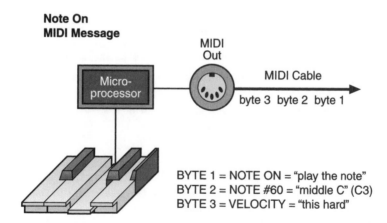

Figure 1.6 MIDI is a language for transmitting performance information (events). Here we see a Note On MIDI event, which is transmitted when you press a key on a MIDI keyboard.

❊ **Note: MIDI Connections**

MIDI is a serial communications protocol. MIDI-compatible devices have 5-pin DIN connectors for MIDI. Your computer requires a MIDI interface to translate between this protocol and its own hardware/software. Many consumer-level Windows soundcards already have a built-in MIDI in/out port, which nonetheless usually requires the separate purchase of a short adapter cable that splits out to two 5-pin DIN in/out connectors. Macintosh computers require an external MIDI interface, generally connected to the USB port on recent models. Windows users requiring *multiple* MIDI inputs/outputs also use an external MIDI interface. External USB MIDI interfaces are the norm for Windows users. (Parallel-port MIDI interfaces also exist for older PCs.)

MIDI interfaces range from simple one in, one out models through 2×2, 4×6, 8×8, 10×10, and more. You can even network certain multiport MIDI interfaces for dozens of MIDI inputs/outputs. Many also provide real-time routing and filtering between their inputs and outputs (handy for larger configurations with multiple MIDI controllers) and synchronization for SMPTE time code. (More about this in Chapter 11, "Synchronization.") Fortunately for Pro Tools, you can start with whatever MIDI interface fits your present needs and budget and then upgrade as required. (Note that the Digi 001 and Digi 002/002 Rack include MIDI in/outs on the Digidesign interface itself, as do many of the M-Audio interfaces that are compatible with the M-Powered version of Pro Tools.)

Many current keyboards, pads, control surfaces, and such use USB connections to the host computer. Some users may not require a MIDI interface at all, especially if their sound sources for MIDI tracks are all software based.

MIDI File Formats

Like MIDI sequencers (Digital Performer, Logic Pro, Cubase SX, SONAR, and others), Pro Tools records these standard MIDI events into its own proprietary file format. Each of these programs offers a wealth of display options for MIDI data (for both musical and mixing applications) and many real-time functions that affect how MIDI events are played back. In the case of Pro Tools, all the MIDI performance data that you record or create is incorporated into the session document itself (as opposed to audio, which is stored into separate files on the disk).

❊ **Tip: Importing Standard MIDI Files into Pro Tools 7**

In Pro Tools 7, two commands in the File > Import submenu bring Standard MIDI files into your session: to the Regions List only, or directly to tracks. An appropriate number of new MIDI tracks will be created as required by the contents of the SMF. This ability existed in previous versions of Pro Tools (although in version 7, import functions for audio and MIDI files are no longer found in the Regions List's local menu). However, in Pro Tools 7, the Digibase browsers now support MIDI files. You can use the Workspace browser window to navigate to the disk location for your Standard MIDI Files (which typically have the .MID file name extension) and then either drag these directly into the Regions List or into the track display area of the Edit window, where an appropriate number of new MIDI tracks will automatically be created.

Occasionally, users need to transfer an entire MIDI file (consisting of multiple tracks, with their note events, controller data, program settings, volume, and other data) from one program to another. The *Standard MIDI File* (SMF) format was defined to facilitate this process. Standard MIDI files are an interchange format that includes all MIDI events, track names, volume and pan settings, and many other parameters, so that (if you properly prepare before exporting the file) none of the MIDI data will be lost or misinterpreted when transferring files between different applications. In Pro Tools, you can also import or export files in SMF format. This ensures compatibility not only with other MIDI sequencing software but also with multimedia applications (such as the Web or interactive CDs and DVDs), which can play back these Standard MIDI files.

❋ **Standard MIDI Files and General MIDI**

If you are creating SMF-format files for multimedia (which in Windows must always have the .MID file name extension in order to be properly recognized!), be sure to use General MIDI (GM) program numbers for designating the sounds you want for each track. (Many current synths and modules have a General MIDI bank. GM is also the norm for assigning sounds to MIDI program numbers on current computer soundcards for Windows, as well as QuickTime Musical Instruments for Macintosh computers. However, these may not actually offer unique sounds for each of the 128 program numbers defined in General MIDI, instead using the same timbre for several acoustic pianos or drum sets, for example.) By using General MIDI program numbers, if you choose sound #14 for your xylophone part, it will still be a xylophone sound of some type when played back by QuickTime Musical Instruments, Windows Media Player, or standard interactive applications. It may not sound quite as good as the xylophone sound you used to compose the piece, but at least it won't be, say, a tuba!

❋ **Tip: Routing External MIDI Gear into Pro Tools**

If you have enough audio inputs on your Pro Tools hardware (for example, with a Digi 002, Digi 002 Rack, HD system, or some of the M-Audio hardware for Pro Tools M-Powered), you might connect each of your external synthesizers to an input pair on your audio interface and create individual stereo Aux Input tracks to monitor each of them in Pro Tools. Having the synths' audio output routed through the Pro Tools mixing environment, as shown in Figure 1.7, offers many advantages. You can apply automation and real-time plug-in processing to these external sound sources and, of course, incorporate their audio when you *bounce* your mix to disk as a stereo file, for example. However, in some cases, the number of channels required for all your external modules exceeds the available inputs on the audio hardware—especially considering that while recording you might want at least an input or two free for your microphones and guitar preamps. Another alternative is to use a small mixer (or even a clean-sounding line mixer) to combine some external sources into a stereo submix prior to the audio inputs on your interface (and then monitor this via a single stereo Aux In track; but we're getting ahead of ourselves!).

Software-Based Virtual Instruments for MIDI

We talk much more about this in Chapters 9, "Plug-ins, Inserts, and Sends," and 10, "MIDI," so let's just mention quickly here that, for the Pro Tools composer, software instruments are one of the most exciting technical developments of recent years. In very simple terms, these are either some sort of *plug-in* (a software construct activated within the host application; we talk more about this especially in Chapters 2 and 9) or a separate program whose audio outputs stream into Pro Tools through a software routing technology called *ReWire*. You can assign the output from any MIDI track (or Instrument track) to any currently enabled software instruments in the Pro Tools session, using MIDI channel assignments and the same MIDI controller messages as with an external MIDI module. Additionally, Instrument tracks (new in Pro Tools 7) are similar to a single MIDI track with an associated Aux In that contains an instrument plug-in. Each virtual instrument presents a software interface for altering its parameters and selecting presets, according to the kind of sound generator being modeled (sampler, analog, FM or wavetable synthesizer, drum machine, and so on).

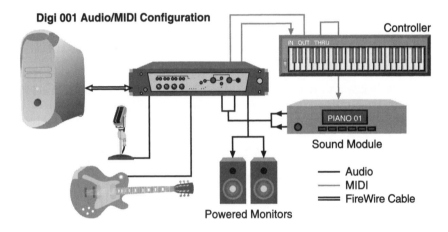

Figure 1.7   A typical configuration with a Digi 002 or one of the M-Audio interfaces with MIDI inputs/outputs. The audio outputs of the external MIDI sound module enter the audio inputs on the interface. MIDI data sent from Pro Tools is passed through the MIDI keyboard to the module.

Re-opening each Pro Tools session can instantly recall myriad settings, effects, and signal-routing configurations for each of its active software instruments. (Of course, if you're using an additional program slaved to Pro Tools via ReWire, its configuration for a given Pro Tools session must be saved and recalled separately, in that program's own format.) If you've ever managed a complex MIDI configuration with multiple external modules, you know what we're talking about—it's practically a full-time job just documenting the setup for each song. Even then, exactly reproducing a given configuration and gain structure months later is often nearly impossible. Better yet, because all the routing is internal within the computer software instead of via multiple cables and outputs from external gadgets...no noise!

Summary

This chapter provides a broad overview of what Pro Tools is, the kinds of system configurations that are possible (although these are reviewed in more detail in Chapter 3), a basic introduction to core digital audio and MIDI concepts, and a general look at the recording process. As mentioned, any one of these subjects alone often fills entire books (some of which are mentioned in Appendix A), so the intent of this review is to provide you with some context and a basic vocabulary for understanding how things work in digital workstations such as Pro Tools.

The next chapter covers more fundamental concepts—especially the key terms that all users must understand in order to effectively use Pro Tools. For more basic information about MIDI and its applications within Pro Tools, see Chapter 10.

2 Pro Tools Terms and Concepts

If you're new to Pro Tools (and even if you have an extensive audio background), take a moment to explore the review of basic concepts in this chapter. These are the conceptual building blocks for your understanding of the Pro Tools program and will provide a good grounding for your exploration of nonlinear audio and the virtual studio. Some of these terms have specific meanings in the Pro Tools environment (for example, tracks versus channels), so even experienced audio users will benefit from taking a moment to review this chapter. If this is your first time around with digital audio workstations and with Pro Tools in particular, this chapter should help you get things sorted out more quickly.

Pro Tools Data and Files

Each Pro Tools session actually consists of multiple files and folders. So, in order to manage your Pro Tools configuration, you need to know where Pro Tools puts things! Let's take a look at the master session document where you store your work, the audio files that Pro Tools creates, and how you actually view and edit these within the Pro Tools software.

Session

The *session* file is the basic document of Pro Tools. After you open the Pro Tools program and select File > New Session, a dialog box requires you to specify a file name for your new Pro Tools session document (as well as the bit-depth, sample rate, file format, and other parameters). A new folder of the same name is created in the disk/folder location you specify, within which this document resides (see Figure 2.1). The session file includes information about the name and appearance of any tracks you create, all mix settings and the appearance of the onscreen mixer, routing of audio between tracks, sends, inserts, plug-in effects, audio inputs/outputs, and other parameters. Any MIDI data recorded or created in Pro Tools is stored within the session document. In contrast, the audio regions that you record and edit from within the session actually are *pointers* to areas within audio files residing separately on your hard disk. As soon as you record any audio in a new Pro Tools session document, a subfolder named Audio Files is automatically created within that session's folder. The session document is essentially where you work—recording audio and MIDI, creating a signal-routing and effects-processing structure, editing your audio, creating a mix, automating the movement of faders, and so on. Session files are relatively small because they don't actually contain any audio. They *refer* to much larger audio files, portions of which are used within the Pro Tools session. These audio files appear as *regions* (see below), whose audio waveforms can be viewed where they have been placed within Pro Tools audio tracks.

Figure 2.1 Pro Tools session document (inside its folder of the same name), with Audio Files, Fade Files, and other folders that it creates.

Audio File

The digital audio data you record to disk from each audio track in Pro Tools is stored into a file (within an Audio Files subfolder that Pro Tools creates for this purpose—see Figure 2.2). Each file name inherits the name of the track where it was recorded, so in Pro Tools it's a very good idea to give your audio tracks meaningful names as you prepare to record in each. (Of course, you can always change the names of audio files later by double-clicking that whole-file audio region in the Region List and choosing the Name Region and Disk File option.) Pro Tools can also import existing audio files (and convert their format or sample rate, if necessary) into the current session. A single audio file may even be used in several different Pro Tools sessions—for example, frequently used items like test tones, station IDs, drum sounds or stock sound effects, and so on. Typically, as you record in Pro Tools, you end up creating a large number of audio files, especially since by default audio recording is nondestructive—*all* the takes are retained on every track. Because digital audio files are very large, file management is an important issue for Pro Tools. It's important to selectively eliminate unneeded audio as your project progresses; the sheer size of these audio files already introduces some pretty hefty data-storage issues without wasting any more space than necessary. (More about this in Appendix C, "Archive and Backup.")

Region

An audio *region* is a segment of audio data of any length—a guitar riff, a four-bar drum phrase, a sound effect, or a phrase of dialog within a longer audio file that is always external to the Pro Tools session document itself. In contrast, the data in all MIDI regions is included within

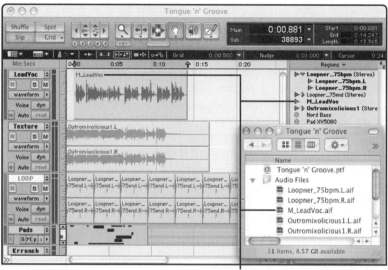

Audio File

Figure 2.2 Audio recordings in Pro Tools create new audio files on your disks (and new audio regions in your Pro Tools session). Regions that correspond to entire audio files (rather than portions within them) appear in bold type in the Region List.

the session document itself, whether the data is recorded or created within Pro Tools or imported from some existing file. New regions are created automatically when you record into any track (and audio files, in the case of audio tracks). Both audio and MIDI regions appear in a single Region List, with distinctive icons for each (while previous versions of Pro Tools had separate region lists for audio and MIDI). Entire audio files—whether created through recording in Pro Tools or existing files imported into Pro Tools from their original disk locations—appear in the Region List, along with other audio regions that represent only specific portions within their parent sound files. (Whole-file audio regions are distinguished by boldface type in the Region List.) Once you place existing audio or MIDI files and regions into Pro Tools tracks, you can *capture* or *separate* additional region definitions (via commands in the Edit menu) for any selected range within them. The edits you perform on the regions in tracks (for example, eliminating a middle portion from the middle of a longer region) often create new, additional region definitions, as do certain processing operations in the Pro Tools menus.

Since audio regions are only pointers to external files (or portions within them), you can string regions together in any order by dragging, cutting, pasting, or duplicating within track(s). Pro Tools handles the seamless, nonlinear playback of these diverse sections within large numbers of separate audio files via the Digidesign Audio Engine's (DAE) read-ahead buffer. This is the essential nonlinear (and non-destructive) nature of digital audio workstations like Pro Tools—no matter how much you chop up and re-order the regions in your tracks, the original audio files are not altered.

Creation of additional audio region definitions occupies very little extra disk space. (Your session document increases somewhat in size as more edits and region definitions are referenced, but this is still extremely small compared to actually duplicating any audio data.) Multiple region definitions within an audio file or MIDI region can overlap or coincide in any manner that is convenient. For example, you could define 16 bars of the bass track as a region named Verse2 and substitute it for the bass in Verse3, where the bass player made some mistake. Or you could select a smoothly looping eight-bar section of a short drum recording, separate a region called DrumGroove, and repeat this region as many times as necessary to build up your layered dance track. (Separating and capturing a new region name involve very similar commands. Both add a new region definition to the Region List, but Edit > Separate Region actually replaces the current track selection with the new region definition, while Region > Capture only adds the region definition to the Region List without replacing the current selection.) No matter how many times you repeat the drum loop, its audio data only occupies those eight bars worth of space on the hard disk.

Figure 2.3 shows how audio regions appear in the Edit window, both as rectangular graphics within audio tracks and in a *bin* at the right side of the Edit window, called the Region List. During playback, Pro Tools takes care of retrieving all the appropriate sections of audio within multiple files. All regions in a track will play back at the correct time—even if they reside within audio files that are on physically separate sections of the disk(s).

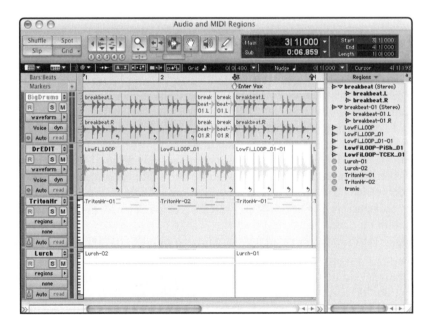

Figure 2.3 Regions are segments of audio or MIDI data; audio regions can represent either entire files or portions within files. Some region definitions are created automatically by Pro Tools in the course of editing.

Track

An audio or MIDI *track* is where regions are strung together. Each horizontal strip in the Edit window (into which you record or drag audio and MIDI regions) represents one of these virtual tracks. The Mix window displays the same audio and MIDI tracks seen in the Edit window, but as vertical *mixer strips*. (Instrument tracks are a sort of hybrid—while they are similar to Aux Ins as seen in the Mix window, in the Edit window MIDI regions can be recorded and edited in an Instrument track.) Each audio, MIDI, or Instrument track has its own *playlist* of regions (see the next section), plus an automation playlist for volume faders, pan, sends, and plug-in parameters. Tracks can be assigned any convenient name and dragged into any convenient order. (On HD systems and other TDM-based predecessors, when tracks are manually assigned to voices rather than the default dynamic voice allocation mode, track positions also affect playback priority. Leftmost tracks in the Mix window, which are also topmost in the Edit window, always have priority access to a voice.) Each track can be muted, soloed, assigned to any audio input/output available on the system, or routed to another destination through Pro Tools' internal mixing busses. Two other classes of tracks that do not contain regions also offer many similar features to audio tracks: Auxiliary Inputs and Master Faders (see definitions of these terms later in this chapter). Lastly, if you import a QuickTime movie (a type of digital video file) as a reference for a postproduction project, a Movie track is created. In Chapter 7, "The Mix Window," we explore the various classes of tracks in Pro Tools.

Playlist

In general terms, an e*dit playlist* is a list of audio (or MIDI) regions strung together in a specific order on a Pro Tools virtual track. Recorded audio used by an audio track is stored within files on the hard disk; a playlist is a list of regions (pointers to portions of the audio data within those audio files) indicating which are to be read for playback, at what time, and in what order.

In some programs, you can order the playback of audio regions or files through a single, text-based list (for example, Steinberg's WaveLab and Sony/Sonic Foundry's Sound Forge—not to mention Digidesign's long-discontinued Sound Designer II and MasterList CD programs, and most CD-burning software, for that matter). In Pro Tools, however, each track you see in the Edit window is actually a graphic playlist. Regions can be viewed as blocks within each track, or when the Waveform view is selected, visual representations of the actual audio waveforms are displayed within these region blocks.

For example, let's say you import a few dozen sound effects from a CD library and then, in the Edit window of Pro Tools, drag them out onto an audio track. You trim their beginnings and ends, and perhaps create a few fades (which are actually separate files; see the section "Fade, Crossfade," later in this chapter) and resize them in other ways. When you press Play, Pro Tools understands that you want to hear a specific section of one file, with a seamless fade on the end, followed by another section from a completely different file. Pro Tools follows every audio track's playlist, making sure to pre-load all appropriate audio data from disk into the DAE Playback Buffer for timely playback.

In the controls for each audio, MIDI, or Instrument track, a pop-up Playlist selector (to the right of each track name in the Edit window) switches between alternate playlists for that track (as shown in Figure 2.4). This is useful for experimentation; you duplicate the current version of the track's region order as a playlist so that you can always go back to it! For users familiar with video-editing systems: Each playlist for a Pro Tools track is similar to an Edit Decision List (EDL). The important point to understand here is that, in both cases, playback order is not restricted to the original physical order of your source material on the recording medium.

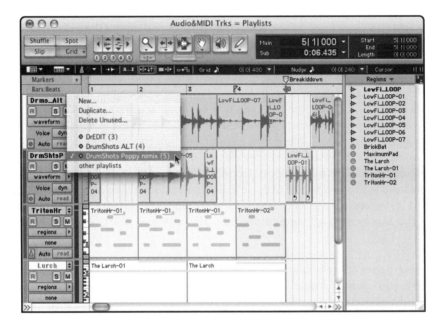

Figure 2.4 Each audio or MIDI track in Pro Tools represents a playlist, indicating which regions of audio or MIDI data should be played and when. You can switch between multiple playlists for each track, using the pop-up Playlist selector shown here.

Note: Track Automation versus Playlists of Regions

There is only one automation playlist for each Pro Tools audio track, no matter which edit playlist (region order) is selected. This is extremely important to keep in mind, for example, if you want to experiment with cutting and pasting audio regions within alternate playlists in the same audio track. By default, any automation data (for example, volume, pan, or effects parameters) overlapping the regions you select will also be copied—and the resulting automation shapes may not always be appropriate when you use the track's Playlist selector to switch to a different edit playlist. If you need to experiment not only with audio region order, but also with automation within a track, it may be a better idea to duplicate it to a new audio track rather than using multiple playlists in the source track for this purpose.

MIDI tracks also allow you to view and edit automation, of course. While the appearance of MIDI volume, pan, and other automation data in MIDI tracks is similar to audio, it is handled quite differently by Pro Tools. The automation shapes in MIDI tracks actually represent MIDI controller messages for these parameters that will be transmitted on the track's MIDI channel along with its note events (in a similar fashion to damper pedal, mod wheel, or breath controller data, for example). The only automation playlist data type that is part of the MIDI track itself are the Mute/Unmute events (which, like audio automation, are part of the track itself). All the other MIDI automation, for volume, pan, pedals, modulation, Aftertouch, and so on, is actually contained within the MIDI regions themselves as MIDI controller information. So except for Mute/Unmute automation events (which affect anything in that MIDI track, no matter which edit playlist is selected), in MIDI tracks you can freely edit the Volume, Pan, and other MIDI controller data types in each alternate playlist without worrying about this affecting any of the other playlists in the same track. In fact, when you duplicate an edit playlist in a MIDI track, Pro Tools automatically creates duplicate MIDI regions to reflect any edits you make to these parameters.

How Pro Tools Handles Audio

Using conventional mixing boards and tape recorders, it's fairly easy to see where your audio enters and exits individual channels, auxiliary inputs or outputs, and so on. For the sake of convenience, Pro Tools uses mixer strips and tracks as familiar metaphors, but in fact it's much more flexible than that. If you look at alternative configurations in Pro Tools with a traditional tape-based mindset, you might think, for example, that for equivalent functionality to a 24-track recorder, you need 24 channels of I/O (input/output) on your Pro Tools audio interfaces. It ain't necessarily so! *Especially* if you're coming to this program from a traditional MIDI or audio background, you need to readjust your thinking about voices, tracks, and channels in particular to truly understand the power of Pro Tools.

Voice, Track Priority

The number of *voices* in a digital audio workstation determines the number of separate audio tracks it can play at any given moment. Voices in Pro Tools are like a pool of digital audio converters, which audio tracks must use to play back the audio regions they contain. By default, Pro Tools dynamically assigns voices to tracks (via the dyn setting in the Voice Assignment selector for each track) to avoid conflicts. In LE and M-Powered versions of Pro Tools (using Digi 002, Mbox 2, or M-Audio hardware, for example), this is the *only* option for managing voice allocation—other than setting a track's voice assignment to "off" so that it doesn't play at all.

On HD and previous TDM systems, however, you can *manually* assign a voice number to each Pro Tools track. Whenever two tracks want to use the same manually assigned voice at the same moment, the one with the highest playback priority will win. The scheme for managing voice allocation is very simple: Whichever track is higher in the Edit window or further left in the Mix window is the higher priority. Wherever the higher-priority track contains an audio region, it will play, even if that means cutting off a region already sounding in another lower-priority track assigned to the same voice number. If you drag tracks into a different order, you're also changing their priority! Multiple tracks can be assigned to the same voice; as long as their regions don't overlap at any point in time, each can play back all required audio. As shown in Figure 2.5, this effectively gives you much more polyphony out of whatever fixed number of voices your Pro Tools system provides. Each track maintains its own completely independent routing, effects, automation, and so on, which is unaffected by that of any other tracks assigned to the same voice.

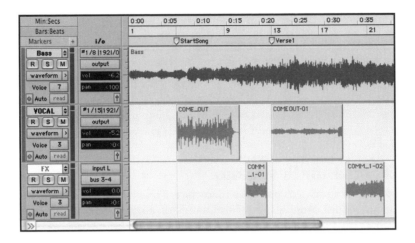

Figure 2.5 In TDM-based versions (including Pro Tools HD), wherever audio regions coincide in tracks manually assigned to the same voice, the higher-priority track always takes precedence—cutting off previously sounding audio in the other if necessary. Setting the voice selector of audio tracks to dyn (dynamic) automatically adjusts voice allocation to minimize conflicts.

Bear in mind that multichannel tracks (stereo and surround) utilize a corresponding number of voices. This is why high-end configurations such as Pro Tools|HD support such high voice counts—for complex soundtrack mixes with many surround submixes, stereo tracks, and so on, the number of voices required for playback can get large very quickly. Also, on HD systems (but not LE/M-Powered versions) each active ReWire channel in your Pro Tools session uses one of your available voices; see "ReWire (and the DigiReWire Plug-in)," later in this chapter, for more information.

Back in the early days of Pro Tools, voice assignment was quite an art form. (Systems with four or eight channels and four or eight voices were the norm, whereas today anywhere from 32 to 192 voices are supported.) On current Pro Tools|HD systems, though, most users leave the default dyn (dynamic) setting for track voice assignments, letting the software automatically handle this. Therefore, unless you inadvertently assign two tracks to the same voice manually (and their audio regions coincide at some point), voice assignment won't necessarily be a daily issue for you—unless, for example, you're specifically using this voice-stealing feature to bleep out certain words in a voice recording or lyric. (You would place the bleep sounds into a higher-priority track, assigned to the same voice as the track you want to bleep.)

Channel

Although the mixer strips in the Mix window of Pro Tools are sometimes called *mixer channels*, this is really more of a holdover from traditional analog mixing boards, where each channel actually does correspond to an audio input. In the Digidesign realm, we prefer to reserve the term *channel* strictly for describing the input/output (I/O) capabilities of the audio hardware itself. For example, Digidesign's 96 I/O audio interface for HD systems simultaneously offers up to 16 channels of input and output, using various combinations of its eight analog inputs/outputs, eight-channel ADAT Lightpipe input/output, and its AES/EBU and S/PDIF digital inputs/outputs. The original Mbox is a two-channel system: two inputs, two outputs (one stereo input, and one stereo output). The Mbox 2 can operate as a 4×4 system *if* you use both the two-channel analog and S/PDIF digital I/O simultaneously. If you're using M-Audio's FireWire Solo or Audiophile interface with the M-Powered version of Pro Tools, four inputs and six outputs are available (including their digital I/O in S/PDIF format). Nevertheless, in the Digidesign manuals (and for that matter, several places in this book!) you will occasionally see colloquial references to the channels or channel strips in the Mix window. Indeed, an audio track *is* a virtual signal path whose input(s) and output(s) can be configured to any physical input/output or internal mixing bus within the software mixing environment.

In Pro Tools, the number of audio *tracks* playing back simultaneously can be significantly greater than the number of audio *channels* that the hardware interface provides, as shown in Figure 2.6. The number of *output* channels on the interface determines your options for the main mix output assignment, for additional sends to external effects or headphone mixes, for looping audio through external audio devices, and so on. Obviously, the number of *input* channels on your audio hardware determines the number of discrete audio sources that can be recorded simultaneously (and the return capabilities from external effects devices, whether these are monitored via Aux Ins, or used as hardware I/O inserts).

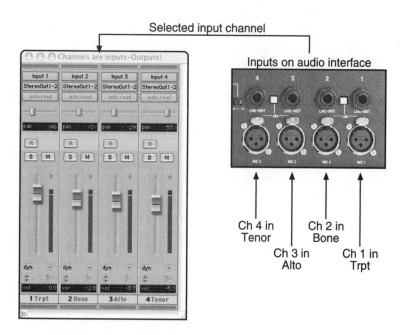

Figure 2.6   In the Pro Tools environment, strictly speaking, *channel* refers to an audio input or output (analog and/or digital) on the audio interface. The number of input channels on this hardware determines how many audio sources you can record simultaneously, even though a much larger number of tracks may play back audio.

❄ **Note: Digidesign Audio Interfaces—Past and Present**

In the past, model numbers given to Digidesign's external audio interfaces for Pro Tools described their input/output capabilities (going back to the original four-channel interface for Pro Tools, later known as the 442 I/O). For example, 882 I/O interfaces had eight analog inputs, eight analog outputs, and two channels of digital I/O (one S/PDIF); the 1622 I/O had 16 analog inputs, two analog outputs, and two digital channels (one S/PDIF); 888 I/O interfaces had eight analog inputs, eight analog outputs, and eight channels of digital I/O (four AES/EBU).

At a certain point, however, this handy (albeit unexciting) nomenclature was abandoned.

The Digi 001 (now discontinued), for example, had eight analog inputs, eight analog outputs, plus up to eight channels of ADAT Lightpipe digital I/O and two channels of digital I/O (two RCA connectors for S/PDIF in and out). Plus, it provides a headphone output, MIDI in/out, and two phantom-powered microphone preamplifiers. So they called it the Digi 001—because it was a catchy name!

The Digi 002 and Digi 002 Rack were the next step up in hardware for Pro Tools LE (hence the name). Like the Digi 001, they include eight analog inputs/outputs plus ADAT Lightpipe and S/PDIF digital I/O and increase the mic preamp count to four (also including phantom power and of higher quality than the Digi 001). These interfaces also offer a dedicated monitor output and second MIDI output. The 002 audio interface doubles as a desktop control surface with motorized faders and can actually be used as a standalone digital mixer with EQ, delay, reverb, dynamics processing, and snapshot recall, while the 002R consists of only a rackmountable unit with the same connections. The original Mbox interface connects to your computer's USB port, offering two channels of audio I/O, switchable between analog jacks—which also include hardware inserts, microphone preamplifiers, and 48V phantom power—and S/PDIF digital connectors. (It's called the Mbox because "222" would have been too too too boring!) The current Mbox 2 model also connects to the host computer via USB, adding the capability to use both the analog and digital I/O simultaneously for 4x4 operation. It also features a MIDI input and output.

The names of external audio interfaces introduced with Pro Tools|HD highlight their most notable characteristic: the capacity for very high-resolution audio. The 96 I/O and 96i I/O offer 24-bit conversion, at sample rates up to 96 kHz. The 192 I/O is also 24-bit, supporting sample rates up to 192 kHz, while the 192 Digital I/O is a digital-only version without the analog input or output sections. Most of these interfaces also incorporate AES/EBU and S/PDIF digital connections, plus simultaneous ADAT Lightpipe (eight Lightpipe channels on the 96 I/O, 16 on the 192 I/O, plus eight *additional* channels of Tascam TDIF on the 192 I/O) for interconnection with digital multitrack recorders from Alesis or Tascam, and any other device compatible with these multichannel optical connection standards. In contrast, the 96i I/O has no Lightpipe or TDIF connectors for multichannel digital I/O but offers 16 channels of analog input and stereo analog output, plus a single stereo S/PDIF digital I/O. You can use various combinations of the available connections on these HD interfaces for a maximum of 16 channels of I/O on any individual interface (and up to two interfaces connected to each HD card installed in the host computer). Chapter 17, "Pro Tools Power: The Next Step," provides more detailed information about hardware options for Pro Tools|HD systems.

Virtual Tracks versus Physical Tracks

On a traditional multitrack tape recorder (analog *or* digital), audio information is recorded physically onto the tape—at a location directly corresponding to its playback time. During recording, audio data entering a Pro Tools audio track is written to a hard disk; a playlist then controls the triggering of audio playback at the appropriate time. The audio tracks in

Pro Tools are virtual tracks. Instead of being recorded to any specific physical location, the source audio files for the audio regions you record and play back could actually reside at widely scattered locations on your computer's hard disk(s). At any moment you can move audio events from one location or audio track to another, regardless of where they were originally recorded or the disk location where they currently reside, in order to experiment with different arrangements.

On a multitrack tape recorder, the assignment of outputs or playback voices to tape tracks is fixed. Its physical audio inputs and outputs 1–8 correspond to tape tracks 1–8, and that's it. In Pro Tools, however, the inputs and outputs on the audio interface are available to many different tracks for diverse purposes during all the phases of a project. One or more *voices* may handle playback for several of the audio tracks that you edit onscreen, but each of these can be independently assigned to different inputs and outputs (any physical input or output or an internal mixing bus). Simply put, voices act as a pool of audio converters enabling tracks to play. Each voice is available to play back a single channel of any audio tracks assigned to it, but it can only service one channel (for example, mono track, or one of the channels in a stereo track) at any given moment.

LE and M-Powered versions of Pro Tools are limited to 32 voices (16 stereo audio tracks, 32 mono tracks, or some combination thereof), and voice allocation is dynamically handled by Pro Tools to avoid conflicts. (The Music Production Toolkit option permits 48 mono/stereo tracks on these systems, as does the DV Toolkit 2 for Pro Tools 7 LE.) In HD versions, voice allocation can also be dynamic or assigned manually, and the total number of tracks can exceed the number of voices. Figure 2.7 provides a simple representation of this concept. Many tracks are assigned to share the same voice, but as long as no two regions of audio within these tracks ever coincide, each can play all its required audio. Wherever they do overlap, though, whichever track is higher in the Edit window (or further left in the Mix window) has higher priority to play the regions it contains, even cutting in on another previously sounding track if necessary and stealing the voice.

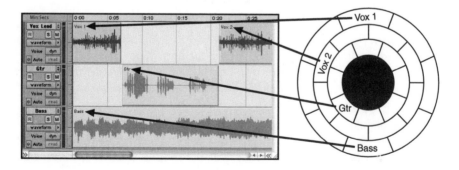

Figure 2.7 The virtual audio tracks in Pro Tools are graphic representations of playlists that determine when audio regions should be played. In HD systems, for an audio region to be heard, the voice assigned to the track must be available at that moment. The rest of the time, that voice is available to any other tracks assigned to it.

It's as if you had many more channels of audio available than the number of voices (or audio polyphony) on your system might otherwise imply. That's where the concept of *virtual tracks* arises in the Digidesign realm—unlike a multitrack tape recorder, the number of available, mixable tracks actually exceeds the number of physical output channels. Again, the selected input and output of each track—and its routing, plug-ins, automation, and other parameters—are completely independent of any other tracks assigned to the same voice.

Destructive versus Nondestructive Editing

Destructive editing is what happens when you cut and splice audio tape! The editing process permanently alters the actual recording medium in order to make changes. Recording on traditional multitrack tape recorders (even digital) is likewise destructive—if you record a new take of a solo or voice-over, the audio previously recorded on that same tape track is gone forever.

In contrast, the nonlinear access provided by Pro Tools and other digital audio workstations permits playing back regions (segments) of audio in any order without altering the original recorded data. Therefore, hard-disk editing is *nondestructive* by nature. No matter how many regions and fades you create or how much you alter their playback order, the original recorded take is still intact on the disk. Even process-based effects (like the AudioSuite version of pitch shifting, for example) are nondestructive by default. They create new audio files to contain the result of the audio processing you apply.

As you record a solo or voice-over in Pro Tools, unless you specifically enable Destructive Recording mode (by choosing Options > Destructive Recording), each take is separately recorded to disk. Sequential numbers are automatically assigned to each region name, so you can tell which takes are most recent. You can even composite together an ideal version using sections of various takes, all recorded on the same Pro Tools track (perhaps in Loop Record mode, in which case all your loop-recorded takes are actually regions within a single audio file).

Fade, Crossfade

As you might guess, a *fade* gradually increases the audio volume from zero at the beginning of an audio region or decreases it to zero at the end. Pro Tools offers a variety of shapes that determine how audio will fade from or to silence at the beginnings and ends of audio regions. (These include a variety of Equal Power and Equal Gain curves, linear fades, S-curves, and so on, as seen in Figure 2.8.) A *crossfade* occurs when the fade in and fade out for two adjacent regions in the same track overlap across the boundary between them.

To create a fade, highlight a portion of audio at the beginning or end of an audio region in a track and select Edit > Fades > Create. The Fades dialog box (shown in Figure 2.8) allows you to audition and select various fade-in or fade-out shapes. (Actually, a new audio file is created in the Fade Files folder and appended to the beginning or end of the region for playback at the appropriate moment. Fades are therefore *nondestructive*—they don't alter the original audio file and can be revised as many times as necessary.) When two regions adjoin each other on the same track and your selection creates a fade across the boundary between them, the resultant *crossfade* actually overlaps each region, using material in each parent audio file beyond the current regions' current boundaries in the track. (If insufficient additional material is available because one of the fades would extend beyond the beginning or end of its parent audio file, Pro Tools will inform you.) Crossfades are very useful for overlapped effects. They can also minimize the audibility of edits—for example, where the decay of a cymbal needs to overlap the beginning of the next drum region in order to sound natural, or when you're duplicating a shorter section of background ambience to fill a given amount of time and don't want the splices to be obvious.

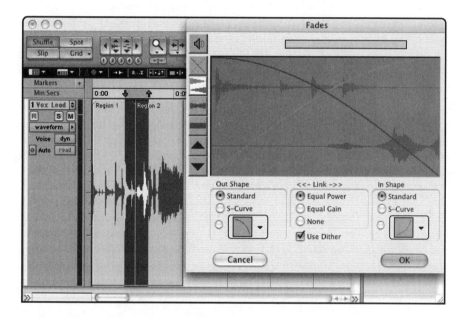

Figure 2.8 When you create a crossfade at the boundary between two adjacent audio regions, additional portions of the audio within their parent audio files are played before and after the transition. This figure shows the Fades dialog box, where fade-in and fade-out shapes are displayed.

Mixing Concepts

Chapter 7, "The Mix Window," and Chapter 9, "Plug-ins, Inserts, and Sends" go into depth about mixing and signal routing in Pro Tools. In this chapter, we'll limit our discussion of these topics to mentioning just a few key terms that acquire more expanded meanings in the Pro Tools environment (versus traditional analog mixers).

Group (Tracks)

In Pro Tools, a *group* is formed when multiple tracks are linked, so that their volume faders (as well as any volume automation you create while the group is active) are "ganged" together. Also, selections made in one track are mirrored in the other tracks in that group. For example, after selecting four backing vocal, drum, or sound effects tracks, you could use the Track > Group command to create a Mix and/or Edit group so that all four tracks can be treated as a unit. (Each group you create can be active in both the Mix and Edit windows or in just one of these.) When a group is active, all changes made to volume, selections, fades, and display format on one track in the group will apply to the others as well (as will the action of Solo and Mutes buttons, as long as this default option remains enabled in the Automation tab of the Preferences dialog box).

As you drag the volume for any one of the tracks in an active group, *all* their faders move up and down together. However, the *relative* volume level of each individual fader, from when the group was created, is maintained. Output assignment and panning for each track in a group remain independent, as do voice assignment and plug-in settings. By default, the mute status and level of any *sends* from individual tracks in a group are also independent. However, you can also link mutes and send level adjustments for grouped tracks by enabling this option in the Automation tab of the Preferences dialog box (which affects *all* groups).

As shown in Figure 2.9, a track can belong to more than one group. Grouping tracks in Pro Tools can also make it easier to manage sessions; for example, clicking the dot next to a group's name selects all tracks belonging to that group. Pro Tools provides a Groups list in both the Mix and Edit windows for enabling or renaming groups and also supports assigning custom colors to each group that make it easier to quickly identify its member tracks.

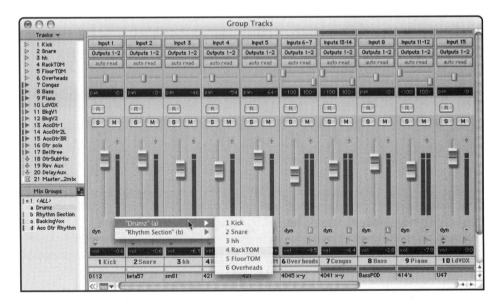

Figure 2.9 Grouping tracks can simplify mixing and editing. In this figure, the Group ID pop-up shows that the Overheads audio track is included in the Drumz (a) mix group, as well as the Rhythm Section (b) mix group displayed in its Mix Groups indicator.

> ### ❋ Note: Grouping Regions
>
> Version 7 of Pro Tools introduced the possibility of grouping regions in the Edit window (via the Region > Group command). First, you might select several regions on a single track (segments of a guitar solo you've just edited together, for example) and then group them so that you can manipulate them as a single unit. A small icon appears in the lower-left corner to indicate that this object contains multiple source regions. You can even create groups across *multiple* tracks. (More about this in Chapter 6, "The Edit Window"; behavior and appearance of multitrack region groups depends on whether they were created with Time Grabber or Object Grabber selections.) In either case, you can also create fades on these region groups, even if they span source region boundaries or consist of multiple tracks. And of course, you can always ungroup regions later for further editing. Cool stuff!

Bus

A *bus* is an audio pipeline used to route signals within Pro Tools and can be used for many different purposes. You can use them individually, in stereo pairs, or in multichannel groups. You can set the input or output of any audio, Auxiliary Input, or Instrument track to one of the many busses that Pro Tools provides, and you can also assign each of its sends to a bus. You can use busses in mono, as stereo pairs, or as multichannel paths in surround mixing. Busses are frequently used to group signals from multiple sources. For example, you could assign the main outputs from multiple tracks to a common stereo bus pair where they are combined and then create an Auxiliary Input track (covered later in this chapter) assigned to monitor that bus pair as its selected input source. This Aux In's level fader now provides a single volume control for all tracks assigned to this bus and its own inserts (see "Insert," later in this chapter) and sends also allow you to use effects that affect this entire submix. (In conventional mixing boards, this is also sometimes known as a *subgroup*—in this book, however, we always use the term *submix* in order to avoid any potential confusion with Edit and Mix groups in Pro Tools, described in the previous section.)

It's also common to use a bus in Pro Tools as the destination for sends from multiple tracks, combining their signals on their way to an Aux In track with a reverb or delay insert, for example (something like the main Aux Send outputs on a live mixing console). Pro Tools HD provides 128 busses, while the LE and M-Powered versions support 32 busses (versus 16 prior to Pro Tools 7 in these versions).

Send

Also known as an *auxiliary send* (or *aux send*) on traditional mixers, a *send* is a secondary audio signal pathway in a mixing console (or for tracks in the Pro Tools mixing environment). In Pro Tools, sends are used to additionally route signal from any audio, Auxiliary Input, or Instrument track to another destination, independently from this track's main output assignment. You can route the 10 send points on each mixer strip (five in prior versions of Pro Tools) either to a physical output on the audio hardware (the signal source for a performer's cue mix or an external effects processor, for example) or to any one of Pro Tool's internal mixing busses. Sends are frequently used from various tracks to a single destination—in order to apply a reverb or delay effect, for instance. Unlike inserts, where a track's entire signal passes through the processor (a typical way to use a compressor or EQ plug-in, for instance), sends are *additional* destinations for a track's signal and have no effect on its main output. So, if you've sent some of your vocal track to an Auxiliary Input where a reverb plug-in was inserted, both the *dry* (unprocessed) signal from the track itself and the reverb's *wet* output from the Auxiliary Input track can be present in the main mix from Pro Tools. Sends can be mono, stereo, or multichannel. Of course, the level, pan, and muting of each send can be automated.

Auxiliary Input (Aux In)

Auxiliary Input tracks (*Aux Ins*) have a similar appearance to other audio tracks in the Pro Tools mixing environment, but they cannot contain audio regions, since their only possible input selections are inputs on the hardware interface or one of the internal mixing busses in Pro Tools. Aux Ins can be mono, stereo, or multichannel. As the name implies, they are extra inputs into the Pro Tools virtual mixer and are for monitoring audio from either *internal* or *external* sources. The Input selector on each Aux In allows you to monitor any of the internal mixing busses in Pro Tools or actual, physical audio inputs on the audio hardware. Like audio tracks, you can insert (pre-fader) plug-in effects on Aux Ins. You can also create sends to other destinations from Aux In tracks and automate their volume, pan, sends, or plug-in parameters. You can assign the output of each Aux In to any internal mixing bus or to one or more physical outputs on the audio hardware. Common uses of Auxiliary Input tracks include the following:

* **Effects busses.** You might insert a reverb or delay plug-in on a stereo Aux In and set its input source to stereo bus 1-2. You would then route stereo sends from various audio tracks to bus 1-2, so that you can feed some of their signal into the reverb or delay effect.

* **Subgroups.** You could assign the outputs of your seven drum tracks to bus 3-4 and then create a stereo Aux In with that bus pair selected as its input. Not only does this provide a single volume fader for the entire stereo drum submix, but it also makes it convenient to, say, insert a single stereo compressor or other effect on it.

* **Monitoring external sources.** As mentioned previously, if you have an external synthesizer or module that is the sound source for MIDI tracks transmitted from Pro Tools, you will want to bring that device's audio output up in the Pro Tools mixer, if possible. This allows you incorporate that device's audio output when you bounce your mix to disk as a new file. Of course, you can also place insert effects (for example, reverb, compression, and EQ) on the Aux In where any external source is being monitored. You can also use Aux Ins to monitor (and process) audio channels from a multitrack tape recorder within the Pro Tools mixing environment.

* **Virtual instrument plug-ins.** Aux In tracks were traditionally used for instantiating software instrument plug-ins in Pro Tools (or the Click plug-in, which can be considered a rudimentary sort of virtual instrument). Although these instrument plug-ins *can* still be used in this way in Pro Tools 7, Instrument tracks (see the next section) provide another option.

* **ReWire.** When you use this virtual signal routing technology—see the section "ReWire (and the DigiReWire Plug-in) later in this chapter—to stream audio channels from virtual synthesizer or sampler programs into Pro Tools, their outputs can also be monitored via Auxiliary Inputs (or on audio tracks in HD versions of Pro Tools).

Instrument Track

This new type of Pro Tools track was introduced in version 7. It can be roughly described as an Aux In with a single, incorporated MIDI track. As seen in the Mix window, Instrument tracks are very similar to Auxiliary Inputs (Aux Ins). However, in the Edit window, an Instrument track looks and acts more like a MIDI track. It contains MIDI notes and regions and provides breakpoint editing for automating volume, pan, and other MIDI controllers. (Details about the elements in MIDI tracks are provided in Chapters 6 and 7.) It is still possible to instantiate virtual instrument plug-ins on an Auxiliary Input or audio track, as in previous versions of Pro Tools. In fact, for multitimbral plug-ins (which respond to incoming MIDI data on more than one channel simultaneously, producing different sounds for each), this may still be your preferred method. However, when a single MIDI track is used for a monotimbral instrument, the ability to manage these directly as a single, combined Instrument track is easier, reducing onscreen clutter. Since Instrument tracks have their own distinctive icon in the Mix window, in larger sessions, this can also make it easier to distinguish them at a glance from Aux Ins being used for other purposes.

Master Fader

Master Faders are a track type used to control the *output stage* of physical outputs or internal mixing busses. Like Auxiliary Inputs, you can insert plug-in effects into the Master Fader's signal chain and automate volume, pan, and plug-in parameters if desired. (On Master Faders, the Inserts section is *post*-fader only, instead of *pre*-fader as on audio, Aux In, and Instrument tracks.) Master Faders appear in the Edit and Mix windows alongside audio, Aux In, MIDI, and Instrument tracks and have a similar appearance and behavior, except that, like Aux Ins, they cannot contain regions. Master Faders—sometimes referred to simply as *Masters*—can be mono, stereo, or multichannel. They have no Record, Solo, or Mute buttons, no pan controls, and of course, no input source selector (because, by definition, Master Fader tracks affect *only* the output of the selected physical output or bus).

A very typical use of a Master Fader track is to provide a final monitoring and control stage for your main mix output. For example, you might use outputs 1 and 2 on your audio interface for this. Creating a Master Fader for that output pair provides a level meter, so you can confirm that your mix output isn't overloading. (Even when you're bouncing a mixdown file to disk—described later in this chapter and also in Chapter 16, "Bouncing to Disk, Other File Formats"—rather than recording to some external device, clipping can still be a problem. You might also apply final EQ, dynamics processing (or dithering, when bouncing from 24-bit audio resolution down to 16-bit, for example), and other finishing effects (again, as post-fader effects) at this last output stage of your mix.

Master Faders have many other uses, however. Many users create Master Faders for the busses they're using for send effects—using its Volume fader or dynamics plug-ins to avoid clipping due to signals being combined from many source tracks, for example. Others find Master Faders extremely useful for the sole fact that their insert section is *post*-fader. Depending on the sound you're after and how you want the effect to interact with any volume fader automation prior to it in the signal chain, this can also be a powerful technique.

To make a very broad recommendation: Before ever bouncing out any mixdown file or recording to an external device from Pro Tools, you should always create a Master Fader—at the very least, so that you can see what's going on with your output levels. (As you will learn in Chapter 7, if you open an Output window for your main output's Master Fader, it can always be visible even when you're working in the Edit window—very handy.) Other potential uses are limited only by your imagination and the degree of cleverness your projects demand!

❈ **Note: Unity Gain**

When you create a new Master Fader track to monitor and/or control the path to an audio output or mixing bus in Pro Tools, its volume fader defaults to 0 dB. This setting for a volume fader doesn't apply any gain change to audio signals passing through it. (That is, their volume isn't increased or decreased.) In professional audio, this is also known as *unity gain*.

Plug-in

Like some other audio-, video-, and image-editing software, the Pro Tools software architecture is flexible and fairly open, allowing you to customize your software mixing environment with additional processing modules according to your needs. One of the significant innovations Digidesign introduced in the digital audio editing field was the ability to incorporate additional effects-processing *plug-ins* into virtual insert points in the Pro Tools mixing/signal-routing environment. These are used for applying real-time effects to audio signals (something like using an insert point on an analog mixing board to patch in a compressor, for example). There are also plug-ins that are process based (that is, instead of working in real time, they create a new audio file to store the transformed results of the selected effect settings). In Pro Tools, these non–real-time effects are usually accessed via the AudioSuite menu.

Generally speaking, a *plug-in* is an auxiliary software program that functions as an add-in *module* within another program; it cannot work by itself. Plug-ins add functionality to the host application and may be provided by the manufacturer or by third parties.

❈ **Note: Third-Party Plug-Ins**

When Digidesign introduced the plug-in concept (in Pro Tools' stereo predecessor, Sound Tools II), the company made the then-revolutionary choice to make the programming code available so that third parties could develop their own compatible plug-ins and market them to Digidesign users. This was a huge success, and today, scores of companies offer plug-in software modules that are compatible with Pro Tools (some of which are complete virtual synthesizers, in addition to a wealth of sophisticated effects processors). Not only does this increase the variety of special-purpose effects available, but it also allows plug-in developers to tailor sound quality and interfaces to suit every taste.

Many plug-in software modules are included with Pro Tools (in AudioSuite, RTAS, and/or TDM format, depending on the system you're using), including equalization, dynamics processing, reverb, and delays. Naturally, the more effects-processing plug-ins you use simultaneously, the more demands this makes on your system's audio signal processing capabilities.

One of the great advantages of using plug-in software processing is that, because the virtual signal routing environment is completely software based, signal degradation problems associated with a traditional analog studio setup (due to each device in a lengthy processing chain having its own input/output stages, digital converters, and other self-generated noise) are a thing of the past. Also, from a user's perspective, having the parameter editing for many different effects accessible from a reasonably consistent interface within a single program means that you spend a lot less time wading through manuals, proprietary operating systems, and jargon! Adding effects processing via plug-ins tends to be less expensive in the long run, too, because you aren't buying stacks of redundant boxes, each with its own inputs/outputs, displays, and so on. Furthermore, a single plug-in can be used simultaneously at several locations in the same mix, so you're getting several effects for the price of one! Figure 2.10 represents the signal flow in an audio track, showing the location of the Inserts section, where plug-in effects are instantiated.

❋ **Note: Instantiate**

Just what does it mean to "instantiate?" The standard dictionary definition of the word goes something like this: "To represent an abstraction by a tangible or concrete example." So when you select a plug-in on an insert slot, you're creating an "instance" of this software process at that point within the host program's virtual signal routing environment—a software object called *EQ III*, for example, that now demands some portion of your system's available processing power. You might instantiate numerous EQ, compressor, and other types of plug-ins on individual tracks.

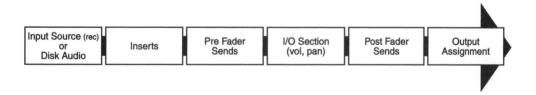

Figure 2.10 Signal flow of an audio track. While recording, an audio track's volume fader has no effect on the recorded level from the input! However, you can apply up to 12 dB of additional gain to the monitoring level.

Insert

An *insert*, also known as an *insert point*, is a feature found in mixing consoles (and in the Pro Tools mix environment). Simply put, an insert is a break in the signal chain—an access point allowing a track's audio to be routed through an external device or even more typically to an analogous software construct in Pro Tools called a *plug-in*. Each audio track, Aux Input track, Instrument track, or Master Fader in Pro Tools offers an Inserts section, with five slots where plug-ins can be enabled (*instantiated*). The pop-up menus for each slot in the Inserts section of a track are used to select and "patch in" a software plug-in—in which case the audio signal passes completely through that plug-in before proceeding through the rest of the track's plug-in slots and eventually to the track's volume/pan controls and output assignment. In Pro Tools, insert points are all pre-fader, *except* on Master Faders, where they are always post-fader.

Hardware I/O inserts can also be created at these same insert points. You can use them to send the audio signal out to an external device and back from an insert point via real physical audio inputs/outputs—either analog or digital—on your audio interface. This is how you might incorporate some specialized external effects processor into the Pro Tools mixing environment, for example. However, if you're using a 2×2 system like the original Mbox, this isn't a practical option because your main outputs are already in use for your stereo mix.

Bounce to Disk

When you issue the File > Bounce to > Disk command, a new audio file is created in real time, incorporating the sum of all the editing and automation information in the current session document (that's passing though the output pair you select). Exactly what you're hearing during the bounce process (muted/unmuted tracks, automation, and everything else currently affecting the mix) is reflected in the resultant audio file. Bouncing to disk is comparable to the traditional studio practice of mixing down multitrack recordings to a stereo master recorder (except that it's a completely digital process, of course; there is no signal degradation, as is the case when recording to an analog master tape!). If you make any selection within the timeline of your Pro Tools session, only that portion will be included in the bounced file; otherwise it includes the entire session from beginning to end. To burn an audio CD from your Pro Tools mix or save out a stereo file when collaborating with a video editor or multimedia author, you use this File > Bounce to > Disk command.

Also, if you've run out of playback voices (or your computer's performance has begun to suffer from too many tracks and plug-ins in the current session), you might bounce down a stereo submix of multiple backing tracks (with effects) so that those voices are again available for record/playback of additional tracks. (Of course, you can always retrieve the original backing tracks and revise that submix; like so many things in Pro Tools, it's a non-destructive process.)

If you have external MIDI modules being triggered by MIDI tracks in your Pro Tools session, their audio output will need to be routed into Pro Tools in order to be incorporated into your bounced mix, usually through Aux Inputs.

❄ **Note: Using Audio from Pro Tools in Other Programs**

The Bounce to > Disk command is one way to export selections of audio for use with other audio-capable programs. As noted, you might bounce out stereo files in order to create an audio CD with Mac programs such as Roxio's Jam or Toast or Apple's iTunes—or with Windows programs such as Steinberg's WaveLab, Roxio's Easy Media Creator, Sony/Sonic Foundry's CD Architect or Sound Forge, and so on. Converting regions or bounced mixes to AIFF, WAV, or MP3 files at various resolutions is also a frequent intermediate step when producing audio for interactive media (CD-ROM, Internet, interactive DVD, and so on), with programs such as Macromedia's Director, Flash, or AuthorWare; Adobe's Premiere; Microsoft's Power-Point or Visual Basic; Asymetrix's ToolBook; 3D Game Studio; and others.

The Bounce to Disk dialog box allows you to choose an audio file format, including AIF, SD2, Broadcast WAV, QuickTime audio, MP3, and others. You can also choose the number of channels, bit-depth (16, 24, and in some cases 8 bits per sample), and sample rate for the bounced file. You may be able to select between 8-, 16-, and 24-bit resolution in the bounced file, but why would you ever want to bounce to a *lesser* resolution than the original recording? One extreme example would be in order to produce 8-bit files for interactive media (multimedia CD-ROMs and such) in situations where limitations on disk space or system throughput don't permit playback of full CD-quality 16-bit, 44 kHz stereo audio. (By all means, though, try reducing the sample rate or performing some form of audio data compression before resorting to 8-bit audio if possible!) For music production, you might bounce from a 96 kHz, 24-bit session down to 44.1 kHz, 16-bit files because that's what you'll need to burn an audio CD for demo or evaluation purposes. For in-depth information about this process, see Chapter 16.

Digidesign Technology

Following are several key technical terms that are constantly referenced in Digidesign's manuals and other documentation. More than simply marketing constructs, these terms refer to important technical innovations by Digidesign and are enabling technologies for Pro Tools in general.

DAE (Digidesign Audio Engine)

An operating-system extension for real-time digital audio processing, DAE automatically operates in the background when you launch Pro Tools. It mediates access between the Pro Tools software and the audio hardware and handles the pre-loading of digital audio data from disk into the DAE Playback Buffer for smooth playback at the proper time. You may occasionally need to change the size of this playback buffer, depending on your hardware configuration and how fragmented or slow your hard disks are.

Occasionally, if something about your system is producing a performance error in Pro Tools, an alert box may appear with a numerical reference to a "DAE error." In the Support area of http://www.digidesign.com, if you type this number into the Answerbase, you will often find useful information about possible causes and solutions for your problem.

TDM (Time-Division Multiplexing)

A Digidesign term, TDM is a 256-channel signal-routing matrix implemented within the Pro Tools software environment (HD version only, not the LE version used with Digi 002 and Mbox 2/Mbox configurations or the M-Powered version used with M-Audio interfaces). TDM operates at a much higher multiple of the audio sample rate so that more than one stream of audio can be routed and processed within a single data bus. TDM requires specific Digidesign hardware configurations, all of which feature dedicated DSP (Digital Signal Processing) chips on PCI cards in the host computer and sometimes an expansion chassis for additional PCI cards in larger system configurations.

TDM is also a plug-in architecture that requires a TDM-capable hardware configuration. TDM plug-ins can often be much more robust (in other words, processing intensive) than host-based effects (the RTAS processing and routing architecture supported by Pro Tools LE and M-Powered) because they can rely on dedicated DSP chips on the Digidesign cards rather than sharing the host CPU's processing power with the operating system and Pro Tools itself. One very important advantage of TDM plug-ins is that they generally introduce much less processing delay (latency) into the signal chain than their RTAS equivalents. (HTDM was another plug-in format that allowed plug-ins to use host-based processing within the TDM environment. It is not supported in Pro Tools 7.) TDM is the plug-in and signal-routing architecture used in Digidesign's high-end Pro Tools configurations (although these also support RTAS and AudioSuite plug-in formats), including all the Pro Tools|HD systems. (Their predecessors—24|Mix, Pro Tools|24, and Pro Tools III—were also TDM systems but don't support current versions of the Pro Tools software.)

TDM II is the revamped version of Digidesign's TDM bus architecture that was introduced with the Pro Tools|HD hardware and used in the current version of the Pro Tools software, Pro Tools HD (versions 7.0 and higher). TDM II doubles the number of timeslots in previous TDM systems, which is essential for handling the higher sampling rates supported by HD hardware. Its redesigned architecture also makes much more efficient use of the available TDM resources. However, for simplicity's sake, this book will often simply refer to *TDM systems* when discussing HD systems (as well as the older 24|Mix systems, which don't support Pro Tools software higher than 6.4.1) using the TDM or HD version of the Pro Tools software.

> ❋ **Note: More About Signal Processing and Routing in Pro Tools**
>
> For more information about how Pro Tools routes audio within its virtual mixing and processing environment, see Chapter 9, which discusses TDM and RTAS plug-ins, ReWire, and other features of the totally integrated virtual studio provided by Pro Tools.

ReWire (and the DigiReWire Plug-in)

ReWire is a technology developed by Propellerhead Software (developers of the Reason program) for routing digital audio, MIDI, tempo, and transport commands between multiple programs running on the same computer. A ReWire application (such as Reason and Ableton Live, for example) is *slaved* to Pro Tools. Any sequences, loops, or drum patterns in the slaved ReWire program will start and stop under the control of the Pro Tools Transport and tempo. Likewise, you can assign the output from any Pro Tools MIDI track to one of the active MIDI-compatible modules within the slave program.

After enabling, say, Reason on a track in Pro Tools, you can then choose which of the virtual output audio channels from that program you want to appear in that particular track. Because these programs have their own mixing capabilities, the channel(s) from the slaved ReWire program that you enable for routing into Pro Tools may represent a single instrument module or a submix that sums many of these together. Bear in mind, however, that with Reason in particular, only one stereo pair can be sent from Reason to Pro Tools (its outputs 1–2); all *other* channels from Reason into Pro Tools must be activated via mono tracks. Some other applications that can work in ReWire slave mode with Pro Tools don't have this limitation. All this is enabled by the DigiReWire plug-in (shown in Figure 2.11), which must be active within your Plug-Ins folder in order for you to use ReWire.

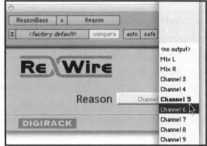

Figure 2.11 Although with Reason in particular only one stereo output pair from Reason can enter Pro Tools, many additional channels of audio from Reason can also enter Pro Tools via mono tracks (each with another instance of this plug-in). Other ReWire programs don't have this limitation.

❈ **Note: About DirectConnect (Now Discontinued)**

DirectConnect technology was developed by Digidesign for Macintosh versions of Pro Tools 5 under Mac OS9. It allowed as many as 32 separate channels of audio to be routed between separate programs in real time. Most importantly, Digidesign's own Soft SampleCell program (the software-only successor to the highly successful SampleCell card) and a handful of other third-party virtual synthesis programs were compatible with DirectConnect. It was never updated for Pro Tools versions 6 and above running under Macintosh OS X (much less version 7), and its functionality is now replaced by the more robust and industry-standard ReWire method.

Summary

We hope you've found this overview of the fundamentals useful. These ideas will become clearer as you work through practical examples in the rest of this book. We believe it's essential to have a good handle on basic concepts and to know the proper names for things in order to organize your thoughts, solve problems, and effectively use this software. *Shameless plug*: In part, we base this belief on user feedback from our series of CD-ROMs dedicated to digital audio concepts (and Pro Tools operation), *Cool School Interactus (CSi)*, published by Thomson Course Technology. The instructional titles in the *CSi Starter* and *Master* series use QuickTime-based movie tutorials to guide you through setup, terminology, and program operations—not only for Pro Tools, but also many other digital audio applications for Mac and Windows. Check 'em out!

The *Pro Tools Reference Guide* also provides a good overview of these concepts and should be thoroughly explored by all users. This is a PDF document that you can access in the Digidesign > Documentation > Pro Tools folder or directly from the Help menu within Pro Tools. As stated elsewhere, this book is *not* intended to be a substitute for the *Reference Guide*! At over 700 pages, when combined with the *Keyboard Shortcuts* (30+ pages) and *DigiRack Plug-ins Guide* (120+ pages), this is the most comprehensive and detailed reference available for Pro Tools. *Pro Tools 7 Power!* distills this wealth of information into the strategic essentials, offers real-world examples and recommendations, explores how Pro Tools interacts with other studio gear, provides practical tips for both new and experienced users, offers primers for specific applications (like postproduction, music, and interactive media), and gets you up and running as soon as possible. Appendix A of this book, "Further Study and Resources on the Web," guides you to other learning resources about Pro Tools and digital audio in general. Chapter 3, "Your System Configuration," provides guidelines for a working computer and audio hardware configuration for Pro Tools, and Chapter 4, "Creating Your First Pro Tools Session," dives right into creating a session in Pro Tools. If you're already a Pro Tools user, you may want to skip ahead to Chapters 5, "The Transport Window," 6, "The Edit Window," and 7, "The Mix Window," which, you guessed it, break down the elements in the Transport, Edit, and Mix windows. Some of it may be review, but you're guaranteed to find some useful tidbits there as well.

3 } Your System Configuration

It can be hard to separate marketing and hype from reality when dealing with computers—or pro audio in general, for that matter. And of course, just as computers evolve from year to year, Pro Tools software and hardware are constantly improved and upgraded, which in turn can increase the system requirements needed to run them. There are some fundamental ideas to keep in mind, though, plus some peculiar requirements for multichannel digital audio and hard-disk recording that are definitely worth reviewing here. You also need to understand the basic peripheral devices required to successfully interconnect Pro Tools with other devices in your studio.

Basic Components

Let's consider the basic hardware components—computer and peripheral gear—you need in order to run any version of Pro Tools.

Computer

Exact system requirements vary widely according to your Pro Tools configuration—audio interfaces, Pro Tools software version, optional hardware and software (including virtual instruments and other processing-intensive plug-ins). But even for shipping LE and M-Powered versions of Pro Tools, the CPU (central processing unit) of your computer needs to be at least a G5 or faster G4 (Macintosh) or a Pentium 4, Xeon, or AMD Athlon XP, Thunderbird or Opteron (Windows), with dual processors recommended for some applications. As you can imagine, requirements for an expanded Pro Tools|HD system are even more demanding, including specific chipsets on the motherboard, CPU models, and voltage capacities in the PCI slots, to name a few. High-powered computer configurations that are excellent for other application types (such as graphics or 3D rendering, for instance) may have serious drawbacks when used for high-resolution multitrack audio. If you're purchasing a system as a first-time Pro Tools user, you would be well advised to distrust the advice of any computer "expert" friends unless they actually use Pro Tools!

The system requirements for Pro Tools evolve over time as newer versions of the program are released and available Digidesign hardware changes. For this reason, before purchasing *any* computer for Pro Tools use, be sure to check the Compatibility section of the Support area at http://www.digidesign.com for current system requirements and detailed compatibility documents. You will also find some links there for companies that provide audio-optimized Windows systems for Pro Tools (such as Terra Digital, Sweetwater, and Guitar Center). Such a system can be an excellent investment for a serious production rig. Although the Digidesign Web site is always your best source for up-to-date information, you might also take a look at the DUC (Digidesign Users Conference) site at http://duc.digidesign.com for test results, advice, and recommendations from other Pro Tools users. Windows users in particular will want to note the ongoing "sticky" threads (which always stay at the top of the list) in the forum for Windows LE versions, where users share their experiences with different CPUs and system components.

Given the unusual demands that digital audio makes on the computer, only very specific operating system versions are supported or recommended for a given release of Pro Tools software. Don't upgrade your operating system until you've confirmed that it works properly with the version of Pro Tools you're using. Here are some general guidelines about Windows/ Macintosh operating systems and Pro Tools:

* **Windows.** Windows XP with Service Pack 2 is the minimum requirement for Pro Tools 7.
* **Macintosh.** Mac OS X version 10.4 (a.k.a. "Tiger") or higher is required for Macintosh versions 7 (or higher) of Pro Tools.

> **Note: OS Requirements for Previous Versions of Pro Tools**
>
> Macintosh: OS X was required for all Pro Tools 6.xx versions (Mac OS 10 or higher, with some version of 10.3.x usually preferred, depending on your software/hardware combination). Pro Tools Free 5.01 and some legacy Pro Tools software/hardware may work on older computer platforms, especially on the faster models among the pre-G3 PowerMac series. Mac OS 8.6 is the minimum for some 5.xx versions of Pro Tools, with Mac OS9 *highly* recommended. All legacy Pro Tools software versions 5.31 and lower are for Mac OS9 *only*; they are not supported under Mac OS X, even in Classic mode!
>
> Windows: Windows XP with Service Pack 1 is required for 6.xx versions of Pro Tools. Note, however, that legacy Pro Tools software versions 5.3 and lower do *not* support Windows XP, and Pro Tools Free 5.01 works with Windows 98 SE or ME *only*.

As with most other software, you may find both minimum and recommended amounts of memory (RAM) listed among the system requirements on Digidesign's Web site. Count on needing the recommended amount in order to truly work comfortably.

By the way, you will want to run a lean machine because, as you can probably imagine, multitrack digital audio is fairly taxing on the computer's resources. Don't clutter up your operating system with a lot of background processes that may interfere (for example, screen savers, file and printer sharing, disk indexers, MP3 and Internet time servers, Norton's File Saver, and so on).

> ❄ **Caution: If It Ain't Broke...**
>
> Users of processing-intensive, real-time applications like Pro Tools should never automatically download operating system updates before confirming that the updates are compatible with their current software version. Admittedly, Digidesign is very cautious and can be somewhat slow to "bless" a given OS update. After seeing a couple dozen users report no problems on the Digidesign User Conference, you may decide to assume a certain amount of risk, installing a minor but not-yet-qualified update. But when the update is a full decimal number on the Mac OS or a Service Pack update on Windows, make *sure* you have an exit strategy thought out (including a full system backup) before potentially debilitating your production system with an incompatible update.

Monitor(s)

For all versions of Pro Tools, the monitor needs to be set at 1024×768 resolution or higher, so even though a 15-inch monitor is definitely workable, you will be much more comfortable with 17-inch or larger model. Most high-end Pro Tools users prefer to use *two* large monitors—for example, leaving the Pro Tools Mix window on one and the Edit window on the other. Guitar and bass players using Pro Tools in their project studios should opt for an LCD flat-panel display because traditional CRT monitors create buzzing through their magnetic instrument pickups unless the instrument is moved a meter or two away from the monitor while recording—not terribly convenient if you're the sole operator! Most users also find that LCD monitors cause less eyestrain. They also produce less heat, which is always a concern in small project studios.

Hard Drive(s)

You need a very large, fast hard drive for recording and playing back multiple tracks of digital audio. We suggest several dozen gigabytes at the very least, especially because larger hard drives routinely also offer better performance. As a general rule, count on using a 7,200 rpm or faster hard drive for recording audio. If you are an HD user recording at higher sample rates, 10,000 rpm drives are definitely worth a look. As with the basic computer model itself, sustained throughput and other performance requirements for drives used on digital audio workstations such as Pro Tools are different from non–real-time applications such as graphics-processing and network servers. For high performance, it is worthwhile to investigate disk drive offerings from companies who specialize in products for audio recording, such as Glyph and Avid, for example. Be sure to consult with your Digidesign dealer or experienced Pro Tools users before making any sizable investment in disks for audio recording. USB hard drives do *not* offer adequate performance for recording audio with any version of Pro Tools!

Some large Pro Tools configurations have traditionally used multiple drives on a SCSI connection (which requires an add-in SCSI card in virtually all current computer models). For example, expanded Pro Tools|HD (or 24|Mix) configurations may use SCSI drives attached to one of the ATTO SCSI accelerator cards that Digidesign supports for audio or Digidesign-certified FireWire drives. Most current Mac and Windows models generally don't incorporate any factory SCSI drives at all, instead using an internal ATA drive where the operating system is loaded. You can add SCSI drives internally and/or connect external drives. Although these systems can also use FireWire drives, in order to obtain maximum track counts on some configurations, a SCSI card and disks may still be desirable—especially if this helps lighten the load on the CPU itself.

FireWire drives have also recently become popular and can be very cost effective for Mac users especially, because recent models include built-in FireWire (IEEE 1394) ports. The drive mechanism *must* be based on the Oxford 911 chipset to work properly with Pro Tools, however. All current LE and M-Powered systems can achieve their maximum track counts using only multiple FireWire drives—SCSI disk subsystems are not obligatory.

SATA drives are also an excellent option for Windows users, offering very high performance to support large track counts of high-resolution audio. One example is the Raptor 10,000 rpm drive by Western Digital, which, when combined with the Intel ICH-5 controller chipset on the computer's motherboard, can deliver levels of performance comparable to UltraSCSI disks.

Users of Mbox 2, Mbox, and even Digi 002/002R systems (as well as the now-discontinued Digi 001 or ToolBox configurations) can sometimes rely on the high-capacity, high-speed internal ATA hard disks in more powerful current computers. However, it is always preferable to dedicate a separate hard drive for audio data even on these systems (although it is obligatory for HD systems, for example). If this isn't possible, you should at least format your large internal drive into two or more partitions, dedicating the larger one exclusively to Pro Tools session documents and audio files and reserving the other for the operating system and programs. Along with the performance benefits, using separate drives or partitions makes maintenance and disk reorganization much easier and allows disk optimization of the audio volume(s) while still booted off the system volume. If you're working at 44.1 kHz sampling rates and audio-track counts typically don't exceed a dozen or so, you may find that this setup provides acceptable performance for your Pro Tools LE or M-Powered system.

Figure 3.1 shows the Workspace window in Pro Tools, where you can view all the hard disks on your system, their capacity, and available free space. You can also specify which are eligible for audio recording and search for audio files by name anywhere on the system. Once you locate the audio or MIDI files you want on your system's hard disk, you can drag them from the Workspace browser into the Edit window's Region List or track display area. To help you see just how much space you'll need on your hard drive, Table 3.1 shows the effects of sample rate and bit-depth on audio file size.

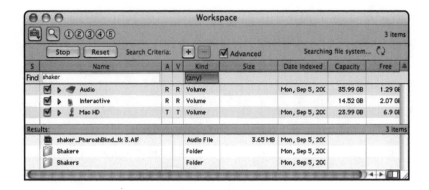

Figure 3.1 The Workspace window in Pro Tools provides an overview of hard disks, available capacity, and which of them can be used for recording or playback (transfer) only. You can also search for files here and drag them into the tracks or Region List of your current session.

Table 3.1 Big and Bigger: The Effects of Sample Rate and Bit-Depth on Audio File Size

Sample Rate	Bit-Depth	1 minute (mono)	1 minute (stereo)
44.1 kHz	16 bits/sample	5 MB	10 MB
44.1 kHz	24 bits/sample	7.9 MB	15.8 MB
48 kHz	16 bits/sample	5.7 MB	11.4 MB
48 kHz	24 bits/sample	8.6 MB	17.2 MB
96 kHz	24 bits/sample	17.2 MB	24.4 MB
192 kHz	24 bits/sample	34.4 MB	68.8 MB

Peripheral Equipment

Pro Tools expansion options and additional peripherals are covered in more detail in Chapter 17, "Pro Tools Power: The Next Step." Here, we take a look at some of the basic equipment that will complement your Pro Tools configuration in a studio setting.

MIDI Interface

If you will use external MIDI controllers or modules with Pro Tools (for example, to record performances into MIDI tracks, to play back MIDI data being sent from Pro Tools, or to connect certain external control surfaces to Pro Tools), some sort of MIDI interface is required. MIDI is a serial communications protocol that uses 5-pin DIN connectors. Your computer's MIDI interface acts as an adapter to convert the MIDI protocol to a format usable within the software environment. Various MIDI interfaces can be purchased, depending on your requirements and the connection methods your computer supports for this optional piece of gear. One example is shown in Figure 3.2.

Figure 3.2 A multiport MIDI interface. (Shown: the MOTU MIDI Express XT, which connects to the computer via USB.)

Mbox 2 and Digi 002/002 Rack systems, like several Pro Tools-compatible audio interfaces from M-Audio (and the older Digi 001 interface), have MIDI In and MIDI Out connectors built into the external interface that can be used in Pro Tools, as does the external USB control surface from Digidesign, Command|8. Otherwise, your options include the following:

* **Windows.** The cheapest MIDI interface option is to use a standard PC soundcard, most of which have a small, built-in port for MIDI. Usually, you must separately purchase a small Y adapter cable, which splits out from a 15-pin D-shaped connector on the card into two 5-pin DIN connectors for MIDI In/Out. However, for more serious applications, you will want a more professional, dedicated MIDI interface. For multiple MIDI ports or SMPTE synchronization, an external MIDI interface is generally required—either a card installed in the computer's PCI slot, a parallel port device, or most commonly among current models, an external device connected to the computer's USB port.

* **Macintosh.** External MIDI interfaces are attached to the USB port.

It's easy to upgrade your MIDI interface as requirements change. The Mac version of Pro Tools interacts with the configuration defined in the Audio MIDI Setup Utility of Mac OS X, a sort of middle software layer that negotiates between programs like Pro Tools and the MIDI interface, along with any external MIDI devices that are connected to it. After changing to another model of MIDI interface and setting it up in this system utility (found in the Utilities subfolder of the Applications folder on your system volume), the new port configuration will appear the next time you access the MIDI output assignments from MIDI tracks within Pro Tools. Again, Digi 002/002 Rack systems and the Mbox 2 feature MIDI In/Out connectors built into the external interface, as do many of the M-Audio interfaces and the Command|8 control surface (as well as the now discontinued Digi 001 interface). If that's sufficient for your needs, no separate MIDI interface may be required for your system.

In Windows, the MIDI Studio Setup window (discussed in Chapter 10, "MIDI," and shown in Figure 10.4 in that chapter) provides very similar functionality. After configuring an external MIDI instrument on the appropriate port of your MIDI interface, its enabled send/receive channels for MIDI and patch name documents (if available) are available for selection from MIDI tracks within Pro Tools.

Digidesign offers its own high-end MIDI interface, the MIDI I/O, which connects to Windows or Macintosh computers via USB. Along with 10 MIDI inputs and 10 MIDI outputs, it also supports MIDI timestamping features in Pro Tools, which use a data buffer within the interface itself to maintain proper timing even when very dense streams of MIDI data from multiple tracks are being sent out through the interface. Chapter 10 includes a section about the MIDI I/O that provides more details and a look at the front and back panels of this unit.

> ✵ **Tip: Direct USB Connections for MIDI Controllers**
>
> Some manufacturers offer controller keyboards (and sound modules) that connect directly to the computer via its USB port. These range from very simple models to full-featured controllers. Particularly if you are relying exclusively on software-based instruments for Pro Tools as the sound source for your MIDI tracks—via ReWire, RTAS, or TDM plug-ins—you may not require a MIDI interface at all.

SMPTE Interface

SMPTE time code is used in the video and film industry to synchronize audio devices to a master video deck and also for synchronizing MIDI and audio software to multitrack audio-tape machines. A series of numbers representing hours, minutes, seconds, frames, and subframes is encoded either into an audio signal (Linear Time Code, or LTC) or within the upper lines of the video frame (Vertical Interval Time Code, or VITC). A SMPTE interface for digital audio workstations translates these encoded signals into MIDI Time Code (MTC), which carries the same information encoded in the MIDI protocol. With SMPTE synchronization, when the Pro Tools transport is in Online mode, it will know what time location is currently playing on the video and correctly play the part of that session's timeline that corresponds to that SMPTE location.

In many cases, multiport MIDI interfaces from manufacturers such as Mark of the Unicorn, M-Audio, and others additionally incorporate audio inputs/outputs for synchronizing to time code in LTC format. Because LTC is a way of encoding SMPTE time code as an audio signal, this is also the most common method for synchronizing Pro Tools with multitrack tape decks (both analog and digital). There are also synchronization peripherals for VITC (time code embedded into each frame of a video signal). More sophisticated units, such as the Sync I/O by Digidesign (shown in Figure 3.3) or Mark of the Unicorn's Digital Timepiece, also allow the internal sample clock of your Digidesign audio hardware to be *resolved* or *slaved* to incoming time code or video sync, so things stay perfectly locked together over long periods of time. For more information, see Chapter 11, "Synchronization."

Figure 3.3 Sync I/O, an SMPTE synchronizer from Digidesign. (Photo courtesy of Digidesign.)

MIDI Instruments/Controllers

Your keyboards, drum modules, MIDI modules, MIDI effects, and other MIDI controllers (guitar, wind, or percussion, for example) usually feature MIDI In/Out/Thru connectors. Multiple MIDI devices can be daisy-chained on a single MIDI output if your MIDI interface only features one In/Out (like the Mbox 2, the discontinued Digi 001 interface, and many of M-Audio's audio interfaces for Pro Tools M-Powered). However, routing tracks from Pro Tools out to several *multitimbral* modules (which are able to respond with different sounds to incoming events on multiple MIDI channels) could be a little tricky in this setup because you've only got 16 MIDI channels to work with, and each module may be listening to all of them. With a larger number of independently addressable MIDI Out ports (such as on Digi 002 interfaces or the Command|8 control surface, which have one input and two outputs for MIDI), you could connect each external module to a separate port, for 32 outgoing MIDI channels with two ports, 96 channels if your MIDI interface has six MIDI Out ports, and so on. Digidesign's own MIDI I/O features 10 MIDI inputs and outputs, for a potential total of 160 MIDI channels.

The important thing to remember is that MIDI events going between Pro Tools and your MIDI devices are *data*, and the MIDI interface connections described here have nothing to do with how all the *audio* outputs of your MIDI modules get back into the Pro Tools mix (so that these sound sources can be bounced to disk together with your audio tracks and software instruments). If you have enough available inputs on your external audio interface, audio from MIDI modules can enter the Pro Tools mix via various Auxiliary Input tracks (or Instrument tracks, which, without instrument plug-ins instantiated on them, behave like Aux Ins). The input source for those tracks would be set to monitor the physical outputs where those devices are attached to your audio interface. Otherwise (particularly if you're using an original Mbox, which provides only two audio inputs) you might use a good small mixing board, pre-mixing all your MIDI modules to stereo before entering the Pro Tools mix via a single stereo Auxiliary Input that is monitoring the stereo inputs on the audio interface where the mixer's outputs are connected. Figure 3.4 shows a typical MIDI configuration for a project studio.

✱ Note: Software Instruments

Software-based *virtual* synthesizers and samplers represent another increasingly popular class of MIDI instrument. Their virtual audio outputs are routed into audio/MIDI programs on the same computer running Pro Tools. Benefits over external physical sound sources for MIDI parts include elimination of noise (because there are no analog connections in the signal path) and the fact that you can use many MIDI sound sources—with superior user interfaces—without stacking up a lot of bulky modules in your studio! If you're just starting to build up your Pro Tools/MIDI studio (and if your computer has sufficient processing power to handle running additional software instrument plug-ins or programs simultaneously with Pro Tools), this is a great way to go. It's much simpler, offers total recall and greater control, and takes up less space!

In Chapter 10, the section titled "Virtual Instruments" provides more information, but among the industry-standard software architectures that emerged in recent years, here are the methods Pro Tools currently supports for using virtual (software-based) instruments:

✱ Many virtual instruments are available in RTAS format (which can be used in Pro Tools LE, M-Powered, and HD versions). Examples include IK Multimedia's SampleTank; Ultimate Sound Bank's UltraFocus and Charlie; MOTU's MX4 (Mac only); Applied Acoustics' Lounge Lizard EP-2; fxpansion's BFD; Ultimate Sound Bank's Charlie; Spectrasonics' Atmosphere; and Native Instruments' B4, Elektrik Piano, Battery, Absynth, Pro-53, and FM7.

❋ Virtual instruments in TDM format (which is not supported on LE or M-Powered systems) include McDSP's Synthesizer One (also available as RTAS), Access Music's Virus Indigo, and Duy's Synth-Spider.

❋ HDTM was another plug-in format that supported virtual instruments on Pro Tools TDM systems using versions 6.xx of the software. It is no longer supported under Pro Tools 7. In most cases, when you open an existing session containing instances of HTDM plug-ins, these will automatically convert to RTAS format.

❋ ReWire is a software architecture that allows audio from other audio programs and virtual instruments to appear in the Pro Tools mix; examples include Propellerhead's Reason, Tascam's Gigastudio3, and Ableton's Live. Various output channels of virtual audio signals from these separate programs can then be routed into the Pro Tools mix via DigiReWire, an RTAS plug-in.

Basic Audio/MIDI Configuration

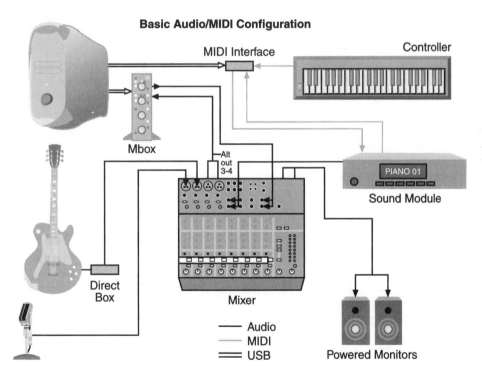

Figure 3.4 The MIDI interface handles transmission of MIDI data between Pro Tools, an external MIDI controller, and an external MIDI module. In order for the audio from your MIDI instruments to be incorporated when you bounce out a mix file from Pro Tools, they are typically routed into the inputs of your Pro Tools audio hardware and monitored via an Auxiliary Input in Pro Tools.

DVD-Recording Drive

A CD- or DVD-recording drive is not officially a system requirement for Pro Tools—but trust us, you need one! First, you're working with audio—so no matter what your area of expertise, you will occasionally need to burn audio CDs from the mixes you bounce out of Pro Tools, right? And if you're creating audio files for interactive media, you will want to throw all those AIF, MP3, or WAV files onto a CD-ROM or DVD-ROM for delivery to developers. And if you're in video production, it can sometimes be simpler and more economical to burn CDs when delivering your OMF or AIF files to Avid, FinalCut Pro, or Media 100 video editors (assuming that you don't share a network server for media files) rather than using some other removable media.

More importantly, however, when your Pro Tools session folders (including the Audio Files folders within them) run into hundreds of megabytes, how are you going to back them up for data security or archive them off the system when projects are completed? CD recorders and media have become very inexpensive, and this may be sufficient for many home studio users. However, the 700MB capacity of a CD isn't so impressive in relation to the typical size of audio projects, and it can be very confusing to split a large project onto multiple CD-R (CD-recordable) discs in order to get it archived off your system. Mind you, this is only getting worse, as most users now record at 24-bit resolution, let alone 96 kHz and 192 kHz sampling rates on some systems! The availability of affordable DVD recorders for computer data has been a real boon for digital audio/video users. Several gigabytes fit onto a single recordable DVD, allowing entire projects to be backed up in a single operation. And the easier it is, the more often you'll do it. Rewritable DVDs are excellent for daily backups, although you might use ordinary write-once DVDs for long-term archival once the project is completed and re-moved from your system. In short, in our opinion all Pro Tools users need a DVD-recording drive on their computer (which can also burn data CD-ROMs and audio CDs, of course). *Whatever your method, you need to back up your data often!*

Audio Mixer or Mic Preamp

Isn't the idea of Pro Tools to be a complete studio in a box? Well, sort of...especially with systems like Digi 002 and many of the M-Audio hardware options for Pro Tools M-Powered, which combine multiple audio inputs/outputs, MIDI In/Out, and microphone preamps into a single audio interface. Digidesign's Mbox 2 (a compact USB audio interface) also incorporates MIDI In/Out and two mic preamps with 48-volt phantom power for studio condenser microphones and supports Hi-Z (high-impedance) input from musical-instrument pickups (which can produce impressive results with a guitar amplifier simulation plug-in like AmpliTube). Typically, though, high-end Pro Tools audio interfaces for TDM systems feature only line-level audio inputs (plus at least one digital audio input, naturally), which means that microphone levels have to be stepped up to this level in order to record their signal. A good mixer with multiple high-quality microphone preamps can be excellent for this purpose and very cost effective. You might even use the mixer's insert points to patch in a compressor on a microphone source prior to recording it at the Pro Tools input, if you happen to really like the coloration that device adds to your sound or have concerns about unexpected peaks in a live situation. The audio mixer can also be handy for other purposes, such as monitoring different sources in your studio (for example, a CD player, DAT, or turntables) or as a pre-mixer for multiple MIDI devices on their way into Pro Tools. Lastly, for certain users it can be more expedient to use the mixer itself to combine all the audio outputs from Pro Tools tracks, external effects such as reverb, and multiple MIDI modules in the studio when mixing in real time to DAT (especially if the audio interface on their Pro Tools system doesn't offer a sufficient number of simultaneous inputs for all the external devices).

Other users opt for one of the extremely high-end microphone preamps available on the market. This can be a very effective choice for project studios, for example. Because single users don't typically require a large number of simultaneous mic inputs (unless a drums set needs to be recorded, for example), a single high-quality microphone preamp can deliver pristine sound on all the microphone sources they record. Other users simply prefer the convenience of having everything rackmounted; there are several eight-channel mic preamps on the market that are very good quality and cost effective. Many even offer digital outputs so that after the mic preamp stage itself, there aren't any additional analog stages in the signal path before entering Pro Tools. These multiple-channel, rackmountable microphone preamps are also very popular for Pro Tools users who do location recording because taking a computer and a single small rack onto location represents the entire recording system. All you have to do is set up the microphones and you're ready to go. Even Digidesign has jumped into the fray, offering their own high-end, eight-channel rackmounted mic preamp. The Digidesign PRE (shown in Figure 3.5) offers the notable advantage of being completely configurable (via MIDI) from inside the Pro Tools (TDM) software, which means that its previous settings will be recalled the next time you open a session.

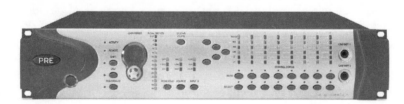

Figure 3.5   PRE, Digidesign's eight-channel microphone preamp. (Photo courtesy of Digidesign.)

Speakers, Amplification

You need to hear the audio you're editing! If you're just setting up your project studio, you should look at some of the small, powered studio monitors that are available. These can be directly connected to the audio outputs you're using for your main stereo mix (on your computer, card, or external audio interface). Here's a special note for you multimedia and video folks: Granted, the cheap speakers that came with your computer are a bonus if you need to start working *today*. But don't kid yourself; all kinds of audio garbage, especially background noise, hiss, and hum, are going to sneak right by you into your final mixes—until you acquire a decent set of speakers and turn 'em up loud! If you have to place the speakers near a CRT computer monitor, make sure the speakers you buy are magnetically shielded so that the magnetic field they produce doesn't interfere with your monitor, distorting the colors of the display or creating interference patterns. A good set of headphones can also be very useful to check the stereo localization (panning) and reverb and to help you be picky about minor edit noises, clicks, and pops that may not be obvious when listening in a room (especially if you have other noisy gear—or human beings—in your studio).

❄ **Caution: Turn Down Your Speakers Before Rebooting**

If you have your Macintosh built-in audio outputs connected to your main speakers at nice, loud monitoring levels, don't forget to turn down the audio output before you shut down or restart the system—that Macintosh startup sound is loud as heck! This also applies to Windows users who have connected their computer's main audio output to studio monitors. Pops from system startup or launching/closing of Pro Tools and other programs can be annoying and even potentially damaging to your speakers.

Pro Tools Hardware Configurations

This section reviews the configurations of Pro Tools that are currently available. (Note that Chapter 17 breaks down hardware configurations and expansions in more detail.) The variety of possible Pro Tools setups means there is a configuration that's right for just about every purpose and budget.

Mbox 2 (Pro Tools LE and External USB Audio/MIDI Interface)

This version consists of Pro Tools LE software, and an external USB audio/MIDI interface with two simultaneous channels of analog I/O, plus two more channels of digital input (S/PDIF connectors) that can be used simultaneously for 4×2 operation (since the S/PDIF output always mirrors analog outputs 1–2). Unlike its Mbox predecessor (which is also compatible with Pro Tools 7 and is described later in this chapter), the Mbox 2 incorporates one MIDI input and output. The 24-bit analog/digital converters on this USB-powered external interface (which are also capable of 16-bit operation) were also improved over the original Mbox (106 dB signal-to-noise ratio versus 102 dB, THD+N significantly reduced to 0.0008% versus 0.003% previously). Its analog inputs incorporate microphone preamps designed by Digidesign with 48-volt phantom power that is enabled/disabled for both channels simultaneously via a button on the front of the unit. Except for the 1/4-inch headphone output, all audio connections are on the rear panel. Separate XLR, TRS (1/4-inch phone, tip-ring-sleeve) balanced, and TS (tip-sleeve) instrument-level (Hi-Z, high impedance, for direct connection from electric guitar or bass) jacks are provided for each of the two analog input channels, reducing the need for recabling when switching sources. On the front panel, buttons for each input channel toggle between these Mic, Line, and Direct inputs. The main studio monitor outputs on the rear panel are also balanced 1/4-inch TRS, and S/PDIF digital in/out (for channels 3–4) is provided via coaxial RCA connectors. Front panel gain knobs are provided for the headphone output and main monitor output. Like its Mbox predecessor, the Mix knob on the Mbox 2 adjusts the relative levels between the interface's input and playback within Pro Tools (to ameliorate monitoring latency during recording). Input gain indicators are provided for each analog input channel, as well as a mono switch, −20 dB pad switches, and single-LED peak indicators. Like the Mbox before it, the unit is exclusively powered by the USB connection itself (no AC power required).

Pro Tools LE software supports 32 tracks (expandable to 48 mono/stereo tracks via the optional Music Production Toolkit) of simultaneous audio playback and syncing to SMPTE time code when the Transport's Online button is enabled. In addition to offline AudioSuite processing, Pro Tools LE supports the RTAS (Real-Time AudioSuite) plug-in architecture, which uses the computer's processing power for audio effects and software instruments. Mbox 2 users can work at 16- or 24-bit resolution and at 44.1 or 48 kHz sample rates. (Bandwidth limitations of the USB connection itself—version 1.1, in the case of the Mbox 2—preclude 96 kHz and other higher sample rates that are available in some AC-powered or FireWire-based interfaces.)

Currently the most basic hardware configuration for the Pro Tools LE software, the Mbox 2 (shown in Figure 3.6) is an excellent choice for location recording with your computer (even an appropriately configured laptop) and is also ideal for the home or project studio. If you generally are recording only one or two channels at a time (as in a home studio), being limited to two analog channels plus two more digital channels (where you might connect another microphone or guitar preamp with digital outputs, for example) is not a handicap at all. The availability of digital I/O on the Mbox interface allows you to transfer DAT recordings into Pro Tools for subsequent editing and mastering or to upgrade to a high-end microphone preamp with digital output as your front-end for recording via the S/PDIF digital input. Being able to use the LE version of Pro Tools, with SMPTE synchronization, Beat Detective LE, and support for the DV Toolkit option, makes the Mbox 2 an excellent choice for any appropriate computer offering a USB port—not only for project recording, but also for video production, broadcast, multimedia, spoken word, location recording, and many other applications.

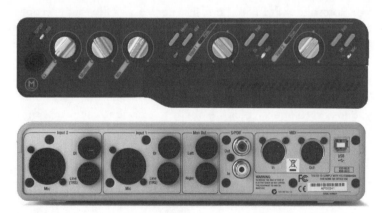

Figure 3.6 Pro Tools Mbox 2 configurations use the Pro Tools LE software plus the Mbox 2 external USB audio/MIDI interface. (Photos courtesy of Digidesign.)

Digi 002 and Digi 002 Rack (Pro Tools LE and External Audio Interface/Control Surface)

The Pro Tools Digi 002 configuration consists of the Pro Tools LE software and an external audio interface/control surface connected to the host computer via its FireWire (IEE 1394) port. It is compatible with Pro Tools version 7. The Digi 002 hardware (shown in Figure 3.7) features eight analog inputs and outputs, ADAT Lightpipe digital I/O (up to eight more channels of audio and is also configurable as stereo optical S/PDIF), plus stereo coaxial S/PDIF digital I/O with RCA connectors. (Be sure to always use proper 75-ohm coaxial cable with all S/PDIF digital connections, especially at cable lengths over three feet.) XLR connectors and microphone preamps with individual gain controls, 75 Hz hi-pass filters, and 48-volt phantom power (switchable by channel pairs) are provided for the first four input channels, as well as balanced TRS connectors for line/instrument level inputs; front-panel switches for these channels allow you to select between the inputs. The TRS inputs for channels 5–8 can be switched (by pairs) between −10 dBV and +4 dBu level. The Digi 002 offers one MIDI input and two MIDI outputs (for 16 MIDI channels in, 32 channels out). There is a front-panel headphone jack, a dedicated monitor output with TRS connectors, and dedicated volume control (which mirrors outputs 1–2 and is switchable to mono), plus a fixed-level output (with RCA connectors at −10 dBV level). The Digi 002 interface also has a −10dBV dedicated Alternate Source input, which can be routed to inputs 7–8 or directly through to the monitor output. This is typically used to monitor playback from CDs, computer audio output, video decks, DATs, and other audio devices in the studio.

The Digi 002 external audio interface is also a dedicated *control surface* for Pro Tools. It includes eight channel strips with motorized 100 mm faders and Solo/Mute buttons; eight soft rotary encoders (for controlling panning, sends, and plug-in parameters, among other things); LED-based scribble strips, which can selectively display various track and plug-in parameters; Transport controls for Pro Tools; and trim controls for the four microphone preamps. There are also a number of other dedicated buttons for Pro Tools functions (for instance, for the Mix, Edit, and current Plug-In windows; F-keys; and a button for activating QuickPunch mode).

One of the most innovative features of the Digi 002 is that you can also use it without any computer (or Pro Tools) at all, as a standalone 8×4×2 digital mixer, complete with EQ, dynamics, delay, and reverb effects, plus the ability to store and recall mix snapshots from its built-in memory.

As mentioned previously, the LE version of Pro Tools (also included with Mbox 2) supports SMPTE time code, Online mode in the Transport, and up to 32 audio tracks. The plug-in architecture is RTAS, which uses the power of the computer's CPU to perform signal processing; process-based AudioSuite effects are also available. The Digi 002 supports 16-bit or 24-bit recording at sample rates up to 96 kHz. (Eight-channel ADAT Lightpipe I/O is limited to 48 kHz sample rate. If this Toslink connector is used as stereo optical S/PDIF instead, sample rates up to 96 KHz are supported over that connection.)

Figure 3.7 Pro Tools Digi 002 consists of the Pro Tools LE software, plus an external, multichannel audio interface connected to the host computer via FireWire. The Digi 002 interface itself is a control surface for Pro Tools LE and can also be used as a standalone digital mixer. (Photo courtesy of Digidesign.)

❊ **Note: More Faders for the Digi 002**

When used in conjunction with the Digi 002, the eight faders on Digidesign's Command|8 control surface can act as an expansion to the Digi 002 itself, as faders 9–16.

The Digi 002 Rack (shown in Figure 3.8) offers the same features as the Digi 002, except without the control surface and in a two-unit high rackmountable chassis. It can be an ideal choice for mobile recording racks and for those who generally create mix automation graphically or by moving onscreen controls in Pro Tools with the mouse. If desired, the Command|8 control surface can also be added to this configuration.

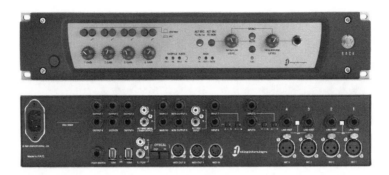

Figure 3.8 Pro Tools Digi 002 Rack consists of the Pro Tools LE software, plus an external, multichannel, rack-mountable audio interface connected to the host computer via FireWire. (Photos courtesy of Digidesign.)

M-Powered (Pro Tools M-Powered and an M-Audio Interface)

Various audio hardware options from M-Audio (which became a subsidiary of Avid, Inc., Digidesign's parent company, in 2004) can be used with the M-Powered version of the Pro Tools software, which is purchased separately. Like the Mbox, the supported M-Audio hardware is compatible with Pro Tools version 7. You can also use M-Audio hardware with many other audio-MIDI programs, via the ASIO2 or DirectX protocols, for example.

The capabilities of the Pro Tools M-Powered software are nearly identical to the LE version, with the following exceptions:

* An iLok copy protection device (USB dongle) provided with the Pro Tools M-Powered software is required to run the program.

* Various third-party programs and plug-ins are bundled with Pro Tools LE systems but not with Pro Tools M-Powered. However, some M-Audio interfaces include bundled software of their own. In either case, the manufacturers vary the exact contents of these bundles from time to time.

* While the Digidesign Dither plug-in *is* included with M-Powered, Pow-R Dither is only available in the LE version.

* Pro Tools M-Powered doesn't support the Control|24 control surface from Digidesign.

* Pro Tools M-Powered doesn't support DigiTranslator (an optional utility for transferring projects between Pro Tools, Final Cut Pro, and other video editing systems via the OMF or AAF file format discussed further in Chapter 14, "Postproduction and Soundtracks").

* The optional DV Toolkit software is not compatible with M-Powered. (This software bundle includes DigiTranslator and DINR LE noise reduction; it also allows Pro Tools LE users to work with SMPTE time code or Feet+Frames in the Edit window timeline and supports pull-up or pull-down sample rates for film-video conversions.)

In this book, therefore, unless specified otherwise, comments about Pro Tools LE will also apply to the M-Powered version.

For detailed specifications on M-Audio's hardware offerings, go to M-Audio's Web site at http://www.m-audio.com (you can also reach this site via the M-Powered page on Digidesign's own Web site). There you will find more information about signal-to-noise ratios, frequency response, software drivers, and so on. What follows are functional descriptions, to help you sort out the general characteristics of the M-Audio hardware that is currently compatible with Pro Tools M-Powered.

FireWire-Based Systems

The following M-Audio hardware systems are all external audio interfaces, connected to the host computer via its FireWire (IEE 1394) port. They are all capable of either 24- or 16-bit resolution for digital audio. While FireWire has been standard on Macintosh computers for a number of years, some Windows computers may require an optional FireWire card. Also, Macintosh OS X or Windows XP with Service Pack 2 is the minimum requirement for using *any* of M-Audio's FireWire-based audio interfaces with Pro Tools M-Powered.

FireWire Solo

The FireWire Solo (shown in Figure 3.9) features two inputs with gain controls on the front panel: one dedicated to microphone sources (and providing 48-volt phantom power) and the other to guitar or bass (also known as Hi-Z, high-impedance) sources. There is also a headphone output on the front panel. The rear panel offers two additional channels of analog input with TS (1/4-inch phone, tip-sleeve, unbalanced) connectors, analog output with TRS (1/4-inch phone, tip-ring-sleeve, balanced) connectors, as well as stereo coaxial S/PDIF digital I/O with RCA connectors. A switch on the front panel of the unit allows you to select between front (mic/instrument) and rear (line-level) inputs. If you simultaneously use both analog and S/PDIF digital I/O, you can use up to four input channels and four output channels on the FireWire Solo at the same time. The FireWire Solo supports 24-bit audio at sample rates up to 96 kHz.

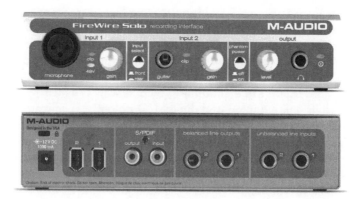

Figure 3.9   M-Audio's FireWire Solo interface is compatible with the M-Powered version of Pro Tools, as well as with other audio/MIDI programs. (Photo courtesy of M-Audio.)

FireWire Audiophile

The FireWire Audiophile (shown in Figure 3.10) has RCA connectors on the rear of the interface, for two channels of analog input, four analog outputs, and stereo coaxial S/PDIF digital I/O. This 4×6 configuration supports 24-bit audio at sample rates up to 96 kHz. Aux sends on all channels and aux output assignments allow for dedicated headphone mixes and sends to external effects (controlled through the provided software utility). The FireWire Audiophile also provides one MIDI input and output on the rear panel. There is no microphone preamp.

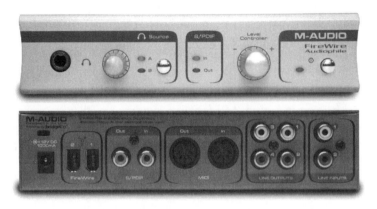

Figure 3.10   M-Audio's FireWire Audiophile interface features RCA connectors for two analog inputs and four analog outputs, plus S/PDIF digital I/O. (Photo courtesy of M-Audio.)

FireWire 410

The FireWire 410 (shown in Figure 3.11) features two front-panel inputs for channels 1–2 with Neutrik combo connectors that are switchable between instrument and microphone levels (with 48-volt phantom power). Alternatively, line inputs (with TRS connectors) on the rear panel can be used for channels 1–2. Inputs and outputs for MIDI and stereo S/PDIF digital I/O are also available on the rear panel via either RCA coaxial or Toslink optical connectors. Additionally, there are eight analog outputs with 1/4-inch TS (tip-sleeve, unbalanced) connectors. If its entire analog and digital I/O potential is utilized, this unit provides 4×10 operation—hence the name. Two headphone outputs with level controls can be switched between different sources within the unit itself. The FireWire 410 also features a MIDI Thru switch so that standalone operation is possible without turning on the host computer or recabling. It supports 24-bit audio with a maximum 96 kHz sample rate for recording and 192 kHz for playback (on outputs 1–2 only), although 192 kHz with this interface is not supported by the M-Powered software.

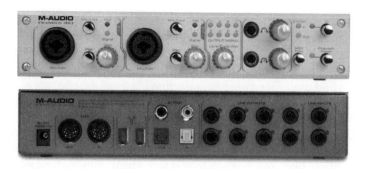

Figure 3.11   M-Audio's FireWire 410 interface features two analog inputs (mic, instrument or line) and eight analog outputs, plus S/PDIF digital I/O. (Photo courtesy of M-Audio.)

FireWire 1814

Like the FireWire 410, the FireWire 1814 (shown in Figure 3.12) features two front-panel inputs with Neutrik combo connectors that are switchable between line and microphone levels (with 48-volt phantom power). On the rear panel are six additional analog outputs (1/4-inch unbalanced TS), four analog outputs (1/4-inch balanced TRS), and ADAT Lightpipe I/O (eight channels of digital audio on each optical Toslink connector, which can alternatively be used for optical S/PDIF digital connections). A breakout cable provides inputs and outputs for stereo coaxial S/PDIF digital signals via RCA connectors, MIDI, and word clock. If its entire analog and digital I/O potential is utilized, this unit provides 18×14 operation. While all inputs are capable of recording at 24-bit resolution and sample rates up to 96 kHz, only inputs 1–2 can record at 192 kHz. All outputs on the 1814 can play back audio at up to 192 kHz with Logic and some other programs, but this highest sample rate is not supported when using this interface with the Pro Tools M-Powered software. On the Lightpipe connectors, S/MUX mode is also supported, for higher sample rates. Using the control panel software provided with the unit, the source for the FireWire 1814's two headphone outputs can be switched between analog outputs 1–2, 3–4, or any of the unit's internal aux output busses.

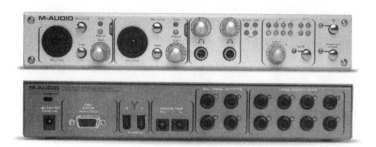

Figure 3.12   M-Audio's FireWire 1814 interface features six analog inputs (two with mic preamps) and four analog outputs, plus S/PDIF and ADAT Lightpipe I/O. (Photo courtesy of M-Audio.)

ProjectMix I/O

The ProjectMix I/O (shown in Figure 3.13) combines a FireWire-based 18×14 audio interface with a control surface. As an audio interface, it is directly supported by Pro Tools M-Powered 7 (as well as several other audio programs). If offers eight analog inputs, each of which has an input Gain knob and a mic/line switch for selecting between its separate XLR (with phantom power) and TRS jacks (plus a selectable instrument-level input on the front panel, for channel 1). Four TRS analog outputs are also provided. Additionally, the ProjectMix I/O has digital input/output in S/PDIF and ADAT Lightpipe formats, two headphone outputs with independent level controls, MIDI input/output, and word clock input/output with BNC connectors. As a control surface, it offers transport buttons and a jog wheel, plus motorized faders for eight channels (each with an assignable rotary encoder, plus dedicated record-enable, channel select, solo, and mute buttons) and the master level. Various other dedicated buttons are provided for functions such as nudging, looping, and so on, plus a footswitch input. It can also be used with many other programs, as it supports Mackie Control, HUI, and Logic Control emulation modes.

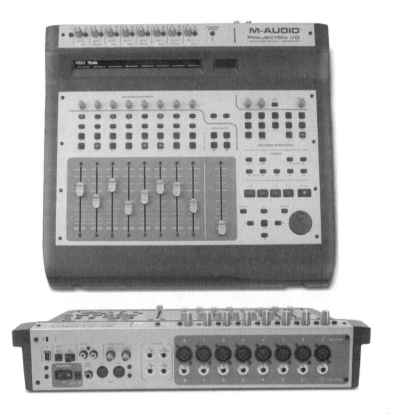

Figure 3.13 M-Audio's ProjectMix I/O combines a FireWire audio interface and control surface. (Photo courtesy of M-Audio.)

> ❋ **Note: Good Audio Cables Are a Sound Investment**
>
> Be sure to always use proper 75-ohm "digital" coaxial cable with all S/PDIF digital connections, especially at cable lengths over three feet.

USB-Based Systems

All of these M-Audio interfaces connect to the host computer via USB (Universal Serial Bus). With the exception of the Ozone and Black Box, most are also powered via this connection; no AC adapter is required. (Three additional interfaces not pictured here are supported by Pro Tools M-Powered versions 7.1 and higher: Audiophile USB, Fast Track Pro and JamLab.)

MobilePre USB

The MobilePre USB (shown in Figure 3.14) is a stereo audio interface that exclusively supports 16-bit audio at a 48 kHz sample rate. This interface has two TS (1/4-inch unbalanced) outputs on the rear panel, which are mirrored by an additional 1/8-inch stereo output. Gain knobs are provided on the front panel for channels 1 and 2. Two TRS (1/4-inch phone, tip-ring-sleeve, balanced) jacks support instrument or line-level sources—one on the front panel, the other on the back. Alternatively, the rear panel of the interface offers balanced XLR inputs for mic/line sources and a 1/8-inch stereo microphone input (with no phantom power available). The MobilePre USB does not feature any digital I/O.

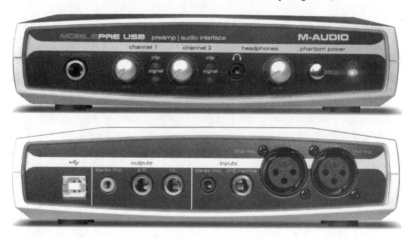

Figure 3.14 M-Audio's MobilePre USB interface. (Photo courtesy of M-Audio.)

Fast Track USB

The Fast Track USB (shown in Figure 3.15) is a compact stereo audio interface that supports 16- or 24-bit audio at sample rates of 44.1 or 48 kHz. The stereo outputs use RCA (unbalanced) connectors. One TRS (1/4-inch phone, tip-ring-sleeve, balanced) input can be switched between line and instrument levels. A second XLR input supports microphone sources, with an associated front-panel gain control for its mic preamp. No phantom power is provided for this microphone input. No digital I/O is provided on this interface. The Fast Track USB features a front-panel Mix knob (similar to that found on Digidesign's Mbox 2 and original Mbox) for balancing direct input levels (in mono or stereo) and playback from the host audio program as a way to circumvent monitoring latency issues.

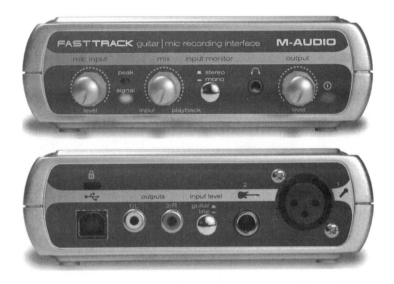

Figure 3.15   M-Audio's Fast Track USB interface. (Photo courtesy of M-Audio.)

Transit

The Transit (shown in Figure 3.16) is another compact stereo audio interface. It has a stereo mini 1/8-inch connector that doubles as line/headphone output, a TOSlink connector for S/PDIF optical output, plus a single input that doubles as a 1/8-inch stereo mini line/mic input or optical input (via a provided adapter). Like the Ozone, 16- or 24-bit audio is ostensibly supported at sample rates up to 96 kHz; however, due to the limitations of the USB 1.1 connection used by these units, this highest frequency would only be possible if you were using the inputs or outputs *only*—not a practical option with Pro Tools.

Ozone

This unit (shown in Figure 3.17) combines a two-octave (25-key) keyboard controller with an audio interface connected to the host computer via USB. The Ozone ostensibly supports 16- or 24-bit audio at sample rates up to 96 kHz, although 48 kHz is the practical limit if you want both the input and output channels to be active simultaneously in Pro Tools. (This is due to the inherent bandwidth limitations of the USB 1.1 connection used by this unit and is also true of the other USB-based audio interfaces from M-Audio that are ostensibly capable of 96 kHz operation if used in unidirectional mode.) Its two-channel operation can use either two TRS (1/4-inch phone, tip-ring-sleeve, balanced) inputs and two TS (1/4-inch unbalanced) outputs and a built-in, phantom-powered XLR microphone input or a 1/4-inch TS instrument-level input. The Ozone doesn't include any digital audio I/O. A headphone jack is also available. The Ozone's Direct Monitor knob allows mixing a certain amount of the signal from the Mic and Instrument inputs directly to outputs 1–2 (in mono or stereo) as a workaround to monitoring latency similar to that offered on Digidesign's Mbox 2 and original Mbox. Because the Ozone is also a MIDI controller, it features a sustain pedal jack and MIDI input/output (not required for communication with the computer, since the USB connection is available), plus eight control knobs that can be assigned to various MIDI parameters. It can operate from either batteries or the provided "wall wart" AC power supply.

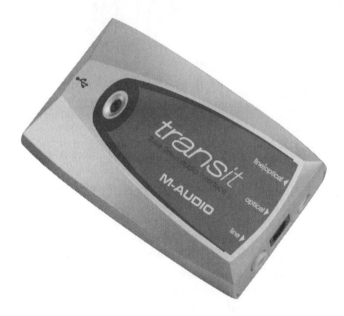

Figure 3.16 M-Audio's Transit interface. (Photo courtesy of M-Audio.)

Black Box

This unit (shown in Figure 3.18) combines a modeling guitar preamp/processor, a pro-grammable drum module, and a stereo audio interface connected to the host computer via USB. The Black Box is the result of a collaboration between M-Audio and Roger Linn Design and supports 16- or 24-bit audio at sample rates up to 44.1 kHz. The rear panel provides two TRS (1/4-inch phone, tip-ring-sleeve, balanced) outputs, plus a single S/DIF digital output (which supports 44.1 kHz sample rate only). No digital audio input is provided. An instrument-level input is provided on the front panel (with a 1/4-inch TS connector), as well as an XLR microphone input on the rear panel. There is also a front-panel headphone output. On the top of the unit, an Input/Playback knob allows for adjusting the balance between the direct input signal and the output through the internal processing and host software to circumvent monitoring latency issues. A "wall wart" AC power supply is required and is included with the unit.

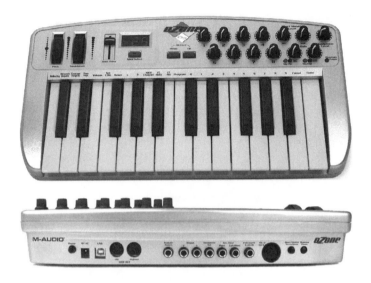

Figure 3.17   M-Audio's Ozone combines a keyboard controller and audio interface. (Photo courtesy of M-Audio.)

PCI Card-Based Systems

The following M-Audio hardware systems use a PCI card installed in the host computer. In some cases, a breakout cable provides some or all of the actual audio connections, while in others, an external box is connected directly to the PCI card. All of these PCI-based systems include M-Audio's Delta Control Panel software, which allows for level adjustments and signal routing between inputs and outputs on the hardware itself (for direct monitoring, for example). As before, all of these interfaces are capable of either 24- or 16-bit operation.

Audiophile 2496

The Audiophile 2496 audio card (shown in Figure 3.19) features two analog inputs and outputs for audio with RCA connectors on the rear of the PCI card itself. Alternatively, stereo coaxial S/PDIF digital I/O with RCA connectors is available via a breakout cable that attaches to a 15-pin D-sub connector on the rear of the card, which also provides one MIDI input and output. As the name implies, the card supports 24-bit audio at sampling rates up to 96 kHz. The coaxial digital outputs are Dolby Digital 5.1 surround sound capable (for sending out to an external decoder).

Audiophile 192

The Audiophile 192 audio card (shown in Figure 3.20) features stereo coaxial S/PDIF digital I/O with RCA connectors on the rear of the PCI card itself. A breakout cable attaches to a

25-pin D-sub connector on the rear of the card. This cable provides TRS (1/4-inch phone, tip-ring-sleeve) connectors for analog audio I/O: two analog audio inputs, two main outputs, plus two dedicated monitor outputs. The monitor outputs can mirror the main output from Pro Tools (or other DAW program) and/or pass through signals from the inputs on the Audiophile 192 itself, whose levels are controlled by a software mixer in the included Delta Control Panel software. One MIDI input and output is also provided on the breakout cable. The Audiophile 192 supports 24-bit audio at sampling rates up to 192 kHz (although this highest sample rate is not currently supported by the Pro Tools M-Powered software). The coaxial digital outputs are Dolby Digital 5.1 surround sound capable (for sending out an external decoder) and also offer a "professional" setting for running the AES/EBU protocol over the S/PDIF connection.

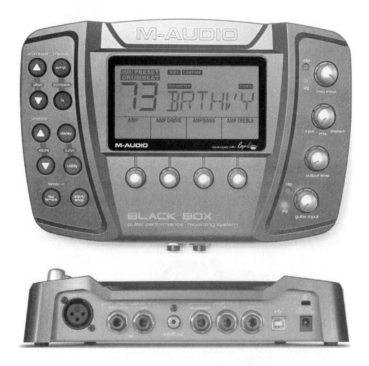

Figure 3.18 M-Audio's Black Box combines a modeling guitar preamp and drum module with an audio interface. (Photo courtesy of M-Audio.)

Delta 44

The Delta 44 PCI card (shown in Figure 3.21) connects to an external audio interface called the Delta series breakout box—which provides all of its audio and MIDI connections—via a cable with 15-pin D-sub connectors. Four analog inputs and outputs use TRS (1/4-inch phone, tip-ring-sleeve) connectors and can be switched between −10 dBV and +4 dBu nominal levels via the included Delta Control Panel software. As with the other M-Audio interfaces listed here, the software allows for routing input audio signals directly to outputs on the interface as a workaround for latency issues when monitoring audio sources being recorded through the host program. No digital I/O is included with the Delta 44. It supports 24-bit audio at sampling rates up to 96 kHz.

Figure 3.19   M-Audio's Audiophile 2496 card has RCA connectors for analog I/O on the card, plus S/PDIF and MIDI I/O via a breakout cable. (Photo courtesy of M-Audio.)

Figure 3.20   M-Audio's Audiophile 192 card supports 4×4 operation if all analog and digital I/O is used. (Photo courtesy of M-Audio.)

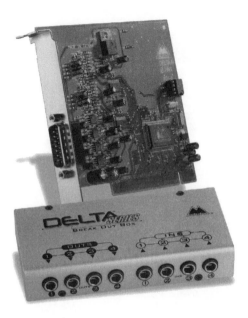

Figure 3.21   M-Audio's Delta 44 card includes analog I/O only. (Photo courtesy of M-Audio.)

Delta 66

The Delta 66 (shown in Figure 3.22) uses the same external breakout box and cable as the Delta 44 (see above) but expands I/O capability to six channels if the RCA connectors on the rear of the Delta 66 PCI card itself are used for stereo coaxial S/PDIF digital I/O (in other words, four channels of analog I/O plus two digital). Other characteristics are similar to the Delta 44.

Delta 1010

The Delta 1010 (shown in Figure 3.23) consists of a PCI card that connects to an external, rackmountable audio interface. This external "rack-mount converter unit" provides all the analog audio, MIDI, and word clock connections, while stereo coaxial S/PDIF digital I/O is available via RCA connectors on the rear of the PCI card itself. The external audio interface provides eight channels of audio input via TRS (1/4-inch phone, tip-ring-sleeve) connectors, with individual switches for choosing −10 dBV or +4 dBu nominal levels independently on each input and output channel. Word clock input and output on the rear of the interface provide for synchronizing the sample rate of the Delta 1010 with external systems, using 75-ohm coaxial cables with BNC connectors. One MIDI input and one MIDI output are provided on the front panel of the external audio interface. The Delta 1010 supports 24-bit audio at sampling rates up to 96 kHz.

Figure 3.22 M-Audio's Delta 66 card adds S/PDIF digital I/O to the capabilities of the Delta 44. (Photo courtesy of M-Audio.)

Figure 3.23 M-Audio's Delta 1010 card with external interface. (Photo courtesy of M-Audio.)

The optional Delta 1010-AI (a separate interface module; not pictured here) adds ADAT Lightpipe digital I/O capabilities to the Delta 1010 (up to eight channels of audio on this optical connection). However, the maximum of ten I/O channels does not change. Instead, the Delta 1010-AI allows you to globally switch between all eight of your analog input channels or all eight Lightpipe channels as the input source. Alternatively, you could route these eight Lightpipe channels directly to the analog or Lightpipe outputs on the interface itself. The Delta 1010-AI is connected between the Delta 1010 external interface and PCI card. ADAT Lightpipe I/O is limited to 48 kHz and 44.1 kHz sample rates.

Delta 1010LT

The Delta 1010LT (shown in Figure 3.24) consists of a PCI card with two breakout cables. The "analog" breakout cable attaches to a 25-pin D-sub connector and provides eight analog outputs with RCA connectors, plus eight analog inputs. Six of the inputs have RCA connectors, while female XLR connectors on channels 1 and 2 can be switched between microphone or line levels via a jumper on the PCI card itself (not accessible from outside the computer). The "digital" breakout cable attaches to a 15-pin D-sub connector and provides stereo coaxial S/PDIF digital I/O with RCA connectors, one MIDI input and output, plus a word clock input and output (for synchronizing sample rates between the Delta 1010LT and external systems, using 75-ohm coaxial cables with BNC connectors). Using the eight analog and two digital channels simultaneously, a maximum of 10 channels of I/O are available on the Delta 1010LT.

Figure 3.24 M-Audio's Delta 1010LT card with its breakout cables. (Photo courtesy of M-Audio.)

With so many choices for compatible audio interfaces for Pro Tools M-Powered, you can see why it is worth the time to investigate all their technical characteristics on the M-Audio Web site. Table 3.2 summarizes how these interfaces connect to the host computer and the number and type of audio inputs/outputs each of them provides.

Table 3.2 M-Audio Interfaces for Pro Tools M-Powered: I/O Channels

Model	Connection	Analog, S/PDIF, ADAT Ins	Analog, S/PDIF, ADAT Outs
FireWire Solo	FireWire	4/2/–	2/2/–
FireWire Audiophile	FireWire	2/2/–	4/2/–
FireWire 410	FireWire	2/2/–	8/2/–
FireWire 1814	FireWire	8/2/8	4/2/8
ProMix I/O	FireWire	8/2/8	4/2/8
MobilePre USB	USB	2/–/–	2/–/–
Fast Track USB	USB	2/–/–	2/–/–
Transit	USB	2/2/–	2/2/–
Ozone	USB	2/–/–	2/–/–
Black Box	USB	2/–/–	2/2/–
Audiophile 2496	PCI	2/2/–	2/2/–
Audiophile 192	PCI	2/2/–	4/2/–
Delta 44	PCI	4/–/–	4/–/–
Delta 66	PCI	4/2/–	4/2/–
Delta 1010	PCI	8/2/–	8/2/–
Delta 1010LT	PCI	8/2/–	8/2/–

❈ **Note: Pro Tools HD Software**

Prior to version 7, the version of the Pro Tools program that supports TDM hardware and plug-ins was known as Pro Tools TDM. This term was used for Pro Tools|HD systems, as well as 24|Mix and various other predecessors that supported the TDM plug-in architecture. Now, the software itself is called Pro Tools HD. The plug-in architecture is still called TDM, however, and current "TDM plug-ins" operate in Pro Tools HD software (along with RTAS plug-ins, which rely on the CPU's processing power rather than on the DSP chips on the HD cards).

Pro Tools|HD

Presently the most powerful generation of Pro Tools, Pro Tools|HD systems support recording 24-bit audio (with 16-bit operation also supported, as with all 24-bit interfaces) at sample rates up to 96 kHz or 192 kHz, depending on the HD audio interface(s) from Digidesign that you purchase separately to complete your system. (For example, the 192 I/O allows you to select sample rates of 44.1, 48, 88.2, 96, 176.4, or 192 kHz.) Pro Tools HD 1, the basic Pro Tools|HD system, consists of one PCI card in the host computer (HD Core), cabled to an external audio interface; it supports up to 32 channels of I/O if available on the audio interfaces. Pro Tools HD 2 Accel systems add the HD Accel card for more mixing and processing power (and up to 64 channels of I/O when using multiple audio interfaces, because each HD Accel card also supports 32 channels of I/O). Pro Tools HD 3 Accel systems have two HD Accel cards (up to 96 channels of I/O). You can expand the processing power and I/O capacity on these systems by adding more HD Accel cards. (Note: For computers with PCI-Express slots—the Macintosh G5 Quad, for example—Digidesign also offers PCIe card configurations for Pro Tools|HD. Conventional PCI/PCI-X cards for Pro Tools|HD are not directly compatible with this newer slot format. However, they could be used via the Expansion|HD expansion chassis on these computers.)

Multiple audio interfaces can be added to expand these systems, including the 192 I/O, 192 Digital I/O, 96i I/O, and 96 I/O. Several interfaces from the 24|Mix hardware family can optionally be connected to the Legacy port of the HD audio interfaces for additional channels of audio I/O. Even more so than with the previous 24|Mix systems, a very high-performance SCSI adapter and SCSI disks are required for the absolute maximum track count at these high resolutions. However, Pro Tools|HD systems also support audio recording on various FireWire drives (with supported track counts per disk decreasing as the sample rate is increased, as is the case with most disks). With fast, latest-generation ATA disks (and especially multiple SATA drives on Windows machines with the ICH-5 controller chipset, for example), disk-performance levels with Pro Tools|HD systems can be comparable with typical SCSI arrays.

Pro Tools|HD systems use DigiLink cabling, allowing audio interfaces to be separated from the PCI cards in the host computer by as much as 100 feet. The TDM II architecture used in HD systems doubles the number of time slots in this signal-routing/processing bus and is more efficient than the original TDM architecture used on Pro Tools 24|Mix and its predecessor, Pro Tools III. (Note that if you upgrade to Pro Tools|HD from a previous TDM system, upgrades are required for your third-party TDM plug-ins.)

Obviously, Pro Tools|HD lends itself to the most demanding audio applications, like music and film or video. Among other things, HD systems support Automatic Delay Compensation in the software, which automatically adjusts for processing delay due to plug-ins and signal routing in order to maintain ultra-precise time alignment in your mixes. (User-configurable amounts of delay compensation can also be applied to hardware I/O inserts to adjust for the latency of external devices and the inputs/outputs on the Pro Tools audio interface itself.) The high-resolution audio-recording formats used by Pro Tools|HD provide excellent forward compatibility with emerging standards—for example, in DVD-Audio. In addition, because of the capacity for 32 channels of I/O on each HD card, in many cases even a low-end HD system makes more economic sense than an expanded 24|Mix configuration, even for recording at 44.1 or 48 kHz—let alone all the enhancements in version 7 of the Pro Tools software.

Chapter 17 explores some of the expansion options for Pro Tools|HD and Digi 002/002 Rack configurations (as well as the older Pro Tools 24|Mix and Digi 001 systems that are not compatible with Pro Tools 7) and provides more specific details about the currently available audio interfaces for Pro Tools|HD systems. Figure 3.25 shows a basic Pro Tools|HD configuration.

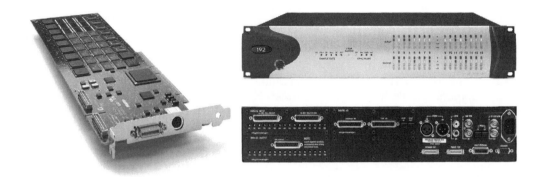

Figure 3.25 Pro Tools | HD systems consist of the HD software and PCI cards in the host computer, plus separately purchased external multichannel audio interfaces. (Photos courtesy of Digidesign.)

Note: Pro Tools|HD Cards: Then and Now

In the original Pro Tools | HD hardware, in addition to the single HD Core card in the HD 1, one or two HD Process cards were included in the more powerful HD 2 and HD 3 configurations. The HD Process was quickly superseded by the current-generation HD Accel card. Using more powerful 321 chips for digital signal processing, HD Accel delivers twice the power of the HD Process card (and quadruple that of the Mix Farm cards used on the older-generation 24 | Mix systems). Among other things, this increases your practical limit for voice counts by up to 50 percent at a given session sample rate, compared to the original Pro Tools | HD configurations. Some TDM plug-ins for HD systems (even using the previous 6.xx versions of the Pro Tools software) actually *require* the HD Accel card in order to carry out their more processing-intensive tasks.

Older PT Configurations

The Mbox (discontinued in fall of 2005) is compatible with the LE version of Pro Tools 7. Some previous incarnations of the Pro Tools hardware (especially 24 | Mix and Digi 001 at the time of this writing) continue to be viable options for many users, even though they don't support version 7 of the Pro Tools software. Be sure to check compatibility on http://www.digidesign.com, though, and once your hardware/software configuration is working, do *not* be in a hurry to upgrade to new CPUs or operating systems before confirming that they will work with your older Pro Tools setup!

Some of these legacy hardware configurations offer excellent audio specs and certainly are as functional today as when they enabled Digidesign to take over the world (at least as far as digital-audio workstations are concerned)! For instance, repurposing older hardware may be an excellent way to use an older Macintosh model that might otherwise be considered out of date. For recording voice-overs, beat mixing in your project studio, and other simple tasks, this can be an extremely cost-effective way to get into the game or have a second workstation in your facility. (Note that Pro Tools TDM 5.0.1cs8 is the highest software version that supports Pro Tools III hardware—Mac OS9 only, on G3/G4 models manufactured up through 2001.)

Used Pro Tools systems can be found for sale on eBay and in Digidesign user forums. You can license your used Pro Tools system with Digidesign so that you are a registered user when the time comes for updates and upgrades (again, these may or may not be compatible with your older hardware or host computer). The Transfer of Ownership Form is available as a downloadable PDF file in the Tech Support area of Digidesign's Web site and must be signed by both you *and* the seller. If the used Pro Tools version you are buying uses an authorization diskette to enable software installation, be sure to confirm with the seller that all authorizations have been restored to that diskette.

Mbox (Pro Tools LE and External USB Audio Interface)

This immensely successful predecessor to the Mbox 2 was discontinued in the fall of 2005. The Mbox (shown in Figure 3.26) was an external USB audio interface with up to two simultaneous channels of analog or digital I/O and included the LE version of the Pro Tools software. The Mbox *is* fully compatible with Pro Tools version 7. The 24-bit analog/digital converters on this USB-powered external interface are good quality, and its analog inputs incorporate Focusrite microphone preamps with 48-volt phantom power and balanced I/O using combo connectors (compatible with both XLR and 1/4-inch phone) from Neutrik. Unlike the Mbox 2, TRS (1/4-inch phone, tip-ring-sleeve) analog insert jacks were provided on the original Mbox—for patching in a compressor/limiter prior to the Pro Tools recording input, for example. S/PDIF digital in/out is supported via coaxial RCA connectors. (The digital output always mirrors analog outputs 1–2, while input for channels 1–2 can be switched between analog and digital output within the Hardware Setup dialog of the Pro Tools software. In any case, the original Mbox is always a 2×2 interface.) Buttons on the front panel toggle either channel between Mic, Line, and Instrument level (Hi-Z, high impedance, for direct connection from electric guitar or bass). The Mbox includes front and rear headphone jacks, plus a mono switch. Front panel knobs allow adjustment of input gain, mix between input and playback (to ameliorate monitoring latency during recording), and output level for the headphone jacks. Mbox users can record at 16- or 24-bit resolution and at 44.1 or 48 kHz sample rates.

❄ Caution: Use the USB Cable That Came with Your Mbox!

The USB supplied with the Mbox incorporates a cylindrical ferrite *choke* to eliminate RF interference. If you substitute some other USB cable (regardless of whether it has a choke or is advertised as very high-quality, shielded, and so on), you will probably hear a high-pitched whining from the Mbox's outputs (not unlike the sound of SMPTE time code, but higher pitched). The same thing will occur if you use a USB extender cable so that you can separate the Mbox further from the host computer. Although this noise is strictly on the outputs and doesn't end up in any mix files you bounce to disk, it can be quite annoying, especially in headphones.

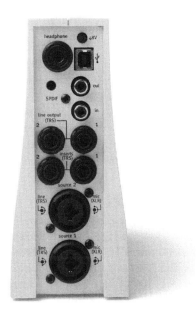

Figure 3.26   Pro Tools Mbox configurations use the Pro Tools LE software plus a two-channel Mbox external USB audio interface. (Photos courtesy of Digidesign.)

Pro Tools|24 MIX, Pro Tools|24 MIXplus, Pro Tools|24 MIX³ (TDM)

This is one of Digidesign's legacy (in other words, now discontinued) high-end systems for more professional applications. It does not support any version of the Pro Tools software higher than 6.4.1 and is therefore not usable with Pro Tools 7. As shown in Figure 3.27, the basic Pro Tools 24|MIX system consists of the Pro Tools TDM software, a Mix Core PCI card with dedicated chips for DSP (digital signal processing) to support the TDM environment, a selection of external audio interfaces (sold separately), plus, of course, the cable to connect them. Mix systems support multiple audio interfaces (up to 16 channels of I/O per Mix Core or Mix Farm card). All require a SCSI adapter card and SCSI hard disks for audio recording (although audio recording is also supported on various FireWire drives). A MIXplus system includes a second PCI card called the Mix Farm, with additional DSP chips for more powerful signal routing and processing within the Pro Tools TDM architecture. Each additional Mix Farm card supports attaching other audio interfaces for 16 more channels of I/O and increases simultaneous playback voices from 32 to 64. MIX³ is a bundled configuration with two Mix Farm cards for even more DSP capabilities and another 16 channels of I/O (maximum of 72, versus 160 in current HD configurations using Pro Tools 7). The TDM version of the Pro Tools software (5.xx and 6.xx versions), included with Pro Tools 24|Mix systems, supports AudioSuite, RTAS, and TDM plug-in architectures simultaneously, as well as HTDM. (HTDM plug-ins are no longer supported in Pro Tools 7.) The predecessor of 24|Mix, Pro Tools III, was also a TDM system, using a different card setup.

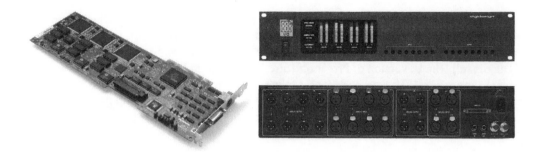

Figure 3.27 Now discontinued, Pro Tools 24|Mix systems consist of the Pro Tools TDM software, PCI cards in the host computer, plus separately purchased external multichannel audio interfaces. (Photos courtesy of Digidesign.)

Although no longer manufactured, the Pro Tools|24 Mix product line is still being used in thousands of professional music and postproduction facilities around the world. Besides supporting the powerful TDM plug-in and signal-processing architecture, these configurations were very expandable. Like the current Pro Tools|HD hardware, one could start from a single-card, single-interface configuration and then, as dictated by requirements and budget, add cards and/or additional hardware interfaces. Be aware, however, that all the PCI audio cards used in Mix systems are *incompatible* with G5 Macintosh models.

Again, Pro Tools TDM 6.4.1 is the highest software version supported by Pro Tools|24 Mix systems—it is *not* supported for version 7. Also, Automatic Delay Compensation for plug-in processing and routing latency is not supported by 24|Mix systems, nor are the D-Control (a large-format external control surface for HD systems) and D-Command control surfaces.

❄ **Caution: G5 Compatibility (Macintosh Versions)**

Due to changes in how card voltages are supported by the PCI bus in these models, several of the discontinued Pro Tools hardware systems listed here are *incompatible* with Macintosh G5 computers, including 24|Mix (the Mix I/O, Mix Farm, and DSP Farm cards), Digi 001, ToolBox (Audiomedia III card), and the d24 card used by Pro Tools|24 systems. None of these hardware configurations are compatible with Pro Tools 7 either, of course.

Digi 001 (Pro Tools LE and Digi 001 Card, External Audio Interface)

The now-discontinued Pro Tools Digi 001 configuration (see Figure 3.28) consists of the Pro Tools LE software, the Digi 001 PCI card and cable, plus the Digi 001 I/O, a rackmountable external audio interface. It is *not* compatible with Pro Tools 7 (or any other Pro Tools version higher than 6.4.1). The Digi 001 I/O has eight analog inputs and outputs, ADAT Lightpipe digital I/O (up to eight more channels and also configurable as stereo optical S/PDIF), stereo S/PDIF coaxial digital I/O (with RCA connectors), two microphone preamps with 48-volt phantom power that can be selected as inputs for channels 1 and 2, one MIDI input and one MIDI output, plus a headphone output. It's possible to use all these inputs/outputs simultaneously for 18 channels of I/O (eight analog audio connections, eight ADAT digital, and two S/PDIF digital). The LE version of Pro Tools (also included with Digi 002, Mbox, and ToolBox systems) supports SMPTE time code and Online mode in the Transport and up to 32 audio tracks. Therefore, the plug-in architecture is RTAS, which uses the computer's processing power to perform signal processing, with AudioSuite processing (non–real-time) also available.

Figure 3.28 Pro Tools Digi 001 (now discontinued) consists of the Pro Tools LE software, a single PCI card in the host computer, plus a single external, multichannel audio interface. (Photos courtesy of Digidesign.)

Digi 001 was a revolutionary product and a great choice for users needing a larger number of simultaneous audio inputs with good specs at a very economical price. For recording a band or for multiple microphones in live theatre, Digi 001 provided a reasonable number of simultaneous recording channels (especially if the ADAT Lightpipe and S/PDIF digital inputs were also used). It's still a very practical companion for editing ADAT tracks that have been digitally transferred into Pro Tools. As an excellent all-in-one solution, the Digi 001 broke important ground in the evolution of digital-audio workstations, combining the audio I/O, MIDI interface, and two moderate-quality microphone preamplifiers into a single rack-mounted interface. Combined with a high-quality mic preamp (especially when this can be connected to the 001 interface digitally, via the S/PDIF or ADAT Lightpipe output, and when using a high-quality clock source), the Digi 001 can produce *very* good-sounding results! (Note that Pro Tools LE 6.4 is the highest software version supported by Digi 001 systems— and again, the Digi 001 is *not* supported for version 7.)

ToolBox (Pro Tools LE and Audiomedia III Card)

This version consisted of the Pro Tools LE software and the discontinued Audiomedia III card (installed into a PCI slot in the host Windows or Macintosh computer). While we include it here for the sake of completeness, this hardware is not supported for Pro Tools 7, nor by more recent versions of the 6.xx software. The Audiomedia III has both analog and S/PDIF digital I/O (all RCA connectors) directly on the card. It can potentially be used as a four-channel system—if you have a digital source or an outboard device to convert audio signals between digital and analog for the card's digital I/O—for example, a DAT or microphone preamp with S/PDIF connections. Even as a two-channel system, it offered higher-quality audio converters than generic soundcards or built-in audio on most computers. Figure 3.29 shows the Audio-media III–based configuration used in ToolBox systems.

Figure 3.29   Pro Tools ToolBox systems were based on the Pro Tools LE software and the now-discontinued Audiomedia III card. (Photo courtesy of Digidesign.)

For older computers that don't support a USB port for attaching an Mbox, for example, a ToolBox system (which is based on the Audiomedia III card) might still be a viable choice. It's directly supported by a number of MIDI sequencers, and in many studios an existing ToolBox system could be productive for many years to come, perhaps in a second editing room or for voice-overs and MIDI preproduction. (Note that AMIII-based systems are officially supported through Pro Tools LE version 6.1.2 on Macintosh and version 6.1.1 on Windows, although we have seen acceptable results with 6.2.3 and Mac OS 10.3.2. Once again, ToolBox systems are *not* compatible with Pro Tools 7.)

Pro Tools Free 5.01 (CPU-Based Audio)
This is a free, downloadable version of Pro Tools for Macintosh operating system 9 and Windows 98 (SE/ME) only. It is *not* compatible with Windows XP or any version of OS X, even under Classic mode! It is limited to eight audio tracks and stereo audio input/output. Like the LE and M-Powered versions of Pro Tools, in addition to AudioSuite effects, Pro Tools Free supports RTAS (Real-Time AudioSuite) plug-in architecture, which uses the computer's processing power to perform audio effects and routing. It doesn't require any Digidesign audio hardware and instead uses the audio capabilities of the host computer (stereo input, stereo output, 16-bit resolution, and 44.1 kHz or 48 kHz sample rate, according to hardware). Audio-recording quality depends on the specs of the audio converters in your computer or soundcard (which, although not outstanding, can be sufficient for many purposes). Some users

upgrade their audio quality with Pro Tools Free either by purchasing a better soundcard or by using an external unit for audio conversion, such as USB audio interfaces from Tascam, Edirol/Roland, and others. In this case, Pro Tools Free is not really aware of the external audio device's capabilities; instead, it's the operating system itself that re-routes *all* audio I/O (input/output) through the device. Pro Tools Free may be an attractive option for owners of an older iMac or laptop because it doesn't require any card slots (but make sure your laptop truly meets the system requirements, especially for disk performance).

If you have a computer running one of these older operating systems (Mac OS9 or Windows 98/SE/ME), Pro Tools Free 5.01 might be a low-cost option for starting your home or project studio. In many cases two audio inputs can be enough when working by yourself. For interactive developers (and some audio-for-video work), the eight audio tracks this version supports may be plenty, and especially if you upgrade your audio input quality by adding a USB audio interface, Pro Tools Free can be sufficient for recording voice-overs—as long as you have a decent mixer or microphone preamp.

iLok USB Smart Key

The iLok USB Smart Key is a USB (Universal Serial Bus) hardware device used for authorizing various programs and plug-ins on both Windows and Macintosh computers, including many plug-ins used with Pro Tools (especially on HD systems). An iLok is also included with the M-Powered version of Pro Tools and must be attached to the host computer in order for the program to run. It's manufactured by PACE anti-piracy, who also developed the authorization diskette copy-protection mechanism used by many previous versions of Pro Tools and other audio/MIDI programs. Many audio and MIDI programs require that a hardware *dongle* (a hardware authorization device that is specific to a single program) be attached to the computer in order to operate (usually via USB, in most current versions). The iLok's important innovation was allowing a *single* device to store the authorizations for multiple programs and plug-ins, even from different developers. An iLok USB Smart Key is shown in Figure 3.30.

Figure 3.30 A single iLok USB Smart Key stores authorizations for multiple programs and plug-ins.

Here are the basics of how the iLok system works: A License Card comes with the plug-in software you've purchased. (The working part of this is actually a smaller GSM plastic chip—a cutout that you remove from the larger protective card. It uses "Smart Card" technology, which is also used on GSM cell phones and some credit cards.) During the process of authorizing a plug-in or program, you insert the License Card into a slot in the end of the iLok USB Smart Key.

iLok owners need to register for a free account on http://www.ilok.com in order to download any new licenses. With an active iLok account, you can purchase plug-ins online, and if the iLok is attached, it can be automatically authorized for the plug-in as part of the purchase process. Alternatively, the plug-in vendor may deposit the license to your iLok account. Digidesign Customer Service also uses this site for processing upgrades from plug-ins using the older authorization diskette method to the iLok system. (Incidentally, authorizations can be obtained by connecting the iLok to any computer with access to the Internet and the iLok Client Software installed, whether it has Pro Tools hardware attached or not.) Be sure to use Internet Explorer while using this site; other browsers are not currently supported!

Another feature sometimes implemented with the iLok are fully functional versions that a plug-in vendor licenses to you for a limited period in "demo" mode. (For many plug-ins, however, this is also a possibility even if you *don't* have an iLok.)

The drivers that iLok requires are automatically installed with current LE, M-Powered, or TDM Pro Tools software. (These are updated periodically, and updaters will sometimes be included when you purchase a plug-in. It is usually necessary to restart the computer after updating iLok and PACE drivers.) Whenever plug-ins are found that haven't been authorized yet, upon launch, a Pro Tools dialog box will prompt you to click the Authorization button in order to begin the process.

So, what's the advantage of all this, you might ask? First, plug-in developers have a right to protect their intellectual property, ensuring that only users who have paid for their product can use it; that's a given. However, if you're a new user and never lived through the drawbacks of diskette-based software authorizations, here's a brief primer. First, you would install the software (from a CD, and in the *really* olden days, from many, many diskettes!). Upon launching the software, you would be prompted to insert a separate authorization diskette. The authorization routine would install invisible key files somewhere on your hard disk that enabled the program to run and then would write onto the diskette, decreasing its available authorization count from, say, two to one. Later, if you needed to install the software on a new disk or machine, you would de-authorize the program on the original machine, which removes the invisible key files and again writes onto the key diskette to restore the authorization count. Among the disadvantages of this system were the following:

❄ If your hard disk crashed—or you reformatted without remembering to de-authorize all the necessary programs and/or plug-ins—you lost that authorization forever, reducing the available count on the diskette.

❋ Given the fragility of diskettes and the necessity to write onto them each time you installed or removed authorizations, the chances of that diskette eventually failing were very good.

❋ You may have noticed that most base configurations for new computers no longer include a diskette drive!

Conventional dongles (hardware authorization devices that are specific to a single program) also work pretty well. Like the iLok, they have the advantage that you can reformat and restore the contents of your hard disk without worrying about any invisible key files or authorizations, move up to a new machine, and simply transfer the dongle for the new software installation, and so on. Obviously, losing or breaking your dongle could be a real crisis—but this is equally a concern with the iLok system. One of the traditional problems has been that dongles from certain programs can be incompatible with others—this was especially true back in the days of SCSI and parallel port dongles—and consequently, using more than one program requiring a dongle could be very problematic. But with the iLok, various manufacturers can use the same programmable device to store authorizations for many different programs and plug-ins, and these conflicts are avoided. Additionally, using the iLok, you can back up your software and do a low-level reformat on your system disks, reload the programs, and then simply re-attach the iLok to get back to work with your previously authorized plug-ins. That's the attraction of the iLok system and the reason why it has been overwhelmingly accepted by plug-in developers in the Pro Tools arena.

The M-Powered version of Pro Tools comes with an iLok that has been "pre-authorized" for the program (no separate License Card is required). This iLok must be attached to the computer's USB port in order to run Pro Tools M-Powered and can also be used to store authorizations for other programs or plug-ins.

Digidesign Control Surfaces for Pro Tools

Many users find that a mouse or trackball and keyboard are all they need to work with Pro Tools. Nevertheless, a physical control surface has its advantages. Among other things, having dedicated faders and buttons that you can actually feel under your fingers can be a productivity enhancement when you're interacting with musicians out in the studio or mixing long sequences for film and video. Also, it's obvious that being able to move multiple faders simultaneously is a must for intuitive, seat-of-your-pants mixing. It all comes down to your personal preference and the main kind of work you do. Appendix B revisits the subject of external control surfaces, including these and other options from Mackie, CM Labs, and other third parties. The following, then, briefly summarizes the current offerings from Digidesign.

Command|8

Command|8 connects to the host computer via USB. Transport controls, eight motorized faders, and eight rotary encoders with LED rings around them indicate current parameter values or metering. These can be assigned to Pro Tools channels in groups of eight. A backlit LCD display (two rows of 55 characters) shows track information and parameter values.

Command|8 incorporates a 1-in, 2-out MIDI interface and a footswitch jack for hands-free punch in/out of recording. Its monitoring section, designed by Focusrite, includes main Pro Tools audio input, External Source input (for CD players and other audio devices around your studio), and dedicated Control Room/Headphones outputs.

The Command|8 (seen in Figure 3.31) can be used with TDM, LE, and M-Powered versions of Pro Tools (and also with Avid Media Composer). It can be used as a fader expander for other tactile control surfaces from Digidesign, such as the Pro Control, Control|24, or the Digi 002 itself. The Command|8 offers a standalone MIDI controller mode for use with other MIDI applications.

Figure 3.31 The Command|8 control surface is compatible with TDM or LE versions of Pro Tools and other MIDI programs and can be used as an expander for the Digi 002. (Photo courtesy of Digidesign.)

Control|24

This external control surface, shown in Figure 3.32, connects to the host computer via Ethernet (10BaseT, RJ-45 connectors). It features Transport controls with a scrub/shuttle wheel; a built-in talkback microphone; an 8×2 analog line submixer; 24 motorized faders with dedicated level meters; and Mute, Solo, Record-Enable, Channel Select, Automation Mode, EQ, and Dynamics buttons on each channel; as well as 16 Class A mic/line preamps by Focusrite, with 48-volt phantom power. The surface also boasts an LED display for Transport locations, plus 26 illuminated scribble strips for names and parameter values. Dedicated modifier keys for use when pressing other buttons include Command, Option, and Control (equivalent to Ctrl, Alt, and Start on Windows). Control|24 is compatible with HD (TDM) or LE versions of Pro Tools but *not* with M-Powered.

Figure 3.32 The Control|24 control surface is compatible with TDM and LE versions of Pro Tools (but not with M-Powered). (Photo courtesy of Digidesign.)

ProControl

The ProControl external control surface connects to the host computer via Ethernet (10BaseT, RJ-45 connectors). It features Transport controls with a weighted scrub/shuttle wheel, eight motorized 100 mm faders, and eight rotary encoders with LED rings around them to indicate current parameter values or metering. An analog monitoring section supports analog I/O via DB-25 connectors. The control surface also features a built-in talkback microphone and input for a listenback microphone; a dedicated Control Room section with its own level controls, source selectors, and Mute/Dim, Stereo/Surround, and Mono switches; a numeric keypad; and Edit/Assign scribble strips that show five insert slots on the selected channel or parameters for the effect currently being edited. A dedicated Send section is usable on any currently selected channel. The base ProControl unit is expandable via the Edit Pack option (featuring a Machine Control section; eight 40-segment level meters; LED displays for Start, End, and Length; two joystick panners; a trackball; and a built-in color-coded keyboard with Pro Tools function labels), or additional Fader Expansion Packs (eight faders each, up to a maximum of 48 channels). While the newer D-Command control surface supplants much of its functionality, ProControl units continue in operation at many professional studios, not only with HD systems but especially with the previous-generation Mix|24 hardware. ProControl (shown in Figure 3.33) can be used only with TDM systems, including Pro Tools|HD.

Figure 3.33   The ProControl control surface is for use with TDM systems (including both HD and Mix|24) only. (Photo courtesy of Digidesign.)

ICON Integrated Console and D-Control

ICON systems are based around the D-Control and D-Command worksurfaces, the rack-mounted XMON monitoring and communications module, and a Pro Tools|HD system. The D-Control is currently Digidesign's most sophisticated external control surface for use with Pro Tools|HD systems in a studio environment. The core D-Control tactile work surface for Pro Tools|HD systems consists of a Master Module, plus a single 16-channel Fader Module, which can be mounted to either side of it. From there, additional Fader Modules can be added, up to 80 channels/faders total. Each channel strip has six rotary encoders, with LED rings around them to indicate current parameter values or metering. LED metering is provided for each channel, plus eight channels of metering for the Master section. Twenty-nine illuminated push-buttons per channel strip are provided for switching channel modes and attributes. LED displays indicate channel names or the currently selected editing parameter for each, and there are also dedicated LED displays for the Main/Sub time indicators and for the Start, End, and Length fields of the Pro Tools software. A Focus channel strip in the center Master Module can be used for editing any selected channel without leaving the center of the console. In addition, the D-Control has dedicated EQ and Dynamics panels, usable on any selected channel. Its Transport section includes separate Pro Tools Transport and Machine Transport switches, a scrub/shuttle wheel, a master Record Enable switch, dedicated buttons for selecting the various Pro Tools recording modes, pre/post-roll, and zoom/navigation controls. There's a built-in alphanumeric keyboard, a two-button trackball, and a swinging arm for mounting a flat-panel display of the user's choosing. The D-Control connects to the core Pro Tools|HD Accel system via Ethernet.

An optional Surround Panner is also available for installation in the D-Control. In addition to hardware and software buttons, it incorporates a color LCD touchscreen and two touch-sensitive joysticks and two rotary encoders with LED rings, any of which can be used for surround panning in the X-Y axis or for controlling plug-in parameters and other mix features that are unrelated to panning.

Completing any ICON system is a rackmounted XMON monitor system. In addition to supporting surround mixing, it provides dedicated outputs for three separate stereo cue mixes, talkback, listenback, studio monitors, and headphones.

The D-Control (shown in Figure 3.34) is for use with HD systems only and does not support 24|Mix systems, M-Powered, or any LE version of Pro Tools.

Figure 3.34 The basic D-Control consists of a Master Module plus a 16-channel Fader Module. This can be expanded up to 80 channels/faders. (Photo courtesy of Digidesign.)

D-Command

The D-Command worksurface offers a more compact alternative to the D-Control. (In its basic 8-fader configuration, D-Command is about 32 inches/82 cm wide by 29 inches/74 cm deep, versus 55 inches/166 cm wide and 42 inches/107 cm deep for a basic 16-fader D-Control console.) The D-Command Main Unit features a central control section with monitoring and communications controls and eight touch-sensitive, motorized channel faders. It communicates with the host Pro Tools computer system via Ethernet. (A separate Ethernet hub is required, to which all these devices are attached.) Each channel strip has two rotary encoders, with LED rings to show either the current parameter setting or metering. The D-Command is expandable up to 24 faders via a single 16-channel Fader Module (connected to yet another port on the Ethernet hub). On each channel, one 6-channel LCD displays information about the current parameter selected for the rotary encoder, while another serves as a scribble strip. Each of these channels can function independently, in a different mode from the others. There are illuminated pushbuttons and bar-graph meters on each channel, plus eight more bar-graph meters in the Master section. The center section has dedicated control panels for editing EQ (with 12 rotary controls) and dynamics plug-ins (with 6 rotary controls). The D-Command includes the same XMON remote, rackmounted analog I/O audio monitoring and communications module (two rack units high) as the D-Control, to which it is connected via a proprietary 15-pin cable. The monitoring section on the D-Command itself provides control for up to two 5.1 surround inputs, three stereo inputs, and two cue sends.

Like the D-Control, the D-Command (shown in Figure 3.35) is for HD systems only and does not support M-Powered or any LE version of Pro Tools.

❈ **Note: Bundled ICON Configurations**

Digidesign also offers bundled configurations for their ICON systems (which include the D-Control and D-Command worksurfaces): D-Control|16 POST, D-Control|32 POST, D-Control|16 MUSIC, D-Control|32 MUSIC, plus D-Command|MUSIC and D-Command|POST. All these include the worksurface (with one or two additional fader expansion modules according to the configuration), a Pro Tools|HD3 Accel system with at least two 192 I/O audio interfaces, a Sync I/O synchronization peripheral, a MIDI I/O interface, a DigiDelivery Serv|LT file exchange server, plus ReVibe, Smack, and the HD Pack 3 plug-in bundle. The post configurations include the MachineControl option, DigiTranslator software, and Avid Mojo video interface (with Avid Media Station|PT software). Instead of these post options, music configurations include Digidesign's eight-channel PRE microphone preamp, Synchronic beat/audio manipulation plug-in, and a third 192 I/O interface (except for D-Command|MUSIC, which includes an 192 AD expansion card for one of the existing 192 I/Os).

Venue

Venue is Digidesign's first offering for live digital mixing consoles. It consists of the D-Show mixing console shown in Figure 3.36 (the Main Unit plus one Sidecar fader module) and its FOH Rack (which contains the computer for its mix engine and also the expandable audio and MIDI I/O), an expandable Stage Rack I/O unit with remote-controlled preamps and recallable settings, plus multichannel digital snakes with BNC connectors that each support up to 48 bidirectional signals over distances of up to 500 feet. A fully expanded Venue system (including two additional Sidecar modules, with 16 faders each) supports up to 96 microphone inputs and routing to 27 audio busses. We won't go into all the Venue features here—snapshot automation, the Personal Q option so that performers can control their own monitor mixes, real-time use of plug-in effects during live mixing/recording with dynamics processing on every input channel, four plug-in inserts and one hardware insert on every input channel and output bus, and many others—that's a subject that would fill another book! We simply mention Venue here because it can also simultaneously act as the front-end for Pro Tools recording in live situations. With the optional FWx card, multichannel recording and playback with Pro Tools LE systems is supported. After recording the live event, the native Pro Tools LE session that results can subsequently be edited and mixed on any Pro Tools system. The optional TDM Record card will support direct connection via DigiLink cables to HD Core and HD Accel cards on a Pro Tools | HD system without any external audio interfaces required on that system in order to record. A native Pro Tools HD session is produced that can subsequently be edited and mixed in the studio.

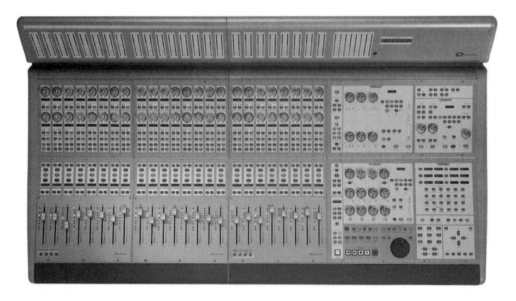

Figure 3.35 This basic 8-fader configuration for the D-Command worksurface has been expanded with a 16-fader Fader Module. (Photo courtesy of Digidesign.)

Figure 3.36 Venue is a live mixing solution that also offers options for direct recording to Pro Tools. Shown here: the D-Show console. (Photo courtesy of Digidesign.)

Summary

As stated at the beginning of Chapter 1, "About Pro Tools," Pro Tools consists of a program that runs on a computer (plus specialized audio cards and/or interfaces, required in every version except the older Pro Tools Free 5.01). So aside from being an audio expert, you need to be on top of the computer game. You *must* back up and archive your data on a regular basis (unless you don't mind losing it)! And try to use some common sense about installing other programs on the same computer (especially older games, background-operation utilities, and operating-system upgrades). Pro Tools makes your hard disks work very hard, so they need to offer good performance levels and be properly maintained. Also, Pro Tools needs much more RAM than, say, your typical spreadsheet. If you need to connect external MIDI devices or synchronize to SMPTE time code or video, additional hardware is generally required—it's not included in Pro Tools because user requirements vary so widely. (The Mbox 2, Digi 002 interface, and the now-discontinued Digi 001 have built-in MIDI I/O, as do many M-Audio interfaces and the Command|8 control surface.) In short, you're probably going to need a more robust computer setup than most of your non-audio friends (with the obvious exception of video editors and 3D designers). But then again, you're going to have a *lot* more fun!

4 Creating Your First Pro Tools Session

So you've installed the Pro Tools program (and completed the appropriate installations and configurations for your MIDI interface and any external MIDI modules), opened the program, checked your settings in the Pro Tools Hardware Setup and Playback Engine dialog boxes, and now you're ready to rock. Let's walk through a new session, take a look at some of the most important features, and get a feel for how you start on a Pro Tools project.

This chapter provides a quick tour of the basic Pro Tools working style for the impatient new user. If you're somewhat familiar with Pro Tools already, you may wish to skip ahead to Chapters 5, "The Transport Window," 6, "The Edit Window," and 7, "The Mix Window," to explore these windows in much more detail. For the sake of simplicity, we're assuming here that all default preferences for a new installation of the Pro Tools program have been left unchanged.

❋ **Tip: Another Way to Learn**

If you're new to all this and would appreciate a more "show me" style of learning for Pro Tools–based music production, you might check out the *Pro Tools 7 CSi Starter* CD-ROM. Several movie tutorial examples from this interactive learning environment are included on the CD-ROM in the back of this book. *Pro Tools 7 CSi Starter* is structured to take you from initial setup and mixer configuration through the recording, editing, mixing, and delivery of a finished music project using any version of the Pro Tools software. There's also a *Pro Tools 7 CSi Master* volume, which covers more advanced applications.

For the sake of simplicity, in this chapter, you're going to record and edit only audio, not MIDI. We assume that you have *some* audio source that can be recorded from the channel 1 input of your audio hardware—a microphone (perhaps via a mixer or preamplifier, unless your Digidesign hardware provides this), a guitar preamp, your kid brother's portable CD player, whatever. We also assume that you have some 16-bit, 44K audio files somewhere on your audio disks—for example, in AIF or WAV format. You can also use Pro Tools to import entire audio CD tracks by dragging them into the Region List from the Workspace browser window.

Otherwise, you could import a small section of audio from within a CD track (for now, it's not important what) using QuickTime Pro (Mac), Peak (Mac), Sound Forge or WaveLab (Windows), Audacity (Mac/Win), or whatever your favorite CD audio extraction program is (MusicMatch Jukebox, CD Spin Doctor, and so on).

❋ **Note: You May See Things Differently!**

As we've explained in previous chapters, not only are there several versions of the Pro Tools software (associated with various hardware configurations), but this program is also being updated fairly regularly by Digidesign. We've been careful to make this example equally applicable for all current versions of the software. For the record, though, most of the screenshots throughout this book were created in Macintosh version 7.0 of the Pro Tools software (HD, M-Powered, and LE versions).

Your First Session

First, you're going to open Pro Tools from the Macintosh Dock (or Windows Start menu) or by double-clicking its icon on the desktop or a window and set up a new Pro Tools session document. Notice that you select the audio file format (including sample rate and bit depth) for each Pro Tools session *before* recording any audio! There are two ways of getting audio into your Pro Tools session: using an audio track's record-enable button in the Mix (or Edit) window and the Record button in the Transport window to record an audio source, or importing existing audio files from other disk locations.

Setting Up a New Session

Unlike some other programs, Pro Tools does not present you with an untitled or default document when you first open the program. Instead, you use the File menu to either create a new session document or open an existing one. As explained in Chapter 2, "Pro Tools Terms and Concepts," when you create a new session document, this file resides within a folder of the same name, which Pro Tools automatically creates on your hard disk. An Audio Files subfolder is automatically created within this folder to store any audio files created by recording in this session. To set up a new session in Pro Tools, do the following:

1. Open the Pro Tools program. Choose File > New Session. In the New Session dialog box (shown in Figure 4.1), name the new session document anything you like, but be sure to create it on the disk drive you will be using for audio recording. The name you specify applies not only to the Pro Tools session document but also to a new folder containing this document. For this test session, let's choose either WAV (BWV) or AIF file format, 44.1 kHz as the sample rate, and a bit-depth of 24 bits.

   Unless there's some specific reason *not* to do so, we recommend 24-bit resolution for all Pro Tools sessions where you plan to record new audio. For one thing, working at this higher bit depth allows you to be less concerned about always recording at relatively high input levels. There's also less quantization noise (error) in proportion to very low-level signals or reverb decays on recorded tracks. At lesser bit depths, this could come back to haunt you if you ever needed to dramatically boost the level of an extremely low-level recording later on. Lower recording levels also leave more headroom for unexpected volume peaks in the source signal you're recording. This is especially handy because, unlike most analog recording situations, an ever-increasing number of Pro Tools users don't use compression or any other dynamic processing prior to the inputs of their audio hardware.

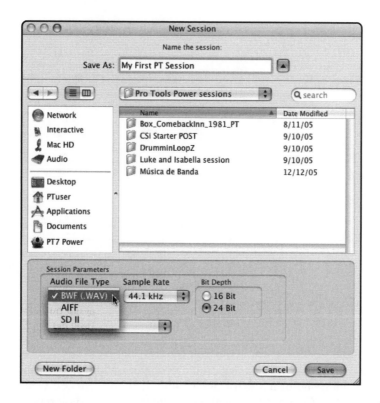

Figure 4.1 The New Session dialog box is where you name the new session file and configure its audio parameters. Some options (such as sample rates) in this dialog box vary according to which version of Pro Tools you're using.

2. There are three main windows in Pro Tools: the Transport (which looks like the controls of a tape recorder and always floats on top of the other two windows), the Mix window (which displays Pro Tools tracks in a similar fashion to traditional audio mixers), and the Edit window (which displays the contents of individual tracks along a horizontal timescale, and in the latest versions of the software can display duplicates of the Transport's buttons). In a newly created session, there are no tracks to display yet (because in Pro Tools, you create tracks as needed). A toolbar with various indicators and buttons

is always visible at the top of the Edit window, while the Mix window is completely blank until you start creating tracks to work in. For the purpose of this quick tour, we want the Edit window to be visible. Note that you can toggle (alternate) between the Mix and Edit windows by pressing Command+Equal (=) (Ctrl+Equal in Windows).

3. Choose Track > New, enter 4 in the Audio field of the dialog box that appears (shown in Figure 4.2) to create four new audio tracks, and then click the Create button.

Figure 4.2   The New Tracks dialog box is where you create new audio or MIDI tracks, Aux Ins, Instrument tracks, and Master Faders in Pro Tools. In this dialog box, hold down the Command key (Ctrl key in Windows) and use the up/down arrows on your computer keyboard to cycle through the various track class options. As shown here, you can create multiple classes of tracks simultaneously.

4. Four new audio tracks appear in the Edit window, named Audio 1, Audio 2, Audio 3, and Audio 4. Because these names aren't terribly descriptive, let's rename them. First, double-click the name of the first track (Audio 1, at the left side of the window) and rename it MyStuff. Click the Next button without leaving this dialog box and then name the second track Drums, the third track FX1, and the fourth track More FX2. (By the way, there's a keyboard shortcut for using the Next button to move from one track to another within this track naming dialog box:
   Command+Return (Ctrl+Enter in Windows) on the alphanumeric keyboard—a very good one to know!) Click OK—or simply hit Return (Enter in Windows) on the alphanumeric keyboard—when you're finished naming tracks.

5. Choose File > Save. (Be sure to also check out Chapter 8, "Menu Selections: Highlights," for information about the AutoSave function in Pro Tools, which is configured in the Operation tab of the Preferences dialog box.) It's important to save as you work!

6. Use the Track > New command again (notice the keyboard shortcut indicated next to this menu selection). This time, though, let's change the rightmost pop-up selector within

the New Track dialog box to create an Auxiliary Input (mono) instead of an audio track. After clicking the Create button to close this dialog box, double-click this Aux In track's name as before and change its name from Aux 1 to Delay.

7. Press Shift+Command+N (Shift+Ctrl+N in Windows) to open the New Tracks dialog box one last time. Create a Master Fader track (stereo), keeping the default name, Master 1. (Actually, you could have used the New Tracks dialog box to create all these tracks in a single operation, as shown in Figure 4.2. Now we tell you!)

8. Now, select View > Mix Window. Here's a convenient keyboard shortcut for toggling between the Edit and Mix windows: Command+Equal for Mac and Ctrl+Equal in Windows (that is, hold down the Command key or Ctrl key while pressing the equal-sign key). Remember that! The Mix window is now the topmost window in Pro Tools, although the Edit window is still open behind it. These are two different views of the tracks you've created.

Your First Recording

Each time you record audio in a Pro Tools session, new disk files are created. Pro Tools automatically creates an Audio Files subfolder within the session's main folder to contain these digital audio files. For our purposes here, it's not terribly important exactly *what* you record—and 30 or 60 seconds worth of material will be sufficient. Our goal here is simply to familiarize you with how to enable individual tracks for recording in Pro Tools. (On the other hand, if you just happen to record a masterpiece your first time out, go ahead and take it all the way!) To record, do the following:

1. Click the R (record enable) button on the MyStuff track to arm (enable) this track for recording. If you have your sound source properly connected, you should see some activity on the track's level meter. (In the Mix window, a pop-up Input Selector for each audio track allows you to select any bus or physical input on the audio hardware that's the source for recording. Again, we're assuming here that Analog Input 1/Left appears as the default selection for your first audio track and that your audio source is connected there.) Test your levels; if the red clipping indicator on this track comes on, click it once to reset it, reduce the volume of your input source (or the source gain control for this audio input, if your audio interface offers one), and test again.

❊ **Note: Audio Record Levels Are Adjusted at the Source (Not via the Track's Fader)**

Unlike conventional mixing boards and tape recorders, Volume faders on audio tracks have *no effect* on the level actually being recorded to disk! You can therefore adjust these to whatever level is convenient for listening purposes. If you see the track's red clipping indicators lighting up when it's record enabled, you must reduce the level either at the source device or on the audio interface itself if this feature is provided (for example, gain controls on the Mbox 2 (and original Mbox) as well as some of the M-Audio interfaces, the gain controls for microphone inputs on the Digi 002 and Digi 001 interfaces, and the gain controls in the Hardware Setup dialog box for the 96i I/O interface).

2. In the Transport window, click the Record button and then click Play. (As mentioned earlier, Transport window controls are similar to those of a tape recorder. Chapter 5 explains the features of the Transport window in much more detail.) If for any reason the Transport window isn't visible, you can always open it via the Window > Transport command or by holding down the Command key (Ctrl key in Windows) as you press 1 on your computer's numeric keypad.

3. Make whatever noises you like using your microphone or guitar/bass preamp. If the Edit window is still visible, you'll notice that a red rectangle within the track gradually increases in length as you record, reflecting the duration of the audio region being created (as shown in Figure 4.3).

4. Click Stop in the Transport window. If you wish, you can now arm other tracks for recording and repeat these steps in order to create additional parts.

Figure 4.3 An audio track during recording in the Edit window. The top segment of the level meter is a clipping indicator. It lights up in red if levels are too high, which causes digital distortion in the recorded audio. Digital clipping is not pretty—avoid it!

❋ **CSi Examples**

The CD-ROM in the back of this book contains sample movie tutorials from Pro Tools-related volumes in the CSi (Cool School Interactus) interactive learning environment. Among these, you'll find one called *Overdubs and Loop Recording*. This movie tutorial walks you through recording multiple takes while listening to existing material, substituting new recordings for certain sections within an existing recording (*punching in*), and recording many alternate takes while the same section loops around. Sometimes it helps to actually see these concepts being put into practice—that's what the CSi series is all about!

Importing Audio into Pro Tools

In some Pro Tools sessions, you want to use existing audio files from some other disk location on your computer. These may be standard elements used in many projects (station identifications, tones, recurring sound effects, and so on) or elements from other Pro Tools sessions being used to create a remix or submix. The File > Import Audio to Region List command is typically used for this. In the Import Audio dialog box, you can probably guess that the Convert button appears when audio files to be imported are not directly compatible with the current session—for example, if their audio file format, sample rate, or bit depth is different. If you use the Convert or Copy button in this dialog box, new copies of any imported files are created within the current session's Audio Files folder.

In Chapter 6, we provide more detailed information about importing existing audio files into Pro Tools, but here's the basic procedure:

1. If necessary, press Command+Equal (Ctrl+Equal in Windows) to switch back to the Edit window.

2. Select the File > Import Audio to Region List command. (You'll notice that the Region List at the right side of the Edit window contains only the single audio region you've recorded so far.)

3. In the Import Audio dialog box (shown in Figure 4.4), navigate through your disks and folders to the audio file you've chosen to import. Double-click the file to copy it into the list of audio to be imported (and converted, if necessary, to match the current session's audio format), and then click the Done button.

4. The imported audio file now appears in the Region List for this session. (If the file you imported was stereo, it will have been split into two new mono files, with the suffixes .L and .R, because Pro Tools doesn't directly support stereo interleaved files for use within tracks. However, it will appear as a single stereo audio region unless you click its triangular icon to reveal the left/right subregions.)

> ❋ **Tip: Creating New Tracks While Importing Audio**
>
> The Pro Tools File menu also offers a command for importing audio: Import > Audio to Track. It opens the same dialog box as the Import > Audio to Region List command. The difference is that, for each region you import, Pro Tools automatically creates a new audio track, with a region corresponding to that audio file already placed at its beginning. The newly created track inherits the name of the source file. This can be a real timesaver. An alternative method is to drag an audio file from the Workspace browser window directly into the Track List (assuming that this pane at the left side of the Edit window is currently visible); in a similar fashion, a new audio track will be automatically created and named after the source file.

Editing and Effects

In this section, you'll edit the audio you recorded and imported and apply some plug-in effects to alter the sound.

Editing

Now you're ready to start editing your audio—where the real fun starts! Unlike tape-based audio systems, where you actually have to cut up your original recording (a risky, destructive

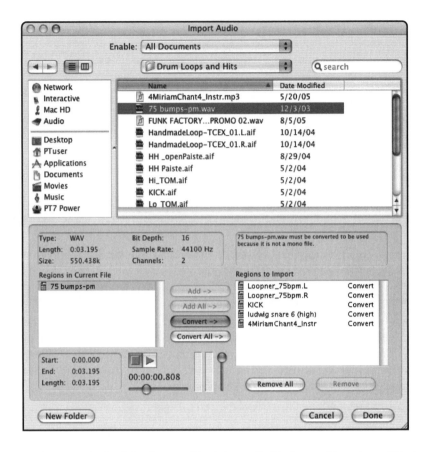

Figure 4.4 Use the Import Audio dialog box to add existing audio files (or specific regions within them) into the current Pro Tools session's Region List. Pro Tools references these files in their original disk locations unless new copies are created if you copy rather than simply add references, or if conversions are required to match the audio file format, sample rate, or bit depth of the current session.

process), in Pro Tools, you can freely move segments of audio around, adjust their length, and so on—without altering the original recordings in any way. So feel free to experiment! To get started, do the following:

1. Click on the Grabber tool to select it. It's the button that looks like a hand in the toolbar at the top of the Edit window, shown in Figure 4.5.

2. Locate the audio region you just imported in the Region List and drag it out into the track display area, releasing the mouse button to drop it anywhere near the beginning of the Drums track. Notice that as soon as you drag this region out onto the track display area, an outline of the region appears, reflecting its duration.

Figure 4.5   Use the Grabber tool to select and drag regions around within tracks (and also to move MIDI notes within MIDI tracks while in Notes display format, or to edit automation data.) Shift-click with the Grabber to select additional regions. If you hold down the Option key (Alt key in Windows) as you drag a selected region with the Grabber, it is copied rather than moved.

3. Again using the Grabber, click and drag the region, pulling it down into the FX1 track. Audio regions can reside in any Pro Tools audio track with the same number of channels, regardless of where they were originally recorded.

4. Now select the Trimmer tool. It's also in the toolbar at the top of the Edit window and looks like part of a rectangle with left/right arrows, as shown in Figure 4.6.

Figure 4.6   Use the Trimmer tool to alter the length of existing regions within tracks. You can also use it to change the duration of fades, lengthen/shorten MIDI notes, and scale automation and MIDI controller data.

5. Click and drag with the Trimmer at a point somewhere near the end of the region you recorded in the MyStuff track. Notice that as you drag back and forth without releasing the mouse button, the region gets shorter or longer (but cannot be stretched any longer than its original length, of course). Because you can see the audio waveform, you can trim the region to a shorter duration to make it end right at the point where you actually stopped playing (or singing or speaking, or whatever noise you made). After you release the mouse button, a new region definition is created, with "-01" added to the end of the original region's name. Both this new region definition (created as the result of an edit) and the original whole-file region it came from now appear in the Region List. Most editing in Pro Tools is nondestructive, meaning that the original audio is unaltered. This gives you a great deal of flexibility for experimentation.

6. Click on the Selector tool; it's between the Trimmer and Grabber tools and looks like an audio waveform with a selection in its middle portion, as shown in Figure 4.7. Click and drag the Selector's I-beam cursor to highlight a portion in the *center* of the region now residing in the FX1 track (the file you imported from disk).

7. Now delete that selection (either by pressing the Delete/Backspace key or by using the Edit > Clear command). Notice that new region names were created for the two remaining pieces at the beginning and end, with the suffixes -01 and -02 appended to the original region name. No matter how many times you delete, cut, or resize audio regions with tools in the Edit window, the process is always nondestructive—the original

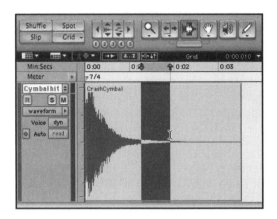

Figure 4.7 Use the Selector tool to make selections within a region or larger selections encompassing multiple regions or tracks. To adjust the boundaries of a currently highlighted selection, hold down the Shift key as you click or drag. Shift-clicking in additional tracks adds them to the current timeline selection. Shift+Tab extends the selection to the end of the current region. Option+Shift+Tab (Alt+Shift+Tab in Windows) extends the selection to the region's beginning.

audio regions and files remain intact in the Region List, and the complete audio file on disk is unaffected by any resizing or deletion in the Edit window.

Note: The Region List

The Region List is a sort of "bin" where all the audio and MIDI referenced by the current Pro Tools session appears. You can drag audio regions directly from here out onto an audio track (but not an Auxiliary Input or Master Fader track, because by definition these cannot contain audio regions). You can also drag MIDI regions onto MIDI or Instrument tracks. As you've just seen in step 7, some region definitions are automatically created by Pro Tools as a result of editing operations (although an option in the Show submenu of the local menu for the Region List allows you to suppress display of these auto-created regions, if preferred). Other chapters will also explain instances where you create your own new region definitions via commands in the Edit and AudioSuite menus, for example. *Whole-file* audio regions (as opposed to others that only represent smaller portions within their parent audio files) appear in bold face in the Region List.

---

8. Select the Zoomer tool; its button features a magnifying glass, as shown in Figure 4.8. The Zoomer changes the magnification of your horizontal (time) view of the contents of Pro Tools tracks, which enables you to be extremely precise when cutting/copying audio data within regions or trimming their length. Click and drag to highlight a very small area of the waveform within any visible audio region. Repeat. Now double-click the Zoomer to zoom out to a level of magnification where the entire session's duration fits in the Edit window.

Figure 4.8   With the Zoomer tool, click anywhere in a track to zoom in. Option-click (Alt-click in Windows) to zoom outward instead of inward. Click and drag to magnify a specific horizontal area within a track. Double-clicking the Zoomer button changes the zoom level so that the entire session's duration fits within the Edit window.

9. Be sure you've trimmed the boundaries of the audio region you recorded into the MyStuff track (with the Trimmer tool) so that it doesn't include any silences at the beginning or end. Now select this region by clicking it once with the Grabber tool.

10. Choose Options > Loop Playback to enable this feature, and then press the spacebar to start playback. Your current *selection* will be looped, rather than the session's entire timeline. (If for some reason the portion of the timeline being played doesn't change no matter *what* you select, confirm that the Options > Link Timeline and Edit and Selections option is enabled. (As you will discover, there will be times during editing when you don't want the play selection to be altered by the current edit selection.) Press the spacebar again to stop playback, but for the moment, leave the current region highlighted.

Inserting Plug-In Effects

Digital Signal Processing (DSP) allows you to shape the sound of your recorded audio in Pro Tools. On conventional mixing boards, effects-processing elements are generally of fixed types and at fixed locations. For instance, each source audio channel may have several equalization stages, while submasters or groups have none, and any external effects (for example, reverbs, delays, and so on) must be connected to the mixer's auxiliary sends and returns or to the insert point of individual channels. Worse, if each song in a project requires a different effects-processing setup, you not only have to change parameters on every external effects unit, but you may also need to reconfigure your whole cabling setup. Even if a patchbay provides flexible access to all the inputs and outputs of these devices (both multiple external effects processors and the mixing board itself), this is a laborious process.

In contrast, within Pro Tools, each virtual signal processor is actually a modular software construct called a *plug-in*. These can be inserted into the signal chain of *any* audio track, Auxiliary Input, Instrument track, or Master Fader. The entire processing and signal routing setup within each Pro Tools session document is recalled when it is reopened. Obviously, with software-based processes, noise is not an issue (unlike when using external effects units). The complexity of any effects treatments that you create is limited only by the available processing power of your system and/or your imagination! Here, you'll take a look at two typical locations for plug-in effects processors in Pro Tools: in the signal chain of an individual audio track and on an Auxiliary Input that is used as a common destination for signals sent from multiple tracks.

1. If necessary, press Command+Equal (or Ctrl+Equal in Windows) to switch from the Edit window to the Mix window. Press the spacebar to start looped playback again.

2. The mixer strip for the MyStuff track includes a Volume fader, a pan slider (a stereo track would have two), and a mute button. Take a moment to experiment with these; you probably won't find them very mysterious!

3. Now you want to create (*instantiate*) an insert effect on this track. In the top section of the track's mixer strip, you'll notice five small rectangles with up/down arrows in them. Click and hold on any one of these inserts to open its pop-up menu, and then choose plug-in > EQ > 4-Band EQ II (mono), as shown in Figure 4.9. The Parameters window for the DigiRack four-band equalizer will open. (DigiRack is Digidesign's name for the standard plug-ins included with the Pro Tools software.)

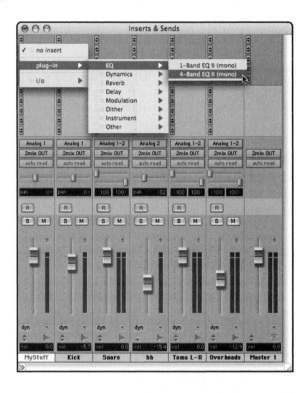

Figure 4.9 Each audio track, Aux In, Instrument track, or Master Fader in Pro Tools has five insert locations. A pop-up menu allows you to route the track's entire signal through a software effect called a plug-in or loop it out through physical audio connectors on your hardware. On audio tracks, Aux Ins, and Instrument tracks, sends allow you to additionally route some of that track's signal to a secondary destination, like a physical audio output or one of Pro Tools' internal mixing busses. Sends can be mono, stereo, or multichannel (if you've created multichannel paths for surround mixing, cue mixes, or broadcast feeds, for example).

4. Press the spacebar to start looped playback again and experiment. Drag the Gain and Frequency sliders around in the various bands of the EQ until you find some settings that amuse you and then press the spacebar to stop playback. As you're doing this, keep in mind that if you Option-click (Alt-click in Windows) on any of these sliders, they return to their default values. You will find that *many* controls in Pro Tools work the same way.

5. Now instantiate a *compressor* plug-in on one of this track's other insert points. Go back to the beginning of the song, start playback, and experiment with the Threshold slider (which determines the level at which gain reduction starts to be applied, per the selected input/output ratio).

6. Now let's go over to the Auxiliary Input you've created (named Delay), and instantiate a plug-in effect on one of its inserts, just as you did for the audio track. Let's choose the Medium Delay effect for this Aux In (choose plug-in > Delay > Medium Delay II).

7. Click and hold on the Input Selector for the Delay Aux In and select Bus > Bus 1 (Mono) as its input source. The Input Selector is at the top of this track's I/O section, just below the Sends section, as shown in Figure 4.10.

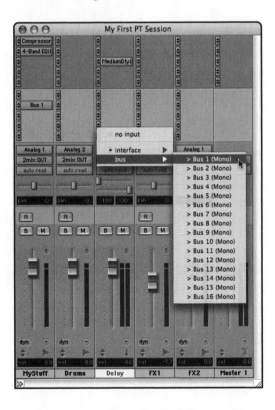

Figure 4.10   Here, we're selecting bus 1 as the input source for the Aux In where we've inserted the delay effect.

8. Option-click (Alt-click in Windows) on the Aux In's main Volume fader to set it to 0 dB. (This is also known as *unity gain* because no gain change is being applied between the fader's input and output.)

9. If you were to click Play now, you wouldn't hear anything passing through the delay because you haven't routed anything to this Aux In yet. Let's do that now. Click and hold on any one of the 10 sends for the MyStuff audio track (located underneath the Inserts section of the Mix window) to open its pop-up menu, and select Bus > Bus 1 (Mono).

10. An Output window opens for the mono send you just created. Option-click (Alt-click in Windows) on the Level (volume) slider to set it directly to 0 dB (instead of −∞).

11. Start playback. You should now also hear the sound of the audio in the MyStuff track being delayed. Reduce the Level slider of your track's send to suit your taste.

12. If necessary, click the Medium Delay insert button in this Aux In track to reopen the delay's plug-in parameters window. Experiment with the Feedback parameter, which determines how much of the delay's output is routed back into its input; this is how you produce multiple repeats.

Mixdown

OK, you're ready to consider the basics of mixing your audio to stereo and saving it. Granted, this may not be the most impressive recording of your career, but don't let that stop you!

Mixing

As we've said elsewhere, *mixdown* is the process by which a large number of source audio tracks are combined into a standard playback format (for example, two tracks for stereo or six tracks for 5.1 surround). For each track, you can adjust volume, apparent spatial placement and ambience, frequency content, and so on to create the desired audio perspective. In a Pro Tools mix, most parameters can change dynamically over time; you can automate the movement of faders, sliders, plug-in parameters, and so on to create an ideal mix or to create special effects. Below, you'll explore the two ways you can create mix automation in Pro Tools: by recording changes you make to mixing controls in real time or by using the mouse to directly create graphic shapes for the automation data within each track.

1. If you wish, take some time in the Edit window to drag or duplicate (choose Edit > Duplicate) some of your existing regions so that you have a longer mix to deal with than what you've been listening to so far.

2. Click the Return to Zero button in the Transport window (to the left of the Rewind button) to make sure the playback cursor is at the beginning of the session's timeline.

3. The Automation Mode indicator for the MyStuff audio track now displays "auto read." Using its pop-up selector, change it to "auto touch" so that any mix changes you make to this track during playback—on any controls that you actually touch—will be recorded as automation. (Pro Tools also has an Automation Enable window, which allows you to globally enable/disable different types of automation. We're assuming here that all automation types are currently enabled, which is the program default.)

4. Start playback and move the Volume fader and Pan control for this track a few times. Then stop playback.

5. Start playback again, and you'll see that Pro Tools repeats the volume and pan moves you just created.

6. Switch back to the Edit window.

7. A display format selector is available among the track controls at the left of each track in the Edit window. Right now, for the MyStuff track, it shows "waveform." Use this pop-selector to switch to displaying volume automation for this track. The volume moves you just recorded appear graphically, as a line with breakpoints.

8. Experiment with using the Grabber tool to drag these breakpoints around. This is one of the most common ways to edit automation data. You can also click anywhere on this line to create a new breakpoint. For many users, rather than recording automation in real time, it's just as easy to draw automation directly in the Edit window—which is exactly what you're going to do next.

9. Change the display format for this track from volume to pan (see Figure 4.11). The vertical ruler at the left edge of the track now shows L and R. With the Grabber, click at several places along the line (near the beginning of the track) to create some new breakpoints and drag them to several extreme left/right positions.

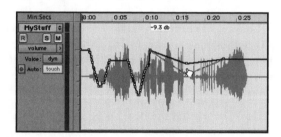

Figure 4.11 By changing the display format on the MyStuff audio track to volume, you can view and graphically edit breakpoint automation data for that parameter. You can also do this for the track's Pan control, the level, pan, and mute for any active sends on the track, and parameters on the track's plug-ins.

❊ **Tip: Automation Breakpoints**

The automation for volume, pan, and many other mix or plug-in parameters can be displayed and edited graphically within Pro Tools tracks. When viewing a track in Volume, Pan, or any other mix-automation format, lines represent the changing values for that automation parameter (superimposed over a dimmed version of the audio waveform, on audio tracks). The *breakpoints* on these lines (also known as *envelope points*, or *automation event points* in some other audio programs) are the handles you use to create automation shapes. Many of these are created automatically when you create automation by moving an onscreen control or by using one of the Pencil tool's drawing modes (like the Line or Free Hand mode, for example). Whether they've been created this way or with the Grabber tool as in steps 8 and 9 of this example, you can always drag breakpoints with the Grabber, select a range of them with the Selector, and copy, delete, or scale their values up or down with the Trimmer tool.

✻ To delete a breakpoint, Option-click it (Alt-click in Windows).

✻ For finer control, hold down the Command key (Ctrl key in Windows) while adjusting (or trimming) breakpoint values.

✻ To restrict movement of breakpoints to the vertical direction while dragging (so that their horizontal position in the timeline is unaffected), hold down the Shift key.

✻ The Nudge value is described in more detail in Chapter 6. To nudge a selected range of automation breakpoints right or left in the timeline (without affecting any audio underneath them in audio tracks), use the + and − (plus/minus) keys on the numeric keypad.

10. Now switch back to the Mix window. Click the Return to Zero button in the Transport window again and then click Play. You will now see the Pan slider moving back and forth according to the automation contours you created.

Bounce to Disk

In traditional audio studios, the mixdown would be performed in real time, and the mix output would be recorded to another audio device (for example, a two-track master recorder). In fact, this is sometimes done with Pro Tools, especially when laying off a mix to a DAT or video tape. More commonly, though, you will *bounce* the results of your Pro Tools mix into a brand-new file (which can then be used to create an audio CD or given to a computer-based video editor, interactive or DVD author, and so on). In Pro Tools, this is a real-time process, so you also have the option of incorporating external audio sources (like MIDI modules, multitrack tape recorders, or effects processors) into the resultant file. To bounce your mix to a new audio file, do the following:

1. Select File > Bounce to > Disk. In the Bounce dialog box (shown in Figure 4.12), change the Format setting to Stereo Interleaved and accept the default values for the other options.

2. Click the Bounce button. In the dialog box that appears next, type the name of whatever file (including its disk and folder location) you like for the bounced mix and click OK. As you hear your session play back in real time, a small window opens that shows a count-down of the time remaining until the bounce is completed. (If you enable the Import After Bounce option—which is only available when bouncing to mono or split mono audio files in the same file format as the session itself—the resultant audio file/region appears in the Region List afterwards. This can be useful, for example, when bouncing out a submix in order to free up tracks or CPU power.)

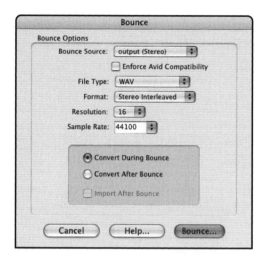

Figure 4.12   The Bounce dialog box creates new audio files based on your current mix. You name the resultant file and select the Pro Tools output that will be the source for the bounced file, the audio file formats and resolution, and so on.

✳ **Tip: What's Included in Your Bounced Mixdown File**

When nothing is currently selected in the Edit window, the entire session (from the beginning of the timeline to the end of the last audible, unmuted region in any track) is included in the resultant file. If you make a timeline selection in any track, however (assuming that Options > Link Timeline and Edit Selections is enabled), only that selected range will be included in your bounced file. Beware: Reverbs, echoes, and so on might need a few seconds to tail out beyond the actual end of the last region. When bouncing to disk, be sure to lengthen your selection enough for these to decay completely to silence before its end.

Summary

Obviously, you would carry the recording, editing, and automation process to much more useful extremes than what's been described here. Hopefully, the rudimentary exercise in this chapter has given you a basic idea of what Pro Tools is about. We'll get into all the details in the rest of this book; you'll especially want to check out the next three chapters about the Transport, Edit, and Mix windows and review the basic concepts laid out in Chapter 2. Read on!

5 } The Transport Window

In this chapter and the next two, we're going to provide specifics about most (but not all!) elements in the Transport, Edit, and Mix windows of Pro Tools. These key windows are where you will spend most of your time. If you get a handle on them, you'll be ready to tackle serious Pro Tools projects. In these three chapters, we highlight the most essential features and techniques you must know in order to be an all-around competent Pro Tools user. For that reason, please note that we don't comment on every selection in every menu—that's what the Pro Tools documentation is for! Two documents, the *Pro Tools Reference Guide* and the *Menu Guide*, provided in PDF format with Pro Tools, are excellent sources for more detailed information.

Other chapters in this book provide additional practical examples for many of the features briefly described here. Although we clarify some concepts and point out many useful tips and shortcuts along the way, much of the material in this chapter, as well as in Chapters 6, "The Edit Window," and 7, "The Mix Window," may be review for readers with significant Pro Tools experience. If that's your case, feel free to browse!

The Transport window (shown in Figure 5.1) includes basic tape-type controls for controlling playback and recording, with numeric displays for the current selection and pre-/post-roll settings and MIDI controls. This chapter reviews each of the elements in the Transport, which is a floating window that can overlap either the Mix or Edit window in Pro Tools, staying in place even as you switch from one to the other. (Unlike most other windows in Pro Tools, it doesn't have a title bar or scrollbars, nor can it be resized.) Many of its functions are also available through menu selections and/or keyboard shortcuts.

❋ **Tip: Pro Tools Documentation**

Be sure to check out the PDF (Acrobat Reader) documents that Digidesign provides in the Documentation folder (Digidesign > Documentation > Pro Tools). These documents (plus the book currently in your hands, of course) will be a great help getting you up to speed. Even more convenient, you can open these documents directly from the Help menu inside Pro Tools.

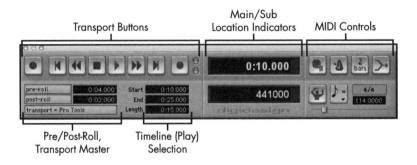

Figure 5.1 The Transport window.

> **※ Note: Keyboard Shortcuts**
>
> Like any complex program, Pro Tools offers many keyboard shortcuts, especially for frequently used features. In this book, we always start from the visible menu command or onscreen control but will emphasize keyboard shortcuts that we find most basic (that is to say, worth the effort to memorize). The *Keyboard Shortcuts* PDF document included with Pro Tools should be printed out and studied by all users. In particular, because the Transport is so essential to the operation of Pro Tools, we recommend that you learn *all* its keyboard equivalents—it will save you time!
>
> Also, for this chapter, we're assuming that, in the Operation tab of the Preferences dialog box (Preferences > Operation), the Numeric Keypad Mode setting is set to Transport (more about this later in this chapter) so that keys on the numeric keypad can be used to control the Transport functions discussed here. We're also assuming that, in the View > Transport dialog box, all three options—Counters, MIDI Controls, and Expanded—are enabled.
>
> Another reminder: Unlike with many Mac and Windows programs, the Return key on the alphanumeric keyboard (a.k.a. the Enter key in Windows) and the Enter key on the numeric keypad are usually *not* equivalent! The Enter key on the numeric keypad is often used for different purposes in Pro Tools—for example, for creating memory locations.

Transport Buttons

Obviously, some of these buttons (shown in Figure 5.2) behave like their equivalent controls on a video, CD, or tape deck. They are used to control playback and recording. As indicated in the descriptions provided here, keyboard shortcuts are available for all the button functions, which are summarized in Table 5.1 at the end of this chapter. If you're just starting with Pro Tools, these should be among the very first keyboard shortcuts you memorize.

Play/Stop

When you click the Play button in the Transport, playback starts at the current position noted by the Main and Sub location indicators seen in the right side of the Transport., (You can link these to the Main/Sub counters at the top of the Edit window via the Options > Link Timeline and Edit Selections command; more about this in Chapter 6.) When the Transport's Start and

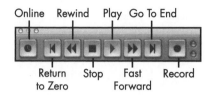

Online Rewind Play Go To End

Return Stop Fast Record
to Zero   Forward

Figure 5.2   The Transport window buttons resemble a tape recorder's controls.

End values are identical (and the length is therefore zero), playback continues indefinitely until you click Stop. Otherwise, playback begins at the Start location and stops when the End value is reached (or loops back around if you've enabled the Options > Loop Playback option). If you prefer using your computer keyboard to issue commands, pressing the spacebar (or pressing 0 on the numeric keypad) is always the same as clicking the Play button; press the same key again to stop playback.

❄ **Tip: Half-Speed Play/Record in Pro Tools**

Using Pro Tools, you can record things at half speed and play them back at double speed. Don't worry, we won't tell your friends you can't really sing that high—hey, Alvin—or shred like Eddie on too much caffeine. To record at half speed, hold down the Shift and Command keys (Shift and Ctrl keys in Windows) as you press the spacebar. For half-speed playback, hold down the Shift key as you press the spacebar.

Rewind/Fast Forward

Like the Play/Stop buttons, the Rewind/Fast Forward buttons are similar to the equivalent controls on a tape deck. You can also repeatedly click either of these to jump forward or back through the session timeline in increments determined by the units currently being displayed in the Transport window's Main location indicator—entire seconds or entire bars, for example. (If you're in the Edit window, however, it may be just as easy to click anywhere in a track with the Selector tool to reset the current play position—as long as the Options > Link Timeline and Edit Selections option is enabled.) You can also click and hold on these buttons to shuttle through the Pro Tools timeline. Keyboard equivalents for the Rewind/Fast Forward buttons are 1 and 2 on the computer's numeric keypad, respectively.

❄ **Tip: Audio During Rewind/Fast Forward**

To *hear* the audio play while using the Rewind and Fast Forward functions (via either the buttons in the Transport or Edit windows or the keyboard shortcuts mentioned previously), enable the Audio During Fast Forward/Rewind option in the Operations tab of the Preferences dialog box. While you hold down either of these buttons, playback skips forward or backward through the timeline, in a similar fashion as using the scan buttons on a CD player. This makes it easy to locate or replay a range within your audio material, and we recommend enabling this option for all users. (During rewind/fast forward in

---

Pro Tools, audio doesn't play back at fast speed or in reverse as on analog tape, and MIDI tracks don't play at all. However, some TDM users opt to change their numeric keypad preferences to Shuttle, as opposed to the more conventional Transport mode generally assumed throughout this book. In that mode, audio *does* play back at accelerated speed while shuttling forward or backward through the timeline. Use either technique—whatever helps you find your way!)

Return to Zero/Go to End

Clicking the Return to Zero button sets the playback position (and the *Timeline selection*) to the beginning of the Pro Tools timeline. Return to Zero sets the current playback position to the left edge of the timeline, regardless of what timeline units are in use or what actual bar number or session start time this corresponds to. Clicking the Go to End button resets the current playback position to the end of the last region in the session (its right edge). If you had anything selected in the Edit window (for example, a region you've been looping as you made adjustments), pressing Return to Zero or Go to End also deselects it. If you have moved the Song Start Marker to some location other than the actual start of the session's timeline, the playback cursor will back to that position the first time you press the Return to Zero button and then move to the actual beginning of the timeline the *second* time you press the same button. The keyboard equivalent for Return to Zero is Return (Enter in Windows) on the alphanumeric keyboard, and the equivalent for Go to End is Option+Return (Ctrl+Enter in Windows) on the alphanumeric keyboard.

Online

Clicking the Online button puts the Transport in Online mode, where playback/recording starts and stops according to SMPTE time code received. (SMPTE time code is explained in Chapter 11, "Synchronization.") In the Session Setup window (opened via the Setup menu), you can set the start time for the current session. This determines what incoming SMPTE time-code value will correspond to the left edge of the Edit window (the beginning of your session's timeline).

When you enable Online mode, if the incoming SMPTE time code values (for example, from a multitrack audio recorder or a video master) correspond to a location *prior* to the Session Start time value for the current session, Pro Tools waits until that position is reached and then starts playback. (Playback then stops after you press Stop on the master device sending time code, and the flow of SMPTE time code values into Pro Tools ends.) If the incoming SMPTE time code values correspond to a location *later* than the Session Start time value, Pro Tools jumps to the corresponding position and commences playback (even if this position is actually beyond the last region of audio in your session). The Command+J keyboard shortcut (Ctrl+J in Windows) toggles Online mode on/off.

❋ **Note: Synchronizing Pro Tools to Video and Multitrack Recorders**

As mentioned in the preceding paragraph, in Online mode, Pro Tools playback is triggered at a position determined by incoming time code values (and the Start Time value specified in the Session Setup window).

An external SMPTE synchronizer is required to convert the incoming SMPTE (encoded into an audio or video signal) to MIDI Time Code (MTC). This, in turn, is communicated to Pro Tools via the optional MIDI/ SMPTE interface in your configuration. For more details about SMPTE time code, MTC, and synchronization in general, see Chapter 11.

Record

Clicking the Record button arms Pro Tools for recording mode. (At least one audio or MIDI track must first be record enabled before Pro Tools will allow you to start recording.) After you click the Record button, it flashes; recording then commences when you click the Play button. If the Pre-Roll option is enabled (discussed later in this chapter, under "Transport Window Fields"), playback begins before actual recording starts by the indicated time interval. If the Post-Roll option is enabled, playback continues after recording ends by the indicated time interval. If Timeline and Edit selections are linked, selections in the Edit window (or directly changing the Start, End, or Length value in the Transport window) can be used to specify where recording will punch in and punch out. Remember that unless you've deliberately enabled Destructive Record mode (in the Options menu), every record pass is saved. A new file/region is created for each take and automatically assigned a name derived from the track name where it was recorded (which is why it's good practice to assign meaningful names to your tracks *before* recording—it saves time later!).

Pro Tools offers various recording modes: Normal, Destructive, Loop Record, QuickPunch (and TrackPunch in Pro Tools HD). The current mode affects the appearance of the Record button itself, as shown in Figure 5.3. You can cycle through these recording modes by right-clicking the Record button (and/or Control-clicking the button on Macintosh). Each of these recording modes is discussed in further detail within the Options menu section of Chapter 8, "Menu Selections: Highlights." If you prefer, you have your choice of several keyboard shortcuts to start recording: Command+Spacebar (Ctrl+Spacebar in Windows), the 3 key on the computer's numeric keypad, or the F12 key. (Mac users see the following Caution about reassigning the shortcut key for Dashboard.)

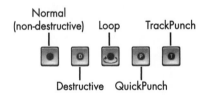

Figure 5.3 The appearance of the Record button indicates the current recording mode: Normal (non-destructive), Destructive, Loop, QuickPunch (and TrackPunch, in Pro Tools HD). You can cycle through these modes by Control-clicking the Record button (or by right-clicking the Record button in Windows).

❄ **Caution: Macintosh, Pro Tools, and Using Function Keys F9—F12.**

In any Macintosh operating system version 10.3 (a.k.a. "Panther") or higher, these F-key shortcuts in Pro Tools won't work properly unless you change your System Preferences settings. Traditionally, F9 selects the Scrubber tool, F10 the Pencil tool, and (if this option is enabled in Preferences) F11 toggles the Wait for Note function of the Transport on and off. Starting with Mac OS 10.3, however, Apple introduced an immensely useful feature called Exposé. From within any program, while holding down certain F keys, you can temporarily view all open windows simultaneously, including folder views, application windows only, or the desktop. While in these temporary views, you can click within another document or application window to switch or even double-click to navigate through disks and folders in the Finder without leaving your original program at all. However, inconveniently for Macintosh Pro Tools users, the default F keys for toggling to these three views are F9, F10, and F11!

In operating system 10.4 (a.k.a. "Tiger"), which is the minimum requirement for Pro Tools version 7, the new Dashboard feature was added for popping open utilities called Widgets. While this can be done from the Dock, there's also a default keyboard shortcut: F12, which is also used in Pro Tools to initiate recording.

Fortunately, both of these conflicts are very easy to fix:

1. Open System Preferences, under the Apple menu.

2. In the Personal section, click Dashboard & Exposé.

3. You will see the F keys currently assigned to the three Exposé options for temporarily switching the view. Use the pop-up menus to reassign them to something else. For example, on our systems, to make them easy to remember, we've simply added the Shift key to the default shortcuts. If you'd like to do the same, simply hold down the Shift key while opening the pop-up menu for each Exposé option, in order to reassign these to Shift+F9, Shift+F10, and Shift+F11. Then do the same for the fourth pop-up menu, reassigning the Dashboard shortcut to Shift+F12.

❄ **Note: About Numeric Keypad Modes (Preferences)**

In the Preferences dialog box, you can switch the mode of numeric-keypad operation in Pro Tools. In Transport mode, the numeric-keypad equivalents shown in Table 5.1 are enabled. We consider Transport to be the most generally useful mode, and throughout this book, we always refer to numeric-keypad shortcuts based on this recommendation. Classic mode emulates how the numeric keypad worked in Pro Tools versions prior to 5.0. On TDM systems, a third mode called Shuttle allows these keys to control Pro Tools playback at extra-slow or extra-fast speeds, stopping once you release the key; many users also find this handy.

Transport Window Fields

This section discusses additional fields that can be displayed in the Transport window (if the View > Transport > Expanded option is enabled). Not only can you directly enter numerical values into these fields (which can be seen in Figure 5.4), but several of them can be directly affected by your actions in the Transport and Edit windows, serving as data displays for your current Timeline selection, play position, and so on.

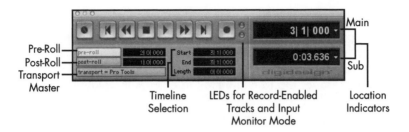

Pre-Roll
Post-Roll
Transport
Master

Timeline
Selection

LEDs for Record-Enabled
Tracks and Input
Monitor Mode

Main

Sub

Location
Indicators

Figure 5.4 Various Transport window fields provide information about your current selection, playback position, pre/post-roll times, and whether the Pro Tools Transport window is master or slave to other devices in your studio.

Main/Sub Indicators for Current Location

The Main and Sub location indicators are counters that display the current play position. They are static while stopped, continually change during play/record, and can be set to different time units. When the Options > Link Timeline and Edit Selections option is enabled, making a selection in the Edit window also resets the Transport's Timeline selection—the current play position corresponds to the beginning of that selection. (The Main and Sub counters at the top of the Edit window represent the Edit selection, which, when convenient, can be unlinked from the actual Timeline selection that will play back when you press the spacebar.) A pop-up menu to the right of each counter lets you change the time units of each indicator. For example, you might choose to display musical bars and beats in the Main counter and minutes and seconds in the Sub counter.

You can change the location value in the Main counter in several ways:

❄ Using the Transport buttons—Rewind/Fast Forward, Return to Zero/Go to End, and so on.

❄ By making a new selection or clicking anywhere in the Edit window's main Time ruler, assuming the Options > Link Timeline and Edit Selections option is enabled.

❄ Recalling a user-defined memory location (more about these in Chapter 6).

❄ Clicking in the field and typing a new value (see the following tip.)

> **Tip: Quick Entry of New Locations in the Main Location Indicator**
>
> Pressing the asterisk (*) key on the numeric keypad selects the Main location indicator for data entry, pressing the period (.) key switches between columns, pressing the up/down arrows lets you increment/decrement the selected value, and pressing the Return key on the alphanumeric keyboard (Enter in Windows) confirms your entry into this numerical field. So if you're using Minutes:Seconds as the time unit in the Main location indicator, to go to 1 minute, 30 seconds, you would press the following sequence on the numeric keypad: *1.30 (Return/Enter). If you were in Bars:Beats mode and wanted to set the playback cursor directly to bar 15, beat 3, you would press the following sequence on the numeric keypad: *15.3 (Return/Enter). Alternatively, if you're working on a musical piece using Bars:Beats mode, you could press the asterisk (*) key, press the up arrow four times, and then press Return (Enter on Windows) on the alphanumeric keyboard to move the play position four bars later.

Play Selection: Start/End/Length Fields

Assuming that the Options > Link Timeline and Edit Selections option is enabled, if you simply click somewhere in the Edit window with the Selector tool, the values in the Start and End fields of the Transport window will be identical. (This is also the case if you use the Rewind, Fast Forward, Go to Zero, or Go to End button to change the playback location, or if you recall a Marker memory location—these are discussed in Chapter 8.) The Start value is the position where playback will begin when you click Play.

On the other hand, if you make a selection, either by clicking and dragging with the selector or highlighting an existing region with the Grabber, the beginning, end, and duration of the current selection are indicated in the Start, End, and Length fields (again, unless you've disabled the Link Timeline and Edit Selections option in the Options menu). You can also click in any of these three fields to manually enter new values. Time units displayed in the Transport's Start, End, and Length fields always match those of the Main location indicator.

The Start and End fields determine where recording stops and starts in Record mode. In both recording and playback, these Start and End points may be preceded or followed by the specified pre-roll and post-roll intervals, if that option is enabled—see the following section in this chapter for more details. When Loop Playback (or recording) is enabled, Pro Tools will continuously cycle the material between the Start and End values until you stop playback.

> ❋ **Tip: Quick Entry into the Transport Window's Start/End/Length Fields**
>
> Hold down the Option key (Alt key in Windows) and press "/" on the numeric keypad to directly select the Start field in the Transport window. Each subsequent press of the "/" key cycles through the Start, End, and Length fields for numerical entry, as well as the Pre-Roll and Post-Roll fields. As with other time value fields in Pro Tools, you can use the period key (or left/right arrow keys) to switch columns as you enter values, type numerical values (or use the up/down arrow keys), and then hit Return or Enter to confirm your entry (or the Esc key to exit without changing the field).

Pre-Roll/Post-Roll

If the Pre-Roll button is enabled, when you click Play, playback actually starts before the current value in the Start field (or the current selection in the Edit window) by the time interval you enter in the Pre-Roll field. Time units in this field always match those of the Main location indicator display (Bars:Beats, Minutes:Seconds, Samples, SMPTE time code, and so on). The Post-Roll button and field work in a similar fashion; playback continues past the current value in the End field (or the end of the current Edit window selection) by the specified amount. In Record mode, however, recording (on record-enabled tracks) will always punch in and punch out exactly at the values in the Start and End fields. Having Pre-Roll enabled therefore facilitates making inserts or drop-ins on previously recorded takes because you can monitor the surrounding audio material as you record the new segment.

Besides double-clicking to manually enter new time values into the Pre/Post-Roll fields, you can use the Pre-Roll and Post-Roll flags in the Edit window's main Time ruler, as shown in

Figure 5.5. (They're white if inactive, green if enabled.) To change Pre/Post-Roll intervals, simply drag the corresponding flag to the left and right of the current Start/End indicators. The Command+K keyboard shortcut (Ctrl+K in Windows) toggles both Pre- and Post-Roll on/off.

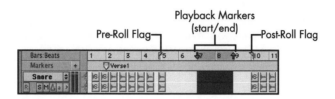

Figure 5.5 The Edit window's main Time ruler in Bars:Beats format. Start and end points for recording are currently at bars 7 and 9, with two bars of pre-roll and one bar of post-roll.

Transport Master

Most users will leave this set to the default option, Pro Tools. However, if you want another machine to directly control Transport functions in Pro Tools (which requires appropriate hardware/software, like the synchronization peripherals discussed in Chapter 11, and optional MachineControl software from Digidesign), you would make that selection here: MachineControl, MMC (MIDI Machine Control), or ADAT. When MMC is selected, the playback position of Pro Tools is controlled by the position values transmitted from an external device via MIDI.

❈ **Note: External Control Surfaces and the Pro Tools Transport**

Transport functions can be remote controlled from external control surfaces. Options include Digidesign's D-Control, D-Command, ProControl, Command|8, Control|24, the Mackie HUI, the J.L. Cooper CS-10^2, and others (see Appendix B, "Add-Ons, Extensions, and Cool Stuff for Your Rig," for more information).

Record Enable Status/Input Status

These small indicators are to the right of the Record button and look like LEDs. The top red indicator is lit whenever any track is record enabled (that is, the R button in its track controls is red). The lower green indicator is lit when you enable Track > Input Only Monitoring so that all tracks monitor their selected input (regardless of whether any regions already reside on the track).

MIDI Transport Controls

The Transport controls discussed in this section are all related to tempos, time signature (meter), metronome settings, countoff settings, recording modes, and other features that are useful for music production, and especially for using MIDI tracks and instruments in Pro Tools. If you don't have any MIDI devices in your studio setup (and don't use meter/tempo changes with the Event > Identify Beat command), you may save screen space by choosing not to view these MIDI Transport controls, which, by default, appear at the right end of the Transport window (shown in Figure 5.6). To hide the MIDI Transport controls, choose View > Transport > MIDI Controls.

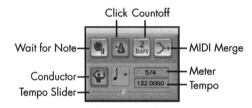

Figure 5.6 The Transport window, with MIDI controls shown.

Wait for Note

When the Wait for Note button is enabled during Record mode, recording on any record-enabled audio/MIDI tracks will not commence until a MIDI event is received from your controller. This option, which you can enable in the Operation tab of the Preferences dialog box, is really handy if you need time to hustle across the room to your keyboard! Naturally, if the Pre-Roll option is enabled, Pro Tools will still begin playback from some earlier point, with actual recording not punching in until the value in the Start field is reached. The keyboard shortcut for enabling/disabling the Wait for Note option is F11. (Mac users should see the note at the beginning of this chapter about changing the default F-key shortcuts for Exposé in System Preferences.)

❋ **Tip: Remote Starting Record in Pro Tools via MIDI**

The Wait for Note function can also be handy while recording audio tracks, likewise giving you time to get across the room to a microphone or instrument without recording a lot of dead air after clicking the Record button. Even if you don't record any MIDI tracks at all, if you have an inexpensive MIDI keyboard and a MIDI interface on your computer, you could stretch a MIDI cable all the way over to the keyboard inside your isolation booth. Click Record in Pro Tools (with Wait for Note enabled). Then, when you're in position and ready to sing or play, pressing any note on the MIDI keyboard will start recording (after the designated Pre-Roll interval, if enabled). You could even use the sustain pedal on this keyboard to activate recording so that your hands stay free!

Metronome Click

Clicking this button turns the metronome click on/off. Double-click the button to open the Click/
Countoff Options dialog box (see Figure 5.8 in the next section), where you can specify
whether this metronome sound should occur only while in Record mode, in Record *and* Play
modes, or only during the countoff bars (see the next section). All Pro Tools versions 6 and
higher include a Click plug-in (shown in Figure 5.7), which can used as an insert on an Aux
In track. The Click plug-in automatically responds to the Pro Tools tempo when the Transport's
Metronome Click button is enabled; no routing to it is necessary from the Click/Countoff
Options dialog box. (Volume levels for accented and unaccented beats are set directly within
the plug-in itself.) Alternatively, some external MIDI device (or software-based instrument)
can be used to produce an audible click sound in response to Note On MIDI events transmitted
from Pro Tools. If you do this, you can configure the MIDI note and velocities, output, and
channel in this dialog box. To toggle the Metronome Click button on and off, you can also
press the 7 key on the computer's numeric keypad.

Figure 5.7 The Click plug-in can be used on a mono Aux In and produces a variety of metronome sounds
according to the current Pro Tools tempo.

Countoff

When the Countoff button is enabled, Pro Tools plays the metronome click sound for the
specified number of measures (according to the current tempo and time signature) before
playback or recording begins. The countoff click sound will play even if the Click button is
turned off (in which case the click sound stops once Play or Record mode begins). Double-
clicking the Countoff button (or Metronome Click button) opens the Click/Countoff Options
dialog box (shown in Figure 5.8), where you can specify how many bars of countoff you
want. (Notice that if you wish, countoff can occur only when you're in Record mode.) To
toggle the Countoff button on and off, you can also press the 8 key on your computer's numeric
keypad.

MIDI Merge

With the MIDI Merge button enabled, when recording MIDI into a track already containing
MIDI regions, the newly recorded MIDI data is combined into the existing material instead
of replacing it as a new MIDI region. For example, to build up a drum track while looping a

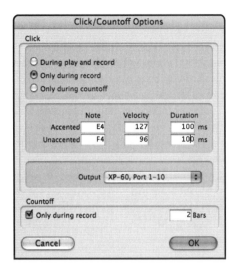

Figure 5.8   Open the Click/Countoff Options dialog box by double-clicking the Click or Countoff button in the Transport window.

couple of bars, make your Timeline selection, ensure that Pro Tools is not in Destructive Recording mode, and enable the Options > Loop Playback option. Then enable the MIDI Merge button. The notes you play in each repetition of the looped selection are *added* to the previous MIDI data instead of replacing it. (In Loop Recording mode, the MIDI Merge button is dimmed because it has no effect. Instead, for every cycle of Loop Record where you input new MIDI data, a new, separate take/MIDI region is always created.) To toggle MIDI Merge on and off, assuming as always that the numeric keypad mode is set to Transport in the Preferences dialog box, press the 9 key on the computer's numeric keypad.

Tempo Ruler Enable

Clicking the Tempo Ruler Enable button (which has a "conductor" icon) enables the tempo map. If the Tempo ruler in the Edit window contains tempo Change events, enabling this button makes these active. (To make the Tempo ruler visible, choose View > Ruler > Tempo.) When the Tempo Ruler Enable button is *not* enabled, the current manual bpm (beats per minute) setting in the Transport's Tempo field applies to the entire session; it can be edited numerically or via the Tempo slider. Conversely, Pro Tools will *not* allow you to make manual changes to the Transport's Tempo field while this button is enabled.

Current Meter

The Current Meter button indicates the musical meter (time signatures of 4/4, 5/4, 6/8, and so on) at the current play position. Of course, different bars can have different meter settings in Pro Tools! You can use the Time Operations/Meter Change window, shown in Figure 5.9, to create Time Signature events in all Pro Tools versions 6.7 and higher.

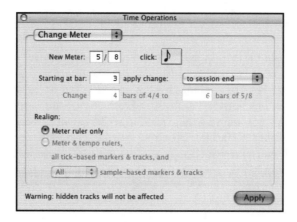

Figure 5.9 You can create changes of time signature (meter) in the Time Operations window.

Alternatively, double-clicking the Transport window's Current Meter indicator (or clicking the + sign in the Edit window's Tempo ruler) opens the Meter Change window, shown in Figure 5.10. The initial location for meter changes can be edited, but it defaults to the current Start position. Be sure to place it at the beginning of Bar 1 (and select To Session End, if using the Time Operations window) if you want this new time signature to apply to the entire session!

Figure 5.10 You can open the Meter Change window by double-clicking the Meter button in the Transport window.

Tempo

In this field, tempo settings appear in bpm (beats per minute). The reference note value for the tempo (1/4 note, 1/8 note, and so on) appears in the pop-up Tempo Resolution selector at the left of the Tempo field. When the Tempo Ruler Enable button is *not* enabled, there are three main ways to manually change the musical tempo setting in the Transport window:

❊ Click in the Tempo field and type tempo values directly. As in many numerical fields in Pro Tools, you can also click and drag with the mouse to scroll these values upward or downward.

❊ Use the manual Tempo slider below the Tempo field. Hold down the Command key (Ctrl key in Windows) for finer adjustments.

❊ Select the Tempo field and tap in the tempo in real time from your MIDI controller or the T key on your computer keyboard—if this option is enabled in the MIDI tab of the Preferences dialog box. Pro Tools computes the average tempo based on your last eight taps. As pointed out in Chapter 13, "Music Production," this is by far the best method for setting up a click track tempo when working with live performers. Just have them play through the song naturally and tap along to set your correct tempo *before* feeding any click track into their cue mix. With bands that are inexperienced in the studio, you should also consider tapping in the tempo based on a cassette of a rehearsal or performance (audio quality is irrelevant), since their sense of appropriate tempo may be unreliable in this unfamiliar context.

Alternatively, the Identify Beat command can be used to create a MIDI tempo setting based on an audio selection. To use this feature, you must first enable the Conductor button (which disables the field for manual tempo settings in the Transport window). As with Meter events, if you use the Tempo Operations window shown in Figure 5.11 to create Tempo Change events, select Bar 1, Beat 1 (1|1|000) and To Session End if you want these to apply to the entire session.

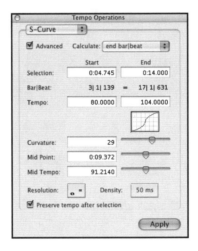

Figure 5.11 Tempo Operations window.

Another method for creating Tempo Change events is to click the + sign in the Edit window's Tempo ruler. Remember, though, that whenever the Conductor button is enabled (so that events in the Tempo and Meter rulers are in effect), you cannot manually make changes to the Tempo setting. You can also *graphically* edit tempo changes in the Edit window, using an editing pane that opens from the Tempo ruler. To learn more sophisticated techniques for managing tempo settings in Pro Tools, see Chapter 8.

Traditionally, tempo changes always affected the position of events within MIDI tracks in Pro Tools. However, version 7 introduced the option to assign the timebase of any MIDI track to Samples, so that the positions of the MIDI events within it will not be affected by subsequent tempo or meter changes. Users of MIDI-based sound effects for soundtrack work will find this especially useful.

Aux In and Master Fader tracks can optionally be set to Ticks (relative) timebase instead of the conventional Samples (absolute) timebase. For all track types assigned to Ticks timebase, positions of all events within them are relative to the session's tempo and will shift when you create or edit tempo changes (manually or in the Conductor track).

❄ **Tip: Punching Recordings In/Out Within Previously Recorded Material**

Do you need to replace one line of lyrics or dialog within an existing recording, or one portion of an instrumental part? Here's a quick how-to. First, in the Edit window, use the Selector tool to precisely highlight the section of the track you want to replace. (We're assuming here that the Options > Link Timeline and Edit Selections option is enabled.) By the way, we recommend that you DON'T use Destructive Recording mode while doing this! Then enable the Pre/Post-Roll buttons and set appropriate times in the Pre/Post-Roll fields so that the performer can match the levels and sound of the material before and after the newly inserted recording. Click on that track's Rec button to record-enable it, click the Record button in the Transport, and then click Play. Repeat as necessary!

Although this technique is useful when you know exactly when recording needs to begin and end, QuickPunch and TrackPunch recording modes allow you to punch in and out of recording mode "on the fly." See the descriptions of these functions in Chapter 8 for more details.

In Table 5.1, we've listed just a few of the Transport-related keyboard shortcuts in Pro Tools. However, there are many more. Among the PDF documents included with the program is one entitled *Keyboard Shortcuts,* which we have mentioned previously. Print it out and keep it handy—consider using card stock or even having it laminated. Learning keyboard shortcuts early in the process is one of the most important things you can do to increase your productivity with Pro Tools.

Table 5.1   Essential Keyboard Shortcuts for Transport Functions

Function	Macintosh	Windows
Play start/stop	Spacebar	Spacebar
	0 on numeric keypad	0 on numeric keypad
Loop Playback On/Off	4 on numeric keypad	4 on numeric keypad
	Right-click Play button	Right-click Play button
	Control-click Play button	
Rewind/Fast-Forward	1 and 2 on numeric keypad	1 and 2 on numeric keypad

Function	Macintosh	Windows
Return to Zero	Return on alpha keyboard	Enter on alpha keyboard
Go to End	Option+Return on alpha keyboard	Alt+Enter on alpha keyboard
Record start	Command+Spacebar	Ctrl+Spacebar
	F12	F12
	3 on numeric keypad	3 on numeric keypad
Record stop	Spacebar	Spacebar
Record stop and discard take	Command+. (period)	Ctrl+. (period)
		Esc key
Loop Record On/Off	5 on numeric keypad	5 on numeric keypad
Toggle through Record modes	Control-click on Record button	Right-click on Record button
	Right-click on Record button	
Pre+Post Roll On/Off	Command+K	Ctrl+K
Show/Hide Transport	Command+1 on numeric keypad	Ctrl+1 on numeric keypad
Online mode On/Off	Command+J	Ctrl+J
	Option+Spacebar	Alt+Spacebar
Online Record On/Off	Command+Option+Spacebar	Ctrl+Alt+Spacebar
Wait for Note (MIDI)	F11	F11
Click On/Off (MIDI)	7 on numeric keypad	7 on numeric keypad
Countoff On/Off (MIDI)	8 on numeric keypad	8 on numeric keypad
MIDI Merge On/Off (MIDI)	9 on numeric keypad	9 on numeric keypad
Select & cycle through time fields for numerical entry	Option + "/" on numeric keypad	Alt + "/" on numeric keypad
Select Main counter for numerical entry	*(asterisk) on numeric keypad	*(asterisk) on numeric keypad
Move between columns during numerical entry in time fields	Period or arrow keys	Period or arrow keys

Summary

The Transport functions are the most frequently used features in Pro Tools, so make an effort to learn these keyboard shortcuts early—they work whether the Transport window itself is currently visible or not. (Once again, throughout this book we're assuming you're using the default Transport mode for the numeric keypad, specified in the Preferences dialog box.) In the next chapter, we explore the most important elements in the Edit window.

6 The Edit Window

The Edit window (Figure 6.1) is the heart of Pro Tools. This is where you can do things like view the contents of your tracks, edit your audio and MIDI regions, edit MIDI notes, create fades and crossfades, and draw automation changes for volume, panning, and plug-in parameters. In most respects, however, the Edit and Mix windows present two views of the same thing. Many items appear in both windows, including track names and the Mute, Solo, and Record Enable buttons. Furthermore, some users choose to have the sends, inserts, instruments, and I/O sections (which appear by default in the Mix window) appear in the Edit window. In any case, this is where you will likely spend most of your time in Pro Tools. The fact that this chapter about the Edit window is by far the longest in this book should give you an idea how essential its features are for mastering Pro Tools!

The basic idea of the Edit window is simple enough. Underneath the toolbar and numerical display area at the top of the screen are the audio, Auxiliary Input, Master Fader, Instrument, and MIDI tracks in your session, stretching along a timeline from left to right. The Region List (including both audio and MIDI regions in versions 7.0 and higher of Pro Tools) is a "bin" that can be displayed at the right side of the Edit window. Segments (regions) of audio or MIDI you've recorded or imported into Pro Tools appear here, including region names automatically created by Pro Tools as a result of editing or processing—whether or not they're currently placed into a track. You can drag regions directly from the Region List out onto tracks (audio, MIDI, or Instrument, as appropriate). You can also rename, export, or delete regions (as well as preview audio regions) right inside the Region List, using its local pop-up menu.

You can change the display format of each track in the Edit window. For example, you can graphically edit changes to each track's volume or panning, viewing this automation as lines and breakpoints. On audio or MIDI tracks, this breakpoint automation is superimposed over a dimmed-out version of the audio waveform (or MIDI notes) within the regions that the track contains.

The four basic editing modes in the Edit window are Slip, Shuffle, Grid, and Spot. Edit modes determine how regions behave as they are moved within tracks, how to move automation and MIDI data, and how editing tools behave. Briefly, the Slip mode allows free

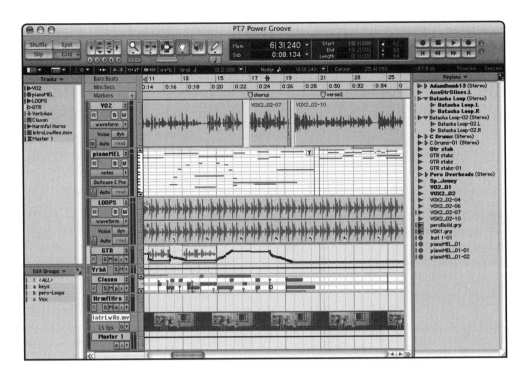

Figure 6.1 The Edit window, showing various track types and display formats.

movement; Shuffle mode snaps regions to each other like magnets; Grid mode adjusts movement to certain increments like the snap-to-grid mode in drawing programs; Spot mode allows locations to be entered numerically. By the way, you can use the tilde (~) key to toggle between the four edit modes, or you can select a mode using the F1, F2, F3, and F4 keys, respectively. Later in this chapter, you will find more specifics on the edit modes and how they affect the behavior of various tools.

Before getting into these specifics, however, this chapter elaborates on edit tools, edit modes, and track types and reviews automation and other important elements in the Edit window.

Edit Tools: The Zoomer, Trimmer, Selector, Grabber, Smart Tool, Scrubber, and Pencil

The editing tools, shown in Figure 6.2, provide a multitude of ways to manipulate regions, automation, and MIDI events within Pro Tools tracks. (You can also use many of these in the graphic Tempo editor.)

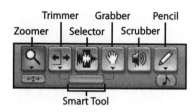

Figure 6.2   Editing tools: Zoomer, Trimmer, Selector, Grabber, Scrubber, Pencil, and the Smart Tool.

Zoomer

When you select the Zoomer tool, the cursor turns into a miniature magnifying glass, as shown in Figure 6.3. Click anywhere in a track to zoom in. Hold down the Option key (Alt key in Windows) to switch from zooming *in* to zooming *out* (the plus sign in the zoom cursor changes to a minus sign). Click and drag over a specific area within a track to magnify it to the current width of the Edit window's track display area. The Zoomer tool has a drop-down selector for two modes: Normal Zoom and Single Zoom (which deselects the Zoomer tool after one zoom, returning to whatever editing tool you previously selected—a good feature to remember!). Later in this chapter, you will find a section about zoom controls and preset buttons, keyboard shortcuts, and the Zoom Toggle icon. Use the F5 keyboard shortcut to select this tool and to switch between the Zoomer modes.

Figure 6.3   The Zoomer's magnifying glass cursor.

Trimmer

The Trimmer tool can be used to shorten or lengthen regions and to scale automation shapes up or down. Depending on where you are within the file, the tool automatically determines whether you are trimming the beginning or end of that region—the cursor changes from a left trim to a right trim as you move across a region's midpoint (see Figure 6.4). To force the Trimmer to flip from one direction to the other, hold down the Option key (Alt key in Windows). In Grid edit mode, the Trimmer snaps to each time increment on the editing grid as you drag, therefore adjusting your region's end or beginning to these grid subdivisions (per the current Grid Value). Think of a region as a window into an audio or MIDI recording, which you can make wider or narrower with the Trimmer. (Obviously, you can't lengthen a region beyond the actual beginning or end of its parent audio file.)

Figure 6.4 The Trimmer cursor is a left or right bracket at the beginning/end of regions and MIDI notes or a horizontal bracket when scaling automation or MIDI controller data up or down.

The Trimmer can also be used to scale automation shapes (such as Volume, Pan, send parameters, and some MIDI controller types) up or down within a track—for example, if you're satisfied with the overall volume changes you've created but want to trim them downward a few decibels. (Abbreviated dB, *decibels* is a measurement unit for power levels, or loudness.) Switch the track's display format to Volume (using the pop-up selector, described later in this chapter), select the entire track (or any portion), and then use the Trimmer to pull the entire volume shape downward. As you drag volume or send levels with the Trimmer, the *delta*, or amount of change, is indicated in dB.

The Trimmer tool has a drop-down selector for different modes: Standard, Scrub (TDM systems only; audio scrubbing as you trim makes it easier to locate events), and the Time Trimmer (time compression/expansion; the audio within the current selection is stretched or squeezed to match the time range you've trimmed).

You can also use the Time Trimmer on MIDI regions, scaling the MIDI data they contain. While the Tempo Operations window offers more practical ways to adjust tempos to specific durations or start/end points, users who compose or arrange music in Pro Tools may appreciate this function's usefulness for creating half-time or double-time versions of selected regions. For example, in Grid edit mode, you could select a four-bar region and then select the TCE mode of the Trimmer tool (the Time Trimmer) to compress it to a two-bar duration. Use the F6 keyboard shortcut to select the Trimmer and to switch between its modes.

Selector

When you use this tool, the mouse cursor changes to an I-beam, as shown in Figure 6.5. Click and drag within a track to select any horizontal range in the timeline within a track (whether or not your selection contains or overlaps any regions). Hold down the Shift key and click (or drag) to adjust the current selection's duration. Shift-click in additional tracks to select the same range in multiple tracks. Whatever range you select is reflected in the Start, End, and Length indicators of the Transport window, and you'll hear it when you press Play (unless you've disabled Options > Link Timeline and Edit Selections). Be aware that the currently selected edit mode also affects the behavior of the Selector (see the next section in this chapter). For example, in Grid edit mode, the beginning and end of your selections are snapped to the nearest time increment. The keyboard shortcut for the Selector is F7.

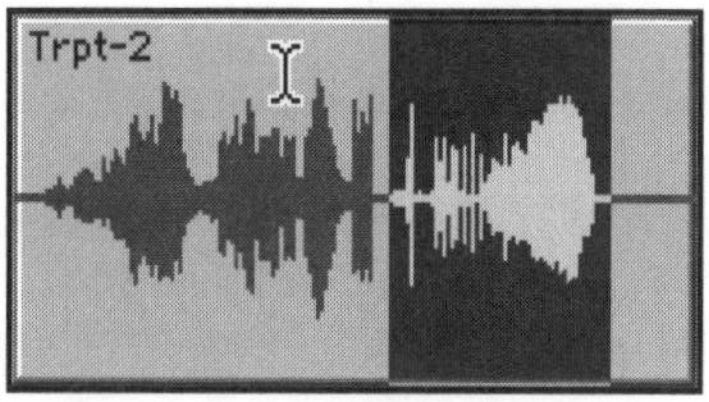

Figure 6.5 You can use the Selector's I-beam cursor to highlight ranges within tracks.

Fine-Tuning Your Selections

Let's say you've selected four bars within a drum or rhythm track because you're going to use that selection to create a tempo setting in Pro Tools (via the Event > Identify Beat command) and then repeat the phrase to start building up a groove. It's extremely important that this selection is precise and loops smoothly back onto itself. We will go more deeply into beat mixing techniques in Chapter 12, "The Pro Tools Groove," but here's a selection method that is also handy for many other situations.

1. After selecting Slip edit mode, click with the Selector tool to locate the playback cursor exactly at the beginning of the four-bar phrase. (Zoom into the sample level, make absolutely sure your cursor is *precisely* at the zero crossing where the downbeat begins, and then zoom back out.) Now, hold down Control+Shift (right-click in Windows or on any Mac with a two-button mouse) to *temporarily* select the Scrubber tool. Click and drag the Scrubber rightward until you locate the downbeat of the bar following the end of your four-bar phrase, then release the mouse button (and the Control+Shift keys, if you used these modifier keys on a Mac). Your selection should now *roughly* correspond to the four bars, and the Selector tool should still be active. (You can also create a selection on the fly during playback: Press the down arrow at the beginning and the up arrow at the end of the desired selection.)
2. Enable Options > Loop Playback, and press the spacebar to play the selection. You'll probably notice a hiccup in your looping phrase, meaning you need to refine your selection. Pressing the spacebar again stops playback. Let's assume for a moment that the beginning point is correct; our only problem is adjusting the end point of the selection to create a smooth loop.
3. Underneath the Main and Sub Counters in the Edit window is a numerical field labeled "Nudge." This sets the increments by which nudging is applied. Open the pop-up menu to the right of the Nudge Value field, select Minutes:Seconds as the reference time unit, and then select 1 millisecond as the initial nudge amount.
4. As you hold down Command+Shift (Ctrl+Shift in Windows) and press the + and – keys (plus/minus) on the numeric keypad, the end point of the current selection moves forward or back by the one-millisecond nudge increment. (To adjust the start point, use the same technique, but hold down Option+Shift or Alt+Shift in Windows instead.) Note that even if you are in Loop Playback mode, the selection to be looped will *not* be adjusted on the fly each time you nudge the selection end with the plus/minus keys. You must stop and then restart playback after making each adjustment to a looped selection's duration.
5. At some point, you will be so close that one millisecond is too large a nudge increment. Open the Nudge Value pop-up menu again, select Samples as the reference unit, and work your way down through 10-, 2-, or 1-sample nudge increments as necessary, until the loop is completely smooth.

6. Go ahead and separate this selection as a new region (using the Edit > Separate Region > At Selection command). Name it "4 bars." If you're ambitious, with this exact four-bar region still selected, try out the Event > Identify Beat command. Then switch to the Grid edit mode. Each time you press Command+D (Ctrl+D in Windows), the selected region is duplicated. Even better, use the Region menu's Loop command (which is Option+Command+L on Macintosh, Alt+Command+L on Windows) to create any number of loop aliases—an extremely useful feature added in Pro Tools 7. Have fun!

Grabber

When the Grabber tool is selected, the mouse cursor turns into a hand shape, as shown in Figure 6.6. The Grabber can be used to click and drag regions to new locations within tracks, drag and create/delete breakpoints in a track's automation, drag notes within MIDI tracks, drag tracks up and down by their name fields to change their order, and drag markers in the timeline ruler, among other things. The currently selected edit mode (see "Edit Modes: Slip, Shuffle, Grid, and Spot," later in this chapter) determines how regions will behave when you move them around within tracks with the Grabber. For example, if you are in Shuffle mode, a region will always snap to the beginning or end of another existing region (or to the beginning of the track). When you are in Grid mode, the movement of regions (and automation breakpoints) is snapped to the nearest time increment, according to the current grid value.

Figure 6.6   You can use the Grabber's hand cursor to drag regions, MIDI notes, and automation breakpoints.

Several important modifier keys alter how the Grabber tool operates:

* Like other Mac and Windows programs, holding down the Shift key as you click additional regions *adds* to the current selection. To clear one of several already-selected regions, Shift-click it again. (These techniques also apply to the Selector tool.)

* When viewing automation, clicking with the Grabber creates a new breakpoint. Option-click (Alt-click in Windows) on existing automation breakpoints with the Grabber cursor to delete them. For finer adjustment of breakpoint levels (for example, volume increments), hold down the Command (Mac) or Ctrl (Windows) key as you drag the breakpoint with the Grabber. (You can also obtain fine adjustment of *many* fader and slider values in Pro Tools by holding down this same modifier key as you drag.)

* Option-drag (Alt-drag in Windows) audio/MIDI regions or MIDI notes with the Grabber tool to *copy* instead of moving them.

❋ When dragging or copying a region from one track to another, hold down the Control key (right-click and drag with the Grabber in Windows or on any Mac with a two-button mouse) to constrain its movement to the vertical direction—meaning that the region will maintain its original timeline location regardless of the current edit mode.

The Grabber tool has three modes: Time Grabber, Separation Grabber, and Object Grabber. The Time Grabber mode is the standard mode for the Grabber tool. You can use this mode to drag entire regions within tracks. In contrast, once you've made any selection with the Selector tool, the Separation Grabber mode of the Grabber tool automatically splits the selection into a new region—as you either drag to move or Option-drag (Alt-drag in Windows) to copy. If your initial selection was across multiple tracks and regions within them, several new regions are created in each track. Finally, the Object Grabber mode allows selection of non-contiguous regions, even on different tracks—this means that as you Shift-click to select additional regions within a track, for example, the range in the timeline between them is not also selected, as is the case with the Time Grabber mode. The F8 keyboard shortcut selects the Grabber and switches between the various Grabber tool modes.

❋ **CSi: Using Edit Tools on Audio Regions**

On the CD-ROM in the back of this book, check out the sample movie tutorial from *Pro Tools 7 CSi Starter*, "Editing Audio Regions." In this sample movie tutorial, you can see the Trimmer and Grabber tools in action: how they interact with Grid edit mode (see the "Edit Modes" section in this chapter) and how to create fades, nudge regions, and other basic Pro Tools edit operations.

Smart Tool

If you highlight the *smart bar* underneath the other tools, you activate the Smart Tool, which enables you to alternate between the Trimmer, Selector, and Grabber without having to click the tool buttons to select them. The Smart Tool guesses which tool you want to use based on the position of the cursor over regions or MIDI notes (see Figure 6.7). To switch to the Smart Tool with a keyboard shortcut, press F6 and F7 simultaneously (or F7 and F8).

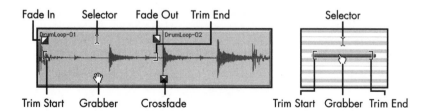

Figure 6.7 When you use Smart Tool mode, Pro Tools selects the appropriate tool according to the cursor's position within a track; the cursor shape changes accordingly. Shown here are cursors and edit operations—within an audio track (Waveform view) and a MIDI track (Notes view).

Here's how the Smart Tool knows what you want:

* When the cursor is over the middle of any region—in Waveform (audio), Regions (MIDI), or Blocks track display format—and in the lower half of the region graphic, the Grabber tool is active. In the upper half, the Selector tool is enabled.

* When the cursor is near the beginning or end of any region in these same views and in its lower half, the Trimmer tool is enabled.

* When the cursor is near the beginning or end of an audio region and in its upper half, when you click and drag, Pro Tools creates a fade in/out instead of trimming the region's duration. (Fades are not applicable to MIDI regions.) If your cursor is near the boundary between two adjacent audio regions and in the lower half of either region graphic, you can drag with the Smart Tool to create a crossfade between them (assuming there is enough additional audio available within their parent audio files to do so).

* On MIDI tracks in Notes view, the cursor changes to the Selector tool whenever you are not directly over any MIDI notes. The cursor changes to the Grabber tool when it's directly over the middle of any MIDI notes and to the Trimmer when over the beginning or end of a MIDI note.

* When you view automation on a track (and certain MIDI controller parameters, such as Volume, Pan, Pitch Bend, Mod Wheel, Mute, Aftertouch, Velocity, and so on), the cursor changes from the Selector to the Trimmer when you're in the upper portion of the track. (Also, when you view the velocity stalks for MIDI note events, the cursor changes to the Grabber when directly over the head of each stalk.)

> **Tip: Using Modifier Keys with the Smart Tool**
>
> Pro Tools provides several options for temporarily switching to other editing tools while the Smart Tool is still selected:
>
> * On audio tracks, to switch to scrubbing mode while using the Smart Tool in Waveform view (for example, to locate an audio event by ear), hold down the Control key (Start key in Windows) or simply right-click and drag.
>
> * On MIDI tracks, to make the cursor change to the Pencil while using the Smart Tool in MIDI Notes view (for example, to insert a note event), hold down the Control key (Start key in Windows).
>
> * To make the cursor change to the Grabber while using the Smart Tool in Automation view (for example, to insert or drag breakpoints), hold down the Command key (Ctrl key in Windows). For finer control, keep this modifier key pressed down as you drag the breakpoint; otherwise, release the key for coarser adjustments.

Scrubber

When you click and drag on an audio region with the Scrubber tool (see Figure 6.8), you hear the audio playing backward or forward, depending on which direction you drag. This is handy for locating audio events. The farther and faster you drag away from the initial click point, the faster the playback. Note that you *cannot* scrub MIDI tracks.

Figure 6.8 The Scrubber's speaker cursor.

So why is it called *scrubbing?* On professional analog tape decks, you can engage the playback head and rock the tape back and forth across the head. The audio on the tape is heard as you drag (or *scrub*) the tape across the engaged playback heads—to locate the beginning of a song before cutting the tape, for example. This was the standard method for locating the boundaries of audio events on magnetic tape prior to physically cutting the tape in order to make edits.

Note that on HD systems, the Trimmer tool has an additional Scrub Trimmer mode. This mode scrubs audio in a similar fashion as you click and drag to lengthen or shorten audio regions. To select the Scrubber tool from the keyboard, press F9.

❋ **Tip: Scrubber Operation Modes—Using Modifier Keys**

If you hold down the Shift key as you scrub audio playback and then release the mouse button, a range within the track is selected—from the previous playback position to the point where you released the Scrubber tool. This makes it easier to find where specific sounds begin or end as you're selecting them for edits.

For finer control and slower playback while using the Scrubber, hold down the Command and Control keys as you click and drag (in Windows, hold down Ctrl while you right-click and drag). You can also combine this modifier key with the Shift-scrubbing technique described in the preceding paragraph. Hold down the Option (Mac) or Alt (Windows) key as you scrub for extra-fast scrubbing (Shuttle mode).

You can also temporarily switch from the Selector tool (or Smart Tool) to the Scrubber by holding down the Control key as you click and drag (in Windows or on any Mac with a two-button mouse, right-click and drag).

Pencil

When you are zoomed in far enough on the Waveform view of audio tracks, you can actually *destructively* (in other words, permanently) draw changes to the waveform with the Pencil tool (see Figure 6.9)—to eliminate clicks, for example. In MIDI tracks, you can draw in note events with the Pencil (and then drag them around with the Grabber, of course). If you draw a series of notes with the Pencil tool, their spacing reflects the current grid value, but you can also set a custom duration if you wish (for instance, to draw notes with an 1/8-note duration, with 1/2-note spacing between them). You can also use the Pencil tool's Line shape to draw new velocity contours for existing MIDI notes (in Velocity display format). When displaying automation on audio and MIDI tracks (such as volume, pan, or send levels, or other parameters), you can also draw new shapes with the Pencil, although the Grabber tool is often more convenient for this purpose. The Pencil tool has a drop-down selector for its various drawing shapes: Free Hand, Line, Triangle, Square, Random, Parabolic, and S-Curve. Use the F10 keyboard shortcut to select the Pencil and toggle through its modes.

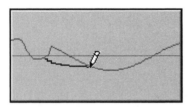

Figure 6.9   You can use the Pencil tool to draw or correct audio waveforms (once you are zoomed into sample level).

Table 6.1 includes the keyboard shortcuts for the various editing tools.

Table 6.1
Keyboard Shortcuts for Editing Tools

Keyboard Shortcut	Tool
F5	Zoomer
F6	Trimmer
F7	Selector
F8	Grabber
F6+F7 (or F7+F8)	Smart Tool
F9	Scrubber
F10	Pencil

For the Zoomer, Trimmer, Grabber, and Pencil tools, you can also repeat their Function key shortcuts to toggle through their operation modes. (Mac users should see the Caution in Chapter 5, "The Transport Window," about reassigning Function keys F9, F10, F11, and F12 for Expose´ and Dashboard.)

To cycle through the editing tools, press the Esc key or click the center mouse button (Windows only).

> ❋ **Tip: Oops!**
>
> If you make a mistake, don't panic! All versions of Pro Tools support up to 32 levels of Undo. (The exact number of undo levels is set in the Editing tab of the Preferences dialog box; users with slower computers can improve system performance slightly by choosing a smaller number.) As a general rule, Pro Tools clearly warns you when a critical action cannot be undone. The Undo History window displays a list of up to 32 recent undoable actions (optionally including their creation times), allowing you to return to one of these previous states—even if you've saved the session to disk several times since then.

Edit Modes: Slip, Shuffle, Grid, and Spot

The four edit mode buttons in the upper-left area of the Edit window (see Figure 6.10) affect the behavior of the editing tools: how regions and MIDI notes respond when moved or placed within tracks (or lengthened/shorted by the Trimmer tool), how selections can be made, and how markers and breakpoints (for automation and Tempo events) can be placed or moved around in the timeline. During the course of a project, you will often find yourself switching between edit modes for specific tasks; we suggest you immediately get used to using Function keys F1–F4 for this.

Figure 6.10 Edit modes affect selection, movement, and trimming of automation, audio, and MIDI regions/notes.

Slip

In Slip edit mode, no restrictions are applied. You can freely drag regions and MIDI notes to any position within tracks, and the exact ranges you highlight with the Selector and Scrubber tools are not adjusted in any way (as is the case in Grid mode, which is explained later in this section). When using the Grabber, you can even place regions so that they overlap existing regions in the track. (An overlap icon can be displayed to indicate wherever a region boundary overlaps another underlying region.) Slip mode allows extremely accurate selection, positioning, and trimming (all the way down to the level of individual audio samples, on audio tracks that are set to this format) with no restrictions. The keyboard shortcut for Slip mode is F3.

Shuffle

In Shuffle mode, regions move more or less like magnets. If you use the Grabber to drag a region from the Region List onto an empty track, it snaps to the beginning of the track. If you drag it into a track already containing a region, the region you're dragging snaps to the beginning or end point of the nearest region already on the track, depending on where you release the mouse button. All regions (and empty spaces between them) following the newly inserted region in the track are then pushed later in time (or *shuffled* to the right) by the new region's exact duration. When using the Trimmer tool in Shuffle mode, as you lengthen or shorten regions in a track, adjacent regions are moved as necessary so that they remain adjacent. When you have regions lined up in a track (for example, sections of a musical arrangement or drum variations) and use the Grabber to change their order in Shuffle mode, they remain stuck together as you move them around, with no gaps between them. The keyboard shortcut for Shuffle mode is F1.

Grid

Grid mode works like the snap-to-grid function in many drawing programs. All selections, trimming, and dragging of regions (as well as drawing of breakpoint automation) are adjusted, or rounded, to the nearest time increment on the grid. You can use the Grid Value indicator and its pop-up menu, underneath the Edit window's toolbar, to adjust the time units and spacing of this grid. The keyboard shortcut for Grid mode is F4.

All Pro Tools versions support Minutes:Seconds, Samples, and Bars:Beats formats for grid increments. As shown in the "Grid Value Display" section later in this chapter, time units in the Grid Value selector can either follow the time scale of the Main Counter or you can set them independently. On LE systems equipped with the DV Toolkit option (which is not compatible with M-Powered versions of the Pro Tools software), you can also use SMPTE timecode format for grid units. HD versions, like previous generations of TDM-based Pro Tools software, also support SMPTE grid units, as well as Feet+Frames for film work.

Below are some key points for understanding how the Edit tools interact with Grid mode:

* Using the current tempo setting (or tempo map), if you set the Edit window's Main Counter to Bars:Beats and the grid value to 1/4 or 1/8 notes, your selections within audio and MIDI regions are automatically corrected to these musical values. If you'd like to use the Grabber to drop a snare sample on the second and fourth beats of each bar, for example, adjust the Grid Value setting to 1/4 notes, and you won't have to squint!

* Grid mode can be very handy when you're dragging (Grabber) or drawing (Pencil) MIDI notes. You might say that Grid edit mode quantizes their movement. As you drag an existing region on a track to a new location, its left boundary (or sync point, if it contains one—these are described further in Chapter 8, "Menu Selections: Highlights," in the section about the Region menu's Identify Sync Point command) is adjusted to the nearest grid increment, snapping from one to another as you drag left or right. Likewise, as you click (or click and drag) with the Pencil tool to create MIDI notes, their beginnings and ends snap to the nearest grid increment. To temporarily suspend Grid mode so that you can freely reposition any event, hold down the Command key (Ctrl key in Windows).

* Grid mode is convenient for snapping the automation breakpoints you create for volume or panning to exact beats and bar lines.

❋ Resizing of regions and MIDI notes with the Trimmer tool is snapped to the nearest grid increment while in Grid mode.

❋ Pro Tools users working on video and film projects will appreciate Grid mode for precisely adjusting the boundaries of audio events to whole seconds or frames. For sound designers, when you know that each button sound or background you bounce out must be exactly 2 seconds, 500 milliseconds, or some other round number, trimming regions or selecting time ranges to bounce to disk in Grid mode can save time.

❋ If you activate the Regions/Markers option in the Grid Value pop-up menu (which is shown in the "Grid Value Display" section later in this chapter), your selections, resizing, and movement of regions and MIDI notes will snap not only to the nearest grid increment, but also to marker locations and the boundaries of any region in any track (or sync points within audio regions). Be sure to explore this feature; it's overlooked even by many experienced Pro Tools users!

❋ **Tip: Getting the Most Out of the Grid Edit Mode**

In the Display tab of the Preferences dialog box, you can enable the Draw Grids in Edit Window option. When Grid mode is active, grid increments are visible as vertical lines in the Edit window. While the Draw grid also appears in the other three edit modes when this preference is enabled, the spacing of their vertical lines changes according to the current zoom level. In contrast, while in Grid mode, the line spacing stays fixed at the current Grid Value setting. We find this feature very helpful and recommend that you use it. To toggle Draw grids on and off without having to open the Preferences dialog box, click in the blue format rectangle (which indicates the time units currently in effect—for example, Min:Secs) at the left end of the current main ruler.

Spot

Spot mode is convenient for placing regions at precise numerical locations—for example, when placing (*spotting*) sound effects during a film or video project. In this edit mode, the Spot dialog box (shown in Figure 6.11) appears as soon as you click on a region with the Grabber, drag it out onto a track from the Region List, or click it with the Trimmer. In this dialog box's fields, you specify time values *numerically* for the Start and/or End, Duration, or Sync Point (Grabber only) of the selected region.

Spot mode is especially handy for audio editors in video facilities. Using a video master tape with a time code window burned into the video image, you can jog the video tape exactly to the frame where an audio hit needs to be placed, click an audio region or drag it onto a track, and then simply type the correct time into the Spot dialog box. Even easier, as time code is received into Pro Tools, if the Spot dialog box is open—and the master video transport is in Play mode using *LTC* (Longitudinal Time Code, which is time code embedded in an audio signal) or even paused or stopped using *VITC* (Vertical Interval Time Code, which is time code embedded into each video frame)—you can press the = (equals sign) key on your computer keyboard to automatically enter the current SMPTE position into its numeric fields. For more information about using SMPTE time code in postproduction, see Chapter 14, "Postproduction and Soundtracks." The keyboard shortcut for Spot edit mode is F2.

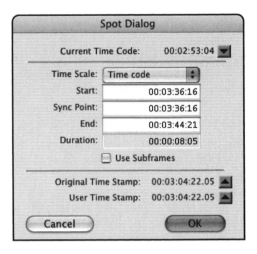

Figure 6.11 You can use the Spot dialog box to specify positions (and selections) numerically; this can be especially powerful when Pro Tools is slaved to an external device via SMPTE time code.

Tip: Quick Entry in the Spot Dialog Box with the Plus/Minus Keys

Here's a quick way to add or subtract a given number of video frames to any of the time value fields in the Spot dialog box when using SMPTE time code as your time scale (available on HD systems or LE systems equipped with the DV Toolkit option): Make sure the pop-up Time Scale selector in the dialog box is set to SMPTE time code. Click in the last segment of the number to select the Frames column, press either + or − (plus/minus) on the numeric keypad, enter the number of frames, and then press Return (Enter in Windows) on the alphanumeric keyboard. You can also use this technique in the Seconds column.

Even on M-Powered and LE systems without DV Toolkit, you can do this in the Seconds column when using Minutes:Seconds as your time scale in the Spot dialog box—as well as any column of the Bars:Beats or Samples time scale.

As with other time value fields in Pro Tools, you can use the up and down arrow keys on your computer to nudge numerical values in the Spot dialog box, and pressing the period or right/left arrow keys lets you move from one column to another. Tab and Shift+Tab toggle forward or backward from one field to another, and the Esc and Enter keys are shortcuts for the Cancel and OK buttons, as in many dialog boxes.

Zoom Controls and Zoom Preset Buttons

The zoom controls and zoom preset buttons, shown in Figure 6.12, change your view magnification for the contents of tracks in the Edit window, either in the horizontal direction for the time scale or vertically for audio amplitude or MIDI pitches. You can store and recall your own zoom presets—an important time-saving habit that you should acquire as early as possible!

You will spend a lot of time zooming in and out as you edit data in your tracks. After reading the following descriptions for each zoom control, be sure to check out the following tip about

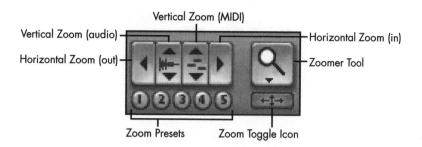

Figure 6.12 Zoom controls in the Edit window.

keyboard shortcuts for zooming. Along with the basic Transport functions, zooming shortcuts should be among the first ones you memorize in Pro Tools!

- ❄ **Horizontal Zoom In/Out.** Clicking these buttons expands or contracts your current view along the (horizontal) time scale of the Edit window. The further you zoom in, the more detail is available while editing (although a shorter duration will fit in the Edit window).
- ❄ **Vertical Zoom In/Out (Audio).** Clicking these buttons affects the displayed range on the amplitude (vertical) axis of audio waveforms within audio tracks. The vertical zoom level for audio has no effect on the view of automation, MIDI tracks, Aux Ins, Instrument tracks, or Master Faders.
- ❄ **Vertical Zoom In/Out (MIDI).** Clicking these buttons does the same thing as with the vertical axis (pitch, or note number) within MIDI and Instrument tracks. Likewise, they have no effect on the view of MIDI controller data, audio tracks, Aux Ins, or Master Fader tracks.
- ❄ **Zoom Presets.** These buttons (1–5) are used to store horizontal (time scale) zoom presets for the current session document. Command-click (Ctrl-click in Windows) on any of these buttons to store the current horizontal zoom settings there, and then later click any Zoom Preset button to recall its stored zoom settings. Take some time to learn how to use the Zoom Preset buttons; it's surprising how many otherwise competent Pro Tools users repeatedly click the zoom buttons to go back and forth between the same two magnifications!

❄ **Tip: Zoom! Faster!—Zooming Shortcuts**

Getting around quickly in your project is essential, not only for building up creative momentum, but also to avoid making your clients impatient! Here are some shortcuts to make navigation a bit easier:

- ❄ Hold down the Command key (Ctrl key in Windows) and press the square bracket keys (] or [) to zoom in and out horizontally.
- ❄ Hold down the Command+Option keys (Ctrl+Alt in Windows) and use the square brackets (] or [) to zoom in and out vertically on all audio tracks.

* Hold down the Command+Shift keys (Ctrl+Shift in Windows) and use the left or right square bracket ([or]) to zoom in and out vertically on all MIDI tracks.

* Hold down the Command key (Ctrl key in Windows) while highlighting an area with the Zoomer tool to simultaneously zoom into an audio waveform both horizontally and vertically.

* Double-click the Zoomer to zoom completely out so that the entire session fits into the Edit window.

* Option-click (Alt-click in Windows) the Zoomer tool itself to horizontally zoom your current track selection to fill the current width of the Edit window.

* You can also use the zoom arrow buttons (and the vertical zoom buttons) to recall the *previous* horizontal zoom setting. Let's say, for example, that you're viewing tracks at a comfortable horizontal zoom level, but just to confirm where you are within the entire session, you double-click on the Zoomer tool so that the entire session's duration fits into the Edit window. Option-clicking (Alt-clicking in Windows) on either of the Zoom In/Out buttons returns you to the previous zoom level.

* Learn how to use the Single Zoom mode of the Zoomer tool (which reselects the previous editing tool after zooming once). This is a real timesaver and all too easy to overlook.

* Memory locations can also store zoom settings as an attribute of any marker or selection. (See the "Timeline Display: Timebase Rulers and Marker Memory Locations" section, later in this chapter.)

Zoom Toggle Icon

This icon, which appears beneath the Zoomer tool, was introduced in Pro Tools 7 (replacing the Zoom Toggle preference settings in previous versions). It allows you to store certain parameters of an Edit window view, to which you can switch at any time by activating this icon. The parameters affected by stored Zoom Toggle settings are track height, display mode, horizontal and vertical (audio/MIDI) zoom, and grid value. Here's how you use it: Click on the Zoom Toggle icon to enable it, and then manually set up your zoom levels, track heights, and grid value. Click it again to disable. After you've changed view parameters, you can simply click again on the Zoom Toggle icon as you work to return to the stored Zoom Toggle settings. To alter these settings, just change these view parameters while the Zoom Toggle icon is enabled (lit).

Event Edit Area (Selection/Position Indicators)

How can you edit your audio if you don't know where you *are*? The indicators in the Event Edit area (shown in Figure 6.13) let you know where you are in the session's timeline, the time values for your current selection, and exactly where your cursor is as you move it around within Pro Tools tracks. You will find these very useful when making edit selections, when selecting audio material for bouncing out mix files to disk, and for controlling playback in Pro Tools.

Edit Selection Indicators (Start/End/Length)

The Start, End, and Length numerical fields display information about the current Edit window selection (in the Main Counter's current time units). As you use the Selector and Grabber tools to make selections within tracks, these will be indicated in the Start/End/Length fields. When

Figure 6.13 The Event Edit area provides information about the current selection and playback location.

using the Trimmer to lengthen/shorten regions, the values here also change in real time as you drag the Trimmer cursor.

You can enter values directly into these fields to modify or create a selection (and/or change the current playback cursor location if Options > Link Timeline and Edit Selections is enabled). Here are a few shortcuts for quick entry into these fields:

❋ Use the slash (/) key to toggle between the Start, End, and Length indicators.

❋ Use the period key (or right/left arrows) to switch from one column to another within these fields.

❋ Use the up and down arrow keys to incrementally increase/decrease the selected value.

❋ As with the Spot dialog box, you can also select a column, press the + or − (plus/minus) key, type a number, and then press Return to increase or decrease its value by a specific amount.

Main/Sub Counters

During playback or recording, the Main and Sub counters display the current play position. If Options > Link Timeline and Edit Selections is enabled, the Start and End fields in the Transport window are also adjusted to match your current Timeline selection in the Edit window. If not, the Transport's "play" selection and Main Location indicator (the playback cursor position) are not altered by the current edit selection. This can be useful while editing: The same four-bar selection would always play when you press the spacebar, for example, even as you edit and drag around regions within that range.

A pop-up menu to the right of the Main and Sub counters allows you to select different time units. The time units you select for the Main counter will affect the time units of the Edit window's main active ruler (and vice versa). The units currently selected for the Main Counter are also reflected in the Cursor Location indicator and in the Start/End/Length indicators for edit selections.

 Tip: Main Counter

To directly highlight the Edit window's Main Counter, press the equals sign (=) key on the numeric keypad. Like other time value fields in Pro Tools, there are several methods for directly entering values here (direct numerical entry, up/down arrows, or plus/minus keys, for example). Press Return or Enter to confirm your entry, moving the playback cursor to the new position. Remember that you can use the period key or right/left arrows to navigate between columns in any time indicator that has multiple segments (for example, minutes, seconds, or milliseconds). Lastly, if you open the Big Counter (via that command in the Window menu), the Main Counter's values are displayed large enough for you see them from across the room while recording takes, and you can also type values directly into this oversized view.

MIDI Note Attributes

When a single MIDI note is selected in a MIDI or Instrument track in Notes or Velocity track view, the editable value fields shown in Figure 6.14 display the note's pitch, attack velocity, and release velocity. The keyboard techniques described for the Main and Sub Counters also work in these fields—once you click within them to enable them for editing values. Additionally, you can enter new values for each of these MIDI note attributes by striking keys on your external MIDI keyboard or other controller. This saves time, because if you record-enable the track while performing this data entry, you hear the result of the new values in real time as you repeatedly strike the key.

Figure 6.14   Additional fields appear in the Event Edit area when MIDI notes are selected.

When multiple MIDI notes are selected, each of these fields initially appears with a zero value and a delta symbol (for the amount of change). As you drag the group of selected notes to a new pitch, the corresponding amount of transposition (in semitones) is displayed in the Pitch field. You select the Pitch field and type in the amount of transposition you want on all the selected notes—for example, +7 semitones to raise them by a perfect fifth, or +12 for an octave. Typing numbers or clicking and dragging also works for altering attack and release velocity values of multiple notes, except that in this case, the amount of change (the delta) is displayed here (compared to whatever the original velocity value was for each note in the selection). As always with MIDI, there are upper and lower limits for both pitch and velocity; values can't exceed these, no matter how much change you apply.

Edit Window Transport Buttons

The Transport buttons in the Edit window (see Figure 6.15) duplicate the buttons in the Transport window, as a convenience while working in the Edit window. Even when the Transport window isn't currently visible, all the same keyboard shortcuts apply; for example, you can press the spacebar to start/stop playback, press Return (Enter in Windows) on the alphanumeric keyboard to return to the beginning of the session timeline, press Command+spacebar (Ctrl+spacebar in Windows) to start recording, and so on.

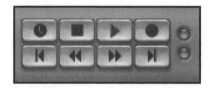

Figure 6.15 For convenience, the Transport buttons are duplicated in the upper area of the Edit window.

❋ **Tip: Get a Scroll-Wheel Mouse for Your Mac!**

Although scroll wheels are commonplace on Windows computers, a single-button, wheel-less mouse is still the factory-supplied option on a Macintosh. Like most Internet browsers, word processors, and other programs on both platforms, however, Pro Tools supports use of the scroll wheel. Trust us, your productivity in Mac versions of Pro Tools will be greatly improved if you upgrade to a mouse or trackball with two buttons and a scroll wheel.

❋ Simply roll the mouse wheel to scroll vertically (in any active window where a scrollbar is currently visible—for example, the Mix, Edit, Memory Locations, Region List, and MIDI Event List windows, whenever their entire contents don't fit in to the current window size).

❋ To scroll your view *horizontally* in the Edit window, hold down the Shift key as you use the mouse's scroll wheel.

❋ For the equivalent of the Edit window's horizontal zoom buttons, hold down the Option key (Alt key in Windows) as you scroll the wheel up or down.

❋ For the equivalent of the Edit window's vertical zoom button for audio, hold down the Option+Shift keys (Alt+Shift keys in Windows) as you scroll.

❋ For the equivalent of the Edit window's vertical zoom button for MIDI, hold down the Control+Option +Shift keys (Alt+Start+Shift keys in Windows) as you scroll.

❋ To scroll the Notes display of a MIDI or Instrument track, hold down Command+Control+Option keys (Alt+Start+Ctrl in Windows) as you scroll.

Other Edit Window Fields

Other useful fields and indicators appear in the black horizontal strip between the toolbar at the top of the Edit window and the track display area below it. Several of these are shown in Figure 6.16.

Edit Window View Selector

Use this pop-up selector to display the Comments, I/O, Inserts, Sends, Instrument, Real-Time Properties, and Track Color sections at the left side of the Edit window's tracks. You can also use it to toggle display of the Edit window's Transport buttons. This selector duplicates options also available in the View > Edit Window submenu.

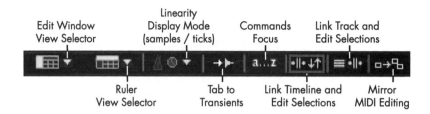

Figure 6.16 Additional fields above the track display area of the Edit window.

Ruler View Selector

This pop-up selector enables/disables the different ruler types in the Edit window and duplicates options in the View > Rulers submenu.

Linearity Display Mode Selector

You can use this display timebase selector to switch the horizontal scale for displaying all track events in the Edit window between Linear Sample Display (absolute time) and Linear Ticks Display (relative to the current tempo settings). In Linear Sample display format, the display corresponds to actual audio samples at the current sample rate, so if you increase the musical tempo, each bar (in the Bars:Beats ruler, for example) occupies less space. Conversely, in Linear Ticks display format, each bar of 4/4 occupies the same amount of horizontal space in the Edit window, even if tempo changes actually mean that each bar corresponds to a different amount of absolute time (as measured in samples).

Tab to Transients

When this button is enabled, pressing the Tab key within an audio track automatically moves the cursor to a location immediately before the next transient peak in the track or to the next audio region boundary (beginning or end). This can be an important time saver, for example, when editing a long voice-over. Within a vocal or guitar overdub, for example, you could also highlight audio waveform data all the way from the current location or selection to the beginning of the next phrase by holding down the Shift key as you tab. (As with when selecting regions within tracks, Option+Tab moves backward, and you can combine it with the Shift key to make selections.) Tab to Transient also works when multiple tracks are selected, moving the playback location (or extending the selection, if you're holding down the Shift key) to the next transient found in *any* of these tracks. This is especially convenient when editing multiple drum or backing vocal tracks!

Commands Focus

In all versions of Pro Tools, a...z Keyboard Focus buttons are available in the upper-right corner of the Region List and the Groups list. Another Keyboard Focus button is underneath the Zoom Preset buttons (and right next to the Tab to Transients button), providing key-focus shortcuts for commands. (This Commands Focus button is shown in Figure 6.16.) When one of these buttons is highlighted, its keyboard-focus commands (single-key shortcuts from the alphanumeric keyboard) are active. For example, when the Keyboard Focus button for the Region List is enabled, you can select regions in that list by typing the first few letters of a name. When Keyboard Focus is active for the Groups list, you can toggle Edit and Mix groups on/off by typing the group ID letter. When Keyboard Focus for command keys is active, you can access many editing and play commands via single keystrokes on the alphanumeric keyboard.

❋ **Tip: The Quest for Speed: Keyboard Shortcuts**

Once you've spent a few hours in Pro Tools, you'll wish for keyboard shortcuts to many of the frequently used commands. Not all of them are identified next to the menu selections!

For example, you can recall memory locations (both markers and selections) from the numeric keypad by typing a period, then their number, followed by another period.

Within the Documentation folder for Pro Tools, you'll find an Acrobat Reader document (Keyboard Shortcuts.PDF) with several pages of keyboard shortcuts. Print this out, and keep it as a handy reference!

Link Timeline and Edit Selections

When the Link Timeline and Edit Selections button is enabled, the selections you make within tracks or rulers—or simply repositioning the playback cursor—will not only reset the values of the Start and End indicators at the top of the Edit window (the edit selection), but also in the Transport (the play selection, which determines where playback starts and stops when you press Play). In the event you wish to unlink the two, simply deselect this button (refer to Figure 6.16). For example, you might want to select and edit individual notes and regions while a longer four-bar selection loops or edit a different part of the session without losing your current Timeline selection for playback. Toggling this button on/off is the same thing as using the Options > Link Timeline and Edit Selections menu selection.

Link Track and Edit Selection

This feature was added in version 7 of Pro Tools. When this option is enabled (via the Edit window button or the corresponding command in the Options menu), selecting any material for editing within the track also automatically selects the track itself (highlighting its track name). This is a convenient way to select one or more tracks for track-level operations, grouping them, making them inactive, or dragging them to a new position in the track list, for example. If you hold down Option+Shift (Alt+Shift on Windows) as you change a track parameter, this change is applied to all currently selected tracks. (In contrast, if you hold down the Option key—Alt key in Windows—without the additional Shift key modifier, the change applies to *all* tracks, whether selected or not.) Used in conjunction with the Link Track and Edit Selection feature, this Option+Shift (Alt+Shift) technique is a convenient way to change track height, view format, Record/Solo/Mute button states, automation mode, timebase format, and other track attributes based on your current selections within multiple tracks.

Mirrored MIDI Editing

This is another feature added in version 7 of Pro Tools. When you use this feature, any changes you make to a MIDI region are also applied to all other MIDI regions with the same exact name. For instance, suppose you start with a very simple four-bar drum figure (for example, a MIDI region called "Drum4") to build your arrangement, and then you want to edit velocities or otherwise embellish this basic pattern after adding a few more instrumental parts. With Mirrored MIDI Editing enabled, as you make each edit in a single instance of this MIDI region, this button blinks red once, reminding you that the same change is being applied to all other MIDI regions called "Drum4."

Grid Value Display

The Grid Value setting reflects the current time increments that govern the selection and movement of regions, trimming, and automation when the Grid edit mode is enabled. As shown in Figure 6.17, the pop-up Grid Units Selector menu to the right of this indicator lets you change this value. Its time units default to those of the currently active ruler, but you can also set time units for the Grid Value field separately. When the Grid edit mode is selected, movement and trimming (resizing) of regions and MIDI notes in the Edit window (as well as the location of automation breakpoints) are snapped (quantized) to the nearest increment on this time grid. When you drag with the Selector tool, the beginning and end values of the selected time range are also snapped to the nearest grid increment. (Refer to the "Grid" section under "Edit Modes: Slip, Shuffle, Grid, and Spot," earlier in this chapter.)

Nudge Value Display

This field's pop-up selector (also shown in Figure 6.17) sets the time increment to be used when you nudge regions and events with the plus/minus keys on the numeric keypad (as discussed previously). As with the grid value, the units for nudging can reflect those of the currently active ruler, or you can set them separately. For example, if you select an audio or MIDI region and use the pop-up display to the right of the Nudge Value indicator to select a one-millisecond nudge increment (or one SMPTE frame or one 1/8 note), each time you press the plus/minus keys (+/−), the region is moved forward or backward from its present position by that amount of time. This lets you make fine adjustments to timing without zooming all the way in to drag regions around. Nudging also works on MIDI note selections within MIDI tracks (as well as selected breakpoints for MIDI controller data, such as mod wheel, pitch bend, aftertouch, and others). Besides the preset Nudge values, you can also type in any other amount. This can be useful, for example, if you are nudging sound effects and you find that 100 milliseconds is too large, while 10 milliseconds is too small.

Here are some other useful techniques for nudging:

❊ To nudge the start and end points of the selection forward or back by the current Nudge value (without altering the selected audio or MIDI data), use the plus/minus keys on the numeric keypad. This works when you use the Selector tool to highlight a selection (either within an audio or MIDI region or across multiple regions).

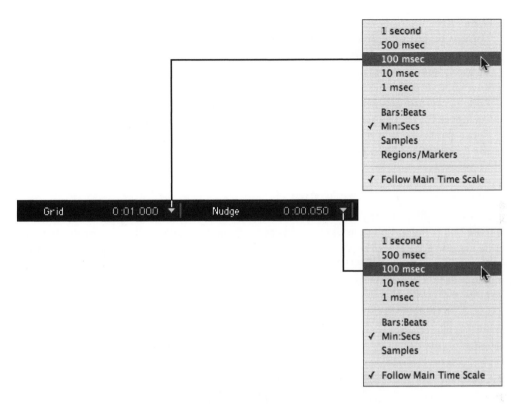

Figure 6.17 The Grid Value and Nudge Value displays incorporate pop-up menus for selecting Grid/Nudge increments. (Options for an LE or M-Powered system are shown here—HD systems additionally support SMPTE time code and Feet+Frames as Grid or Nudge time units.)

❋ **To nudge only the end of the selection, hold down the Command key (Ctrl key in Windows) as you nudge with the plus/minus keys on the numeric keypad.**

❋ **To nudge only the beginning of the selection, hold down the Option key (Alt key in Windows) as you nudge with the plus/minus keys on the numeric keypad.**

❋ **To nudge the waveform contents of an audio region without affecting the region's current start/end points in the track, hold down the Control key (Start key in Windows) as you nudge with the plus/minus keys on the numeric keypad. (Additional audio must be available within the region's parent audio file for this to work.) This is handy, for example, if you have some excess silence on the beginning of a region containing a cymbal sound, which you've already placed exactly on the 1/4 note. You can nudge this region's definition further back in the parent audio file so that it doesn't include the silence prior to the cymbal attack. The result is that the cymbal attack ends up at the beginning of the region, right on the 1/4 note.**

❋ When Commands Focus mode is enabled (the a…z button next to the Tab to Transients), you can nudge selections—regions, notes, and ranges of automation, for example—using your computer keyboard (as well as many other time-saving shortcuts; be sure to read about Commands Focus in the Keyboard Shortcuts PDF document!). The period and comma keys move the selected events forward or back by the current Nudge value. To nudge forward or backward by the next-largest Nudge value (e.g., 1/4 notes if your current setting is 1/8 notes), use the / and M keys. In fact, as with many other Commands Focus shortcuts, you don't necessarily have to enable this mode at all—just hold down the Control key (Start key on Windows) as you use these same keyboard shortcuts for nudging.

Cursor Location/Cursor Value

The Cursor Location display reflects the (horizontal) time location as you move the cursor within the Edit window (in whatever units the Main Counter is using). The Cursor Value display reflects the current vertical position of the cursor within a track. For example, while moving your cursor vertically over a MIDI track in Notes view, the Cursor Value shows note numbers to indicate its current position. But if the display mode of a track is set to Volume, the value shown for the current cursor position is decibels (dB) for audio or 0–127 for MIDI track volumes. Both of these fields are shown in Figure 6.18. They're not editable fields but instead provide feedback about the current position as you move the cursor (while dragging automation breakpoints up and down, for example, or resizing notes and regions).

Figure 6.18   These fields indicate the cursor is currently within a MIDI track at 44 seconds, 768 milliseconds, and a vertical position corresponding to MIDI volume 120.

Region List

This "bin" at the right edge of the Edit window (shown in Figure 6.19) lists all the MIDI and audio region names that are referenced within the session—whether they have been placed into tracks or not—as well as region group names. When you create a new session, of course, the Region List is empty. As soon as you record into any audio, MIDI, or Instrument track, a new region name is created based on the name of the track where it was recorded. You can also import external audio files directly into the Region List by dragging from the Workspace browser window or Desktop or by using the File > Import > Audio to Region List command. (The File > Import > Audio to Track command is identical, except that it additionally creates a new audio track for each file you import.) Imported audio files and regions appear with their original names in the Region List; double-click to change any region's name. Many of your edits in Pro Tools will cause additional regions to be created. For example, if you cut the middle out of an existing audio region, there will now be three region definitions (all referring to different selections with the same parent audio file): the original region, plus two additional region definitions for the portions before and after the cut. An option in the local menu of the Region List allows you to choose whether these auto-created regions should be shown—if you import Acid and REX files directly into the Region List by dragging directly from the Workspace browser window, you will definitely want to see auto-created regions, since that's how the time slices within them appear in Pro Tools!

As elsewhere, you can Shift-click to select multiple adjacent items in the Region List, and/or Command-click (Ctrl-click in Windows) to make non-contiguous selections. If you wish, you can also choose to display the source file names, full directory paths, and/or disk locations in the Region List, although doing so will make the displayed region names much longer.

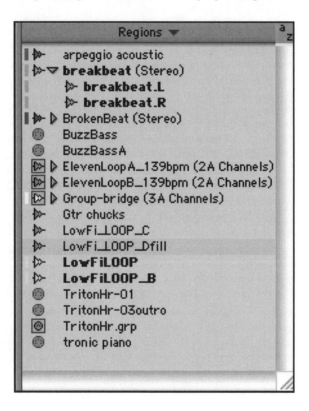

Figure 6.19 The Region List.

✳ **Tip: Renaming Regions**

Double-click to rename any region in the Region List. (Using the Grabber to double-click regions directly within tracks also opens the renaming dialog box.) Remember that as you record into audio and MIDI tracks, the region names created are based on the track name where they were recorded. So take a moment to name your tracks as you prepare to record; it will save time and confusion later!

Many region names represent portions of longer "parent" audio files. Other region names represent entire audio files; if so, their names appear in bold type inside the Region List. When you rename any of these whole-file audio regions, an additional option appears in the dialog box, asking whether you want to also rename the source disk file or only the region name as it appears within the current Pro Tools session.

❋ **Note: How Pro Tools Creates Region Names as You Record and Edit**

As mentioned previously, when you record the first audio (or MIDI) region into a track, a new region name is created based on that track's name. For example, say you create a new Pro Tools session and then create some new audio tracks (using the Track > New command). Here's what happens:

1. In the Edit window, double-click the name field of track Audio 1 and rename it something else (like "Cornet"). Click this track's Rec button to arm it for recording.

2. Click Record, and then click Play on the Transport. Let Pro Tools roll in Record mode for a few seconds (you'll see your recording in progress as a red rectangle within this track). Now click Stop. The region name "Cornet_01" (or "Cornet-01-00" in Pro Tools Free and versions 5.1 and earlier, which used a slightly different naming convention for regions) appears in the Region List, and a similarly named file is created inside your session's Audio Files folder. (We're assuming you're seeing Pro Tools' default options for region display here—that is, you haven't opted to also display the lengthier file names, disk names, or directory paths within the Region List.)

3. Click Play and Record again, and let it run a couple of seconds longer. A second region, "Cornet_02" (or "Cornet-02-00" in versions 5.1 and earlier), appears in the list and replaces the previously recorded region in the Cornet audio track. Are you getting it so far? The first part of the numerical suffix automatically numbers successive recordings.

4. Use the Selector tool to highlight a portion anywhere in the middle of the second region you just recorded, and press the Delete key on your keyboard. Pro Tools automatically assigns two new region names to the segments remaining before and after the cut (assuming that this default option is enabled in the Editing tab of the Preferences dialog), appending "-01" and "-02" to the original region's name—in this case, "Cornet_02-01" and "Cornet_02-02". Pro Tools will often create new region definitions as a result of editing operations, using these numerical suffixes to identify them.

If you get confused about what regions are used where, select any region name within the Region List, and it will also be highlighted everyplace it occurs within a track, and vice versa. (This assumes that these default options are enabled in Preferences > Editing; some users prefer to have Region List and Edit selections be independent of each other.) Even better, start double-clicking to rename your regions—call the flute solo "flute solo," and so on!

Using the Region List's Local Menu

Audio files are very large, and no matter what your system's disk capacity is, it is still important to limit your audio projects to a reasonable amount of disk space. For one thing, this will make the backing up and archiving of your project data more efficient. Many of the commands in the Region List's local menu (shown in Figure 6.20) are self-explanatory, but here are a few that are useful for making sure your Pro Tools projects don't needlessly occupy disk space for unused audio data. As you will be reminded many times in this book, it is extremely important to assign meaningful names to regions as you work in Pro Tools. (Always naming tracks *before* recording into them is a good start, by the way.) When you're sorting through a hundred or more regions from dozens of tracks and takes in order to delete unused files and reduce the amount of disk space utilized by your session folder, think how much easier this will be if the region for your tenor sax solo is actually named "TenorSax_02" rather than, say, "Audio 17_12"!

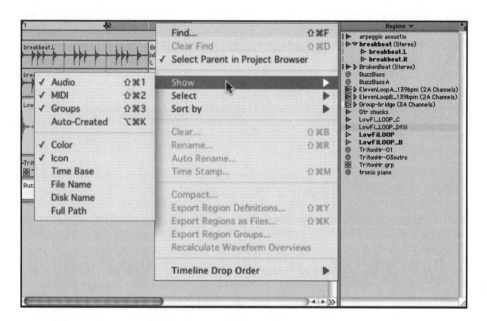

Figure 6.20 The Region List's pop-up local menu helps manage regions (and region groups) as well as MIDI and audio files in Pro Tools projects.

❋ **Note: Importing Audio Files and Regions**

Besides recording audio directly into Pro Tools, you may often import existing files into a Pro Tools session—for example, sound effects (or drum grooves) that you've created yourself or copied from a CD library to your hard disk. Or you might want to use an audio file that resides within another Pro Tools session's Audio Files folder. Current versions of Pro Tools can directly import the following file formats:

❋ AIFF (.AIF)

❋ WAV, including Broadcast WAV

❋ Acid WAV files

❋ REX (Recycle)

❋ Sound Designer I & II (.SD2)

❋ QuickTime (audio only)

❋ Sound Resource (Mac versions only)

* WMA, Windows Media (Windows versions only)
* CD-DA (audio tracks on standard, "red book" audio CDs
* MP3
* AAC (a variant of MPEG-4)
* MXF (Material eXchange Format)

Of course, if you need to import a 44.1 kHz file into a session set to a 48 kHz sample rate or vice versa, the Import Audio dialog box will alert you that conversion is required (and enable the Convert/Convert All buttons instead of Add/Add All). The same will apply if the file format or bit-depth doesn't match that of the current session. By default, Pro Tools stores converted files in the current session's Audio Files folder (although this is not mandatory).

If no conversion is required, files (or regions within them, which can be imported instead of the entire parent audio file) that you import into Pro Tools can remain in their original disk locations. If you want to be absolutely certain that a duplicate copy of the file is added to your session's Audio Files folder even if conversion is not otherwise required, click the Copy or Copy All button in the Import Audio dialog box (instead of clicking Add/Add All).

Pro Tools must convert any imported stereo files into two new, separate mono files in your session's Audio Files folder. In this case, Pro Tools not only shows you a stereo region group in the Region List, but also two subregions underneath it, with the suffixes ".L" and ".R" added to the original file name.

If you already know that multiple files on your hard disk need to be imported into the currently open Pro Tools session, you can batch-import them by selecting one or more files from the desktop or the Workspace browser window and then drag them into the Region List or directly onto a track. Pro Tools will automatically handle any necessary conversions for the session's audio format. Repeat as necessary!

Lastly, when the Automatically Copy Files on Import option is enabled in the Operations tab of the Preferences dialog box, new copies are made of all imported audio files in your session's Audio Files folder—whether conversion is required or not. This is one way of ensuring that all the audio files that a session requires reside within its own folder and reduces the possibility of accidentally deleting or altering source files if they happen to also be used in a different session.

Select (Unused Regions, Unused Regions Except Whole Files)

The Select Unused Regions and Select Unused Regions Except Whole Files commands highlight all regions in the list that are not currently placed into any audio tracks in this session. Audio regions that represent entire audio files appear in bold type within the Region List. (These may have been created by new recordings, importing audio files into the session, menu commands such as Consolidate Selection, or any function in the AudioSuite menu with the Create Continuous File or Create Individual Files option enabled.) It's common to exclude whole-file regions (via the Select > Unused Regions Except Whole Files option) if you're going to use the Clear Selected command. That way, the whole-file regions representing the parent audio files for smaller regions actually residing in your tracks will remain in the Region List (making it easier to compact these later on to recover disk space; see the section "Compact Selected" in this chapter for more information).

Clear Selected

When the selected audio regions represent portions within larger parent audio files, the Clear Selected command simply removes this reference from the current Pro Tools session document. For whole-file regions that correspond to entire sound files (and therefore appear in bold type within the Region List), you have the option to either simply remove the session's reference to the file (leaving it intact on your disk) or to delete the file from the disk entirely. Obviously, the second option is potentially dangerous, especially if you've forgotten that you also use this audio file in a different session. (Be sure to pay attention to what you're doing!) After using the Select Unused Regions command, you can always Shift-click to deselect several of them before executing the Clear Selected command.

Compact Selected

Applying the Compact Selected command to selected regions in the Region List eliminates any portions within the selected audio file that are not actually being used in any region definitions in the current session document. Say you pressed Record at the beginning of a song for some backing vocal harmonies the singers want to put down. Out of the four minutes you've recorded, they only sing two lines at the bridge, plus another few lines at the closing refrain. No problem; use the Edit window tools to cut and trim, leaving only the regions in the track where vocal lines are actually sung. At this point, however, your original four-minute recording is still taking up many megabytes of disk space! After eliminating all the unused region names created as a result of your editing (with the Select Unused Regions Except Whole Files and Clear Selected commands), select the whole-file region that corresponds to that complete four-minute file for the backing vocal take (whole-file regions appear in bold type within the list) and then execute the Compact Selected command.

The Padding setting in the Compact dialog box determines how close to the actual boundaries of currently used regions the Compact function will eliminate excess audio. It's nice to have a little extra, in case you inadvertently trimmed the attack or release of a region too much and later need to lengthen it by a few fractions of second. The other advantage of compacting your audio files is that, because your overall project size is reduced, it's somewhat quicker to back up and archive your audio data. One drawback is that compacting often frees many small increments on many files, which will increase disk fragmentation over time. (Of course, since you'll be defragmenting/optimizing your disks on a routine basis, that won't be a problem.) As with the Delete option in the Clear Selected dialog box, keep in mind that the Compact Selected command only looks at usage of this audio file in the current session. Beware if you are also using the same audio file in other sessions, because applying the Compact Selected command in the current session could eliminate portions of audio in those files that you actually still need in other sessions!

Export Region Definitions

The Export Region Definitions command incorporates the selected region definitions used in this session into their parent audio files. This is necessary if you want the option to view and import those regions into a completely different Pro Tools session. For example, you might find this useful after chopping up a drum loop into useful segments, or if you've taken the time to define regions for specific events within a much longer sound-effects file. (The Bias Peak Pro program and several others also recognize region definitions exported into their parent Sound Designer II or AIF audio files from Pro Tools. There is also a very useful Windows utility available, Region Synch from Rail Jon Rogut, that converts these Pro Tools region definitions exported into parent audio files to Sound Forge regions, which are recognized by CD Architect, WaveLab, Vegas, Adobe Audition, and other audio programs.)

Export Regions as Files

The Export Regions as Files command batch exports the currently selected audio regions to external files. (Shift-click to select multiple regions in the list.) In the Export Selected dialog box, you can select the destination directory, file formats, number of channels, sample rate, bit-depth, and other attributes. However, the results of this operation will not reflect any automation or plug-in effects processing applied where these regions appear within a Pro Tools track. For that, you might consider soloing the track (and any send destinations to which it may be routed) and bouncing to disk instead.

Tip: Previewing Audio and MIDI Regions in the Region List

Option-click (Alt-click in Windows) and hold on any audio or MIDI region in the Region List to listen to it without having to drag it out onto a track. (MIDI regions will be previewed via the default Thru instrument defined in the MIDI tab of the Preferences dialog box—this can be configured to always follow the MIDI output assignment of the first selected MIDI/Instrument track.)

Tip: Importing Audio from CDs

There are handy utilities out there for extracting audio tracks from audio CDs into various hard-disk file formats, and these are especially useful when you only want a specific portion within a given CD track. For Macintosh, you can open the CD icon on your desktop and drag entire tracks to any disk location or use iTunes and the QuickTime Player itself (if you upgrade to QuickTime Pro). For Windows, other programs including Roxio's CD Spin Doctor, the MusicMatch Jukebox, and the Windows freeware program CDex can extract CD tracks onto the hard disk as WAV files. (Be aware that MP3 or AAC formats are undesirable if you intend to import these files into Pro Tools because they compress the audio data in a lossy manner.) Many audio-editing programs, such as Bias' Peak (Mac), Steinberg's WaveLab (Windows), and Sony/Sonic Foundry's Sound Forge (Windows) can also extract audio directly from CDs.

You can also use the File menu's Import > Audio to Region List and Import > Audio to Track commands to import from audio CDs, using the same preview and selection options as with audio files residing on your computer's hard disks.

However, there's a much easier way to accomplish this in Pro Tools, especially if you want to bring the entire track into your session. Simply place the audio CD in your computer's drive, open it either in the Workspace browser window or in the operating system itself, open the CD's icon to view the tracks it contains, and then drag any of these into the Edit window. You can drag them into the Region List directly onto an existing stereo audio track. You can also drop them into the Tracks List (a panel at the left side of the Edit window) if you want new audio tracks automatically created in the process. The CD track's audio data will be converted to the current session's audio file format, bit-depth, and sample rate and stored in its Audio Files folder.

Edit Groups List

Chapter 2, "Pro Tools Terms and Concepts," discussed groups. You can use the pop-up local menu in the Edit Groups List (shown in Figure 6.21) to choose whether Edit or Mix groups are displayed in the list area below it, delete or create new groups, or suspend all groups. (See Chapter 7, "The Mix Window," for further details about the Mix Groups selector.) By default, Edit and Mix groups are linked, but you can change this in Preferences > Operation > Link Mix and Edit Group Enables.

You can also assign colors to Edit and Mix groups. If it helps you keep track of your material while editing, an option in the Display tab of the Preferences dialog box allows you to automatically reassign the colors of audio and MIDI regions in the Edit window according to the group assignments of the tracks where they currently reside.

Figure 6.21   Local menu for the Edit Groups List.

Track List

The Track List—which was known as the Show/Hide Tracks List in previous versions of Pro Tools—can be displayed at the left edge of the Edit (and Mix) window. To conserve screen space, you can enable/disable display of individual tracks by highlighting them in the Tracks List. Hidden tracks will still play (unless they're muted, of course)! The pop-up menu at the top of the Tracks List offers other options for controlling the display of tracks. The Show Only Selected Tracks command in this selector's local menu is especially handy when you briefly need to focus only on a small number of tracks (perhaps increasing their height for detailed editing), or when you're running out of room to display all tracks at their current sizes. Another especially useful feature here is to hide or show all audio tracks, MIDI tracks, Aux In tracks, Instrument tracks, or Master Faders.

> ❊ **Tip: Another Way to Create New Tracks in Pro Tools 7**
>
> If you drag and drop an audio or MIDI region from the Region List into the Tracks List at the left edge of the Edit window, a new track is automatically created with a similar name (minus any audio file name extensions).

Track View Selector for Track Data

The Track View selector for each track enables you to change how its contents appear in the Edit window. This selector opens a pop-up menu, as shown in Figure 6.22. Available display format options for the data contained in a track depend on its type (audio, Auxiliary Input, Master Fader, Instrument, or MIDI).

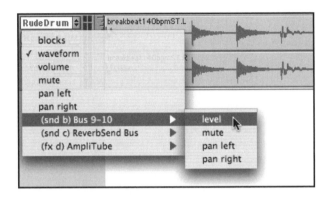

Figure 6.22 Display options for an audio track (with two active sends and one plug-in insert).

Audio

The Track View pop-up menu for audio tracks offers the following options:

※ **Waveform.** Audio regions appear as rectangles (containing the region name, if View > Region > Name is enabled), with a graphic representation of the audio waveforms they contain. (If a sync point has been defined within any region, this also appears as a small inverted triangle at the bottom of the rectangular region graphic.)

> ※ **Note: Region Layers**
>
> You can layer regions to overlap within a track (although only the topmost, visible region plays at any given point) and then change their order via the Region > Send to Back/Bring to Front commands. A dog-ear graphic on the corner of a region rectangle indicates where its boundary overlaps another region in the same track (if the View > Region > Overlap option is enabled).

※ **Blocks.** This is similar to the Waveform track view, but the waveform is not displayed inside the region rectangles. Because redrawing audio waveforms as you zoom in and out (or create new regions through recording and editing) requires some of your computer's processing power, this option is useful for users on underpowered systems who find that screen redraws are slowing the operation of Pro Tools.

❈ **Volume.** This track view format represents volume graphically. Lines and movable break-points represent how values for the Volume parameter on this track (corresponding to its main Volume fader) change over time. You can draw volume changes directly with the editing tools or record volume automation in real time (using onscreen faders or an external control surface, such as Command|8, ProControl, Control|24, D-Control, and D-Command, as well as other third-party options) and then edit it graphically afterward. For example, you can use the Grabber tool to insert, delete, or drag existing breakpoints, while you can use different modes of the Pencil tools to create automation for a track's volume. You can highlight automation events with the Selector tool and cut, paste, and so on without affecting the audio waveforms shown underneath. You can also use the Trimmer tool to scale existing automation events up or down.

❈ **Pan.** Pan view also shows lines and moveable breakpoints for creating or editing this kind of automation data, which affects the audio track's left/right position. A single pan control is provided for mono tracks; the Left Pan and Right Pan controls are separate for stereo tracks. (Note that even if your source audio region is mono, inserting a stereo plug-in on a track makes its output and panning controls stereo.) On multichannel surround channels, availability of multiple pan views depends on the surround format in use. For example, on a 5.1 track, separately editable pan automation includes Front Position, Rear Position, Front/Rear Position, Front Divergence, Rear Divergence, Front/Rear Divergence, and Center.

❈ **Mute.** This view shows the mute/unmute status of a track, Not Muted and Muted being the only possible values.

❈ **Sends (Level/Mute/Pan).** For each of the sends currently enabled on an audio, Aux In, or Instrument track, you can record and graphically edit automation for the send's Level, Mute, and Pan parameters—in a similar fashion to the Volume, Mute, and Pan parameters for the track's main output (as described previously). For each of the track's active sends, a submenu appears where you can select which of these send parameters should be displayed as breakpoint automation within this track in the Edit window.

❈ **Plug-in parameters.** Many parameters can be automated. The Plug-in window for each plug-in has an Auto button, which opens a dialog box where you can individually enable its parameters for automation. Each enabled plug-in automation parameter then appears as another track view option in the pop-up selector for the track where you enabled that plug-in. For example, if you instantiate the 7-band EQ 3 included with Pro Tools as insert effect "a" on a track and enable the Gain parameter of its high band filter for automation, an option called (fx a) 7-Band EQ 3 > Hi Band Gain appears among the track view options for that track.

Auxiliary Input

The Track View pop-up menu for Auxiliary Input tracks features the same options as the pop-up for audio tracks, minus the Block and Waveform options because Aux In tracks contain no regions.

Master Fader

The only available view for a Master Fader track is Volume unless any of the plug-ins inserted on the track have parameters currently enabled for automation, in which case those parameters appear as well (as with audio plug-ins on audio, Auxiliary Input, and Instrument tracks). There are no pan controls or sends on Master Faders.

MIDI and Instrument Tracks

As mentioned, MIDI tracks and the regions within them contain MIDI *events* (note events, data for pedals, modulation, pitch bend, and other types of MIDI controllers) rather than audio data. This is also true of Instrument tracks (although they behave more like Aux In tracks in the Mix window; see Chapter 7). Accordingly, the display format options shown in Figure 6.23 for MIDI and Instrument tracks are rather different from those offered for audio, Auxiliary Input, and Master Fader tracks. In fact, on MIDI tracks, the only data type that *is* the same kind of track-based automation as on these other track types is Mute/Unmute. The volume and pan shapes you view and edit as breakpoint automation on MIDI tracks actually represent a type of MIDI controller data that is stored as part of the MIDI regions themselves. In contrast, Instrument tracks offer all the same track view options as MIDI tracks, plus the parameters for audio volume and panning—plus any plug-in parameters on the instrument plug-in or any others that you instantiated on the track—that you enabled for automation. Both MIDI and Instrument tracks offer the following display format options:

* **Regions.** In this display format, MIDI regions appear as rectangles, with the region name and bars representing MIDI note events within each. The Grabber and Trimmer tools work on the region boundaries, but when viewing a track's contents as MIDI regions, you cannot edit individual MIDI notes.

* **Notes.** This display format enables you to edit MIDI notes with the Grabber (to move or copy a note) and Trimmer (to change a note's length). As you edit notes in this view, you will often find it useful to switch your main Time ruler to Bars:Beats format and enable the Grid edit mode (changing the Grid increments as necessary to different note values to facilitate accurate positioning of notes and breakpoints for controller data). You can also draw notes with the Pencil tool while in Notes view—click once to create notes whose duration corresponds to the current Grid value (whether or not Grid mode is currently active), or click and drag to extend the note you're creating to some longer duration.

* **Blocks.** Blocks display format is the same as Regions format but without MIDI note events shown within each rectangular region graphic.

* **Velocity.** If you use MIDI and Instrument tracks in Pro Tools, you will find yourself using Velocity display format fairly often (as well as the Notes view). Velocity stalks appear for each MIDI note event, which you can scale with the Trimmer or drag up and down with the Grabber. Click any MIDI note to highlight its velocity stalk. You can also use the Pencil tool to draw across multiple velocities—for example, using its Line drawing mode to create a decrescendo at the end of a phrase.

❋ **Volume, Mute, Pan.** These views of mix parameters work pretty much the same way as described for audio regions, but with one important difference: Volume and Pan data are sent out as MIDI controller messages to the external MIDI device (or software synthesizer), rather than being audio mixing events. Volume and Pan data are part of the contents of each region, rather than pertaining to the MIDI track itself. (On MIDI tracks, only automation events that are actually part of the MIDI track itself—as opposed to MIDI controller messages contained within the regions—are Mute/Unmute. In contrast, since Instrument tracks are like an Aux In with an associated MIDI track, they also include all the audio-related track view options that you would find in an Aux In.) You should be aware that some MIDI devices (or patches) don't respond to incoming Volume and Pan messages. For example, most drum patches won't respond to MIDI panning because the elements of a drum set are already spread across the stereo field as part of the patch's design.

❋ **Other (Pitch Bend, Aftertouch, Mod Wheel, Program Change, and so on).** You can also view additional MIDI controllers as breakpoint automation in the Edit window and edit them with the same tools. Pro Tools automatically detects when a MIDI controller type is recorded that doesn't already appear in the pop-up list by default and adds it accordingly.

❋ **Single Note.** This display option for MIDI and Instrument tracks is useful for MIDI drum parts where each drum sound is on a separate track. Notes actually present within regions already on the track automatically appear in the top level of the note selection pop-up, although you can also select any note in any octave.

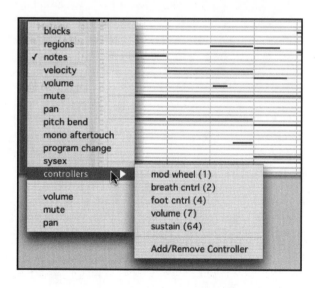

Figure 6.23 Display formats for a MIDI track.

About Instrument Tracks

As mentioned in the previous section, all MIDI-related options in the Track View pop-up menu for Instrument tracks are identical to MIDI tracks. However, an Instrument track combines the functionality of an Aux In (especially as seen in the Mix window) with a MIDI track in the Edit window. Accordingly, in additional to MIDI parameters, it offers the same display options as an Auxiliary Input track, for Volume, Pan, and any plug-in parameters that you enabled for automation.

Track Height Selector

The Track Height selector is fairly self-explanatory: It's a pop-up menu (shown in Figure 6.24) that allows you to change the height of each track. The basic options are Mini, Small, Medium, Large, Jumbo, and Extreme. As your sessions get larger, you will tend to minimize the size of the tracks you're not currently editing in order to save screen space. (Options in the Tracks List are also useful when you start running out of space in the Edit window.) On MIDI tracks, you have the additional option of displaying only a single note (the MIDI note value D1 for all snare hits, for example).

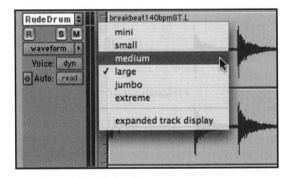

Figure 6.24   Click an audio track's Height Selector button, or anywhere in its amplitude ruler, to open this pop-up menu.

On stereo and multichannel tracks only, an Expanded Track Display option is available in the Track Height selector that shows each audio channel on the track in a separate editing lane with its own mono level meter (although these are all linked; edits in any channel are reflected in the others). Hold down the Option key (Alt key in Windows) as you change any track's height to simultaneously change the height of all tracks.

> ✻ **Tip: Simultaneously Changing a Parameter on All Tracks**
>
> With many track parameters in Pro Tools, if you hold down the Option key (Alt key in Windows) as you make a change on the current track, the new value is applied to *all* tracks. For example, to set the data

display view for all tracks to Volume, hold down this modifier key as you change this option for any individual track. (This also works with the Mute and Solo buttons, Input and Output selectors, track heights, and other items.)

Playlist Selector (Audio and MIDI Tracks)

As explained in Chapter 2, a *playlist* is a list of the regions to be played back by each audio or MIDI track. This pop-up selector, immediately to the right of the track name (as shown in Figure 6.25), enables you to create and duplicate any edit playlists for the track and to quickly change from one playlist to the other. If you want to experiment with different arrangements, edits, and so on—but still be able to quickly change back to the original version—this feature is important to master. The automation (for example, volume, panning, or send levels) on audio tracks is global for the track, so a single automation playlist applies no matter which edit playlist (arrangement of audio regions and their fades on a track) is currently active. MIDI Volume and Panning events actually comprise part of the data within MIDI regions, so these can be different in each edit playlist on a MIDI or Instrument track (Mute events in these tracks are the only exception; these are Pro Tools automation events, so they apply no matter what edit playlist is selected for the MIDI/Instrument track). Feel free to experiment; playlists are nondestructive and don't occupy significant disk space! In fact, if you change the notes and other events within a MIDI region that Pro Tools knows is used in another playlist, it automatically creates a new MIDI region name for the altered version.

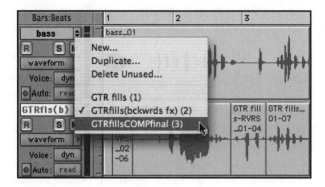

Figure 6.25 The Playlist selector opens a pop-up menu, where you can select between alternate playlists for each audio or MIDI track, create new playlists, and duplicate or rename existing ones.

Samples/Ticks Timebase Selector

The pop-up Samples/Ticks Timebase selector, shown in Figure 6.26, enables you to choose whether the time references for location of events on this track are to be treated as *absolute* (samples) or *relative* (ticks—subdivisions of the musical beat—in thousandths). When these are absolute, changing Pro Tools tempos (whether via events in the Tempo ruler or manual settings in the Transport window's Tempo field) will not affect the location of events already placed into this track. On the other hand, if a track's timebase is relative (ticks), when you make tempo adjustments, events move to a new position in order to maintain the same bar/beat location relative to the new tempo.

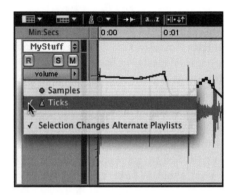

Figure 6.26   The timebase for event locations in audio, MIDI, and Instrument tracks can be absolute (samples) or relative (ticks).

When Ticks timebase is chosen for an audio track, the regions it contains will shift if you apply a tempo change afterward (either manually, via the Tempo Operations window, or by using the graphical Tempo Editor that you can open beneath the Tempo ruler). Any crossfades between audio regions on the affected tracks will be re-rendered if their positions are altered as a result of tempo changes, but durations of fade ins and fade outs will be unaffected.

Existing automation data on tick-based tracks will also be remapped to reflect any tempo changes. With this capability, for example, any shots from a send to a reverb or delay effect, or the Master Fader's volume fade at the end of a song, will automatically have their locations adjusted for the new tempo so that they still occur at the same bar and beat relative to the new tempo.

In previous versions of Pro Tools, MIDI tracks could *only* be ticks based. However, Pro Tools 7 introduced the option of setting MIDI and Instrument tracks to a samples timebase. This is useful not only for MIDI-based sound effects design, but also when recording free-form MIDI performances.

Track Color Indicators

You can toggle the display of this color strip to the left of all tracks in the Edit window (visible in Figure 6.27) using the View > Edit Window > Track Color option. You can reassign colors for selected tracks via the Color Palette window to conveniently flag groups of tracks that are related. For example, you might assign a color to all percussion tracks, whether MIDI or audio, or use different colors for basic tracks versus instrumental overdubs—whatever helps you keep track of things in a complex session. You can also display Track Color indicators at the top and bottom of the Mix window, as discussed in Chapter 7. Some users prefer *not* to display Track Color indicators in the Edit window in order to conserve horizontal screen space for displaying track data.

Timeline Display: Timebase Rulers and Marker Memory Locations

You can display various timeline rulers along the top of the Edit window: Time (Minutes: Seconds, Bars:Beats, Samples, SMPTE Time Code, or Feet+Frames), Tempo, Meter, and Markers. Enable these rulers via the View > Rulers submenu or the Ruler Options pop-up menu beneath the Edit mode buttons in the Edit window. The available rulers are shown in Figure 6.27. (Note: the Feet+Frames ruler is only available on TDM systems; on LE systems, the DV Toolkit option—which is not compatible with M-Powered versions—must be installed in order to use the Time Code ruler.) The display units for the main Time ruler reflect those of the Main Counter at the top of the Edit window. Conversely, you can click the title area at the left end of any Time ruler to switch the Main Counter to that ruler's time units (and display its Grid Line increments in the Edit window, if this preference is enabled). This main, active ruler is always indicated by the blue background behind its title (versus the gray background on other visible rulers) and determines the default time units that will appear in the selectors for Grid and Nudge values. Click and drag rulers by their titles to change their vertical order in the Edit window.

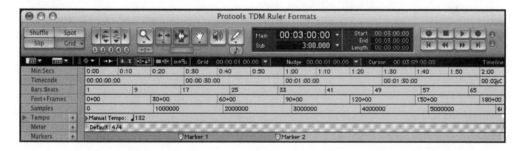

Figure 6.27   You can display multiple timeline rulers at once: Bars:Beats, Minutes:Seconds, Samples, SMPTE time code, and Feet+Frames. Additional rulers display markers, tempo events, and meter events.

No matter which editing tool is currently selected, the cursor changes to the Selector's I-beam shape when the pointer is over any of the rulers in the Edit window. Click and drag here to highlight a timeline range in all tracks.

✳ ✳ ✳

Markers Ruler

The Markers ruler displays all Marker memory locations (but not Selection memory locations) that were created in your session. Markers identify single points in time. Among other things, you can use markers to identify parts of a song, scenes, punch in/out points that you expect to use again, or any other location that you might want to quickly find afterward. Click the button at the left end of the Markers ruler—or simply press the Enter key on the numeric keypad—to create a new memory location (marker or selection) based on the current position or selection. (Incidentally, you can do this even while in Play or Record mode! Many users drop markers into the Pro Tools timeline while recording a performer to identify song sections or spots where punch-ins may be necessary.)

A marker specifies a single time value (and appears in the Markers ruler with the name you've defined), while a selection represents a range of time (for example, the verse of a song or a portion within a longer session that you may bounce to disk more than once). Selection memory locations recall not only the timeline range, but also *which* tracks were highlighted. Both markers and selections can be displayed and recalled in the Memory Locations window (shown in Figure 6.28). Since the stored attributes of any memory location can optionally include zoom settings, pre- or post-roll times, group enables, track show/hide, and other track display options, some users create memory locations with no time reference at all, for the specific purpose of storing and recalling these customized views.

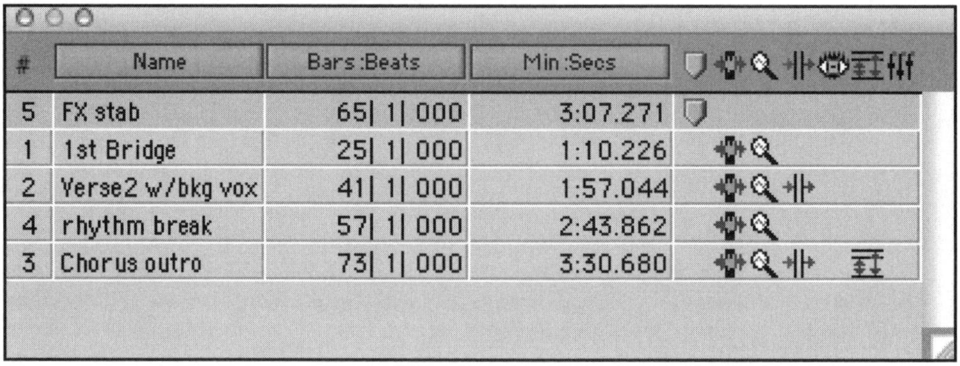

#	Name	Bars:Beats	Min:Secs	
5	FX stab	65| 1| 000	3:07.271	
1	1st Bridge	25| 1| 000	1:10.226	
2	Verse2 w/bkg vox	41| 1| 000	1:57.044	
4	rhythm break	57| 1| 000	2:43.862	
3	Chorus outro	73| 1| 000	3:30.680	

Figure 6.28 The Memory Locations window displays markers and selections with their absolute or relative position. The icons in the right-hand column indicate additional view properties stored with each memory location.

Markers and selections can reference either an absolute position in the session's timeline or a relative position in Bars:Beats:Ticks (whose absolute time position is affected by tempo changes in the session). In the New Memory Location dialog box, the default reference type reflects the time units currently displayed in the Main Counter.

Colors can be manually or automatically assigned to each marker (using the Color Palette window). If the Always Display Marker Colors option is enabled in the Display tab of the Preferences dialog box, fill colors in the Markers ruler reflect each marker's assigned color until the next marker is encountered (and from that point on, switches to that marker's color). This is useful, for instance, for keeping track of what section of the song or soundtrack you're currently seeing, even while editing track data at a very high zoom level.

You can drag marker memory locations to new positions within the Markers ruler (and their movement will affected by Grid mode, if enabled). You can also use markers to make timeline selections in the Edit window: Shift-clicking a marker highlights the range between the current Main location and that marker. To delete a marker in this ruler, Option-click it (Alt-click in Windows). Double-click a marker to edit its properties (for example, to change its time reference or to restore the current pre- and post-roll times every time this marker is recalled). To redefine an existing selection memory location, highlight a different range, open the Memory Locations window, and then Control-click (or right-click in Windows or Macintosh) that selection's name. (This technique also works on Marker memory locations; the current Start value replaces the marker's original time reference.) Memory locations are explained in more detail in the "Memory Locations" section of Chapter 8. They're often an underused feature of Pro Tools; take some time to learn how to use them!

❈ **Tip: Recalling Memory Locations from the Keyboard**

You can also recall memory locations (both markers and selections) from your computer's numeric keypad. Press the period key on the numeric keypad and then the desired memory location number, followed by another period.

❈ **Note: Pro Tools Gives You Ticks!**

Memory locations can be absolute (time) or relative (Bars:Beats). An *absolute* time reference is a specific number of minutes, seconds, and samples from the session's start and is unaffected by tempo settings. In contrast, the actual time location of a *relative* Bars:Beats reference depends on musical tempo. If the tempo is set to 60 beats per minute (bpm), each beat lasts one second; therefore, the ninth beat (the downbeat of the third bar, if you're in 4/4 time) occurs precisely eight seconds into the session's absolute timeline. But if you double the tempo setting to 120 bpm, the downbeat of that third bar is now only four seconds into the session timeline.

In the Bars:Beats time scale, Pro Tools subdivides each 1/4 note into 960 pulses, or *ticks*. Of course, the actual time represented by each tick depends on the tempo. So a full 1/4 note has a duration of 960 ticks (one second at 60 bpm, but only 500 milliseconds at 120 bpm), an 1/8 note is 480 ticks, a 1/16 note 240 ticks, and so on.

If you need to tie the markers or selections you create to musical events and the Pro Tools tempo, use the pop-up selector in the New Memory Location dialog box to make their positions relative (Bars:Beats). That way, if you change the tempo settings, the memory location's absolute time position will also be altered such that it stays in the proper musical location.

Tempo and Meter Rulers

In Pro Tools, changes of tempo and meter (how fast the beat is and how many beats per bar) are represented by tempo and meter events. Clicking the buttons next to the Tempo and Meter rulers creates new tempo/meter events at the current position. (Another button at the left of the Tempo ruler opens the Tempo Editor, where you can use the editing tools to graphically edit tempo events, as discussed in the "Tempo Editor" section later in this chapter.) Click and drag to change the position of an event in these rulers, or double-click to alter its properties. Option-click (Alt-click in Windows) to delete any event in the Tempo or Meter ruler—or simply drag it vertically in either direction to remove from the ruler.

Song Start Marker

By default, the Song Start marker appears at the beginning of the timeline within the Tempo ruler. Double-click this marker to enter a new bar number or time signature in the Edit Bar| Beat Marker dialog box. If you want bar 1 of the song to begin at some other point in the timeline (for example, at exactly seven seconds), drag the Song Start Marker to that location within the Tempo ruler—its movement will be affected by Grid mode, if enabled. By default, the location of events (regions, automation, and so on) within any track set to Ticks timebase will be also be displaced to maintain their previous positions relative to the song start. However, you can also hold down Control+Shift while dragging (Start+Shift in Windows) if you want the position of events in tick-based tracks to be unaffected by moving the Song Start marker. (Prior to version 7, MIDI tracks were ticks-timebase only; now, however, you can also set MIDI and Instrument tracks to samples timebase, in which case the locations of MIDI events within them are unaffected by changes to the tempo and song start point.)

The Move Song Start page of the Time Operations window provides an alternative method to dragging the Song Start marker in the Tempo ruler. The Time Operations and Tempo Operations windows are discussed further in the corresponding sections of Chapter 8. Using this window to move the Song Start marker provides more precise control. For example, you can specify its new position numerically, using any timeline units available in your version of Pro Tools, regardless of which main ruler is currently active in the Edit window, or simultaneously assign any bar number to the Song Start marker's new location.

Managing Multiple Takes

When you've recorded multiple takes with the same start and end times within a track—perhaps by using Loop Record mode or because you've used a Timeline selection and pre-/post-roll fields to automatically punch in a series of recordings at the exact same place—Pro Tools offers several features to help you keep track of these. As mentioned elsewhere, new region names are automatically created for each take (Trackname_01, Trackname_02, and so on), and these all appear in the Region List. Additionally, though, there's a really quick way to review and select among these alternate takes. Using the Selector tool, Command-click (Ctrl-click on Windows) within the region. A pop-up Takes List appears (shown in Figure 6.29), allowing you to choose among all regions in this track with exactly the same start and end times. As you do this, take some time to edit these region names to organize your thoughts (for example, "Gtr fill OK," "Gtr fill bad," "Gtr fill best," and so on). Don't just leave the default numeric suffixes; big sessions get confusing enough as it is!

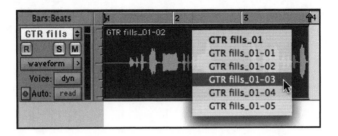

Figure 6.29 Here, we've used the Selector tool to Command-click (Ctrl-click in Windows) on the topmost region of several that were recorded in Loop Record mode. The Takes List pop-up menu allows you to select between multiple takes recorded in this mode.

Assembling a Comp Track

Comping multiple takes together (that is, assembling a composite take using segments of each) is very easy to do in Pro Tools. There are many possible approaches, but here's a very simple method:

1. Select the original track containing your multiple, layered takes, and then use the Track > Duplicate command. (If you're using an HD system, you should then drag the duplicate track immediately *above* the original track, as you will see in step 5 below. The track order doesn't matter on LE and M-Powered systems.)

2. Confirm that this new track is exactly the same format (mono/stereo) as the original track and assigned to the same output path (or MIDI output/channel).

3. After you've reviewed the alternate takes in the original track, use the local menu of the Region List to eliminate the takes you will definitely not use via its Clear Selected command.

4. Using the Takes List pop-up menu, select a take with alternate bits that you want to cut into the basic take. Then drag this up into the new, second track, holding down the Shift key to constrain its movement in the vertical direction.

5. Use the Selector and other tools to slice up the alternate take in the new track, leaving only the keeper parts. Cut holes into the basic take in the original track by selecting and then pressing the Delete (or Backspace) key. (On an HD system, manual voice assignments can make this even easier: Just assign both tracks to the same voice number as soon as you create the duplicate track in step 1, and the upper track will always steal that voice wherever regions in the two tracks coincide. There's no need to edit the basic take in the lower track at all.)

6. Select and Shift-drag the regions from the upper work track down into the main track. Then delete the work track if you no longer need it.

If you've already instantiated some plug-ins or created sends on the basic audio track, however, you might find that differing sounds on the basic and work track are a distraction during this comping process. If so, here's one easy workaround. Create a new Aux In—mono or stereo as per the original track, and assigned to the same output path. Assign the input of this Aux In to any unused bus (or bus pair) in Pro Tools, and then assign the main outputs of both source tracks to that same bus. You can drag the plug-in inserts and sends directly from the original track to the Aux In.

❊ Tip: Colorful Comp Tracks

The ability to manually assign colors to selected regions is extremely useful when assembling a comp track, as in the preceding example. Use the Color Palette to select and assign a distinct color to each of the takes (regions) in your source tracks before cutting and pasting it all together into a single composite track. Later, this will make it easier to see at a glance which segments came from which source take.

Real-Time MIDI Properties on MIDI/Instrument Tracks

This feature was introduced in version 7 of Pro Tools and is immensely useful for anyone who composes and edits MIDI performances. Real-time MIDI properties are nondestructive, real-time versions of many of the MIDI processes already available via the MIDI menu in previous versions of Pro Tools. You can apply Quantize (including the same parameters available in the "destructive" version, including swing and groove quantize), duration and velocity changes, delay offset, and transposition—without altering the contents of the MIDI regions on the track. (You also have the option of permanently incorporating the result of the current real-time MIDI properties into the affected region or track.) You can enable display of these parameters (as seen in Figure 6.30) via the View > Edit Window > Real-Time Properties command. Using real-time properties on MIDI and Instrument tracks is discussed further in Chapter 10, "MIDI." There we also discuss how you can apply real-time properties to individual *regions* on MIDI and Instrument tracks, as well as applying real-time properties to the track itself, that will affect all MIDI data played back through it (including regions that already have their *own* real-time properties).

Figure 6.30 The Real-Time Properties column for MIDI and Instrument tracks.

More About Automation in Pro Tools

As mentioned previously, there are two ways to create mix automation in Pro Tools:

❋ Record your automation moves in real time, using either the mouse and the onscreen controls in the Pro Tools software or an external control surface (such as Digidesign's D-Control, D-Command, Command|8, ProControl, Control|24, CM Labs' MotorMix, the HUI, or Mackie Control Universal, by Mackie).

❋ Draw breakpoint automation directly in the Edit window, using the Grabber or Pencil tool.

Of course, you can use any combination of these two techniques during a project. Indeed, many new Pro Tools users coming from a background in old-school mixing consoles and tape tend to place a lot of priority on the real-time automation recording capabilities. But with time, they often find that in some cases it's just plain faster to draw in volume, panning, and other automatable parameters by hand using the Grabber tool (or the Pencil and Trimmer tools). Nevertheless, there will always be times when you prefer to record (or revise) automation by ear, in real time, either with the mouse—or even better, with an external control surface.

Automation Modes

Mix automation is so essential to Pro Tools that by default, the Automation Mode selector for each track appears in both the Edit and the Mix windows. It is a pop-up menu, with these options:

❋ **Auto Off.** This mode disables all automation in the track.

❋ **Auto Read.** This mode plays all enabled automation types in the track.

❋ **Auto Touch.** This mode records automation only while any of the faders for the track are touched, moved with the mouse, or moved via a touch-sensitive fader on one of the control surfaces that can be used with Pro Tools. When you release the fader, it returns to its position according to the previous automation values for this track. Auto Touch is handy for punching in a section within the track's existing automation data. (Note: The Touch Timeout and AutoMatch Time settings under Preferences > Automation determine how quickly faders ramp up or down to their previously automated levels once Pro Tools determines that you have released the fader in Auto Touch mode.)

❋ **Auto Latch.** Like Auto Touch mode, automation recording in Auto Latch mode doesn't start until a fader is moved. However, when you release the fader in Auto Latch mode, it *stays* at its current level, recording new automation data for that fader until playback is stopped. This mode is especially handy for automating plug-in parameters, for example, or other situations where you want to overwrite existing automation data from a certain point forward.

❋ **Auto Write.** This mode records automation for a track from when playback is started until it's stopped, regardless of whether you move any faders. (You'll notice that tracks automatically switch from Auto Write mode to Auto Touch mode when you stop playback, which reduces the danger of accidentally overwriting the data you just recorded when you press Play again!)

❋ **Trim (HD/TDM systems only).** This mode applies to volume and send-level automation only. Trim mode works in conjunction with other automation modes—but the fader changes you make in Trim mode apply *relative*, rather than *absolute*, value changes to the existing automation data in the track. While recording automation in Trim mode, onscreen faders show the delta value (the amount of increase or decrease to their level) rather than the usual absolute value.

❋ **Tip: Trimming Automation Data**

You can use the Trimmer tool to scale existing automation data up or down within Pro Tools tracks, as shown in Figure 6.31. For example, to reduce the overall level of a send from an audio track (which perhaps you've routed to an Aux In with a delay effect inserted), first change the display format of the track to show the level for the send you want to edit. Then use the Selector tool to highlight the portion of this send's level automation you want to alter. Then drag it upward or downward with the Trimmer; you'll notice that as you do so, the amount of change being applied (that is, the *delta*) is indicated in dB. The contour of your send-level changes will be retained, but the overall level will be louder or softer. If necessary, you can even squash the selected automation shape against the top or bottom of the track to flatten out peaks or valleys!

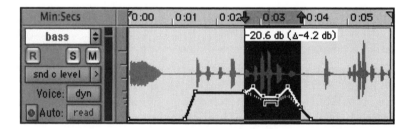

Figure 6.31 You can use the Trimmer tool to scale selected automation data up or down.

❋ **CSi: An Automation Editing Tutorial**

In the CD-ROM at the back of this book, check out the sample movie tutorial from *Pro Tools 7 CSi Starter*, "Automation Overview." In this sample movie tutorial, you can see the automation modes in action—not only for pan and volume, but also for pre- and post-fader sends. Use of the automation Safe button in Output windows is shown, as well as the features in the Automation Enable window.

Automation Enable Window

The Automation Enable window (opened via the Windows menu and seen in Figure 6.32) enables you to suspend playback of *all* animation in a Pro Tools session or to individually enable/disable entire categories of automation data for recording (volume, pan and mute for track outputs; any enabled plug-in parameters; or level, pan, and mute for sends).

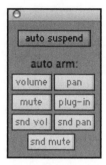

Figure 6.32   The Automation Enable window globally affects how automation is recorded/played back in the entire Pro Tools session. (LE/M-Powered version is shown here; TDM offers additional options.) If recording or playback of automation on your tracks doesn't seem to be working, check here to make sure automation isn't suspended!

❋ **Note: Basic Rules for Cutting and Pasting Automation Data**

Editing automation is somewhat different from editing audio/MIDI regions. Knowing how any region editing you do interacts with existing automation data in the same area of the track will help you unlock the power of editing tracks to further shape your projects. Here are some of the most basic rules to keep in mind:

❋ In Pro Tools versions prior to 6.7, when you cut, copy, paste, or drag audio waveform selections/ regions (in Waveform or Blocks view for audio tracks) or MIDI data (in Regions, Blocks, Notes, or Velocity view), their automation data accompanied them to the new location. However, the Options >Automation Follows Edit option allows you to disable this if necessary.

❋ Trimming audio regions to change their length does *not* affect any overlapping automation data.

❋ When an audio track's display format is set to any of the automation types, you can select, cut, copy, and paste automation data without affecting the audio regions visible underneath it.

❋ You can't paste automation from an audio track into a MIDI track, or vice versa.

Tempo Editor

The Tempo Editor was first introduced in version 6.7 of the Pro Tools software. Clicking the button to the left of the Tempo ruler opens this resizable, horizontal pane beneath it, as shown in Figure 6.33.

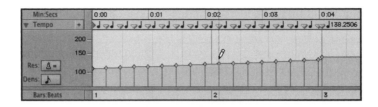

Figure 6.33 The Tempo Editor allows you to graphically edit the tempo track. (You can also use the Tempo Operations window.)

In a manner similar to automation, you can use the edit tools to create (Pencil), select (Grabber and Selector), or scale (Trimmer) tempos graphically. As you can see in the figure, each tempo change in Pro Tools is a discrete event that stays in effect until another tempo change event is encountered. Even if they are drawn with the Pencil tool, the end result of graphically editing tempos is a series of separate tempo events, which are visible in the Tempo ruler even after this graphic editor is closed.

Use the Grabber tool to drag a tempo event vertically to a new bpm (beats per minute) setting or horizontally to a new position in the timeline. If enabled, Grid edit mode snaps the horizontal movement of tempo events to the nearest grid increment as you drag them. As with automation breakpoints within tracks, you can delete existing tempo events in this editor by Option-clicking (Alt-clicking in Windows) with the Grabber. While dragging or trimming tempo events in the Tempo Editor, you will notice that the units in the Cursor Location Display switch to bpm.

You can use the Trimmer tool to scale multiple tempo events up or down—either within a previously highlighted range or with the entire session timeline when no range was previously highlighted.

You can use the Pencil tool to create a series of tempo events in this editor, using the freehand, line, or curve drawing modes (you cannot use the triangle, square, and random drawing modes in the Tempo Editor). The pop-up Density menu gives you control over the spacing of these newly created tempo events, specified in either note-value or millisecond time units. The pop-up Resolution menu determines the note value that will be the basis for all beats-per-minute settings created when you draw tempo curves with the Pencil tool. When you have just created a tempo curve using the Pencil tool, blue adjustment handles appear, which allow you to adjust its beginning and end points (and also the midpoint, if you used the S-curve drawing mode). You can only do this immediately after creating the curve, however; as soon as you apply any other editing command, select another editing tool, or switch the drawing mode of the Pencil tool, these adjustment handles are no longer available.

If you move the Song Start marker (either by dragging in the Tempo ruler or using the Time Operations window), the locations of existing tempo events usually shift accordingly. (This is not obligatory, though; in the "Time Operations" section of Chapter 10, you will find more techniques and applications for moving the Song Start Marker, renumbering bars, and so on.) To extend the currently selected range in the Tempo Editor to the next tempo event in the Timeline, press Shift+Tab. To instead extend the current tempo selection to the previous tempo event, press Option+Shift+Tab (Ctrl+Shift+Tab in Windows).

You can use the Tempo Editor instead of, or in conjunction with, the Tempo Operations window (discussed in the "MIDI Menu" section of Chapter 10). However, in some situations, using the Tempo Operations window instead may allow you finer control—especially when adjusting tempos in order to match musical events with absolute time references in minutes, seconds, and frames while scoring video or film, for example.

You can switch the main timebase for the Edit window between Linear Samples (absolute) and Linear Ticks (relative). This will affect how tempo events are displayed in the Tempo Editor. For example, in Linear Samples format, tempo events at bars three and five would appear more closely spaced after increasing tempo settings, since the absolute time difference between their positions has been reduced.

You can set the timebase that controls references to positions of regions and/or automation events in each track to Samples or Ticks. Here's a brief summary of how these are affected by tempo changes in Pro Tools:

❋ If your session is set to Linear Sample Display (absolute), as you trim or otherwise alter tempos in this editor, you will see bar numbers shifting in the Bars:Beats ruler if it's visible. Events inside any tracks whose Timebase selector is set to Ticks will shift in relation to this absolute (Samples) timeline. This means that if you use individual audio samples in conjunction with tick-based MIDI or Instrument tracks (for example, individual drum hits or cymbal crashes), you would set their timebase to Ticks so that individual region locations will be automatically adjusted to the same relative musical position if you ever change the Pro Tools tempo.

❋ If your session is set to Linear Tick Display (relative; there are 960 ticks per 1/4 note), you will instead see the markings for units in the rulers for absolute time formats (like Minutes:Seconds, Samples, SMPTE, or Feet+Frames) shifting around as you alter tempo events, while the horizontal size of each MIDI bar stays fixed throughout all tempo variations.

❋ Likewise, events in individual tracks set to the Ticks timebase format won't slide around onscreen as you alter tempos, but tracks set to Samples timebase format *will*.

❋ Even though they cannot contain regions, you can also set Auxiliary Input and Master Fader tracks to either Ticks or Sample timebase. As with other track types, when using Ticks timebase, any existing automation breakpoints in these will be automatically adjusted to the same relative musical location as you alter tempos. The best display format for the Edit window depends on where your editing focus is, and you can change the display back and forth at any time.

❋ Previous versions of Pro Tools only supported Ticks timebase for MIDI tracks. However, Pro Tools 7 supports setting MIDI and Instrument tracks to Sample (linear) timebase as well.

Summary

Be sure to consult your Pro Tools *Reference Guide* (a PDF document included with the program) for further details about the Edit window. There are many more time-saving shortcuts and tips to find there. Also, print out *Keyboard Shortcuts*, another PDF document provided with the program, and keep it handy!

7 } The Mix Window

To a certain extent, the Mix window is an alternative view of the same material you deal with in the Edit window. In fact, you can view many track parameters in both the Mix window and the Edit window (including comments, track I/O, inserts, sends, and other options via the View > Edit Window submenu). However, it's usually more convenient to deal with audio and MIDI mixing via the familiar metaphor of a conventional mixing board. Therefore, in the Mix window, the same tracks that appear as horizontal strips in the Edit window are shown as vertical mixer strips, with the familiar Volume faders, Level meters, Pan controls, effects sections, and sends. This "virtual mixer" metaphor is especially relevant for those who prefer to use external control surfaces, such as the Command|8, Control|24, ProControl, D-Control, D-Command, and so on, while others find that using a mouse or trackball—combined with Edit window automation—is quite sufficient for their needs. Most users alternate between the two techniques, frequently switching back and forth between the Mix and Edit windows. Having two monitors on the computer you use for Pro Tools is a huge productivity boost, especially because you can leave the Mix window (and perhaps an Output window or two; these are discussed later in this chapter) open on the second monitor as you work in the Edit window. Although Chapter 9, "Plug-ins, Inserts, and Sends," will go into more detail about the use of inserts, sends, signal routing, and plug-in architectures, this chapter mainly focuses on the elements of the Mix window's user interface. If any of the basic Pro Tools terminology you see here is unfamiliar, check back with Chapter 2, "Pro Tools Terms and Concepts."

Mixer Strip Elements

Every track you create in Pro Tools appears in the Mix window as a vertical mixer strip. (These are also sometimes called *channel strips* in Digidesign's documentation; although this isn't strictly incorrect, we prefer to reserve the term "channel" for actual input/output channels on the audio hardware, and call these *mixer strips* to avoid confusion.) Again, each mixer strip in the Mix window corresponds to a horizontal track in the Edit window—they're two different views of the same thing (although Instrument tracks have somewhat of a dual personality, as discussed later in this chapter). The controls available for each track in the Mix window depend on its type: audio, MIDI, Auxiliary Input, Instrument track, or Master Fader. Let's start by reviewing the track classes in Pro Tools and the elements that can appear in the mixer strip for each track type.

Audio Tracks

Audio tracks contain *playlists* that designate which audio regions should be played and when (and, like Aux Ins, Instrument tracks and Master Faders, audio tracks also contain automation data). Mixer strips for audio tracks in the Mix window are shown in Figure 7.1. The main output from an audio track can be routed either to any physical audio output path on the system, or to any one of Pro Tools' internal mixing busses. Audio tracks can be mono, stereo, or multichannel. An audio track can record from any physical audio input path (that is, mono, stereo, or multiple channels on your audio interface, according to the track's channel format) or from any one of Pro Tools' internal mixing busses. Only audio tracks can record audio and contain audio regions.

Track Name and Comments

Double-click the track name field to enter a meaningful name for your audio tracks. This is important, not only for keeping tracks in your session properly labeled, but because the new regions created by recording into each track are automatically assigned names derived from the track's current name. This is also true of regions created as a result of the Edit > Consolidate command, for example, as well as any AudioSuite processes that create new regions. Because you can change track names at any time, some users take advantage of this feature so that each set of new recordings into the track creates a group of similarly named regions in the Region List. For instance, if you recorded scratch lead vocals during the basic tracks session and are about to record keeper versions in the same track, you might change the track name from "ScratchVox" to "VoxGood." The region names created by your subsequent recordings will begin with the text "VoxGood" and can appear grouped together in alphabetical order within the Edit window's Region List.

The Comments area (beneath each track name field) is for your own reminders, recording notes, and so on and has no effect on audio recording or playback. Use this scribble strip however you like; it's the equivalent of that strip of tape that people use for writing on conventional mixing boards. For example, you might make note of which microphones were used and how they were positioned; settings or patches on a source guitar amplifier, MIDI device, or effects unit; notes about the settings and other information about additional programs being used with Pro Tools via ReWire; or reminders about items on that track that need to be fixed before mixdown. It's also a great idea to type the names of the performers you're recording into the Comments area for each track. This provides some historical data in the archived session document (in case you ever want to contact that talent again, for example; having a phone number or e-mail address here might be handy). More importantly, anyone who has ever recorded bands has probably experienced that awkward moment when you need to address the bass player, for example, and can't remember his name! Besides the technical information, wouldn't it be convenient if you had also typed "Larry" or "Curly" (because Moe is the drummer) into the Comments area when introductions were made during setup?

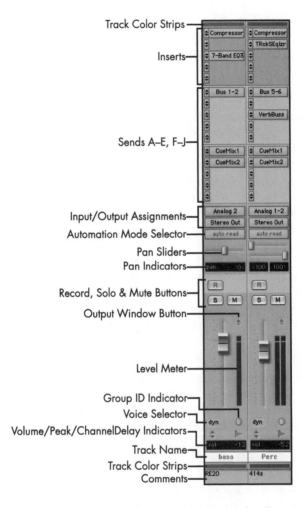

Figure 7.1 Mixer strips for mono and stereo audio tracks in the Mix window (in a stereo mix), showing the Inserts, Sends, I/O, Track Controls, Comments, and Color Strip sections.

Track Color Strips

You can toggle display of these color strips above and below all tracks in the Mix window using the View > Mix Window > Track Color option. You can reassign colors for selected tracks using the Color Palette window, so that you can immediately identify groups of tracks that are somehow related. (For example, to help keep track of a complex session, you might assign distinct colors to all your vocal tracks, guitar tracks, drum and percussion tracks, or sound effects.) You can also display assigned track colors at the left edge of the Edit window, as discussed in Chapter 6, "The Edit Window." Double-click any track's color strip to open the Color Palette and re-assign its color. (Version 7 of Pro Tools added a Hold button in the

Color Palette. When enabled, you can preselect a specific color, regardless of the current color of the track you're modifying. Additionally, the Color Palette's Apply to Selected option allows for independent color-coding of regions in the Region List, which can be useful for complex sessions.)

Volume Fader and Level Meter

The Volume fader adjusts the output level of this audio track on whatever output path(s) you've assigned to it—which may be either a physical audio output or any internal Pro Tools mixing bus. The track's Level meter appears to the right of its Volume fader. If the topmost, red segment (the clipping indicator) lights up while you record, your input level to this track is too high, and you need to adjust it to avoid distortion. The clip indicator may also light up during playback due to gain changes applied in one of the track's inserts or its main Volume fader setting (assuming that the Options > Pre-Fader Metering option is not enabled—this option *should* always be enabled while recording, however!). Click to clear a track's clipping indicator, or Option-click it (Alt-click in Windows) to clear this indicator on *all* tracks. (There's also a keyboard shortcut for clearing all clip indicators: Option+C on Mac, or Alt+C on Windows versions.) Volume faders can boost the track's level by as much as +12 dB. For finer adjustment of any Volume fader (and many other onscreen controls), hold down the Command key (Ctrl key in Windows) as you drag the control. To return a track's Volume fader to its default setting of 0 dB (Unity), Option-click (Alt-click in Windows) on the fader. If the sends on this track are set to post-fader, their level is also affected by the track's main Volume fader level (see "Sends," later in this section, for more information).

In the Mix window, each track's class is indicated by a distinctive color icon (audio, MIDI, Aux In, Instrument, or Master Fader), just below its main Level meter. You can hold down Command+Control and click on this icon (or hold Ctrl+Start and click on Windows) to make that track inactive, which conserves CPU power. (This duplicates a function in the Track menu and is not available for MIDI tracks.) Repeat the same action to make a track active again. You can also use the Group ID indicator, which is underneath the Level meter for each track, as a pop-up display that indicates all the Mix groups to which this track was assigned and what other tracks are also assigned to those groups.

> ### Caution: Setting Input Recording Levels
>
> Volume faders on audio tracks affect the track's output, *not* the input recording level! On most Pro Tools hardware configurations, if you want to change the input signal level to a Pro Tools audio channel (either to avoid clipping or to increase its level in order to take full advantage of the dynamic range offered by your audio hardware and selected recording resolution), you must do this *prior* to its input (for example, in your mic preamp, mixer, or guitar preamp that's connected to the selected audio input on your interface, and/or some Aux In track you're using as the front end for an audio track while recording). Exceptions to this include the Mbox audio interface and many of the M-Audio interfaces, which have input level knobs on their front panels. The Digi 002 and 002 Rack have gain controls on their four microphone preamps, as does the 96i I/O interface for HD systems. Unlike analog tape recorders, on digital audio recording systems, when input recording levels go "into the red" and the track's clip indicator lights up while recording, the results are decidedly *not* warm or pleasant sounding! While recording on a track, feel free to

change its main Volume fader level—whatever's convenient for your listening requirements. This has no effect on the actual audio level being recorded to disk.

It's highly recommended, however, to always enable the Options > Pre-Fader Metering option while recording into audio tracks. That way, you see what the levels are at the selected input for each track, regardless of its current fader setting or the effect of any of its plug-ins.

Pan

In a stereo mix, a *panner* determines the left-right position of each track's audio output. Mono tracks have a single left-right Pan slider. If the track is stereo—or you inserted a stereo plug-in on a mono track that converts its output to stereo (for example, a mono/stereo delay)—the track will have two separate Pan sliders for the track's left and right channels. In surround mixing, on tracks whose outputs are assigned to multichannel paths (more about this in Chapter 14, "Postproduction and Soundtracks"), you can use an XY panner to move the track left/right and front/rear in the surround field. You can always Option-click (Alt-click in Windows) Pan controls to return the track's position to center.

❋ **Tip: Setting Each Audio Track to a Separate Output**

Sometimes it's convenient to set the output from each audio track in Pro Tools to a separate mono path (for example, the individual physical outputs on your audio interface). This might be useful when transferring all your individual Pro Tools tracks to the inputs of a multitrack digital tape recorder in real time. You *could* set the output assignments one-by-one, but there's a quicker way: After using the I/O Setup dialog box to create individual mono paths for each output on your audio interface, hold down the Command and Option keys (Ctrl and Alt keys in Windows) as you set the Output selector of the first track (leftmost in the Mix window) to Output #1. The remainder of the audio tracks will be automatically assigned to consecutive output paths.

Track Controls: Solo, Mute, Record Enable, Voice Selector, Track Input Enable

While the basic functionality of the Solo, Mute, and Record Enable buttons is familiar to anyone who has used a multitrack tape recorder, Pro Tools offers a few enhancements for these. The Track Input Enable button has a rough equivalent in the selector on traditional recording consoles that switches a channel strip to its mic/line inputs instead of the tape input, while the Voice selector represents a digital audio workstation-only concept.

❋ **Solo button.** Enables playback for this track only, muting all others (although you can always solo additional tracks, because more than one track can be soloed at the same time). Command-click (Ctrl-click in Windows) a track's Solo button to put it in Solo Safe mode; the Solo button will be dimmed. In Solo Safe mode, the track will not be muted even if other tracks are soloed.

❋ **Mute button.** Disables audio output from this track on its main output assignment. This also mutes any *post*-fader sends (the default send type; a track's *pre*-fader sends are unaffected by muting the track, however). You can mute more than one track at the same time. Option-click (Alt-click in Windows) on any track's Mute button to mute/unmute all tracks at once.

✳ **Record Enable (Rec) button.** Enables an audio track for recording (and when in the default Track > Auto Input Monitor mode, switches the track to monitoring audio signals at its selected input source—either a physical input path or a bus). When you press the Record and Play buttons in the Transport window, all record-enabled tracks start recording their selected sources. (Only audio, MIDI, and Instrument tracks have Record Enable buttons.)

✳ **Voice Selector.** Determines which of Pro Tools' floating pool of voices this track will use to play back its audio regions. Ordinarily, you leave this set to dynamic (dyn) so that Pro Tools will automatically make a voice assignment according to your system configuration—and that's the *only* voice assignment mode in LE or M-Powered versions of Pro Tools. Dynamic voice allocation is usually the most convenient choice even if you have an HD system or some other TDM configuration providing a relatively large number of voices—unless you are deliberately using *voice stealing* so that regions in one track interrupt playback in another (when bleeping dialog, for example). Alternatively, in the HD software (as on all previous TDM systems), you can manually assign voice numbers to each track. Wherever two tracks attempt to use the same voice for playback, the higher-priority track (because its current position is farther left in the Mix window or higher in the Edit window) always "wins," even if this means cutting off the previously playing audio in that track. Within the Voice Selector pop-up menu for each audio track in these versions, voices already in use by other tracks appear in bold type.

✳ **TrackInput Enable (HD systems only).** Switches an individual audio track to monitoring its input, whether record-enabled or not, and regardless of whether the Track > Input Only Monitor setting is enabled.

✳ **Tip: Record-Safe Your Tracks**

Record Safe mode disables recording on an audio, MIDI, or Instrument track. Especially when working with large sessions and/or viewing tracks at small sizes, this simple technique can help you avoid mistakes as you record new takes into additional tracks. When you are finished making new recordings in a track, Command-click (Ctrl-click in Windows) its Rec button to put it in Record Safe mode (the button will be dimmed; see Figure 7.2). Repeat this if you ever need to reenable recording on the track.

Automation Mode Selector

The Automation Mode pop-up selector determines how mix automation will be recorded and played back on this track; options are Auto Off, Auto Read, Auto Touch, Auto Latch, and Auto Write (plus Trim mode on TDM systems only). For more details about these automation modes, see Chapter 6. Remember that you can also use the Automation Enable window (again, discussed in Chapter 6) to *globally* enable or disable recording and playback of entire classes of automation for the entire session.

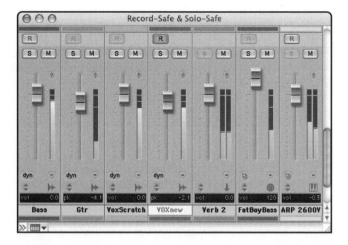

Figure 7.2 Dimmed Rec buttons in several of these tracks indicate they are in Record Safe mode. Dimmed Solo buttons in the Instrument track "ARP 2600 V" and Aux In "Verb 2" indicate they are in Solo Safe mode (so they won't be muted when other tracks are soloed).

Input/Output Section: Volume/Peak/Channel Delay and Pan Indicators, Output Selector, Input Selector

As you can imagine, the I/O section of each track's mixer strip provides selectors that determine where its audio is coming from, and where it's going! The numerical value displays in this section are also essential for keeping an eye on the level and position (for example, left–right in a stereo perspective) of each track in your mix.

❈ **Volume/Peak/Channel Delay indicators.** These fields display current values for the Volume fader, peak level, or channel delay. (See the following tip, "Volume/Peak/Channel Delay Indicator Modes," for more information.)

❈ **Pan indicators.** Numerical display for the current positions of the Pan sliders—either a single value for mono tracks or dual values for stereo tracks. Displayed values change in real time as you make adjustments and, during playback, continuously reflect the changing values for any pan automation on this track.

❈ **Output selector.** Determines the main destination where a track's audio is to be routed within the Pro Tools mix environment. You can choose any of the available physical audio output paths on your system (which depend on the hardware in use) or any of Pro Tools' internal mixing busses. You can even assign audio tracks and Aux Ins to *multiple* output paths. After you've made the main output assignment, hold down the Control key (Start key in Windows) as you open the track's output selector again to choose additional paths. When you assign tracks to multiple output destinations, a + (plus) sign appears in front of their main output assignments within the Output selector button's pop-up menu. The output paths available in this pop-up selector—and especially the grouping of their mono subpaths—depend on the track's channel format (mono, stereo, or multichannel), your I/O setup configuration, and your audio hardware.

❋ **Input selector.** Determines what physical input or internal bus will be monitored when this track is record-enabled (and recorded to disk when you click Record and Play on the Transport) or when the Track > Input Only Monitor option is enabled. (Software instrument plug-ins can have auxiliary outputs enabled. If this is the case, these will appear among the options in the Input selector for audio and Aux In tracks.)

❋ **Tip: Volume/Peak/Channel Delay Indicator Modes**

The Volume/Peak/Channel Delay indicator for any Pro Tools track has three modes (except MIDI tracks, which display only MIDI volume):

❋ **Volume (the default).** Reflects the current level of the track's main Volume fader. Values displayed here change in real time as you move the fader, or display Volume fader automation values during playback.

❋ **Peak.** Displays the most recent peak playback or input level in the track. (In other words, if the audio on this track reached a maximum level of −3 dB during playback, that value is displayed.) Click it to reset it. This setting is useful for managing your session's gain structure and lets you know exactly how much headroom is left on the track—especially since its output level may be affected by level changes made in its plug-ins or hardware inserts. For both the Peak/Hold and Clipping Indicator functions, you can choose whether you want these to hold their values infinitely (for instance, the most recent peak level during playback, or after you hit Stop), for three seconds, or not at all in the Display tab of the Preferences dialog box. You can clear the red clip indicators on *all* tracks simultaneously by Option-clicking any one of them (Alt-click on Windows).

❋ **Channel Delay.** On HD systems, this setting indicates the total processing delay introduced on this track by whatever plug-ins you've added, in samples. Obviously, the absolute amount of delay time is proportionate to your session's sample rate and is progressively smaller at higher rates. Note that on LE and M-Powered systems, this indicator may display a delay of zero samples on certain third-party plug-ins—even when that's audibly not true! For most RTAS DigiRack plug-ins supplied with LE and M-Powered systems, however, the effective latency is indeed very small and correctly displays as (almost, but not quite) zero. At any rate, for fine adjustment of time alignment on tracks in LE and M-Powered, the Time Adjuster plug-in is very useful. On Pro Tools|HD systems using any Pro Tools software version 6.4 or higher, you can adjust the Automatic Delay Compensation feature to eliminate delays caused by processing latency in the plug-ins on your tracks.

To toggle between these modes, click on the indicator while holding down the Command key (Ctrl key in Windows).

On HD systems, you can expand this panel to additionally display the current amount of Automatic Delay Compensation (if any) being applied to each track. There is also an editable field where you can manually enter a negative or positive offset value for each track if you feel that additional adjustment for time alignment is necessary. To show this expanded view, choose View > Mix Window > Delay Compensation View.

Sends A–E, F–J

As explained in Chapter 2, *sends* are access points in a track's signal chain from which you can additionally route its audio signal to other destinations independently from the track's main output assignment. In a traditional mixing console, this is how you route part of a vocal track's signal to an external reverb—for instance, using a knob on each channel strip that feeds an output labeled "Aux Send" or something similar. In Pro Tools, you can enable up to 10 sends (grouped into two sections labeled "A" through "E" and "F" through "J") from each audio (or Aux In, or Instrument) track. Each send can be either mono or stereo (or multichannel on HD systems), as shown in Figure 7.3. You can assign the destination of each send to any of the physical outputs available on your system—used for an external effects device or a performer's headphone mix out in the studio, for example. Most frequently, you'll route sends to one of Pro Tools' internal mixing busses. When you create sends, they default to post-fader, but you can switch them to pre-fader if required. (Pre-fader send levels are unaffected by the track's main Volume fader and Mute buttons.) Controls in the Output window for each send include Output Assignment, Pre/Post selector, Level, Pan (stereo and multichannel surround sends only), and Mute.

Whether you choose the pre- or post-fader position for each send depends on how it's being used, and this varies a lot from one session (and Pro Tools user) to another. Here are two typical examples:

❄ *Post-fader sends* are often used for sends to effects: In addition to the level of the send itself, the amount of signal entering the send (and consequently arriving to its assigned destination) also varies in proportion to the track's main Volume fader. When you mute a track, all its post-fader sends are also muted.

❄ In contrast, a *pre-fader send* routes audio from the track to the specified destination, strictly according to the send's own level (volume) setting. Even if you mute the track or lower its main Volume fader, the level reaching the send's destination remains the same. Pre-fader sends can be very useful, for example, for creating an independent headphone mix for performers out in the studio. Even if you change volumes or mute tracks while you're monitoring the recording session in the control room, this won't affect what they hear in the headphone mix.

❄ **Caution: Send Compatibility with Older Pro Tools Versions**

Pro Tools 7 increased the number of sends from each track from 5 to 10. However, if compatibility with older versions is a concern (for example, when using the File > Save Copy In command to create a 6.xx version of your session for a Digi 001 or 24|Mix user), be aware that sends F–J and their associated automation data will be dropped in the process of converting to the older .pts session format.

Example: Creating an "Aux Send" to a Delay Effect

If you'd like to send audio from multiple tracks to a single mono delay (although stereo sends and delays are equally common), you might do the following:

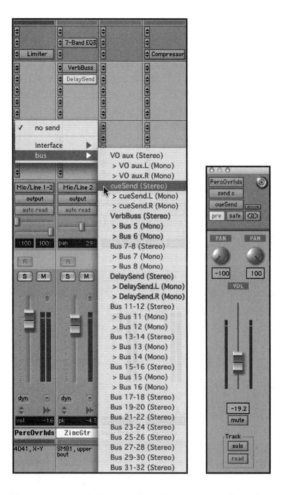

Figure 7.3 You can enable up to 10 sends from each audio, Aux In, and Instrument track. If you enable the Target button in a send's Output window, it remains open even as you select other tracks or sends.

1. Create a mono, post-fader send (the default send type) on each track, assigned to bus 1.
2. Create a mono Auxiliary Input whose input is set to bus 1.
3. Insert a delay plug-in on this Aux In (100% wet, meaning that that no direct, unprocessed signal passes through it).

Now you can use the send levels on each source audio track (each track's send level can of course be automated) to determine when and how much of that track's signal will be delayed, delayed, delayed, delayed...

> ✳ **Tip: Don't Be Afraid to Name Names!**
>
> The I/O Setup dialog box (which you can open via the Setup > I/O command) allows you to assign names to your inputs, outputs, inserts, and busses. Although you *can* set the name assignments you create as a default for all other new sessions, it's also useful to create name assignments only for the current session (and we're amazed at how few users actually do so!). For example, in the preceding example, you're using a Pro Tools bus as a send destination because you've got a delay effect on an Aux In whose input is assigned to monitor that bus. So why not go into I/O Setup and change the name of Bus 1 to "Delay"? That way you can see at a glance where the sends in each track are going, instead of having to remember a lot of bus numbers. Afterward, when you open any output assignment pop-up to select a bus (either from a send or track output), it comes right up by name instead of a number. Simple, right? So why don't more people do it? The I/O Setup dialog box is also where multichannel paths for inputs, outputs, busses, and sends are managed. This enables surround mixing, of course—templates for this are provided with Pro Tools TDM systems. Speaking of templates, as you get more adept at using the I/O Setup dialog box, be sure to learn how to import/export its settings so that you can reuse them in other sessions. (The default I/O Settings subfolder of the Pro Tools program folder is a good place to store your collection, although you might split this up even further if a single folder gets unwieldy.) In the long run, your life will be *much* simpler if you use a consistent set of configurations for I/O setup in all your sessions, especially if you start using distinct names and path groupings during record and mix phases of your projects, for example.

Inserts

As explained in Chapter 2, a track's entire signal passes through each of the five insert points in series. Using the insert selectors "a" through "e" that Pro Tools provides, you can patch in a plug-in (a software-based effects processor) at any insert point. Alternatively, you can loop the track's signal through external outputs and inputs on your Pro Tools hardware before it continues out through the main output assignment for the track. For example, you might use such a hardware insert to route the track through some favorite high-end compressor or signal processing device in your studio.

These five insert points are always *pre*-fader on audio tracks, Aux Ins, and Instrument tracks but always *post*-fader on Master Faders. Bear in mind that a track's audio passes through each insert in series, from "a" through "j." The order in which you place effects in these inserts makes a difference in the resultant sound; for example, placing the EQ (equalization) after the compressor (a dynamics processor) sounds different than doing it the other way around. To move the insert effects on a track into a different order, drag their buttons in the Mix window. Any existing automation for these inserts is adjusted accordingly as you do this. If you instead Option-drag (Alt-drag in Windows) the plug-in buttons, they are copied instead of moved to the new location—either on the same track or any other track with the same number of audio channels.

Using RTAS Plug-Ins in HD Versions of Pro Tools 7

Previous TDM 6.xx versions of Pro Tools had more constraints on where RTAS plug-ins could be instantiated. While you can place RTAS and TDM plug-ins on any track type (except MIDI tracks) in the current HD version, there are still some points to keep in mind about usage of playback voices:

❋ The first instance of an RTAS plug-in on Aux In or Master Fader tracks takes up two additional voices per channel (for example, two voices for input/output on a mono track or four voices for stereo).

❋ On *any* track type, wherever an RTAS plug-in follows a TDM plug-in in the track's signal chain, it also takes up two additional voices per channel.

❋ When RTAS plug-ins are used on any track, any use of sidechaining (on a dynamics plug-in, for example) or multiple output assignments for the track also uses additional voices.

❋ Given these limitations, and especially if running out of playback voices is already an issue on your system, try to use TDM equivalents on Aux Ins and Master Faders when they are available; place RTAS plug-ins *prior* to TDM plug-ins on all track types if practical.

❋ There may be one exception to this: When an audio track is record-enabled (or switched to Input Monitor mode), any RTAS plug-ins that precede other TDM plug-ins in the track's signal chain are bypassed. If you really need to hear these as you record on that track, you might want to place these *after* the TDM plug-ins, despite the voice-usage considerations.

❋ **Tip: Selecting Favorite Plug-Ins**

Plug-ins are now grouped within hierarchical submenus in the pop-up selector menu for each insert on a Pro Tools track (as long as you don't disable this in the Display tab of the Preferences dialog for some reason). Alternatively, you can also group plug-ins by manufacturer. This may be handy for users with large collections of plug-ins. However, you can also select some favorite plug-ins to always appear at the top of this pop-menu, *before* the categorized submenus. Just Command-click (Ctrl-click in Windows) on any insert button in any track, and while still holding down this modifier key, select the plug-in you want to add as a favorite. Repeat this procedure to add more plug-ins to the favorites list or to remove your existing favorites. (Stereo favorites won't appear on mono tracks, and vice versa.)

Auxiliary Inputs (Aux Ins)

Aux Ins behave much like audio tracks; they cannot, however, record or contain audio regions. They act in real time upon incoming audio in their selected audio input(s)—either a physical input path on your system or one of Pro Tools' internal mixing busses. You can automate the controls on Aux Ins, and place hardware and software inserts into their signal paths. You can also route a portion of their signals to one of the sends they provide. Like audio tracks and Master Faders, Aux Ins can be mono, stereo, or multichannel, and you can assign the output of each Aux In track to any physical audio output path or internal mixing bus. Figure 7.4 shows how Auxiliary Input tracks appear in the Mix window.

Typical uses of Auxiliary Inputs include:

❋ **Global send effects.** An effects plug-in (like a reverb or delay, for example) is placed as an insert on the Aux In. The selected input for the Aux In is a bus, which is used as the destination for sends from various source audio tracks.

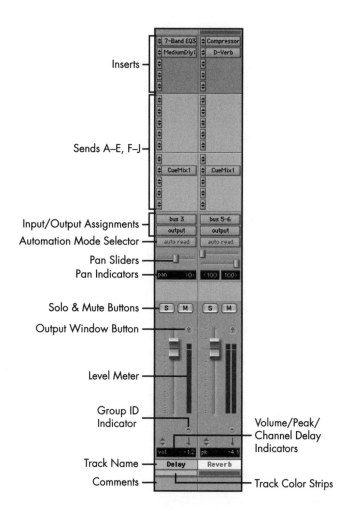

Figure 7.4 Auxiliary Inputs (mono and stereo) in the Mix window (in a stereo mix).

❄ **Subgroups/submasters.** The main outputs from multiple source audio tracks are assigned to a common bus, which is selected as the input source for an Aux In. A single Volume fader on the Aux In thereby controls the entire submix—for example, multiple drum microphones, a wind section, multiple backing vocals, or a complex sound effects background. Also, you can apply plug-ins to the entire submix by placing them on this Aux In. This not only makes more efficient use of available DSP resources but may also produce more appropriate-sounding results—for example, applying a single stereo compressor plug-in to a backing vocal submix instead of many individual compressors on the mono source tracks. Some people route the same source audio through multiple subgroups (generally called *mults* when used in this fashion) so that they can apply radically different effects treatments to each. During mixdown, you can blend them together, or drop them in and out at strategic points in the arrangement—a popular technique for processed drum loops, for example.

* **Monitoring external sources.** You can use Aux Ins to monitor the input from external MIDI instruments, tracks from a multitrack audio recorder, and so on. You can even use Aux Ins to premix multiple external input sources during the recording process (the outputs from multiple Aux Ins would be assigned to a single bus, which is selected as the input for an audio track in Record mode).

* **Software instruments.** You can instantiate software instruments (including the Click plug-in itself, which functions in a somewhat similar manner) as inserts on Aux In tracks (as well as on Instrument and audio tracks).

* **Monitoring audio from ReWire sources.** If you're running a ReWire application concurrently with Pro Tools (with the ReWired application in slave mode so that its transport and tempo are controlled by Pro Tools), you can instantiate a plug-in that allows you to monitor that program's output through an Aux In (or Instrument track).

Subsequent sections review the available controls and indicators for Aux Ins. (Refer to Figure 7.3.) For some individual elements, we make no comment—in these cases, you should assume that the element behaves exactly as already described for audio tracks.

Track Name, Color Strip, and Comments

These elements behave the same way here as they do in audio tracks, described earlier in the chapter.

Volume Fader and Level Meter

These elements behave the same way here as they do in audio tracks, described earlier in the chapter.

❋ Caution: Don't Overload the Bus

When you route sends (or main output assignments) from multiple tracks to the same bus and Aux In destination, beware of exceeding the maximum input level of that bus! If the clipping indicator lights up on the Aux In track (assuming that Options > Pre-Fader Metering is enabled), you may need to slightly reduce levels being sent to it from all these tracks in order to avoid unpleasant digital distortion. One strategy is to create a Master Fader for that bus (mono or stereo, as appropriate) in order to display what kind of levels are being produced as the audio sent from all its audio sources are combined into the same bus. Master Faders have very little impact on system resources, so don't hesitate to create them for such purposes!

Pan

The elements behave the same way here as they do in audio tracks, described earlier in this chapter. Naturally, for stereo and multichannel Aux Ins, the original Pan values on the individual sends or main outputs from other tracks routed to the Aux In also predetermine how they are affected by the Pan control on the Aux In itself.

Aux In Track Controls: Solo, Mute

The elements behave the same way here as they do in audio tracks, described earlier in this chapter. Remember, however, that if you solo an Aux In, the output from other tracks (and any post-fader sends) routed to this Aux In are muted!

❋ **Tip: Solo-Safe Your Auxiliary Input Tracks**

In Solo Safe mode, a track cannot be muted even if you click the Solo button on other tracks. Command-click (Ctrl-click in Windows) any track's Solo button to put it in Solo Safe mode (the button will be dimmed). This is *especially* useful for Aux Ins. Whether you're using the Aux In as a send destination with an effect plug-in or as a stereo subgroup to which various audio tracks' output assignments have been routed, you probably won't want the Aux In to be muted just because you momentarily solo some other track.

Automation Mode Selector

This element behaves the same way here as it does in audio tracks, described earlier in the chapter.

Input/Output Section: Volume/Peak/Channel Delay and Pan Indicators, Output Assignment, Input Selector

You can set the Input selector on an Aux In to any appropriate physical audio input path (or internal mixing bus) available on your configuration. Aux Ins can be mono, stereo, or multi-channel, and this pop-up Input selector will only display input paths that match the format of the Aux In itself. For mono Aux Ins, you select single audio inputs or mixing busses; for stereo Aux Ins, you select stereo pairs of physical inputs or busses; and for multichannel Aux Ins, you select matching multichannel input or bus paths. If any software instrument plug-ins have auxiliary outputs enabled, these will also appear among the input options for an Aux In track.

You can also assign the output of an Aux In track to any physical audio output path (providing a cue mix for your performers' headphones, for example) or internal mixing bus. Again, the available selections depend on your system configuration and whether the Aux In is mono, stereo, or multichannel.

Sends

Sends behave the same way here as they do in audio tracks, described earlier in the chapter. Like audio tracks, sends from Auxiliary Inputs can be either *post*-fader or *pre*-fader.

Inserts

Inserts behave the same way here as they do in audio tracks, described earlier in the chapter. Like audio tracks, the Inserts section on Auxiliary Inputs is always *pre*-fader.

> **Tip: Pro Tools, the Ultimate Digital Mixer**
>
> You can also use Pro Tools configurations with multichannel audio hardware as an automated digital mixer, even if you don't record any tracks to hard disk. For example, the Digi 002/002R, 96 I/O, and 192 I/O audio interfaces (as well as the M-Audio 1814) feature not only analog audio inputs, but also an eight-channel Lightpipe connector compatible with ADAT multitrack digital recorders. (Lightpipe is an eight-channel digital audio connection standard, using optical cables that terminate in a Toslink connector.)
>
> Connect the Lightpipe output from the ADAT (or compatible device) to the Lightpipe input on your audio interface. Create eight mono Aux Ins in your Pro Tools session, and set each of their inputs to a separate ADAT Lightpipe channel. (Alternatively, you could group some of these as pairs on stereo tracks, if appropriate.) Option-click the Volume fader for each Aux In to set its level to 0 dB (also known as *unity gain* because no gain change is being applied). The tracks recorded on the ADAT are now digitally routed into the Pro Tools mixing environment. (Hey, you could also use *analog* audio inputs to bring multiple tracks into Pro Tools—for instance, if your audio interface is a 1622 I/O or 96i I/O. Just between us, it will still sound great!)
>
> You can insert plug-in effects onto these Aux Ins in order to apply signal processing to the audio coming in from the digital tape source, and use sends to route part of their signal to other effects (such as reverb and delay) within the Pro Tools mixer. Then either bounce it all to a disk file or mix in real time to a DAT recorder to create your stereo "master." (Obviously, the simple method we're describing here doesn't address synchronizing Pro Tools to the tape source, so you wouldn't be able create real-time automation without purchasing one of several synchronization peripherals that are available for this purpose.)

Master Faders

Like Auxiliary Inputs, Master Fader tracks cannot contain regions. Master Faders can be mono, stereo, or multichannel. Figure 7.5 shows mono and stereo Master Faders as they appear in the Mix window. They act as a master gain stage and control for the audio signal going through a physical output path on your audio hardware (mono, stereo, or multichannel) or through one of Pro Tools' internal mixing busses. For example, Master Faders are very useful as a final level control over the physical outputs being used for the stereo (or surround) mix—or for the output pair that is the source for mix files bounced to disk. Not only does this provide a Volume fader, but more importantly, the Master Fader's Level meter facilitates final adjustment of your session's gain structure, making sure the Master Fader's clipping indicator is not being lit. Creating a Master Fader for your main mix output also provides insert points, where you could apply compression, limiting, EQ, or other effects to an entire mix (especially dithering, used when bouncing down to a lower resolution or recording digitally to a lower-resolution device). You should never bounce a mix to disk (or record to an external device, for that matter) without first creating a Master Fader where you can monitor and optimize the levels on your main mix output!

Although you can place inserts (both hardware inserts and software plug-ins) into a Master Fader's signal path, sends are *not* available from Master Faders. Also, keep in mind that, unlike audio tracks and Auxiliary Inputs, the inserts on Master Fader tracks are always *post-fader*. You can automate volume on Master Fader tracks, as well as the parameters for any plug-ins inserted into their signal paths. As before, if we make no particular comment about an element below, assume that it behaves the same as in audio tracks.

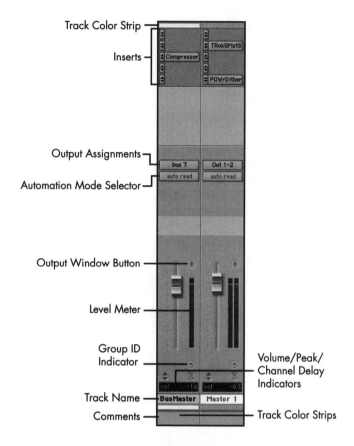

Track Color Strip
Inserts
Output Assignments
Automation Mode Selector
Output Window Button
Level Meter
Group ID Indicator
Track Name
Comments

Volume/Peak/ Channel Delay Indicators
Track Color Strips

Figure 7.5 Master Faders (mono and stereo) in the Mix window. (These can also be multichannel on HD systems.) Master Faders have no sends or Pan controls, and their inserts are post-fader.

Track Name and Comments

The elements behave the same way here as they do in audio tracks, described earlier in the chapter.

Volume Fader and Level Meter

The elements behave the same way here as they do in audio tracks, described earlier in the chapter.

Automation Mode Selector

This element behaves the same way here as it does in audio tracks, described earlier in the chapter.

Input/Output Section: Volume/Peak/Channel Delay Indicator, Output Selector
Unlike audio tracks and Aux Ins, Master Faders have no Input selector—only a selector for the output path (or internal mixing bus) whose signal path they control. Master Fader tracks also have no Pan controls.

Sends
Master Faders do *not* have sends!

Inserts
Inserts behave the same way here as they do in audio tracks, except that as mentioned earlier, the inserts on Master Faders are always *post*-fader. (In other words, the input level to the Inserts section is affected by the Master Fader track's main Volume fader—as opposed to audio tracks, Auxiliary Inputs, and Instrument tracks, where inserts are always *pre*-fader.)

Tip: Wide Meters View

You can change the width of all the track Level meters if this helps you keep an eye on what's going on in your mix. To switch to wide meters view, hold down the Command, Option, and Control keys (Start, Alt, and Ctrl on Windows) as you click on the Level meter for any track. Repeat the same operation to switch back to normal meter width.

MIDI Tracks

MIDI tracks contain MIDI regions. The output assignment for each MIDI track determines where the MIDI data contained in its regions will be transmitted—to one of the MIDI outputs available on your system (as determined by your current MIDI setup) and on a specific MIDI channel. Remember that MIDI is data, not audio! If you want to route the *audio* outputs of your external MIDI devices through Pro Tools, you must connect them to physical audio inputs on your Pro Tools audio hardware and monitor their audio via Auxiliary Inputs (or record them to audio tracks). If the sound sources used by your MIDI tracks are synthesizer and sampler plug-ins or external programs via ReWire, these are generally also instantiated on and/or monitored through Aux Ins (or Instrument tracks).

Track Name and Comments
As on audio tracks, the MIDI regions created as a result of recording into MIDI tracks inherit the current track name. So again, it's much better to assign meaningful track names as you record (for example, "bass," "drums," or "strings")—it will save confusion later. On *all* track types, take advantage of the Comments field to make notes to yourself—for instance, any manual settings that must be restored on one of your external MIDI devices the next time you open this session (see Figure 7.6).

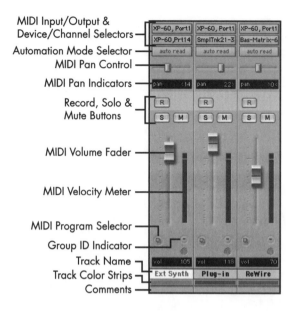

MIDI Input/Output &
Device/Channel Selectors
Automation Mode Selector
MIDI Pan Control
MIDI Pan Indicators
Record, Solo &
Mute Buttons

MIDI Volume Fader

MIDI Velocity Meter

MIDI Program Selector
Group ID Indicator
Track Name
Track Color Strips
Comments

Figure 7.6 MIDI tracks contain MIDI data. Each track is assigned to a MIDI channel, program number, and output (either a physical port on the MIDI interface or a virtual instrument).

MIDI Volume and Velocity Level Meters

The Volume fader on MIDI tracks sends out values for MIDI Controller #7, Main Volume, which range from 0 to 127, on the MIDI channel selected for each track. The Level meter on MIDI tracks displays Note On velocities of the MIDI note events being played back—*not the output audio volume of whatever instrument (physical or virtual) is playing back the MIDI events being sent from this track!*

❋ Note: MIDI Volume and Pan Are Controller Data

Volume and panning (and other MIDI Controller events) work differently in MIDI tracks than in other Pro Tools tracks— especially in relation to automation and alternate playlists on the same track. On MIDI tracks, both Volume and Pan are numerical MIDI values, from 0 to 127, transmitted like any other MIDI controller type. It is actually your MIDI device that responds, changing the volume on some sound that's responding to the same MIDI channel where this MIDI controller information for Pan values is being received.

When you record fader automation or draw volume changes into to MIDI track, these become part of the data actually contained in each affected MIDI region. In audio tracks, there's only one automation playlist for the track. Therefore, when you choose between alternate edit playlists (the list of audio regions and fades to play), the same automation data for that track still applies (for example, breakpoint automation you've created for Volume or Pan). Also, if cutting and pasting of audio regions in one playlist also causes overlapping automation events to be moved, this underlying automation affects *all* playlists on that audio track. In contrast, because on MIDI tracks the controller data for volume, pan, and other types of MIDI controller data is part of the MIDI regions themselves, the automation data for these can be completely different in each playlist on the same track. If you alter the MIDI data within MIDI regions after switching to an alternate track playlist for a MIDI track, a new MIDI region is automatically created.

MIDI Pan

The Pan slider on MIDI tracks sends out values for MIDI Controller #10, Pan, on the channel selected for each track. Values range from 0 to 127 (0 = hard left, 127 = hard right, 64 = centered).

> ### ❋ Caution: Who's the (MIDI) Boss?
>
> If you assign two MIDI tracks to the same MIDI output and MIDI channel, that external MIDI device or software instrument will respond to MIDI volume, pan, and other controller messages arriving on either channel. This can get confusing, especially if you're using automation! If you ever do need to assign multiple MIDI tracks to an identical destination (for example, to create and edit left- and right-hand keyboard parts separately, or to use separate tracks for the individual elements in a MIDI drum kit), it's better to choose beforehand which track to use for controlling volume and pan—and for automation—and stick to it. Otherwise, things can get very confusing!

MIDI Track Controls: Solo, Mute, Record Enable, MIDI Program Selector

On MIDI tracks, the Solo, Mute, and Record Enable buttons work in a comparable way to audio tracks.

The MIDI Program selector (below and to the left of the track's main Volume fader) opens a dialog box displaying patch numbers from 1–128. The program number you choose (for example, an electric piano sound, program #005 on your synthesizer) is sent as a MIDI Program Change message on the MIDI channel number currently selected for the track.

Once you have the patch name file for your synthesizer properly configured with the Audio MIDI Setup utility provided with the OS X operating system, you can use the Change button shown in Figure 7.7 to load a .midnam file. (This feature is also available in Windows XP versions, working in conjunction with the MIDI Studio Setup window of Pro Tools rather than a separate operating system utility.) This is a list of program names and numbers that, when active, allows you to select sounds on that particular synth (a device that was previously defined, attached to a specific port on your computer's MIDI interface) by name rather than program numbers in this dialog box. Once you import a patch name file for an instrument that's available in your MIDI setup, it is also available in any other Pro Tools session.

Automation Mode Selector

The Automation Mode selector for MIDI tracks behaves more or less like the one for audio tracks, as described earlier in this chapter; you select between Auto Off, Auto Read, Auto Touch, Auto Latch, and Auto Write (plus Trim mode for Volume and Pan, on TDM systems only). However, automation on MIDI tracks (with the exception of Mute/Unmute events) is

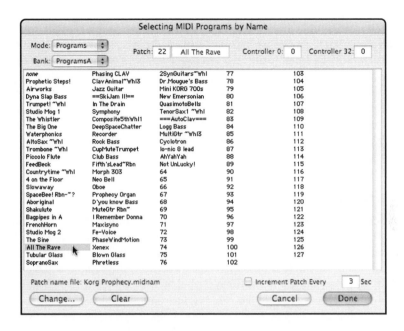

Figure 7.7 Loading a .midnam file for the external synth this track is using allows for selection of sounds by name rather than by MIDI program numbers.

recorded into the current MIDI regions as MIDI Controller events (and the MIDI module or software synthesizer responds to incoming volume or pan data on each MIDI channel, for example, rather than the automation controlling an aspect of audio signal flow or processing within the Pro Tools mixer).

Input/Output Section: MIDI Volume/Pan Indicators, Device/Channel Selectors for MIDI Input/Output

Again, remember that changes in MIDI volume and pan are actually MIDI *controller* messages, sent on that track's currently assigned MIDI channel! The values Pro Tools displays for Pan range from <64 (100% left) to 63> (100% right). MIDI Volume values range from 0 to 127.

You can change the MIDI device (and output path) and channel for each MIDI track's input and output via a pop-up selector. Available choices depend on your configuration, per the Audio MIDI Setup utility for Mac users or the MIDI Studio Setup window in Windows versions 6.7 and higher—and, of course, the MIDI interface and devices on your system. For editing convenience, you may occasionally assign more than one track to the same MIDI destination (device and MIDI channel). Bear in mind, however, that volume, pan, and program changes will affect other tracks assigned to the same MIDI output and channel.

You can also assign a single MIDI track to *multiple* devices/channels. Once you've made the main assignment, hold down the Control key (Start key in Windows) as you open the track's MIDI Device/Channel selector again to choose additional destinations. This is a down-and-dirty way to double the current part you've created within a MIDI track, using some completely different MIDI device or channel with a distinct timbre. You could also simply duplicate the current MIDI track (using the Track > Duplicate command) and assign that duplicate track to its own output destination—in fact, in many cases, you will eventually do so anyway in order to have separate control over its volume and panning, for example. But while still creating your arrangement, the big advantage of using multiple output assignments from a single track is that you can easily make changes to note values, velocities, and so on without having to copy these each time from the flute to the clarinet part, for example. The Automatic Delay Compensation feature available on HD hardware also extends to MIDI tracks that are routed to software instrument plug-ins.

Instrument Tracks

This type of track was added in Pro Tools 7. You might say that Instrument tracks are like an Aux In with a MIDI track caboose. When you create a new Instrument track in the Mix window, except for the distinctive "keyboard" icon at the bottom of the mixer strip, it looks and acts almost identically to an Aux In (except that it has a Record button and a MIDI patch selector). However, when you view the same Instrument track in the Edit window, it looks and acts like a MIDI track. Among other things, unlike Aux Ins, Instrument tracks can contain MIDI regions. Once you instantiate a software instrument in one of the insert points on an Instrument track, this can be selected as the MIDI output destination for MIDI events recorded (or placed) on the Instrument track itself in the Edit window. As with software instruments residing on ordinary Aux Ins, however, you can select software plug-ins on Instrument tracks as the output assignment from any other MIDI (or Instrument) track. Instrument tracks save screen space—especially when using monotimbral instrument plug-ins, which can only respond to events on one incoming MIDI channel at a time.

In the Mix window, the topmost Instrument panel (which can be seen in Figure 7.8) shows MIDI input/output selections for each Instrument track, plus MIDI Volume, Pan and a Mute button (while the main I/O selection, down by the main Volume fader, is identical to an Auxiliary Input track). In the Edit window, the track view selector for an Instrument track shows the usual options for MIDI tracks (including MIDI volume and pan and other controllers, which are really part of the controller data contained in the MIDI regions on that track), plus Volume, Pan, Solo and Mute buttons (identical to the ones on Auxiliary Input tracks) that affect the audio output of the Instrument track itself. If you enable any audio plug-in parameters for automation in that track, these will also appear in the track view selector.

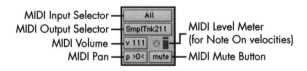

Figure 7.8 On Instrument tracks in the Mix window, the Instrument panel offers controls for input/output, volume, pan, and mute.

Track Name, Color Strip, and Comments

These elements behave the same way here as they do in audio tracks and Aux Ins, described earlier in the chapter.

Volume Fader and Level Meter

These elements behave the same way here as they do in audio tracks and Aux, described earlier in the chapter. Bear in mind, though, that volume settings and levels here are related to the audio output of the track, not to the MIDI data being sent from that track (to its own instrument plug-in or elsewhere).

Pan

Pan behaves the same way here as it does in audio tracks and Aux Ins, described earlier in the chapter, but again, this affects the audio output of the track (and doesn't send MIDI pan data, like the Pan control on MIDI tracks).

Instrument Track Controls: Solo, Mute, Record Enable

The Solo and Mute buttons on Instrument tracks work as on Aux In tracks, described earlier in the chapter—affecting their audio output only. (These buttons don't affect playback of any MIDI data the Instrument track contains. If its MIDI output is assigned to some MIDI destination other than the track's own instrument plug-in, that MIDI data still sounds even when the track's main Mute button is engaged.) In contrast, the Record Enable button on an Instrument track (which is *not* available on Aux Ins) arms the track for MIDI recording, just as on MIDI tracks.

Automation Mode Selector

This element behaves the same way here as it does in audio tracks and Aux Ins, described earlier in the chapter.

Input/Output Section: Volume/Peak/Channel Delay and Pan Indicators, Output Selector, Input Selector

These elements behave the same way here as they do in audio tracks and Aux Ins, described earlier in the chapter. Note that some software instrument plug-ins may require that *something* be selected as the audio input for the Instrument track on which they reside—even if they don't use that incoming signal in any way! Unlike MIDI tracks, there is no MIDI output selector in this section of Instrument tracks. Instead, the Instrument section at the top of the Mix window is used for this (it's also available for other track types, except Master Faders). You can toggle display of the Instrument panel in the Mix window either via the View > Mix Window submenu or (more conveniently) by using the Mix Window View selector at the bottom left corner of the Mix window itself.

Sends

Sends behave the same way here as they do in audio tracks and Aux Ins, described earlier in the chapter.

Inserts

Inserts behave the same way here that they do in audio tracks and Aux Ins, described earlier in the chapter. However, remember that most software instrument plug-ins don't use the input signal. In those cases, don't place any plug-ins in insert slots prior to the instrument plug-in itself. Only effects plug-ins that you place *after* the instrument plug-in in the track's signal chain will affect that instrument's output.

Instrument Section

This area at the top of the Mixer window is blank on every track type except Instrument tracks. When any virtual instruments have been instantiated on an Instrument track (but not audio or Aux In tracks, for example, even if they *do* have software instruments on their inserts), parameters including MIDI Volume, MIDI Pan, plus MIDI input and output assignments are displayed here. This is discussed further under the "Instrument Tracks" heading earlier in this chapter, as well as in Chapter 10, "MIDI."

Mix Window View Selector

This pop-up selector at the lower-left corner of the Mix window (shown in Figure 7.9) provides the same options as the View > Mix Window submenu, allowing you to enable/disable display of the following sections for each channel strip: Instrument, Inserts, Sends A–E, Sends F–J (none of which are applicable for MIDI tracks), Track Color strips, and Comments.

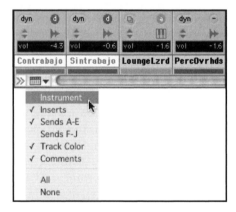

Figure 7.9 The Mix Window View selector offers the same options as the View > Mix Window submenu.

Output Windows

Just above the Level meter for each track (except MIDI tracks) is an icon that opens its Output window (see Figure 7.10). This floating window (which stays open and in place even as you switch between the Mix, Edit, and other windows) provides a secondary set of controls for the track's Volume fader, Pan controls (including surround panners, if appropriate), and

Mute, Solo, and Automation Mode selectors. Output windows also feature an automation Safe button, which prevents writing of automation data on the track in question.

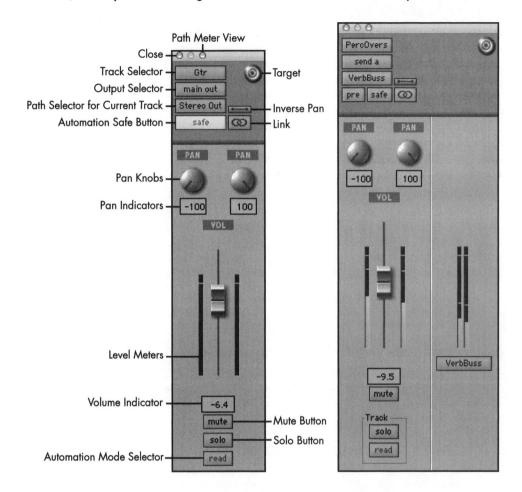

Figure 7.10 The Output window for a track or send can stay anchored in place regardless of whether the Mix or Edit window is currently visible, and you can toggle between a track's main output and any of its send assignments. If you disable (dim) the Target icon, this Output window remains open as you open others. In the right half of this figure, the Path Meter View has been opened so that you can simultaneously view levels for both the PercOvers track's reverb send and the VerbBuss mixing bus being used as the input for that reverb.

For stereo audio tracks, Aux Ins, and Instrument tracks, Link and Inverse buttons are also provided. In Link mode, both Pan knobs in the Output window move left and right in sync, with identical values. If you additionally activate the Inverse buttons, the two Pan knobs are linked but move in opposite directions. This is useful for adjusting the width of a stereo track, for example—as you move the right Pan control toward the middle (using either the knobs in the Output window or the pan sliders in the Mix window itself, whose operation is also affected by this inverse linking function), the left one automatically moves in by a corresponding amount.

Clicking on any send in the Sends section of the Mix window (or Edit window, if you choose to display them there) also opens an Output window. Output windows for sends have an additional Pre button for selecting whether the currently viewed send should be pre- or post-fader. A Path Meter View button in the upper bar of the Output window (next to its Close button) is of particular interest when viewing sends, as it opens a side panel showing a level meter for the send's destination (a bus used to route audio to a reverb or delay effect, for example). This expanded view of an Output window can be seen in the right half of Figure 7.10. As a matter of fact, without leaving the Output window, you can switch between displaying the track's main output section to displaying any of its 10 sends using the pop-up Output selector in its upper panel.

You can leave Output windows open to provide quick access—regardless of whether the Mix window or even the track itself is currently visible. By default, the Target icon is lit in an Output window, which means that clicking the Output icon for a different audio track replaces the contents of the current Output window. However, if you click on an Output window's Target icon to disable (dim) it, the window stays open; clicking other sends or the Output icon for another track will open an *additional* Output window.

> ### ❄ Tip: Using Output Windows
>
> By default, the Target icon in the first Output window you open is enabled. As you click on other sends or track Output window buttons, their contents are swapped into the Output window that is already open. As mentioned, disabling the Target icon lets the current Output window stay open, even as you open others. Especially for large sessions, keeping several Output windows open can make your life *much* simpler, with frequently accessed controls always immediately available even as you scroll through huge numbers of individual source tracks in the Mix or Edit window. Here are a few convenient uses for Output windows:
>
> ❄ Reverb sends from key vocal and soloist tracks. (Don't forget to open the Path Meter view so that you can also avoid overloading by monitoring levels on the send bus!)
>
> ❄ Auxiliary Inputs used as mixer subgroups for multiple source tracks routed through a common bus—for instance, the entire rhythm section, a drum set, a bed of backing vocals or guitars, a set of choir microphones within a larger ensemble, or submixes of dialog, effects, or music for postproduction.
>
> ❄ The Master Fader for the main mix output—having this visible in an Output window makes it easier to keep an eye on your levels, since in very large sessions, this track might not always be visible as you scroll back and forth in the Mix window.

Safe Button for Automation

When enabled, the automation Safe button prevents writing of automation data on the track currently displayed in this Output window. This can save a lot of hassle; get in the habit of using the automation Safe button to avoid accidentally overwriting your mix automation.

Linked Panners (Multichannel and Stereo Tracks Only)

When the Link button is enabled in an Output window, pan changes in one channel are immediately mirrored in the other (in both the Output window itself and the Mix window).

Inverse Pan (Multichannel and Stereo Tracks Only)

The Inverse Pan button is used on stereo or multichannel tracks in conjunction with the Link button, described earlier in the chapter. For a stereo track, for instance, enabling both Panner Linking and Inverse mode provides a convenient way to reduce the stereo width. As counter-intuitive as it may seem, sometimes it's desirable to *narrow* the stereo image of a track—for example, reducing clutter by having a stereo drum loop not extend as far out to the edges of the mix as other loops and other percussion tracks that are layered over it. As you move the Pan control for one channel toward the center, the other automatically mirrors it in the opposite direction. However, in surround mixing, inverse linking of panners acquires a whole other dimension—literally!—because you can link the two front channels, the two rear channels, or front and back.

❊ **CSi Example: Using Output Windows for Sends**

In the CD-ROM at the back of this book, check out the sample movie tutorial entitled "Automation Overview" from *Pro Tools LE 7 CSi Starter*. In this sample movie tutorial, an Output window is used to control both pre- and post-fader sends and also to enable the automation Safe button for a track.

Tracks List

The Tracks List (shown in Figure 7.11) appears in both the Mix and Edit windows, allowing you to enable/disable display of individual tracks. (It was known as the Show/Hide Tracks List in previous versions of Pro Tools.) Only tracks that are currently highlighted in this list will appear in the window. This can help you conserve screen space, especially if the tracks in your current mix don't fit in its current width. Hidden tracks will still play (unless they're muted, of course)! As shown in the figure, the pop-up menu for this list also includes commands for showing or hiding all tracks, the currently selected ones, or even audio, MIDI, Aux In, Instrument, or Master Fader tracks by category.

Here's a typical scenario for hiding tracks: You're posting a video project and have built up a fairly complex mix for the background ambience and sound effects for a scene, involving many tracks. You're ready to work on several tracks of dialog, but your Mix and Edit windows now contain such a huge number of tracks that they take up excessive screen space, making your work cumbersome. Change the output assignment of each sound effects track to one of Pro Tools' internal bus pairs and create a stereo Aux In that monitors that same bus as its input. Now you can hide all these sound effects tracks (by unhighlighting their names in the Tracks List) and use this Auxiliary Input's fader to control their overall level.

Figure 7.11 The Tracks List and its pop-up menu.

❋ **Tip: Slimming Down Your Mix Window**

When the number of tracks in your Mix window exceeds what will fit in the current screen, you have several options:

❋ Scroll back and forth, and live with not being able to see all the tracks at once.

❋ Use the Tracks List to view only certain tracks or track types.

❋ Enable the View > Narrow Mix option, which squeezes each vertical mixer strip into a smaller space.

❋ Purchase a *much* larger monitor, which is always nice!

Lastly, in the Tracks List, you can also drag tracks around to change their order. This has the same effect as dragging tracks around by their names, either horizontally in the Mix window or vertically in the Edit window.

Mix Groups List

This area displays the Mix groups you've created with the Track > Group command; however, the group name "All" always exists. When a group's name is highlighted in the Mix Groups List, it's active. Muting, soloing, and volume changes on any track belonging to the group will be mirrored in the others in the group (maintaining their original relative levels, of course). However, record-enable, panning, and output assignments for these grouped tracks will remain independent.

When you unhighlight a group name, it is inactive—you can make changes on any of its tracks without affecting the others in the group. By default, Pro Tools creates groups that are active in both the Mix and Edit windows (although for each new group, you can also specify that it should be Edit or Mix window only). In that case, enabling of groups in either window affects the other. However, if you ever need to deal with Mix and Edit groups separately, click the Edit or Mix button (instead of clicking the Edit *and* Mix buttons) in the dialog box as you create each group and deselect the Preferences > Operation > Link Mix and Edit Group Enables option.

❋ **Tip: Color-Coding Mix Groups**

You can use the Color Palette window to assign colors to selected Mix or Edit groups (independently of color assignments for the tracks that pertain to them and/or audio and MIDI regions *within* those tracks). Not only will these colors appear in the Mix Groups List shown in Figure 7.10, but also in the pop-up Mix Groups display for each track within the Mix window.

Double-click the dot to the left of any group in this list to change its name and properties (for example, to convert a Mix and Edit group into a Mix-only group). The pop-up menu at the top of the Mix Groups List (see Figure 7.12) also allows you to delete any group or *suspend* all groups. Remember that underneath each track's Level meter, a pop-up Mix Groups display allows you to confirm which active Mix group(s) that track is assigned to and what other tracks share that same group assignment.

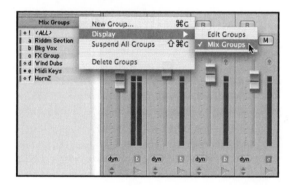

Figure 7.12   Mix groups allow you to select or mute/solo multiple tracks with a single operation and change their volumes simultaneously.

❋ **Tip: Adjusting Individual Volumes on Grouped Tracks**

When tracks are grouped in the Mix window, moving any one of their Volume faders changes the levels of the other tracks in the group by a corresponding amount. Their *relative* levels are maintained, however, from when they were first grouped. In this way, for example, you could group together all the drum tracks so that you can drag all their faders up and down together without altering the relative balance of the elements within the drum set. However, you can always make independent volume adjustments on individual tracks within a Mix group—it's not strictly necessary to suspend the group. Just hold down the Control key (Start key or right mouse button in Windows) as you drag the fader for any grouped track; other tracks in the same Mix group won't be affected. (As always, if you hold down the Command key—Ctrl key in Windows—as you drag *any* fader, its value changes in smaller increments, allowing for fine adjustments.) You can use this fine-adjustment modifier key in conjunction with the previously mentioned modifier key for temporarily suspending a group, if that's ever necessary.

Summary

Whether you control (and automate) your mixes in Pro Tools mainly through graphic break-points in the Edit window or using the controls in the Mix window depends on the nature of your work and on personal preference. Although this chapter focused on the onscreen elements of the Mix window and how they behave, the issue of signal routing within Pro Tools is explored in more detail in Chapter 9. For a more technical view of Pro Tools signal-routing architecture, see the illustrations in Appendix E, "Signal Flow in Pro Tools."

8 Menu Selections: Highlights

This chapter does *not* review every selection in every menu. Most of the functions are well documented in the *Pro Tools Reference Guide*, and especially in the *Pro Tools Menus Guide* (PDF files provided with Pro Tools, located inside the Digidesign > Documentation > Pro Tools folder). Plus, we're guessing you might already have a pretty good idea what, say, Cut, Copy, and Paste are for! Instead, the intent of this chapter is to highlight menu items that are key to Pro Tools' operation, have specific characteristics in the Pro Tools environment, are new, or simply are ignored by too many Pro Tools users.

File Menu

Most commands in the File menu concern creating new session files, opening existing ones, or saving the current session under a different name. Other commands allow you to import audio or MIDI files *into* your Pro Tools session (although this is often more efficiently accomplished via the Workspace browser window) or bounce mixes out to disk as new audio files. You can also import data from other Pro Tools session documents or send items via DigiDelivery (if you have an account on a DigiDelivery server). Remember that by nature, most Pro Tools projects consist of *multiple* files—the audio files that you use and create are not actually part of the Pro Tools session document itself. Again, here we will mention only some of the items under this menu.

Save, Save As, Save Copy In, Revert to Saved

These commands concern saving to disk the session document you currently have open, either under the current name or to a different name and location.

Save

This File menu command saves the current session document, including all edits, settings, and MIDI recordings up this point, under the existing file name. Remember: You must save *often* as you work; get used to using the Command+S (Ctrl+S in Windows) keyboard shortcut as soon as possible!

❋ **Tip: Oh No! My Computer Crashed Before I Saved My Session!**

If the unthinkable should happen as you record audio—that is, your computer hangs before you can save the session—don't despair! Although all MIDI recording, automation, parameter changes, and region edits you've performed since the last save will be lost, you don't necessarily lose all the recorded audio takes. The particular recording in progress when the computer hangs may not be retrievable, but other completed audio recordings will probably be usable. In Pro Tools, each time you press Stop on the Transport after recording, the resultant audio files are left intact within your session's Audio Files folder—*whether you save the session file or not.*

So even though you will have to restart from the last saved version of the session—which won't have these new recordings placed into their audio tracks—you can do the following:

1. Re-create the audio tracks if necessary, and then use the Import command in the local menu of the Region List to import these files from your session's Audio Files folder. (Aren't you glad you always give your tracks meaningful names, so you can easily identify files and regions, and that Pro Tools automatically numbers your takes?)

2. Now, drag these regions out onto the appropriate tracks, but don't worry about the exact position for now—the cool part is coming next.

3. Switch to Spot edit mode and click on one of the regions you've just dragged out onto the tracks; the Spot dialog box opens. Click the button next to the Original Time Stamp value in the lower half of this dialog box. That value is automatically entered into the Start field. Click OK; your region has now been spotted to the exact time location where it was originally recorded! This is possible because Pro Tools automatically timestamps regions as they are created by recording.

You still may have lost a good amount of work done since the last time you saved the session—because automation, MIDI recordings, region edits, plug-in or software instrument settings, assignment of sends, enabling of hardware or plug-in inserts, and so on are all stored within the session document itself. That's why you must be sure to save your session often (Command+S on Mac, Ctrl+S on Windows) as you work! This also might be a good time to become acquainted with the AutoSave feature of Pro Tools, which is described in the "Operation Preferences" section later in this chapter.

Save As

This command saves the current session document under a new file name. From that point on, you're working on (and saving to) that new session name. (That said, the same Audio Files and Fade Files folders are being used in this new copy as under the previous name. All additional audio recordings or fade files that you create will continue to be stored inside these same folders.) The File > Save As command is useful for saving different versions of a session—for example, if you want to try some extended experimentation but maintain the possibility of returning to a previously saved session document.

❋ **Tip: Saving Iterations of Your Pro Tools Session**

In addition to using the AutoSave feature (discussed under "Preferences," later in this chapter), many experienced operators use the Save As command as a backup strategy, in case the current session document should become corrupted for any reason. They append the date, time, or version number into file names as they save successive versions of the same session (for example, "MySession_01," "MySession_02," or "MySession_Sept20," "MySession_Sept21"). This not only protects you against file damage (although you need to be saving incremental backups of your important work files anyway!) but also gives you a specific "go back" state for your project, in case you make any mistakes, bad decisions...or clients change their minds!

For users with very limited tracks or DSP on their systems, it can be practical to bounce out submixes from a session, create a new copy using Save Session As, import the submix, eliminate source tracks bounced to disk in the submix (or merely disable them using the Track > Make Inactive command), and then start recording more overdubs. Because you created the session using the Save Session As command, both previously existing and new audio files reside together in a single Audio Files folder.

❄ **Tip: Creating Your Own Session Templates**

Most users will repeatedly work on certain kinds of projects, creating many sessions with similar configurations. To save time, you should create your own templates. These serve as starting points for new sessions (Mix window configuration, including plug-ins, inserts, and sends; track names; Edit window display format; window arrangements; zoom presets; session sample rate; bit-depth and start time; and so on). Here's a brief how-to, assuming that you want to use an existing session already containing audio and/or MIDI regions as the basis for creating your template:

1. Use the File > Save a Copy In command to save this session under a completely new name and in a different location (perhaps onto your Desktop, where it will be handy later). Give it an obvious name, like "30-second spot template." Do *not* enable any of the other copy options in the Save dialog box (Copy Audio Files and Session Plug-In Settings Folder, Copy Root Plug-In Settings Folder, or Copy Movie/Audio files)! Close your current session, and then open the copy you just created.

2. In the local menus for the Region List, use the Select All and then Clear Selected commands to *remove* all existing regions from the current session. (Caution: Click the Remove button, *not* the Delete button, which would permanently eliminate these source audio files from disk, trashing your previous session!) Delete any existing memory locations, and if you were using a Movie track, delete that from this new session copy as well.

3. If necessary, clean up your track names, display formats, and other settings until they exactly reflect how you want them to initially appear in all newly created sessions based on this template. Save this session, and then close the session or quit Pro Tools.

From this point on, the procedure is slightly different on Mac versus Windows systems:

❄ **Macintosh (Method A):** In the Finder, highlight the template session document you've created and then select File > Get Info. In the General tab of the Get Info dialog box, click to enable the Stationery Pad check box and then close this dialog box. From now on, whenever you double-click this session document (or open it from within Pro Tools), a dialog box gives you the choice of editing the Stationery Pad file itself, or creating a new session based upon it. Clicking the New Session button (and entering a session file name in the subsequent dialog box) creates a new folder and session file, based on the Stationery Pad (but as yet containing no audio or MIDI regions). Alternatively, you can use Method B, which is convenient for importing track setups from *any* existing session without requiring that it be saved previously as a Stationery Pad (read-only) file.

✹ **Windows or Macintosh (Method B):** From Windows, locate the template session document you've just created on your hard disk, right-click the file, and select Properties from the pop-up menu. Click the Read-Only check box and then click OK to close the Properties dialog box. This isn't strictly necessary for the method we're recommending, but it does help prevent accidentally overwriting this template session document if you ever open it again. Create a new, empty Pro Tools session and then use the File > Import > Session Data command (which is discussed later in this section). In the Source Tracks area at the bottom of the Import Session Data dialog box (which can be seen in Figure 8.2), choose New Track as the destination for whichever source tracks from the template session you want to import. Leave the default settings for the rest of the options in this dialog box and then click OK to bring the imported track setup into your existing session. Save your session, and now you're ready to get to work.

Save Copy In

This command saves a snapshot of the current session document (even in a completely different location) without leaving the session document that's currently open or changing its name. When you open that other session document copy, any subsequent audio recordings or fade files will be stored within that session's own Audio Files and Fade Files folders (so be sure to create a new folder for that session copy to reside in, to keep things orderly). You can use the Save Copy In command simply as a method for saving snapshots of the work in progress without changing the main session file name you're still using (as is the case with the Save As command). This is also the command you will use for saving sessions from Pro Tools 7 format (with the .PTF extension on the session file name) to earlier session formats for Pro Tools 6.xx (with the .PTS extension) or Pro Tools 5 (with the .PT5 extension).

However, the Save Copy In dialog box (shown in Figure 8.1) also provides several other important options for saving a copy of your current session document. For example, you can choose to save the session copy in 24-bit or 16-bit format, or a different sample rate for the target session copy. Enabling the Enforce Mac/PC Compatibility option when saving back to Pro Tools format 5.1–6.9 facilitates opening this session and its audio files in Pro Tools from either Mac or Windows, especially in versions prior to 6.7. If saving to Pro Tools version 5.1–6.9, you can also choose whether the maximum gain boost permitted by track Volume faders in the new session copy is +6 dB (only necessary if session compatibility with versions prior to 6.4 is a concern) or +12 dB. You can also save sessions back to Pro Tools version 5.0 or 4 (and 3.2 on Mac versions) for compatibility with older Pro Tools systems. In this case, the total track count in your session may change, since these older versions don't support stereo or multichannel tracks.

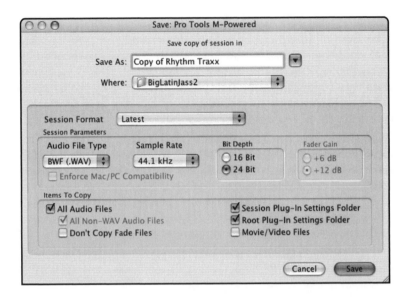

Figure 8.1 Options in the Save Copy In dialog box.

The Items To Copy section at the bottom of this dialog box provides further options:

❊ **All Audio Files.** Duplicates the Audio Files folder *and its entire contents* to the folder where you save the session copy. However, if you choose a different sample rate or bit-depth from the current session, this option is automatically enabled because the new session copy will require all audio files it references to be at the same resolution. (Hint: When copying all audio files from a source session, it can save time and disk space if you take a moment beforehand to identify unused files/regions and apply the Clear Selected command in the local menu of the Region List, as well as apply its Compact command on some of the remaining whole-file regions.)
The new session file will now reference the new Audio Files folder created by this operation—that is, all audio regions in the new session's audio tracks and Region List refer to the new file copies, rather than to the originals. However, whether you enable this option to copy the audio files or not, in the new session created by the Save Copy In command, all subsequently created audio files or fades are stored into their own Audio Files and Fade Files folders.

❊ **Session Plug-In Settings Folder.** Copies plug-in settings in the current session to a new folder, which will be referenced in the new copy. This ensures that the plug-in presets for that session continue to appear by name (and are available for assignment to additional instances of those plug-in types) when you open this session on another system supporting the same plug-in architecture.

❊ **Root Plug-In Settings Folder.** Copies the main Plug-In Settings folder into a subfolder of the disk/folder location where you create your session copy, named Place in Root Plug-In

Settings Folder. This is also useful when moving sessions from one Pro Tools system to another, because all saved plug-in settings (for example, a favorite compressor or EQ setting that you generally use for the same voice) can then be recalled by name on the new system whether used in the current session or not. (The same plug-in and plug-in architecture must be available on that system. TDM plug-ins, for example, are omitted when an HD or TDM session is opened on a system that only supports RTAS plug-ins, such as Pro Tools LE, M-Powered, or Pro Tools Free 5.01.)

❋ **Movie/Video Files.** If you have imported any digital video file into your Pro Tools session, enabling this option copies it into the new session's folder (and the new session will point to this new copy of the video). Otherwise, the new session copy continues to reference the video file in its original location.

❋ **Note: Saving Pro Tools 7 Sessions to Older Formats**

Obviously, you can't retain some of the features in Pro Tools 7 when you save a session back to 6.xx format (much less 5.xx or earlier). When you use the Save Copy In command to save a Pro Tools 7 session to 5.1–6.9 format, the following occurs:

❋ Pro Tools 7 allows you to use file names with as many characters as the operating system supports, but for previous versions, those file names are shortened to 31 characters, including the file name extension. This affects the session file name; more importantly, names for any source audio files that exceed this limit are truncated and placed into a new folder called Converted Audio Files.

❋ Sends F–J are dropped, along with any associated automation (since versions 6.9 and earlier only support five sends per track).

❋ In LE and M-Powered sessions, busses 17–32 are omitted, since only 16 busses were supported in previous versions (versus 128 in HD and TDM versions of Pro Tools).

❋ Region Groups (another Pro Tools 7 feature) are omitted, as are Region Loop aliases.

❋ Markers/Memory Locations 201–999 are dropped (only 200 are supported in 6.9 and earlier).

❋ Sample-based MIDI regions and tracks (a feature introduced in version 7) are dropped—both the track and the regions it contains are completely deleted from the session.

❋ Instrument tracks, a Pro Tools 7-only feature, are split into separate Aux In and MIDI tracks.

Revert to Saved

This command reverts the session to its previous state as saved on disk, undoing all changes since the last time you saved it. (In previous versions of Pro Tools, you had to close the session file without saving changes and then reopen it.) However, as Pro Tools will warn you, you cannot undo some operations. For example, if while using the Region List menu's Clear Selection command you opt to delete a selected audio file completely from disk, you can't use the Revert to Saved command to get it back!

Bounce to > Disk

This command mixes the entire Pro Tools session (or the current selection) into a single new audio file (or multiple mono files) in real time—including all plug-in processing, automation, auxiliary inputs, and other factors that affect the mix you're currently hearing. You select the bus or output pair to use as the source for the bounced mix, and you can specify a variety of file formats and resolutions for the resultant file. (See Chapter 16, "Bouncing to Disk, Other File Formats," for more detailed information.) You will often use Bounce to Disk to save out stereo files for CD mastering, stereo or mono mix files for video editors, interactive authors, and so on.

If you've chosen a multichannel path as the source for your bounce (for example, a surround mix), in addition to stereo and mono, the pop-up Format selector in the Bounce dialog box has a multiple mono option. One audio file is created for each mono subpath in your surround mix. When you select a stereo bus or output pair as the source for the bounce, you can also create split stereo files (pairs of mono files, with .L or .R inserted into their file names) using the multiple mono option. This is the best choice if you're planning to enable the Import After Bounce check box to automatically re-import bounced files into your current session (for instance, if you're bouncing in order to submix tracks, freeing up voices or DSP resources); interleaved stereo files must be split into separate left and right mono file copies to be usable from within a Pro Tools session anyway.

You can use the Bounce to Disk function to "print" tracks to disk (after soloing them or muting other unwanted tracks), incorporating all their current effects processing and automation. In very large or complex sessions, you might max out the digital signal processing (DSP) capacity your CPU and/or Pro Tools HD hardware provides. Bouncing one or more tracks to disk (or submixing multiple tracks) and then re-importing the bounced files into your session is one way to free up DSP resources for additional tasks on a slower system.

❋ Tip: Loud Is Good, Louder Is Better?

Careful use of gain-optimization plug-ins like Digidesign's Maxim and L1, L2, or L3 from Waves can ensure that your mixes are peaking at the maximum possible output level without digital *clipping* (signal overload, which distorts the audio waveforms by clipping off their peaks). Nevertheless, for most users, it is convenient and prudent to normalize bounced mixes before burning CDs or turning them over to a video editor.

Peak-mode normalization (as opposed to RMS mode, an alternative that was added in Pro Tools 7) is very straightforward: It finds the peak level within an audio file, and adjusts that to whatever level you designate. (If 100% is "full code" or 0 dB, 94.4% is equivalent to −.5 dB. For bouncing out music mixes, it's recommended to normalize somewhere between this and a more conservative −2 dB, which is just under 71% on an absolute scale, in order to prevent clipping during sample-rate conversion. This is also good advice for avoiding potential distortion on some older CD players!) As a result of the normalization process, the level in the rest of the audio file changes proportionally... including any previously inaudible background noise if the specified normalization parameters dramatically increase the file's level (beware!). Still, if you're trying to get gigs, local airplay, or 30 seconds of attention from an agent or record-company rep, it's always a good thing if your CDs aren't much softer than everyone else's!

However, contrary to what you might hear, normalizing does *not* "decrease your dynamic range" or make everything slam up against maximum level all the time (which *can* be the case when gain optimization, maximizer plug-ins, or even conventional limiters are abused!). As a matter of fact, as pointed out in Chapter 15, "Sound Design for Interactive Media," normalization can be used to make the peak levels of entire batches of files more consistent, often effectively *reducing* their original level—for example, when creating button sounds or background effects that should be uniformly lower in volume than accompanying voice-overs. Again, Chapter 16 goes into much more detail about bouncing files to disk in other formats and the use of normalization. Incidentally, if someone else will be doing the final mastering on your mix, mastering engineers always prefer that you *not* normalize or apply your own aggressive dynamics processing to the supplied mixes, because this severely limits their options!

Here's one way to normalize a bounced mix without leaving Pro Tools:

1. Enable the Import After Bounce check box in the Bounce dialog box. (The audio file format and resolution selected for the bounce must match that of the source session for this option to be enabled. Also, Pro Tools doesn't support re-importing stereo audio tracks; you should select the multiple mono option in this case.) After the bounce is completed, the new file appears in the Region List; click to highlight it.

2. Select AudioSuite > Normalize. In the Normalize dialog box, select Region List (instead of Playlist) and Overwrite Files (instead of Create Individual Files). You could leave the Max. Peak value at 0 (0 dB = 100%), but as mentioned earlier in this section, we recommend you adjust it to 94.4% (−.5 dB) or less, to leave a little bit of headroom and possibly avoid distortion on older CD players. Then click the Process button. Your original bounced files are normalized right in place. (Whenever you have chosen to permanently overwrite file contents with an AudioSuite process, the Destructive Mode OK dialog box appears to warn you that you cannot undo this and offers you the option to apply the process non-destructively instead by creating a new file copy to store the processed result. In this case, you click the Continue button to proceed with this *destructive* edit.)

3. If the audio CD recording program you're using doesn't support split mono source files, you still have to convert these two mono files into a stereo file. With the .L and .R split audio files still selected in the Region List, select Export Regions as Files in the Region List's local menu. Choose AIFF or WAV file type, stereo format, 44,100 (44.1 kHz) sample rate, and 16-bit-depth (unless you're using one of the more sophisticated CD-creation programs that include their own options for sample-rate and bit-depth conversion, in which case you would bounce at the native resolution of your source session).

For those who prefer to normalize their stereo or mono bounced mixes in a separate program, here are some common options (which also offer many other processing and conversion features):

* Mac: Peak Pro (Bias), Cleaner (Autodesk), Audacity (freeware), and Cacophony (shareware by Richard F. Bannister)

* Windows: Sound Forge (Sony; formerly Sonic Foundry), WaveLab (Steinberg), Nero Ultra (Nero AG), Cleaner XL (Autodesk), and Audacity (freeware originally developed by Dominic Mazzoni, with subsequent contributions from many others)

Bounce to > QuickTime Movie

In a similar fashion to the Bounce to > Disk command, this command bounces the session's audio mix (or currently selected range) directly into a new copy of the QuickTime video file currently in use in this session. 48 kHz is the most common sample rate for professional video applications. For multimedia applications, interactive authors often request a lower sample rate for the audio in their QuickTime movies (like 22,050 Hz or even 11,025 Hz) in order to keep file size and throughput requirements to a minimum. 44.1 kHz is the lowest sample rate directly supported here, however, so you would have to perform that conversion afterward in another program. See Chapter 15 for further information.

Import Submenu

This menu offers options for importing audio files and regions, MIDI files, QuickTime video files (and audio soundtracks from within QuickTime video files), as well as region groups (a feature added in Pro Tools 7). You can also import track data from other Pro Tools sessions. (In previous versions of Pro Tools, some of these options were in the local menu of the Region List or in the Movie menu.)

Import > Session Data

Use this command, which opens the Import Session Data dialog box (see Figure 8.2), for importing tracks and other data from other Pro Tools sessions into the current one. You can reference the source audio and video files for tracks you're importing from the other session at their original location (via the Refer to Source Media selection in the pop-up selector for Audio Media Options), or copy those files into the current session's Audio Files folder (via the Copy From Source Media option). The Consolidate From Source Media selection, also under Audio Media Options, has an effect similar to the Compact command in the local menu for the Region List. It copies only the utilized portions of the imported track's audio files, with the "handle" size providing a padding factor in case you need to slightly lengthen any of its regions afterward. If necessary, you can convert the sample rate and bit-depth of source audio files to those of the current session.

Location of regions and events in the newly imported tracks can be identical to the absolute time references in their original session, adjusted relative to those of the current session, or offset by a given amount. For music and soundtrack work, you can even import the tempo/meter map from the source session. This could be handy, for example, when you bring together various work sessions for musical segments into the final master session for a film or video soundtrack.

❄ **Tip: A Better Way to Use Session Templates**

Granted, using read-only (Stationery) documents via the File > Open Session command is the method you will find discussed in the Pro Tools Reference Guide—and this works more or less OK in Mac versions. However, in Windows versions, the newly created session will use the template's Audio Files folder for any new recordings—not at all what you want! After opening a read-only template in the Windows version, you would then have to use the Save Copy In command to make sure that your new session uses its own unique Audio Files folder. To avoid this inconvenience, we recommend that you use Method B, described in the tip earlier in this chapter about creating your own session templates. Not only does this avoid the Audio Files folder problem for Windows users, but on either platform *any* existing session could be used as a template—whether previously saved as a read-only (Stationery Pad) file or not. (If you *do* import tracks from an existing session containing audio regions, though, choose Link to Source Media in the Audio Media Options selector. You usually *don't* want to import any audio regions contained in the source session into your new Audio Files folder, and it will be easier this way to simply remove those audio regions from your session afterwards (without deleting them, since they are being used in the other Pro Tools session!).

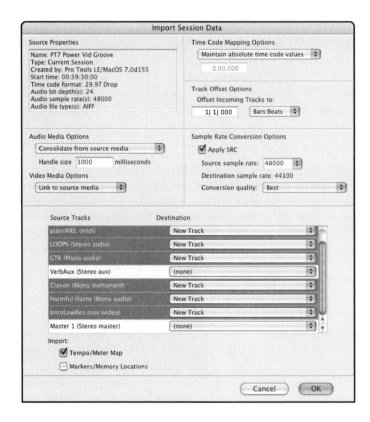

Figure 8.2 The Import Session Data dialog box.

Import > Region Groups

Region groups were introduced with version 7 of Pro Tools. Once you create a group from currently selected regions (via the Region > Group command), you can treat it as a single object while editing. Region groups can span multiple tracks, even if they are not in contiguous order in the Edit window. Other commands in the Region menu allow ungrouping and re-grouping regions. As soon as you create any region groups, a Region Groups subfolder is created for the current session. You can use a command in the local menu of the Region List to export region groups as separate files, which you can then export into other sessions via this File menu command.

Import > Audio to Track, Import > MIDI to Track

When you use these commands under the File menu, a new audio track is created for each imported audio file, or a new MIDI track for each MIDI channel within an imported Standard MIDI File. The imported audio or MIDI regions are automatically placed into these new tracks; the new track names reflect the source file names. See Figure 8.3.

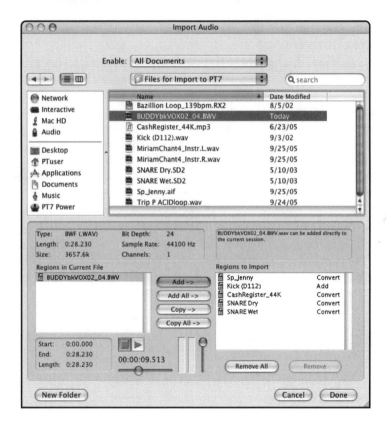

Figure 8.3 The Import Audio dialog box allows you to import entire audio files or regions within them. You can also preview audio files here.

Import Audio from Current Movie/QuickTime Movie

As mentioned, the Import > QuickTime Movie command by itself does not bring in the audio contained in the selected QuickTime/MPEG movies. These commands allow you to import the audio track(s) from the session's current QuickTime movie or any other QuickTime file on your system. (Pro Tools cannot import audio from MPEG video files.) If necessary, the movie's audio is converted to the current session's bit-depth and sample rate (although when working with video editors, you should always try to work in session formats matching their audio resolution anyway).

You can view digital video within Pro Tools, which will play back in sync with the Pro Tools Transport. Users who create video soundtracks and interactive sound designers who create audio for QuickTime movies will definitely appreciate these nonlinear video-playback features. You can jump around in the session's timeline, with the Movie window and Movie track (with small thumbnails of individual video frames) serving as a frame-accurate reference for *spotting* audio events to specific locations.

Import > QuickTime Movie

Use this command to import digital video files in QuickTime format into your Pro Tools session. The Movie window displays this video during Pro Tools playback and freezes the movie's current frame wherever you stop the Transport. A Movie track is also created in the Edit window, where the movie can be seen as a region block or as individual video frames. (Be aware that the system overhead for redrawing all these thumbnails—called *picons*, or picture icons by Digidesign—as you zoom in and out can slow your pace in the Edit window. If so, you can improve the speed of screen operations by setting the Movie track to Blocks display format most of the time, except when you specifically want to use these thumbnails for spotting events.) Many professionals prefer to dedicate a separate video card/monitor and hard drive for video playback.

As you can guess, using an onscreen digital video file as your master can be extremely useful when collaborating with video editors (for example, users of Avid Media Composer, Media 100, Adobe Premiere, or FinalCut Pro). This is all discussed in more detail in Chapter 14, "Postproduction and Soundtracks," and also in Chapter 15, "Sound Design for Interactive Media." Here's a brief overview of a typical work process:

1. The editor exports a low-resolution video for you to use in Pro Tools. This should be full frame rate, but with the image compressed to a much smaller size throughput so that video playback doesn't clobber your Pro Tools performance; generally 320×240 pixels or less is fine.

2. Bring this digital video file into your session via the File > Import > QuickTime Movie command. A Movie track is automatically created, and the Movie window opens.

3. Import the soundtrack from that video file into your session using the File > Import > Audio from QuickTime Movie command (also discussed under this heading), because the previous Import Movie command only imports the image portion of source video files. Obviously, you want the video editor to provide full-resolution, uncompressed audio inside the video file. If you're a newcomer to audio for video, don't overlook the fact that audio soundtracks in video-editing systems (and PCM audio tracks in professional video-tape formats) use a 48 kHz sampling rate! Generally, your session should also be set to this rate.

4. You can now do a complete audio postproduction on their project—music, sound effects, and dialog or voice-over—without requiring a video deck in your setup at all. Furthermore, because of the frame-accurate display in the Movie track, extremely precise placement of sound effects and other audio events is easy.

5. After you finish the soundtrack, there are several options for returning this finished mix to the video editor. You could simply use the File > Bounce to > Disk command to give the video editor stereo, 48 kHz files for the entire soundtrack (in AIF or Broadcast WAV audio file format, for example). If you have the optional DigiTranslator program (which is not compatible with Pro Tools M-Powered), you might instead export an OMFi file if the video-editing system supports this interchange format. A third option is to bounce your audio mix into a new copy of the original QuickTime movie, using the File > Bounce to > QuickTime Movie command, also discussed in this section.

Edit Menu

Obviously, you're going to find the Cut, Copy, Paste, and Clear commands here, plus Select All and your best friend in the whole world—the Undo command! The Edit menu also includes many of the key functions you will use for editing regions. Here we will review only recently changed or most essential selections.

Cut/Copy/Paste/Clear Special

The "special" versions of these basic editing commands allow you to apply them only to automation in the Edit window, or even more specifically, to only pan or plug-in automation.

Duplicate, Repeat

Everybody seems to overlook these commands. Duplicate makes one copy of the current selection, immediately following its current position, even if the selection is on multiple tracks. Repeat does the same thing but lets you specify *how many* copies you want—for example, 15 more copies of a four-bar drum loop you've just dropped into the track. If the currently highlighted selection in any track is only some portion within a longer region, a new region definition is created in the process. In contrast, if an entire region is selected, these commands simply create additional instances of the same region within their tracks. Naturally, if you're in Shuffle edit mode, any material that follows the current selection within the track(s) will be pushed back later in the track by a corresponding amount.

However, for repeating ambient or musical loops, the Region > Loop command (discussed later in this chapter, under the Region menu) offers a much more effective method. If you're new to Pro Tools or to version 7 in particular, be sure to learn how to use this feature.

Shift

Shift is another underused command. It opens a dialog box for moving the current selection (even on multiple tracks) earlier or later in the track. You can specify the amount of displacement for the selection in either the Bars:Beats, Minutes:Seconds or Samples time-scale format (and SMPTE time code and Feet.Frames, if these time-scale formats are available in your version of Pro Tools). If your selection is within an existing region, or if its new location will overlap existing regions in the track, new region definitions are created as necessary. Although you can use the Shift function on all the tracks in your session simultaneously, the Insert Time page of the Time Operations window offers a much more effective and flexible way of achieving this.

Trim Submenu

The Trim to Selection command (whose keyboard shortcut is Command+T, or Ctrl+T in Windows) replaces the current region with a new region definition based on the currently highlighted portion within it. On MIDI tracks in Notes display format, you can also use Trim to Selection to crop beginnings or ends of MIDI notes to the boundaries of the current selection. The Trim Start/End to Insertion commands are fairly simple: The left or right boundaries of the current region(s) are trimmed (cropped) to the current location of the Selector tool's insertion cursor. You can use the Trim Start/End to Fill Selection commands when multiple regions are selected in the same track(s). Each region's start/end is extended to adjoin the boundary of the previous/next region in the track. Alternatively, highlight an additional range of time before or after a single region, and the Trim Start/End to Fill Selection command extends the boundary of the region definition up to that point.

Separate Region Submenu/Heal Separation

After making a selection within an existing audio or MIDI region, you can give that selection a name (create a new region definition) using the Separate Region > At Selection command. A new region name is inserted within the existing region on the track. (As required, additional region names are created for portions of the existing region before and after the newly separated region name.) This command is handy when you're planning to drag the new region elsewhere. You will also notice two variations on the basic Separate Region command in this submenu. On Grid splits the new regions at the nearest grid value increment, while At Transients creates the split at the nearest transient peak in an audio region.

Note that the Capture Region command, in the Region menu, serves a similar function. The only difference is that, while the Separate Region commands insert the new region definition into the track, Capture Region merely adds it to the Region List. (It should also be noted that copying any track selection within an existing region also automatically creates a new region definition in the Region List, even if you don't copy or paste it afterward. This can be a very quick way to create a series of new region definitions, with the Command+C shortcut, or Ctrl+C on Windows.)

Heal Separation restores an audio selection that was split using the Separate Region command—as long as its segments are still in their original, adjacent locations and haven't been moved or trimmed. Separate Region operations are nondestructive; the original region name still exists and resides in the Region List. Region definitions are merely pointers (references) to sections of audio within the parent sound files.

Strip Silence

The basic Strip Silence mode breaks up currently selected audio regions into smaller ones, omitting any sections where the audio level falls below the specified Audio Threshold value. (This threshold is typically *not* complete silence, because there may be low-level background noise, bleed from other microphones, and so on). In the Strip Silence window (shown in Figure 8.4), the Min Strip Duration setting establishes the minimum size, in milliseconds, of the regions to create when the Strip Silence function is applied to the selection (because an excessive number of extremely short regions would be cumbersome). The Region Start Pad and Region End Pad leave that specified amount of "silence" appended to the boundaries of the resultant regions, providing a cushion factor to make sure that you don't drastically cut off soft attacks, low-level breath intakes, finger noise, decays, or other low-level sounds that might otherwise get completely eliminated at the specified threshold audio level for the Strip Silence function. As you adjust all these parameters, you'll see a preview of the results in the Edit window. Because Strip Silence is a *non-destructive* process (it merely creates new region definitions—the original, longer region is still intact in the Region List), you can always make adjustments afterward by trimming or editing the new regions it has created on the track.

While the Strip and Rename buttons were present in previous versions of Pro Tools, the Extract and Separate modes are new in Pro Tools version 7. Extract is the inverse of the ordinary Strip Silence mode: Only those portions of audio that *aren't* above the threshold (and within the minimum duration or padding amounts) are left in the track. As the *Pro Tools Reference Guide* points out, this can be useful for extracting room tone, amp buzz, or background noise for some other use. The Separate mode leaves everything intact in the track but applies a variant of the Separate Region command so that the "keeper" and "stripped" portions are split into separate, adjacent regions.

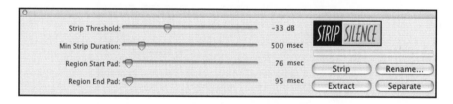

Figure 8.4 The Strip Silence window. The basic function breaks longer regions into a greater number of smaller ones by eliminating sections where the audio level falls beneath the specified threshold.

Consolidate

The Consolidate command is very useful: It creates a new region (and a new audio file on audio tracks) based on the current track selection (containing multiple regions) and substitutes it for the original selection. If multiple tracks are selected, Consolidate creates new regions in each. Because the new region also contains any silence that was between regions or preceded them, Consolidate also can be handy for creating new region definitions that begin (or end) right on a bar line or 1/4 note, even if they contain silence at the beginning. This simplifies dragging regions around in Grid edit mode, for example, or using the Edit menu's Duplicate and Repeat commands if their duration corresponds to an even number of bars or beats. You should bear in mind that any fade-ins or fade-outs (but not automation) on the selected regions will be permanently incorporated into new regions created by the Consolidate command. If you're dealing with an audio event that consists of numerous short regions strung together in a track (maybe a four-bar drum phrase cobbled together out of various sections, or a sound-effect sequence) and will be used at various other locations in the session, it can be a hassle to select and drag around so many small pieces. Instead, you could select the whole event and then consolidate it into a single region using the Consolidate command. (However, the Region > Group command introduced in Pro Tools 7 offers a more efficient alternative for this scenario.)

Fades

Creating fade-ins, fade-outs, and crossfades on audio regions is discussed in many places in this book. New Pro Tools users very quickly learn to select the first or last portion of audio regions and then use the Command+F (Ctrl+F in Windows) keyboard shortcut to create fades using the dialog box shown in Figure 8.5. (Fades are actually separate audio files; each session has a subfolder where these are stored. If the contents of this folder are ever missing or damaged, the next time you open that session a dialog box offers you the option to re-create the missing fades.) Later, of course, fades can be lengthened or shortened with the Trimmer tool, double-clicked with the Grabber tool to edit their fade curves, and so on.

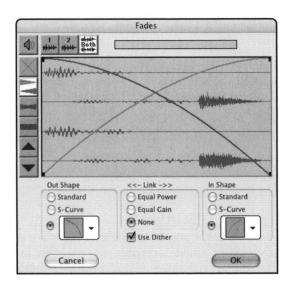

Figure 8.5 The Fades dialog box. Shown here, a crossfade between two adjacent audio regions.

Creating fade-ins, fade-outs, and crossfades for audio regions is a fundamental technique for working in Pro Tools. However, even many experienced users overlook the other commands in the Edit > Fades submenu—and especially their keyboard equivalents. Although the submenu itself is a good way to start, you will save a lot of time by assimilating the following shortcuts:

❋ When a portion of an audio region that includes its beginning or end is selected, Command+F (Ctrl+F in Windows) opens the Fades dialog box with a single fade-in or fade-out shape.

❋ When the selection crosses the boundary between two contiguous (adjoining) regions in the same track, this same keyboard shortcut also opens the Fades dialog box, but with both the fade-in and fade-out shapes (and the ability to link the two shapes, so that changes in one are reflected in the other). You can use this for creating crossfades between those regions.

❋ After clicking with the Selector tool's I-beam cursor anywhere within an audio region, the Fade to Start command creates a fade from the region's beginning up to that point, using the default fade-in shape (which you can edit anytime afterward by double-clicking with the Grabber tool). The keyboard shortcut for Fade to Start is Option+D (Alt+D in Windows).

❋ The Fade to End command does the opposite, creating a fade from the insertion point to the *end* of the region, using the default fade-out shape. The keyboard shortcut for Fade to End is Option+G (Alt+G in Windows).

❋ Default in, out, and crossfade shapes for fades can be changed in the Editing tab of the Preferences dialog box. Be sure to alter these preferences if the current default shapes aren't what you use most frequently!

View Menu

Options in the View menu allow you to optimize your view during each phase of a project. You can select items to be viewed in the Mix, Edit, and Transport windows; how sends are displayed; which Timebase rulers are visible; and what time units are used for the Main counter and main Timebase ruler. You can also choose whether you want names and/or various time values to be displayed within the regions on your Pro Tools tracks. All this merely serves to help you work more comfortably and efficiently and to manage the content of your sessions with ease. Some of the options are fairly self-explanatory or only need to be tried once for their purpose to be clear; for that reason, like others in this chapter, this section discusses only the key items in this menu.

Narrow Mix Window

As mentioned in Chapter 7, "The Mix Window," this option makes all the mixer strips in the Mix window narrower, allowing more tracks to fit on the screen.

Mix Window/Edit Window Submenus

You can use these submenus to change your view in these windows. You may do this often, during different phases of your work on each project. Like other items in the View and Options menus, the most recently selected options here will also be enabled initially in sessions that are created with the File > New Session command (as opposed to opening a template document, for example). For instance, if the last session you saved displayed the MIDI section of the Transport window, Transport buttons in the Edit window, and Comments in the Mix window, the next new session you create will also have these options enabled.

By default, the Instrument section, in the upper part of the Mix window, is not displayed. When using Instrument tracks, you will use the Mix > Instrument command to enable these track controls (which include MIDI Volume, Pan, Solo, and Mute and affect playback of the MIDI data that the Instrument track contains, as seen in the Edit window).

In addition to (or instead of) their default location in the Mix window, some items can optionally be displayed in the Edit window—for instance, the Instrument, Inserts, Sends, Comments, I/O, and Real-Time Properties sections for each track. For example, if you rely mainly on *drawing* automation shapes for creating your mixes, displaying these track controls in the Edit window may allow you to spend almost all your time there—as long as your monitor is wide enough that the added width this requires won't cramp your style. Otherwise, use the options in these submenus to optimize your use of screen space according to your own needs at each phase of a project.

This submenu is also where you choose whether the Transport controls should be visible in the upper area of the Edit window. On HD systems, you can enable Delay Compensation View here to display—and adjust for—the total amount of plug-in delay on each track.

You can also toggle display of track color strips for all tracks (in the Mix and/or Edit window) in this submenu.

Rulers Submenu

You can use this submenu to select which Timebase ruler types are visible in the Edit window, in addition to the main Timebase ruler: Bars:Beats, Minutes:Seconds, Samples, SMPTE Time Code (HD and DV-equipped LE systems only), Feet.Frames (HD only), Markers, Tempo, and Meter. Remember that the format indicator at the left end of the ruler that represents the main time scale is always blue; by default, its units always correspond to the Main counter—changing units for either the main ruler or the Main counter also affects the other. (Time units for the Sub counter can always be set separately, however.) When multiple rulers are enabled, just click in any one of their name plates to make it the main ruler (which determines the default units for the grid value and nudge value, among other things). Another method is to use the Main Time Scale pop-up selector, just below the Grid edit mode button in the Edit window.

You can also open the Tempo Editor (a pane underneath the Tempo ruler where you can graphically edit tempo events) from the Ruler View Shows submenu, although it's quicker to just click the triangular Expand/Collapse button at the left side of the Tempo ruler's name plate.

Region Submenu

Here, you can choose what information is displayed within the regions in your Pro Tools tracks: the sync point symbol, region name, "dog-ear" overlap icon, current time, and the original/user timestamp.

Sync Point

When this option is enabled, a small triangle indicates the location of sync points within regions in the Edit window. If a region has a sync point at a location other than at its beginning, this is the "hook" that will be adjusted to the nearest time increment in Grid edit mode (or to a specified time location in Spot mode) rather than the default sync point location at the left boundary of the region itself.

Overlap

Enabling this option displays a "dog-ear" edge (i.e., the corner is cut) on each region graphic that overlaps the boundaries of another region. Even though regions can be layered over each other, only one of them can sound at a time. Two Region menu commands, Send to Back and Send to Front, are used in conjunction with this feature; the topmost region at any point is the one that is heard.

Track Number

Pro Tools assigns numbers to tracks in ascending order from the top of the Edit window—or from the left of the Mix window, which amounts to the same thing. If you drag tracks into a different order in either window, numbers are reassigned automatically. Making track numbers visible is convenient when using the Track > Scroll to Track command.

Transport Submenu

The Transport submenu enables/disables three sections aside from the basic Transport buttons: counters (Main and Sub location indicators), MIDI controls (Metronome, Wait for Note, Countoff, Tempo, Meter, and others), and Expanded (if disabled, the lower section, with Pre/Post-Roll, Start, End, and Length fields, as well as the Sub counter and some MIDI controls, is not displayed).

Disk Space Submenu

The Disk Space window (opened via the Windows menu) displays the remaining capacity on the disks attached to your system in gigabytes, as a percentage of free space, and as available track minutes of record time at the current session's bit-depth and sample rate. Options here in the View menu determine whether this is shown as text or graphically, in a horizontal "gas gauge" format. The Workspace window, however, provides a much more detailed view of audio and MIDI files and folders on your disks, with columns for the total capacity and current free space on each. For more information, refer to the section titled "Workspace Browser Window," later in this chapter.

Main Counter Submenu

These last selections in the View menu change the format of the main time scale for the session (Bars:Beats, Minutes:Seconds, Samples, and HD system Time Code, Feet+Frames). If the desired ruler for one of these time formats is already visible, you can accomplish the same thing by clicking its format indicator—the name of the ruler that represents the main time scale is highlighted in blue.

Track Menu

Options here have to do with creating, duplicating, and grouping tracks, as well as deleting them or making them inactive. There are also options for splitting stereo tracks into mono, changing their input monitoring mode, and so on.

New (Tracks)

The New command (Shift+Command+N, or Shift+Ctrl+N on Windows; learn this keyboard shortcut!) opens the New Tracks dialog box (shown in Figure 8.6), which is used for creating audio, Auxiliary Input, Instrument, and Master Fader tracks (mono, stereo, or multichannel), as well as MIDI tracks. The timebase for events in any track can be either *absolute* (Samples) or *relative* to musical bars and beats (Ticks). In the latter case, events will be shifted to maintain their relative musical position if you ever alter the tempo of your Pro Tools session. You can change the timebase of tracks in the Edit window at any time, as well as the timebase for display of events for the session in general. However, a selector in the New Tracks dialog box assigns the initial timebase for tracks as they're created.

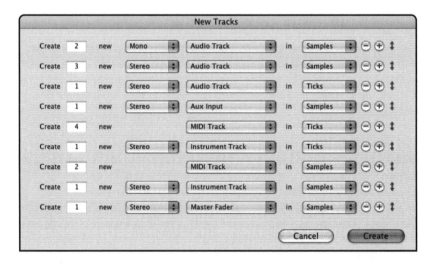

Figure 8.6   The New Tracks dialog box allows you to create multiple track types simultaneously.

❄ **Note: New Tracks Dialog Box**

The New Tracks dialog box allows you create many different types of tracks *simultaneously*—for example, multiple mono/stereo audio tracks, Aux In tracks, Instrument tracks, Master Faders, and MIDI tracks. Just click the button with the plus sign (+), and a new row of fields appears for creating additional tracks of a different type.

Note also that newly created tracks in your session are initially in the same order that they appeared in the New Tracks dialog box. Within the dialog box, you can use the button on the left end of each row to drag them into your preferred order before pressing the Create button. Keep this in mind; it may save you some time dragging your tracks around into the proper order afterwards.

Group (Tracks)

When you group two or more selected tracks, their faders move together in the Mix window. Changes in track view, Solo/Mute button states (but not the record-enable button), and track selections in one track of the group are also made in the others. Any automation that you draw within a grouped track is also reflected in the others. Groups can be active in the Mix or Edit window only or both (the default), and are managed in the Groups List at the left edge of the Mix and Edit windows. (This command, whose keyboard shortcut is Command+G, or Ctrl+G on Windows, also appears in the local menu of the Groups List.) Be sure to give your track groups meaningful names!

Split Into Mono

Sometimes you need to separate a stereo track into two separate mono tracks. For example, even though you may have recorded a source into a single track with a stereo pair of microphones (a piano or acoustic guitar, for instance), there may be occasions when you would like to apply different plug-in processing to each side. This command creates the two new mono tracks but leaves the original stereo track intact until you disable or delete it.

Make Inactive/Active

Even if you mute a track in Pro Tools, its audio/automation data—and especially its sends and insert plug-ins—still consume the same amount of your system's processing capacity for audio (in other words, the same proportion of the available DSP, or digital signal processing, of your CPU and/or TDM audio cards). If you use the Make Inactive command to make the track completely inactive, however, the processing power for the selected track's plug-ins, sends, and audio playback is now available for other Pro Tools tracks.

If your system is underpowered for the task you need to accomplish (hey, it can happen to everyone sooner or later), you might find the Make Inactive command very useful. For example, say you're near the end of a fairly complex project and have just decided that layering up 9–10 additional backing vocal parts is just the ticket. However, you quickly discover that, with all the existing tracks and effects you've already got going, after laying down just a couple of vocal parts, you're already getting audio glitching and choppy playback. Your system simply can't keep up with the demand. Of course, the first thing to check is your

Hardware Buffer size in the Setup > Playback Engine dialog box, especially if you're an LE or M-Powered user. You may find, however, that it is already at the maximum, or that increasing this buffer setting induces a delay for input monitoring that is unacceptable for the singers, who are hearing themselves back through the Pro Tools mixer (on LE and M-Powered systems where low-latency monitoring or the Mix knob on the Mbox 2/Mbox isn't available, or where direct input monitoring from an external mixer, mic preamp, or through the interface itself isn't a practical option). Take a look at which of your tracks is using the most processing-intensive plug-ins. Reverbs are obvious candidates, especially some of those gorgeous-sounding, CPU-hungry ones from third parties. Try making the Aux In tracks where these reverbs are instantiated inactive while tracking the backing vocals. Perhaps you have a complex chain on some instrumental part—such as a third-party amp simulator, compressor, EQ, and the flanger on a lead guitar part. If you can do without hearing that part while tracking these voices, deactivating that track might free up enough DSP capacity to get this accomplished.

Next, bounce your backing vocals to disk as a stereo file (checking the Import After Bounce selection to bring them right back into this session on their own stereo track). Then select all those source backing vocal tracks and apply the Make Inactive command. If you ever change your mind about the balance in this vocal submix, these (currently inactive) tracks are right there in your session so that you can simply use the Make Active command on those tracks again and repeat the process.

Delete

This command deletes the currently selected track(s) and any playlists (audio, MIDI, or automation) that they contain. However, after using the Delete (track) command on audio, MIDI, or Instrument tracks, any regions they contained will still remain in the Region List.

Write MIDI Real-Time Properties

This command permanently alters the MIDI data within regions on the affected track, applying the net results of the track's current real-time property settings to the MIDI events themselves. On MIDI and Instrument tracks, *track*-level real-time properties apply non-destructive changes to all MIDI played back through the track—for example, quantization, transposition, changes to velocity and duration, and so on. There are also *region*-level real-time properties, which are prior to—and have an effect on the action of—any real-time properties assigned to a MIDI or Instrument track. When you open the Real-Time Properties window for a selected MIDI region (via the Event menu), a Write to Region button also allows you to permanently alter the contents of the currently selected region(s), incorporating the results of the current real-time properties settings. However, the Apply To selector in this window lets you toggle back and forth between region- and track-level properties. Its Write to Region changes to Write to Track if that's what you have selected in the Apply To field and has the same effect as this Track menu command.

Input Only/Auto Input Monitoring

Input Only Monitoring, as the name implies, monitors *only* input signal on any record-enabled tracks, regardless of whether a punch-in point exists and whether Record mode is engaged. In Auto Input Monitoring mode, when playback is *stopped*, you hear the input signal on record-enabled audio tracks. Likewise, if you simply start recording without making any selection for punch in/out, you will always hear that record-enabled track's audio input. However, when recording a punch-in in ordinary monitoring mode, before and after the punch-in point, you hear the pre-existing audio in the track (which helps you match its level and timbre) and then the input source during the punched-in segment. Note that in the HD version of Pro Tools, individual audio tracks have a TrackInput button, which toggles the track itself between Input Only (with the button enabled) and Auto Input (button disabled) modes. The effect of the TrackInput button is not affected by which mode you choose here in the Track menu.

Scroll to Track

Each track is assigned a number reflecting its current position (ascending from left to right in the Mix window, or top to bottom in the Edit window); to display these numbers, enable that option in the View menu. The Scroll to Track Number command scrolls the Edit or Mix window as necessary, so that the specified track is visible. This helps you get around in large sessions. Of course, in Pro Tools, you can drag tracks into any order, at any time, which changes their track numbers! The keyboard shortcut for the Scroll to Track Number command is Command+Option+F (Ctrl+Alt+F in Windows).

Clear All Clip Indicators

As mentioned in Chapter 7 and elsewhere, when the red clipping indicator lights up in the Level meter for any track or Plug-in window, this indicates that excess signal level may have overloaded and distorted its source audio, clipping off the top of its waveform at that channel's maximum level. Aside from individually clicking clip indicators with the mouse to clear them and Option-clicking (Alt-clicking in Windows) any clip indicator to clear *all* of them simultaneously, you can also use the Track > Clear All Clip Indicators menu command. Even more convenient (and worth memorizing!) is its keyboard equivalent: Option+C (Alt+C on Windows).

Don't forget that, aside from the track output level determined by the main Volume fader itself, the settings for each active plug-in on a track affect the level entering the next plug-in in the track's signal-processing chain. Additionally, the audio signal entering all sends is subsequent to the entire Inserts section in a track's signal chain. Be sure to watch for clipping at your send destinations also, if your insert effects end up applying a significant amount of gain increase—for example, if you radically boost some frequency range with an EQ plug-in.

Region Menu

Region menu options affect both audio and MIDI regions currently placed in Edit window tracks. Learn their keyboard shortcuts early; you will probably be using at least some of these commands quite often.

Mute/Unmute

Muting and unmuting individual regions within a track (rather than the entire track) allows you to experiment without making the commitment of removing these regions from their original track locations. In the Edit window, muted audio regions appear dimmed (grayed out) in Waveform or Blocks data display format, while muted MIDI regions appear dimmed only in Regions data display format. You can use the keyboard shortcut Command+M (Ctrl+M in Windows) to mute/unmute selected region(s).

Lock/Unlock

When a region is locked, a small padlock graphic appears in its lower-left corner. You can't drag, trim, or delete locked regions. Also, locked regions won't be pushed aside as a result of moving other regions in Shuffle edit mode. You can still edit the automation that overlaps a locked region, though, or record over it (so always be especially careful when recording in Destructive Recording mode). As you can guess, locking a region protects you from yourself and is definitely a feature you want to be familiar with. You can use the keyboard shortcut Command+L (Ctrl+L in Windows) to lock/unlock selected region(s).

Send to Back/Bring to Front

Pro Tools allows regions to be layered with a track (although only one audio region can play at a given time within a single track). With the View > Region > Overlap option enabled, a dog-ear icon on the upper corner of regions indicates where their boundaries overlap another region underneath. The topmost region always has priority; they can't both sound at once. The keyboard shortcuts for sending regions to the back/front are Option+Shift+B and Option+Shift+F (Alt+Shift+B and Alt+Shift+F in Windows), respectively.

Group/Ungroup/Ungroup All/Regroup

The ability to group regions is one of the more important features introduced in Pro Tools version 7. As you will discover, a new region group graphic is created, with a waveform representation of the regions it contains. This allows you to move a more complex group of audio events around as a single unit. By the way, it isn't even necessary for grouped regions to reside on adjacent tracks. As you can see in Figure 8.7, a rectangular region group graphic helps to distinguish region groups from individual regions on a track.

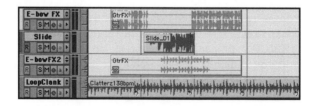

Figure 8.7   The "broken" region group graphics here indicate that the members of the "GtrFX" region group are on non-adjacent tracks. The looped arrows indicate that the region in the last track was looped via the Region menu command.

Loop/Unloop

You can use this command on audio regions, MIDI regions, and region groups. A specified number of loop *aliases* are created, which mirror the original source region. In the Region Looping dialog box (seen in Figure 8.8), you can specify a duration and shape for crossfades between loop repetitions; this is especially useful for ambient, sustained, and background loops. Note that unlike the Duplicate and Repeat commands (when the Options > Automation Follows Edit option is enabled), the automation coinciding with the source loop is *not* copied along with the loop aliases.

The Unloop command presents you with a dialog box where you can choose to simply revert back to a single instance of the source loop (Remove) or to Flatten the loop, which creates individual regions for each loop alias.

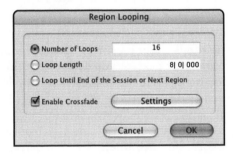

Figure 8.8 Options in the Region Looping dialog box allow you to control how many times the region or region group will repeat.

Capture

This command creates a new region definition based on the current track selection. However, unlike the Edit > Separate region command, the new region(s) created by the Region > Capture command don't take the place of the current selection and split existing regions. Like Separate Region, you can use this command on mono, stereo, or multichannel tracks, as well as on multiple tracks simultaneously.

Identify Sync Point/Remove Sync Point

A *sync point* is a precise location within a region that will be used as the positional reference whenever that region is snapped to the nearest time increment in Grid mode (rather than the beginning of the region, which is the ordinary mode of operation). Likewise, in Spot mode, it's the sync point that's moved to the specified position (a SMPTE time-code location, for example), along with the rest of the region surrounding it. You might think of the sync point as the "hook" used for positioning that region at specific timeline positions in Grid or Spot mode. By default, the sync point is always at the region's beginning. Identifying a new sync point within a region moves this hook to a new location. In the Edit window, sync points within regions appear as small inverted triangles at the bottom of each rectangular region graphic.

You can drag sync points with the Grabber tool to alter their locations within the region. You can also use the Scrubber tool to drag a sync point, providing audible feedback as you drag it within the audio waveform for audio regions.

Sync points are relevant both for music and during postproduction. Say you've got a spunky little backward-reverb snare sound you'd like to drop on the occasional backbeat. (Of course, it needs to actually begin *before* the backbeat and fade up to it.) Position the Selector tool precisely at the peak of the backward sound (somewhere near the end), and then select the Region > Identify Sync Point command. You now see a small triangle at the bottom of the region, which indicates the location of the sync point within it. Now switch to Grid mode and select 1/4 notes as the Grid value. When you drag this region to a specific 1/4 note, the sync point, rather than the beginning of the region, is snapped into position. The backward snare ramps up to its loudest point right on the 1/4 note, regardless of how much sooner this region's sound actually begins to fade in.

With regard to postproduction, one classic sync point example is a train (or plane) passing through the video frame. You should hear it coming *before* the SMPTE time-code location where it actually enters the frame. However, as you position this sound effect, the point inside the audio region that interests you is that loudest moment, where the Doppler effect changes pitch. You want *that* point to coincide with where the train enters the picture. Again, use the Selector to position the cursor right at that loudest spot in the region and create a sync point. Based on your video master's time-code location (visible in its Transport or time-code window), use Spot mode to enter the exact reference where the train enters the frame. The sync point itself will be spotted to that time-code position, although the audio region for the oncoming train sound actually begins sooner.

> ❈ **Note: Sync Points in the Edit Window**
>
> The View > Region > Sync Point option allows you to choose whether sync points are visible within regions in the Edit window. You can drag sync points with the Grabber or the Scrubber tool.

Quantize To Grid

Moves the *beginning* of all currently selected regions (audio or MIDI) to the nearest grid increment, according to the current grid value. For any region that contains a sync point, the sync point itself is moved to the nearest grid increment, instead of the region's actual beginning (left boundary). The Quantize To Grid command does not alter region durations, it simply moves the regions. When used on MIDI regions, the command does not apply any quantization to notes contained *within* the MIDI region; they just get repositioned along with the region itself, maintaining their relative locations within its boundaries. (The Event > MIDI > Grid/Groove Quantize command is used for adjusting individual note positions within MIDI tracks!)

Event Menu

This is where you will find the commands related to time and tempo operations, setting tempos according to track selections, creating time slices and groove templates for quantization, plus most of the MIDI-related operations in Pro Tools.

Time Submenu: Change Meter, Insert Time, Cut Time, Move Song Start

All four of these operations open the Time Operations window (within which you can switch directly from one to the other). These features may be useful when the song you're going to record has multiple time signatures, when you need more room in the timeline for an intro, or you need to move a music cue to a different time location while scoring a video or film. Because these are explained in more detail in Chapter 10, "MIDI," the following descriptions are relatively brief.

Change Meter

Use this command to insert a meter change into the Meter ruler. Meter settings can stay in effect through the end of the session, during the current selected range in the Pro Tools timeline only, or until the next bar only. The Change Meter page of the Time Operations window also provides a pop-up selector to change the note value for the metronome click in the new meter. For example, the click could change from 1/4 notes in a 4/4 time signature to 1/8 notes during a section in 6/8 time and then revert back to 1/4 notes for the remainder of the song. If a range of time is selected when you open the Change Meter page of the Time Operations window, you can also use this dialog box to change a given number of bars at one time signature to a different number of bars at another. Depending on what combination of bar numbers and time signatures you enter in these fields, some bars in the timeline may be added or deleted as a result. See the "Time Operations" section in Chapter 10 for more information.

> ❋ **Note: Another Way to Insert Meter Changes in Pro Tools**
>
> You can also insert meter changes using the Meter Change dialog box, which you can open by clicking the "plus" sign (+) in the Meter ruler or double-clicking the Meter field in the Transport window. Like the Change Meter page of the Time Operations window, you can either accept the current Start value as the location for the new meter change event or type another location, and also change the note value for the metronome click.

Insert Time, Cut Time

The units for inserting or cutting time in the pages of the Time Operations window opened by these commands reflect those of the main Timebase ruler. You can choose whether the time shift is applied to tick-based (relative) and/or sample-based (absolute) tracks.

Move Song Start

This feature is especially handy for film and video scoring. For instance, if you've created an entire musical arrangement starting at the left edge of the Pro Tools timeline, in this window you can quickly move the song beginning to a specific location—perhaps the Minute:Second or SMPTE time-code reference where this musical cue needs to begin in relation to the picture. Events in the Meter and Tempo rulers will shift accordingly. The Move Song Start page of the Time Operations window (shown in Figure 8.9) also allows you to specify that any bar number be assigned to the song start at its new location. This is useful if you've worked out a musical arrangement but later decide you need to insert some pick-up bars (or a full intro) while still designating the beginning of the song proper as bar one, beat one.

If the timebase in this dialog box is set to Bars, you additionally have the option to move only the song start without affecting the positions of any events in your tracks. Also, note the pop-up selector that lets you choose whether the positions of sample-based (absolute) markers and events in sample-based tracks should also be affected by the Move Song Start operation.

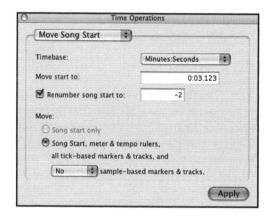

Figure 8.9   The Move Song Start page of the Time Operations window.

The Move Song Start function is also described in more detail in the "Time Operations" section of Chapter 10. As described there, you can also drag the Song Start marker to a new location in the Tempo ruler. Its movement will be affected by Grid edit mode, if enabled. When you change the Song Start setting by dragging this marker, events in all MIDI, audio, Aux In, Instrument, or Master Fader tracks whose timebase is set to Ticks will be adjusted to new positions in the timeline in order to maintain their previous relative position to the Song Start Marker (the previously mentioned option to move only the Song Start setting without affecting tick-based events is only available via the Move Song Start dialog shown in Figure 8.9. Any markers whose reference is set to Bars: Beats (relative) rather than absolute will also change positions accordingly.

> ❋ **Note: Additional Information About Time and Tempo Operations**
>
> More details about changing meter and tempos, renumbering bars, and other music-related options are provided in Chapter 10.

Tempo Submenu

The options in this submenu all open the Tempo Operations window. We discuss it only briefly here because more details are provided in the "Tempo Operations" section of Chapter 10.

You can use the Tempo Operations window to create a single tempo event or to apply a constant tempo over the currently highlighted range in the Edit window's timeline. Alternatively, you can apply a variety of curve shapes (line, parabola, s-curve, and so on) for increasing or decreasing the tempo over a range of time, in which case the result is a series of tempo events at the density specified in this window (shown in Figure 8.10). You can use the Scale page of the Tempo Operations window to increase or decrease an existing series of tempo events by percentage. The end point in minutes and seconds (or other ruler time units available on your system) are automatically calculated. As you can imagine, this can be very useful for soundtrack or jingle work! Lastly, the Stretch page of the Tempo Operations window can also affect an entire tempo map (a series of tempo events) within the currently selected portion of the session's timeline, adjusting all these relative tempos so that this selection's start or end point coincides with a desired time location. This is how you might adjust a complex underscore, with multiple tempo and time signature changes, so that it ends at precisely the end of a scene, minutes later. Remember that the location of events (including automation) in all MIDI, audio, Aux In, Instrument, or Master Fader tracks whose timebase is set to Ticks are affected by tempo changes—as are any memory locations whose Reference attribute for Time Properties is set to Bars|Beats (rather than Absolute).

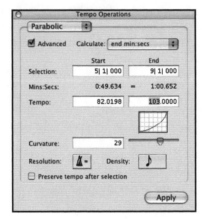

Figure 8.10 In the Tempo Operations window, you can create a variety of shapes to increase or decrease musical tempo over time.

MIDI Submenu

Obviously, many of the functions here, along with several other commands in the Event menu, are of most interest for people who use MIDI instruments (either external or software-based) with their Pro Tools configuration.

MIDI Operations: Grid/Groove Quantize, Change Velocity, Change Duration, Transpose, Select/Split Notes, Input Quantize, Step Input, Restore Performance, Flatten Performance

All these menu selections open the MIDI Operations window. A pop-up field allows you to switch directly from one function's page to another, and this window doesn't close after you apply each function—or successive iterations of the same function, like some percentage of quantization, for instance. Obviously, these commands act only upon MIDI data, within MIDI regions! Because there is an entire section dedicated to the MIDI menu in Chapter 10, we include just a few brief descriptions here.

Grid/Groove Quantize

This command snaps all notes within the current selection to a specified rhythmic value. Make special note of the Strength parameter; if you set it at less than 100%, notes are not moved all the way to the specified quantization grid increment. This preserves some of the natural feel of your performance (assuming that's a good thing). The Swing parameter is also very useful for making your MIDI performances sound in time but not completely mechanical. For a subtle effect, start at about 10% and work from there. Being able to add a swing factor to a straight quantization is great (1/16 notes, for instance), but for some music, you really need a more complex sort of grid for adjusting timing in order to accomplish specific feels. Various preset DigiGrooves are included in the pop-up Quantize Grid selector, along with the more conventional straight, dotted, and triplet note values. With Beat Detective, you can extract DigiGroove templates from audio selections, saving these either to the Groove Clipboard or as a DigiGroove template. Groove information can also be extracted from MIDI selections and applied to audio material (and vice versa).

> More details about the Quantize feature and other options in the MIDI menu are provided in Chapter 10.

Change Velocity and Change Duration

These transformations of MIDI notes are frequently used, especially the Add, Subtract, and Scale By methods.

Transpose

MIDI users will use this feature often. For example, you might select a group of notes or an entire region and select Transpose to transpose it up or down an octave (plus or minus 12 semitones), either because you're doubling another part at the octave or simply because you've changed to another sound on the MIDI module or software instrument plug-in playing this track's data, and it's pitched in a different octave. For applying transposition to entire tracks or regions, however, the Real-Time Properties feature introduced in Pro Tools 7 will usually be the better choice. When used in conjunction with Mirrored MIDI Editing, if you change note events or controllers within the original MIDI region, these will be reflected immediately in other identically named copies of the same region—each with its own region-level transposition (and/or other real-time properties).

Select/Split Notes

Select and Split Notes functions are combined into a single dialog box, shown in Figure 8.11. Select Notes mode allows you to select only notes within a given pitch range, or top/bottom notes of each chord. After making this selection, you can drag the selected notes, copy them, apply velocity or duration changes, and so on. You might be able to accomplish the same thing by drawing a rectangle around many different notes with the Grabber tool (holding down the Shift key to select/deselect additional notes), but it would be awfully cumbersome!

The Split Notes feature is also useful for composing and arranging. The options for Split Notes are identical to Select Notes, except for the additional options in the lower half for either cutting or copying notes that meet the pitch criterion. This places those note events onto the Clipboard so you can paste them elsewhere: directly into a new track or split onto multiple new tracks by pitch (useful for splitting drum parts onto separate drum tracks, for example).

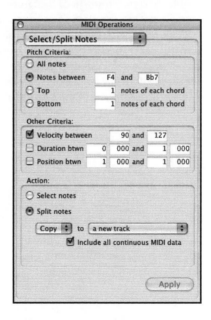

Figure 8.11   The Select/Split Notes page of the MIDI Operations window.

Input Quantize

This feature is also known as "Auto Quantize" on many MIDI sequencers. It destructively applies quantization upon input. The options in the Input Quantize page of the MIDI Operations window are identical to those in the Quantize page, except for an additional check box that enables or disables this feature. In truth, however, you may never use this, because it's just as easy—and a *lot* more flexible—to experiment with quantization after the fact (especially through the non-destructive method of using real-time properties on the region or track), instead of entirely discarding the original timing in your performance during the recording process.

Step Input

The Step Input feature will be familiar to users of other popular MIDI sequencers. In this step-entry mode, you can enter MIDI notes or chords one by one, with the input cursor advancing by the specified increment each time you enter something. Not only can this non–real-time entry of note events be just the thing for creating "impossible" rapid-fire arpeggios and so on, but can also be useful for entering certain types of drum parts.

The "Step Input" section of Chapter 10 goes into the details of Step Input mode for MIDI notes, but here's the basic idea behind the Step Input window (shown in Figure 8.12): First, you select which MIDI track in your current Pro Tools session to use as the destination for the note events created in this mode. You can then choose the step increment (the rhythmic spacing between the notes that will be created), a percentage of that note value to use as the duration for notes created in each step, and whether the velocities for these note events should be a fixed value or represent how you actually struck the keys during step input. Finally, Undo Step and Next Step buttons (which, if desired, you can assign to keys on your MIDI keyboard) allow you to back up and redo a step or skip a step entirely in order to create rests for syncopated rhythms. You can change all of these parameters while you continue to create notes, and you can even switch from one target MIDI track to another within this window.

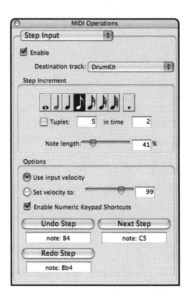

Figure 8.12 The Step Input window, for non–real-time creation of MIDI events.

Restore Performance

This command restores the selected MIDI region to its original recorded form (or to the most recent flattened version; see the next paragraph) with respect to timing, duration, velocity, and/or pitch.

Flatten Performance

Flattening a selected MIDI region freezes it at its current state, and it will return to this state the next time you apply the Restore Performance command. You can select timing, duration, velocity, and/or or pitch parameters for flattening. In Chapter 10, "MIDI," you will find a practical example of the Flatten/Restore Performance commands.

MIDI Event List

The MIDI Event List window (shown in Figure 8.13) displays MIDI events in a track as numerical data in a table format, as opposed to the standard graphical representation of these same events within MIDI tracks in the Edit window. Some MIDI editing operations are easier to perform in this list view. In a sense, this is the most accurate view of what is recorded and played back in your MIDI performances—even though it may not be especially intuitive, musically speaking! The MIDI Event List window is also the only place where you can view and edit Polyphonic Pressure data (sometimes called *polyphonic aftertouch*—MIDI data for the pressure applied to each individual key, as opposed to the more common *monophonic* aftertouch data sent from most keyboards, which is more properly known as *Channel Pressure*). When you enable real-time MIDI properties on the regions or tracks containing the selected MIDI data, the display in the MIDI Event List will reflect this. As you can see in the figure, an R indicates events that are affected region-based properties, while a T indicates those affected by track-based properties.

MIDI Track Offsets

Some MIDI devices (especially older ones) have a certain latency time before they respond to incoming MIDI events, but this is not the most common reason for using MIDI track offsets. More typically, when you are using Auxiliary Inputs (and audio inputs on your hardware) to monitor audio coming from your external MIDI devices, this must be digitized and brought into the Pro Tools mixing environment. On any Pro Tools LE or M-Powered system, there is a certain latency factor involved (a processing delay due to the analog-to-digital conversion process and the overhead of the operating system itself). Additionally, you will find that the external MIDI modules themselves take a certain amount of time to respond to incoming MIDI note events. The MIDI Track Offsets window allows you to individually specify a negative offset, in samples or milliseconds, for each MIDI track in the current Pro Tools session. You can also set a global MIDI offset (also accessible via the MIDI tab of the Preferences dialog box), which is probably all you need if there is only one external MIDI synth in your configuration. Bear in mind that the offset for each MIDI track is a playback parameter only; it doesn't affect where MIDI events are displayed within Pro Tools tracks. In the following Tip, we provide a fairly simple technique that will get you in the ballpark for calculating your system's MIDI-to-audio latency factor. In Pro Tools HD, however, the Automatic Delay

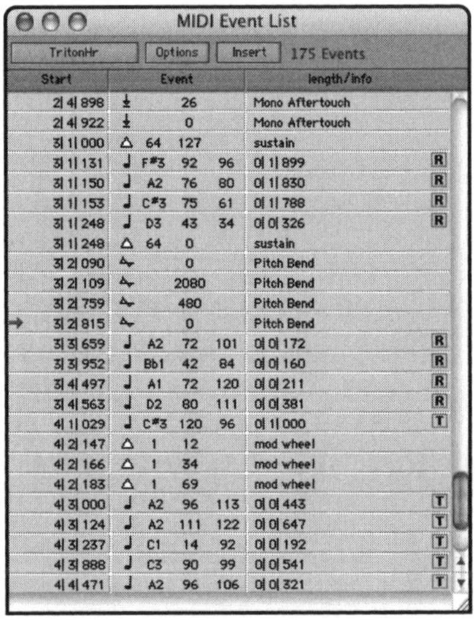

Figure 8.13 The MIDI Event List displays the actual data that selected MIDI parts contain and transmit out to their selected destination.

Compensation feature also applies to MIDI tracks; so especially when using software instrument plug-ins as the sound source for MIDI tracks, this sort of manual adjustment may not be required.

Tip: Calculating Monitoring Latency for MIDI Track Offsets

Create a MIDI track with a cow bell or wood block sound playing 1/4 notes, and then record the output of that synth into an audio track. Switch your main time scale to samples (activating that Timebase ruler), and select one of these MIDI notes; make note of the precise sample number shown in the Edit window's Start field. Now, zoom in on the corresponding attack in the audio track you just recorded, click the Selector precisely at the initial attack of the audio waveform, and note the (higher) sample number now shown. The difference between the sample numbers approximates the total amount of monitoring latency (between MIDI transmission of the note event from Pro Tools, the MIDI device's response time, and then the redigitization into Pro Tools via whatever Auxiliary Input or audio track is monitoring this external MIDI device). This time setting would be the ideal negative offset amount (in samples) for MIDI tracks played through this particular device.

Here's a typical situation in which a negative MIDI track offset is required: Say you're doubling a MIDI snare sound with a snare sample in a Pro Tools audio track whose attack is *precisely* on the 1/4 notes. If you hear a flam effect (closely spaced double attacks), you could empirically adjust the MIDI snare part's negative offset until you hear the two attacks converge.

MIDI Real-Time Properties

Real-time properties apply non-destructive changes to the contents of MIDI regions or tracks—for example, quantization, transposition, changes to velocity and duration, and so on. They can be track based (affecting all MIDI events on the track) and/or region based (affecting only the currently selected instance of that region). The Real-Time Properties window has a pop-up Apply To selector that defaults to region based if one or more MIDI regions are selected when you launch this command or to track based if a MIDI or Instrument track is selected but not any regions within it. However, you can use the Apply To selector to switch between these two modes without leaving this window. (By the way, a third choice in this selector, Default Track Properties, is a handy way to toggle the entire set of real-time properties off and on for the affected track or region.) There is also a real-time properties column that can be displayed in the Edit window, for track-based properties only. Real-time Properties assigned to a selected region take effect prior to any real-time properties that may be assigned to the track on which it resides. You will probably use both types, in various combinations. In the Real-Time properties window for a selected MIDI region, you can also permanently incorporate the effect of these parameters into the actual MIDI data a region contains. (For example, note locations would be changed according to the quantization settings, velocities and durations would be altered, and transposition applied.) Figure 8.14 shows the Real-Time Properties window for a selected MIDI region.

Figure 8.14 Here, real-time MIDI properties are being applied to individual MIDI regions. The pop-up Apply To selector also lets you apply track-based real-time properties to the current MIDI or Instrument track(s).

Remove Duplicate Notes

Especially when loop recording a MIDI part, it is all too easy to create duplicate notes at a given location. This can also occur as a result of quantization. This command resolves the problem.

Beat Detective

This feature conforms an audio region to the session's tempo by breaking it up into multiple regions and aligning these to the beats—or conversely, generates a tempo map based on transients contained within the selected audio (by creating a *beat trigger* map). You can also use Beat Detective to extract DigiGroove templates from audio and MIDI selections. You can use these templates with the Groove Quantize function for MIDI parts, for example, effectively applying the feel extracted from an audio selection in the Beat Detective window to a MIDI performance. The Analysis button in the Beat Detective window allows you to specify whether low or high frequencies should have more weight for the beat-detection process in the source audio selection (for example, whether the kick drum or the hi-hat may be a more reliable tempo indicator). Collection mode, for analyzing multiple tracks simultaneously, is included with Pro Tools HD and can be added to LE or M-Powered versions (which already have the basic Beat Detective LE feature) via the Music Production Toolkit option. The Beat Detective window (shown in Figure 8.15) is a fairly complex subject; Chapter 12, "The Pro Tools Groove," provides more discussion of its basic modes.

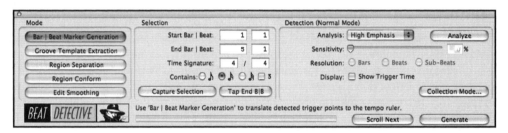

Figure 8.15   The Beat Detective window is immensely useful for beat mixing and dance production, allowing you to utilize source audio with differing tempos to deconstruct beats and build entirely new arrangements.

> ❋ **CSi: Beat Detective in Action**
>
> In the CD-ROM at the back of this book, you'll find a sample movie tutorial excerpted from the *Pro Tools 7 CSi Master CD-ROM* by Steve Thomas that provides a great overview on using Beat Detective. It's actually one of three separate movie tutorials dedicated to the Beat Detective (*Overview, Collection Mode,* and *Creating DigiGrooves*) on this interactive CD-ROM learning environment for advanced Pro Tools concepts and techniques.

Identify Beat

Use the Identify Beat command to indicate the current position (or selection), in musical bars and beats, which creates a tempo/meter event in the Tempo ruler based on the bar number(s) and meter you indicate. If you do dance mixing (or something similar), the Identify Beat function is very important—be sure to check out Chapter 12 for more information! (The Pro Tools tempo map must be active in order for the Identify Beat command to be available; click to enable the Conductor button in the MIDI section of the Transport.) You can also use Identify Beat to (rather painstakingly) create a tempo/meter map for music that was not recorded with a click, or even at a strict tempo.

Let's say you've imported an interesting drum groove or a musical phrase under which you will build a rhythm groove in Pro Tools. Select *exactly* four bars of the phrase. If necessary, enable Options > Loop Playback, and then press Play. If the four bars don't loop around smoothly, you could zoom in and adjust the selection length (while holding down the Shift key) with the Selector. Alternatively, you could nudge your selection using Command +/– (Ctrl +/– in Windows) to adjust the end point of the current selection until you get a sample-accurate, smooth loop. (Be aware that every time you adjust the selection (or nudge it), you must press Stop and then Play again to reset the timeline selection for looped playback.)

After you've created an *extremely accurate* four-bar selection that loops in correct rhythm (take the time to get this right!), select Event > Identify Beat. In the Add Bar | Beat Markers dialog box shown in Figure 8.16, enter the correct meter (4/4, for example) and bar numbers for the beginning and end of the selection. For example, if the beginning of the four-bar phrase is 1|1|00, the end is 5|1|00, right? Now set your Grid time units to Bars:Beats, set the Grid value to 1/4 notes or 1/8 notes, and activate Grid mode. Also, change the Main location counter to Bars:Beats (which will also enable the Bars:Beats ruler). You're ready to start chopping up the longer musical piece (assuming it was recorded at a steady tempo in the first place); selections and trimming of region lengths will also be snapped by Grid mode to the nearest note value. As you start dropping drum sounds or recording and quantizing additional MIDI or Instrument tracks, everything can be snapped to the tempo grid you created based on that first phrase, which is why it was so important to be so precise before using the Identify Beat command. See Chapter 12 for more examples.

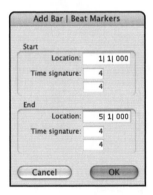

Figure 8.16 You can use Identify Beat to create Pro Tools tempos based on timeline selections corresponding to a precise number of bars and beats (such as audio files containing drum loops or phrases within musical arrangements).

Renumber Bars

This command assigns a new number to the first bar of your session; all subsequent bars are renumbered accordingly. Negative numbers are supported, in case you prefer bar one to be somewhere farther into the session's timeline if that helps you keep better track of song structure.

All MIDI Notes Off: The Panic Button!

Use the All Notes Off command if you ever need to turn off stuck MIDI notes on your MIDI instruments. The keyboard shortcut for the All Notes Off command is Shift+Command+period (Shift+Ctrl+period in Windows). If you're a MIDI user, memorize this now!

AudioSuite Menu

AudioSuite plug-ins appear in this menu, grouped into categories when you use the default preferences in Pro Tools (although you can group them by manufacturer and then by category, if you prefer). By default, the following plug-in categories appear: EQ, Dynamics, Pitch Shift, Reverb, Delay, Modulation, and Other. (Additional categories may also appear if these types of optional plug-ins are installed on your system.) AudioSuite effects are strictly file based. In other words, they create new audio files (or *destructively* overwrite the current selection within the audio file, if you wish) when you click the Process button and cannot operate in real time.

In addition to the AudioSuite plug-ins supplied with Pro Tools, you can purchase third-party plug-ins for RTAS (and TDM, of course) separately. Some RTAS plug-ins also function as AudioSuite plug-ins, while you can only use others (like software instruments and the Click plug-in) as real-time effects on tracks, so they won't appear among these AudioSuite menu selections.

> ※ **Tip: Favorite Plug-ins**
>
> By designating any plug-in as a *favorite*, it always appears at the top of the hierarchical plug-in menu. Just hold down the Command key (Ctrl key in Windows) as you open the pop-up menu for selecting plug-ins in the AudioSuite menu or insert slots on the tracks, and select the item you want to add to your favorites. Repeat this procedure to remove a plug-in from your favorites. This is a very useful feature; creating your own "hot half-dozen" plug-in favorites will save you a lot of time!

The precise contents of the parameters window differ for each AudioSuite effect, but a Process button is always available; clicking that button creates new regions that are placed into the affected track instead of the current selection (unless you select Overwrite Files, in which case the data in the source file itself is destructively overwritten). AudioSuite Plug-in windows frequently also include a Preview button and a Bypass button so that you can toggle the preview between the processed and unprocessed version. The Use In Playlist button, if enabled, substitutes the processed result for the selected original in the track. Most importantly, a pop-up menu enables you to copy and save settings for each plug-in, or import them from another session's plug-in settings folder. Additionally, if any part of the current selection includes multiple audio regions in a single track, you can choose whether the result of the AudioSuite processing creates a single new region (with processing applied) for that entire track selection or individual regions/files corresponding to each original region.

❋ **Tip: Free Up Your DSP Resources**

For users with limited DSP capacity, a point may come in your project where Pro Tools tells you that you are low on DSP resources and won't allow you to add any more plug-ins, Aux In tracks, Instrument tracks, or sends, for example. At that point, it may be practical to commit some of your real-time effects to new regions to free up that signal-processing power for the rest of your mix. Fortunately, most DigiRack RTAS effects are available both as inserts and also as process-based functions in the AudioSuite menu. You can copy settings from the insert version of the effect (via a pop-up menu in its Plug-in window), remove the plug-in from the audio track, select all audio in the audio track, and then paste these settings into the corresponding file-based (non–real-time) AudioSuite effect before clicking the Process button.

For real-time plug-in effects, or to "print" (permanently incorporate) several effects to a new file in a single operation (something you frequently do if your Pro Tools sessions will later be used by someone who doesn't have the same plug-ins available as you do), you can alternatively use the Bounce to > Disk command, muting all tracks but the one(s) you want incorporated into the bounced file. (The Bounce dialog box's Import into Session after Bounce option is also very useful in these cases.)

Options Menu

As you might guess, the selections in the Options menu affect the operating modes of Pro Tools: recording modes, monitoring modes, synchronization status, pre/post-roll, and looped playback—how edit selections affect play selections, for example. Here, we concentrate on the selections in this menu that we consider essential for *any* Pro Tools user. For information about other commands not discussed here, see the *Pro Tools Menus Guide*, provided in PDF format with the program; it describes every selection in every menu of Pro Tools, including those in the Option menu.

Destructive Record

In Destructive Recording mode, any new audio recorded into an existing region *replaces* and *erases* the previously recorded audio data in the same location. Ordinarily, recording in Pro Tools is *nondestructive*; even if you record right over a region already in the track, replacing it with a new region, the previous region is still intact and can be dragged out from the Region List (and returned to its original timestamp location via the Spot dialog box). Saving every take of audio uses more disk space (until you delete the unwanted audio regions/files, of course), so users who are obliged to be extremely conservative about disk space will occasionally use the Destructive Record command to switch over to Destructive Recording mode. (Books on tape might be a typical situation for using Destructive Recording mode, especially if your disk capacity is relatively limited.)

Loop Record

Hey, musicians! This cool feature is of special interest to you! When this recording option is enabled, you can keep looping the same timeline selection (between the Start and End locations) as you record multiple takes. Every take you record is saved within a single audio file, which contains all the takes. If you want to discard all takes since you last began loop recording at any point while still in Loop Recording mode, press Command+period (Ctrl+period in Windows). Each take recorded in Loop Recording mode appears in the Audio Regions List after you stop recording and is numbered sequentially.

After recording multiple takes, you may want to listen to each to decide which one is the keeper. Click with the Grabber to highlight the most recent take currently appearing within the track, and then switch to the Selector tool and Command-click and hold (Ctrl-click and hold in Windows) on that region. A pop-up Takes List appears, where you can toggle between all the takes matching that timeline selection. (Note that several selections in Preferences > Editing affect behavior of the Takes List.) Incidentally, the Options > Loop Record option only affects how audio plays while in Record mode; the Options > Loop Playback option is used to enable looping during normal playback.

❊ CSi: Loop Recording

The CD-ROM at the back of this book contains a sample movie tutorial excerpted from the *Pro Tools 7 CSi Starter CD-ROM* called *Overdubs and Loop Recording*. Here, you can see how Loop Recording mode is used for both for audio and MIDI, how to use the pop-up Takes List, and how to use Grid mode and pre-roll or post-roll to determine where Pro Tools will record and what gets looped.

QuickPunch

This menu command toggles the QuickPunch recording mode for audio on and off. When QuickPunch mode is enabled, you can manually click the Record button on and off during playback to punch recording in and out on any record-enabled audio tracks. Owners of Digi 002 systems can connect a footswitch to drop in and out of recording when using QuickPunch mode.

Using QuickPunch

What do you do when the performer hasn't given you a clue about when you will need to punch in recording? (Hey, maybe he or she doesn't have a clue yet either!) The QuickPunch feature enables you to avoid having to record a lot of dead air before you get the high sign. It allows you to turn the Record button on and off while Pro Tools is playing back, to activate recording into any record-enabled tracks. Here's how you do it:

1. Choose Options > QuickPunch.
2. Record-enable one or more tracks where you want to record by clicking its Rec (Record Enable) button. Notice that the Record button in the Transport now has a P in it and starts flashing when you click Play.
3. When your helpful performer gives you the signal that he or she is about to do something great (hopefully), click the Record button. Pro Tools will start recording in all record-enabled tracks.
4. Once the greatness is over, click Record again to exit Record mode. Pro Tools continues playback, and you can click the Record button again to punch in at a different section (backing vocals in the second verse of the song, for example). Alternatively, click Stop or press the spacebar when the performer is finished.

Of course, the Command+Spacebar (Ctrl+Spacebar in Windows) keyboard equivalent for the Record button also works for dropping in and out of QuickPunch mode, as does the F12 key—although Mac users must be careful to assign this Exposé shortcut key to something else. (Again, on Digi 002 systems, you can connect a footswitch to the appropriate jack on your audio interface to achieve the same effect as pressing the Record button in the Transport window—nice!) Only those portions of time when the Transport's Record button was enabled will have created new audio region(s).

Be aware that while using QuickPunch mode on Pro Tools LE and M-Powered systems, the total number of tracks and available DSP power are reduced. Also, although the number of tracks on which you can simultaneously record in QuickPunch mode is determined by the current number of free voices, on LE and M-Powered versions, you are limited to punching in a maximum of 16 audio tracks in QuickPunch mode.

QuickPunch is *not* required on MIDI tracks! Any record-enabled MIDI tracks will go in and out of Record mode as you turn the Record button on and off during playback, even during *normal* Play mode. QuickPunch is only required for audio tracks.

Note: QuickPunch, TrackPunch, and Delay Compensation

On HD systems, you should disable the Options > Use Delay Compensation option while recording in either QuickPunch or TrackPunch mode.

TrackPunch (HD Systems Only)

This menu command toggles the TrackPunch recording mode for audio on/off. TrackPunch lets you independently use Record Enable buttons in up to 16 different individual tracks, punching each one in and out of Record mode in real time during playback.

Using TrackPunch

Imagine for a moment that you're recording a jazz session, where multiple soloists will each take a few choruses, but it's not clear exactly when. You have individual microphones on each solo instrument, and you want to avoid recording multiple takes of the entire song on six tracks simultaneously. With TrackPunch recording mode, you have the option to drop in and out of Record Enable mode on the fly on individual tracks—enabling microphones for each player at the opportune moment. (You might also use this technique for a Foley artist, expansive percussion setups with numerous microphones, conference recordings, and so on.)

1. First, Control-click (Start-click in Windows) the Record Enable buttons on all the individual tracks that may be required to make them active for recording in TrackPunch mode. Up to 16 tracks can be in TrackPunch mode simultaneously. These Record Enable buttons turn blue, as does the Record button in the Transport window itself. (This button now displays a "T," for TrackPunch.)

2. Press the spacebar to start playback.

3. When you're ready to punch in recording on any TrackPunch-enabled track, click its Record Enable button. The Transport button turns solid red while recording is in progress.

4. Click the track's Record Enable button again to punch it out of Record mode. The Transport button turns blue again.

5. Repeat as many times (and on as many tracks) as necessary.

To punch in simultaneously on all TrackPunch-enabled tracks, hold down the Option key (Alt key in Windows) as you click any of their Record Enable buttons, or click the Record button in the Transport window.

Video Track Online

When this option is enabled, contents of the Movie window scroll according to cursor position and selections (and as you drag regions back and forth in the timeline, to spot them to video events). When disabled, playback of the video is frozen at its current point. If you find that playback in the Movie window is significantly affecting performance on your system configuration, you might occasionally take the movie offline to free up system overhead for metering and other display tasks, or while editing a sequence when you don't need the video as a reference.

QuickTime DV Movie Out FireWire (Mac Only)

If you have a DV-compatible video deck, camera, or monitor with a FireWire input (which Sony calls "iLink"), enabling this command sends playback of the current QuickTime movie file in your Pro Tools session out that port on your computer.

Loop Playback

This command loops the current Timeline selection (displayed in the Start/End/Length fields of the Transport window) until you press Stop or the Spacebar. This is really handy for repeating a section while you make mix and effects adjustments. You can also loop playback while refining a musical phrase selection so that it loops exactly at a precise number of bars or beats, either to capture/separate a new region definition or to establish a precise selection as the basis for the Identify Beat command. The keyboard shortcut to enable looped playback is Shift+Command+L (or Shift+Ctrl+L in Windows).

Link Timeline and Edit Selection

When this option is enabled (the default), selections you make in the Edit window immediately change not only the values in the Edit window's Start, End, and Length indicators (the Edit selection) but also those of the Transport window (the Timeline Selection). The Timeline selection in the Transport window (whether currently visible or not) determines what happens when you press Play, what loops in Loop Playback mode, and punch-in/out points for recording, for instance. In other words, when Options > Link Timeline and Edit Selections is enabled, values in the Transport's Start, End, and Length fields are always slaved to the current Edit selection (identically named fields, up in the Event Edit area at the top of the Edit window) and will change as you select regions and MIDI notes or highlight any area of the timeline within the tracks or Timebase rulers.

Sometimes, however, you *don't* want track selections in the Edit window to alter the Transport window's Start, End, and Length values. For example, you might want the same portion of the timeline to keep looping around, even as you select, drag, or trim regions and notes within the Edit window. In this case, you would temporarily disable the Link Timeline and Edit Selections mode (either using this Options menu selection or the Link Selection button located just underneath the Zoomer tool and Zoom Toggle button).

Note that the Edit > Play Edit Selection command plays back your current track selection, even when the Timeline and Edit selections are not linked.

Link Track and Edit Selection

When enabled, this option automatically selects the track itself whenever you make any selection within it, highlighting its name in the Edit/Mix windows. This feature was added in Pro Tools 7 and facilitates applying track-based commands as you edit. For example, with this option enabled, you might group the tracks that get selected or use this keyboard shortcut for changing track heights only on currently selected tracks: Control+Up/Down arrow key (or Start+Up/Down arrow key in Windows). Also, if you hold down the Option+Shift key combination (Alt+Shift in Windows) when changing a track parameter (track view, automation mode, or track timebase, for instance), the same change will be applied to all currently selected tracks, as applicable. Even better, when Commands Focus mode is enabled (via the a...z button below the five zoom preset buttons—learning the shortcuts in Commands Focus mode is *well* worth your effort!), pressing the minus (–) key on your alphanumeric QWERTY keyboard (*not* the numeric keypad) toggles any currently selected tracks between two pre-defined track views: Waveform (regions) and Volume on audio tracks, Regions and Notes on MIDI or Instrument tracks.

Mirror MIDI Editing

When mirrored MIDI editing (another feature introduced in Pro Tools 7) is enabled, the edits you perform on a MIDI region are automatically applied to all MIDI regions of the same name, in any track. (This would apply, for example, to changing notes or drawing new MIDI controller automation.) For example, say you've created a very basic 4-bar drum pattern named "Groove," which you've copied to various places in a MIDI or Instrument track as you start laying down parts. Once you have a couple more instrumental parts working and you've enabled Mirror MIDI Editing, you can tweak any instance of the MIDI region "Groove" (altering the hi-hat, for instance, or adding a kick drum accent), and that change is immediately reflected in the other instances of the same region. Being able to mirror MIDI regions is important not only in this linear sense, but also for simultaneously doubling parts in separate tracks (with different output assignments and real-time MIDI properties applied to each).

Automation Follows Edit

When this option (available in all versions 6.7 and higher) is enabled, the effect of editing operations on Pro Tools data is exactly the same as in all previous versions: Dragging or pasting regions to a new location also moves or copies all their overlapping automation data.

For example, you may have created automation for the send level to the delay effect in a track, so that a single note in a lead vocal or guitar line spikes the delay. In the default Automation Follows Edit mode, if you copy or drag this region to a new location, it still has that automation event at the same relative note. However, if you disable Automation Follows Edit, the automation on tracks stays in place, even as you drag, cut, copy, and paste regions within it.

MIDI Thru

Generally, the MIDI Thru option should be enabled. Here's the typical setup: You turn Local mode off on the keyboard (or MIDI guitar, wind, or percussion controller, of course) that you're using for the MIDI performance. This cuts the internal connection between the keyboard and its own internal sounds. Otherwise, every note you play is doubled; your synth would not only play the note in response to its own keyboard but also when the note event comes echoing back from the record-enabled track in Pro Tools (perhaps on a different channel, and with a different sound).

On record-enabled MIDI tracks, the MIDI data received from your keyboard (usually via one of the MIDI inputs on your MIDI interface, unless you're using a keyboard with a direct USB connection) is echoed back out through the MIDI interface or USB connection—redirected to the MIDI port, channel, and MIDI program number assigned to this track.

Why use MIDI Thru? Without changing anything on your keyboard, you can switch from one MIDI channel and program setting to another (or even play while using a software instrument or the sounds of some other external MIDI module connected to a different port on your MIDI interface, as shown in Figure 8.17), changing volumes, pan, and other parameters on the Pro Tools track rather than on the controller itself.

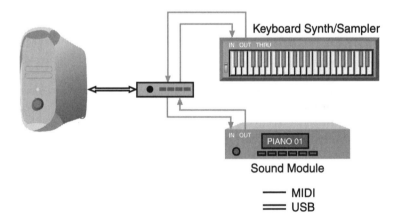

Figure 8.17 A simple MIDI setup for a Pro Tools system: one keyboard synth/sampler, one multitimbral MIDI module, and a multiport external MIDI interface connected to the computer's USB port.

Pre-Fader Metering

When the Pre-Fader Metering option is enabled, Level meters in the Edit or Mix window display the level for each track prior to its main Volume fader (which of course can apply gain changes of its own). Pre-fader levels are therefore unaffected by the Volume fader's current position and more accurately reflect the levels for whatever audio source is feeding the track (disk-based audio data, a hardware input, a bus, or the output from a software instrument). However, because pre-fader metering derives from a point in the track's signal chain immediately after the Inserts section, the pre-fader levels *do* reflect gain changes resulting from any plug-ins on the track. This is actually quite useful. When track meters are displaying *post-fader* levels (in other words, when Options > Pre-Fader Metering is disabled), a lowered main volume setting on a track's output makes it all too easy to overlook the fact that, between the compressor and boosted EQ settings you may have going on a track, clipping (overload) is occurring on its main output. This book will remind you many times that digital clipping is not pretty; you need to manage the gain structure of your session (that is, the amount of boost or cut at the various stages in the signal chain from track inputs and outputs to the Master Fader track for your final mix output) so that clipping doesn't occur at any point. Experienced users will switch back and forth many times between pre- and post-fader metering at different stages of the work process (generally using pre-fader metering while recording into tracks, for example, but occasionally switching to post-fader to confirm that any plug-ins or especially hardware I/O inserts are at appropriate levels).

Auto-Spot Regions (HD Versions Only)

This feature is especially useful when using VITC or the MachineControl option (or with LTC while the transport of the master device is in Play mode). When Options > Auto-Spot Regions is enabled, clicking on any region with the Grabber *spots* its beginning (or the sync point within it) to the current time-code location. With Machine Control or VITC synchronization, you can jog or shuttle the master video transport itself in order to spot a selected region to the desired location.

Low-Latency Monitoring (Digi 002/002 Rack Only)

On these Pro Tools systems, this Options menu item is extremely useful while laying down tracks. Instead of a relatively long monitoring delay (latency) between the input signal and when it is heard back through the Pro Tools mixer (especially noticeable when larger Hardware Buffer sizes are selected in the Playback Engine dialog box), this feature reduces latency to a minimum—on tracks whose output is assigned to outputs 1–2 only. When Options > Low-Latency Monitoring is enabled, all plug-ins and sends are automatically bypassed on all record-enabled tracks assigned to outputs 1–2.

❄ **Caution: Bouncing to Disk on Digi 002/001 Systems**

Don't forget to disable the Options > Low Latency Monitoring option before bouncing to disk! Although this feature is very handy while tracking, if you forget to turn it off, only the output from *audio* tracks will be included in your audio mixdown file and none of the Instrument or Aux In tracks (where you might have instantiated plug-ins for reverbs, delays, or software instruments, for example).

❄ **Note: "Zero-Latency" Monitoring on the Mbox 2 and Mbox**

Digidesign documentation and marketing materials often refer to this feature of the Mbox and Mbox 2. This somewhat misleading term refers to a very useful feature of this particular audio interface for Pro Tools LE. A knob on the front panel of these units adjusts the proportional volume of the input (whatever signal is entering the interface's analog inputs) and playback (the main stereo output from Pro Tools LE). Because this input source monitors the interface's analog input via a direct analog signal path to its outputs, there's no latency. When recording a mono source in this mode, don't forget to press the Mono button on the front panel of these units so that it comes out both sides of your headphones or speakers.

Use Delay Compensation (HD Systems Only)

In Pro Tools HD, this Options menu item enables Automatic Delay Compensation (ADC). ADC adjusts for the processing latency (delay) of each plug-in insert and any audio routing (for example, internal bussing, external hardware used as inserts), which consequently improves your mix by maintaining better time alignment between its various tracks. For most DigiRack plug-ins, the delay for each is only on the order of four samples or so. This can accumulate to a noticeable amount, however, when several are used in series and also when a given track's audio passes through its own plug-ins, those of an Aux In, plus a couple more in the Master Fader prior to the main output, for example. Third-party plug-ins and processing-intensive plug-in types such as reverb or noise reduction can have much greater amounts of inherent latency. Expert operators on pre-HD TDM systems have long compensated for accumulated latency manually, using the Delay indicators at the bottom of tracks in the Mix window and the Time Adjuster plug-in, for example. Maintaining proper time alignment between all the tracks in your mix keeps it more phase-coherent. This is especially important when the same signal is somehow present in several tracks with different routing or processing setups (for example, because it bleeds into two different microphones in a drum set or in live-performance situations). Small time-alignment discrepancies can create phase cancellation in high frequencies, and even very tiny amounts can affect the overall coherency of your mix. You can adjust the parameters for Delay Compensation in the Setup > Playback Engine dialog box.

If you're just getting started with audio recording, however, we should mention that when recording from multiple simultaneous microphone sources, your first time-alignment concern should be with microphone placement and acoustical isolation of each sound source. To cite a common example, if you have a snare or cymbal crashes bleeding into a vocal microphone 12 feet away, you've already got time-alignment and phase cancellation issues on your tracks—before even using any plug-ins!

Setup Menu

Selections under the Setup menu pertain not only to the hardware on your system, but also allow you to control how available disks on your system are used for recording on each audio track in the current session. It is also here that you establish your preferences and your MIDI setup and tell Pro Tools what sort of external hardware peripherals are attached to your computer for use by Pro Tools (for example, synchronization peripherals, external control surfaces, and devices linked via the Machine Control protocol). Another extremely important feature you can access via the Setup menu is the I/O Setup dialog box, where you can define and select audio paths for use within Pro Tools, representing inputs, outputs, inserts, and busses, from simple mono and stereo paths to multichannel configurations for surround mixing.

Hardware (Setup)

The contents of the Hardware Setup dialog box (shown in Figure 8.18) depend on your Pro Tools hardware configuration. On Pro Tools LE hardware like the Digi 002, for example, you may be able to set your audio hardware's sample rate and input gain (although not on the Mbox 2/Mbox, since they have front-panel knobs for this), select between analog or digital input, use Sync mode for the digital input, use DAT-compatibility features, and set other options specific to the audio hardware. On M-Powered systems, however, control of all these parameters for your M-Audio interface is turned over to the device's own setup application. Only a single button is available in the Hardware Setup dialog box, which then launches this external program that is included with the M-Audio interface. On Pro Tools TDM configurations prior to HD, the Hardware Setup dialog box was also used to specify which audio interfaces are connected to the system (however, these are automatically detected on HD systems). Additional options for HD systems may include some of the following:

- ❋ Selection of digital or analog connectors for various input channels on the audio interface.

- ❋ Reference levels for analog connectors (+4 dBm or −10 dBV, respectively, associated with pro and consumer equipment).

- ❋ Clock source for sample rate and external clock output.

- ❋ Level sensitivity and peak hold characteristics on the audio interface's front-panel display (if applicable).

Pro Tools|HD systems offer auto-configuration features, so that you don't have to manually select the interface when installing or expanding the hardware configuration. Users of the 96i I/O (but not the 96 I/O) with Pro Tools|HD can also use the Hardware Setup dialog box to adjust gain on the inputs of the audio interface itself.

Playback Engine

As with the Hardware Setup dialog box, the contents of the Playback Engine dialog box (shown in Figure 8.19) depend on your hardware configuration. On HD (as on any other TDM system using version 6.4 and higher), a Delay Compensation Engine setting in the Playback Engine dialog box lets you specify how much of your DSP resources should be dedicated to this task. Options are none, short, and long (which may be required on slower systems or when using relatively high-latency plug-ins).

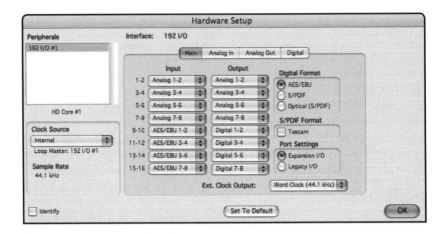

Figure 8.18 The contents of the Hardware Setup dialog box depend on your Pro Tools hardware. Shown here are the options for a Pro Tools|HD system, with a 192 I/O audio interface.

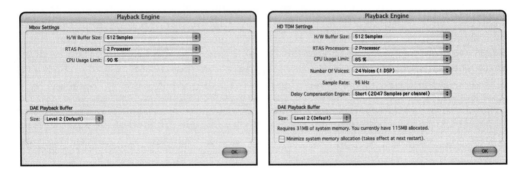

Figure 8.19 Contents of the Playback Engine dialog box depend on your Pro Tools hardware. Shown here are the options for M-Powered and HD software.

Pro Tools LE and M-Powered users, however, should be especially aware of three all-important settings in the Playback Engine dialog box (which also affect HD systems):

⁜ If you hear glitching or choppiness during playback, especially due to intensive use of plug-ins or virtual instruments (even with only a dozen or so tracks, for example), try increasing the value in the H/W Buffer Size parameter. The larger this hardware buffer, the more plug-ins are supported; this can be especially beneficial when using more processing-intensive plug-in types like reverbs and software instruments, for instance. Additionally, larger hardware buffer sizes allow you to record a larger number of tracks simultaneously on LE and M-Powered systems. However, larger buffer sizes also increase latency (processing delay) issues when monitoring input signals through the Pro Tools mixer during recording (unless you're circumventing this by enabling the Low-Latency

254
⁜ ⁜ ⁜

Monitoring option on a Digi 002/002 Rack, the Mix knob on an Mbox 2/Mbox, or one of the direct input monitoring options provided by M-Audio hardware). You might therefore start with smaller hardware buffer sizes when recording relatively small numbers of tracks, increasing these as necessary if activating lots of plug-ins during mixdown causes your system to hiccup during playback.

✸ The CPU Usage Limit setting controls how much of the CPU's processing power can be devoted to audio processing tasks for Pro Tools. Larger settings allow smooth playback of sessions with more numerous or processing-intensive RTAS plug-ins. However, higher percentages of CPU usage take away processing power from screen redraws (including moving faders and real-time displays in track Level meters), video playback, and any other program running concurrently with Pro Tools on the same computer, which could consequently seem sluggish. A good initial setting for the CPU Usage Limit option on single-processor systems is 85%, although in Pro Tools 7, you can increase this parameter up to 99% on any computer, whether single- or dual-processor. For dual-processor systems, the RTAS Processors parameter lets you choose how many of the computer's CPUs to allocate to processing tasks for RTAS plug-ins. Choosing a larger number—and yes, configurations with more than two CPUs are supported—spreads the processing load. Along with the H/W Buffer Size, increasing your CPU Usage Limit is another possible strategy if you start to hear choppy playback or other artifacts while using many software instrument tracks. The System Usage window provides a graphic display of how heavy the combined load is on *all* the currently enabled processors. In sessions with many processing-intensive RTAS plug-ins (reverbs and software instruments, for example), there will be a notable difference when you switch between one and two RTAS processors. The CPU Usage Limit and number of RTAS processors interact, and requirements vary according to the particular session, computer model, and your working style, so it's impossible to make a blanket recommendation for these values. Generally speaking, however, if you're using a lot of RTAS plug-ins and hear glitching or get an alert box from Pro Tools about "CPU Usage" (and increasing the H/W Buffer Size doesn't help), try increasing your CPU Usage Limit. Conversely, if your onscreen fader movement and Movie window updates seem sluggish during playback, reducing the CPU Usage Limit might help.

✸ The DAE Playback Buffer setting affects how much of your computer's RAM is used to manage disk buffers for audio playback. Generally, you should start out with the default setting of 2. If you find that your hard disk can't keep up with playback and recording in complex sessions (with lots of tracks, regions, and automation), try the next larger size. Of course, also make sure that your disks for audio recording and playback are properly maintained and defragmented in the first place! The tradeoff is that with larger DAE playback buffer sizes, Pro Tools takes a moment longer to start playback or record after you press Play.

Disk Allocation

If you have multiple hard drives available for audio recording on your system, you can use the Disk Allocation dialog box to specify which drives and folders are used to record new audio for each individual track. This helps to spread out the load on your disks (although it could make manual backup of a session's audio data more confusing if you don't have a Pro Tools–savvy backup program like Mezzo). Alternatively, in some sessions you may choose to record all tracks onto a single drive, while using a different drive for other sessions, clients, or users. (For convenience, you can highlight multiple tracks in this dialog box and simultaneously assign them to the same destination.) The Disk Allocation dialog box offers a pop-up disk destination selector for each audio track where you can even choose specific *folders* for new recordings from each track. Another option is round-robin allocation: For each new track you create, a different audio-recording drive on your system is selected in rotation.

❄ Caution: Make Your System Volume/Partition Transfer-Only

If you can avoid it, try not to include your startup system volume (the drive with the operating system and programs such as Pro Tools) among the eligible disks for audio recording! If you must use a single drive in your computer for both the operating system and audio recording, at the very least, create two separate logical partitions (for example, using Apple's Disk Utility, or Computer Management > Disk Management in the Administrative Tools control panel of Windows XP). Of course, you will need to reload your operating system and programs after doing this! For one thing, this permits running disk optimization or simple defragmentation on the audio volume (partition) while still booting from the system volume and makes your disk-management routines a little simpler in general. In Pro Tools' Workspace window (discussed later in this chapter), you can designate each drive (or partition on a physical drive, which will appear as a disk volume) on your system as Playback and/or Record or Transfer only. Volumes set to Transfer only won't appear in the Disk Allocation window at all and will never be used during round-robin allocation for new tracks.

Peripherals

The Peripherals dialog box (shown in Figure 8.20) includes choices for SMPTE time-code source (port and device type, such as Digidesign's USD or Sync I/O), MIDI Machine Control (MMC) settings, and Machine Control (the MachineControl software option is required for use of 9-pin controller connections with video decks, DATs, and other compatible devices). External MIDI controllers for Pro Tools are also configured here, such as the Mackie Control Universal or its predecessor, the HUI (which is also emulated by several other controllers including the wireless TranzPort); the CM Labs MotorMix; or the J.L. Cooper CS-10, as are Digidesign's Command|8 USB controller for Pro Tools and the company's Ethernet-based controllers: the D-Control, D-Command, ProControl, and Control|24.

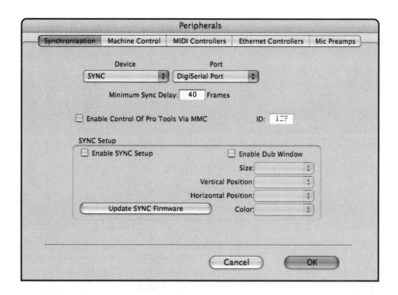

Figure 8.20 The Peripherals dialog box, where you identify external sources for SMPTE time code, MIDI Machine Control, and external controllers for Pro Tools functions. (Options for an HD system with a Sync I/O shown here.)

I/O

The I/O Setup dialog box (shown in Figure 8.21) is where you manage signal paths (also known simply as *paths*) for inputs, outputs, inserts, and busses (plus inputs on Digidesign's optional PRE microphone preamplifier for HD systems, as well as Hardware Insert Devices), assigning them meaningful names to match how you're actually using them. On larger system configurations and for surround mixing, this can be a fairly complex subject—in the *Pro Tools Reference Guide* PDF document included with the program, an entire chapter is dedicated to I/O setup—so only a brief overview and some general recommendations are provided here.

The I/O Setup dialog box is organized into various tabs (Inputs, Outputs, Inserts, and Busses, plus Mic Preamps and Hardware Inserts on HD systems), each of which contains a channel grid that varies according to the audio interface(s) available in your configuration. A *path* is essentially a label for one of these audio pathways, which can be either mono, stereo pairs, or multichannel. The available choices for input and output selectors on audio, Aux In, or Instrument tracks, output selectors on Master Fader tracks, send assignments, and Hardware I/O inserts are all determined by the paths that have been defined in the I/O Setup dialog box. Stereo and multichannel *main paths* are logical groupings of multiple mono *subpaths*; use the dialog box's Channel grid to specify exactly which physical inputs and outputs correspond to each of these mono subpaths. (Templates are provided for the common surround formats, and of course, you can create your own configurations. In Chapter 14, we provide more information about surround mixing in Pro Tools.) Note that you can use the checkboxes in front of each main path in the channel grid to toggle their active/inactive status. This can reduce clutter in pop-up menus, when selecting inputs, outputs, and send destinations.

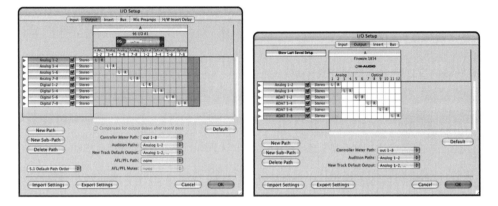

Figure 8.21 The I/O Setup dialog box lets you define named paths for inputs, outputs, inserts, and internal mixing busses. (Shown here: an HD system with a single 96 I/O, and an M-Powered system using the ADAT Lightpipe outputs on a FireWire 1814 interface.)

Especially if your audio hardware has multiple inputs and outputs, it's often a good idea to assign meaningful names to the inputs, outputs, Hardware I/O inserts, and busses on your Pro Tools system. For example, you might have your Focusrite microphone preamp more or less permanently connected to inputs 1–2 of the audio interface and a Korg Triton synth connected to inputs 7–8. Why not create two stereo input paths named "Focusrite" and "Triton" (each consisting of two mono subpaths for the corresponding physical inputs) so that these names always appear when you pop open the input selector on audio tracks or Auxiliary Inputs? Likewise, if you have an external reverb more or less permanently looped into outputs 5–6 so that it can be used as a Stereo I/O insert from Pro Tools tracks, go ahead and assign this insert path a default name. On Pro Tools|HD systems, you can also manually set a latency amount for each Hardware I/O insert. This delay time (representing how long it takes for audio to get out through that external device and back into the Pro Tools mixing environment) is compensated for when the Automation Delay Compensation engine is enabled on Pro Tools|HD systems. If outputs 3–4 on the audio interface are always connected to an audio tie line or studio feed, go ahead and set a default name for this stereo output path that will always be obvious.

Alternatively, you may use the I/O Setup dialog box to assign names that are only pertinent to the *current* session, simply to make a complex routing scenario easier to manage. When you use internal mixing busses to route multiple sends to a stereo Aux In with an effect, it can make life simpler, for example, if you name that bus pair "Delay." The bus pair will appear by this name in the output selectors for each stereo send and also the input selector for the Aux In track where you've instantiated this effect—a heck of a lot easier to remember than, say, "bus 7–8," right?

Another good habit is to create default names for a couple of your busses (or stereo bus pairs), perhaps "Verb Send" or "Delay Send" (or "Drum Sub," if you frequently submix drum sets to a single stereo Aux In track), by clicking the Set Default button so these bus names appear automatically in new sessions. As already mentioned, when you select busses with descriptive names as the source for send or output destinations and inputs on Aux In tracks with effects, it's much easier to see at a glance what's going on in your session. Consistent naming conventions and regular habits like these save you time later on and become *extremely* important when more than one operator has a hand in the same session document!

Click the Default button in the I/O Setup dialog box to reset the channel grid for the path type (Input, Output, Insert, or Bus; plus Mic Preamps and HW Insert Devices on HD systems only) displayed in the current tab to a factory-defined default configuration, where all possible main stereo paths are created for your audio hardware, plus two mono subpaths for each.

❋ **Tip: Use as Many (or as Few) Paths as You Require**

If you're using an M-Audio audio interface with ADAT Lightpipe I/O, you may be surprised to discover that, by default, these inputs and outputs don't appear in the I/O Setup dialog box. If you don't have Lightpipe devices in your studio configuration, that's appropriate; otherwise these unnecessary selections would appear every time you select track inputs and outputs. If you do want to use this type of I/O on your interface, however, two steps are usually required. First, in the device's own setup application, be sure to activate the ADAT input/output. Then in the I/O Setup dialog box of Pro Tools, click the Default button in both the Input and Output tabs to automatically create all possible stereo paths (with mono subpaths) for the ADAT I/O.

In Pro Tools 7, the maximum number of busses available for LE and M-Powered versions was increased from 16 to 32. However, when opening existing sessions, users may be surprised when only the first 16 busses appear, as in previous Pro Tools versions. No problem: Just use the Bus tab of the I/O Setup dialog box to create additional busses as required, or simply click the Default button to create them automatically.

In either of these cases (and also after assigning names to busses you will habitually use for certain types of effects sends or for input/outputs where you always have a given hardware device connected), after configuring I/O Setup to your taste, click the Export Settings button (seen in Figure 8.21) so that you can recall this setup at any time. Experienced users will have many different I/O configurations stored this way as presets for various tasks.

Session

Some of the parameters displayed in the Session Setup window are fixed when you first create the current Pro Tools session—audio file format, sample rate, and bit-depth, for example. The Session Start time setting, however, is important when synchronizing to incoming SMPTE time code (converted to MIDI Time Code by your SMPTE synchronization peripheral), because this is how Pro Tools knows what time-code position corresponds to the beginning of the session's timeline. The frame rate (number of frames per second) you specify for your Pro Tools session must match that of the incoming time code in order for Pro Tools to synchronize properly to the video (or audio) master. As you can see in Figure 8.22, Pro Tools can also *generate* time code with certain peripherals, as well as MIDI Time Code. (See Chapter 11, "Synchronization," for more detailed information about synchronization.) In the HD version of Pro Tools, you can select the Sync I/O or a digital audio input here as the external clock source that will control the sample rate of your audio hardware, as well as internal clock. Clock source changes here are reflected in the Hardware Setup dialog box and vice versa. However, in the M-Powered version of Pro Tools, you instead select this in the audio interface's own control panel software.

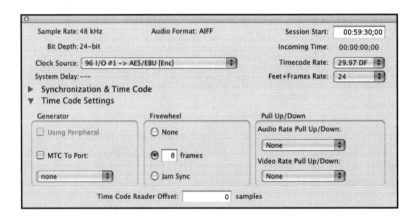

Figure 8.22   Use the Session Setup window to specify a session's frame rate and other options for SMPTE time code. (The HD version is shown here; options vary in LE or M-Powered versions.)

Reminder: When you record from a digital input (S/PDIF coaxial or optical, AES/EBU, TDIF, or ADAT Lightpipe—according to the audio interface you're using), it's common to switch the clock source from internal to the source digital input (unless you're using a central, high-quality clock source as the master; see the following paragraph). This slaves the sample clock of your Pro Tools hardware to that of the specified incoming digital audio signal. OK—so far, so good. Then, as you continue working, maybe your DAT powers itself off (or perhaps you leave it turned off the next time you open this session). If the clock source is still set to the digital input, your audio hardware tries to synchronize to a non-existent external timing reference, and your playback speed may be very slow and peculiar or simply non-existent on M-Powered systems! Just switch the clock source back from the digital input to internal, and you'll be back to normal. (Don't laugh—it may happen to you!)

In larger studios with multiple digital audio devices, however, it's common to use a highly stable, centralized clock source to which the sample rates of all the devices are slaved, in a sort of star configuration. Not only does this improve synchronization as these devices play back together, but the better units can noticeably improve audio quality by reducing jitter and other irregularities in the clock that controls audio sample rates. The "Word Clock and Sync Generators" section of Appendix B, "Add-ons, Extensions, and Cool Stuff for Your Rig," provides a few examples of these master clock devices.

> ❆ **Note: Time Code Formats Around the World**
>
> We discuss SMPTE Time Code in greater detail in Chapter 11, but if you're configuring the Session Setup window, here's a quick reference for where the various frame rates are commonly used:
>
> ❆ For audio-only applications, 30 frames/second non-drop is very common throughout the world (although theoretically you could use any frame rate for syncing two MIDI or audio-only devices).
>
> ❆ For video in North America, parts of Latin America, and the Caribbean, South Korea, Taiwan, and Japan, 29.97 drop or non-drop is the norm for video work (and it makes a *difference* whether it's drop or non-drop; be sure to ask!) because this frame rate is associated with the NTSC color television format used in these countries.
>
> ❆ 25 frames/second is used for video projects in Europe, Africa, Brazil, Argentina, Paraguay, Uruguay, Australia, parts of the Middle East, and most of Asia. The 25 fps frame rate corresponds to the PAL and SECAM television formats common in these regions.
>
> ❆ 24 frames/second is used for film everywhere.

MIDI Submenu

These options affect how MIDI data is sent and received from Pro Tools in general.

MIDI Studio Setup (Mac)

Audio MIDI Setup is a utility included in Mac OS X (that is, any Mac operating system 10.0 or higher) that manages your MIDI configuration—what kind of MIDI interface you're using and how many ports/channels it has, which MIDI controllers and modules are available on your system, where they are attached to the interface, and so on. In Mac versions, the Setup > MIDI Studio menu selection in Pro Tools launches the operating system's Audio MIDI Setup utility. You indicate where your MIDI keyboards and modules are connected by dragging cables between symbols for input/output ports to those of your MIDI interface. You specify whether each is a controller, is multitimbral, what channel it transmits/receives, and other attributes. You can also assign logical names to each MIDI device, which then appear as you select MIDI destinations for tracks within Pro Tools (and any other MIDI-compatible program under Mac OS X). Lastly, in Pro Tools you can also subscribe to a patchname document for your MIDI device so that you can use the MIDI Program Selector button for each MIDI track in the Mix window to select programs for MIDI tracks on the destination device—by *name*, rather than by program number. Note that if your MIDI device doesn't appear in the preconfigured list included with Audio MIDI Setup or Pro Tools itself, there are user-supported Web sites where you can download patchname documents.

MIDI Studio Setup (Windows)

The MIDI Studio Setup window in Windows versions of Pro Tools serves a similar function to the Audio MIDI Setup utility for Macintosh and is discussed further in Chapter 10. Briefly, you can define instruments for each of the external MIDI controllers or modules, also indicating where each is connected to the available ports of your system's MIDI interface. (You can also daisy-chain multiple devices on a single port of the interface, of course, via their In/Out/Thru ports.) You can also assign a descriptive name to each port on your MIDI interface.

All Pro Tools versions 6.7 and higher for Windows allow you to click the MIDI Program Selector button on each MIDI track in the Mix window and assign a MIDI patchname file (.MIDNAM) so that you can select sounds on its destination device by *name* instead of by program number. (The ability to select patchname files is also available in all Mac versions via the Audio MIDI Setup utility provided in the operating system.) As with the patchname files on Macintosh, these are simple text files containing data in the XML language. You can very easily edit these files' contents in Notepad, WinPad, or any word processor capable of saving back to TXT format. This is highly recommended if you've altered the contents of the user banks on the device, for example.

MIDI Beat Clock

Some external drum machines, sequencers inside keyboard workstations, and arpeggiators can synchronize to Pro Tools using this method. Part of the original MIDI data specification, MIDI Beat Clock doesn't contain any absolute time-code (location) information. Instead, it's tempo related, at 24 pulses per 1/4 note (PPQN). In the MIDI Beat Clock dialog box, you simply indicate the MIDI device/output where you want MIDI Clock data to be transmitted. In Appendix D, "Power Tips and Loopy Ideas," you will find a tip about transferring sequences from external MIDI workstations (or drum machines) into Pro Tools.

Input Filter

In this dialog box, you select what types of MIDI data Pro Tools will record and/or pass through. For example, you may choose to disable polyphonic aftertouch received from your MIDI controller if you know that none of the MIDI modules or plug-ins you're using respond to this type of data (especially since polyphonic aftertouch dramatically increases the number of MIDI events recorded on the track). Or, in a scenario where you're recording keyboardists via MIDI during a live performance, you might choose not to record their changes to the master volume control (MIDI controller 7) made for the purpose of onstage monitoring levels.

Input Devices

In larger MIDI configurations, there may be many MIDI devices that you could potentially use as controllers. To minimize the number of selections that appear each time you select the MIDI input source for MIDI and Instrument tracks, you might use this dialog box to disable display of some of those devices.

Click

This menu command simply turns the metronome click on or off—which can also be done by clicking the Metronome Click button in the Transport window. To set up what kind of click sound you want and how it will behave, open the Click/Countoff Options dialog box (shown in Figure 8.23) by double-clicking the Metronome Click or Countoff button in the MIDI Controls section of the Transport window. If you instantiate the Click plug-in on an Aux In (or audio, as well as Instrument) track, it produces a metronome click sound per the tempo map or manual tempo setting in Pro Tools. The Click plug-in itself allows you to choose what sound to use for the metronome click and the relative levels of accented and unaccented beats. If you instead prefer to use some external MIDI device as the source for your click sound, in the

Click/Countoff Options dialog box you'd select its MIDI output and channel and the MIDI note numbers, velocities, and durations to use for accented and unaccented beats. As you can see in the figure, you can enable the click always, only during record, or only during countoff bars. You can also set the desired number of countoff bars (during which only the metronome click sounds) in this dialog box.

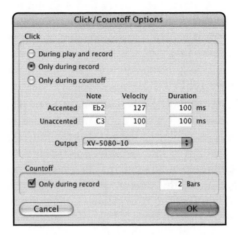

Figure 8.23 You can also open the Click/Countoff Options dialog box by double-clicking the Metronome Click or Countoff button in the Transport window.

Preferences

Many of the items in the Preferences dialog box are self-explanatory, so this section mentions only a few of the most important or poorly understood selections.

Display Preferences

Options in this tab of the Preferences dialog box affect how track data is displayed, and how peak levels and clipping indicators are handled in Pro Tools.

- ❋ **Draw Grids in the Edit Window.** Provides vertical lines as a useful reference while editing. In every edit mode except Grid (where the spacing of these lines is fixed, according to the current grid value), the spacing of the Draw grid depends on the zoom setting and current time units for the main Timebase ruler. For example, as you zoom inward in Minutes:Seconds format, the Draw grid spacing changes from a vertical line every minute to every 30 seconds, 10 seconds, 5 seconds, 1 second, .5 seconds, .1 seconds, .05 seconds, and so on. (Note that you can also toggle Draw grids on and off in the Edit window without going into Preferences; just click the blue title area at the left end of the main Timebase ruler, where its units are indicated.)

- ❋ **Default Track/Region Color Coding.** These two options determine how colors are assigned to tracks and regions. Color-coding for tracks and especially the regions within them helps you keep track of what's going on in a large session. Tracks and MIDI Channels is perhaps the best initial setting; then, as you experiment with use of colors to keep track of your session material (such as Mix and Edit groups, MIDI devices, or location of regions between markers in the timeline), you will discover other useful settings for specific editing tasks or project types.

* **Always Display Marker Colors.** Most users find it useful to enable this option. In the Markers ruler, the color assigned (automatically or manually) to each marker fills the ruler until the next marker is reached in the timeline. If you're using markers to identify sections of a song or scenes in a video, this helps you see at a glance where you are in the session. If the colors simply bother you or you're using a large number of markers for a different purpose, disable this option.

* **Peak Hold.** A small, horizontal yellow line within the Level meters on tracks indicates the highest peak level reached during playback. Three modes can be selected for this feature: 3 Second, Infinite, and None. For most uses, the 3-second setting is practical, although you can also set this to Infinite. The Peak Hold feature helps you monitor how close your levels are getting to maximum, for example. Another approach to monitoring peak levels on audio, Aux In, Instrument, or Master Fader tracks is to Command-click (Ctrl-click in Windows) the Volume/Peak/Delay indicator at the bottom of each track in the Mix window to display peak levels. This peak indicator holds the maximum level attained during playback infinitely until you Option-click (Alt-click in Windows) to clear it. Because it provides an actual numerical value, the peak indicator field is usually a more practical tool than the Level meter display when you are interested in monitoring peak levels.

* **Clip Indication.** Level meters on audio, Aux In, Instrument, and Master Fader tracks feature a top red segment that indicates when 100% is exceeded (which causes clipping, distorting the original audio waveform passing through that track). Some people prefer the 3 Second setting. When set to Infinite, however, the clipping indicator remains lit until you reset it (by clicking it). But remember, you *never* want to see the red clipping indicator light up—on any track (or in any Plug-in window)! Be especially sure to check for this before bouncing out any mixes. This digital type of distortion is undesirable, and you should adjust your gain structure (the audio levels going in and out of each component in the mixing environment) to avoid it.

Operation Preferences

As you become more adept with Pro Tools, you will find it convenient to change some of the options in the Operation tab of the Preferences dialog box for specific projects or even for different phases of the same project.

* **Timeline Insertion Follows Playback.** Ordinarily, when you press Stop after recording or playback, the Transport's Start value (and therefore the position in the timeline where playback will commence next time) remains the same. When you enable Timeline Insertion Follows Playback, the Start value (where playback or the next recording will start) always updates to wherever you last pressed Stop. This is very useful, for example, when

recording spoken-word projects like long narrations or books on tape. When recording live speakers and theatrical presentations, you could stop during pauses and then simply press Record again to pick up recording at the exact point in the session's timeline where you left off.

❈ **Edit Insertion Follows Scrub/Shuttle.** If you frequently use the Scrub tool or a scrub wheel on an external controller to scan through audio regions, there may be situations where you want to enable this item. Similar to the Timeline Insertion Follows Playback option, the time value for the Edit insertion point (indicated by the Main/Sub location indicators of the Edit window) is updated to wherever you stopped scrubbing. When you hold down the Rewind or Fast Forward key (or the 1 or 2 key on the numeric keypad—a very good shortcut to know!), Pro Tools shuttles quickly through the timeline. In a similar manner, when you enable Edit Insertion Follows Scrub/Shuttle in Preferences, the Edit insertion point ends up at whatever point you stopped shuttling.

❈ **Automatically Copy Files on Import.** If the audio files you import into a session already match its bit-depth and sample rate (and don't need to be split into mono pairs), they don't necessarily have to be copied into its Audio Files subfolder unless you deliberately click the Copy button instead of the Add button in the Import Audio dialog box. However, users quickly learn that they can simply double-click source files in this dialog box to add them to the list of regions currently chosen for import. If you generally *do* want to copy files rather than import them from their original locations (especially if they're on a CD-ROM or some other removable media, for example, or in order to avoid potential risk when the same source files are used in multiple sessions), enable this option.

❈ **Use F11 Key for Wait for Note.** As mentioned in Chapter 5, "The Transport Window," when the Wait for MIDI Note function is enabled, after you press Record on the Transport, recording still doesn't begin until the first MIDI event is received (even if you are recording on an audio track). This option enables the F11 key as a shortcut for turning the Wait for Note button on and off. However, Macintosh users should see the caution in Chapter 5 entitled "Macintosh, Pro Tools, and Using Function Keys F9–F12" about reassigning the default function keys for Exposé, which otherwise interfere with the Wait for Note feature in Pro Tools.

❈ **Link Record and Play Faders.** When enabled, any volume changes you make on a track during recording (remember that these do not affect the actual levels recorded to disk!) are retained in Playback mode. Generally, most users prefer to leave this disabled. That way, you can adjust volumes while recording (for example, to hear a part better, or to *reduce* its level if you're otherwise hearing some of the direct signal during recording anyway) without having to worry about this affecting this fader's level in the mix during playback.

❈ **Numeric Keypad Mode.** Although a minority of users prefer the Classic or Shuttle mode for controlling Transport functions with the numeric keypad, try leaving this set to Transport for now; otherwise, all the cool numeric keypad shortcuts given for Transport functions in this book won't work!

❋ **AutoSave.** When the Enable Session File Auto Backup option is enabled, backup copies of your session files are automatically saved while you work. Here, you specify how often this happens and how many auto-saved copies should be saved. These are stored inside your session folder in the Session File Backups subfolder, which is created automatically. Backup copies are numbered, and .bak is added to your session's file name. If your main session file ever becomes corrupted—or if you completely mess it up yourself!—this feature could save a lot of frustration. You can open any auto-saved backup copy of your session with the File > Open Session command. (Pro Tools will add "recovered" to the title bar for this session document to prevent you from confusing it with the original file when/if you save this backup version of the session to disk.) This is a very important feature of Pro Tools that can save the day or your reputation. Unless you have overpowering reasons not to (such as marginal system performance), it is always *strongly* recommended that you enable AutoSave!

❋ **Open Ended Record Allocation.** Unless you are recording extremely long performances (as in live theater or a symphonic piece) and are not sure how long they may last, it is generally prudent to limit the number of minutes here instead of enabling Use All Available Space. For one thing, Pro Tools jumps into Record mode slightly faster because it doesn't have to pre-allocate *all* the free space available on the hard drive being used for each track (assignable via Setups > Disk Allocation) before starting to record. But there's an additional advantage: If Pro Tools should ever hang catastrophically during recording, an entire audio drive can appear full upon restart (on rare occasions), even though you don't see files to account for all that space. (The recording work files that were in progress when the computer froze up may still have disk space allocated, even though they are invisible to the operating system.) With effort, you can remedy all this, but limiting this hard-drive allocation in the first place may help you get Pro Tools back into Record mode more quickly, before your clients get too peevish!

Editing Preferences

You will change some of the settings in the Editing tab of the Preferences dialog box to suit your working style. As with previous tabs in Preferences, only several of the most critical options are mentioned here; more details for the other selections are always available in the *Pro Tools Menu Guide,* supplied with Pro Tools as a PDF document.

❋ **Auto-Name Memory Locations While Playing.** Ordinarily, when you use the numeric keyboard's Enter key to create markers during Play or Record, a dialog box appears. You enter a marker name, specify its properties (absolute or relative, zoom settings, track heights, and other attributes, including comments), and then click OK. If you don't want to go through these steps (for example, because you're creating frequent markers while recording or listening back to a performance and don't want to be distracted), enable this option. Pro Tools automatically assigns new marker names each time you hit the Enter key—"Marker 1," "Marker 2," and so on, *without* the dialog box appearing each time. You can always change marker names, properties, and locations afterward.

- ❊ **Default Fade Settings.** This is fairly self-explanatory; change the default fade shape display format for the fade-in, out, and crossfade types to match the settings you use the most. It's mentioned here only because too many users never seem to get around to changing this preference!
- ❊ **Levels of Undo.** The default setting is 32, and this is best for most users. The Undo History window also greatly facilitates the process of stepping back through many editing operations to a previous state of the session. The number of steps available in the Undo History window is also determined by this Preference setting.

MIDI Preferences

Most users will find the default settings here to be a good starting point—although you may eventually set your own default Note On velocity for when you create notes with the Pencil tool, for instance, or enable Use MIDI to Tap Tempo. Here, we mention just two key options in the MIDI tab of the Preferences dialog box.

- ❊ **Global MIDI Playback Offset.** Especially when using external MIDI instruments, you may find that there is a more or less fixed amount of delay with respect to the actual start point of the note events on your MIDI and Instrument tracks. It does take some small interval of time for MIDI events to be transmitted from your MIDI interface, plus some degree of analog-to-digital conversion delay that is added when you monitor these external sources through inputs on your audio interface. More significant, however, is that, after receiving a Note On event, many MIDI keyboards and modules can take quite a few milliseconds to actually get around to triggering an actual sound in response. Setting a negative playback offset globally for MIDI tracks here in Preferences can be the easiest way to compensate for this. Nevertheless, remember that the MIDI Track Offsets dialog box (discussed in this chapter, under the Event menu) always allows you to set offsets for each MIDI or Instrument track individually.
- ❊ **Default Thru Instrument.** Here you select the MIDI output and channel that appear by default in new MIDI and Instrument tracks. This is also the destination that is used when you preview MIDI regions. This feature was introduced in Pro Tools 7—just as you can Option-click (Alt-click in Windows) on an audio region to preview it in the Region List, doing this on a MIDI region will play it through the Default Thru Instrument destination. Perhaps the most useful option is to enable Follows First Selected MIDI Track in this pop-up menu. That way, you can first select a MIDI or Instrument track that is assigned to a destination with an appropriate-sounding patch, and that will be used for previewing MIDI regions in the Region List.

Window Menu

The selections in this menu are for showing/hiding the various windows of Pro Tools. Many are discussed elsewhere in this book and won't be covered here, but several are worth special mention.

Task Manager Window

Many tasks in Pro Tools occur in the background—for example, fade creation, relinking to files that are missing or were moved since the last time a Pro Tools session was saved, copying source files as you import track data from other Pro Tools session documents, and so on. All of these have some effect on your system's performance at any given moment, so it's handy to be able to check what's going on. Be sure to check out the options in the pop-up menu in the upper-left corner of the Task Manager window. For one thing, you can cancel, pause, or resume individual tasks.

If a complex project is already heavily taxing the capabilities of your system as you edit and play audio, pausing or canceling these background tasks may be a short-term solution. In particular, though, notice the last item in this pop-up menu, Pause During Playback. This is a global preference that prevents background tasks from diverting resources while in Record and Playback modes. If your system is already underpowered for the kind of projects you work on, be sure to enable this option.

Be sure to explore the *DigiBase Guide*, a PDF document provided with Pro Tools, which covers features of both DigiBase (all versions) and DigiBase Pro (included with HD and previous TDM versions–can be added to LE via the DV Toolkit 2 option). It provides much more detailed explanations (over 80 pages worth) of the Task, Workspace, Project, and Catalog browser windows.

> ❄ **Tip: Status Indicators for Timeline and Session in the Edit Window**
>
> Above the Audio Regions List in the Edit window, two indicators appear for Timeline and Session. When the Timeline indicator is green, it means that all files used by regions within track playlists are properly linked and available for playback. Otherwise, this indicator is red, meaning that some files need to be located and relinked. When the Session indicator is green, it means that all source files referenced by the session (both audio or video) are properly linked and available for playback, whether they are currently being used within a track or not.

Workspace Browser Window

This window is used together with the Project browser window, discussed in the next section. The Workspace and Project browser windows are the two "browsers" for the DigiBase technology, an audio (and video) file database engine that is an integral part of the Pro Tools platform. (The DigiBase Pro version included with HD systems and the DV Toolkit 2 option for LE systems offers additional features, including a third Catalog browser window.) At the simplest level, the Workspace window provides a bird's eye view of all eligible disk volumes for audio playback and recording on your system, their capacity, and how much space is currently available. You can also specify whether each of your disk volumes should be used for playback, record (and playback), or for transfer only—meaning that you can view and copy files from that disk but not play back audio files from it in real time. Within this window, you can browse the entire folder/file hierarchy on each disk without leaving Pro Tools, as well as view audio file attributes and audition audio files. You can rename, duplicate, and delete folders and files in the Workspace window. You can even add comments about these audio files that will be visible in this window, within this or other Pro Tools sessions.

From the Workspace window, you can drag the audio files (seen in their original disk locations) directly to the Region List or onto an audio track with a matching number of channels (for example, mono or stereo). You can import audio files into Pro Tools from audio CDs by dragging tracks directly from the Workspace window to the Region List or onto a stereo audio track in the Edit window. If you want to automatically create a new track, either drag the file from the Workspace window into the Tracks List at the left edge of the Edit window or hold down the Shift key as you drag it directly into the Edit window's track display area.

You can also view standard MIDI files in the Workspace window and import them by dragging them into the Region List. If you instead drag the MIDI file into the Tracks list (when visible at the left edge of the Edit window), an appropriate number of new MIDI tracks is created. An Import MIDI Settings dialog box allows you to choose whether to import the existing tempo map in that file, and whether to delete existing MIDI/Instrument tracks and/or MIDI regions. There's a Search button (the one with the magnifying glass) in the Workspace and Project browser windows. You can search for files by name on multiple volumes (including searches with wildcard characters and the Boolean operators OR/AND), by kind (folder, audio, video, session, OMF, AAF, MIDI, or region group), and by modification date. You can constrain searches to certain volumes and folders, or you can scan the entire system simultaneously. With DigiBase Pro in Pro Tools HD (or with the DV Toolkit 2 option for Pro Tools LE), you can additionally search by attributes in the other columns of these windows, such as file format, sample rate, bit-depth, creation date, and comments. This is powerful stuff!

> ❋ **Tip: Don't Use Your System Volume for Audio Recording**
>
> In the Workspace browser window, you can designate each of the disk volumes on your system (whether entire disks or logical partitions on a single physical disk) for audio playback and/or recording (P or R), or transfer only (T). Be sure that your system volume (the disk or partition containing the operating system used to boot up the computer and usually most of the program files as well) is set to Transfer to prevent session audio files from ever getting stored there as the result of recording or editing operations.

Project Browser Window

This window (shown in Figure 8.24) provides powerful features for organizing complex projects and for working in collaboration with other people on large Pro Tools sessions. It also helps you keep track of which files are used in the current session, including their disk locations and other attributes. For example, for each source audio file, columns in the Project browser window can display its name, a waveform graphic with an Audition button, its absolute duration, a user-editable file and database comments, creation and modification dates, the number of channels, file size, format, sample rate, bit-depth, and the original and user timestamp information. Very importantly, the full disk/folder path to this file's location on your computer system is shown in the Project browser window, with a unique file ID assigned by

Pro Tools. When you find audio files missing upon reopening a Pro Tools session (perhaps because you changed their disk or folder locations or moved this project from one Pro Tools system to another), the Project browser window provides tools for relinking references from regions used in that session to the correct source files. The unique file IDs that Pro Tools assigns to each audio file you import make it much easier to locate them afterward in the Project browser window, even if there are other files on the same disks with similar or identical names.

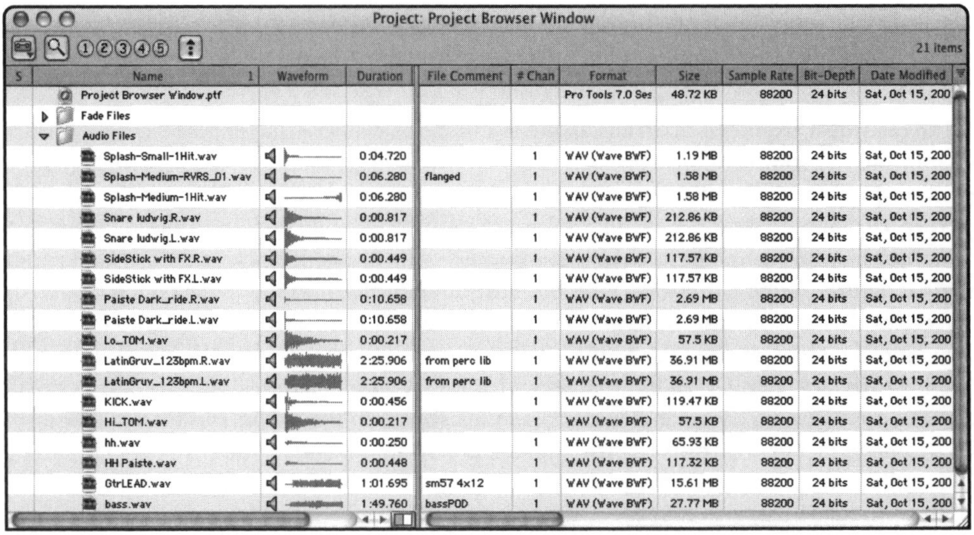

Figure 8.24 The Project browser window.

❄ **CSi: The Project Browser in Action**

Check out the movie tutorial by Steve Thomas on *Pro Tools 7 CSi Master* about the Project browser for a real-life example of how the Project browser window helps you relink to missing files (that is, files that have changed locations or were transferred from a different disk or system).

❄ **Tip: Find and Import Files Directly from Workspace, Project Browser Windows**

After you locate an audio file you want to use, you can drag it from either one of these DigiBase browser windows directly into the Region List or a Pro Tools track (with a matching number of channels) to import it into your current session. To create a brand-new audio track at the same time (similar to using File > Import Audio to Track), either drag the audio files into the Tracks list, or hold down the Shift key as you drag the region to a specific timeline location in the track display area. (You can also preview and import source tracks on audio CDs from these windows in the same manner.)

Catalog Browser Window (HD Versions Only)

Catalogs are a feature of DigiBase Pro, included only in HD/TDM versions of Pro Tools (or via the Music Production Toolkit option for LE and M-Powered). Items in a catalog represent references to files (like a list of favorite shortcuts or aliases) that reside in many different disk/folder locations. You can store and recall many different catalogs for convenience when locating files in your Pro Tools sessions. You can add files (or entire folders) to the currently displayed catalog by dragging them directly into the Catalog browser window from either of the other two DigiBase browser windows. Alternatively, you can create a new catalog by selecting a group of files in one of these other browser windows and then using the Create Catalog from Selection command in the browser window's pop-up local menu. You can also copy all the files referenced in a catalog to a new disk location by dragging the catalog in the Workspace browser window onto another disk volume. Lastly, like the other two DigiBase browser windows, you can also drag and drop catalog items directly into the Region List or Track List, or onto audio, MIDI, or Instrument tracks in the Edit window.

Big Counter

This item opens a large display of the current playback location, visible from across the room as you perform. Time units in the Big Counter window reflect those of the main time scale (the active ruler, whose time units are also reflected in the Main location indicator). You can type new values into the Big Counter window's fields to change the play location, or click and drag to scroll numerical values in any of its columns up or down. For some reason, a lot of users seem to overlook the Big Counter; this is a shame, because it's *very* convenient!

Automation Enable

This window (shown in Figure 8.25) allows you to suspend *all* automation in a Pro Tools session or to individually enable/disable recording for each type of automation data (volume, pan, mute, and plug-in parameters; level, pan, and mute for sends).

Figure 8.25 Here, we've used the Automation Enable window to disable automation completely in this session. You can also separately enable or disable each type of automation data for recording.

> ❄ **Tip: Disabling Automation on Individual Tracks**
>
> As described in Chapter 6, "The Edit Window," you can set the Automation Mode selector for any individual track to Auto Off, disabling *all* automation on that track. You can also suspend any *specific* automation parameter on individual tracks. Use the track's Display Format selector to view that type of automation (for example, the level of send "a," which you may have routed to a bus and Aux In where a delay effect was inserted). Next, Command-click (Ctrl-click in Windows) on this track's Display Format selector (containing the name of the currently displayed automation parameter—send "a" in this case). The name will be dimmed, indicating that this type of automation data no longer plays back. Command-click (Ctrl-click in Windows) the selector again to re-enable playback of that automation type on this track.
>
> Reminder: In the Output window for any track, a Safe button for automation helps prevent accidental writing of automation into that track.

Memory Locations

Take some time to master the use of memory locations, even if you're already a Pro Tools user! Memory locations are timeline positions; they can be either *marker* memory locations (a single point) or *selection* memory locations (a range). Additionally, both these types of memory locations can store any of the following properties: current zoom settings, pre-/post-roll times, track show/hide state, track heights, or Mix/Edit group enables. (You can even create General Properties memory locations with their time properties set to None, just to recall these other types of properties.) Both markers and selections can refer to absolute time locations or Bars|Beats values (whose location in absolute time varies according to the current tempo settings). Memory locations support adding comments up to 255 characters long, which you can optionally display in the Memory Locations window.

Markers

Markers are memory locations that identify single points in time. They appear on the Markers ruler (in the timeline at the top of the Edit window)—yellow diamonds for absolute time references, and yellow chevrons for relative time references to Bars:Beats. You might use markers to flag the verses and choruses of a song or a scene transition in a video or film project. Click the button at the left end of the Markers ruler to create a new marker (or selection) at the current position, or simply press the Enter key on the numeric keypad. Clicking on any marker symbol in the Markers ruler moves the playback cursor to that position and also recalls any view properties stored with that marker. You can click one marker and then Shift-click another to select the entire range between them on all tracks. You can also drag markers to new positions within the Markers ruler (and their movement is affected by Grid mode). You can reposition markers numerically by clicking them while in Spot edit mode. You can change the properties of a marker by double-clicking it, either in the Markers ruler itself or in the Memory Locations window (look ahead to Figure 8.26).

> ❋ **Tip: Creating Markers on the Fly**
>
> In either Play or Record mode, you can create marker memory locations by pressing Enter on the numeric keypad. This is handy, for example, to mark sections of a song or narration even as it's being recorded. (Remember, you can always drag markers around in the Markers ruler to change their locations afterward or use Spot edit mode to click and change marker locations numerically.) While recording a performer, you may notice mistakes, noises, or other items that you'll need to fix afterward. When this happens, create markers on the fly so that you can easily locate those locations later. If you don't want to deal with the New Marker dialog box as you do this, enable the Auto-Name Memory Locations When Playing option in the Editing tab of the Preferences dialog box.

Selections

This type of memory location stores the currently highlighted range in the Edit window's timeline as either an absolute time reference or as Bars:Beats relative to the current Tempo setting. A selection can include multiple tracks. For example, if you need to bounce a selection to disk more than once, create a Selection memory location for it and call it "Bounce." Or if you find yourself repeatedly highlighting a section of music for editing, perhaps the bridge of a song, and like to view it at a specific zoom level (for detailed vocal editing perhaps, or so that eight bars fits into the Edit window), create a Selection memory location that also recalls the current zoom setting. While recording punch-ins by selecting the range within the track where recording should occur, it is also a good idea to create a Selection memory location for the punch-in range. If you accidentally deselect the punch-in range while recording and listening back to multiple takes, you can simply recall the Memory Location. Unlike markers, selection memory locations do not appear in the Markers ruler. The Memory Locations window (shown in Figure 8.26) lets you view all markers and selections in your session, change their properties, rename them, or double-click to move the Pro Tools playback cursor directly to that location.

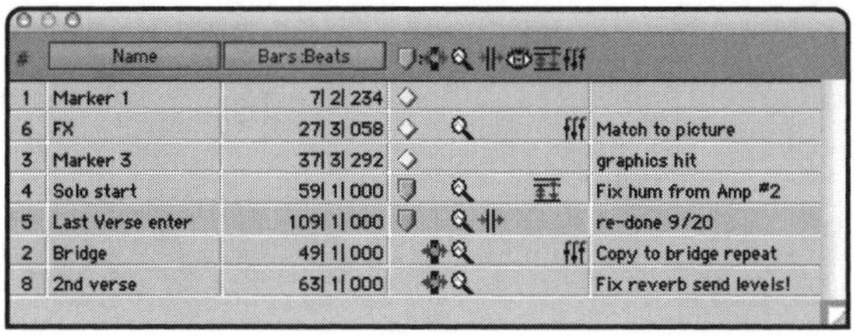

Figure 8.26 You can use Memory Locations to create markers or to recall selections (along with their zoom settings, track heights, and other attributes, if desired).

Universe (HD Systems Only)

The Universe window is a graphical overview of all the tracks in the current session, for quick navigation to any point. Audio and MIDI regions appear as horizontal lines. (Aux In and Master Fader tracks simply appear as blank strips.) The shaded area indicates what's currently shown in the Edit window (as determined by the current zoom setting, track size, and so on). If your tracks don't all fit into the Edit window at their current sizes, clicking in the Universe window scrolls the current contents of the Edit window horizontally or vertically.

Color Palette

You can open the Color Palette window (shown in Figure 8.27) via this command in the Windows menu. When color strips are visible in the Mix and/or Edit windows, double-clicking these strips also opens this floating window. You can also assign colors to currently selected tracks and to regions and region groups, either within tracks or in the Region List. You can also assign colors to Mix and Edit groups; these color assignments will appear in the pop-up group indicator for each track in the Mix window.

Color-coding options in the Display tab of the Preferences dialog box allow you to automatically assign colors to tracks according to track type, group assignments, MIDI device, and channel assignments. For regions, you can also automatically assign colors per all of the above plus track color, Region List color, and marker locations.

Figure 8.27 Use the Color Palette to assign colors to tracks, individual regions, groups, or markers.

If you assign colors to marker memory locations (but not selection memory locations), these colors are shown in the Markers ruler of the Edit window. (Always Show Marker Colors, in the Display tab of the Preferences dialog box, must be enabled in order for marker colors to be displayed.) The range from one marker until the next (or until the end of the session timeline, if it's the last marker) is highlighted in the preceding marker's color, and Pro Tools automatically assigns different colors as adjacent markers are created in the timeline (which you can change afterward). This is especially useful when editing large sessions, because even when you're at a high zoom level for editing events, you'll know you're within a specific scene or song section because you can see the color you assigned to that marker in the Markers ruler.

Most useful, perhaps, is that in the Edit window, you can use the Color Palette to manually assign colors to selected *regions* within tracks. This is a huge productivity booster—as anyone who has managed sessions with scores of individual loops, sound effects, vocal, or guitar segments within a single track can tell you. For example, by assigning colors before copying and pasting regions around, it's much easier to identify at a glance all the occurrences of a repeated item or the smaller regions created by cutting up a much longer one. Color-coding your source regions is also very helpful when *comping* (compositing) a vocal track from multiple source takes. Again, in Preferences you can choose to automatically color-code regions by track and/or MIDI channels/devices, by what group their track belongs to, or by location between markers.

Undo History

Another very welcome feature! The Undo History allows you to step back through various operations (edits, menu commands, and so on—anything that is immediately reversible via the Edit > Undo command). Pro Tools supports 32 levels of undo. In this columnar display, you can also choose to display the hours and minutes for each editing and recording action you've carried out (the Creation Time), as shown in Figure 8.28. Backing up to a previous state can be as easy as clicking the appropriate position in the Undo History window's list of actions.

The Options selector allows you to manually clear the Undo Queue; however, certain editing actions also clear it automatically, such as deleting or importing tracks or using one of the Select Unused Regions commands in the local menu of the Region List.

Figure 8.28   The Undo History window lets you step back through multiple editing operations rather than only one step backward as with the Edit menu's Undo command.

Disk Space, System Usage

The System Usage window shows approximately how much of your system's processing capacity the current session is using: the CPU, disk usage, and the computer's PCI bus (which is relevant if your system includes Pro Tools audio cards). On HD systems, the System Usage window (shown in Figure 8.29) can also show how DSP resources on any HD audio cards are currently allocated to mixing and plug-in processing tasks.

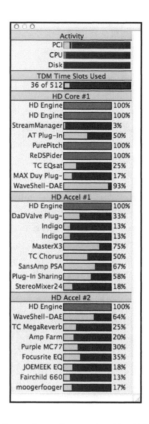

Figure 8.29 The System Usage window—shown here, a Pro Tools | HD 2 system with two HD Accel cards.

Summary

As stated at the beginning of this chapter, only the most important menu selections are high-lighted here. Further information about these menu selections (and others we've omitted) is available in PDF documents provided with the program, including the *Pro Tools Reference Guide, Keyboard Shortcuts, DigiBase Guide,* and especially, the *Pro Tools Menu Guide.* It is well worth your time to explore these.

The next chapter explores plug-ins, inserts, and sends in more detail; the general topic of digital signal processing (DSP); RTAS and TDM audio plug-in architectures and ReWire; plus some tips for getting the most power out of the audio resources your Pro Tools system provides. Read on!

9 } Plug-ins, Inserts, and Sends

This chapter looks a little more closely at how audio can be processed and routed within Pro Tools' software-based mixing environment. Plug-ins, inserts, and sends are discussed in Chapter 2, "Pro Tools Terms and Concepts," and especially in Chapter 7, "The Mix Window," but this chapter will help deepen your understanding of how audio moves around in the virtual signal-routing environment of Pro Tools. If you are completely new to Pro Tools, be sure to read Chapter 7 first, which introduces you to the elements in the Mix window; this chapter expands further on the concepts presented there.

Signal Routing in Pro Tools

Appendix E, "Signal Flow in Pro Tools," provides diagrams of audio signal flow within Pro Tools. While recording audio onto a track in Pro Tools, the signal flow is often as simple as this: An input source is connected to one of the analog or digital input channels on your audio hardware and then is recorded straight to hard disk by a record-enabled audio track that was assigned to that channel.

Notice that unless your Pro Tools audio hardware has physical controls for input gain, you must adjust your levels *at the source*. The Mbox 2 (like its predecessor the Mbox) has two front-panel gain knobs for its two analog inputs, because these incorporate microphone preamps prior to the ADC (analog-to-digital converter). For similar reasons, the Digi 002 and 002 Rack have individual gain adjustment on the four mic/line inputs, while their line inputs 5–8 are switchable between fixed +4 dBu and 10 dBV levels. Among the M-Audio audio interfaces for Pro Tools M-Powered, all the current FireWire models provide front-panel knobs for preamp gain adjustment on at least some of their channels.

❋ **CSi: Overdubs and Loop Record**

In the CD-ROM at the back of this book, the *Overdubs and Loop Record* sample movie tutorial, excerpted from the *Pro Tools 7 CSi Starter* CD-ROM, discusses input selection, source gain, and monitoring levels on audio tracks. It then walks you through the basic steps of recording a new audio part, punching in a

> new section within existing material, and looping a range of bars while you record multiple takes (as well as how to use the pop-up Takes List in the Edit window).

As far as what you *hear* on a track, the signal path is pretty much the same whether its signal source is an audio track's input in record-enable mode, an audio file from disk, or the selected input on an Aux In. It goes like this: Input audio goes through the Inserts section (after which it can optionally be directed to *pre*-fader send destinations), then through the track's main Volume fader (*a gain stage*), and then optionally to any *post*-fader send destinations, through the Pan control, and finally to the track's current output assignment (either physical outputs or a mixing bus within Pro Tools).

Figure 9.1 shows typical signal flow for an audio track in Record and Playback modes. There are also several ways audio tracks can be set to monitor their selected input even when *not* in Record mode. For example, enabling Track > Input Only Monitor affects all audio tracks, and on TDM systems, a Track Input Enable button on each audio track switches it to Input Monitor mode during normal playback, even if it already contains audio regions.

> ❊ **Note: Track Volume Faders Do Not Affect Record Level**
>
> While recording on an audio track, its Volume fader and Mute button have *no effect* on the input level to the audio hardware. This gives you the freedom to adjust monitoring levels while recording, either for your control-room mix or for the comfort of the performer(s). Unless Preferences > Operation > Link Record and Play Faders is enabled, when the track is no longer record-enabled, its Volume fader returns to its previous playback level. The Volume fader on audio tracks (as well as Aux In, Instrument, and Master Fader tracks) can either decrease the track's level or apply as much as +12 dB of gain boost.

> ❊ **Note: About the Level Meters in Pro Tools**
>
> When Options > Pre Fader Metering is enabled, during *playback*, Level meters on audio tracks, Aux Ins, Instrument tracks, and Master Faders always reflect *post-insert, pre-fader* levels. In Pre-Fader Metering mode, the displayed levels on tracks *will* reflect any gain changes resulting from their inserts or plug-in effects but are unaffected by current Volume fader settings (or the track's Mute button).
>
> When Pre-Fader Metering is *not* enabled (the default), meters are post-fader. In this metering mode, if you reduce a track's main Volume fader, this is reflected in its Level meter.
>
> Whenever tracks are *record-enabled,* (or when Track > Input Only Monitor is enabled), the track Level meters display *pre-insert* levels at the track's input.

Input Channels

As explained in Chapter 2, to avoid confusion, this book distinguishes between channels for input/output of audio on the audio interface and tracks within the software itself—even though in the Mix window, tracks look like channel strips on a conventional mixing board. (Even

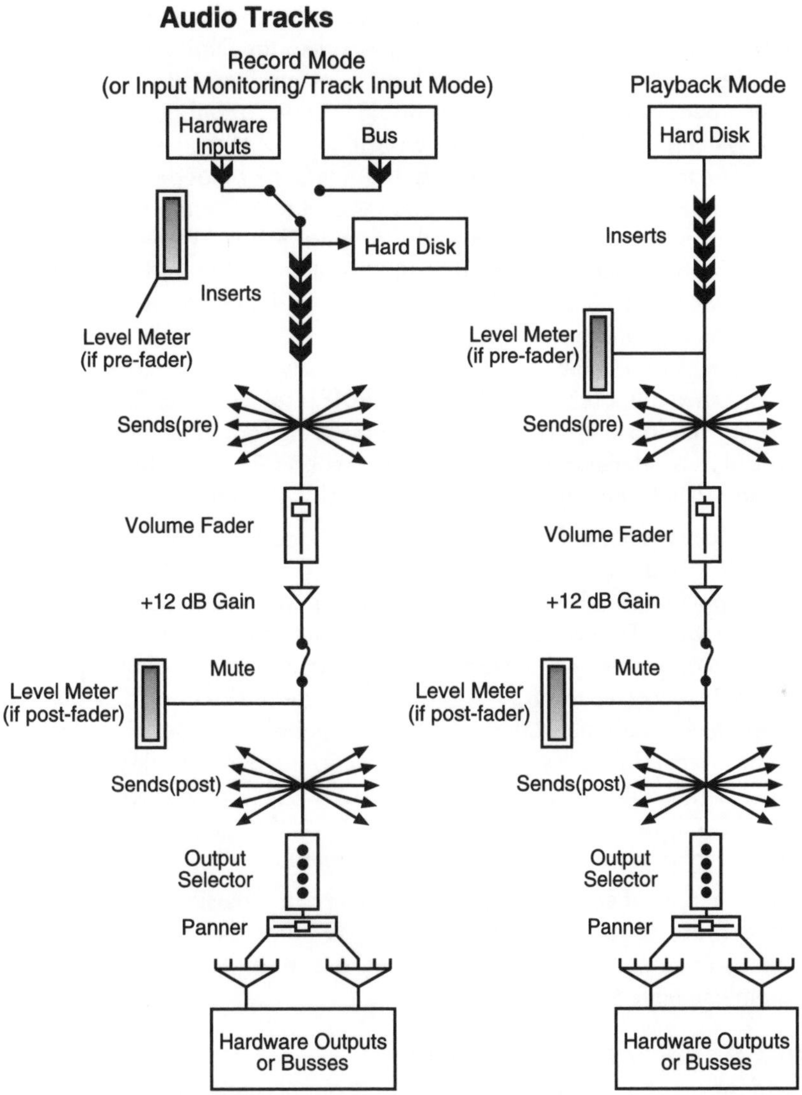

Audio Tracks

Figure 9.1   Virtual signal path for an audio track, in Record mode versus Playback mode.

though the Pro Tools documentation often refers to "channel strips" in the Mix window, when describing Pro Tools and other digital audio workstation software, we make an effort to call these "mixer strips" so that it's clear that we're talking about a view of a track's virtual signal path and not necessarily an input/output path to or from the outside world.) Every Pro Tools system has some finite number of actual audio input channels on the hardware (either digital or analog). Some systems, such as the original Mbox (or the Mbox 2 and M-Audio FireWire

Solo, if you aren't set up for using their S/PDIF digital I/O simultaneously with the analog I/O), only offer two input/output channels. Others, like the Digi 002/002 Rack and some other M-Audio hardware, provide a larger but still predetermined (non-expandable) maximum number of inputs. Finally, greatly expandable hardware configurations are possible with Pro Tools|HD systems (and the previous generation of 24|Mix systems for Pro Tools 6). Whatever system configuration you're using, the number of independent channels on your audio hardware determines the maximum number of discrete audio sources you can record simultaneously. For example, even though the original Mbox has two analog audio inputs plus digital input and output in S/PDIF format, it is still a 2×2 interface. The digital output always mirrors channels 1–2, and either the analog or digital inputs can be selected in the Hardware Setup dialog; unlike the Mbox 2 or FireWire Solo, you can't use both at the same time. In contrast, the 96i I/O for Pro Tools|HD systems is a 16×2 interface; it offers 16 input channels and only two output channels (digital S/PDIF is selectable for inputs 1–2 and always actively mirroring analog outputs 1–2). Of course, Pro Tools|HD supports multiple audio interfaces (as did its predecessors, Pro Tools 24|Mix and Pro Tools III); they're expandable systems that can reach large numbers of I/O channels by adding more audio interfaces.

Some audio interfaces—such as Digidesign's Digi 002 and Digi 002 Rack, Digi 001, 96 I/O, 192 I/O, and 192 Digital I/O, as well as M-Audio's FireWire 1814—offer ADAT Lightpipe connectors for input/output of digital audio. Each Lightpipe connector supports up to eight channels of audio via a Toslink optical cable. These input channels can be used *simultaneously* with any analog inputs on the interface. For example, on a Digi 002 or FireWire 1814 interface, you could record up to 18 separate source channels by using all eight analog inputs, the eight Lightpipe channels, plus the stereo S/PDIF digital input. But of course, digital inputs require a digital source. Unless the device you're recording or monitoring is already equipped with a Lightpipe digital output (like some keyboards, effects, and multichannel mic preamps), an additional device is required to convert its signal to Lightpipe prior to your Pro Tools interface if you need to take advantage of all these simultaneous optical and analog/digital inputs.

Remember that the input of each audio track or Aux In can be assigned to any available audio input path on your Pro Tools system, and that the I/O Setup dialog box allows you to define these input paths (mono, stereo, or multichannel, according to which system you're using) and assign them convenient names.

Audio and Auxiliary Input Tracks

Tracks are discrete audio pathways in the virtual signal-routing environment of Pro Tools. Obviously, in ordinary Play mode, an audio track's source signal derives from the playback of audio data (within files on one of your system's disks) that is referenced by the audio regions within the track. With Track > Auto Input Monitor enabled, whenever an audio track's Record Enable button is lit (or during punch-in recording), the selected input source is monitored through it.

For audio and Aux In tracks, the input source can be either a physical audio input path on your hardware or one of Pro Tools' internal busses. (A *bus* is a utility pathway for routing audio signals around within Pro Tools; for more information, see the "Busses" section later in this chapter, and also Chapter 2 for a basic definition.) Figure 9.2 shows the signal path for an Auxiliary Input.

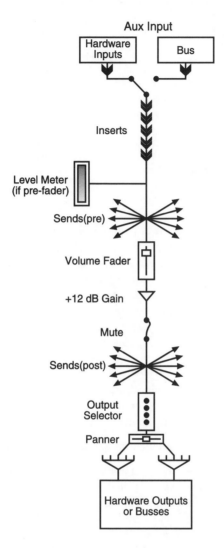

Figure 9.2 Virtual signal path for an Auxiliary Input track. If available, you can select any enabled auxiliary outputs from software instrument plug-ins in the session as an input source.

❄ **Tip: Input Sources for Audio Tracks**

In addition to hardware inputs (or audio regions from hard disk during normal playback, of course), a Pro Tools mixing bus can also be the selected input for any audio track or Auxiliary Input track. On audio tracks, the bus can be used as a front end during recording, combining a larger number of inputs from external sources (if you have a multichannel audio interface, as opposed to the stereo-only Mbox). Here's an example: You might create a stereo Aux In for each pair of physical audio inputs on your audio interface where external MIDI modules are connected. If you like, compression, EQ, or any other insert effect could be instantiated on each Aux In. Assign the main outputs from all these Aux Ins to bus pair 15–16, for instance. Select that bus pair as the input source for a stereo audio track, and record to disk. Creating this stereo audio submix from your MIDI instruments could have several advantages. First, this session will be usable on another Pro Tools system without the MIDI gear attached. Second, you don't have to worry about reestablishing audio connections, gain structure, and so on if you ever reopen this session in the distant future. Lastly, using this submix instead of monitoring the outputs from these external MIDI devices (either temporarily or permanently) frees up all those inputs on your audio interface for recording other sources.

Whatever the source of the audio (audio data being read from disk on an audio track, an audio input or bus being recorded and/or monitored on an audio track, the selected audio input or bus being monitored on an Aux In, or a software instrument via an RTAS or DigiReWire plug-in in the track's Inserts section), the controls on audio and Aux In tracks are otherwise very similar. An Aux In track has no Record button, of course, because it cannot contain audio regions. Both track types can be mono (one audio channel), stereo, or multi-channel (for surround mixing, on TDM systems only). If you insert a mono-to-stereo plug-in at any point on a mono audio track or Aux In, however, the remainder of its audio path becomes stereo, including both the subsequent insert slots and its main output stage. The main output from each audio track or Aux In can be assigned to one or more physical output paths or, again, to any of Pro Tools' internal mixing busses. As a matter of fact, if you hold down the Control key (Start key in Windows) as you reopen the pop-up selector, you can assign *additional* output destinations from any of these tracks.

Instrument Tracks

Instrument tracks (which didn't exist in versions prior to Pro Tools 7) combine aspects of an Aux In and a MIDI track. As seen in the Mix window, Instrument tracks look fairly similar to Aux Ins—with a keyboard icon that indicates their track type. (However, like MIDI tracks, they have a Patch Select button and a record-enable button for MIDI instead of audio.) Instrument tracks also have an audio input selector. Many instrument plug-ins don't actually use this input audio signal, in which case it is simply cut off at the point where an instrument plug-in is instantiated in that track's signal chain. In the Edit window, however, Instrument tracks are treated much like MIDI tracks. (Some of their audio-related view options in the Edit window, like Inserts, Sends, and so on, aren't available on a MIDI track. Also, audio parameters such as pan and volume can be graphically edited on an Instrument track, as on an Aux In.) One of the main reasons the Instrument track feature was created was so that, for single-timbre instrument plug-ins, a single track would allow MIDI event display in the Edit window and a channel-strip view of its signal path in the Mix window. For multitimbral plug-ins, however, you would route the MIDI output from various conventional MIDI tracks to that plug-in—whether it resides on an Instrument track, Aux In, or audio track.

In addition to the traditional I/O , Inserts, Sends, and Delay Compensation views for tracks in the Mix or Edit window, version 7 added yet another: Instrument. This section, which is the topmost in the Mix window, affects the active software instrument plug-in on each track (Instrument, audio, or Aux In). It provides selectors for the track's MIDI input and output (allowing the Instrument track's MIDI data to be additionally routed to another destination), volume, pan, and mute, plus a small LED and velocity meter for MIDI data on that track. On an Instrument track, inserts and sends (which are mentioned in the next two sections) work identically to Aux Ins and audio tracks. (Unless the instrument plug-in actually uses the track's selected input audio signal in some way, however, you wouldn't place any insert effects prior to it in the track's signal chain.)

❄ **Caution: Enable Audio Inputs on Your Instrument Tracks**

Some instrument plug-ins actually use the selected audio input for the Instrument track as part of their processing (although most won't). In some cases, however, you may find that if you *don't* select some physical input on your interface (instead of None—even if you know that the selected instrument plug-in doesn't use that source audio in any way), the instrument plug-in won't sound.

Inserts

From each track's selected input (or disk-playback source, in the case of audio tracks), the signal pathway passes through five insert points. Effects can be placed onto these inserts, in the form of software modules called *plug-ins*. Alternatively, hardware I/O inserts can be spliced into these access points, using physical inputs and outputs on the audio hardware to route a track's audio to and from external devices at this point in its signal path. (This is obviously a more practical alternative on a multichannel audio interface than one of the 2×2 configurations!) In either case, for audio tracks, Aux Ins, and Instrument tracks, inserts are always *pre*-fader, which means that the level of the signal passing through the Inserts section is entirely unaffected by the track's main Volume fader or volume automation. In contrast (as mentioned in Chapter 7), inserts on Master Faders are always *post*-fader.

A track's entire signal passes through each of the inserts, and each insert on the track affects the signal level entering the following one; they're in a series designated "a" through "e." It is possible to overload any one of them and produce clipping if you are careless about the levels on the previous insert!

Sends

As explained in Chapter 2, a *send* is an access point from which a track's audio can be routed to a secondary audio pathway, independently of the main output assignment for the track. In Pro Tools, ten sends are available for each audio track, Aux In, and Instrument track. They're organized into two groups of five: "a" through "e," and "f" through "j," whose display in the Mix and Edit windows can be enabled separately. Sends can be mono or stereo (even from a mono source track); stereo sends incorporate a Pan slider. On TDM systems, sends can also be created to multichannel paths. The destination of each send might be a single physical audio output on your hardware (or multiple outputs, if the send is to a stereo or multichannel path), or more typically a mono or stereo (or multichannel) bus within Pro Tools. If a send is set to *pre*-fader (that is, its Pre button is enabled), its signal source is directly after the output of the Inserts section in the track's audio pathway. The level of a pre-fader send is therefore not affected by the main Volume setting or Mute button for the track. In contrast, the level of a post-fader send (the default send type) is also reduced whenever the track's main Volume fader is lowered, because it follows the fader in the track's signal path.

Typically, when you enable a new send in Pro Tools, its level is automatically set to the absolute minimum, −infinity; no level is sent at all (although you can change this setting in Preferences). In the Output window that automatically opens for this new send, drag the Level slider upward to increase the audio volume being sent to that send's destination. Option-click a send's Level fader (or Alt-click it in Windows) to set it directly to 0 dB (instead of the initial default on a new send, −∞). In Pro Tools 7, the capability was added to Option-drag (or Alt-drag on Windows) to copy sends from one track to another.

Again, the send's audio source can be either directly after the Inserts section of the source track on pre-fader sends (and therefore after any software instrument or ReWire channels in that track's signal path) or after the main track Volume fader (and Mute button) on post-fader sends. Each option has its uses, as you will see elsewhere in this book. An Output window (see Figure 9.3 for mono and stereo versions) opens when you click on any send to edit its parameters.

> ✳ **CSi: Sends Can Be Automated, Too**
>
> In the CD-ROM at the back of this book, the sample movie tutorial excerpted from *Pro Tools 7 CSi Starter*, "*Automation Overview* shows you the process of automating a send, switching a send from post-fader (the default) to pre-fader, using the Output window's Safe button to avoid accidentally overwriting a send's automation data, and graphically editing the automation for a send.

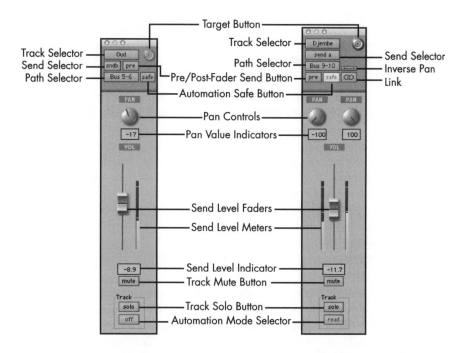

Figure 9.3 Output windows for sends: Track Selector (switches to any other audio track or Aux In without leaving this window), Send Selector (switches among 10 sends on the current track), Path Selector (destination for each send—busses or physical outputs). When the Target icon is dimmed (as in this mono Output window), an Output window remains open even as you open others. The source track's Solo and Automation Mode Selector buttons are duplicated in its Output windows.

Busses

A *bus* is an auxiliary audio pathway available in Pro Tools. Among other things, you can use it as a sort of pipeline for combining or routing audio signals from multiple inputs, track outputs, or sends to a common destination. Pro Tools LE and M-Powered versions provide 32 busses (compared to 16 in versions prior to 7.0), while TDM versions have 128 (64 busses in versions prior to 6.9). You can use busses individually in mono or as stereo pairs: 1–2, 3–4, 5–6, and so on. Additionally, you can use multichannel paths for surround mixing (among other things) on TDM systems. Common uses of busses are reviewed in Chapter 7.

Some people use them like subgroups or submasters on a physical mixing console. For example, you might reassign the outputs from multiple drum tracks to bus pair 3–4 and then select that bus as the input for a stereo Aux In or Master Fader track. This lets you use a single fader to control the overall volume of the drums, and stereo inserts where a single EQ or compressor plug-in could be applied to this stereo drum mix. This would be equally useful for stacks of backing vocals, walls of backing guitars, or in audio for video, an entire foundation of sound effects and ambience.

Other people use busses like Aux sends to create effects on a mixing console, where sends from several tracks are used to route a portion of their signals to a common bus. In Pro Tools, you could then select that bus as the input for an Aux In track where a delay or reverb effect has been inserted, or that is the source of a performer's headphone mix out in the studio.

You can also use busses to route the output from an Aux In to the input of an audio track while recording. A tip earlier in this chapter entitled "Input Sources for Audio Tracks" alludes to this possibility and provides the example of using multiple Aux In tracks to combine audio from several external MIDI modules before recording this to a stereo audio track. However, you can also do this with a single audio source, if you want to "print" it to disk with effects already incorporated. Create an Aux In track, with the appropriate input source selected. Instantiate whatever plug-in effects are required. Next, assign the main output from this Aux In track to a bus (either mono or a stereo pair, as appropriate). Create a new mono/stereo audio track, select this mono/stereo bus as its input, and click its Record Enable button. If you need to adjust the input recording level to the audio track (perhaps because some of the plug-in effects you're using are affecting the gain of the original input signal), use the Aux In track's main Level fader.

The possibilities are immense, but keep in mind that essentially, a bus is nothing more than a convenient pathway for you to move audio around inside Pro Tools. You can assign the output from any audio, Aux In, or Instrument track or the destination of any send to any bus, bus *pair* (if it's a stereo track output or send), or multichannel bus path (TDM only) that was previously defined in the I/O Setup dialog box. But if no Aux In or Master Fader is listening to that bus (because the bus hasn't yet been selected as the *input* to be monitored by anything), you won't hear it!

❋ Caution: Clipping, Overload, and Distortion

Clipping is a form of distortion caused when the top of the audio waveform is cut off (clipped) because it reaches amplitude levels that exceed the capacity of a channel or device the audio is passing through. On some gear, like tube guitar amplifiers and magnetic tape recorders, a controlled amount of this kind of distortion can be desirable and warm sounding. But digital clipping is nasty, rude, and butt-ugly, and should always be avoided.

Audio tracks, Aux In tracks, Instrument tracks, and Master Faders have clipping indicators—the topmost, red segment on their Level meters. As a general rule, if you ever see these red indicators light up as you play back your mix, you should adjust your gain structure so that they don't. (Remember, you can use the Trimmer to scale any existing volume automation up or down.) Click on a Level meter to reset its clip indicator; Option-click (Alt-click in Windows) to reset the clip indicators on *all* tracks simultaneously. (Note: The behavior of the clip indicator can be changed in Preferences—for example, if you only want it to stay lit for three seconds after a peak is detected.)

Obviously, clipping is a critical issue while recording audio tracks, but also be careful when using plug-in effects during mixdown that can increase gain—such as EQ and compression, and especially when routing multiple sends or track outputs to the same destination. Many of the DigiRack plug-ins (for dynamics and reverb, for example) include Volume meters with clipping indicators within the Plug-in window itself. Keep an eye on these!

Master Faders

A Master Fader track controls the output stage for a physical output (or output *pair*, if it's a stereo master, and multiple channels if it's for a multichannel output path). Master Faders can also control a mono, stereo, or multichannel bus. Master Faders have no sends and no Pan controls. Like audio tracks and Auxiliary Input tracks, Master Fader tracks have five inserts. However, Master Fader inserts are *post-fader only*—the input level to these inserts will always be affected by the Master Fader's main Volume fader. Master Faders are also convenient for placing post-fader plug-in effects or hardware inserts on the entire mix output, such as limiting, compression, EQ, and others, or *especially* dithering plug-ins (which are discussed in Chapter 16, "Bouncing to Disk, Other File Formats").

Because you can use a Master Fader as a final gain stage for your mix output, it is a very convenient place to monitor your final levels. For example, you will often create a stereo master fader for outputs 1–2 on your audio interface, if that's the source for the stereo mix you're hearing through your studio monitors (and perhaps the selected output path when you bounce a mixdown file to disk). If you see that your levels are clipping on this Master Fader—or conversely, if they're way too low—your solution might be as simple as adjusting the Volume fader on that Master Fader track. Of course, another possible approach to taming the dynamics in your mix is placing a compressor, limiter, or some more sophisticated gain optimization plug-in on the Master Fader to affect the entire mix (such as Digidesign's Maxim, the multiband compressor in IK Multimedia's T-Racks, or one of the well-known maximizer plug-ins from Waves). As always, the best choice depends on the sound you're after. However, when you do use a dithering plug-in on the Master Fader for your mix output (because you're bouncing or recording digitally to a lesser bit-depth), always make sure it's the *last* plug-in on the Master Fader.

Output Channels

As with inputs, the number and type of output channels available to you (selectable as send destinations, or track or mix outputs) depends on the audio interface used in your Pro Tools configuration. For many users, a stereo output pair is the source for mixes they bounce to disk (or record to DAT). Even if your final mix is going to be bounced to disk as a stereo file, in the Bounce dialog box, you still must choose the stereo output (either a pair of physical outputs or a stereo bus pair) that will be the source for this bounced mix. For stereo mixing, you would generally use the same pair of physical audio outputs you've been monitoring during the edit process (that is, a stereo output *path*, configured in the I/O Setup dialog box). Some users record their mix in real time to another device instead of bouncing mix files to disk. For example, they might record their Pro Tools output digitally to a DAT (be sure to read about dithering plug-ins in Chapter 16). In typical video postproduction scenarios, real-time output from Pro Tools is used when performing a layback of mixed audio to master video tape—although with computer-based video-editing systems like Avid, Media 100, and FinalCut Pro, it's more common to bounce out a mixdown file or use the OMF interchange format for audio data.

For some situations, *direct-out routing* from individual tracks to output channels can also be handy. You can use each output on a multichannel audio interface as a separate mono output path, assigning each of these directly as the output for individual tracks, rather than some common stereo output pair as in more typical mixing scenarios. A tip in Chapter 7 describes how to set these track assignments quickly. Individual track outputs to audio interface channels can be useful when transferring an entire session to a multitrack tape recorder, for instance, or when you use an external mixing board for mixing and processing, and Pro Tools essentially acts as a multitrack playback machine. Some postproduction operators will assign many individual outputs from the Pro Tools audio interface to physical inputs on hardware-based digital surround mixers with dedicated joystick controllers. However, with the availability of Digidesign's Surround Mixer plug-in and Dolby's Surround Tools plug-in for surround encoding/decoding on TDM-compatible systems (not to mention the joystick controllers on several of Digidesign's external control surfaces), many Pro Tools users create their surround mixes completely within Pro Tools (in LCR, Quad, LCRS, 5.1, 6.1, and 7.1; for Dolby Surround/Pro Logic, Dolby Digital, DTS, and SDDS formats).

You use the Pro Tools I/O Setup dialog box to configure multichannel routing in Pro Tools. Multichannel tracks (for example, six channels for Dolby Digital 5.1) allow you to edit regions in their native multichannel format. Multichannel sends, Auxiliary Input tracks, Instrument tracks, and Master Faders can also be created for any multichannel bus or output path. In the I/O Setup dialog box, you define main *paths*—logical groupings of input or output channels, inserts, or busses. This may be as simple as the main stereo output pair you use to monitor a mix, or six physical outputs on your audio interface that are your 5.1 path (the five surround speakers plus the LFE subwoofer channel). Each mono signal path that comprises a stereo or multichannel main path is known as a *subpath*. For example, even in stereo, the main output used for your mix consists of two mono subpaths—perhaps outputs 1 and 2—on your audio interface. After creating a new stereo or multichannel path, if you also want the possibility to individually address the subpaths within it, you would use the I/O Setup dialog box's New Subpath button to enable these. This might be handy, for instance, if you wanted the LFE (Low Frequency Effects) channel in a surround path to also be available as a send destination.

Plug-in Architectures

So what's a plug-in again? As explained in Chapter 2, a *plug-in* is a software component that acts as an add-in module for processing audio within Pro Tools or other digital audio workstations. Many plug-ins are included with Pro Tools by Digidesign—for example, the AudioSuite and DigiRack (RTAS) plug-ins provided with all systems and a similar DigiRack collection of TDM plug-ins provided with TDM-capable systems. There are also many plug-ins available from Digidesign and numerous other manufacturers for the TDM and RTAS plug-in architectures directly supported by Pro Tools version 7.

Unlike AudioSuite plug-ins (*offline*, or processed-based effects in the AudioSuite menu, which save the results of their processing to an audio file), real-time plug-ins (RTAS and TDM) can be placed into the virtual signal path of Pro Tools at any one of the five inserts provided for audio tracks, Aux Ins, Instrument tracks, and Master Faders. A track's signal passes through each insert in turn (from "a" through "e") and therefore through any real-time plug-in effect placed at any of these insert locations.

❋ **Note: Virtual Instrument Plug-ins**

Because this chapter is mainly concerned with signal flow and effects processing in Pro Tools, it discusses plug-ins specifically in that context. However, most software-based instruments are also used within Pro Tools as plug-ins (except for some standalone applications that communicate with Pro Tools via ReWire, like Reason, Live, and Gigastudio3). Instrument plug-ins are discussed in Chapter 10, "MIDI."

AudioSuite

AudioSuite effects are not real-time processes; they are file based. After adjusting the effects parameters of an AudioSuite effect and using the Preview button in its window (if available) to hear a short sample of how its current settings will affect the final audio, you click the Process button. Generally, a new file is then created, wherein the effect is applied to whatever audio was selected. (If you wish, the results of the processing can instead be destructively written over the data in the original file.) Some of Digidesign's own DigiRack plug-ins are available both as offline AudioSuite processes and RTAS real-time effects. This can be useful if you need to conserve your real-time DSP resources by printing effect treatments to new disk files. Figure 9.4 shows the AudioSuite window and the parameters for the Normalize process (which now includes an RMS mode, in addition to the traditional Peak mode for calculating target gain levels).

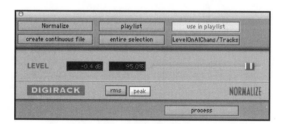

Figure 9.4 The AudioSuite window for the Normalize function.

RTAS (Real-Time AudioSuite)

The Real-Time AudioSuite (RTAS) plug-in architecture was developed by Digidesign for Pro Tools. RTAS plug-ins operate in real time as insert effects on audio tracks, Aux In tracks, Instrument tracks, or Master Faders. DigiRack plug-ins in RTAS format are provided with Pro Tools LE (Mbox 2/Mbox, Digi 002/002 Rack) and Pro Tools M-Powered. (Some of these are also available as non–real-time effects that process audio files, under the AudioSuite menu.) These same RTAS plug-ins are also included with HD systems, along with TDM equivalents for most of them and additional TDM-only plug-ins.

RTAS plug-ins are *host based*; that is, they rely on the computer's CPU for their effects-processing power, rather than relying on specialized DSP chips on a Digidesign card within the computer (as is the case with TDM plug-ins). In addition to the DigiRack plug-ins for RTAS included with all Pro Tools versions, many more are available from Digidesign and other manufacturers. Like TDM plug-ins, you can enable many parameters of an RTAS plug-in for automation (for example, feedback, which affects the number of repeats on a delay) by clicking the Auto button within their Plug-in window, allowing you to build up some very complex and interesting mixes. Lastly, many virtual instrument plug-ins are also offered in RTAS format that can be used as destinations and sound sources for MIDI tracks in Pro Tools. The Click plug-in that provides a metronome sound (typically inserted on an Aux In track) is also a sort of RTAS instrument plug-in. Figure 9.5 shows a typical plug-in window.

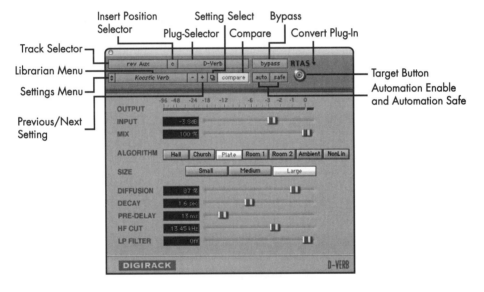

Figure 9.5 Plug-in windows have these common controls. Seen here: D-Verb, which is provided in RTAS, TDM, and AudioSuite formats.

❄ **Tip: Maximizing RTAS Plug-in Capacity**

Obviously, you want to avoid any other system tasks (background processes, energy savers or "sleep" functions, other open programs, and so on) from competing with Pro Tools for access to the computer's CPU. Here are a few more tips:

❄ The capacity of your system to handle larger numbers of simultaneous RTAS plug-ins (especially more intensive types such as reverbs and software instruments) is also proportional to the Hardware Buffer size (accessed from Setup > Playback Engine). Because LE and M-Powered systems only support the RTAS plug-in format, this is an important system-performance issue, but it also affects TDM users who rely heavily on RTAS software instruments, for example. If you start hearing choppy playback or get a "CPU is too busy" message (or, on the Mbox 2 and Mbox, "CPU Usage is holding off USB Audio"), try increasing this setting. However, on LE systems, larger buffer sizes increase monitoring latency during recording, which can negatively affect timing of performances unless you're using low-latency monitoring on the Digi 002 or the Mix knob on the Mbox 2/Mbox (or features in the control panel for your M-Audio interface) to circumvent this problem.

❋ For host computers with two or more processors, another selection in the Playback Engine dialog box allows you to assign more than one CPU to RTAS processing. For instance, on a dual G5 or G4 Macintosh configuration, this is usually desirable. (However, when multiple RTAS processors are used in combination with a 99% CPU usage limit, you may notice some sluggishness in video playback or screen response.)

❋ The CPU Usage Limit selector in this same dialog box can be set up to 99% on all systems when using Pro Tools version 7 and higher (whereas it was previously limited to 85% on single-processor systems). Especially on slower, single-processor systems, this highest setting may affect video playback or screen response. Otherwise, the maximum setting is usually desirable when you're using a lot of RTAS plug-ins—especially software instruments—and want to dedicate more of your CPU's processing power to RTAS.

❋ **Note: Using RTAS Plug-ins in TDM Versions of Pro Tools**

RTAS plug-ins are compatible with LE, M-Powered, and TDM versions of Pro Tools. The basic set of DigiRack RTAS plug-ins is also included with Pro Tools HD software (along with TDM versions of the DigiRack plug-ins).

On HD systems, for most DigiRack plug-ins, the Plug-in window will have a Convert Plug-in button that switches the current TDM plug-in to its RTAS counterpart (if available) or vice versa. Look for a small inverted triangle to the right of the TDM or RTAS text and the Target icon (as seen in Figure 9.5). With the DigiRack plug-ins, switching these from TDM processing on your DSP cards to host-based RTAS processing might be a contingency if you ever max out the available DSP resources on your TDM cards. As a general rule, to avoid excessive use of playback voices, you should avoid placing TDM plug-ins between two RTAS plug-ins in the same track. Also, be aware that side chaining on an RTAS plug-in uses an extra voice.

TDM (Time-Division Multiplexing), TDM II

TDM is a high-performance effects-processing and signal-routing architecture, introduced by Digidesign for Pro Tools in the early 1990s. (TDM II is a redesigned version, with much more robust capabilities, developed for the high-resolution Pro Tools|HD family of systems that was introduced in 2002 and the current Pro Tools HD version of the software. For the sake of simplicity, we often refer to both variants as TDM in this book, because they both support TDM plug-ins.) Unlike AudioSuite and RTAS architectures, TDM enables the use of specialized Digidesign hardware, providing a more stable platform that is less dependent on the host CPU and support for more demanding-signal routing and processing capabilities in expanded, high-resolution systems. Specifically, the HD Core and Accel (or HD Process) cards in Pro Tools|HD systems (as well as the now-discontinued Mix Core and Mix Farm PCI cards in Pro Tools 24|Mix systems) all contain DSP (digital signal processing) chips, which are required to support TDM.

TDM can therefore count on specific hardware resources to support its audio-processing needs and doesn't have to share the processing power of the computer's CPU with the operating system and other tasks (including the Pro Tools program itself) in order to process audio in real time. This generally allows plug-in developers to create more calculation-intensive effects-processing algorithms, often achieving sonically superior results. Also, the monitoring latency during recording (the delay between the selected source and when it is heard back out through the mixer) is much less significant on TDM systems than on host-based LE and M-Powered systems. In addition, the processing latency induced by each TDM plug-in is much smaller than its RTAS counterpart (for each of the DigiRack TDM plug-ins, for example, usually only either four or three samples at the current session sample rate). Not only are effects-processing plug-ins available in TDM format, but so are software instrument plug-ins such as Access Virus Indigo, SOLID, and others. TDM-based Pro Tools systems support a larger number of voices and I/O channels than non-TDM configurations and support audio hardware expansion by adding multiple audio interfaces. Figure 9.6 shows an example of a reverb TDM plug-in for HD systems, while Figure 9.7 shows a dynamics processing plug-in available in both TDM and RTAS formats.

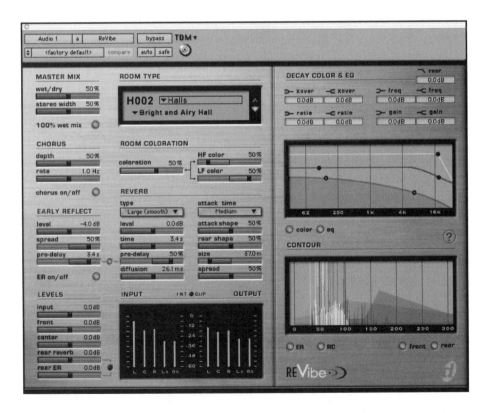

Figure 9.6 ReVibe, a TDM reverb plug-in for Pro Tools|HD systems only.

❊ Note: About HTDM Plug-ins

HTDM plug-ins can only be used on 24|Mix and HD (not LE or M-Powered) systems using Pro Tools software versions prior to 7.0. HTDM is *not* supported in versions 7.0 and higher. Like RTAS plug-ins, HTDM plug-ins relied on the processing power of the host computer's CPU to carry out their tasks (rather than DSP chips provided on the PCI cards in a Pro Tools TDM configuration). Digidesign's StreamManager technology used one of the available DSP chips in a TDM system to handle streaming up to 32 mono channels (or 16 stereo channels) in and out of the TDM mixing environment for these *native* (host-based) HTDM plug-ins. Particularly because of the enhanced RTAS support for multiple-CPU configurations in Pro Tools 7, direct support for HTDM was dropped. When you open an older session containing HTDM plug-ins, with few exceptions, these will automatically be converted to their RTAS equivalents.

Figure 9.7 Smack!, a TDM/RTAS compressor/limiter plug-in, supports multichannel tracks and can emulate tube and analog tape saturation with second- and third-order harmonic distortion.

❊ Tip: Duplicating Plug-ins

You can Option-drag (Alt-drag in Windows) plug-ins (and inserts) to copy them from one track to another, along with their current settings, as long as the number of channels match at the source and destination you're dragging to. Also, if you hold down the Option key (Alt key in Windows) as you enable a plug-in on an audio track, it will simultaneously be created in the same insert slot on all other audio tracks. (You can use this same shortcut to simultaneously create a plug-in on multiple Aux Ins.) Bear in mind, though, that the digital signal-processing resources of even more powerful Pro Tools systems have some practical limit. You might *instantiate* (that is, create an instance of) equalization or compression plug-ins on numerous audio tracks (which typically make relatively small demands on your system's processing power). However, it can often be more DSP efficient (and also simpler to manage) if you place delays and reverbs on Aux Ins, using these as a common send destination from multiple source tracks.

Wrapped Plug-ins

An exciting development in recent years is the emergence of *wrapper programs* that allow plug-ins originally created for one architecture (for example, VST) to be used within a different architecture (like Apple's Audio Units or the RTAS format supported by all current Pro Tools versions). One example is the VST to RTAS Adapter for Mac/Windows by fxpansion.

> ❄ **Tip: Multiple Outputs from Software Instrument Plug-ins**
>
> In addition to the main output from a software instrument plug-in that continues on through the other insert slots in its host track, plug-ins supporting this feature allow you to enable mono or stereo auxiliary outputs. Whenever any of these are active in a session, they appear as options in the track input selector for audio and Auxiliary Input tracks (mono or stereo, as appropriate). For example, this would allow you to route the drum parts from a software instrument plug-in through a separate Auxiliary Input track, so that different reverb or compression treatments could be applied than on the instrumental parts played by this plug-in through its main track output.

Plug-in Effects

In addition to the plug-in software modules included with Pro Tools, many more are available from third parties. Digidesign's Web site always includes updated information about plug-ins available for the various versions of Pro Tools—from Digidesign and many other companies. These range from familiar effects such as reverb, delay, dynamics, processing, EQ, and so on to much more exotic processes. In order to provide a little context, this section briefly reviews just what digital signal processing *is* and groups the various types of audio-processing effects into a few broad categories.

About Digital Signal Processing (DSP)

For the purposes of Pro Tools users, *digital signal processing* means the use of special computational algorithms to alter the data that represents audio waveforms. These algorithms can simulate classic analog audio-processing devices such as equalizers (which change the frequency content of the original material); dynamics processors such as compressors, expanders, and limiters (which alter the level of the audio over time, in response to loudness changes in the original signal or some secondary source assigned as the key input); delay and modulated delay effects (which reproduce some or all of the original signal at some later point in time); and so on. Other plug-ins simulate actual devices, such as tube amplifiers and analog tape, and there are also many other special effects plug-ins that are hard to categorize!

Categories of Audio Effects

Many effect types can be grouped into several broad categories. Plug-ins appear within hierarchical submenus according to their category (assigned by the plug-in's manufacturer) or subgrouped by manufacturer if you enable that option in Preferences. This grouping is much more general, however, and not limited to Pro Tools. There are of course many variants within each effect category, but this overview should provide a conceptual framework.

For experienced audio professionals, much of this may be review; however, some of the Pro Tools–specific aspects mentioned here are worth keeping in mind.

Frequency-Based Effects

These affect the frequency content of the audio input, usually by applying increases and decreases to the gain (level) in various frequency ranges. Equalization, or EQ, is a common frequency-based effect. There are two main types of equalizers:

❀ **Parametric EQ.** These are so named because the characteristics of one or several bands of boost/cut can be modified per various *parameters*, such as the amount of boost/cut (gain setting), the center frequency of the affected frequency band, and the rate that the boost/cut decreases at frequencies progressively further from the band's center frequency (known as the slope, or Q; this describes the shape of the curve of boost/cut around that band's center frequency).

❀ **Graphic EQ.** Divides the frequency spectrum into a fixed number of bands and allows you to boost or cut each frequency band. When the individual bands correspond to octaves or subdivisions of an octave, as is common, the absolute frequency range of each band gets progressively larger, because each higher octave is double the frequency of the previous one. Traditional graphic equalizers were essentially banks of band-pass filters at set frequencies and a fixed Q, with a Volume slider on each.

Figure 9.8 shows an example of an EQ plug-in.

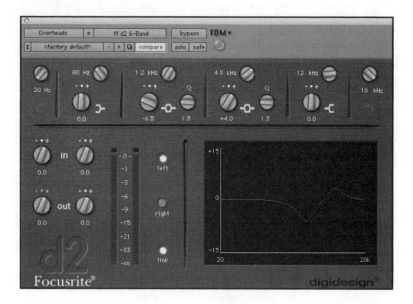

Figure 9.8 D2 by Focusrite, a 4- or 6-band EQ plug-in for TDM.

Gain-Based Effects

Dynamics processors apply gain changes to the original audio over time. Examples include compressors, limiters, expanders, gates, and de-essers. You can use them in many ways to decrease or increase the dynamic range of the input audio. Figure 9.9 provides two examples of compression plug-ins. Compressors (and *limiters*) are often used, for instance, to reduce peak levels in an audio track so that the entire track's level can be increased after compression for a louder, in-your-face sound throughout the track (usually essential in contemporary music mixes for bass, guitars, and vocals, for example). A compressor reduces the signal level by a specified ratio whenever it exceeds the threshold setting. (A limiter completely prevents the audio from exceeding a specified threshold, like a compressor with an extremely high ratio—or banging your head against the bottom of a table!) *Expanders* do the opposite—audio levels *beneath* a specified threshold are even further reduced, again by a specified ratio. For example, they can be useful for decreasing noise from the pickups or amplifier between phrases on an electric guitar or room noise between sentences during a voice-over. A *gate* is like an expander at an extremely high ratio—any audio levels under the threshold are completely closed off by the gate (which might be very handy when other drums can be heard leaking into your kick drum microphone, for example).

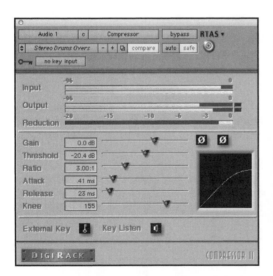

Figure 9.9   Two compressor plug-ins from Digidesign: the DigiRackDynamics II compressor, and the optional Impact compressor for TDM.

A *de-esser* is technically a specialized type of compressor. Instead of reacting to the entire frequency range of the input signal to determine how much gain reduction to apply, only a narrow frequency band—adjustable within a range roughly corresponding to "s" sounds in the human voice—is used as the key input for the compression effect, which then acts upon the full frequency range of the input signal. By using a de-esser to clamp down on the track's level where the "s" and "ch" sounds are in a voice, for example, you can apply more high-frequency boost to the track in general without this sibilance becoming too prominent. (Like any other effects, however, de-essers have many other uses. For example, they can be useful to control sibilance on vocals entering a reverb or occasionally for reducing the prominence of finger squeaks on an acoustic guitar.)

The amount of gain change applied by a dynamics processor is typically based on the level changes within the input audio itself. Alternatively, gain changes on the current track can be keyed by level variations within a completely different audio source, a technique called *side chaining*. To side chain (or *key*) a dynamics plug-in in Pro Tools, you activate its External Key mode (if it offers this feature) and designate some other Pro Tools bus or input as the key source. This could be handy with a compressor for slightly *ducking* (reducing) the level of background music (or rhythm guitars, in a rock mix) whenever the voice is present, or with an expander to help the bass guitar bump a little harder wherever there's a beat in the kick drum track.

Time-Based Effects

Delays store and then reproduce all or some of the input signal at a later time. Sometimes, a portion of the delayed signal is re-routed back to the input to be delayed again. (This is called *regeneration* or *feedback* and is used to create multiple repeats, or echoes.) For plug-ins, as a general rule, longer delays require more processing power than short ones to store and process a potentially longer amount of delayed audio in digital memory.

Modulated delays additionally apply a varying amount of change to the delay time, usually controlled by the values of a low-frequency oscillator, or *LFO* (or its software equivalent). You can adjust the frequency of the LFO, as well as the degree of effect it has on the amount of delay. When such an oscillation is applied to very short delays, and the delayed signal is then mixed with the original audio, a characteristic sweeping, comb-filtered sound is produced, especially when the Feedback (regeneration) value is increased. This is the basis of so-called *chorus* and *flange* effects (whose base delay times may be 20–30 or 2–10 milliseconds, respectively). Figure 9.10 shows one example of such an effect. The effect can be even more dramatic if differing delay times and/or modulation speeds are applied in the left and right channels. Pro Tools includes Chorus and Flanger plug-ins among its AudioSuite (non-real-time) effects, under the Modulation category of the hierarchical AudioSuite plug-in selection menu. Novice Pro Tools users should be wary of overusing chorus and flanging on rock and pop rhythm tracks, however. As many a rock guitarist or bassist will attest, these tend to soften or diffuse the visceral impact of the track to which they're applied—which may or may not be desirable, according to the musical style.

Figure 9.10 TC|Chorus•Delay, by TC|Works, a time-based plug-in with Chorus and Delay sections that is included in their TC|Tools TDM bundle.

In current versions of Pro Tools, the DigiRack medium, long, and extra long delay plug-ins can be synced to the current Pro Tools tempo so that repeats can be easily set to specific rhythmic intervals (musical note values) without making any calculations. This tempo-syncing feature is enabled or disabled by a button in the plug-in window that looks like a metronome.

Reverb Effects

Reverberation is technically another type of time-based effect. In practice, though, it's complex enough to merit its own heading because it involves aspects of all the above categories. In technical terms, *reverb* is the persistence of a sound within an acoustical space—multiple reflected sound waves that continue after the original sound has ceased.

Reverb processors simulate the reverberant characteristics of an acoustic space—the myriad reflections/delays and persistence of ambient sound following the original sound, early reflections, resonances, and other acoustical aspects of the environment. Various spaces can be modeled (halls, rooms, cathedrals, and so on), as well as classic electronic reverb units (plate, spring) and special-effect reverb types (non-linear, gated, reverse, and others). Most sophisticated reverb processors include elements similar to delays (for introducing pre-delay prior to the reverberation or early reflections) and EQ (for high-frequency damping and tailoring the resonances of the modeled reverberant space). In fact, for many mixes, the reverb can often have more influence over the mix's overall character than any other single effect processor, especially as it is applied to the snare or lead vocal track in rock or dance mixes.

Compared to most compressor, EQ, and delay plug-ins, though, reverb is a much more intensive form of digital signal processing. It consequently makes greater demands on the processing power of your CPU (or the DSP chips on the cards of your Pro Tools TDM system). D-Verb is included with all Pro Tools systems, but other more sophisticated or specialized reverbs are available from Digidesign (ReVibe and Reverb One for TDM) and third parties. One of these is shown in Figure 9.11.

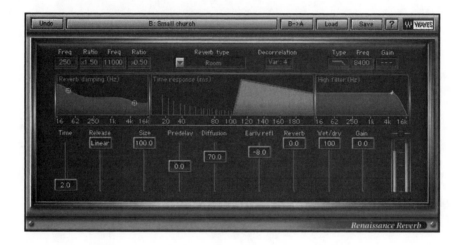

Figure 9.11 Renaissance Reverb, by Waves, a reverb plug-in available for TDM or RTAS.

❋ **Tip: More Information About Effects on the Web**

If you want to explore more technical details, Scott Lehman has published an excellent series of articles about common effect types on Harmony Central (including circuit diagrams, waveforms, graphs, and audio examples). Go to http://www.harmony-central.com, choose the Effects link, and then "Effects Explained."

Pitch-Based Effects

Pitch plug-in processors apply real-time pitch changes to the input audio. This may be a fixed amount (for example, an octave up or down, or just a few cents—1/100 of a semitone—in order to achieve more subtle doubling effects through detuning). Other, more sophisticated pitch-based processors offer more intelligent correction to a specific musical scale, such as the example shown in Figure 9.12, where the notes of a vocal track are being tuned to the notes of an A minor scale.

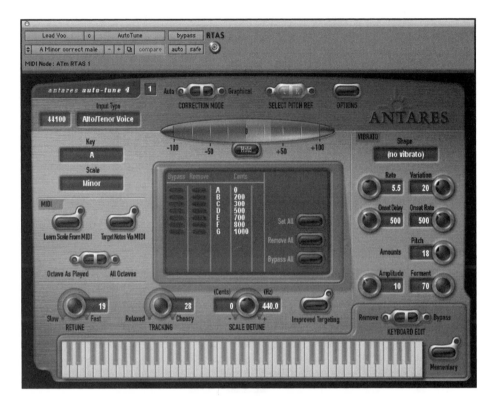

Figure 9.12 Auto-Tune, by Antares, a pitch-processing plug-in for TDM or RTAS.

Modeling Effects

Some effects seek to emulate an existing physical device (or sometimes, one that could never exist). Although these processes certainly involve frequency, dynamics, and time-based elements, the overall result is much more complex. Examples of physical modeling among digital plug-ins and processors include simulators for guitar amplifiers (such as the one shown in Figure 9.13), speaker cabinets, rotary speakers, microphones, tube preamplifiers, tape saturation, previously existing analog effects, and so on.

Other: Special FX

Many special effects defy categorization. For example, phase shifters, vocoders, and exciters (such as the one that appears in Figure 9.14) incorporate aspects of several of the preceding categories, making them hard to pin down. On the other hand, some effects are just too odd to classify (and that's why we love 'em!), such as Digidesign's own optional plug-ins. The D-Fi bundle includes Sci-Fi (various combinations of effects related to ring modulation and resonance), Lo-Fi (a sort of digital bit crusher and distorter), Recti-Fi (harmonic processing and additive synthesis effects, rectification), and Vari-Fi (varispeed effects, including changes

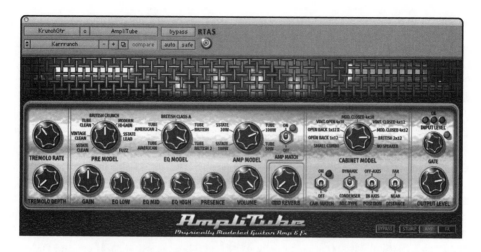

Figure 9.13 Amplitube, by IK Multimedia, an RTAS amp-simulation plug-in.

over time). The Bruno and Reso bundle for TDM offers cross-synthesis, with time-slicing and resonance effects.

Figure 9.14 MaxxBass, by Waves, a psycho-acoustic bass extension plug-in.

❊ **CSi: The X-Noise Noise-Reduction Plug-in**

In the CD-ROM at the back of this book, the sample movie tutorial from Waves *Plug-Ins CSi Master* by John Hughes shows the X-Noise noise-reduction plug-in in operation.

RTAS (DigiRack) Plug-ins Included with Pro Tools

The precise selection of RTAS plug-ins included with each Pro Tools configuration tends to change over time. Digidesign periodically also promotes certain bundled configurations, including one or several additional plug-ins at a reduced price. For the moment, though, count on any current LE, M-Powered, or TDM version of Pro Tools including at least the following RTAS plug-ins:

* **Frequency-based effects:** EQ3 (equalizer with up to seven bands), 4-band EQ (equalizer), and 1-band EQ

* **Gain-based effects:** Compressor, Limiter, Expander-Gate, Gate, De-esser (essentially a compressor with a band-pass filter on its key input, useful for reducing the prominence of sibilant "s" sounds in vocal tracks, among other things), and Trim (provides simple gain adjustment and polarity inversion); via the Dynamics3 and older Dynamics2 plug-ins

* **Time-based effects.** Short Delay (shortest), Slap Delay, Medium Delay, Long Delay, Extra Long Delay (these last three delays can be synced to note subdivisions per the current tempo), Time Adjuster (formerly TDM-only, for manually compensating latencies due to plug-in processing, multiple microphone placement; also provides gain adjustment and phase inversion)

* **Reverb effects.** D-Verb

* **Other effects.** Digidesign Dither (can improve the quality of conversion to lower bit-depths, especially for low-level signals and fades in Pro Tools; see Chapter 16), POW-r Dither (HD and LE versions only), Signal Generator (generates test tones, with control over frequency, waveform, and amplitude, to calibrate Pro Tools with other devices in your studio), DigiReWire (enables sending MIDI to and streaming audio from ReWire-compatible programs on the track where it's instantiated; see the "ReWire" section, later in this chapter), and Click (generates metronome sounds according to the current tempo setting)

Tip: Making a Plug-in Inactive

Every plug-in window has a Bypass button, which allows input audio to pass through without any processing applied. (Hardware I/O inserts cannot be bypassed.) To bypass any plug-in directly from the Mix window, Command-click (Ctrl-click in Windows) its plug-in button in the Inserts section. However, even in Bypass mode, the plug-in is still in the signal chain and utilizes the same proportion of your system's DSP resources. (On HD systems, the Show System Usage window provides an overview of how the DSP resources on your PCI cards are currently allocated to plug-ins, mixing, and other Pro Tools tasks.)

To make a plug-in *completely* inactive, thereby freeing up its demands on your system's resources, hold down the Command and Control keys (Ctrl and Start keys in Windows) as you click on the plug-in's button in the Mix window. As opposed to simply removing the plug-in from the track, making it inactive retains its current settings for whenever you choose to re-activate it. Use the same key combination to make a plug-in active again.

TDM (DigiRack)Plug-ins Included with Pro Tools HD

The selection of TDM plug-ins included with Pro Tools varies as successive versions of Pro Tools and promotional bundles are released. The RTAS plug-ins listed previously are also included with HD versions. Count on current Pro Tools systems including at least the following:

- ❊ **Frequency-based effects:** EQ3 (equalizer with up to seven bands), 4-band EQ (equalizer), and 1-band EQ

- ❊ **Gain-based effects:** Compressor, Limiter, Expander-Gate, Gate, De-esser (essentially a compressor with a band-pass filter on its key input, useful for reducing the prominence of sibilant "s" sounds in vocal tracks, among other things), and Trim (provides simple gain adjustment and polarity inversion)

- ❊ **Time-based effects:** Short Delay (shortest), Slap Delay, Medium Delay, Long Delay, Extra Long Delay (these last three delays can be synced to note subdivisions per the current tempo), Extra Long Delay (which also includes tempo-related delay time settings), and Time Adjuster (can be used to manually compensate for latencies created by TDM routing, plug-in processing, or multiple microphone placement; also provides gain adjustment and phase inversion—for example, each instance of most DigiRack TDM plug-ins typically introduce about four samples of delay into a track's signal path, while other plug-ins may induce much longer processing delays)

- ❊ **Reverb effects:** D-Verb

- ❊ **Other effects:** Digidesign Dither (can improve the quality of conversion to lower bit-depths, especially low-level signals and fades in Pro Tools), POW-r Dither (a more powerful dithering plug-in), Signal Generator (generates test tones, with control over frequency, waveform, and amplitude, to calibrate Pro Tools with other devices in your studio or to provide a reference level for analog recording devices and/or video decks), and Pitch (for real-time pitch shift)

The Acrobat Reader (PDF) document *DigiRack Plug-ins Guide*, included with your system, provides details about all the plug-ins included with Pro Tools and is well worth exploring.

Third-Party Plug-in Developers

There are separately purchasable plug-ins available from Digidesign itself (including the Focusrite and Bomb Factory plug-ins that Digidesign distributes). Another Acrobat Reader (PDF) document, the *Digidesign Plug-ins Guide*, comes with some versions of Pro Tools (and the current version can always be downloaded from the Support area of http://www.digidesign.com); it explains how to use all these Digidesign-distributed plug-ins.

In addition to Digidesign, many other companies also offer plug-ins that are compatible with TDM or RTAS architectures (for example Duy, URS, Waves, Antares, TC|Works, Sonic Solutions, Native Instruments, Aphex, Serato, Arturia, Line 6, Trillium, Audio Ease, Synchro Arts, Sound Toys, and McDSP, to name a few). The Plug-in Finder section of Digidesign's Web site will help you seek them out. Additionally, the "Audio Plug-ins CSi Master" volume of our *Cool School Interactus* series of instructional CD-ROMs focuses specifically on plug-ins for digital audio workstations, including Pro Tools.

Tips for Using Sends (to External I/O, to PT Busses, and to Aux Inputs)

When it comes to effects processing and building a creative mix, you should of course feel free to break all the rules! However, to avoid some of the common pitfalls, and to get a good start on designing a coherent soundscape, keep these basic observations in mind when using sends to additionally route part of a track's audio to a secondary destination from a Pro Tools track:

❉ As a general rule, unless they're unique to a single track, delays and reverbs are usually better placed on Aux Ins because it's typical to create sends from more than one audio track to common delay or reverb destinations. This also simplifies controlling the mix of wet (processed output from the effects) to dry audio. Obviously, it's a more efficient use of your system's DSP resources to send a little bit of five vocal tracks to one reverb, versus five reverbs, one on each track! Even if you aren't terribly concerned about running out of DSP power, using one or several common reverb destinations for multiple tracks can be the glue that helps a mix hang together. It contributes to the impression that the sounds all share a common space. This all depends on what you're trying to achieve, of course, and personal taste. But when you're overdubbing multiple parts and need some help making them sound cohesive, try it—you'll see what we mean!

❉ Remember that when you send audio from multiple tracks to a common bus, you can exceed its maximum level and create some nasty digital clipping. If you find that the clipping indicators on your Aux Ins are lighting up, reduce the send levels from each track (and remember that you can use the Trimmer to scale down any existing automation for each track's send level).

❉ Sometimes your sends are routed to physical outputs (for external effects processors, cue mixes for performers, and other uses). Be careful to watch your gain structure here as well. Creating a Master Fader for that output pair is a good way to monitor its levels.

❉ Signals can pass through more than one bus within Pro Tools. Here's one example: Say you create a send from a track that should eventually pass through a reverb or delay plug-in placed on an Aux In (whose input is assigned to a bus). However, for the effect you want, you'd like the track's audio to be filtered before it hits the delay (while audio sent from other tracks to the same delay should *not* be filtered). Just set the source track's send destination to another bus, create a second Aux In track that monitors that bus as its input, and place the EQ on that Aux In. Then assign the output of that second Aux In to the bus already being used as the input source for the Aux In where the delay or reverb is inserted.

ReWire

ReWire is a standard for real-time routing of digital audio between separate programs that was developed by Propellerhead Software (the manufacturers of Reason, which is shown in Figure 9.15). Compatible ReWire programs can be slaved to Pro Tools so that they follow

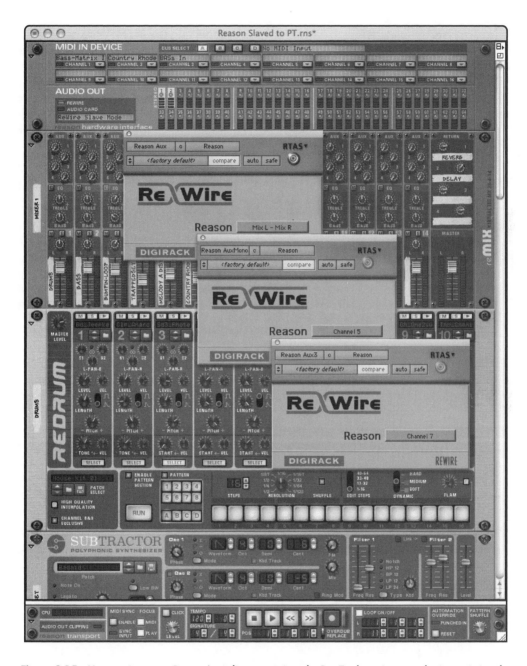

Figure 9.15 You can integrate Reason's audio outputs into the Pro Tools environment by instantiating the DigiReWire plug-in.

the Pro Tools tempo and Transport functions. After instantiating the DigiReWire plug-in in Pro Tools (typically on an Aux In, Instrument track, or audio track), you can select which of the virtual audio channels coming from the separate ReWire application you want to be streamed into the Pro Tools mixing environment. From that point, those channels are subject to the same options for plug-in processing, mix automation, and send routing as any other input signal passing through this track. Many users will find it convenient to instantiate ReWire plug-ins on Instrument tracks (with no instrument plug-in enabled on this same track). That way, not only is it immediately clear from the track's Mix window icon that this mixer strip represents an instrumental sound source, but you can also use that Instrument track's "MIDI track" functionality in the Edit window to record and edit a MIDI performance for that ReWire destination.

> **❋ Note: Rewired Programs and Voice Allocation in Pro Tools**
>
> On TDM systems, each ReWire channel you enable on an audio track occupies one voice out of your system's total pool of voices for audio playback. This is *not* the case when the ReWire plug-in is enabled on Auxiliary Input or Instrument tracks of LE and M-Powered systems, however. Depending on how the slaved ReWire application is used—especially considering that several of them support not only virtual instruments but long samples and audio tracks—this may present some interesting possibilities for overcoming the 32-voice limitation in Pro Tools LE and M-Powered.

Additionally, many ReWire applications include their own virtual instruments (for example, the synthesizers, samplers, and programmable drum machines in Reason, or Gigastudio3 itself, a sampler instrument with many additional features). When a slaved ReWire application is detected, you can choose any of these as output destinations from your MIDI tracks within Pro Tools.

Any ReWire setup requires one program to act as the master and another as the slave—being controlled via the other program's transport and tempo and also relying on the other program for access to the audio hardware and mixing environment. Some programs—including the current version of Apple's GarageBand, many MIDI sequencers, and Pro Tools itself—must be the ReWire "master" (or "host") program and therefore can't be slaved to Pro Tools via ReWire. Examples of ReWire applications that *can* work in slave mode with Pro Tools include:

- **❋ Reason.** Virtual instruments, effects, mixing, and sequencing, from Propellerhead Software. The limited-feature version, Reason Adapted, has been bundled with certain Pro Tools configurations. Unlike some other ReWire applications, Reason supports only one stereo pair; the remainder of its channels must enter Pro Tools via mono instances of the DigiReWire plug-in. (Refer to Figure 9.15.)

- **❋ Live.** Sophisticated looping tools, recording, mixing, and effects from Ableton; available for both Mac and Windows.

- **❋ Soundminer.** Catalog-management and auditioning tool for audio files from Soundminer.

❋ **Gigastudio3.** A sampler program for Windows from Tascam that includes streaming samples, sequencing, mixing, convolution effects, custom sample recording, and mapping. Versions 3 and higher support ReWire.

Getting the Most Out of Available DSP

Especially if you don't have an unlimited budget, in complex Pro Tools sessions, you may eventually get one of those dreaded messages from Pro Tools, such as "CPU is too busy" or "CPU Usage is holding off USB Audio" on an Mbox or Mbox 2, meaning that you've reached the limit of your system's DSP resources. At that point, you have several choices (besides hustling out to buy another HD Accel card, if you have a Pro Tools|HD system!). Obviously, the first thing is to look at whether you're really using the routing and plug-in processing of Pro Tools in the most efficient manner. It's typical to add effects and sends on an ad hoc basis during the edit process. Once a session becomes sufficiently large and complex, though, it can definitely be worth taking a moment to re-examine how you have the signal routing and processing set up. It might even make the final mix much easier later!

Here are some strategies to try if you ever slam into this limit on your projects:

❋ Check your CPU Usage Limit setting (under Setup > Playback Engine). This can be set as high as 99%. Even though you might notice this highest setting slowing down screen redraws on slower, single-processor computers, it might just be enough to get your project finished and bounced to disk!

❋ If your computer has two or more processors and you're a Pro Tools LE or M-Powered user, or for Pro Tools HD sessions that use a lot of RTAS plug-ins, open the Playback Engine dialog box and confirm that the RTAS Processors parameter is set to two or more processors.

❋ Try increasing the setting for the Hardware Buffer size, under Setup > Playback Engine. Higher settings allow more intensive use of RTAS plug-ins. However, on LE and M-Powered systems especially, the amount of latency (monitoring delay between the track's input and output while recording, and real-time response of software instruments to MIDI performances from your external controller) is also directly proportional to the size of the Hardware Buffer. You will therefore usually want this at a smaller setting while still recording tracks, perhaps increasing it during mixdown as you activate a lot of RTAS plug-ins (especially reverbs and software instruments).

❋ On TDM systems, there is a pop-up selector in the Setup > Playback Engine dialog box for Number of Voices. Setting this to a lower number (although still high enough to support the voices required by your mono, stereo, and multichannel audio tracks and RTAS plug-ins, of course) also frees up some processing power for plug-ins.

❋ Where appropriate, try placing a single instance of a plug-in on Aux Ins where multiple tracks are routed, rather than placing similar plug-ins on each individual track. For example, if you have four or five backing vocal tracks, instead of putting a compressor on each one, route all their outputs to a single stereo bus and then place a compressor on the stereo Aux In monitoring that bus. You might even find this makes the parts sound tighter once a single dynamic shape is uniformly affecting them all.

❋ Bear in mind that every active bus, send, and hardware insert also uses some of the available DSP resources on your system. For this reason, try not to create an excessive number of these in any template (stationery) documents, and also be sure to eliminate them after they are no longer needed. For example, if you only required a send, a bus, and an Aux In for a headphone mix during the recording process, consider eliminating these if your DSP resources are running short during the final mix.

❋ Take a look at how you're using your plug-ins and DSP resources. On TDM systems, the first instance of a given plug-in type acquires more of your DSP resources than subsequent instances of the same plug-in. Therefore, from an efficiency standpoint, it makes fewer demands on your available DSP to use the same compressor type in two different places (with different settings, of course) rather than using, say, a Digidesign compressor on one track and a Focusrite compressor on another—as long as the sound you want can still be achieved.

❋ With Digidesign's EQ, it's the *total* number of bands of EQ used that determines usage of your DSP resources on TDM systems. If you're only boosting or cutting one band in any of your 4-band EQ plug-ins, try making them 1-band EQs instead. Likewise, on all Pro Tools systems, the longer the delay, the larger the demand on available DSP resources. It's inefficient to use the Long Delay plug-in if its current delay time setting is short enough for the Medium or Slap Delay instead. Fortunately, with DigiRack delays, when you change from one type to another, their settings are maintained—including the delay time, as long as it fits into the maximum duration of the new, shorter delay type.

❋ You could bounce out some of your tracks to disk with effects and then re-import them into the session (via the Import After Bounce check box in the Bounce to Disk dialog box). Afterward, use the Track > Make Inactive command to completely disable the original tracks containing the plug-in effects, so that they no longer make any demands on your system's DSP resources. For some projects, you could also bounce out the entire mix and import it into a brand-new session with no plug-ins at all—so far!

❋ If you're reasonably sure you can live with the current settings of a DigiRack plug-in for a while, use the Plug-in window's pop-up Settings menu to copy its settings and then paste them into the AudioSuite version of the same effect. First, make a duplicate of the track's current playlist (using its pop-up Playlist selector in the Edit window) and then select the entire audio track and process it with the AudioSuite plug-in. Don't worry, when you click the Process button to apply the effect parameters, new region(s) will be created, leaving your original audio regions still available should you have second thoughts at some later point (assuming you *don't* enable the Overwrite Files option in the AudioSuite window). If the Use in Playlist button is enabled, the new, processed regions will take the place of the original regions in the track (which will still be available in the Region List). If you ever need to revert back to the original state of the track in order to readjust the processing, just use the track's Playlist selector to restore its original form (containing the original, unprocessed versions of the regions).

Where to Place Plug-ins

Plug-ins can be placed on any track type except MIDI tracks. The best option depends on what you're trying to achieve, but here are a few basic thoughts:

✳ As mentioned already, there will be times when it's more efficient to assign the main outputs of multiple tracks to a single bus and place a single plug-in on the Aux In that monitors that bus, rather than inserting redundant plug-ins into each individual audio track. If you're layering up a dozen tracks of the same vocalist, it's an inefficient use of DSP capacity to instantiate identical EQ plug-ins on every one of those tracks and also makes adjusting your settings more laborious later. As an added bonus, in many cases—such as multiple backing vocals or rhythm guitars, for example—having a single compressor apply its dynamic shaping to that entire submix can also contribute to a tighter, more coherent sound.

✳ As a general rule, except when they are an integral part of a single track's sound, get into the habit of putting delays and reverbs on Aux Ins rather than in any single audio track's signal chain. It gives you more control and flexibility later if you decide it might be handy to send some other track's signal to that same delay.

✳ EQ affects gain! Therefore, the amount of gain or boost you apply in an EQ plug-in not only affects audio levels on the track's main output (and any post-fader sends) but also the level entering any plug-ins that follow the track's signal chain. If EQ is followed by a compressor or limiter, for example, a dramatic boost in some frequency range would cause that dynamics-processing effect to clamp down harder—because as a result of the increased gain coming out of the EQ plug-in, the track's peak audio levels exceed the specified threshold more often. With high-frequency boosts, the result may darken the sound somewhat. There are no set rules for effects processing, of course, but as a general guideline for a more transparent sound, you might start by placing the EQ *after* any dynamics-processing plug-ins on the track.

✳ Speaking of EQ, remember that if you can't quite achieve the sound you're looking for with a delay or reverb plug-in, you always have the option of placing an EQ plug-in before and/or after it in that Aux In track. For example, reducing the amount of high frequencies entering the effect can solve problems with vocal sibilance or other bright transients in the source tracks that might otherwise clutter up your mix. (To avoid confusion, note that in general, the Low-Pass Filter or High-Frequency Cut controls in reverb and delay plug-ins apply to the effect's output or delay regeneration, *not* its input signal.) Compressors or even de-essers can also be effective for taming dynamics of the signal entering a delay or reverb—allowing you to increase the effect's overall level without worrying about occasional peaks in the source tracks creating splashes of reverb that are too prominent in the mix, for example.

✳ Reverb plug-ins often don't have gated reverb presets, and novice users often seem to consider this an omission. If you're overcome by 1980s nostalgia (and long to see monster snares again stalk the land, terrifying peaceful villagers everywhere!), here's a quick pointer: In Pro Tools, you can instantiate up to five plug-ins on any track, right? Among the plug-ins included with any Pro Tools configuration, you have a reverb and also a gate that could follow it in the same track's signal chain. You can figure out the rest!

❊ Remember, the inserts on Master Fader tracks are always *post*-fader, while on audio tracks, Aux Ins, and Instrument tracks, the inserts are *pre*-fader. The input level to plug-ins on a Master Fader is therefore affected by the Master Fader's main Volume fader. If you're using a limiter or compressor plug-in on the Master Fader for your main mix output, therefore, you could use the track's main Volume fader to adjust how hard you're driving the input of that plug-in, as with many traditional hardware compressors. When using dithering plug-ins for bouncing to disk or recording digitally to another device at a lower bit-depth, these should always be the *last* plug-in on the Master Fader (or other track controlling a selected bus) that is the source for your mix output.

❊ **Tip: Copying/Moving Plug-ins**

Option-drag (Alt-drag in Windows) any plug-in to copy it to a different track, along with all its current settings. (The source and destination track must have the same number of inputs and outputs, however.) You can also drag plug-ins among the different "a" through "e" insert locations within the same track, which changes their signal-processing order and the resultant sound. (Remember that on HD systems, RTAS plug-ins must always be placed *before* any TDM plug-ins in the same audio track.)

In addition to saving and recalling plug-in settings from disk (as shown in Figure 9.16), you can also copy and paste them directly. For example, to copy current settings from the 4-band EQ plug-in on one track to another, use the Copy Settings and Paste Settings commands in the pop-up plug-in settings menu within the Plug-in window.

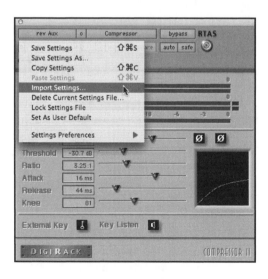

Figure 9.16   Settings for each plug-in type can be saved, recalled, cut, pasted, or imported from other sessions and systems.

AudioSuite Effects versus Real-Time Plug-ins

AudioSuite processing is discussed in Chapter 8, "Menu Selections: Highlights." As stated there, two basic classes of software effects are available in Pro Tools. First there are plug-ins that function in real time as inserts on audio, Aux In, Instrument, or Master Fader tracks. Depending on your system configuration, these may be in RTAS or TDM format. In contrast, the effects in the AudioSuite menu are file based—they must either destructively alter the data in the original file or, more typically, create a new file to store the result of the processing. As previously mentioned in the section "Getting the Most Out of Available DSP" earlier in this chapter, if your system's DSP resources are extremely limited (for example, if you're using a Pro Tools LE or M-Powered version on one of the earliest Macintosh G4 models), there may be times when you start off using one of the DigiRack RTAS plug-ins and eventually copy and paste its parameters into the corresponding AudioSuite plug-in. This is one way to free up that DSP power for subsequent mixing tasks. Even on the more current LE/M-Powered versions of Pro Tools and contemporary computers, there will be cases where you hit the limit for processing capacity on your system—it will be good to know you still have some options for getting your project completed!

Bouncing Effects into Tracks and Submixes

We've already mentioned bouncing out mixes in order to free up DSP resources. Here are a few more observations that may be helpful during this process.

Managing Multiple Session Documents

Remember that the Select > Unused Regions command in the Region List only looks at the *current* session document! If you have bounced out a submix and created a new session (perhaps through the File > Save As command) in order to keep adding more tracks, be cognizant that this new session knows nothing about how any audio files and regions may be used in *other* sessions. Also, remember that when Save Session As creates a new session document, that new copy still uses the same Audio Files and Fade Files folders as the previous session (not to mention the Region Groups and Session File Backups folders, plus the cache file for waveform overviews), as shown in Figure 9.17.

Session copies created by the File > Save Copy In command also continue to use the original audio files in the current session's folder, *unless* you specify in the Save Session Copy dialog box that source audio files should be copied to a new folder along with the session file itself. However, any session created by the Save Copy In command will subsequently use its own subfolders for any new audio or fade files created by recording or editing.

Keep in mind that audio regions and bounced files are automatically timestamped by Pro Tools with their original location information. This allows you to use the Spot dialog box to make sure that the bounced files you import into other session copies are placed exactly in their original location.

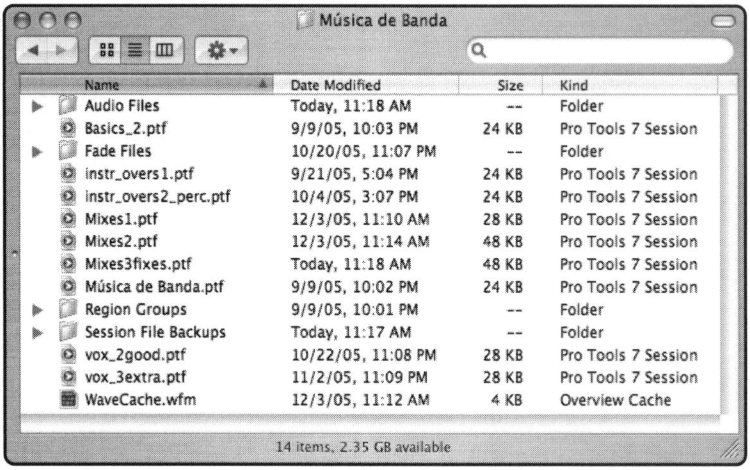

Figure 9.17 Multiple versions of this session (created with the Save As command) all share the same Audio Files and Fade Files folders.

Turning Voice Assignment Off

After turning a track's voice assignment to Off, as opposed to Dynamic (or in certain cases, a manually assigned voice number on TDM systems), it is inactivated. It no longer competes with other tracks for voices and, of course, won't be heard. It's usually more effective to use the Track > Make Inactive command, discussed in Chapter 8. You might do this on multiple source tracks after they have been bounced to disk as part of a submix and re-imported into another track.

Track Muting, Voice Allocation Within a Session (TDM Only)

Generally, you will always want the Options > Mute Frees Assigned Voice option enabled, especially if you are going through this process of bouncing out effected tracks and re-importing them into the session to free up DSP resources. That way, when you mute the original track, that voice is now available to play other tracks.

Summary

The possibilities for signal routing in Pro Tools are as varied as the working styles of each operator. You will see another example in Chapter 13, "Music Production," which includes setting up cue mixes for performers. Multichannel tracks and surround mixing are discussed in Chapter 14, "Postproduction and Soundtracks." Also, if you've skipped Chapter 7, you may want to flip back to it now for more insight into the virtual mixing, signal-routing, and processing environment that Pro Tools provides for your virtual studio.

10 MIDI

As explained in Chapter 2, "Pro Tools Terms and Concepts," *MIDI* stands for *Musical Instrument Digital Interface*. MIDI devices transmit and receive data about a performance—how you struck a key, pressed a pedal, applied pressure to the keyboard, turned a knob or pushed a slider, and so on. MIDI is a communications language; it transmits instructions rather than audio signals. To put it another way, although sound does not travel though MIDI cables, the data MIDI cables carry can be used to *control* things that can make sound.

A Technical and Historical Overview of MIDI

The MIDI standard is maintained and expanded on an ongoing basis by the MIDI Manufacturer's Association, a consortium of hardware and software companies (http://www.midi.org). In technical terms, MIDI is a 31.25 kilobaud serial communications protocol that uses 5-pin DIN connectors to cable together MIDI-compatible devices. MIDI event messages and timing references are transmitted as binary code.

MIDI was introduced in 1983 to address incompatibility issues between electronic musical instruments from different manufacturers (synthesizers, samplers, and so on). The MIDI specification defines data events and timing references to be commonly recognized by all devices that support the standard. For example, a Note On event includes two additional parameters: the note number (from 0–127) and the velocity with which the key was struck (from 1–127). For common performance controllers such as the damper (sustain) pedal on a keyboard, the modulation wheel or lever, the pitch bend wheel or lever, or the main volume control and panner, standard controller numbers and their range of possible values were also agreed upon. The result was that you could connect the MIDI Out of one keyboard to the MIDI In of another, and it would more or less respond with the same notes. This was quite an improvement over the voltage-controlled synthesizers and early digital-connection protocols from different manufacturers, all of which were mutually incompatible!

Fortunately, the developers of the MIDI specification were much more ambitious than this. MIDI sequencers (data recorders that capture MIDI performance events in real time) needed a common timing reference, called MIDI Clock, so that events could be timestamped in order to play back in proper order and timing, as well as to synchronize one MIDI sequencer to another. Naturally, as personal computers became commonplace in the early 1980s, MIDI interfaces were developed so that MIDI cabling could be connected to personal computers, and software sequencers could receive and retransmit MIDI performance data. Later enhancements to the MIDI specification included the following:

* **MIDI Time Code (MTC).** This encodes the same time location information as SMPTE time code (more about this in Chapter 11, "Synchronization").

* **MIDI Show Control.** This added event and controller message types relating to lighting, special effects, hydraulics, audio level controls, and so on.

* **MIDI Machine Control (MMC).** This protocol is used for remote control and interlocking of audio or video tape deck transport functions with other devices (including Pro Tools) via MIDI. This is the MIDI counterpart of an even more prevalent machine control method based on serial connections between hardware devices. As discussed in Chapter 14, "Postproduction and Soundtracks," with the Digidesign MachineControl option, you can use DigiSerial ports on HD cards or 9-pin serial ports on the Sync I/O to slave external devices such as video decks and DAT recorders together with Pro Tools, if these don't support MIDI Machine Control.

For Pro Tools users, MIDI Time Code and MIDI Machine Control are especially relevant. Additionally, it's worth mentioning that all parameters of PRE, Digidesign's microphone preamplifier, are controllable via MIDI (and therefore can be restored when a session is reopened), as are many external effects processors.

MIDI Data

Chapter 1, "About Pro Tools," touched on some basic MIDI concepts. We're not going to go into all the technical details here—that is, the communications protocol, interfacing, and the low-level structure (status bytes, data bytes, most- and least-significant bits, and so on) that actually comprise the messages transmitted from one MIDI device to another. There are many excellent relevant resources in both book and online form. Some MIDI messages represent actual performance events—a key or pedal was pressed, a lever or slider was moved, and so on. Other message types are more system level, perhaps telling the receiving device to switch to a different sound or operating mode, controlling its internal sequencer, or even loading sound-parameter data that is specific to that device alone. At any rate, however MIDI tracks may appear onscreen (for example, horizontal bars for note events or data curves for modulation, aftertouch, and other types of continuous controllers within Pro Tools), what is actually recorded and played from your MIDI tracks is a series of numerical MIDI messages. Figure 10.1 shows the MIDI Event List window in Pro Tools, which gives you a simplified view of what's actually going on.

Although there are many types of MIDI messages, they can all be classified into five basic categories:

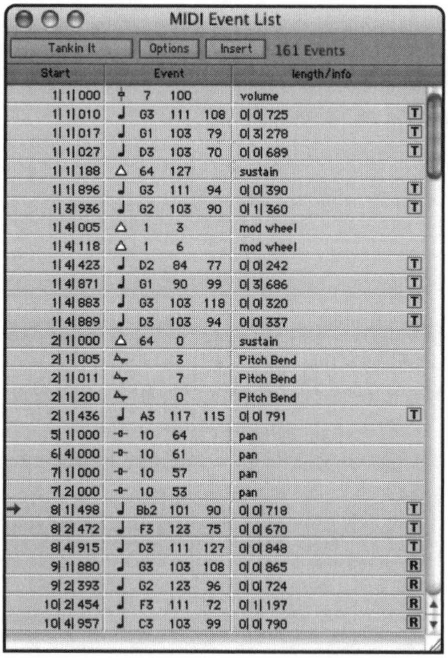

MIDI Event List

| Tankin It | Options | Insert | 161 Events |

Start	Event			length/info	
1| 1|000	✤	7	100	volume	
1| 1|010	♩ G3	111	108	0| 0| 725	T
1| 1|017	♩ G1	103	79	0| 3| 278	T
1| 1|027	♩ D3	103	70	0| 0| 689	T
1| 1|188	△ 64	127		sustain	
1| 1|896	♩ G3	111	94	0| 0| 390	T
1| 3|936	♩ G2	103	90	0| 1| 360	T
1| 4|005	△ 1	3		mod wheel	
1| 4|118	△ 1	6		mod wheel	
1| 4|423	♩ D2	84	77	0| 0| 242	T
1| 4|871	♩ G1	90	99	0| 3| 686	T
1| 4|883	♩ G3	103	118	0| 0| 320	T
1| 4|889	♩ D3	103	94	0| 0| 337	T
2| 1|000	△ 64	0		sustain	
2| 1|005	⌁	3		Pitch Bend	
2| 1|011	⌁	7		Pitch Bend	
2| 1|200	⌁	0		Pitch Bend	
2| 1|436	♩ A3	117	115	0| 0| 791	T
5| 1|000	-○- 10	64		pan	
6| 4|000	-○- 10	61		pan	
7| 1|000	-○- 10	57		pan	
7| 2|000	-○- 10	53		pan	
→ 8| 1|498	♩ Bb2	101	90	0| 0| 718	T
8| 2|472	♩ F3	123	75	0| 0| 670	T
8| 4|915	♩ D3	111	127	0| 0| 848	T
9| 1|880	♩ G3	103	108	0| 0| 865	R
9| 2|393	♩ G2	123	96	0| 0| 724	R
10| 2|454	♩ F3	111	72	0| 1| 197	R
10| 4|957	♩ C3	103	99	0| 0| 790	R

Figure 10.1   The MIDI Event List window displays MIDI events as numerical data. For the most part, you will deal with Channel Voice messages in Pro Tools (although other types of MIDI messages, such as System Exclusive messages, are also supported).

✳ **Channel Voice messages.** These represent performance events such as Note On/Off, Volume, Pan, Modulation, Pitch Bend, Aftertouch, pedals or breath controllers, and so on. Each Channel Voice message is transmitted specifically on one of the 16 MIDI channels (a Note On message on channel 5, for example). Program Change messages are also in this category—usually causing whichever part or patch that is listening to that MIDI channel to switch to a different sound for responding to the MIDI note events it receives.

✳ **Channel Mode messages.** These include messages for switching between operating modes on the receiving devices, which determine how the device will respond to incoming notes and other MIDI events. In Omni mode, the device responds to incoming note events on any channel; in Poly mode it responds to incoming MIDI events on multiple channels, each with an independently selectable timbre; and Mono mode responds to a single channel only. All Notes Off is also a Channel Mode message, used for stuck notes (and there's a command for this in the MIDI menu of Pro Tools).

✳ **System Common messages.** These include Song Position Pointer, Song Select, and Tune Request messages.

✳ **System Real Time messages.** These are used for messages such as MIDI Clock, Start/ Stop, Active Sensing, and so on.

❋ **System Exclusive messages.** These messages contain manufacturers' proprietary control data, and are ignored by all units that don't respond to the unique manufacturer ID at the beginning of each message. They're used for editing, loading, or archiving sound parameters that are specific to that instrument.

For the most part, when you're editing data in Pro Tools MIDI tracks, you will be dealing with Channel Voice events, although each of the other types can come into play in given situations.

❋ **Aftertouch: Can Pro Tools Handle the Pressure?**

In addition to registering attack and release velocity (that is, how rapidly you strike or release each key on your MIDI controller), the MIDI specification includes two types of Aftertouch controller data: Channel Pressure and Polyphonic Pressure.

Channel Pressure, or Aftertouch data, generates a series of values as you change the amount of pressure applied to the entire keyboard. On many synthesizer patches, for example, pressing harder on the controller keyboard as you hold a note or chord may increase the filter cutoff frequency, amount or speed of low-frequency modulation, volume, and so on.

Polyphonic Pressure data (sometimes called "polyphonic aftertouch") reflects the pressure applied to each individual key. Only some MIDI controllers are capable of generating this type of data, and you should be aware that many sampler programs and synth patches may not respond to it. Generation of Polyphonic Pressure events can also dramatically increase the density of your recorded MIDI data, since a stream of pressure events is generated for each key as you press on the keyboard, instead of a single value for the entire keyboard as in the case of Channel Pressure. If none of the MIDI modules or software synths you're using respond to this type of controller data, consider using the MIDI menu's Input Filter selection to disable recording of Polyphonic Pressure into Pro Tools.

Although Channel Pressure (mono aftertouch) is one of the standard Data Display options for MIDI tracks in the Edit window, the MIDI Event List window is the *only* place you can view/edit Polyphonic Pressure events in Pro Tools.

MIDI Interface Options

As mentioned in Chapter 3, "Your System Configuration," a MIDI interface is a sort of adapter that translates the MIDI data communications protocol to a format that your computer can understand. MIDI interfaces can be external devices—generally connected to the computer via USB in current models (especially when interfaces with numerous MIDI connections are required). Many generic Windows soundcards have built-in connectors for MIDI, where you can attach a simple break-out cable with one DIN-5 connector for MIDI In and another for MIDI Out.

Digi 002 and Mbox 2 systems have MIDI input/output connectors integrated into the external Digidesign audio interface itself (although in some cases, you may not be able to use them from programs other than Pro Tools), as do many of the M-Audio interfaces compatible with M-Powered. The Command|8 control surface communicates directly with Pro Tools via USB (unlike some other external control surfaces that communicate via MIDI or Ethernet); it also includes a 1-in, 2-out MIDI interface.

Whichever MIDI interface you're using in your Pro Tools configuration, the number of independently addressable MIDI inputs or outputs (ports) it provides will determine the total number of MIDI channels available for communicating with external MIDI devices—16 MIDI channels per port. For example, if you have a 1-in, 2-out MIDI interface (this 1×2 MIDI configuration is what's built into the Mbox 2 and Digi 002/002 Rack), that's 16 MIDI input channels and 32 output channels that can be selected for external MIDI communication to or from a Pro Tools MIDI (or Instrument) track. Of course, many different types of MIDI interfaces are available, with varying numbers of ports. Additional features in the more sophisticated units might include routing or filtering capabilities for the MIDI data passing through them, stored presets and operation in standalone mode without a computer, SMPTE time code synchronization, word clock features for slaving your audio hardware's sample rate to external sources, slaving multiple MIDI interfaces together to expand the number of independently addressable MIDI ports, and so on. Pro Tools supports most external MIDI interfaces currently available, including units from MOTU, M-Audio (another division of Avid, the parent company of Digidesign), Steinberg, Emagic, and others.

Several of the M-Audio audio interfaces that are compatible with Pro Tools M-Powered also incorporate MIDI inputs/outputs, which you can use with Pro Tools as well as with other programs.

Digidesign MIDI I/O

The MIDI I/O (shown in Figure 10.2) is the first external MIDI interface under the Digidesign name. It features 10 MIDI inputs (with two of these on the front panel) and 10 outputs and connects to the host computer via the USB port (which also powers the device). The MIDI I/O is supported both under Pro Tools for Windows (via WDM) and Macintosh and features a standalone "hardware thru" mode. You can daisy-chain up to four MIDI I/Os together, for up to 640 MIDI channels (16 channels per MIDI port).

Figure 10.2   Digidesign's MIDI I/O (a multiport MIDI interface) connects to the host computer via USB. Two of its 10 MIDI inputs/outputs are available on the front panel (photo courtesy of Digidesign).

Although there are various options for multiport MIDI interfaces, a unique feature of the MIDI I/O is support for the Digidesign MIDI Time Stamping feature for MIDI data in Pro Tools. This addresses an inherent timing problem when you transmit many channels of dense MIDI data in real time over a single connection. Imagine you're sending or receiving 30–40 separate channels of MIDI data, each containing constant pitch bend and polyphonic pressure events or fader and knob movements recorded from an external control surface for Pro Tools that communicates with the computer via MIDI. The sheer volume of MIDI events could exceed the real-time capacity of a single USB connection. Even more likely, a conventional MIDI interface may not be able to receive, convert, and reroute all this information between multiple ports and the data connection to the computer itself without some kind of processing delay, or latency. The result will be random timing discrepancies that become an audible problem in your project. Via the MIDI Time Stamping feature, each incoming MIDI event is timestamped during recording; during MIDI playback, data sent from Pro Tools is *preloaded* into a buffer in the MIDI I/O in real time in order to ensure more timely playback.

MIDI Setup

Pro Tools handles MIDI setup slightly differently in Macintosh than in Windows. In Mac OS X (operating system version 10.0 and above), you do all the configuration of the MIDI interface and external MIDI devices (for example, keyboards, guitar, wind, and percussion controllers; drum machines; and sound modules) in the Audio MIDI Setup Utility, and the possibilities you see for MIDI input/output (I/O) within the Pro Tools software reflect your current configuration in that utility. Once you've run the installer program for whatever drivers an external MIDI interface requires (if any), it automatically appears in Audio MIDI Setup.

Older Windows versions of Pro Tools generally relied on the MIDI configuration settings from the MIDI interface's own driver software (usually accessible via the Sound, Video, and Game Controllers category of the Device Manager window). From version 6.7 on, the MIDI Studio Setup window automatically finds MIDI interface drivers and translates that information into XML-based documents that allow you to assign custom names for the MIDI ports on the interface and also use XML-based patchname documents (which are also customizable, as in Mac OS X) for selecting sounds on your external MIDI devices. However, as with MIDI interfaces for Mac systems, you must always first run the installer program provided with the unit itself, and the proper procedures on Windows can be highly variable from one model to another—read the instructions before installing *anything*!

The Digi 002/002 Rack includes one MIDI input and two MIDI outputs. (Its predecessor, the now-discontinued Digi 001 interface, included one MIDI input and one MIDI input.) Some of the current M-Audio interfaces for Pro Tools M-Powered also offer a single MIDI input and output, as do Digidesign's Mbox 2 (which includes the LE version of Pro Tools) and the Command|8 control surface. For any other Pro Tools hardware configuration, the MIDI interface is a separate hardware peripheral (or possibly a port commonly found on generic Windows soundcards, if the modest performance offered by this option is sufficient for your needs).

Macintosh (Audio MIDI Setup)

The Audio MIDI Setup Utility (shown in Figure 10.3) is part of Mac OS X. You can launch it directly from within Pro Tools using the Setup > MIDI Studio Setup command and use it to configure what type of MIDI interface (if any) is connected to your computer, as well as where and how your external MIDI controllers and sound modules are connected to it. Many devices are already preconfigured so that you can select by manufacturer/model. However, you can manually configure any other device; the most important issues are how many MIDI ports the device has, which MIDI channels it transmits/receives, whether it receives or transmits MIDI Beat Clock and MIDI Time Code, and whether it's General MIDI compatible. You then simply drag onscreen "cables" between each MIDI device's MIDI inputs/outputs and the corresponding ports on the MIDI interface (to mirror their actual physical connections).

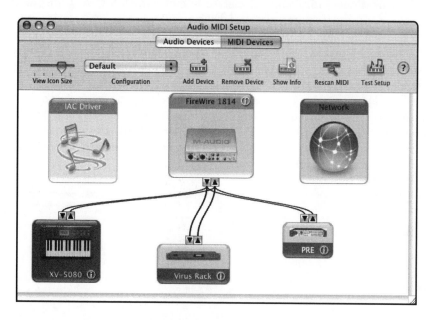

Figure 10.3 The Audio MIDI Setup program, under Macintosh OS X, provides a uniform method for configuring the communication between all MIDI-capable programs and any MIDI interfaces, external keyboards/controllers, and modules attached to your system.

Windows

Most MIDI interfaces come with their own driver installer disks. MIDI drivers are installed via INF files for Windows Device Manager (WDM), which instruct the operating system about how and when to use those driver files. For common (SoundBlaster-compatible) PC soundcards, an optional cable converts a DB-15 data connector on the card into MIDI In/Out 5-pin DIN connectors. However, for professional applications, USB is currently the most common connection for attaching external MIDI interfaces to Windows computers. Installation procedures can vary widely, according to the manufacturer and model of your MIDI interface. Be sure to carefully read the manufacturer's instructions before beginning to install software for a new MIDI interface on your system—doing so takes much less time than trying to undo an improper installation!

Starting with versions 6.7 and higher of Pro Tools for Windows, it became much simpler to manage a complex MIDI configuration, including the external MIDI devices and the sounds within them, thanks to the MIDI Studio Setup window (shown in Figure 10.4). Here, you define *instruments* for each of your external MIDI devices by clicking the Create button. Properties appear in the right-hand panel of this window for each selected instrument. A list of predefined instruments is provided in your Pro Tools installation—these MIDI device files are written in a language known as *XML* (Extensible Markup Language). If the MIDI device you're defining as a new instrument is included in that default list, you can select it in the pop-up fields here for manufacturer and model number. Otherwise, you can leave these fields set to None and simply enter your own name for the instrument. You can also define where this instrument is connected for input and output to and from Pro Tools by indicating the port on your MIDI interface where it is connected. Lastly, you indicate which MIDI channels the device is sending on and the output MIDI channels from Pro Tools to which the device responds. (For example, your keyboard may be configured to transmit only on MIDI channel 1, while it can respond to all 16 MIDI channels. A MIDI module may not transmit on any channels at all but respond to all of them. A MIDI guitar controller may transmit on six MIDI channels simultaneously, while some MIDI percussion controllers transmit on an even larger number of simultaneous channels.)

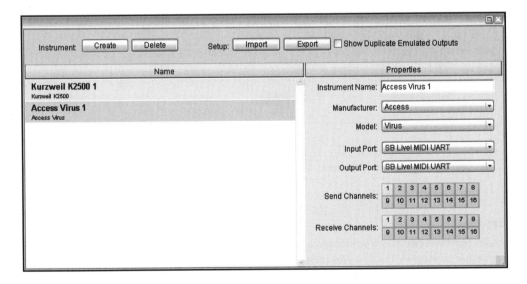

Figure 10.4   The MIDI Studio Setup window is available in Pro Tools on Windows, versions 6.7 and later.

The active instruments in your current MIDI Studio Setup configuration then appear in the MIDI Input and MIDI Output selectors on MIDI tracks. (To make an instrument not appear without having to delete its definition from MIDI Studio Setup, change its input and output port assignments to None.)

Another major MIDI enhancement introduced back in version 6.7 of Pro Tools on Windows was support of patchname files (which are also written in XML and use the .MIDNAM extension on their file names). As with MIDI device files, a collection of predefined patchname files is included with the Pro Tools installation (and reside in the Program Files > Common Files > Digidesign > MIDI patchnames > Digidesign subdirectory). MIDI tracks have a Program button in both the Mix and Edit windows, which opens the Patch Select dialog box. (This functionality had been available in Mac versions for quite a while.) In this dialog box, you can select a patchname file for the current track (using the Change button) from among the .MIDNAM files residing in that directory. If you choose a Korg Triton, for example, all the factory internal programs and banks for that device will now appear *by name*—rather than simply by program number—each time you open the Patch Select dialog box. This is a huge boost to productivity, making it much quicker to select and experiment with different sounds for your MIDI parts. These patchname files are ordinary text files, however (as are the patchname files used with the Macintosh Audio MIDI Setup utility). If you've edited program names or customized the contents of the user bank on your external synthesizer, you can edit the program names inside the corresponding patchname file on your computer using any text editor program. Be sure to make a backup copy of the original first, however! Some third-party librarian or patch editor programs also provide tools for creating your own patchname files from scratch. You can find many of these patchname files on the Web, if your particular device isn't included in the predefined list provided with Pro Tools.

External MIDI Devices

There are many types of external MIDI devices, including standard synthesizers, samplers with keyboards, MIDI sound modules with no keyboards, and MIDI controllers that feature no internal sound-generation capabilities at all (keyboard controllers, guitar controllers, wind controllers, and so on). Of course, many other devices also support MIDI. For example, you can control parameters of many effects processors via MIDI, as well as control automated mixers or, for that matter, some lighting gear and amplifiers.

Besides using a MIDI controller for performance (keyboard, guitar controller, wind controller, electronic drums, and so on), there are also MIDI peripherals that you can use as control surfaces for Pro Tools itself. The Mackie HUI and Mackie Control Universal, the J.L. Cooper CS-10^2 and CS-32 MiniDesk, the Penny & Giles MM-16 (and its predecessor, the DC-16), the CM Labs Dashboard and MotorMix, and the Peavey PC-1600 are all examples of external devices that you can use to externally control Pro Tools faders, sliders, and/or the Pro Tools Transport via a MIDI connection.

Lastly, there are other alternatives for connecting musical peripherals to your computer: USB controller keyboards are available (for example, from M-Audio and others), as well as USB modules and keyboards from Roland, Korg, and others, that don't require a MIDI interface at all for you to use with your computer and MIDI programs. These alternatives are especially attractive for laptop users—some of the smaller keyboard controllers can even run off batteries! For users who rely exclusively on software instruments as MIDI sound sources—and as time passes and computers become more powerful, this is an increasingly common option—a full-featured keyboard controller with a USB connection and no internal sounds may be all that is required.

The following sections discuss software-based virtual instruments. You can use them in conjunction with, or instead of, any external sound modules for MIDI. In the Pro Tools session shown in Figure 10.5, MIDI track output assignments include an external MIDI module, plus two virtual MIDI instruments. SampleTank2 is a software sampler, used here as an RTAS plug-in. The audio signal from *external* MIDI devices enters the mixing environment via an Aux In track's selected input path on the audio hardware. Reason is a separate program, and you can enable its audio outputs within Pro Tools via the DigiReWire plug-in. Once audio from external devices enters an Aux In track's signal path, plug-in processing and Pro Tools mix automation can be applied, sent, created, and so on.

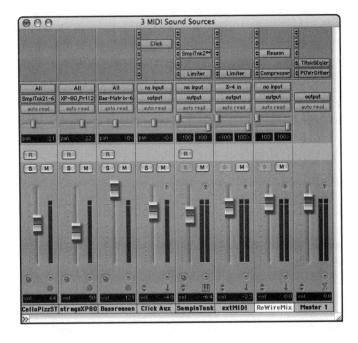

Figure 10.5 A Pro Tools session with external MIDI devices and software-based instruments (an RTAS plug-in on an Instrument track, plus a separate program connected via ReWire).

Virtual Instruments

Software-based MIDI instruments are among the most exciting tools that have emerged in recent years. Virtual instrument plug-ins have been around for a while in RTAS and TDM formats (as well as VST, AU, DirectX, and additional formats used by other audio programs), and the fact that Pro Tools supports ReWire technology enables many more options for integrating software-based synthesizers and samplers into the Pro Tools environment. Virtual instruments for Pro Tools can be broken down into five general classes:

❋ RTAS synthesizer/sampler plug-ins (for Pro Tools LE, M-Powered, and TDM).

❋ TDM synthesizer/sampler plug-ins (for Pro Tools HD and its Pro Tools TDM predecessors).

❋ HTDM synthesizer/sampler plug-ins (for Pro Tools TDM versions prior to 7.0 only). HTDM is no longer supported; when you open older sessions containing HTDM plug-ins in Pro Tools 7 or higher, they are automatically converted to their RTAS counterparts, if possible.

❋ Separate synthesizer/sampler programs such as Reason, Gigastudio3, or Ableton Live, whose virtual audio outputs can be routed into Pro Tools via the DigiReWire plug-in (Pro Tools TDM, LE, and M-Powered).

❋ Plug-ins in other formats that are not native to Pro Tools, which you can use via so-called "wrapper" programs. One example is the VST to RTAS Adapter program by fxpansion, which allows you to use VST effects and instrument plug-ins within the RTAS plug-in environment of Pro Tools on either Mac or Windows.

Typically you would instantiate a virtual instrument plug-in in one of the insert slots of an Instrument (or Aux In) track (although you can also place them on an audio track or Master Fader). If the virtual instrument instead is a separate program communicating with Pro Tools via ReWire (like Reason, Gigastudio3, or Ableton Live), you would select that program as an insert (made possible by the DigiReWire plug-in) and then use its ReWire plug-in window to select which of that program's outputs you want to stream into Pro Tools at this insert point on the track. From there, the audio output of any virtual instrument on a track can be treated identically to other signal sources in Pro Tools, applying mix automation and plug-in processing, or creating sends and other routing assignments. Not only does using software-based instruments simplify working with multiple projects and MIDI sound sources, but the virtual signal path from these synths and samplers into Pro Tools is as clean as it gets!

Why Use Virtual Instruments Instead of External MIDI Gear?

Software-based instruments have numerous benefits over physical MIDI devices. They're less noisy because they have no inputs/outputs, cabling, digital converters, and so on—all of which are subject to whatever compromise in quality the manufacturer had to make in order to sell the instrument at a given price. Secondly, virtual instruments can be more cost effective because you aren't buying RAM, disk storage, and so on for, say, an external sampler that may not be of a type that is as readily available and inexpensive as its counterpart for standard desktop computers. The whole routing and reconnection scenario becomes immensely simple as well: There are no cables to reconnect (or induce noise). In the case of ReWire, you can launch the separate virtual instrument application, reloading its patch and entire routing configuration, the next time you open that Pro Tools session—without touching any cables or adjusting levels. For sampler virtual instruments, the fact that these use standard PC or Mac disk and file formats (as opposed to the proprietary formats used by many standalone samplers) means that you can much more easily create or acquire new audio files for them. (The sound-generation method in samplers relies on playing back digital audio recordings from RAM, varying their playback speed as required to produce different pitches and sometimes looping shorter audio segments in order to produce sustained tones.) You may even decide midway through a Pro Tools session that you'd like to use a particular audio region sampler-style, triggering its playback at different speeds/pitches via MIDI note events. No problem; you bounce out the region as a file (in the same standard SDII, AIFF, or WAV format you're already using with Pro Tools) and load it up into a SampleTank2, Kontakt2, or Gigastudio3 instrument so that it can be played from the keyboard, for example. Need to apply some editing to that sample so that it works better in the software sampler? Open it again in Pro Tools, make your changes, save again to disk, and reload.

Virtual Instrument Programs (ReWire)

Most ReWire programs support both audio and MIDI processing, and many also offer robust sequencing and composing tools. Not only can you route MIDI from ReWire applications into Pro Tools, but you can also use the MIDI-capable sound modules within them as sound sources by assigning them as the output from your MIDI or Instrument tracks in Pro Tools. Third-party programs that are compatible with ReWire and can work in slave mode under the control of Pro Tools include the following:

* Reason (Propellerhead Software).
* Live (Ableton).
* Gigastudio3 (Tascam; Windows only).
* ACID by Sony (originally developed by Sonic Foundry; Windows only).
* Bidule (Plogue).
* VST to ReWire Adapter (fxpansion). This hosts VST instruments in Mac or Windows so that they can be controlled by Pro Tools MIDI tracks and multiple outputs from them routed back into Pro Tools via ReWire.

Virtual Instrument Plug-ins for Pro Tools

A new approach for software-based synthesis and sampling in Pro Tools was opened with the proliferation of virtual instrument plug-ins over recent years. These software-based samplers, synths, and drum modules are completely accessible from within the Pro Tools program. (These must be in RTAS format in order to be used directly by Pro Tools LE and M-Powered systems, while HD systems additionally support software instrument plug-ins in TDM format.) Their parameters (and reference to any external sample files on disk, if applicable) are stored and recalled along with the session document. This is a huge productivity advantage, as any veteran user of multiple external modules can attest. The sound-generation parameters of these software instrument plug-ins can also be enabled for Pro Tools automation (like most other plug-ins)—even from an external control surface.

Virtual instrument plug-ins for Pro Tools|HD systems can be either TDM format (utilizing the DSP chips on Digidesign's PCI cards), RTAS format ("host-based" processing, relying on the computer's CPU), or accessible via separate ReWire programs that communicate with Pro Tools. The audio output from the virtual instrument is incorporated into the Pro Tools mixing environment at whatever insert point you place the plug-in. You can use other standard plug-in or hardware I/O effects on the insert slots following the instrument plug-in in a track to further process its output. You can also create sends from any track containing an instrument plug-in.

Pro Tools LE and M-Powered users use RTAS virtual instrument plug-ins (and of course, separate software-based instruments that stream into Pro Tools via ReWire, as described in the previous section). The performance of these virtual instruments depends on your system's resources (CPU type and speed, available RAM, and so on), as does the Pro Tools LE or M-Powered program in general. If your computer is already having a hard time with the number of tracks, plug-ins, and so on that you're using in Pro Tools, this may set a practical limit on how many voices, channels, and the like that you can actually use on your virtual instrument. Figure 10.6 shows SampleTank2, an RTAS-based sampler instrument for Mac and Windows versions of Pro Tools (which is also available in VST, MAS, and AU plug-in formats supported by other Macintosh audio programs).

Figure 10.6 SampleTank2, by IK Multimedia, is a sampler virtual instrument that uses digital audio samples and sophisticated synthesis features to produce its sounds. Each of the 16 instrument slots has five insert points for internal effects, many of which you can sync to the Pro Tools tempo.

Recording into MIDI and Instrument Tracks

Pro Tools MIDI and Instrument tracks can record from any active port on your MIDI interface on whatever channel(s) your controller is transmitting. Ordinarily, you will have the MIDI Thru function enabled (via a selection in the Options menu). That way, regardless of which MIDI input you record *from*, the MIDI output (and/or port on your external MIDI interface), channel, and program number you've chosen for the currently record-enabled track will be echoed through to the correct instrument, channel, and program.

However, if the selected output for the current track happens to be the same MIDI keyboard controller you're currently playing, the MIDI Thru function can present some issues. In this situation, the sound generation within your synth can end up not only responding directly to its own local keyboard but also to the same note and controller events echoed back around through Pro Tools via the current track assignment. You will hear doubled notes, and typically the external keyboard will lock up due to the infinite loop you've set up via the output assignment on your MIDI/Instrument track and the global MIDI Thru feature in Pro Tools. As with other MIDI-capable programs, when using MIDI Thru, you can avoid this problem by simply turning Local Mode off on your external keyboard. When a MIDI controller's Local Mode is off, its internal sound-generation capabilities no longer respond to its own keyboard; instead they respond only to incoming MIDI events at its MIDI input. (Hey, and if you need to use this MIDI keyboard later in standalone mode, don't forget to turn Local Mode back on!)

MIDI Recording Modes

In addition to the four standard recording modes in Pro Tools, a button in the Transport window enables MIDI Merge mode (more about this in a moment). Let's take a look at how these modes affect MIDI recording, because there are some differences compared to audio:

* **Normal mode.** Non-destructive. If you record anywhere into a MIDI or Instrument track where MIDI regions/data already exist, a new region is created for the newly recorded MIDI data. The region(s) replaced by the new MIDI recording in the track are still available and unchanged in the Region List.

* **Destructive mode.** In MIDI and Instrument tracks, there is no difference between Normal and Destructive modes; they work in exactly the same way. In contrast, in audio tracks, Destructive Recording mode actually overwrites any existing audio data at that track location.

* **QuickPunch mode.** Not required for MIDI and Instrument tracks, because for all record-enabled MIDI tracks, you can *always* use the Transport's Record button to drop in and out of recording mode.

* **Loop Record mode.** Works similarly to loop recording on audio tracks. A new MIDI region is created and auto-numbered for every pass through the looped selection (although in MIDI tracks, if you don't play anything on a pass, Pro Tools waits until the next time you play something before creating and auto-numbering additional regions). As with multiple audio takes recorded in Loop Record mode, you can Command+click with the Selector (Ctrl+click in Windows) near the beginning of the region currently in the

track to view the Takes List pop-up menu. MIDI Merge mode (see the next bullet) cannot be used in Loop Record mode; its button in the Transport is dimmed whenever Loop Record mode is active.

❊ **MIDI Merge mode.** When this button in the Pro Tools Transport window is enabled, as you record over existing MIDI regions, the new MIDI data is *added* to the MIDI data already in the track instead of replacing it.

❊ **Tip: Loop Record**

You can record MIDI and/or audio in Loop Record mode! Simply set pre- and post-roll parameters, make a timeline selection, and enable Loop Record mode (in the Options menu, or by right-clicking the Record button in the Transport window to cycle to this mode). After you click Record and Play, the portion of the session's timeline between the Transport window's Start and End indicators (the play selection) is looped until you press the spacebar to stop it. A new region is created for each pass. To discard all takes recorded so far, while still in Loop Record mode, press Command+period (Ctrl+period in Windows).

If you Command-click (Ctrl-click in Windows) with the Selector at the left edge of a loop-recorded region, the pop-up Takes List appears, which allows you to switch between multiple takes.

❊ **CSi Example: Loop Recording MIDI, MIDI Merge Mode**

In the CD-ROM at the back of this book, check out the sample movie tutorial "Overdubs and Loop Recording," excerpted from *Pro Tools 7 CSi Starter*. This volume in the *CSi* series includes various movie tutorials specifically about MIDI. In this sample movie tutorial, though, you'll see loop recording of audio and MIDI in action, using MIDI Merge mode to build up a loop drum-machine style.

Editing MIDI and Instrument Tracks in the Edit Window

When MIDI and Instrument tracks are in Regions or Blocks view, you can drag MIDI regions with the Grabber. You can also use the Selector to highlight areas within them for cut/copy/paste operations more or less like audio regions. But even here, there's one important difference: If the part of any MIDI note event that is actually inside the region's current boundaries is the initial Note On message itself (the left edge of the rectangle representing each individual MIDI note event), after trimming the end of this MIDI region, those notes that begin before the region's new end point will extend beyond the region's right edge (and sound for their full lengths). Conversely, if you trim a MIDI region's left edge so that it no longer includes a note's beginning, that note is no longer part of the region (and won't play).

In addition to using the standard Trimmer mode to shorten/lengthen the boundaries of MIDI regions, you can also use the Time Trimmer (the "TCE" mode of the Trimmer tool). This affects not only the length of the regions themselves but also the spacing of all the MIDI events within them. As always with the editing tools, the currently active Edit mode affects this kind of trimming as well—so Spot mode opens the Spot dialog box, Slip mode allows free adjustment of the duration, Grid mode snaps the duration from one grid increment to another as you drag, and Shuffle mode always leaves the beginning of the new compressed/expanded MIDI region at the same start point as the original region, whether you trimmed its beginning or end. In particular, using the Time Trimmer in Grid mode may be handy for composers—compressing a four-bar region to two bars creates a double-time version of the events it contains, while expanding it to eight bars creates a half-time version.

Things get more interesting in Notes and Velocity data-display formats. Here are some specific tricks you should know when using the different Edit window tools on MIDI tracks while in Notes view:

- ❋ **Grabber.** You can drag individual notes or multiple selected notes around. Use the Shift key to select/deselect additional notes and Option-drag to copy notes instead of moving them (Alt-drag in Windows). When you click between notes in the track, the Grabber cursor turns into a selection rectangle so that you can select ranges of notes.

- ❋ **Trimmer.** Trims note lengths (end or beginning). Hold down the Option key (Alt key in Windows) to force the Trimmer to change direction (that is, to trim the note at its beginning or its end), regardless of which half of the note graphic you're in.

- ❋ **Pencil.** Inserts new note events. Hold down the Option key (Alt key in Windows) to change the Pencil to an eraser so you can delete notes. The velocity of newly created notes is set in MIDI Preferences. When the Pencil is in Freehand mode, click and drag as you create new MIDI notes to stretch them out to a desired length. In the other Pencil drawing modes, if you click and drag, a series of notes is created at a single pitch whose spacing corresponds to the current grid value. If you use the Line drawing mode, all these notes will have the default Note On velocity value (defined in your MIDI Preferences). In the Triangle, Square, and Random drawing modes, you still can only create notes of single pitch. (Parabolic and S-Curve shapes can be used for adjusting velocities and editing controllers but *not* for creating new notes.) However, the *velocities* of these new notes created by dragging will vary: every eight notes for a full cycle of the triangle shape, alternate notes for the square shape, and, well, *random* for the random shape!

  In Pro Tools 7, the pop-up selector for Pencil drawing modes has a Custom Note Duration option that wasn't available in previous versions. When enabled, an additional pop-up selector for note durations (it looks like a musical note, as shown in Figure 10.7) appears below the Pencil tool itself. This allows you to create various combinations of note spacing and durations as you draw with the Pencil tool: for example, a series of 1/8 notes (the Grid value), each with a duration of a 1/32 note (the Custom Note Duration), would produce a more staccato effect.

❋ **Tip: Zooming Shortcuts for MIDI Tracks**

You can use the Edit window's MIDI vertical zoom buttons to change how much of a MIDI track's pitch range fits into the track at its current height. You can also use the keyboard shortcut Command+Shift (Ctrl+Shift in Windows) and the square bracket keys ([and]) to zoom in/out vertically on MIDI and Instrument tracks.

- ※ **Selector.** No mystery here, although you will notice that a MIDI note isn't selected unless the highlighted range includes its beginning (the Note On event). And no, you cannot select the tail end of a MIDI note and press the Delete key to shorten it; use the Trimmer tool instead.

- ※ **Scrubber.** You *can't* scrub playback of MIDI and Instrument tracks!

※ Tip: Edit with Your Ears

As a general rule, Pro Tools operators who use MIDI should enable the Play MIDI Notes with Grabber and Pencil Tools option in the MIDI tab of the Preferences dialog box. That way, as you drag or create notes, you will hear the notes echoed out to that track's MIDI destination.

※ Tip: Selecting MIDI Note Ranges in Pro Tools 7

Each MIDI/Instrument track in the Edit window has a mini-keyboard at the left edge of the display area. You can use this to select all instances of a single note on the track, or a range of notes by Command+Shift+clicking the desired notes (Ctrl+Shift+click on Windows). You can also click and drag in the mini-keyboard while holding down the Control key (Start key in Windows) to select a range of notes, after which you can Control+Option+click (Start+Alt+click on Windows) a single note within that range to deselect it.

In Velocity view (shown in Figure 10.7 and also discussed in Chapter 6, "The Edit Window"), velocity stalks appear for each MIDI note. You can drag these stalks up and down with the Grabber, draw contours with the Pencil tool (especially in its Line drawing mode), and trim the attack velocities of selected note ranges. Bear in mind, of course, that each program (or *patch*) on a MIDI instrument may respond differently to variations in attack velocity. Whether the sound actually gets louder (or softer) at higher attack velocities, adds another sound layer, or switches to a completely different sound depends entirely on how that program is designed on the currently selected destination instrument. If you switch a MIDI track's output assignment to a different MIDI instrument or program number, you may have to occasionally adjust the velocities of MIDI notes.

※ Tip: Editing MIDI Note Velocities

Here's another easy way to edit individual note velocities that's especially handy when several notes coincide: Hold down the Command key (Ctrl key in Windows) as you click and hold directly on a note; dragging up and down changes its velocity value.

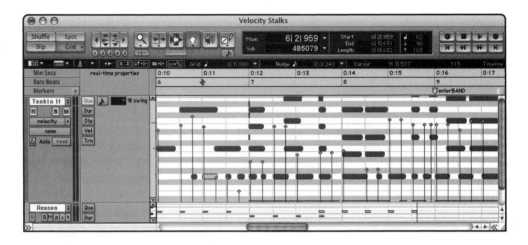

Figure 10.7 You can edit these stalks, which represent the attack velocity for MIDI notes, with the Grabber, Trimmer, and Pencil tools.

Tip: Editing MIDI Note Names, Attack/Release Velocities

As shown in Figure 10.8, when a single MIDI note is selected in Notes view, the Start, End, and Length indicators reflect these values for that note. Three additional fields display the pitch (Note Name), attack velocity, and release velocity. Click in any of these fields to enter a new value. (A fairly large proportion of MIDI controllers do not transmit release velocities, in which case all note events recorded into Pro Tools appear with the default value of 64. Likewise, many sampler and synthesizer patches do not respond to variations in the release Velocity values that are received.)

Any time you press the / key on the numerical keypad while in the Edit window, the Start field is selected. Repeatedly pressing / toggles through these six fields. So you could press / five times until the Attack Velocity field is selected, type in a new number, and press Return (Enter in Windows).

You can also enter values in most MIDI note and velocity fields throughout Pro Tools from your MIDI controller. For example, you could select the MIDI Note field and play the correct note, again pressing Return (or Enter in Windows) to confirm your entry.

If multiple notes are selected, the amount of change (or *delta*) is displayed in these fields. For example, if you type 15 into the Attack Velocity field and press Return (or Enter in Windows) on the alphanumeric keyboard, the velocity values of all currently selected notes are increased by that amount.

Figure 10.8 When MIDI notes are selected, Note Name, Attack Velocity, and Release Velocity fields appear to the right of the Start, End, and Length indicators.

The Event Menu

Chapter 8, "Menu Selections: Highlights," reviews the selections in the Event menu. If you are a composer, arranger, or performer who uses MIDI in Pro Tools, however, you will want to explore all these options in much more detail. We will start with a discussion of the Time, Tempo, and MIDI submenus (see Figure 10.9).

Figure 10.9 The Event menu.

Time Operations

All the functions listed here, which appear in the Time submenu of the Event menu, are also accessible as pages within the Time Operations window, which you can open in this submenu by double-clicking the Meter indicator in the Transport or by pressing Option+1 on the numeric keypad (Alt+1 in Windows).

Change Meter

Selecting the Change Meter command opens a window for inserting a meter change event into the Meter ruler (and optionally in the Tempo ruler). A pop-up selector lets you choose whether this new time signature should remain in effect through the end of the session, the current bar only, or only to the selected range of bars. This Change Meter page of the Time Operations window also provides the option to change the meter of the click.

To better understand how this function works, imagine that the bridge of your song needs to change from 4/4 to 3/4 time signature—for four bars beginning at bar 33, followed by 32 more bars of 4/4, and then another 3/4 section at bar 69 when the bridge is repeated. Before you start recording your audio and MIDI parts, take a moment to set up the song structure using the following steps:

1. Switch to Grid edit mode. If you haven't already done so, switch your main ruler to Bars:Beats format (via the Display menu). Using the pop-up selector in the Edit menu, change the Grid Value setting to 1 bar.

2. Using the Selector tool, highlight bars 33–37, either within an existing track or in the ruler itself if you haven't yet created any tracks in this session.

3. Select Event > MIDI > Change Meter. The Time Operations window opens with its Change Meter page displayed, as shown in Figure 10.10.

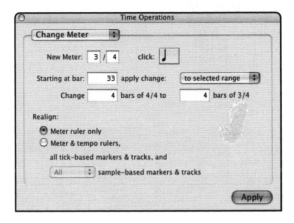

Figure 10.10 The Change Meter page of the Time Operations window. Here, we're changing a four-bar selection to 3/4 time signature.

4. Change the new meter to 3/4. (For this example, leave the pop-up click selector at 1/4 notes. However, if this section was in 3/8—not to mention 5/8, 7/8, or 11/8!—you would usually have the click change to 1/8 notes during this section only and then revert back to 1/4 notes when the song returns to 4/4.)

5. Bar 33 is already selected as the starting bar for this meter change. Use the pop-up selector to the right of this field to choose To Selected Range (rather than To Session End or Until Next Bar).

6. Be sure to specify that you want these four bars of 4/4 changed to *four* bars of 3/4 (and not some other number) because in this case, you want the tempo to remain constant—that is, the 1/4 notes should be equivalent between the two sections.

7. In this case, the Realign option will be fine set to its default, Meter Ruler Only.

8. Click the Apply button.

9. If the Meter ruler is currently visible (enabled either using the Ruler Options pop-up selector in the Edit window or via the View >Ruler submenu), two new Meter Change events now appear: one for the beginning of the 3/4 section and another where it returns to 4/4.

10. Highlight bars 69–72 (the next occurrence of the 3/4 section) and repeat these steps.

Insert Time

The time units displayed in the Insert Time page of the Time Operations window always reflect those of the currently active main ruler. Even if you're not a MIDI user and don't edit music at all, the Insert Time and Cut Time functions will occasionally be useful. For example, when creating soundtracks for video or multimedia, somewhere along the line, you may need to add more time at the beginning of the session because the segment needs a longer intro. When creating music with MIDI, of course, this command is essential, allowing you to work in Bars:Beats time units, adding bars at the beginning of the song or at any point within its timeline as shown in Figure 10.11. Usually, you will choose to have this command affect locations of all the subsequent markers, tempo, and meter events; they are then pushed later in the timeline by a corresponding amount. (One exception might be when working on a video or film soundtrack, where you add bars to the music but don't want the positions of sample-based markers—absolute time locations—that reference dialog or sound effects to be affected by the time insertion.)

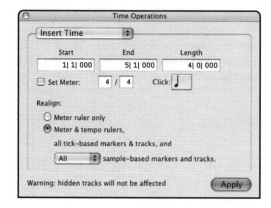

Figure 10.11   The Insert Time page of the Time Operations window. Here, we're inserting four bars at the beginning of the song.

Cut Time

Options in the Cut Time page in the Time Operations window are similar to those for Insert Time. Time units here also reflect the currently active main ruler and, if desired, you can adjust all subsequent markers, tempo events, and meter events to an earlier position in the session's timeline after the specified range is cut.

Move Song Start

In the Move Song Start page of the Time Operations window, choosing musical bars as the time units (timebase) for this function allows you to move the beginning of the session's timeline to a specified bar location and, at the same time, assign a new bar number to that new location (if desired). Whether you choose to have this operation apply to marker locations and audio tracks that are sample based (that is, their positional references are based on absolute time, rather than being relative to musical bars and beats) depends on the situation. As with the Insert Time function, when scoring a soundtrack, you might use Move Song Start to move a music cue to a later position. Using the Minutes:Seconds time units here, for example, allows you to specify that bar one should now start at exactly five seconds into the timeline while leaving sample-based markers and tracks unaffected. This is shown in Figure 10.12.

In the Tempo ruler of the Edit window, a Song Start Marker appears (a small red diamond-shaped icon, which appears at the beginning of the session's timeline by default). The Song Start Marker's position changes as a result of applying the Move Song Start function. However, you can also accomplish more or less the same thing by dragging this marker directly in the Tempo ruler, if you prefer. As with most events in the Edit window, if Grid edit mode is active, the current grid value governs the movement of the markers you drag in the rulers—they will snap from one grid increment to another (for example, seconds might be convenient in Minutes:Seconds format, or frames on system configurations supporting SMPTE time code format for Grid mode). When moving the Song Start in this manner, it's important to note that, by default, the position of regions and other events in all tick-based tracks will also be affected. If instead you only want tick-based events to be affected (including all MIDI track events and regions or automation event locations in audio tracks, Aux Input tracks, and Master Fader tracks whose timebase is set to Ticks), hold down Shift+Control (Shift+Start in Windows) as you drag the Song Start Marker.

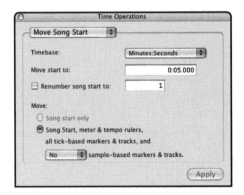

Figure 10.12 The Move Song Start page of the Time Operations window. Here, we're inserting five seconds at the beginning of the song, without affecting bar numbering or the position of any markers or regions within tracks whose timebase is set to samples (absolute).

Tempo Operations

The tempo-related functions in this submenu all open the Tempo Operations window. Whichever option you choose, the end result is that one or more tempo events are inserted into the timeline of your session. You can view tempo events in the Tempo ruler and graphically edit them in the Tempo Editor window, which you can open underneath the Tempo ruler. You can also drag existing tempo events around in the Tempo ruler itself (even when the Tempo Editor is not visible)—if Grid edit mode is enabled, this will affect their movement.

When you adjust tempos in Pro Tools, the positions of all events in all tracks that are set to Ticks timebase are displaced by a corresponding amount. In contrast to the absolute time references in tracks set to Samples timebase, the positions of events in Tick-based tracks are defined by musical time references—bars, beats, and ticks (subdivisions of a 1/4 note)—and consequently, are always *relative* to the current tempo. If you're using audio regions for cymbal crashes, individual drum hits, or sound effects in conjunction with MIDI or Instrument tracks, for example, using Ticks timebase for those tracks will keep them in sync with the MIDI tracks even after a tempo change is applied.

Following are brief descriptions of each tempo operation. Incidentally, when you are concerned about where the selection will end in real time (minutes, seconds, and milliseconds, for example), you will almost always want to enable the Advanced checkbox in the Tempo Operations window. Lastly, although we cannot dedicate space to the subject here, several of these options can be useful for building tempo maps in the event you ever need to build a MIDI orchestration based on a recorded performance with constantly changing tempos.

❋ **Constant.** Applies a single tempo setting to the currently selected range. A single tempo event is created at the beginning of the range, and any previously existing tempo events within it are deleted. If the Preserve Tempo after Selection option is enabled, a second tempo event returns the tempo to its previous setting at the end of the selection.

❋ **Linear.** Creates a series of tempo events to create a ramp-shaped progression from one tempo setting to another. As with some of these other tempo operations, if you enable the Advanced option, you can specify the density and resolution of the resulting series of tempo events. A pop-up selector among the Advanced options (also available for the other shapes here for tempo change) allows for the automatic calculation of the new real-time end point that will result from your tempo change settings (in minutes and seconds, for example).

❋ **Parabolic.** Instead of a straight ramp up or down between the two tempo settings, you can adjust the curvature of this parabola shape with a slider or numerical field. A zero curvature is a straight ramp identical to the Linear tempo operation. Larger positive values push most of the tempo acceleration toward the end of the current selection, while negative values push it toward the beginning.

❋ **S-curve.** With this shape, you can specify the exact time location for the midpoint (in time units corresponding to the currently active main Time ruler, as with all these other tempo operations). You also specify exactly what tempo (somewhere between the starting and ending tempo values for the range) should be in effect at that midpoint. The Curvature value determines how steeply the tempo increases or decreases between the midpoint and the start/end points of the range. Larger positive values push most of the tempo acceleration from the midpoint value toward the start/end points of the current selection, while negative values bunch most of the acceleration to/from the midpoint tempo around the midpoint itself.

✼ **Scale.** Unlike the other tempo operations here, scaling tempos doesn't overwrite existing tempo events. Instead, scaling is used to relatively increase or decrease the value of all tempos within the currently selected range. You can specify this either as a percentage or by altering the average tempo within the current selection (which is automatically calculated for you).

✼ **Stretch.** Figure 10.13 shows an example of using the Stretch function to automatically adjust the tempo of the current selection to match a specific duration.

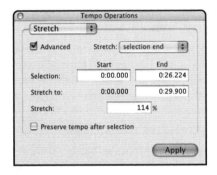

Figure 10.13 The Tempo Operations dialog box. Here, we're automatically adjusting the tempo so that the selected musical segment will match a given length of time.

Using the Tempo Change Dialog Box

Bear in mind that the tempo operations described here must be used on a currently selected range in your session's timeline (either within any track or in a ruler). You could also insert a single tempo event—either at the beginning of the timeline or at some specific point in the timeline. (Tempo events remain in effect until the end of the session or until another tempo event is reached.) After setting the Start value to the desired location—either by clicking a region with the Grabber tool or by clicking somewhere with the Selector tool—click the + (plus) sign at the left end of the Tempo ruler. The Tempo Change dialog box (shown in Figure 10.14) opens.

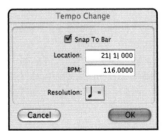

Figure 10.14 The Tempo Change dialog box.

MIDI Operations

All the options in the Event > MIDI submenu (shown in Figure 10.15) open the MIDI Operations window: Grid/Groove Quantize, Change Velocity, Change Duration, Transpose, Select Notes, Split Notes, Input Quantize, Step Input, Restore Performance, and Flatten Performance. In fact, this window contains a pop-up selector you can use to switch between these options for altering the currently selected MIDI data. You can click the Apply button repeatedly to apply the settings you've adjusted for each function without leaving this window (which stays open until you choose to close it). You can find brief descriptions of each of these operations in Chapter 8, but the next section explores in more detail the Pro Tools Grid/Groove Quantization features for MIDI note events, use of Flatten/Restore Performance, and the Step Input feature.

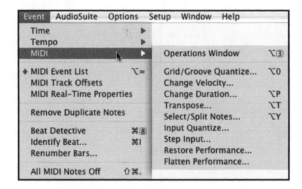

Figure 10.15   The Event > MIDI submenu.

The MIDI Operations window, shown in Figure 10.16, provides options for transforming selected MIDI data. You can leave this window open (space permitting) and use its Apply button to alter the currently selected MIDI data. Like many other windows in Pro Tools, pressing the Tab key cycles through the fields (press Shift+Tab to move backward), and you can use up/down arrows to increase/decrease selected field values. When any pitch or velocity field is selected, you can also enter new values by playing a note on your MIDI controller. As you use the pop-up selector to select this window's pages for Grid/Groove Quantize, Transpose, Change Velocity/Duration, and other MIDI-related functions, the available parameters change accordingly.

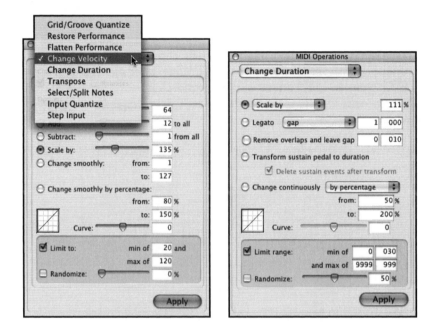

Figure 10.16 Without leaving the MIDI Operations window, you can use a pop-up selector to switch between Change Velocity/Duration, Grid/Groove Quantize, Transpose, Flatten/Restore Performance, and other functions.

Grid/Groove Quantize

As explained in Chapter 8, quantization snaps all notes within the currently selected MIDI data to a specified rhythmic value. The attacks and/or releases of MIDI notes (beginnings or ends) are moved to the nearest increment on a horizontal time grid, whose spacing is determined by the selected note value in this window. As you might guess from its location in the MIDI submenu, this command applies only to MIDI data within MIDI regions. This MIDI quantization function doesn't affect the beginning and end positions of MIDI regions—and of course doesn't apply to audio at all! Many of the options in this window (see Figure 10.17) are self-explanatory, so this section mentions just a few items of special interest. Note that the Option+0 (zero) keyboard shortcut (Alt+0 in Windows) opens the Grid/Groove Quantize window.

Quantize Grid

In this pop-up selector, you can choose among note values that will serve as the increments for the quantization grid (the basis for adjusting MIDI event positions, in conjunction with the other parameters in the Grid/Groove Quantize window). Along with standard note values (whole/half notes, 1/4 notes, 1/8 notes, and so on), you can also choose dotted values and triplets.

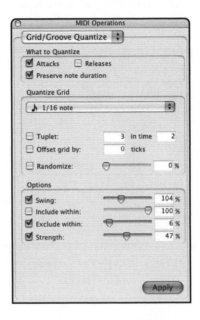

Figure 10.17 Use the Grid/Groove Quantize window for adjusting time locations of MIDI notes. It can be useful for cleaning up rhythmic timing or conforming multiple recordings by some percentage toward a common feel.

You can also choose among various DigiGroove templates that are provided with the program or others that you created with Beat Detective. Groove templates are irregular grids that you can use for quantizing MIDI events. Sometimes, these can produce more human-sounding results than simply adding a swing factor to a straight (symmetrical) time grid for quantization. For example, try manually creating a straight MIDI drum part with a constant 1/16-note hi-hat pattern and applying various grooves to get a feel for the effects they produce. For recorded MIDI parts, one trick is to use the percentage sliders to reduce the effect of quantization on note position somewhat, relying more on velocity patterns from the groove template to produce a more subtle transformation.

As discussed in Chapter 12, "The Pro Tools Groove," you can create your own DigiGroove templates based on audio or MIDI selections and use these as the template for quantizing MIDI events and audio regions. If you combine live MIDI performances (and especially MIDI parts created with the Step Input feature), this is an essential technique for obtaining a tighter groove between multiple overdubbed parts.

Tuplet

A *tuplet* (see Figure 10.18) is a rhythmic grouping where some irregular number of notes fits into the normal duration of two (or four, and so on) notes. For example, 1/8 note triplets are a 3:2 tuplet because three 1/8 notes fit into the duration of two normal 1/8 notes (three notes at 1|000, 1|320, and 1|640 instead of only two at 1|000 and 1|480). So all you folks creating dance music, just quantize everything to some funky 1/8 note quintuplets and sep-tuplets; we promise to be the first ones on the dance floor!

Figure 10.18 Tuplets allow you to create rhythmic groupings of the main beat that aren't multiples of 2 or 3. For example, here we've selected 1/16-note quintuplets as our basis for quantization (with a small degree of randomization).

Randomize

Marketing types like to claim that *randomizing* is the way to humanize MIDI parts that have been over-enthusiastically quantized. Pardon us for getting on the soapbox for a moment here, but generally speaking, while the timing of good musicians is indeed irregular, we contend that it's actually more *complex* than that—not simply random. Nevertheless, if your completely quantized parts really do sound stiff, some *small* amount of randomization (less than 10%) can sometimes help. However, on a drum part, for example, you may get better results applying the randomness only to one element (say, the hi-hat or small percussion parts) rather than the entire groove. And even in these cases, try a very small amount of random-ization on the *velocities* first (using the Change Velocity command), rather than the actual position of the note events in time. Here's another recommendation: In our experience, the stiffness of over-quantized parts usually has more to do with the upbeats, rather than the downbeats, being too rigid. For this reason, try using very small amounts of swing—10% or less—to loosen up a drum groove rather than randomizing the timing in general. To our ears, it usually sounds better.

Swing

Any swing factor greater than 0% delays every upbeat of the specified musical value. In other words, if you're swinging 1/8 notes, the ones that coincide with 1/4-note divisions are unaffected by the swing factor, but the ones between 1/4 notes are moved somewhat later than exactly halfway between the 1/4 notes. This can go from a very subtle groove factor (<10%) through various degrees of shuffle to a full triplet feel (100%), or even more. Very small amounts of swing (for example, 2–5% on 1/8 notes or 1/16 notes in drum and/or bass parts) can make a huge feel improvement on quantized MIDI parts that sound a little stiff compared to the audio tracks you've laid down.

Swing quantization is very musically useful, but many users find its parameters a bit confusing in Pro Tools. Here's how it works:

- ❋ **0% swing.** Applies no swing at all. If we're quantizing a series of 1/8 notes, each 1/4 note downbeat in a measure is obviously 1|000, 2|000, and so on, and each 1/8 note upbeat is 1|480, 2|480, and so on. (Because there are 960 ticks, or subdivisions, for every 1/4 note in Pro Tools, each 1/8 note corresponds to exactly half of that: 480 ticks.)

- ❋ **100% swing.** A full triplet (or 12/8) feel. Each 1/8 note upbeat is quantized to the third note of a 1/8 note triplet, 1|640, 2|640, and so on. 960 ticks per 1/4 note divided by 3 equals 320, so the three notes in an 1/8 note triplet are at 1|000, 1|320, and 1|640. The effect of 100% swing is the same as quantizing to a 3:2 tuplet (see the definition for this quantization parameter below). As always, the 1/4 note downbeats (the first note in each triplet group) stay at 1|000, 2|000, and so on and are unaffected by any 1/8 note swing percentage.

- ❋ **150% swing.** Quantizes each 1/8 note upbeat to the fourth 1/16 note: 1|720, 2|720, and so on. (960 ticks divided by 4 equals 240, so the four 1/6 notes are at 1|000, 1|240, 1|480, and 1|720. It's the same thing as quantizing to dotted 1/8 notes, in this example.)

- ❋ **300% swing.** If 100% swing moves each 1/8 note upbeat one-third of the way (160 ticks) toward the following downbeat, 300% swing moves it *all* the way there. It's as if you quantized to 1/4 notes, except that notes are always moved to the *following* 1/4 note.

In Table 10.1, you can see how progressively greater amounts of swing gradually move the timing of offbeat notes toward a full triplet value (or even beyond it, at swing factors greater than 100%). There are no hard and fast rules here; you will have to experiment with all the values to achieve the feel you want. However, you will find that this is one of your most important tools for achieving a more natural feel in heavily quantized MIDI parts.

Table 10.1   It Don't Mean A Thing… Quantizing with Swing (1/4 Note = 960 Ticks)

Note Value	0% Swing	25% Swing	50% Swing	75% Swing	100% Swing	150% Swing
1/8 note	1|480	1|520	1|560	1|600	1|640	1|720
1/16 note	1|240	1|260	1|280	1|300	1|320	1|360

Include Within

This quantization parameter is worth exploring; it only quantizes notes within a certain distance of the specified note value. For example, you might use this if you want to make sure the downbeats of the hi-hat part coincide exactly with kick and snare 1/4 notes (which are strictly quantized) without changing any of the looser upbeats between them. Select the hi-hat notes only, and then set the Quantize grid to 1/4 notes, changing the Include Within parameter to 50% or less (which leaves anything further than a 1/16 note in either direction from the nearest 1/4 note unaffected). Your hi-hat downbeats are moved to exactly 1|000, 2|000, and so on (unless you set the Strength parameter to less than 100%, of course), while the upbeats remain at their original locations.

Strength

When this parameter is set to anything less than 100%, notes are moved only that percentage of the distance between their current location and the nearest quantization grid increment. This improves timing, while preserving some of the natural feel of your performance.

> ### ❋ Quantizing Regions
>
> The Region > Quantize to Grid command does *not* apply quantization to individual MIDI notes, even when MIDI regions are selected. A more accurate description of this function would be "Snap Regions to Grid." It moves selected regions and all their contents by snapping their left boundaries—or the sync point within them if they contain one—to the nearest grid increment per the current grid value. Quantizing Regions to Grid predates the relatively sophisticated MIDI editing features in current versions of Pro Tools. However, because the underlying idea of quantization is that a phenomenon (in this case, possible time positions of MIDI notes or regions) doesn't permit a continuous range of possible values, but can only jump from one discrete increment (quantum) to another, the Quantize Regions command *is* correctly named. We mention it here because many novice Pro Tools users (including veterans of other MIDI programs) might otherwise think this is the obvious way to quantize their drum part to 1/8 notes, for instance. Not so!

Restore Performance

Pro Tools "remembers" the original recorded MIDI performance in MIDI regions, even after you've made multiple edits, saving and reopening the session many times. This command opens the Restore Performance window (shown in Figure 10.19), where you restore selected MIDI regions to their original recorded form (or to the most recent flattened version; see the next section), choosing one or all of the following attributes for restoration: Timing, Duration, Velocity, or Pitch.

Flatten Performance

The window opened by this command is shown in Figure 10.20. It enables you to freeze the current state of the selected MIDI region. This flattened version will now be the state this region returns to the next time you execute the Restore Performance command. As before, you can choose Timing, Duration, Velocity, or Pitch as the parameters for flattening.

Here's a typical scenario for using the Flatten Performance command: Imagine that you've applied some basic note corrections, global velocity changes, or other edits to a drum part you've previously recorded on a MIDI or Instrument track. Now you will apply some quantization before recording additional parts, because the timing seems a little too loose.

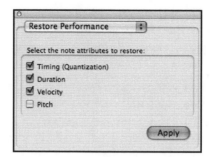

Figure 10.19   Restore Performance let you return parameters of a MIDI recording to their original, "as recorded" state.

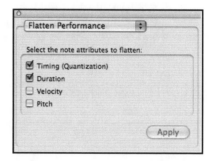

Figure 10.20   Flatten Performance establishes the current state of a MIDI recording as the condition it will revert to if you later apply the Restore Performance command.

However, a common pitfall of quantization is that you can "correct" all the humanity right out of a piece by applying too much of it. Once you've added a few more instrumental parts, you may discover that the original timing in the drums really wasn't as bad as it once seemed when heard all by itself (or with only one or two other parts). The Restore Performance function is great because it lets you go all the way back the original performance—but what if you'd really rather not lose all those changes you made *before* starting to quantize? No problem: At any point in the process when you know that all changes made so far to the selected MIDI region are keepers, apply the Flatten Performance command. This now becomes your new go-back state for that region, should you ever decide to retrace your steps and apply a different set of edits to it from that point forward.

Step Input

Even if you're not severely keyboard challenged, non–real-time entry of a sequence of MIDI notes or chords can sometimes be a useful technique. The important thing to understand about Step Input mode is that you can enter one or several notes simultaneously. Some people use step entry when creating specific drum patterns, for example. Of course, you can also use this feature to create "impossible" *ostinatos* (rhythmic, persistently repeating musical figures) and arpeggios.

Following are some basic rules and techniques for using Step Input to create sequences of MIDI notes in Pro Tools:

✻ Step input begins at the Edit window's current Start position, so you should set this to the correct time location before you begin entering notes.

✻ As you can see in Figure 10.21, options in the Step Input window allow you to either fix the note velocities at a specific value or use the velocity data created as you strike notes on the keyboard (or other MIDI controller).

✻ A destination MIDI or Instrument track must be selected as the target for step entry. If you want to hear these notes as you're entering them, you will also usually want to record-enable that MIDI track. In fact, though, Pro Tools allows you to change the destination MIDI track for the note events you're creating in Step Input mode on the fly—which opens up some interesting possibilities for *hocketing* (rapid alternation of notes or very short phrases) or call-and-answer effects between two different tracks, for example.

✻ Set the Note Length percentage to less than 100% if you want a more *staccato* style (that is, each note ends before the next one begins, as opposed to *legato*, where the

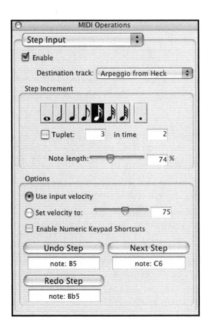

Figure 10.21 The Step Input window allows non–real-time entry of MIDI notes. Note that in this example, keys on the MIDI controller have been mapped to the Undo Step, Next Step, and Redo Step functions.

end of each note joins with the beginning of the following note). Note: You can also use length percentages greater than 100%, if you instead want each note to overlap the beginning of the one following it.

❄ When the Step Input window's Numeric Keypad Shortcuts option is enabled, the Transport commands for these keys are temporarily suspended, and you can use them for Step Input functions. The shortcuts are as follows:

— The numeric keypad's Enter key is the same as the Next Step button; it skips the insertion point for new notes forward to the next step. Therefore, you can use it to create rests, for example.

— The 0 key on the numeric keypad is the same as the Undo Step button; it undoes the previously entered step and moves the insertion point for step-entering a new note back to its previous position.

— While still holding down the key(s) on the MIDI controller during Step Input, you can also use the Next Step and Undo Step buttons—or their keyboard shortcuts—to lengthen or shorten these notes by the current step increment value.

— The 1 key on the numeric keypad selects whole-note step increments.

— The 2 key on the numeric keypad selects 1/2 notes.

— The 3 key on the numeric keypad enables tuplets in relation to the selected step increment (for example, 3:2 tuplets with an 1/8-note step increment creates 1/8-note triplets; 5:2 creates quintuplets; 7:2 creates septuplets; and so on).

— The 4 key on the numeric keypad selects 1/4 notes.

— The 5 key on the numeric keypad selects 1/8 notes.

— The 6 key on the numeric keypad selects 1/16 notes.

— The 7 key on the numeric keypad selects 1/32 notes.

— The 8 key on the numeric keypad selects 1/64 notes.

— The decimal point key on the numeric keypad enables dotted note values (half again as long as the ordinary note value—so a dotted 1/8-note increment is 720 ticks instead of 480, for example).

MIDI Real-Time Properties

This feature was added in version 7 of Pro Tools. MIDI Real-Time Properties allow you to apply real-time, non-destructive changes to the events in MIDI tracks and regions. These types of MIDI note data transformation are supported: quantization of note positions, changes to the duration and velocity of MIDI notes, transposition of their pitches (in octaves and/or semitones), and delay (which supports making the MIDI events in the affected track or region play back either sooner or later than their original position).

In Figure 10.22, you can see the Real-Time Properties window for a selected MIDI region. Note that unless you click the Write to Region button, these changes are applied in real time and don't affect the actual contents of the affected region. In fact, unless you specifically enable that option in the MIDI tab of the Preferences dialog box, Pro Tools always displays the original "source" location of MIDI events and not their position as modified by MIDI Real-Time properties applied to the region or track where they reside.

Figure 10.22   From the Event menu, you can open the Real-Time Properties window for a selected MIDI region.

There is also a Real-Time Properties column in the Edit window that affects entire tracks. As you can see in Figure 10.23, many of the options here are similar. It's important to understand that region-level properties always override track properties. That is, if a particular region already has its own real-time properties, the track-level properties will not affect it. Region-level properties can be a powerful compositional tool, especially when combined with Mirrored MIDI Editing (which you can enable via a button in the Edit window or via a selection in the Options menu). For example, if you want to double a part at the octave, one method is to copy the MIDI region to another track (by Option-dragging, or Alt-dragging in Windows while in Grid editing mode) and then apply a transposition value of +12. If you enable Mirrored MIDI Editing, any note changes you make in the original copy of the region are immediately reflected in the copy. You might apply additional real-time property changes to the transposed part, such as velocity or duration changes, according to the characteristics of the sound used on the MIDI destination for each track.

Within a single track, you might use Mirrored MIDI Editing to apply region-level properties to various copies of a single MIDI region—perhaps repeating a bass line or melody shifted by an interval of a fifth or octave higher, for example.

At the beginning of this chapter, Figure 10.1 shows the MIDI Event List (which is also briefly described in Chapter 8). You will note that where MIDI events are affected by real-time properties, a T or R appears to indicate whether these are track- or region-level.

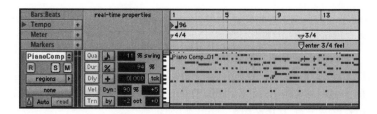

Figure 10.23 Parameters in the Real-Time Properties column of the Edit window affect the entire MIDI or Instrument track (which in turn may contain regions with their own real-time properties).

Remove Duplicate Notes

Especially when you are layering up parts in Loop Record mode (drum-machine style), it is all too easy to end up with duplicate notes. Especially after quantizing, these duplicate notes may not be easy to see, and they can cause phase-cancelled, flanger-like effects as notes are double triggered. While the MIDI Event List might also be handy for these instances, this command makes the process much easier.

Beat Detective

Beat Detective is discussed in more detail in Chapter 12. You can extract DigiGroove templates from either audio or MIDI selections (to be used by the Grid/Groove Quantize command in the MIDI Operations window).

Identify Beat

This command is one of the ways you can tell Pro Tools what the starting and ending bar/beat positions should be for the current selection. One things you can do with this command is to use a precise audio selection (four or eight bars that you've precisely selected using Looped Playback, for example) to establish a Pro Tools tempo so that you can effectively edit in Grid mode. (Steps for this technique are also described in Chapter 12.)

Renumber Bars

The Renumber Bars command is very straightforward; selecting it simply renumbers the bars in your song. A typical scenario for renumbering bars is when your song begins with a drum fill of some kind, but it's much easier to keep track of its structure (with four- and eight-bar sections, and so on) if bar 1 corresponds to the point where the band enters. Similarly, for songs with a slow or *rubato* introduction (freely played, without a strict tempo), you may prefer to have the point where the groove kicks in numbered as bar 1. (In either of these cases, all the bars before bar 1 will have negative numbers after renumbering.)

All MIDI Notes Off

This command silences any "stuck" MIDI notes (caused by system malfunction or interruption of MIDI data transmission—a Note On is transmitted, but a Note Off is never received). The keyboard shortcut for this command is Command+Shift+period (Ctrl+Shift+period in Windows). If you are a MIDI user, memorize it now!

Other Commands Relating to MIDI

These are also discussed in Chapters 5, "The Transport Window," and 8, "Menu Selections: Highlights." Briefly, however, a few are defined here:

* Options > Click turns transmission of MIDI metronome click on and off. This command is also accessible from the Transport.

* Setup > Click opens the Click/Countoff Options dialog box. This command is also accessible from the Transport.

* Options > MIDI Thru enables what you play into a record-enabled MIDI track in Pro Tools to be echoed back out of Pro Tools, according to that track's settings (MIDI port and channel, program number, volume, pan, and so on).

Summary

Pro Tools has some reasonably powerful tools for editing MIDI events and for creating musical arrangements based on MIDI performances mixed with digital audio. Be sure to check out Chapter 12, "The Pro Tools Groove," and Chapter 13, "Music Production," for more musical applications of Pro Tools. Obviously, there are some other audio-savvy programs whose emphasis is more strongly on MIDI and composition—Digital Performer, Logic Pro, Cubase SX, and SONAR, to name just a few. Whenever required, Pro Tools can import and export Standard MIDI Files (for which using the .SMF file name extension will facilitate recognition of the file type on Windows systems). Nevertheless, we know many people who use nothing *but* Pro Tools for their projects, regardless of whether their emphasis is more on MIDI or audio. Especially with all the MIDI features added in recent versions, Pro Tools is certainly up to the job!

11} Synchronization

If you need to synchronize playback and recording in Pro Tools to some external device (such as a video deck or a multitrack tape recorder), this chapter will be of special interest to you. It includes both basic concepts and some fairly technical information—not that you will necessarily absorb it all at first reading, but to provide some context for dealing with synchronization issues when they arise.

As you will see, there are various levels of synchronization possible with Pro Tools. Your synchronization requirements may be no more complicated than simply triggering playback at the correct position in the session's timeline, when the corresponding time code location is received from the master device (trigger sync). More sophisticated techniques lock the internal audio clock of Pro Tools to a very stable external reference (for example, video sync, word clock, or a timing reference generated by an external synchronization peripheral such as Digidesign's Sync I/O). When Pro Tools and the master device share a common *reference sync*, they can stay perfectly locked together over longer periods of time. Sample-accurate sync is also extremely important when Pro Tools audio channels are combined with others playing simultaneously from another source, especially where there might be some shared information in these audio signals (like microphone leakage!). Otherwise, phase cancellation might occur due to slight differences in playback speed on the two devices (for example, between Pro Tools and a multitrack tape recorder).

Synchronization Defined

By *synchronization*, we mean the technology and operational techniques required so that two (or more) devices that record and play back information will work together in a consistent fashion over time. One device always has to start at the same position relative to the other—and ideally, *stay* in the same relative position as both devices continue to operate over time, so that the two devices don't drift apart.

> ## ✳ Note: Synchronization Theory: The Basics
>
> We don't want to overwhelm you with pure theory in this book; our focus is always on practical applications of the concepts in Pro Tools. But in the interest of being clear, here's just a bit of theoretical perspective, drawn from Vol. 3 (Desktop Audio) of our *CSi* (*Cool School Interactus*) CD-ROM series published by Thomson Course Technology, which includes interactive examples that further explain synchronization concepts.
>
> For synchronizing (audio and video) devices, three fundamental time attributes come into play:
>
> ✳ A defined unit of measurement for the information storage method (for example, time units such as hours, minutes, seconds, frames, samples, or inches on a moving tape)
>
> ✳ A nominal rate at which these measurements are taken (how many measurements per unit of time; for example, how many frames, samples, or inches per second)
>
> ✳ A stable timing reference that ensures measurements are recorded and reproduced at a precise rate, maintaining their correct time relationship (for example, video sync, sample clock or word sync, capstan tachometer)
>
> In short, we require a *measurement*, a *speed*, and a *reference* that keeps that speed consistent.
>
> Lastly, for time code work, we add a fourth element, timestamp, or location information. Like the address of your house, a *timestamp* is a precise numerical reference. It's used for positioning devices for playback from specific time locations or to indicate exactly where an event (a video edit, a sound effect, the beginning of a musical cue, and so on) should occur.

SMPTE time code (and its equivalent in the MIDI protocol, MIDI Time Code) is the standard timestamping (addressing) method used to get playback from two devices to start from the correct point in time. For digital audio, some sort of digital clock sync should also be used as a timing reference if these devices need to stay precisely locked together over longer durations. (Both continuous resync and reference sync methods use an external timing reference to control the playback sample rate of Pro Tools—these are discussed later in this same chapter.)

In any synchronization setup, one device is designated as the *master*. The other devices in the setup, the *slaves*, get their location information from this master and start (trigger) playback at the appropriate location. Figure 11.1 shows a simple configuration where Pro Tools is slaved to another device via an external SMPTE interface on the host computer. Pro Tools can instantly begin playback after analyzing the received timestamp information, unlike analog or digital tape machines that first have to rewind or fast-forward the tape to reach the appropriate location. In certain situations, a master also provides a speed reference for the slaved devices (for example, two synced analog tape machines, or a digital audio device whose sample rate is continuously adjusted to that of an external source).

In audio-for-video production, the video transport is typically the master (although MachineControl users often reverse this relationship; see Chapter 14, "Postproduction and Soundtracks"). The master provides a location reference (in the form of SMPTE time code) that triggers where audio playback begins, so that audio events can be correctly placed in relation to the picture. In most professional facilities, a speed reference is also provided—in the form of a stable video signal called *black burst* or *house sync*. With the appropriate

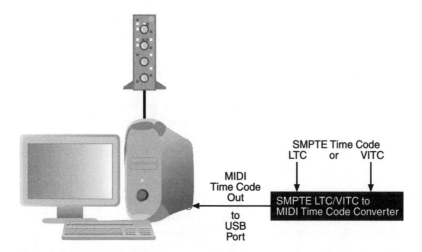

Figure 11.1 A typical SMPTE synchronization setup. An external SMPTE interface translates the incoming SMPTE data from its audio or video encoded format to MIDI Time Code (MTC), which is routed to Pro Tools via the computer's USB port.

synchronization peripheral (like the Sync I/O or Digital Timepiece), this external timing reference can be converted in order to control the audio sample rate of the external Pro Tools hardware interface itself.

SMPTE Time Code

Named for the Society of Motion Picture and Television Engineers, the organization that standardized the format, SMPTE time code is used throughout the video and film industries for cameras, switchers, editing systems, and audio postproduction. Time-location data is encoded into a data "word" that consists of 80 bits, representing hours, minutes, seconds, frames, and subframes. The number of frames per minute depends on the application or geographical location (see the "Frame Rates" section later in this chapter). SMPTE time code provides a standard language for identifying time locations among various operators and devices in an audio, video, or film project. *Edit Decision Lists (EDLs)* are text documents that contain time-code locations for edits made from multiple source tapes; they can be automatically generated by some video-editing systems (and are comparable to *playlists* in Pro Tools tracks). Hit points for audio events (events in the video to which specific sounds or music cues are synchronized) are also sometimes listed in similar format.

SMPTE time code allows events to be properly placed during edit and permits multiple devices to maintain a correct time relationship during recording and playback. When Pro Tools is in Online mode (that is, playback location is controlled by incoming time code), it looks at the incoming SMPTE timestamp information (from a separate SMPTE peripheral attached to your computer) and then calculates the proper position to start playback within the session's timeline. (This offset for the timeline of your Pro Tools session, known as the Session Start time, appears in an editable field of the Session Startup window, which is opened via Setup > Session.)

If the incoming SMPTE location is *prior* to the start of the session, Pro Tools waits until the Session Start time is reached before starting playback. If the first time-code location received is *later* than the Session Start time (for example, if you press the Play button on the video deck that's serving as the master device when it's somewhere in the middle of the tape), Pro Tools will jump to the appropriate position in its timeline and start playing back—regardless of whether the session actually contains any regions and so on at that point. (So make sure you get your SMPTE references right!)

Synchronization Example with an External Video Deck

Let's say a video editor provides you a BetaCam SP master tape containing a 30-second spot. She tells you that the time-code location for the beginning of the program is one hour, zero minutes, zero seconds, zero frames (01:00:00:00), and most importantly, that the time code format is 29.97 frames per second, non-drop. You pop the tape into your BetaCam deck, and you notice that prior to the actual beginning of the spot, there are color bars, audio tones, and so on. (The LTC time code output of the BetaCam deck, a BNC connector for audio, is connected to the time-code audio input of your computer's SMPTE/MIDI interface, which you indicate as the synchronization source for Pro Tools.)

1. Create a new Pro Tools session. Set the sample rate of this session to 48kHz (standard for professional video).

2. Open Setup > Peripherals. Set the Session Start time to 01:00:00:00. Use the pop-up Timecode Rate selector to choose 29.97 fps.

3. Create a stereo audio track. You want to record the original sound from the video master into Pro Tools—not only because it will inevitably require your audio engineer's magic touch (to correct inconsistent levels, background noise, and so on), but the finished stereo mix you lay back onto the video tape must contain not only your music and sound effects, but also the original spoken dialog and ambient sound!

4. Arm your track(s) for recording, and check your levels—if your video editors have been doing their jobs, you can trust that the reference tones prior to the spot truly represent zero dB (but better check, just in case). If you get no level at all, check to see if the audio outputs of the Beta deck are really connected to your audio hardware inputs—it happens!

5. Open Setup > Peripherals, and select the Synchronization tab. Confirm that the configuration is correct for the synchronization hardware you're using (as seen in Figure 11.2).

6. Also, in the Preferences dialog box, under the Operation tab, confirm in the Online Options section that Record Online at Time Code (or ADAT) Lock is enabled.

7. Now, enable the Online button in the Pro Tools Transport window (so that recording of Pro Tools will be engaged when time code is received, at the corresponding location in the session's timeline, according to the Session Start time you've specified in the Session Setup window).

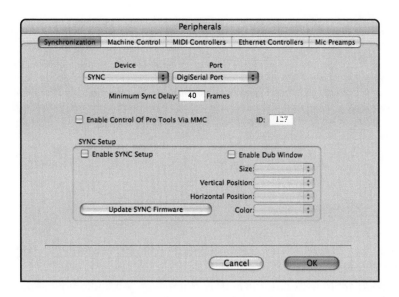

Figure 11.2 The Synchronization tab of the Peripherals dialog box, accessed from the Setup menu, allows you to configure what type of external synchronization device(s) you're using.

8. Click the Record button in the Pro Tools Transport window.

9. Roll the video master back perhaps 9–10 seconds prior to the top of the hour, and press the Play button on the video deck. After a few seconds, you should see Pro Tools kick into Record mode at the beginning of the session's timeline, 01:00:00:00.

10. Once the spot has finished playing, press Stop on the video deck.

11. Click the Record button again in Pro Tools to disable recording mode. However, keep Pro Tools in Online mode so that time code arriving from the video continues to determine where Pro Tools starts playback as you're placing sound effects and music in your session.

12. At the end of the edit process, you can record the stereo mix from Pro Tools back onto the video deck, while still locked to time code (that is, with the Online button enabled), a procedure known as *layback*.

One final note: In many video facilities, when you lay your audio back to the master, you might actually be locking playback of Pro Tools to SMPTE time code arriving from a video deck in a completely separate room. You would route your audio through either analog or digital tie lines, to be recorded directly onto the first-generation master tape in the video-editing suite, rather than the tape copy you've been using while editing. This layback procedure is typical in "online" video editing suites (that is, real-time and tape-based suites). However, when collaborating with Avid or other computer-based video editing systems, it's much more common to either bounce out an audio mixdown file they can use directly or export a file in either the OMF or AAF interchange format. See Chapter 14 for more details.

> ❊ **Tip: Spotting Sound Effects and Music to Time-Code Locations**
>
> Remember to use Spot mode when Pro Tools is slaved to a master video transport! Use the video transport itself, rocking its jog/shuttle wheel to locate the precise frame location where an audio effect should be placed. Then, in Spot mode, click regions with the Grabber (or drag regions out into the Edit window from the Region List), and type their target time position directly into the Spot dialog box's Start Time field. Or, once the Spot dialog box is open, roll the video tape, and press the = key at the desired location (or click the Current Time Code field in the dialog box). That time-code position will be automatically entered into the Start field of the Spot dialog box, and the beginning (or sync point) of the selected region will be moved there once you click the OK button. If you're using VITC (SMPTE time code that is encoded into each video frame), you can capture the current time code even when the master video transport is stopped!

SMPTE Time Code Formats: LTC, VITC, and MTC

There are three ways to encode and transmit SMPTE time-code information. Pro Tools can work with any of these time-code formats, depending on the optional synchronization hardware you add to your Pro Tools rig.

- ❊ **LTC (Longitudinal Time Code).** The most common type. An audio signal encodes the time data through biphase modulation (encoding that rapidly alternates a carrier signal between two tones). The audio signal containing the time-code information might be recorded onto an audio track of a video deck or onto one track of a multitrack audio recorder. LTC may also be directly generated by either of these (possibly via some additional device) in real time, based on the device's own internal timing reference. Because an audio signal is conveying the SMPTE data, the master device's transport has to be in Play (or Record) mode for SMPTE information to be sent to Pro Tools as the slave device.

- ❊ **VITC (Vertical Interval Time Code).** Incorporates time-code data into a video signal within the *overscan* area (that is, the first few lines at the top of each video frame, which are not usually visible on consumer televisions). Figure 11.3 shows a video frame where the VITC information is visible in line 22 of the video image. VITC is used in video post applications; it has the great advantage that time-code values are sent even when paused in a frame or while jogging from one frame to another with the video transport paused. Obviously, a synchronization peripheral that supports VITC will have a video input.

- ❊ **MTC (MIDI Time Code).** Conveys SMPTE information as MIDI data. MTC is in fact the SMPTE format that Pro Tools eventually receives, no matter what type of external SMPTE synchronization peripheral you're using (audio, video, or MIDI). Some digital multi-tracks and computer programs can transmit MTC directly through their MIDI outs. In this scenario, the MTC could be received by Pro Tools even with a standard (that is, non-SMPTE) MIDI interface. MTC should not be confused with MIDI Clock, whose 24 pulse per quarter note (ppqn) subdivisions represent longer or shorter absolute time values, depending on the current musical tempo, and which is sometimes transmitted by the onboard MIDI sequencers in MIDI keyboards. MTC is exactly the same absolute-time reference as SMPTE; it has no relation to the current musical tempo.

Figure 11.3   Here, we've pulled down the top fields of a video frame so that the VITC (Vertical Interval Time Code) in video field 22 is visible.

Frame Rates (30/29.97 Drop/Non-Drop, 25, 24 Frames per Second)

As we've said, various SMPTE frame rates are used, depending on the application or the television standard in use at your geographical location. In the Session Setup window of Pro Tools, you select the SMPTE time-code format. Obviously, if your selection doesn't match the actual time code being received, Pro Tools will start playback at the wrong place or drift out of correct synchronization!

* **30 frames per second (fps).** The original SMPTE format developed for monochrome (black and white) television in North America. 30 fps is still standard for audio-only applications in North America. It's also sometimes (though rarely) used for short-duration, industrial video. (29.97 non-drop is much more common and recommended even for these applications, however.)

* **30 fps drop frame.** Used only for film sync pull-up applications—and even then only infrequently—for correcting transfer errors between film and video.

* **29.97 fps drop frame.** Used in NTSC color video broadcast applications. (*NTSC* refers to the National Television Standards Committee standard, used in North America, most of Latin America and the Caribbean, South Korea, Japan, Taiwan, and so on.) 29.97 drop frame format is especially indicated for longer-duration projects, where SMPTE time-code values need to exactly match absolute time. Also, as a general rule, "29.97 drop" is mandatory for any video submitted to broadcast stations in countries using the NTSC standard. (As stated before, many industrial video production houses in North America use 29.97 fps *non-drop* SMPTE for short durations—corporate and marketing

videos and the like—in spite of the gradual discrepancies, simply because it makes calculating event timings less complicated than when using drop frame format.)

❋ **Note: How Drop-Frame Format Works**

Because the 29.97 frame rate used in NTSC color television doesn't evenly divide into minutes and seconds, certain frames are dropped in order for SMPTE to keep pace with actual time as measured by the clock. By skipping two frames at the beginning of every minute—specifically, skipping from :29 to :02 frames (except with minutes that are multiples of ten—00, 10, 20, 30, 40, 50, and so on)—a total of 108 frames are dropped per hour. This compensates for the accumulated discrepancy between 30 fps and 29.97 fps, which amounts to 3.6 seconds per hour. (Two frames skipped times 60 minutes, less a total of 12 extra frames for the six minutes per hour that don't skip two frames, equals 108 skipped frames per hour.)

❋ **29.97 fps non-drop.** Used in NTSC color video applications, especially for broadcast and shorter-duration pieces. This format makes no drop-frame adjustments in its frame-numbering scheme, and for each hour that passes, accumulates an approximate 3.6-second timing discrepancy (108 frames; the equivalent of 3 seconds plus 18 frames), compared to actual time. For this reason, the use of 29.97 fps non-drop is common in NTSC video projects of shorter duration, such as consumer and industrial videos, where precise durations with respect to the wall clock don't have to match exactly. (In contrast, 29.97 drop frame is required when producing a 30-minute video program for broadcast.)

❋ **25 fps.** Used with the European PAL (and SECAM) video standards, which run at 25 frames per second. The PAL television format is also known as EBU (European Broadcast Union). The 25 fps rate is used for video throughout Europe, Africa, Brazil, Paraguay, Uruguay, Argentina, the Middle East, Australia, and most of Asia. 25 fps is commonly used in Europe for many audio-only applications. Converting between video frames and real time is elegantly simple in this environment: 1 frame equals 40 milliseconds—end of story!

❋ **24 fps.** Used for film applications. At 24 frames per second, each frame of time code exactly corresponds to one frame of film. There is also a 24 fps frame rate used for "24P" high-definition video.

❋ **23.976 fps.** Another frame rate used for high-definition video. Supported in Pro Tools versions 6.4 and higher. (DV Toolkit is required to support this frame rate in Pro Tools LE—and since DV Toolkit doesn't support Pro Tools M-Powered, this frame rate is not available for those users.)

MIDI Time Code (MTC)

MIDI Time Code (MTC) is the MIDI equivalent of SMPTE time code. The MTC addendum to the MIDI specification became official in 1987. The timing formats are identical, but the timestamp information is conveyed as MIDI data, rather than being carried in an audio or video signal.

Like SMPTE, MTC is an absolute timing reference and is independent of musical tempo. Generally, in order to synchronize to an external time-code master, Pro Tools requires an external interface (translator) that converts SMPTE (LTC or VITC) to MIDI Time Code, which is the format that Pro Tools directly understands. Often a single device performs both of these functions; for example, some MIDI interfaces feature an audio or video input for receiving SMPTE time code from a master audio or video master device, which is then translated to MTC for the Pro Tools software. This information then enters the computer via the port where that peripheral is attached (typically USB in current configurations).

> **❋ Note: Digital Clock Sources for Pro Tools**
>
> This chapter focuses on synchronization as a means of sharing location information between devices in a studio configuration. On a more basic level, however, it's also common to sync devices together on more of a hardware level. For example, video sync is used to ensure that the boundaries between frames in the video signals generated by two separate devices correspond exactly (even if their current locations within the material are unrelated). For digital audio devices, word clock (a.k.a. word sync) serves a similar function, ensuring that the audio sample clocks (which control the *rate* of audio playback) of the devices are exactly in sync. (Again, because word clock alone transmits no *location* information, this doesn't ensure that the multiple devices will start playback at the appropriate point. That's what SMPTE time code is for!) Simply put, you might think of word clock as a way to keep digital audio playback from multiple devices in phase. The Hardware Setup dialog box in Pro Tools allows you to select the AES/EBU, S/PDIF, or ADAT Lightpipe digital input on your audio hardware (if available) as the clock source for your Pro Tools session (or word clock, if your audio interface supports this connection, usually via a BNC connector on the rear panel). The clock source defaults to "Internal," where audio playback rate is determined by the audio interface's own internal sample clock. When you are digitally transferring audio tracks from a DAT or ADAT into Pro Tools, it's often desirable to also designate that source audio device as the clock source. Just make sure that, in addition to slaving their clocks together, you specifically set the source and destination to the same nominal sample rate. Also, after completing a digital transfer into Pro Tools, if you later disconnect or power off the external device, be sure to set the Clock Source option in Pro Tools back to Internal—otherwise you may hear some fairly strange playback! Conversely, when you are transferring audio *from* Pro Tools to another device, you would typically set the Clock Source option in Pro Tools to Internal and configure the destination device to slave its sample clock to the incoming digital audio signal from Pro Tools. Again, after the transfer is completed, set that device back to its internal clock source— unless you are using a separate, external clock source for all these devices (such as the Digidesign Sync I/O, Apogee Big Ben, and so on). As discussed later in this chapter, a central clock source is highly recommended when using multiple sources and destinations and frequent two-way transfers in your studio configuration.

SMPTE Peripherals

Of course, the Pro Tools program understands these time-code values, which are received by Pro Tools via whatever SMPTE synchronization device you're using. The Pro Tools hardware itself doesn't feature any inputs for audio or video SMPTE sources; you purchase an SMPTE peripheral separately, according to your requirements. Most include other features; for example, there are many MIDI interfaces for computers that also offer SMPTE-synchronization capabilities, especially LTC (SMPTE information encoded within an audio signal). Various degrees of precision are possible, according to your requirements and budget. To help you get a handle on the capabilities of the units out there, here's a theoretical breakdown of the three basic methods for synchronizing Pro Tools with external devices:

* SMPTE/MIDI interface (Trigger Sync)
* SMPTE/MIDI interface plus separate hardware clock
* Synchronizers that include reference sync

SMPTE/MIDI Interface (Trigger Sync)

Most MIDI interfaces that include only an audio input for LTC (SMPTE information encoded into an audio signal) fall into this category. Along with the MIDI data that they transmit/receive from their MIDI ports, they also translate the audio time code into MIDI Time Code (MTC) and communicate this to Pro Tools (via whatever connection the device has with the computer—USB, serial, parallel, and so on). However, once playback starts from Pro Tools (after it figures out the appropriate location based on the time code received), the program no longer attempts to keep strict pace with the SMPTE location data being received (other than eventually stopping once the SMPTE *stops* arriving). Therefore, a certain amount of drift could result. This sync relationship is represented in Figure 11.4. For MIDI-only projects, for example, this degree of precision may be sufficient. But for audio, especially where the audio from Pro Tools must maintain a precise, sample-accurate level of precision with audio or video from some other device over a more extended period of time, a more sophisticated synchronization method is called for. Trigger Sync simply starts playback when the correct timestamp (location) value is received. Once playback starts, the slaved device doesn't again calibrate its position to the incoming time code (other than to stop when time code stops being received), and the playback speed of the slave device is not governed by the incoming time-code information.

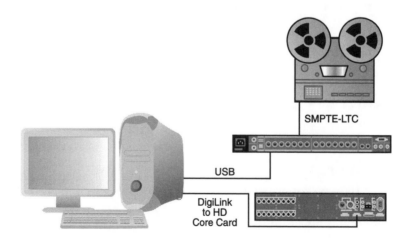

Figure 11.4 LTC (encoded as an audio signal) from a multitrack audio recorder is "translated" for Pro Tools by a MIDI interface that also has SMPTE synchronization capabilities.

SMPTE/MIDI Interface Plus Separate Hardware Clock

In these configurations, in addition to the timestamp (location) information being received as MTC from the SMPTE/MIDI interface, a separate connection links the internal clock that controls the sample rate for audio playback in the Pro Tools hardware (that is, its speed) to an external source. In some situations, both timestamp and clock information may come from the same master device, but often it does not. For example, in video-production houses, it is common to use a single, stable video signal known as *black burst* or *house sync* as the timing reference for all devices in the facility, providing speed information for all video decks, switchers, and Pro Tools systems equipped with the appropriate hardware. (Otherwise, it wouldn't be practical to use a video switcher to combine video signals from various sources because their scan rates would be out of sync.) This signal contains no timestamp (location) information (although it does help Pro Tools lock up to incoming time code somewhat quicker). Because both the video master and the sample clock of your Pro Tools hardware are slaved to the same speed reference, they remain in frame-accurate synchronization over long durations. This is shown in Figure 11.5.

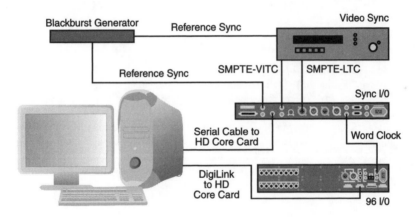

Figure 11.5 Often, as shown here, a single unit can perform both functions (SMPTE for location reference, plus various methods for resolving the sample clock of the audio hardware to an external source).

There are some devices, including Digidesign's own Video Slave Driver (now discontinued), whose only purpose is to translate this video-sync reference to various digital word clock input formats (including the higher-frequency Loop Sync and SuperClock used by Digidesign audio interfaces) so that the audio clock of the hardware itself is locked to the master video sync (the speed reference). Digital clock references in common use for audio hardware are called *word sync* or *word clock*. The advantage of using a common speed reference for both the video and audio hardware is that the beginning of each received SMPTE time-code frame and the beginning of each actual frame in the reference video signal correspond *exactly* (that is, they're *edge aligned*). This helps Pro Tools determine the correct location and lock up to SMPTE time code more quickly and reliably and also maintains more precise sync with the video master over extended periods of time. In fact, many synchronization units combine both SMPTE synchronization (location) and hardware clock sync in the same unit (see the following section in this chapter).

However, there are situations where the sample clock of your Pro Tools hardware (which governs audio playback speed) may be slaved to an external source. (Keep in mind that this doesn't necessarily have anything to do with whether playback of audio inside Pro Tools is coordinated to the location reference provided by SMPTE time code.) In the Hardware Setup dialog box, you can switch the Sync Mode option from Internal (the internal sample clock of your audio hardware) to Digital (where your audio hardware's sample rate is slaved to that of a digital audio signal arriving on the specified input). For example, you would usually switch to digital sync mode while transferring audio from a DAT machine via S/PDIF or AES/EBU digital inputs or transferring from an ADAT via the Lightpipe input (or from one of Tascam's digital multitrack tape recorders via TDIF) on some audio interfaces. In fact, if you forget that you left digital sync mode on, it can make for some, er, *interesting* listening—if the DAT is missing or powered off the next time you open Pro Tools, it still tries to sync playback speed to a nonexistent clock source!

✱ Note: More About Digital Audio Clock Sources

A single digital clock reference for multiple devices can be a very useful tool for audio production facilities. Just as house sync provides a single reference for video gear, using a single device as the digital clock reference for all your audio devices can make it much easier to route audio among digital mixers, multitrack recorders, Pro Tools, DAT recorders, digital patch bays, digital effects, and so on. One example is Apogee's Clock I/O card for the Mackie Digital 8-bus mixer. It supports a variety of sample rates (including pull-up and pull-down; see Chapter 14) and generates a very stable, low-jitter clock reference usable by all these devices. Lucid, Aardvark, HHB/Rosendahl, Apogee, and Session Control also make some excellent master clock generators; see Appendix B, "Add-Ons, Extensions, and Cool Stuff for Your Rig," for more details.

Synchronizers That Include Reference Sync

These devices combine the SMPTE and sample-clock synchronization duties into a single unit. Examples from Digidesign include the Sync I/O (shown in Figure 11.6), a high-end synchronization peripheral, and Universal Slave Driver (and its predecessor, the SMPTE Slave Driver). With these units, not only can you control Pro Tools playback according to the location references arriving via SMPTE time code, but you can simultaneously synchronize the speed of the sample clock in your audio hardware to various external sources. In addition, these devices feature an additional *continuous resync* mode, where the audio hardware's playback rate is resolved to the incoming time code (rather than to some hardware-based speed reference), making continuous and minute adjustments to the playback rate so that it stays phase-locked to the incoming timestamp information. In other words, in continuous resync mode, these units generate a speed reference that is derived from (and continually adjusted to) the location references being received as SMPTE time code.

Figure 11.6   Digidesign's Sync I/O features SMPTE (location) synchronization in LTC (audio), VITC (video), and MTC (MIDI) format; hardware-level synchronization through video sync (black burst); word clock (audio hardware sync); and two 9-pin serial ports (for interlocking transport functions with video decks via the MachineControl option for Pro Tools). It can also add time-code window burns to passed-through video signals.
(Photo courtesy of Digidesign.)

Types of Synchronization

Now that you've taken a brief look at the physical methods for synchronizing Pro Tools to external sources, let's review some general synchronization concepts. Remember, our objective in synchronization is simply that events on multiple devices happen consistently over time, at the appropriate places! Relationships between the master and slave device(s) for dealing with location and speed references roughly break down into the following categories:

- ❋ Trigger Sync
- ❋ Continuous Resync
- ❋ Reference Sync

Trigger Sync

Trigger sync has a master/slave relationship for start or trigger information but has no resolving capabilities, relying instead on each device's internal speed reference and stability for them to play in sync. Figure 11.7 is a simplified representation of this synchronization relationship. Once the slaved device receives time code, it calculates the correct place for playback to commence, and then after playback starts (possibly following some rewind/fast-forward action on a tape transport), the slave's playback speed is not affected by time code that continues to be received.

Continuous Resync

Continuous resync also has a master/slave relationship for start or trigger information, plus resolving capabilities through the use of a device known as a *synchronizer*. The synchronizer provides the ability to compare the time-code location of the devices and adjusts the speed of the slave so that it continuously matches the location of the master. After the master machine provides a start command (trigger) and location information, the synchronizer compares the

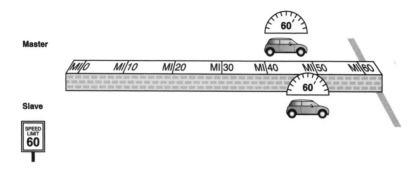

Figure 11.7 Trigger sync. Both vehicles start out at an agreed-upon speed of 60 miles an hour after the master provides the start command, or "trigger." But the slave device can't monitor the master's speed in order to keep pace with it. (It relies on its own speedometer—its internal speed reference.)
Therefore, some drift may accumulate over time.

master and slave locations and tells the slave where to go to match the master. Once *lock* (matched locations) is reached, the synchronizer continues to compare the two locations. If the two drift apart, the synchronizer tells the slave(s) to speed up or slow down to match the master's location (hopefully rather smoothly). Figure 11.8 illustrates the basic idea of continuous resync. In this situation, the SMPTE location information being received from the master provides a constant speed reference for the slave.

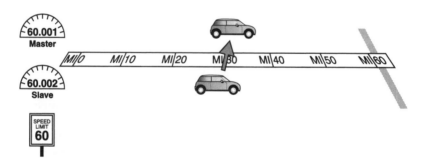

Figure 11.8 Continuous resync. After receiving the trigger to start, the slaved device continually adjusts its speed to keep pace with the master, matching the location information that the master continues to send to the slave. The slave can watch and compare its speed with the master and resolve its own speed to it, so that they stay synchronized over extended periods.

Reference Sync

Reference sync (see Figure 11.9) has a master/slave relationship for start, or trigger, information and additionally utilizes a common clock or reference signal to resolve the speed of the two devices (sometimes from the master itself or from an external source, as in the case

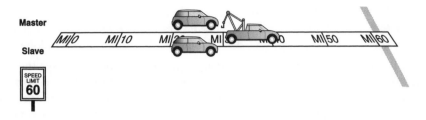

Figure 11.9 Reference sync. Trigger (location) information received from the master starts the slave into motion, while an external device controls the speed of both vehicles. They resolve to it instead of to each other.

of house sync). In larger studio configurations, it can often be best to sync all digital audio devices to a single, highly stable clock source that will be the common timing reference for their sample rates. In Appendix B, under "Word Clock and Sync Generators," we mention a few of the current options.

Using QuickTime

For Pro Tools users who collaborate with nonlinear video editors, importing QuickTime movies into a session opens up some exciting possibilities because using QuickTime movies as your video "master" allows you to do audio postproduction for video projects without having a video deck in your studio at all. Video editors who work with systems such as Avid Xpress, Avid Media Composer (and other Avid video-editing systems), Media 100, Apple FinalCut Pro, and Adobe Premiere can export a video project for you as a QuickTime file (an industry-standard format for video files). Ordinarily, the original video frame rate and audio sample rate (48kHz in professional video) should be retained in the file you use in Pro Tools. But in the interest of this QuickTime file not being huge (and consequently slowing down operation of Pro Tools during record and playback, especially if you're not using a video accelerator card and/or have an underpowered system), you might ask the video editor to reduce the image size of the QuickTime video—perhaps to 320×240 pixels or smaller.

You can then import the QuickTime video into your Pro Tools session (File > Import > QuickTime Movie). This creates a Movie track in the Edit window. Like VITC, using a QuickTime video inside Pro Tools as your video master allows frame-accurate positioning of audio events with respect to video frames (which you can zoom in to view individually in the Movie track) even while video playback is stopped. Another advantage of QuickTime is nonlinear access—you can jump immediately from any point in the video program (that is, the session timeline) to another. When using QuickTime movies, you're free of the hassle and expense of shuttling a video transport back and forth as you edit your audio.

The Movie window is also enabled after you import a video file into your session, where the video will play in real time. Keep in mind that playing back video files makes additional demands on your computer's processing power, though. For serious postproduction work, a video accelerator card with a separate monitor and/or a separate hard disk dedicated to video playback is highly recommended. However, on any Pro Tools system, you will find that changing the Movie track to Blocks view (or even closing the Movie window) will greatly reduce the overhead from video playback and improve the speed of operation in Pro Tools.

Some audio facilities also have their own video-capture hardware—perhaps the same card that will accelerate video playback in the Pro Tools computer—so that outside clients can simply submit video tapes, even on VHS! (The AVoption|V10 video hardware consists of a rack-mountable unit, connected to the computer via FireWire cable. It can capture video and also send out a standard video signal for your NTSC monitor or video projection system. For serious professional work, viewing the video master on large-format monitors makes the postproduction process more comfortable.)

When you've finished assembling all the audio for the project, you have several options:

* Bounce out a stereo file (or multiple mono files for surround mixing), which the video editor with whom you're collaborating can then import and place into his or her video-editing software.

* Using the File > Bounce to > QuickTime Movie command, bounce your mix directly into the QuickTime movie. You might do this, for example, when the final destination is in fact CD-ROM or Internet playback, and your audio work is the last stage in the process (because the video data in the QuickTime file has already been compressed to the final size for playback). However, it is often a good idea to use this option even when your audio is going to be used on a video-editing system. Most video-editing software can import just the audio tracks from the QuickTime file you've provided. However, if there's ever any question about how you thought things were supposed to sync up between the audio and video, the video editor has the file you provided as a reference.

* Export the session as an OMFI (Open Media Format Interchange) file (sequence), supported by video-editing systems such as Avid, FinalCut Pro, Media 100, and others (not to mention other many digital audio programs such as Digital Performer, Cubase SX, Logic Pro, and SONAR), using the optional DigiTranslator program from Digidesign (which is not compatible with the M-Powered version of Pro Tools).

* Use the optional DigiTranslator program to export your session as an AAF (Advanced Authoring Format) sequence to be used by Avid and other video-editing systems. AAF sequences always refer to external media files (as opposed to OMFI files, which can optionally have media files embedded within them) and may in turn refer to OMF media files. While AAF is a newer and more versatile format than OMFI, for most situations you will simply provide whichever the video editor requests.

Summary

Hopefully this gives you a bit of grounding for synchronizing Pro Tools with other devices. We revisit some of these concepts in Chapter 14 and also discuss MIDI MachineControl technology and the Pro Tools MachineControl option. In Appendix B, you'll find further information about synchronization peripherals. Sync or swim!

12 } The Pro Tools Groove

This chapter looks at some specific techniques for basic beat mixing—that is, combining samples from various sources with MIDI performances and additional audio recording to build up a groove—in the dance, trance, or pop style, for example. If you talk with seasoned dance mixers who use Pro Tools, you will discover that they usually supplement the program with numerous synthesizers and samplers (either the software or external hardware variety) and/or dedicated programs for manipulating beats and loops such as ACID Pro by Sony/Sonic Foundry (Windows), Live by Ableton, and so on—some of which can work in tandem on the same computer with Pro Tools via ReWire. In particular, if you're involved in this genre, we urge you to investigate the sampling/synthesis plug-ins for Pro Tools mentioned later in this chapter. Having your entire complex synthesis and signal routing setup tightly integrated into a single Pro Tools session is an enormous benefit and allows you to experiment, continually perfecting previous mixes.

As you can imagine, every Pro Tools user has his or her own methods, and you can make things as simple or as complicated as you like. This is definitely a subject that, by itself, could fill an entire book! This chapter focuses on the basics, limiting its discussion to techniques available to *all* Pro Tools users, and lets you build from there.

Combining MIDI and Audio

We promise this is the last time we'll remind you: MIDI is *not* audio! MIDI is a communications language—that is, a way to represent performance events (such as pressing a key or pedal on your MIDI controller) and transmit these from one device (or program) to another. With a MIDI interface connected to your computer, you attach MIDI cables (In to Out, Out to In) between the interface's ports and those of any external MIDI controllers and/or sound modules (or a MIDI-controllable effects processor, recorder, and so on). MIDI tracks in Pro Tools record incoming MIDI data, and provide you editing tools to alter or create MIDI information in each track. As we mentioned Chapter 10, "MIDI," software-based synthesizers and samplers are a very powerful alternative. These can be RTAS plug-ins (all systems), TDM plug-ins

(HD and previous TDM-based systems only), or separate programs whose audio output is streamed into the Pro Tools mixing environment via ReWire technology (all systems).

Let's assume for a moment that your setup consists of a single MIDI keyboard sitting beside your Pro Tools rig, and you're using that keyboard's internal sounds for some of your MIDI tracks. What are your options for combining the audio output(s) of this external MIDI device with audio tracks playing back from hard disk within Pro Tools?

❋ You could connect the audio outputs from the external MIDI keyboard to available inputs on your audio interface and configure Auxiliary Input tracks to monitor those inputs within Pro Tools. If your audio interface has numerous inputs available (as opposed to just two or four, as is the case with some interfaces for LE and M-Powered), the audio outputs from *several* MIDI modules can stay more or less permanently connected, while still leaving other inputs free for simultaneous audio recordings (guitar or vocal tracks, for example). This is simple to set up. For example, you might create a stereo Auxiliary Input in Pro Tools, selecting input pair 7–8 on your multichannel audio interface as its source (where you've connected the audio outputs from your MIDI keyboard). This incorporates the keyboard's audio output into the Pro Tools mixing environment during playback (with whatever plug-ins or additional audio routing you require on that Aux In), and it will also be included when you bounce a mixdown to disk in real time.

> ❋ **Tip: Instrument Tracks Can Also Be Used for External MIDI Devices**
>
> Most people will immediately associate Instrument tracks with software instrument plug-ins. A single track serves as the output audio channel (similar to an Aux In) whose sound source is an instrument plug-in in its insert slot, and also as the track where you record and edit MIDI performances—saving space and making your session easier to manage. However, Instrument tracks are very useful for external MIDI modules. As the audio input for your Instrument track, select the ports on your audio interface where the external MIDI device is connected. Then, in the Instrument controls section of the Mix window (or the corresponding column in the Edit window, if that's currently being displayed), select the appropriate MIDI port and channel to configure the external device as the MIDI destination for this track. Even if you end up using additional MIDI tracks for a multitimbral external module, having separate Mute and Solo buttons for the Instrument controls section (MIDI) and the Instrument track itself (audio) makes it easy to manage this "hybrid" track.

❋ If you're using a small mixer to monitor your Pro Tools outputs, you could also monitor the audio output from your MIDI keyboard(s) directly through the mixer. In this scenario, you'd have to record the mixer's stereo output to some other device in real time—for example, a DAT. Mixing to an external recorder has some operational disadvantages (not to mention the expense of buying a DAT recorder if you don't already own one). For one thing, once you've bounced out a series of mixes, you may have to record them right back onto hard disk if you're going to use Pro Tools or another program to sequence them and apply any other mastering processes before burning a CD-R (or recording to DAT once again). Some users may find themselves in this situation anyway—for instance, if the number of external, real-time audio sources entering their mix exceeds the available inputs on their Pro Tools audio hardware. This would be the case, for example, if you have stereo outputs coming from five different MIDI modules, plus several external effects processors used as send destinations from Pro Tools outputs, and only eight analog inputs available on your audio interface. Even so, it can often be a practical alternative to use your external mixer to *submix* audio from these devices, perhaps entering the Pro Tools mixing environment via a single stereo Aux In (see the next bullet). In this scenario, it's usually preferable to take the time to record the stereo audio output from each of your MIDI modules to a separate audio track before final mixdown. That way, you have mixable tracks even if those modules are no longer connected in the future. Aside from the obvious hassle of recabling multiple modules if you need to remix the project months or years later, even the most organized users will have difficulty precisely reproducing the original session's gain structure from all these external devices that were submixed into Pro Tools.

❋ You could also record the outputs of your MIDI modules onto audio tracks, one by one. Certainly, this consumes more disk space and has to be repeated if you alter the MIDI data for parts that were already recorded to disk. On the plus side, though, if your audio hardware has only stereo analog inputs, this technique offers important advantages. For one thing, if you're using a single keyboard for all your MIDI tracks, having the parts on separate audio tracks (or on a separate Aux In, if you have a multichannel audio interface and a keyboard with more than just stereo audio outputs) allows you to apply separate plug-in processing to distinct instrumental parts, which typically results in superior quality to the built-in effects on the MIDI keyboard or module itself. For example, you might use compression, or a small-room reverb on the drums, and a completely different Pro Tools effect setup on the tracks for other instrumental parts coming from this MIDI sound source. Again, having an audio version of your MIDI parts saved with the final mixdown session also guarantees that the project will sound the same in the future if the original MIDI gear is no longer available.

❋ Tip: No MIDI Interface Required (?)

Some users rely completely on software-based virtual instruments as sound sources for their MIDI tracks. As discussed in Chapter 10, this offers many advantages: total recall when re-opening sessions, complete and hassle-free integration into the Pro Tools mixing environment for more routing and processing, full automation for most sound parameters, no cables (and no audio inputs occupied, which is especially useful if you're using an audio interface with only two inputs, for instance!), and no background noise. If your system configuration is powerful enough to go this way, it may not be necessary for your external MIDI keyboard (guitar, drums, wind controller, and so on) to have its own internal sounds at all. For that matter, there are now many MIDI controller options that connect directly to the computer via USB—eliminating the need for a separate MIDI interface. Current USB keyboard controllers range from smaller, economical models (which are great, by the way) to others with more sophisticated features—88-key weighted keyboards with aftertouch, for example. Worth checking out!

Building Percussion Parts from Individual Audio Elements

Grid mode is your best friend! If you have some great-sounding samples of drum-kit and percussion elements, you can use multiple Pro Tools audio tracks to build up a drum part. If you're diligent, you can even use volume automation to create some dynamics—on successive snare or tom hits, for example. And remember that, because you can automate the pan, volume, sends, and plug-in parameters, you can often use a single track for several distinct sounds if available playback voices is a concern. For example, if ride and crash cymbals don't need to overlap, they might share a single track—you can pan the occurrences of each cymbal type further toward the left or right to simulate the appropriate stereo image of a drum set. You can also use this method to make multiple tom sounds in the same mono track sound like they're at different positions in the stereo field.

To keep all these source drum element tracks from cluttering up your screen afterward during mixdown, route them to a single Aux In (providing a single volume control and permitting plug-in inserts on the entire drum submix) and then hide the source tracks. Alternatively, if you hit the basic 32-voice limit in LE or M-Powered (expandable to 48 mono/stereo tracks via the Music Production Toolkit), you could bounce a stereo drum submix to disk as split stereo, enabling the Import After Bounce option to bring the resultant mix into a new Pro Tools track and leaving those audio voices available again for new audio tracks. Because Pro Tools timestamps any bounced mix files, you can repeat this process as many times as necessary as you refine your project, using the Spot dialog box if necessary to place your new, revised drum submixes into the correct position.

Grid edit mode will be essential for this process. Another handy command is Region > Quantize to Grid, which moves the beginning of audio regions to the nearest grid increment (as selected in the Grid Value field, at the top of the Edit window underneath the Pencil tool). If a sync point exists within the region (see Chapter 8, "Menu Selections: Highlights" for a description of the Region > Identify Sync Point command), the sync point itself is moved to the nearest grid increment instead of to the region's beginning (handy for a snare sample with backwards reverb on the front end or certain turntable scratch and vocal effects, for instance).

When you're using individual samples to build a drum groove in Grid mode, be sure to set their Timebase selector to ticks (as shown by the metronome icon on the tracks seen in Figure 12.1). With this feature, if you subsequently alter the tempo, all the regions in these tracks (with the Ticks timebase) are automatically repositioned to maintain their same relative Bar: Beat locations in relation to the new tempo.

❋ **CSi: Editing Audio, Slicing Up Drum Loops**

In the CD-ROM at the back of this book, check out the sample movie tutorial from *Pro Tools 7 CSi Starter*, "Editing Audio Regions." You'll see the Trimmer and Grabber (in both Normal and Separation modes) used to move and reorder audio regions on a rhythm track, the Duplicate/Repeat commands, and regions being previewed before dragging them out into tracks. Grid mode and audio fades/crossfades are also used while assembling drum grooves. Notice how in this sample movie tutorial, the Nudge feature is used to experiment with different locations for cymbal or drum hits that are layered over another drum groove—while looped playback continues.

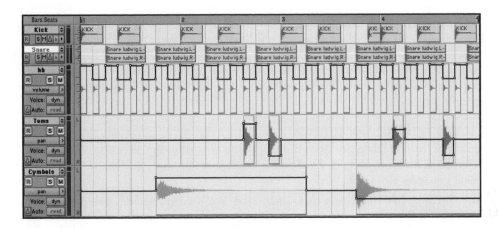

Figure 12.1 In Grid mode, you can build a multitrack percussion part from audio regions containing individual drum elements. Since these tracks are set to Ticks timebase, bar/beat locations of these regions are maintained if the tempo changes.

Using Region Groups for "Assembled" Percussion Parts

The multitrack percussion constructions described here provide an excellent example of how region grouping (introduced in version 7 of Pro Tools) can facilitate the editing and composing process. To create a region group, simply select the regions you want to include, on one or several tracks. Then choose the Region > Group command. The entire selection now appears as a single region, with a region group icon in the lower left-hand corner. Region groups can be looped, duplicated, trimmed, and so on. Since the composite beat we've constructed for our current example is on a tick-based track, if the Pro Tools tempo changes, the start point for each instance of the region group *and all the source regions within it* will adjust accordingly to maintain their previous bar/beat locations. (This feature is also key when you're working with REX and ACID files, by the way.) Later on in this chapter, Figure 12.4 includes our composite percussion track as a region group that was, in turn, looped.

You can use the Region > Ungroup command on a selected region group, so that you can re-edit the regions it contains. If a region group (such as the "assembled" percussion groove we're discussing here) is being used elsewhere in the current session, you can use the Region > Regroup command after making your edits to its ungrouped components. In this case, a dialog box will present you with two choices: to modify the original region group (affecting all other instances) or to create a new copy (leaving other existing instances of this region group unchanged). Alternatively, if you use the Region > Group command again, Pro Tools will simply create a new region group definition for the current selection.

Looping Audio Regions

Certain styles of music involve repetition of rhythm loops, drum beats, and other sounds. For that matter, in postproduction, it is not uncommon to loop certain background sounds, especially the source audio from an effects library may not be long enough to fill the required duration. The Duplicate command (in the Edit menu) has been available in Pro Tools since the beginning, and the Repeat command (for creating multiple duplicates of selected regions in a single operation) has also been around for while. Here we will take a look at some other aspects of looping audio in Pro Tools, starting with how you set your Pro Tools tempo based on the current selection.

The Identify Beat Command

As you know from reading previous chapters, you can loop any selection via the Options > Loop Playback menu command. Pro Tools will keep cycling between the start and end locations until you stop playback.

Let's say that, instead of importing an existing loop, you've imported a full-length stereo rhythm groove from CD (at a single, steady tempo), and you want to use bits and pieces to create a completely new rhythm track. You can use the Event > Identify Beat command to generate a Pro Tools tempo based on any audio selection. Here's the most basic method:

1. Drag the original rhythm groove region onto a stereo audio track. Click the Selector tool anywhere in that track prior to the beginning of the section you want to loop, and then press the spacebar to start playback in Pro Tools.

2. Press the down-arrow key on your computer keyboard at the beginning of the four-bar phrase you want to loop. Then, press the up-arrow key on the next downbeat *after* the end of the phrase.

3. Stop playback. A portion of that track's audio waveform is selected, exactly where you pressed the down- and up-arrow keys.

4. Make sure the Options > Loop Playback option is enabled, and then click the Play button (or press the spacebar) again. No matter how nimble your fingers are (and rock-solid your sense of rhythm), chances are that your loop is not exactly smooth yet. Let's refine our selection to create a sample-accurate loop.

5. Use the Zoomer to click and drag immediately around the beginning of your current selection. Then switch to the Selector tool and, while holding down the Shift key, adjust the beginning of your selection until it exactly matches the downbeat of the phrase (with no excess audio selected before the attack, but without omitting any of the attack). You may need to zoom in and out several levels in order to zero in on the proper position. (Remember: You can hold down the Command key, or Ctrl key in Windows, and use the left/right bracket keys to zoom in/out.) After each adjustment, click Play to confirm that your phrase correctly starts *exactly* at the beginning of the selection. Next, we will adjust the end point of the selection.

6. Once you've precisely defined the beginning, press the right-arrow key on your computer keyboard once, which moves the waveform display to the end of the current selection. Now, while holding down the Shift key, adjust the end of your selection so that it ends immediately *before* the downbeat of the following phrase. Press the spacebar to play your selection after making each adjustment; you'll know you have the end point exactly right when the selected phrase loops around smoothly.

7. Choose Edit > Separate Region > At Selection. Name this new region "4 bars," and click OK to close the dialog box.

8. Eliminate the audio preceding the region "4 bars" in this track by selecting it with the Grabber and pressing the Delete or Backspace key on your computer keyboard. Now, drag the "4 bars" region all the way to the beginning of the track.

9. With this region still selected, enable the Tempo Ruler Enable button (conductor icon) in the Transport window, and then select Event > Identify Beat. Indicate to Pro Tools that the beginning of the current selection is bar 1, beat 1 in 4/4 time and that the end of the selection is bar 5, beat 1.

10. Switch to Bars and Beats as your main time ruler units (View > Main Counter > Bars:Beats). Enable Grid mode, and set Grid value to 1/4 notes.

11. If you've made an accurate phrase selection for the Identify Beat command, you can highlight anywhere within the rest of the drum groove that remains on the track, and your selection will automatically snap to the nearest 1/4-note increment. You're ready to start carving up some phrases out of the groove and put them back together into a different arrangement.

❄ **Note: Another Way to Adjust Looped Selections**

In Chapter 6, "The Edit Window," under the discussion of the Selector tool, we describe an alternate method for making precise phrase selections: using the Scrubber tool and then nudging the selection with the plus and minus (+/−) keys. (You can also hold down the Option or Command modifier key—Alt or Ctrl in Windows—to nudge only the end or beginning of a selection without affecting its other boundary.)

The Region > Loop/Unloop Commands

The ability to loop regions and region groups was introduced in Pro Tools 7. Figure 12.2 shows the dialog box for the Region > Loop command. You can choose a specific number of repetitions, a total duration (in which case the last loop "alias" may be truncated if the target duration for the entire set of loops isn't an exact multiple), or that the region should continue looping until it reaches either the end of the session's timeline or the next region boundary within that track. You can also specify a crossfade time between adjacent loop repetitions. (However, as always with crossfades, there must be enough additional material before and/ or after the boundaries of the region proper within its parent file to fill the desired crossfade duration.) This can often produce smoother transitions, especially when cymbal decays or reverb at the end of the loop might otherwise be abruptly cut off at the splice point.

Loop *aliases* are created, following the original source region. This entire series of loop repetitions can be dragged, copied, and so on, much like a single region or region group. If you drop some other region somewhere within an existing looped region (as seen in Figure 12.4), that topmost region sounds, and then the remainder of the underlying loop repetitions continues. This is obviously very useful when you're building up an arrangement from a simple repeating beat, for example.

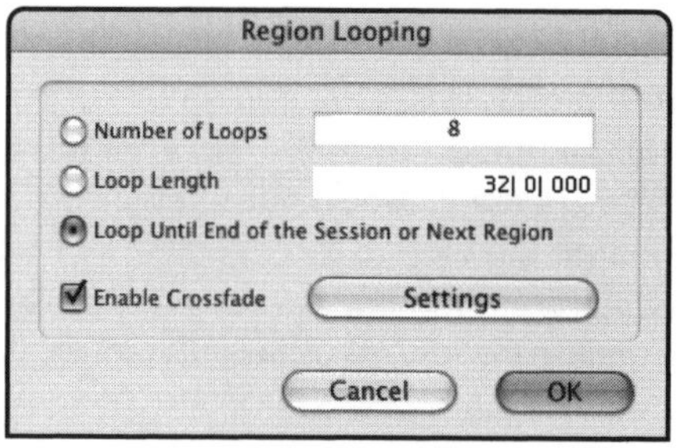

Figure 12.2 Options for looping a selected region (or region group). The crossfade option shown here doesn't apply to looped MIDI regions.

Using the Trimmer tool on looped regions allows you to increase or decrease the number of repetitions. The last repetition may be truncated by this operation, for example, if you wanted to shorten it to a lesser number of bars of beats in order to make room for a fill or transition. If you hold down the Control key (Start key on Windows) while trimming looped regions (but not necessarily region groups), the total duration changes by even multiples of the source region's length. This is one of the quickest ways to create additional repetitions of the entire loop.

The dialog box for the Region > Unloop command (shown in Figure 12.3) lets you either revert back to a single instance of the source region (or region group) or "flatten" the current looped set into separate regions. (Unless you've used the Loop Trimmer—see the next section—the result is similar to having used the Edit > Repeat command in the first place; however, if the last loop repetition was truncated in order to match the desired duration, a separate region definition is created for it.)

Figure 12.3 Options for unlooping a selected region (or region group).

We should add that the usefulness of region looping isn't limited to musical applications. In audio post, it frequently occurs that background ambience and walla, wind, water, or traffic sounds pulled from sound effect libraries may not be long enough to fill the required duration. Using region looping (instead of the Edit menu's Duplicate and Repeat commands) provides a more convenient method for building a base over which you will layer other background sounds.

Loop Trimmer

When the Trimmer tool cursor is over the loop icon within either the source region or any of its aliases (as seen within the top track in Figure 12.4), it changes shape to indicate Loop Trimmer mode. If you are in Grid editing mode, for example, you could use this mode to trim a two-bar loop down to a single bar, for example. The number of loop aliases is adjusted accordingly (exactly double, in this case), to maintain the same total duration. If you are in any other editing mode when using the Loop Trimmer, if the total duration isn't an even multiple of the new loop length, the last loop alias is truncated accordingly.

Note that the Loop Trimmer does *not* apply time compression/expansion, it merely redefines the boundaries for the looped region. If you *do* use the Time Trimmer on looped audio regions or audio region groups, a single, consolidated region is created that contains the results of that time compression/expansion operation, including the effects of any fades on the source region(s).

Duplicating Automation in Your Loop Aliases

If there is any automation data associated with your source region or region group, this is *not* copied into the loop aliases. The idea in Pro Tools is to provide flexibility for creating automation that extends across multiple loop repetitions. Copying and pasting automation (once you have changed the track view to a specific automation parameter) has always been possible in Pro Tools. In version 7, however, there are submenus for Cut Special, Copy Special, and Clear Special, each with options for applying the operation to all automation types, pan data only, or plug-in automation only. After you copy automation data to the Clipboard with the Cut Special or Copy Special command, you can paste it elsewhere with the normal Paste command without affecting any overlapping regions at the track destination and even if no automation parameters are currently visible.

There is also a Paste Special submenu. These Paste Special modes are especially relevant for our current region looping examples. Merge is self-explanatory; the pasted data is combined with existing automation data. The Current Automation Type allows you to paste an automation shape from one type of automation to another; for example, you could paste pan automation into a reverb send. You can use Repeat to Fill Selection to paste a shorter area of automation to fill a larger duration. Since our loop aliases don't include any automation that may have accompanied the source region or region group, you could use Edit > Copy Special > All Automation, highlight all the loop aliases (in multiple tracks, in the case of the multitrack percussion groove we've been dealing with so far in this chapter), and then use Edit > Paste Special > Repeat to Fill Selection. Now the same automation shapes from the source region are repeated, along with all the loop aliases.

Using the Time Trimmer for Conforming Tempos

When you change the Trimmer tool to TC/E (Time Compression/Expansion) mode, its cursor changes to the Time Trimmer. In this mode, as you trim any audio or MIDI region, its contents are adjusted to fit into the new duration. For instance, using this mode to reduce a MIDI region from a duration of four bars to two bars produces a double-time version. By default, using the

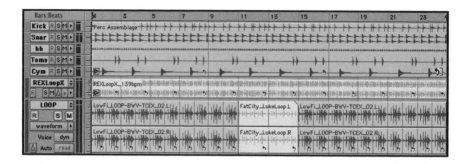

Figure 12.4 Loop icons appear in the source regions or region groups and their respective loop aliases. Shown here, the same multitrack percussion part shown in Figure 12.1, a looped REX file, plus a looped audio region with a different looped audio region dropped within it.

Time Trimmer on audio regions applies the same time compression/expansion algorithm used in the Audiosuite menu's Time Compression Expansion dialog box. (However, if you have some other time-stretching plug-in installed in Pro tools, an option in Preferences > Operation allows you to choose this as the default for the Time Trimmer instead.)

Let's suppose you import some four- or eight-bar drum loops that don't match the current session tempo. Using the Time Trimmer is one quick way to conform their durations to the equivalent number of beats. Switch to Grid editing mode, and drag the four-bar loop to exactly four bars at the current session tempo. Easy! Naturally, the more extreme the ratio of time compression/expansion, the more artifacts will be heard in the results. Be aware, though, that whatever default settings are selected for time compression/expansion in the AudioSuite plug-in window are also used for these Time Trimmer operations. Later in this chapter, a tip explains how to select your own default settings, which is extremely important for users who manipulate musical material with the Time Trimmer.

Working with REX and ACID Files

Both of these formats are optimized for time-sliced loops—that is, audio files that have been analyzed and broken down into their rhythmic components. The REX/REX2 format (which typically uses a .REX or .RX2 file name extension) was developed for the ReCycle program by Propellerheads. ACID format (.WAV files containing additional metadata about tempo, time slices, and other parameters) comes from a program of the same name (originally developed by Sonic Foundry, now owned by Sony). Many loop-oriented programs (Reason, ACID, Ableton Live, and Cubase SX) support REX and/or ACID files and can play loops at any tempo without pitch changes. With version 7 (both Mac and Windows versions), Pro Tools users can also use these time-sliced audio file formats. As with files analyzed by Beat Detective in Pro Tools, having individual rhythmic components automatically sliced up makes it much easier to rearrange them into new rhythmic patterns.

Importing REX/ACID Files into Pro Tools

Import REX and ACID files into Pro Tools by dragging them from the Workspace browser window or desktop directly into the Region List or into an existing track—or into the Track List if you want a new track automatically created to contain them. As you preview these files in the Workspace window using the speaker icon for each, their tempo is automatically adjusted to match that of the current Start time in the Pro Tools timeline. When you import these files into Pro Tools, a new region group is created, with the name of the original REX or ACID file. (Any time slices within these files can also appear as regions in the Region List if the option to view "auto-created" regions is enabled in its local menu. On the other hand, if you use a lot of REX or ACID files in your session, you can reduce clutter by *not* displaying auto-created regions in the Region List.)

Using REX/ACID Region Groups in Your Tracks

When you drag a region group created from a REX or ACID file from the Region List (or from the Workspace browser window or the desktop itself) onto an audio track, make sure the timebase for that track is set to Ticks. That way, if you create any tempo changes, the locations of the time slices within these region groups (derived from the original REX/ACID files) are automatically adjusted to maintain the same relative bar/beat locations. (Nothing stops you from dragging them onto any audio track with a Samples timebase, but Ticks timebase is more convenient and flexible for most musical applications.) For consistency and flexibility when working in this manner, we also recommend enabling the Transport window's Conductor button, rather than using manual tempo settings.

You can cut, copy, paste, and trim these region groups, just as you would any other region in Pro Tools. The Region > Loop command will naturally be of particular interest when using these types of files. In fact, if you want access to the individual slices within them in order to rework the beat itself, just use the Region > Ungroup command. (If during import the ACID/REX loop was speeded up from its native tempo in order to match the current tempo in your Pro Tools, you will notice that some of these time-slice regions will overlap.) Among other things, you could use the Region > Quantize to Grid command to pull the time slices into a more rigid rhythmic alignment and then regroup.

Building a Better Groove

Okay, you've chopped out enough good phrases to build a basic arrangement, and you've even overdubbed a few additional MIDI and audio parts (perhaps some vocals and an instrumental part or two). Now you want to add some nuances to the rhythmic arrangement. Up until now, you've left it fairly repetitive, stringing the same few phrases together many times, almost like a click track or drum loop. What are your options for making it sound less mechanical? Here are just a few ideas:

❋ Use audio regions containing individual drum elements (as described in the section "Building Percussion Tracks from Individual Audio Elements," earlier in this chapter) on an additional audio track, to add appropriate accents on key beats or beginnings of phrases. Discreet cymbal crashes at song transitions and accented beats can go a long way toward making your drum track sound less looped. Unless your MIDI sound source is a high-resolution sampler (including software instruments like SampleTank 2, Kontakt 2, Mach5, Gigastudio3, Reason, and so on), you will generally get more realistic results using high-quality files of individual cymbal hits for this purpose, compared to triggering cymbal sounds from the average MIDI keyboard or module. Make sure these fit in with the existing groove, though, and don't make the novice mistake of making them unnaturally loud!

* Your original rhythm groove may contain some isolated, individual hits on the kick, toms, or snare (if you're lucky) in the intro or breaks. Select these and capture new region definitions so that you have regions in the audio bin called "Kick," "Snare," "LowTom," and so on. (You'll probably need to temporarily turn off Grid mode while precisely highlighting the beginnings and ends of these sounds.) The Tab to Transients button is invaluable for this purpose. Place the cursor fairly closely before the drum hit you want to select—and hitting the Tab key will automatically move the cursor precisely to its attack. Back in Grid mode, you can drag these out onto a track in order to add some accents—and because they came from the same source track, their timbre will match the groove. (Even if your kick sample, for example, has a little bit of extraneous hi-hat, judicious use of the AudioSuite menu's four- or seven-band EQs might help you eliminate most of the hi-hat frequencies. Just make sure you've selected Create Individual Files and not Over-write Selection in the AudioSuite dialog box!)

* Use some of the drum sounds in your MIDI modules, especially small percussion such as shakers, maracas, cabasa, and so on, to layer more variation into your drum groove. Unless you're deliberately seeking a full-blown Latin or world music groove, try mixing this down underneath the drum track's level—too loud, and it will sound cheesy. The idea is to add some varying patterns, changing up velocities and swing factors, to create some longer phrases overlaid on the repetitive four-bar base. Even better, if you have a microphone and some hand percussion (and enough rudimentary technique to not just make matters worse!), you can also perform some of these subtle texture parts yourself for a guaranteed human feel. As a general note, you may be surprised to see how much difference just one human-played part, even mixed at a very low level, can make toward a good groove feel—*especially* with quantized MIDI arrangements!

* Use AudioSuite functions to process some of the existing phrases in your groove (using the Create Individual Files option, so that your original file is unaffected). For example, you might use the EQ to perform some radical EQ on some of the phrases, or extreme compression/gate settings. You can then drop fragments of these processed regions into an additional audio track, trimming their beginnings and ends to create effect "fills" in fiendishly clever locations.

* Use the AudioSuite menu's Expander-Gate function on a rhythm phrase selection, activate the External Key function, and choose one of your other audio tracks (or busses) as the side chain input. The signal that controls the opening/closing of the gate on your selected phrase is whatever occurs simultaneously in that other track/bus. (In other

words, you're imposing the gain/envelope changes of the side chain's audio on your selection.) Depending on where you do this, what source you select, and of course, how extreme your Expander-Gate settings are, some interesting rhythmic effects can be created. Again, a new audio region is created for your results, and you can trim out bits and pieces to use as rhythm accents over your basic groove.

❋ Take advantage of Pro Tools' ability to automate sends (and plug-in parameters, too, of course). Create a send (at send position C, for example) from your drum tracks; route its output to an internal Pro Tools bus (#3, for example). Then create an Aux In, with bus 3 set as its input, and drop a reverb plug-in on one of that Aux In's inserts. Choose a nonlinear or gated reverb setting (or small room, snare room, and so on). Now, switch the Data Display format on the audio track where your drum track resides to Send C > Level. In Grid mode, set at perhaps 1/8 note increments, use the Grabber to create breakpoints that outline 1/8 note–long spikes in the send level right on the snare backbeats—for example, 2 and 4 of each bar (or wherever amuses you). Remember, when viewing breakpoint automation in Pro Tools, you can hold down the Option key (or Alt key in Windows) and click on a breakpoint to delete it. And don't bother drawing your shapes in every single bar. Get it right in a couple of bars, and then copy and paste this automation data into subsequent bars! Also remember that you can trim automation data to scale it up or down. Yes, we know: You're sending the whole drum mix to the reverb, which would sound pretty rude if it was enabled all the time. But by keeping the volume of your Aux In fairly low (and occasionally by using an EQ plug-in on the insert prior to the reverb to reduce high and low frequencies so that the hi-hat and kick drum aren't overly prominent), these rhythmic shots to the reverb can blend into the track, creating subtle dynamic pushes on certain beats. Of course, if subtlety is not your intention, the technique is equally applicable for creating dramatic, dub-style shots to a delay or reverb.

❋ Try routing some of your percussion grooves (drum loops, for example) through a second channel where extremely aggressive dynamics processing is applied. For example, hold down the Control key (Start key in Windows) as you reopen the output assignment selector on your drum loop track, and choose one of the bus pairs in Pro Tools as a secondary destination. Create a new Aux In track with that bus pair selected as its input source. Use plug-in inserts to apply large amounts of compression or limiting to that Aux In track (plus some EQ, if you choose). You can now blend this with the main, unprocessed version of that percussion groove, having it drop out or enter at key points in your arrangement. An even larger number of these *mults* or alternate submixes could be used for creative effect. Also consider applying this "iron fist in a velvet glove" approach with lead vocals, when you want them to sound more powerful or aggressive than your singer may be capable of delivering naturally. A solid, dynamics-processed "backbone" may be just the thing you're looking for.

> **❄ Tip: Thinking Outside the Bar Lines**
>
> A common problem you may encounter when stringing together rhythm phrases is that they may contain events that hang over the exact bar lines at the beginning or end of the phrase. For example, if the drummer hits the crash cymbal on the fourth beat of the last bar, it sounds unnatural for it to get cut off abruptly when the following phrase begins. The Fades dialog box is your best ally for dealing with these situations. A post-splice crossfade after the boundary between the two adjacent regions allows you to smoothly extend the cymbal's decay across the beginning of the next phrase (as long as it's similar to the preceding one—remember that the two regions will overlap during the crossfade, including whatever else is in the first phrase's drum mix).
>
> Select two adjacent regions with the Grabber, and then select Edit > Fades > Create (Command+F in Mac, Ctrl+F in Windows). In the Batch Fades dialog box (shown in Figure 12.5), set the Link option to None (so that you can select the Fade In and Fade Out shapes independently). Then, select the Post-Splice option under Position, Preset Curve 1 for the in shape of the second region (so that it starts immediately, with no fade-up) and one of the more gradual curves for the first region's out shape. Select about 200–300 milliseconds for the fade's initial length; you can always adjust this later with the Trimmer tool.

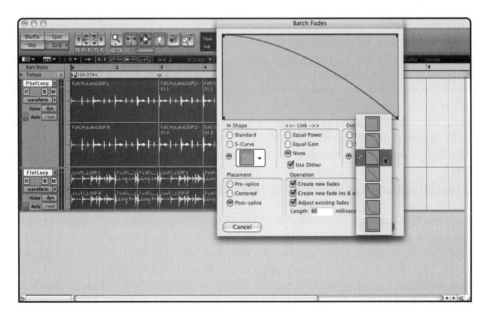

Figure 12.5 Here, we're creating a post-splice fade between the selected regions. At the splice point, the second region begins immediately at full volume, while additional material after the end of the first region fades out over it.

Time Compression/Expansion

In the situation described here, the obvious use of time compression/expansion is to adjust the length of an audio region you've imported from elsewhere to the tempo of the current session (and/or to some other phrase selection). Let's say you've imported a two-bar drum loop, but when you place it on an audio track, it's slightly too long to fit into two bars at the current session's tempo. Because HD systems offer an Edit menu command that makes this especially easy, we'll show you two methods, both with and without this command.

Adjust Phrase Length to Current Tempo: Method A (TDM Only)

In all TDM-based Pro Tools systems (using the current Pro Tools HD 7 software, for example), the TCE Edit to Timeline Selection command in the Edit menu makes it really easy to adjust the duration of a selection. This will be your principal method for adjusting multiple musical phrases, breakbeats, and so on so that they all match a single tempo.

1. In the Edit window, confirm that you're in Grid mode, using Bars:Beats (at your current tempo setting) as the units for your main timeline ruler, and 1 bar, for example, as your Grid value. Also make sure that the Link Timeline and Edit Selections icon is enabled.

2. If necessary, click the region containing the phrase with the Grabber tool to select it and drag its beginning exactly to the first beat of a bar.

3. While holding down the Shift key, use the Selector tool to adjust the end of the currently highlighted selection to exactly two bars. (In this hypothetical case, where our phrase is slightly too long, you will be *shortening* the selection.)

4. Click to disable the Link Timeline and Edit Selections icon in the Edit window toolbar, immediately below the Zoomer tool and zoom preset buttons, so that the track selections you make in the Edit window won't alter the Transport's play selection (an identically named command in the Options menu also duplicates this function).

5. Click the phrase region again with the Grabber tool (notice that the Start and End values in the Transport window do not change).

6. Select TCE Edit to Timeline Selection. The duration of your current Edit selection (what's selected in the tracks) will be adjusted to the length of the current Timeline selection (between the current Start and End values shown in the Transport window).

Adjust Phrase Length to Current Tempo: Method B (TDM, and LE or M-Powered Versions)

Another option is to use the Trimmer in Time Compression/Expansion mode (commonly referred to as the *Time Trimmer* or *TCE Trimmer*). When used in Grid mode, this mode of the Trimmer tool makes is very easy to stretch or squeeze an audio segment to a given duration.

1. In the Edit window, confirm that you're in Grid mode, using Bars:Beats (at your current tempo setting) as the units for your main timeline ruler, and 1 bar, for example, as your Grid value. If necessary, drag the source region (which is slightly too long to fit exactly into two bars at the current session tempo) so that it begins exactly on the first beat of a bar.

2. If necessary, click the phrase region with the Grabber tool to select it (again), and drag so that it begins exactly on the first beat of a bar.

3. Select the Trimmer tool and use its pop-up selector to switch to TCE mode. (In Time Trimmer mode, a clock appears within the Trimmer tool's icon, as shown in Figure 12.6.)

4. Shorten the region so that its end corresponds to the beginning of the following bar. A new region is created where the duration of the original audio was time-compressed to match two bars at the session's tempo.

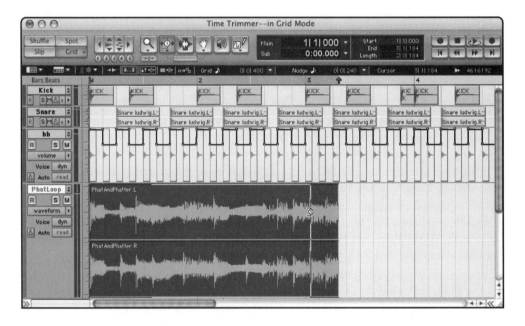

Figure 12.6 You can use the TCE mode of the Trimmer tool to compress/expand the duration of an audio selection.

❄ Tip: User Settings for the Time Trimmer

When looping drums, percussion, and rhythmic material in general, the position of the Accuracy slider in the Time Compression/Expansion window will make a difference in the sonic results. For dialog, sound effects, and ambience loops, you generally want this slider all the way to the left (towards Sound) for maximum quality and retention of transients in the original file—even if this means that the relative positions of some events within the original audio selection aren't precisely reproduced in the time-stretched version. For drum/percussion loops, on the other hand, the original feel is better retained with the Accuracy slider all the way to the right (Rhythm). Fair enough... but this slider defaults to the middle position, and that's the setting that will be used for the Time Trimmer—unless, that is, you change the default to your own setting! Here's how you do it.

1. Select AudioSuite > Time Compression Expansion. Adjust your settings in the dialog box shown in Figure 12.7. For our present purpose, we're mostly concerned with the Accuracy slider, since the ratio, length, and other time-related fields are affected by how the Time Trimmer is used. Assuming

you mostly work with drum/percussion loops, set the Accuracy slider all the way to the right, to favor rhythm over sound.

2. In the local plug-in settings menu within the AudioSuite window, select Save Settings As to store a name for the current settings.

3. Reopen the same menu and select Set As User Default.

4. Open the menu one last time, and choose Settings Preferences > Set Plug-In Default To > User Setting.

That's it! From now on, whenever you first open this AudioSuite function, these settings appear by default. More importantly, this Accuracy slider setting applies whenever you use the Time Trimmer on audio regions. If you ever want to change this, repeat the above steps; even simpler, in the plug-in settings menu, choose Settings Preferences > Set Plug-In Default To > Factory Setting.

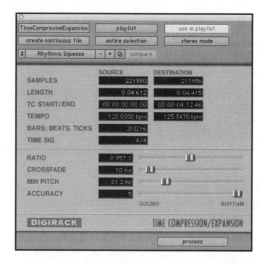

Figure 12.7   The Time Compression/Expansion dialog box opens when you select the Time Compression Expansion option from the AudioSuite menu.

Beat Detective

You open Beat Detective (shown in Figure 12.8) via the Event menu of Pro Tools. The Beat Detective LE version included in current LE and M-Powered versions lacks the Collection mode shown in this figure but is otherwise identical to the full version in Pro Tools HD. (However, the Music Production Toolkit bundle adds Collection Mode to these versions.) Beat Detective automatically identifies the transient peaks within the current selection to generate tempo information (bars and beats) and largely eliminates the need to use the Identify Beat command described in this chapter.

You provide the starting and ending Bar|Beat locations and the time signature and then adjust Sensitivity and other parameters. The four *mode* buttons allow you to choose whether Beat Detective a) simply generates Bar|Beat markers in the Tempo ruler; b) separates the selection into multiple regions based on the detected beats (beat triggers); c) *conforms* (moves) the separated regions to the session's tempo; and d) when conforming separated regions to the tempo, eliminates gaps or clicks between separated regions with crossfades and so on.

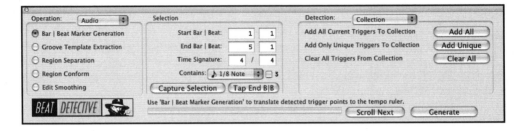

Figure 12.8 Beat Detective includes Collection mode in HD versions, while the Beat Detective LE version in Pro Tools LE and M-Powered does not.

Obviously, you will get best results with rhythmic material, at steady tempos and with well-defined attacks on the beats (drum loops and mixes with rhythm sections, for example).

It's extremely important that your initial selection be exact! Before applying Beat Detective to a four-bar phrase selection, for example, use the Zoom features while using the Selector to precisely adjust the beginning and end of your selection to the correct downbeats.

Beat Detective is also useful for situations where one rhythm loop has a distinctly different amount of swing than another. By using Region Conform (and usually Edit Smoothing, for best results) you could force sub-beats within the region more toward the straight 1/8-note feel of the current tempo, for example.

Beat Detective Modes

There are various Beat Detective modes, as follows:

* **Bar|Beat Marker Generation.** Generates these tempo events and beat triggers based on transients in the audio waveform. You tell Beat Detective how many bars long this selection is (by specifying start and end bars), the time signature, and what note values generally make up the smaller subdivisions of this beat (because generating too many or too few Bar|Beat markers is inconvenient). You can fine-tune the detection mode. As seen in Figure 12.9, the Sensitivity slider adjusts how it reacts to dynamics (although setting this to 0% allows you to generate only a single tempo event in the Tempo ruler, thus enabling you to avoid using the Identify Beat command described earlier in this chapter). You can adjust whether Beat Detective looks more toward low frequencies (Low Emphasis, useful when kick drum is the main defining element of the beat, for example) or high frequencies (when hi-hats, acoustic guitar arpeggios, and so on should be the elements that key the generation of beat subdivisions). You then click the Analyze button so that Beat Detective examines the selected audio data. If you see that the bar or beat lines in the display are at improper locations, adjust the Sensitivity slider—it's

possible, for example, that a softer snare or tom accent on beat four-and-a-half is falsely "triggering" Beat Detective, causing it to think the downbeat should be there. If you want even more control, especially when working with higher sub-beat resolutions like 1/16 or 1/32 notes, you can also manually drag the beat marker to a precise location in the waveform. (Option-click, or Alt-click in Windows, to delete any of these beat triggers. Command- click, or Ctrl-click in Windows, to "promote" a beat trigger from a subdivision to a main beat or bar trigger.)

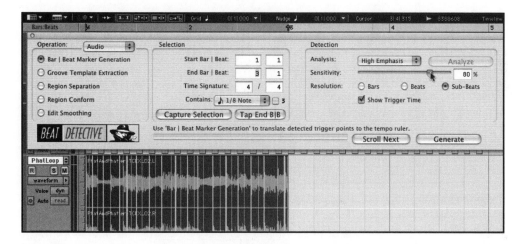

Figure 12.9 In Bar | Beat Marker Generation mode, greater sensitivity increases the number of beat triggers that will be detected in this drum loop.

❋ **Region Separation.** Based on the beat triggers you've defined using this analysis and detection, this function splits the audio selection into multiple regions.

❋ **Groove Template Extraction.** This function creates a DigiGroove template, based on the current beat trigger analysis of your selection. This can be either stored temporarily in the Groove Clipboard or saved to disk (as seen in Figure 12.10), where you could use it with the Grid/Groove Quantize function for MIDI data—a great way to impart the feel of one audio or MIDI part to other MIDI parts.

❋ **Region Conform.** In Standard mode, Region Conform adjusts the location of the multiple regions created by the Region Separation command ("quantizes" them) according to the session's current tempo settings. Further options include Strength (less than 100% retains some of the region's original feel by not moving the separated regions all the way to the nearest grid increment in the session's timeline), Exclude Within (if already within a certain distance of the nearest grid increment, the event won't be moved), and Swing. Once an audio selection is converted to multiple regions, you can also conform region locations either to one of the predefined DigiGrooves in Pro Tools or to the current contents of the Groove Clipboard. This is a practical method for matching the feel of the current selection to existing MIDI parts or to DigiGroove information you've extracted from another audio selection (so that two drum loops sound tighter when played simultaneously, for example).

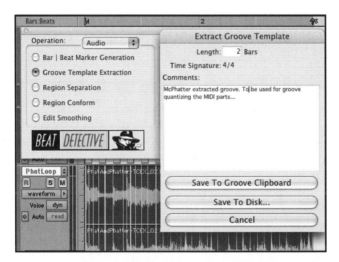

Figure 12.10   Here, we've saving a DigiGroove that was extracted from an audio selection to disk.

* **Edit Smoothing.** This mode applies trimming and crossfades so that there are no gaps left between the regions at their new locations after they've been conformed. Otherwise, after the separated regions are repositioned, you may hear some clicks or choppiness wherever there's silence between two regions, or where their boundaries overlap. You can specify the length of any required crossfades.

* **Collection (HD version only).** With Bar | Beat Marker Generation and Region Separation modes, Collection mode allows you to apply Beat Detective to multiple tracks with individual detection settings to build up a composite *beat trigger* map. Useful for multiple drum set tracks, for example. This is available for LE/M-Powered via the Music Production Toolkit.

You can also use Beat Detective with MIDI tracks. You can generate groove and tempo information from MIDI tracks and apply it to audio tracks, or vice versa. For example, you could extract a groove template from a drum loop and then apply this to a MIDI part you created through step input. MIDI chord recognition parameters included among the options in the Analysis pop-up menu (shown in Figure 12.11) allow you to control how Beat Detective interprets the location of beats in relation to the varied timeline positions of the various notes that make up a chord (since in a real-time performance, these are rarely identical). You can establish the beat trigger according to the first, last, lowest, highest, loudest, or average note position in the chord.

If you're a beat mixer using loops and other "found" audio to build grooves, it will be well worth your while to explore Beat Detective. Although we've provided only a superficial overview here, the *Pro Tools Reference Guide* PDF document dedicates an entire chapter to Beat Detective.

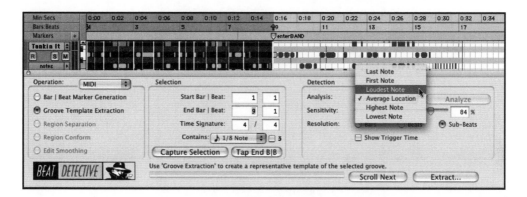

Figure 12.11 When analyzing MIDI with Beat Detective (or extracting a DigiGroove as shown here), options in this pop-up menu allow control over how notes within chords are interpreted.

> ❋ **CSi: Beat Detective in Action**
>
> In the CD-ROM at the back of this book, you'll find a sample movie tutorial by Steve Thomas from *Pro Tools 7 CSi Master* that provides a great overview of using Beat Detective. That CD-ROM actually contains three movie tutorials dedicated to Beat Detective (*Overview, Collection Mode,* and *Creating Digi-Grooves*), plus others about Groove Quantize, Sound Replacer, and many more advanced Pro Tools functions.

Pitch Shift

Ever have difficulty getting samples from different sources to be in tune (assuming that you're musically inclined, and it bothers you if they're not)? This AudioSuite function can help. Unlike samplers, where the sample playback rate is raised or lowered to change the pitch of a sound (which also affects the sound's duration), Pro Tools can change the pitch of a selection *without* changing its duration (as long as the Time Correction check box in the Pitch Shift dialog box is enabled).

One of the features we like in the Pitch Shift dialog box of Pro Tools (shown in Figure 12.12) is the Reference Pitch option. If this is enabled, when you click the dialog box's Preview button, the specified note/frequency sounds so that you can adjust the amount of pitch correction by ear until it sounds in tune. This is really helpful, for example, for adjusting imported samples to the same key as your current session. (So go get your old LP collection out of your mother's basement and start mining some beats!)

You can also use pitch shift for special effects, of course—silly vocal effects, transposed pitches on toms for melodic fills, and our personal favorite: destroyed drum parts (either way up, or

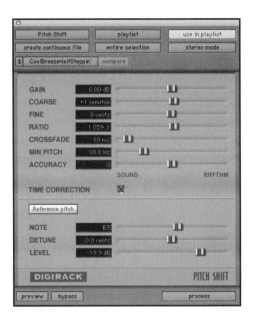

Figure 12.12 The Pitch Shift dialog box allows you change the pitch of an audio selection without changing its duration.

way down; use small parts/pieces as occasional overlays for the normal percussion parts). As you probably know, however, there are limits to what you can do with pitch shifting (and time expansion, for that matter) before digital artifacts appear in the resultant audio.

And yes, you can use pitch shift to correct some out-of-tune vocals. However, if the singer wavers or swoops in pitch (rather than steadily holding a sharp or flat note), it may be difficult to get convincing results. Should you have the misfortune to require pitch correction for vocalists quite often, we suggest you might look into dedicated pitch-correction plug-ins, such as Antares Auto-Tune, Serato Pitch 'n' Time, SoundToys (formerly Wave Mechanics) PurePitch, Eventide Octavox, and so on, which are much more effective—even applying automatic correction in real time.

Tip: Dumb Tricks with Pro Tools Automation

The Pencil tool in Pro Tools has several interesting drawing shapes (in addition to Free Hand, the default, and the Parabolic and S-curve shapes), as seen in Figure 12.13. In particular, Triangle, Square, and Random modes can provide some amusing results when drawing automation. Each shape creates steps (individual automation breakpoints) whose spacing is determined by the current Grid value, and whose amplitude is determined by the vertical mouse position. For example, let's say your Grid mode is set to 1/2 notes, you're viewing a track in Pan Data Display mode, and you've selected the Triangle mode for the Pencil tool. As you click and drag rightward in the track, repeating triangle shapes occur every two beats; the distance between their upper and lower apexes (the *amplitude* of the triangle shape) is determined by how far you drag the mouse up and down as you draw. This is one way to create panning (or send levels, volume, and so on) that is synchronized to the beat. The spacing between the resultant breakpoints is always determined by the current Grid value. The Square mode works the same way, as does Random (keep in mind that the *range* of random values also depends on the vertical movement of the Pencil tool as you draw). And remember, you can always scale automation up or down later with the Trimmer. This technique might be a little radical for a classical piano recording, but can be just the ticket when you're trying to create an unusual mix!

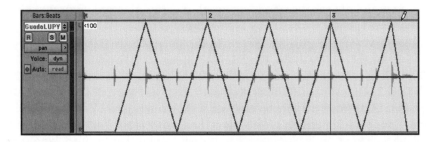

Figure 12.13 You can use the Pencil tool's drawing shapes for creating automation (and audio waveforms, at the appropriate zoom level). In this example, we've set the Grid value to 1/4 notes and are drawing pan automation within our audio track using the Pencil tool's Triangle shape.

❊ **Automation as a Creative Tool**

On the CD-ROM at the back of this book, check out the sample movie tutorial excerpted from *Pro Tools 7 CSi Starter* called "Automation Overview." Among other operations, you will see the Pencil tool used to draw automation, copying and pasting automation breakpoints from one section of a song to another, and how the various automation modes work in Pro Tools. In fact, the entire structure of *Pro Tools 7 CSi Starter* is based upon starting from an imported drum loop and eventually building up a finished arrangement.

So What About Samplers?

A sampler is a different animal than an audio editing environment like Pro Tools. Essential to the idea of a sampler's operation is that it plays back samples (also digital audio recordings, but stored in RAM in order to be used during real-time performance) at different pitches, in response to incoming MIDI note events. Samplers accomplish this by varying each sample's playback pitch—this naturally affects the sample's duration as well. For smoothly looping samples, this is not much of an issue, within limits. However, for rhythm loops, you can only change a sample's playback speed by so much (that is, in order to adjust its tempo) before it starts to sound quite a bit different. For that reason, current samplers also offer time-stretching features.

If what you'd like to do is trigger samples in some kind of musical fashion, maybe even picking out melodic figures and so on, a sampler can be just the ticket. Building percussion tracks from individual elements can be much faster and more flexible with a sampler because overlapping sounds are not a problem, and editing is done in ordinary MIDI tracks within Pro Tools. But you don't have to lug around a keyboard or rack module in order to enjoy the benefits of sampler instruments (or, strictly speaking, sample *playback* instruments in many cases). There are also many other synthesizer and sampler plug-ins for Pro Tools, which can be immensely valuable tools for your dance, trance, and beat-mixing arsenal:

* **Standalone synthesizer and sampler applications compatible with Pro Tools via ReWire.** Reason (by Propellerhead Software), Live (by Ableton), Gigastudio3 (by Tascam), Unity DS-1, and Phrazer 2 (by Native Instruments).

* **Synthesizer and sampler plug-ins for Pro Tools.** SampleTank, Unity DS-1, Unity Player, Unity AS-1, MachFive, MX4, B4, Pro-53, FM7, Battery2 (shown in Figure 12.14), BFD, DR-008, Charlie, Moog Modular V, ARP 2600 V, Orange Vocoder, Synthesizer One, SampleTank 2, Atmosphere, Reaktor, Kontakt 2, Lounge Lizard EP-2, Trilogy, and Access Virus|Indigo TDM (the V40 version of which is shown in Figure 12.15). Check the "Plug-In Finder" page on Digidesign's Web site to find many more synthesis plug-ins that are compatible with your particular operating system and hardware. Also, fxpansion offers the VST to RTAS Adapter, a "wrapper" program that allows VST plug-ins to be used within Pro Tools. (Not all VST plug-ins are supported; check the fxpansion Web site and forums for the most recent information.)

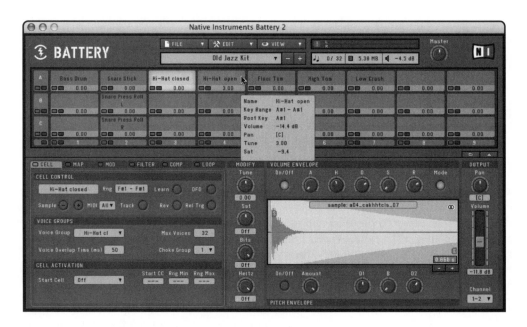

Figure 12.14 Battery 2, by Native Instruments, is a drum sampler available for the RTAS plug-in format (as well as others).

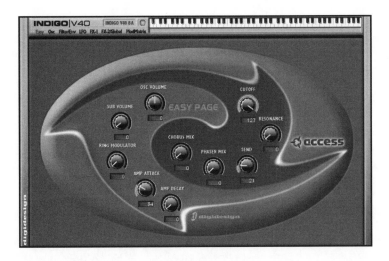

Figure 12.15 Access Virus IndigoV40 is an analog synthesis plug-in in TDM format. You can also use its DSP effects for the synthesis engine for effects processing (including the resonant filters) from other Pro Tools sources, via the Input Mode feature.

❋ **Tip: Set Your Delay Times in Relation to the Current Tempo**

Sometimes you might want the delay time to correspond to a specific note value (say an 1/8 note or a 1/4-note triplet) in relation to the current tempo of the music. Although you can automatically sync the DigiRack delays included with Pro Tools (and some other third-party delay plug-ins) to the session's tempo, it's also fairly easy to accomplish this manually. Some people also like to use tempo-related time settings for predelays on reverbs—LFO (low-frequency oscillator) speeds on flangers and chorus effects, for example. Setting these additional time factors in a mix to some logical relationship with the tempo can sometimes help avoid clutter—*especially* with delay repeats:

❋ The DigiRack delays include short, slap , medium, long, and extra-long variations (with maximum delay times of 43, 171, 341, 683, or 2726 milliseconds, respectively; longer delay types utilize a larger fraction of your system's processing capacity, even if their current delay time value is short). Except for the short and slap versions, you can sync these DigiRack delays to the current Pro Tools tempo, as you can see in Figure 12.16. This makes it easy to set repeat times to some rhythmic value without needing to make any calculations. The tempo-syncing feature is enabled or disabled by a button that looks like a metronome in the Delay Plug-in window (shown in Figure 12.16). The Meter and Tempo fields are disabled when Tempo Sync is active; otherwise, you could use these to manually specify your delay times in terms of a musical tempo and time signature. The Groove slider is useful for adding some swing factor to delay repeats; that is, each offbeat is progressively later—or earlier—as you increase/decrease the amount of swing.

When using the medium and long versions, you can set delay times in musical values for a specific meter and tempo setting using the Meter, Tempo, and Groove controls.

❋ Unfortunately, some older delays (especially the external, hardware variety and some third-party plug-ins) only allow you to specify delay times in milliseconds, not note value/bpm, and so on. Okay, so stop complaining, already; it's easy!

To start, simply change the Main counter (either in the Transport window or at the top of the Edit window) from Bars:Beats to Min:Secs. Switch to Grid mode, and use the Grid Value selector to choose Bars:Beats as the grid time units and the desired note value as the grid increment. The increments of the grid (at your specified Grid value) now appear as blue vertical lines in the Edit window.

Then use the Selector tool to highlight a duration of only one increment anywhere within a track. The Length field now displays the duration of your selection in milliseconds. Now you can open up the Plug-In window and type that number into the Delay plug-in's Delay field.

If you were in 4/4 time, for example, with the tempo cranked up to 180 bpm (beats per minute), an 1/8 note would be 166 milliseconds (ms), and a 1/4 note triplet would be 222 ms. (Although Min:Secs timings are only accurate to the nearest millisecond, note that the delay times can actually be adjusted as fine as hundredths of a millisecond. If you need greater precision—perhaps because you're going to use high Feedback values in the delay, so that a large number of repeats will stay in time to the tempo without drifting—you may have to break out the calculator!)

Besides helping your mix sound less cluttered when multiple delays are used, synchronizing your delays to a subdivision of the musical beat has another advantage: When bouncing out loops from selections that contain delays (for example, for an interactive CD-ROM background, sampler, or loop-based audio program), you'll get smoother loops when your selection doesn't end randomly between two delay repeats.

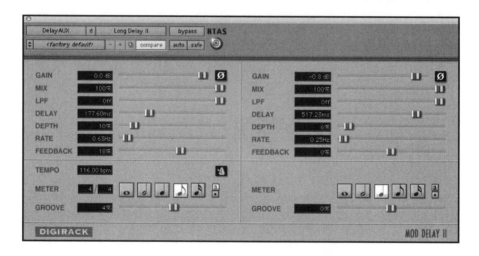

Figure 12.16 The DigiRack delays support setting delay times in relation to musical tempos. Often a good idea!

❋ Note: BPM...The Not-So-Secret Formula

Sixty divided by the beats per minute equals the duration of each beat in seconds (but you knew that). If you prefer to calculate the duration of each beat in milliseconds, it's 60,000 divided by the beats per minute, of course.

If your tempo is 120 beats per minute (bpm) in 4/4 time, each 1/4 note is 500 milliseconds (each 1/2 note is a full second, and each 1/8 note is 250 ms). If your tempo is 150 bpm in 6/8 time, each 1/8 note is 400 milliseconds.

Hey, what about ticks, you say? Pro Tools divides every 1/4 note into 960 ticks... or every 1/8 note into 480 ticks, if you're in 6/8 time, for example. The actual duration of each tick depends on the tempo setting. If the tempo is 120 bpm, each tick actually represents 500ms/960, or about .520833333 milliseconds. Aren't you glad you asked?

Summary

Obviously, the suggestions in this chapter barely scratch the surface. The power is there to create remarkable mixes, and as you surely know, thousands of hit records have been created in Pro Tools. Get in there, and start working!

13 } Music Production

In this chapter, we take a look at using Pro Tools with multiple live musicians in the studio (as opposed to working alone in your project studio). This presents some particular challenges—for example, providing multiple cue mixes for performers (because they won't all want to hear the same headphone mix), monitoring latency issues with Pro Tools LE and M-Powered hardware configurations, and configuring the Pro Tools mixer to easily switch modes from tracking to editing to mixing. (Unlike the analog recording process, in Pro Tools, you're often doing all three things at once.) We won't exhaustively explore all the aspects of music production with Pro Tools... that's a topic to fill an entire book! Finally, we will also provide a brief overview of strategies for live recording with a basic Pro Tools system (that is, without a complete Venue configuration).

Your own studio projects will be different, but for the sake of our hypothetical session, let's assume that the input source requirements for our studio recording mirror those shown in Table 13.1.

Table 13.1 Sample Input Source Requirements

Input	Instrument	Description	Location
Audio inputs 1–8	Drums	Eight microphones: kick, snare, hi-hat, two rack toms, floor tom, plus two left/right overheads	In drum booth
Audio input 9	Bass	Direct mono signal from bass preamp	In main room
Audio input 10	Electric guitar	Microphone on amplifier	In main room

Input	Instrument	Description	Location
Audio inputs 11–12	Acoustic guitar	Two microphones: one on the bridge of the guitar, another over the fingerboard where it meets the body (and angled slightly back toward the soundhole)	In isolation booth #1
Audio inputs 13–14	MIDI keyboard	Two direct audio outs for monitoring only (because you're recording this MIDI performance data on a Pro Tools Instrument track, to facilitate subsequent sound selection and editing)	In main room
Audio input 15	Saxophone	Microphone	In isolation booth #2
Audio input 16	Lead vocal (reference track while recording)	Microphone	In isolation booth #3
MIDI input	MIDI In from keyboard		

This band wants to record all at once (rather than layering tracks one by one), although they will later overdub a replacement vocal and perhaps some backing vocals or a solo. We're obviously assuming here that you have a MIDI interface on your Pro Tools configuration and that your audio hardware allows recording 16 simultaneous analog audio inputs—for example, the 96i I/O. Other interfaces with only eight analog inputs, like the Digi 002/002 Rack, 96 I/O, and 192 I/O, could also have an eight-channel mic preamp plugged into their ADAT Lightpipe digital input. (The 192 I/O alternatively supports the eight-channel TDIF digital input, and can also be expanded up to 16 channels of analog input via a 192 AD card.)

We're also assuming that you have got sufficient microphone preamps for recording all these microphone sources. As a general rule, analog audio inputs on most Digidesign audio interfaces for Pro Tools|HD systems (and their TDM-based predecessors) accept only line-level signals. On Digidesign's Mbox, there are only two mic-level inputs, four on the Digi 002/002 Rack, one on M-Audio's FireWire Solo, two on the FireWire 410, FireWire 1814, and Delta 1010LT... and you're going to need 12 for this session! You can use a good analog mixer with direct channel outputs or, even better, a couple of dedicated multichannel microphone preamplifiers, like Digidesign's PRE high-end mic preamp (see Figure 13.1); Focusrite's OctoPre eight-channel mic preamp with optional digital outputs; PreSonus' DigiMAX, an eight-channel mic preamp with ADAT Lightpipe output; or any larger number of single and dual-channel mic preamps—whatever your budget permits!

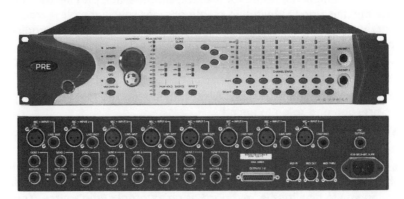

Figure 13.1 You can configure Digidesign's PRE, an eight-channel high-end microphone preamp, from within the Pro Tools software (via MIDI). Its settings are recalled when you reopen the session.

Track Setup and Click Track for Recording

First of all, you need to create a new session with audio tracks for all the sources you are going to record! You'll also create a mono Auxiliary Input to monitor the audio output of the Click plug-in, plus a stereo Instrument track to monitor the keyboard. As you will see, you will not only create some Aux Ins to use as send destinations for effects (even during recording, to provide a less sterile-sounding headphone mix for the performers), but you will also use several Aux Ins strictly during the recording phase of this project to provide different cue mixes for different groups of performers. (This will require multiple headphone amplifiers; you will feed a different mix from a Pro Tools output pair to each.)

Track Setup for Recording

This is one of the remarkable things about working with Pro Tools: Within the limitations of your system configuration and the design of the software itself, you configure your mixer with exactly the number of tracks and effect sends that the project requires—no more, no less. You can even reconfigure the mixer during different phases of a single project—for example, recording, editing, and mixdown.

Create Audio Tracks and Auxiliary Inputs

For the recording phase of this project, you need to create audio tracks to record input signals and an Instrument track for the external keyboard. Auxiliary Inputs will also be used to provide effects in the performers' headphone mix. The initial positions of new tracks reflect their order in the New Tracks dialog box; using the creation order described here will help you avoid having to drag tracks around afterwards.

1. Create a new Pro Tools session. Then choose Track > New (Shift+Command+N in Mac, Shift+Ctrl+N in Windows); see Figure 13.2. Use the pop-up selectors to specify five mono audio tracks in Samples timebase for the kick, snare, hi-hat, plus the rack and floor toms. Then click the plus sign (+) button to create another row in the New Tracks dialog box. (As you create the following tracks, you will repeat this process for adding a new row in the dialog box.)

2. Create a single stereo audio track for the drum overheads. (Even though the two acoustic guitar microphones will be panned hard left and right, you're going to keep these separate on two of the mono tracks you've already created so that you can apply different EQ, compression and so on to each.)

3. Create four mono audio tracks, for the bass, electric guitar, and two acoustic guitar microphones.

4. Create one stereo Instrument track to record your keyboard player's performance. (It will default to Ticks timebase.) The Instrument track will serve a similar function to an Aux In, allowing you to monitor the keyboard as an external audio source. You will also use the Instrument Track to record the MIDI output from the keyboard, giving you flexibility to edit or expand this part later—but don't forget to record the result to an audio track if the performer is going to walk out of the studio with this keyboard before you finish mixing!

5. Create two more mono audio tracks for the saxophone and lead vocal.

6. Create one mono Auxiliary Input where you will instantiate the Click plug-in to produce a metronome sound.

7. Create one stereo Master Fader (we're assuming output pair 1–2 will be the source for your stereo mix).

8. Click the OK button to close this dialog box and create the new tracks.

9. Save your session! If you don't save often, don't complain later if you lose your work!

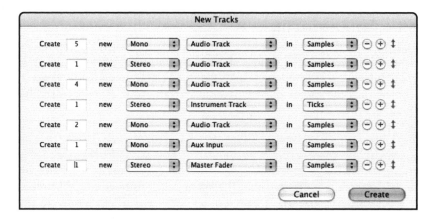

Figure 13.2 You can create multiple track types simultaneously in the New Tracks dialog box.

Name Your Tracks; Select Their Input Sources

Next, you should edit all your track names. Not only does this make it easier to see what's going on in your mix, but it also affects how region names are created once you start recording.

1. If necessary, switch to the Mix window. Rename tracks Audio 1 through Audio 6 "kick," "snare," "hi-hat," "rack tom," "mid tom," and "floor tom." While you're doing this, notice the Next and Previous buttons in the Track Name/Comments dialog box. Holding down the Command key (Ctrl key in Windows) as you press the right or left arrow key is the keyboard shortcut for these buttons. Get in the habit of naming all your tracks and Aux Ins before closing this dialog box!

2. Change the stereo audio track's name (currently Audio 7) to Overhead. Click the Create button to close this dialog box for now.

3. Use the input selectors of the mono drum tracks to select inputs 1–6. The following order is typical for mic inputs in drum tracks: kick, snare, hi-hat, toms from higher to lower pitch, and then overheads, left-right. (You can drag the drum tracks into any order that's convenient, regardless of their input assignments.)

4. Using the Input selector for this stereo Overheads track, specify input pair 7–8 as its input source for recording.

5. Rename the next track (currently called Audio 9) to Bass, selecting input 9 as its source.

6. Continue to rename the remainder of your audio tracks, selecting the appropriate input for their recording sources. Pan the two acoustic guitar tracks hard left and right while you're at it. (Again, the reason we're using two mono tracks for the stereo-mic'ed acoustic guitar—rather than a single stereo track—is so that we can place different EQs and such on the signal from each microphone.)

7. Rename the stereo Instrument track to Kybd. Select input pair 13–14 as its source (where you've connected audio outputs from the MIDI keyboard out in the studio); see Figure 13.3. Also select the MIDI input and channel where the keyboard is connected.

> ✳ **Tip: Name Your Tracks at the Beginning!**
>
> Naming tracks before you begin recording is *important*—in Pro Tools, all the audio regions created by recording inherit the name of their source track. In a session this large, if all the original audio files and auto-created regions in the Region List (and within the tracks, for that matter) have cryptic names like "Audio 6_01," you *will* eventually get confused!

8. Rename your mono Aux In to "Click."

9. Save your session! You're now ready to start record-enabling audio tracks so that you can check input levels. Remember that input levels have to be adjusted *at the source* (the line output, the mic preamp, and so on) if you see any clipping indicators. (Don't stress about recording the absolutely hottest possible levels, either—especially when you're

recording at 24-bit resolution. You're not fighting to overcome hiss and other limitations of analog tape, and digital clipping *always* sounds very nasty, not at all like the warm tape saturation that's sometimes a desirable effect.) It's also worth mentioning here that performers tend to hold back a little while checking levels. Inevitably, when the record light is on, they sing a little harder and play a little louder. Leave yourself some head-room. Also remember that volume faders on audio tracks have no effect on the audio signal level being recorded to disk!

10. As you are checking input levels, adjust your tracks' main Volume faders to obtain an approximate mix for the song. (We will use this later as the basis for our cue mixes; see the section "Setting Up a Cue Mix with Effects," later in this chapter.)

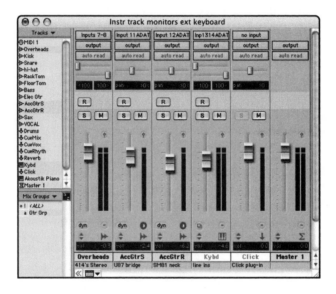

Figure 13.3 At this point in the session, we're using an Instrument track to monitor the keyboard (instead of recording its audio to disk, since we expect to use its recorded MIDI data with a software instrument plug-in later). Overhead microphones for the drum set are on a single stereo track. We're using two microphones on the acoustic guitar but recording them to separate mono tracks.

Click Track

The band wants to record this song with a click track (which, incidentally, is going to make it very easy to edit in Grid mode afterward), so we need to set this up before recording. For this example, we're going to use the Click plug-in on an Aux In track as the source for our metronome sound. (Some people opt for using an external MIDI source for click sounds, or even use audio regions on a track if they're extremely concerned about conserving DSP resources and/or extremely precise metronome timing.) The options in the Click plug-in window are shown in Figure 13.4.

Figure 13.4 The Click plug-in lets you choose from a variety of metronome sounds.

If you prefer, however, the metronome click from Pro Tools (based on the current tempo and meter settings) could also be transmitted as a MIDI note event so that some external MIDI device produces the click sound. This can be any drum machine or synthesizer with any appropriate percussive sound. Most users will opt to use the Click plug-in rather than an external MIDI device, however. For the sake of simplicity, let's assume our entire song is in 4/4 time (Pro Tools' default time signature), and the musicians want 1/4-note clicks.

1. In the Transport window, double-click the Metronome button to open the Click/Countoff Options dialog box (shown in Figure 13.5).

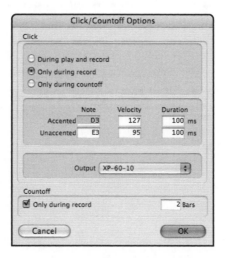

Figure 13.5 The Click/Countoff Options dialog box. Here, a MIDI output (device) and channel are selected as the MIDI metronome destination. If an external MIDI device is generating the metronome sound (instead of the Click plug-in, which is generally the preferred method), its audio output must be connected to an input on your audio hardware if you want to monitor it via a Pro Tools Aux In track.

2. Because you're going to use the Click plug-in in this session, leave the MIDI output selector in this dialog box set to None (instead of selecting any other MIDI destination).

3. Click and hold on any of the insert selectors on the Click Aux In. Under the Instrument submenu, choose the Click plug-in. Option-click the main fader for this Aux In (or Alt-click in Windows) to set its level to 0 dB.

4. If necessary, click the Transport window's Metronome button to enable the metronome click.

5. Press the spacebar to start playback in Pro Tools. You should now hear the click sound (from the plug-in) in the Click Auxiliary Input at your session's current tempo. In the pop-up Presets selector for the Click plug-in, notice that you can choose from various metronome sounds.

6. Now you need to adjust the tempo, with the assistance of your performers. Be aware that musicians' perceptions of appropriate click tempos are notoriously unreliable while they are not actually playing. You can always set the tempo manually (in the Transport window's Tempo field), but you'll probably find that tapping in a manual tempo setting is usually much more reliable. Have the band run through the song until they get their groove on. First, make sure that the Tempo Ruler Enable button is disabled (in the MIDI Controls section of the Transport window). Click the Current Tempo field and use the T key on your computer keyboard to tap in the tempo. (Alternatively, you can enable Use MIDI to Tap Tempo in the MIDI tab of the Preferences dialog box, and use a MIDI keyboard controller—such as a key on a keyboard or pad on a drum module—to tap in a manual tempo.)

❄ **Tip: Grooves on Tap**

When setting click-track tempos for musical groups, tapping in a manual tempo is *always* the most reliable method! As described previously, have your musicians simply play through the song a couple of times while you set an appropriate tempo—before you even let them hear a click track. Be aware, however, that bands with less studio experience often lose sense of appropriate song tempos when they're in cold and unfamiliar studio conditions (typically ending up slower, when the adrenaline rush of live performance isn't there). In that case, ask the band to bring a tape of any good live performance or rehearsal version and use *that* for tapping in your manual tempo setting. (Sound quality doesn't matter; a cassette is fine.) Even if you do end up backing the tempo off slightly from there (because live tempos are sometimes too fast for studio recordings), everyone will be happier in the long run!

❄ **Caution: In the Beginning, There Was a Drum Fill...**

You might figure that once you calculate the proper tempo, activate the Click plug-in, and enable the Precount button, you're all set to record—all the musicians will jump in at bar 1, beat 1. Wrong! The drummer plays a couple of pick-up notes to lead into the first bar. (Some crack about famous drummer "pick-up" lines could be made here, but we promised we wouldn't make any musician jokes—or drummer jokes!)

When recording bands to a click track in Pro Tools, get in the habit of using the Event > Renumber Bars command (see Figure 13.6) to establish some point further into the Bars:Beats timeline (bar 5, for example) as bar 1. That way, besides capturing pick-up notes (or any studio chatter you may later decide to leave in the final mix), this also leaves you some room to drop in some sort of effect before the song's beginning. You can also use the Move Song Start command in the Time Operations window for this purpose. (If the Tempo ruler is visible in the Edit window, another method is to enable Grid edit mode and simply drag the Song Start Marker to the desired position.)

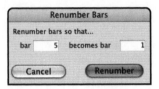

Figure 13.6 The Renumber Bars dialog box enables you to establish some point further into the timeline as bar 1 to allow for pick-up bars, anticipated notes, intro fills, and so on.

Creating Effects and a Drum Submix

As we've laid out in previous chapters, the typical location for reverb and delay effects is on an Auxiliary Input track whose input is set to one of the internal mixing busses in Pro Tools. You then use sends from individual tracks to add their audio to the input bus for the Reverb Aux In, for example.

The other typical use of Auxiliary Ins is to create mix subgroups for multiple source audio tracks. In this example, we're also going to bus the outputs of all the drum tracks to a single stereo Auxiliary Input. This simplifies adjusting the overall level of the drum mix and also allows placing effects on the entire drum submix (rather than on each individual drum track).

1. In the Mix window, create two stereo Auxiliary Input tracks. Name them Reverb and Drums. Option-click (or Alt-click in Windows) on their volume faders to set them to 0 dB.

2. Set the input of Reverb to bus pair 1–2 and the input of Drums to bus pair 3–4.

3. Place a Reverb plug-in on the Aux In track named "Reverb" (so that sends from any track to bus pair 1–2 pass through its Reverb plug-in).

4. Use the output selectors of your six drum tracks to change all their current output assignments to bus 3–4, which is the selected input source for the Drums Aux In track you just created. Now you can control the overall volume of the drums in the mix with a single volume fader, as seen in Figure 13.7. (While you're at it, you could also choose Setup > I/O and rename stereo bus pairs 1–2 and 3–4; call them RevSend and DrumSub, for example.)

5. Create a stereo send to bus pair 1–2 (the Reverb Aux In's input) on send A of the vocal track. (You'll probably end up creating additional sends to the reverb from other tracks, as the musicians request it.)

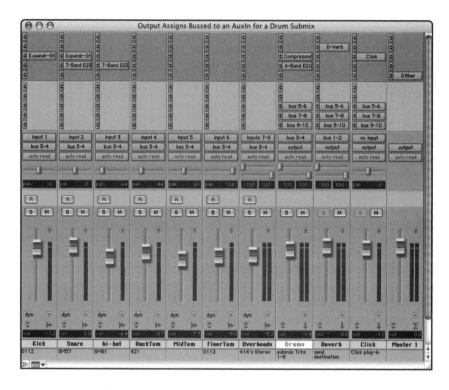

Figure 13.7 The outputs of all these drum tracks are assigned to stereo bus pair 3–4, the selected input source for the Drums Aux In. We have also inserted a compressor and EQ plug-in on this Aux In track for the drum submix.

❋ Caution: Overcompressed Cymbals (Don't Smoosh Your Crashes!)

In the current example, we've assigned all drum tracks to a single stereo Aux In track, mainly for the convenience of having a single volume fader (and Mute/Solo buttons) to control the entire drum submix. The other advantage of doing this is that you can apply a single stereo effect to the entire drum submix—for example, a Compressor plug-in on this Drums Aux In track. Be careful, though—with a large amount of compression, you may not like what this does to the sound of your cymbal crashes. We generally prefer to submix everything *except* the stereo overhead microphones (presumably your primary source for cymbals) to a stereo Aux In when heavy stereo compression is to be applied. You could always assign the output of this Aux In (and that of the stereo overheads) to yet *another* stereo bus/Aux In if you still want a single volume fader to control the entire drum submix.

❋ Tip: Recording Modes

The Destructive Recording mode of Pro Tools is discussed in Chapter 8, "Menu Selection: Highlights," and you can toggle it on and off by choosing Options > Destructive Record. Unlike the default Non-Destructive Recording mode (which creates new regions for each additional take, leaving previous ones intact), Destructive Recording mode erases any previously recorded audio data in the area of the track being recorded. When recording rhythm sections, for example, you may occasionally work in Destructive Recording mode to conserve disk space—if you already know that your available disk space is barely enough for a project, it doesn't always make sense to retain numerous false starts, especially at higher resolutions and using 16 or 24 tracks each! (Of course, you can always use the Select Unused and Clear Selected commands in the Region List submenu at any point to eliminate unwanted audio files and recover disk space.) Especially when recording vocal and instrumental overdubs, however, Non-Destructive Recording mode offers more flexibility and the very useful possibility of compositing together an ideal version from several takes at some later point in the process. (Always using non-destructive recording allows for the possibility of rediscovering some brilliant earlier take that no one recognized as a "keeper" at the time.) Loop Recording mode (also described in Chapter 8) and the Takes List pop-up menu are other invaluable tools during the overdubbing process; be sure to learn about these.

Setting Up a Cue Mix with Effects

At this point, you've created audio tracks for every input and Aux In tracks to monitor the Click plug-in and external MIDI keyboard (whose audio output is not currently being recorded). You can hear all the tracks, even adjusting the volumes and pans for each (without affecting the levels recorded to disk) to get an idea of how the mix will start to take shape. You're almost ready to record. But you still need to provide a cue mix so that the musicians can hear each other in their headphones as they play. Not only does the cue mix need to be unaffected by your volume changes, mutes, solos, and so on as they're recording, but different musicians are going to require different mixes to be comfortable during the recording process.

Let's assume you have three stereo headphone amps out in the studio, so you can provide up to three distinct cue mixes (from three different stereo output pairs on your Pro Tools audio interface). Here's a typical scenario:

❉ The guitars, keyboards, sax, and trumpet want more or less the entire, balanced mix in their headphones. (The source for this mix will be outputs 5–6 on the audio interface.)

❉ The vocalist wants to hear the vocals a little louder than in the band's mix, and would like plenty of reverb. (The source for this cue mix will be outputs 7–8 on the audio interface.)

❉ The bass player and drummer want lots of their own instruments so they can lock up a groove; they also want the click track extra loud in their headphones. (The source for this cue mix will be outputs 9–10 on the audio interface.)

We're going to create Auxiliary Inputs for each of the three cue mixes, and then use sends from source audio tracks so that you can create distinct mixes for each group of instrumentalists. As with many things in Pro Tools, there are many ways to accomplish this, and not all the options presented here will necessarily be appropriate for your own working style.

One of the simplest methods is to use multiple output assignments for each audio track and Aux In. For example, while using physical outputs 1 and 2 on your audio hardware for monitoring in the control room, you can create an additional output assignment from individual audio tracks and Aux Ins to outputs 3 and 4 (where you've connected the headphone distribution amplifier for the performers).

> ❄ **Tip: Creating Multiple Output Assignments on Audio and Aux In Tracks**
>
> As you know by now, the Output selector for each audio track and Auxiliary Input track determines the main destination for its audio. To create an *additional* routing assignment for the main output from an audio track or Aux In, hold down the Control key (Start key in Windows) as you reopen the track's Output selector. Afterwards, a plus sign (+) in the Output selector indicates tracks that have more than one output assignment. In the current example, if you additionally hold down the Option key (Alt key in Windows) as you select the extra output assignment, it is simultaneously added to all tracks. Incidentally, you can also assign each send on a track to multiple destinations, using the same Control key (or Start key in Windows) technique.

This method (multiple output assignments from tracks) isn't very practical for control room/ studio situations—you can't solo/mute tracks or change their levels during recording, because it would also affect what the performers hear in their headphone mix. In most recording situations, therefore, it's usually preferable to create a separate cue mix for the performers' headphones that won't be affected by any changes you make to the control room mix while recording (for example, soloing a bass track during recording because you think you're hearing a buzz from the instrument's pickups).

In the following sections, we'll walk you through two methods:

- ❄ **Method A.** This method uses individual sends from each track for each of the three cue mix busses/Aux Ins. This is the most common method and works fine for most situations. However, it can sometimes be more laborious for making adjustments—to raise the volume of the bass track in all cue mixes, for example, you would have to adjust the levels of three different sends from that track.

- ❄ **Method B.** This approach uses one main cue mix as the basis for the other two (each of which includes the main cue mix, plus a little more of this or that). This method simply describes another way of approaching things (not necessarily better or worse) to hopefully get you thinking differently about using sends, busses, and Auxiliary Inputs for creating cue mixes in Pro Tools.

Method A: Individual Cue Mix Sends

This is the classic approach, most similar to the method used on traditional mixing boards. It can be very effective and offers maximum flexibility for adjusting the level and pan position of individual instruments in each separate cue mix.

1. Create three stereo Auxiliary Inputs. Name them CueMix, CueVox, and CueRhyth.
2. Set the input of CueMix to busses 5–6, the input of CueVox to busses 7–8, and the input of CueRhyth to busses 9–10.
3. Create a stereo send C on each audio track *except* the drum tracks to bus pair 5–6, clicking the Pre button in the Output window for each send as it is created to make them all *pre-fader* sends (so that they are not affected by the source track's main Volume fader or Mute button). In other words, you're routing all these pre-fader sends to the input of

the CueMix Aux In via bus 5–6. (If you like, choose Setup > I/O Setup and change the names of busses 5 and 6 to Cue-L and Cue-R, respectively. Just a thought....)

4. Create a similar stereo send C (to bus 5–6, or Cue-L/Cue-R) on the Kybd stereo Auxiliary Input that you're using to monitor the keyboards, on the Click mono Aux In, on the Drums stereo Aux In, and on the Reverb stereo Aux In so that these can also be heard in the cue mix.

❅ **Tip: Creating Sends on All Tracks, Copying Sends and Plug-ins**

If you hold down the Option key (Alt key in Windows) while creating a send on any track, the same send is created in that position for all audio tracks, as well as Auxiliary Input (and Instrument) tracks. This can be a real timesaver, but in our example, keep in mind that you would then have to *un-assign* some of these send copies because you don't want both the original drum tracks and their drum submix to go to the same send, nor would you want to create sends from one Aux In to the other two (or to itself, in this case). While it's a slightly more advanced tip, one way around this is to previously create a Mix Group for all the tracks that will need sends created for the cue mix. Then use the Mix Groups list to display only this "needs cue send" group of tracks before using the Option (Alt) key technique described in this tip.

Additionally, one of the enhancements introduced in version 7 of Pro Tools is the ability to Option-drag (Alt-drag in Windows) to copy sends from one track or position to another.

---

5. In order to quickly adjust the pans/levels of our stereo sends to bus 5–6, change the view in the Mix window. Ordinarily, all sends appear as buttons, and you click any one of them to open the Sends Editor window. Choose View > Sends A–E and select Send C. Send C's Pan, Level, Mute, and Pre/Post buttons are now simultaneously visible on all tracks. (Figure 13.8 shows the two different views available for sends in the Mix window of Pro Tools.)

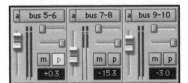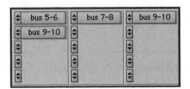

Figure 13.8 By default, the Sends section of the Mix (or Edit) window displays up to 10 possible send assignments—sections A–E and F–J for each audio Aux In or Instrument track—with a bus or physical output assignment for each. Under View > Sends, you can also choose to show individual controls for one send position (globally, on all tracks), including Level, Pan, Mute, and Pre/Post Selector.

6. In order to manually adjust your send levels from each track to the cue mix, you also need to mute all audio tracks, but not the CueMix Auxiliary Input. Because your sends are all pre-fader, they're unaffected by track Mute buttons. Also, if you Command-click

(Ctrl-click in Windows) on the Solo buttons for all your Aux Ins, they will be "solo-safe"—that is, they won't be muted even if you solo an audio track.

7. Repeat steps 1–6, creating a send D from all these tracks to bus 7–8 and a send E to bus 9–10.

> **Tip: Creating Sends on All Tracks, Copying Sends and Plug-ins**
>
> If you're working on an HD system, you could select all the audio tracks for which you've created a send and choose Edit > Copy to Send. (This command isn't available in LE or M-Powered versions of Pro Tools.) Specify send C as the destination for copying each track's current main Volume and Pan values (then D, then E). This will automatically adjust the track's main Volume fader level to that specified send. Of course, you will able to fine-tune these levels afterwards. Otherwise, on LE and M-Powered systems, you must adjust the Volume and Pan settings manually.

8. Now let's get our three cue mixes routed out into the studio so you can start to record! Switch the output of CueMix to outputs 5–6 on the audio interface, CueVox to outputs 7–8, and CueRhyth to outputs 9–10. (You can use any output pairs you like; we chose these because they might be easier to remember since they match the bus pair assignments for each separate cue mix.) See Figure 13.9 for how your Mix window ends up when using Method A for individual sends to three different cue mixes.

9. Unmute all your audio tracks; you're ready to record! First, though, have the band do another run-through not only to confirm your input levels, but to accommodate their requests for changes in the cue mixes.

Method B: Main Cue Mix, Plus Enhanced Versions

In this approach, all the musicians hear the same basic cue mix, with an extra level of certain sources added for the vocalist and for the rhythm section. If the basic cue mix is complex enough and the other versions are simply the base mix plus a little more of certain instruments or effects, this can be the way to go. For instance, if *everybody* would like a little more acoustic guitar in the mix, using this method, you only make that adjustment once to the main cue mix send; the change is automatically reflected in the other two cue mixes (which are based on this main headphone mix). Again, either method gets the job done; it all depends on your situation and preferred working style.

1. Follow steps 1–7 of method A to create a send C from all tracks to the CueMix Aux In.

2. We will use this main cue mix as the basis for alternative headphone mixes for the vocalist and the drums/bass. First, create sends from the CueMix Aux In to the other two Auxiliary Inputs—two stereo, pre-fader sends on send D (to bus pair 7–8, the input for CueVox), and send E (to bus pair 9–10, the input for CueRhyth). Option-click the Level slider for both sends (Alt-click in Windows) to set it to 0 dB, also known as Unity gain.

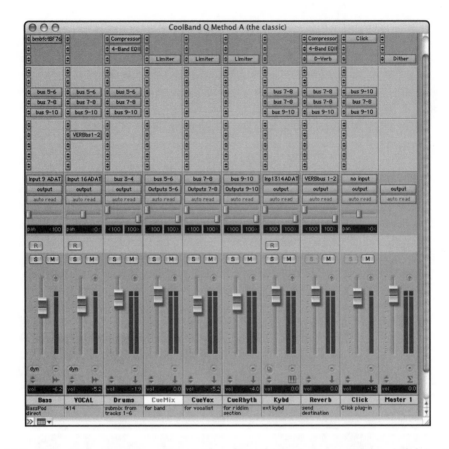

Figure 13.9 Method A for creating cue mixes: Each audio track (plus the Drums, Kybd, and Click Aux In tracks) has a separate pre-fader send for each cue mix destination. This takes a minute to set up but provides the greatest degree of control. (Notice that in the second, F–J send section, we have also created a post-fader send from the vocal track to the bus selected as the input for our reverb Aux In.) You can store a basic track, send, and Aux In setup for cue mixes as a session template for your studio.

3. Mute CueMix and CueRhyth so that you're now only listening to CueVox. Then, suppose that in addition to the general mix, the vocalist wanted some extra reverb. Create a pre-fader stereo send D on the Reverb Aux In, routed to bus pair 7–8 (input for CueVox). Adjust its level to add just a little more reverb to CueVox.

4. Now we will adjust the rhythm section's mix (CueMix, plus more click track and more drums/bass). Mute the CueVox Auxiliary Input, and unmute CueRhyth. Create an additional stereo, pre-fader send E on the Bass audio track, plus the Click and Drums Aux Inputs, routed to bus pair 9–10 (the input for CueRhyth). Adjust these send levels to add just enough additional drums and bass, and click to CueRhyth.

5. Unmute the Aux In tracks for all three cue mixes (CueMix, CueVox, and CueRhyth).

6. Switch the output of CueMix to outputs 5–6 on the audio interface, CueVox to outputs 7–8, and CueRhyth to outputs 9–10 to send them out the headphone amps in the studio. (Again, you can use any output pairs; we chose these because they match our bus-pair assignments for each separate cue mix and so might be easier to remember.)

7. Unmute all your audio tracks. Your Mix window should now look something like Figure 13.10. Again, have the band do one more run-through not only to confirm input levels but to accommodate any requests for changes in the cue mixes.

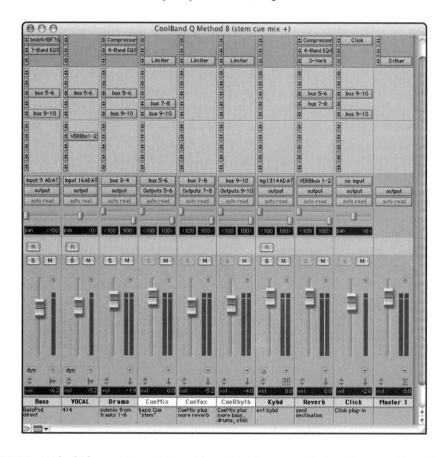

Figure 13.10 Method B for creating cue mixes: A basic "stem" cue mix is the basis for two additional cue mixes (to which additional amounts of certain tracks have been sent). This approach is a bit more complicated but offers the convenience of making only one send level adjustment on each track if, for example, everyone would like a little less electric guitar in their headphone mix.

❋ Tip: Markers and Selections

As mentioned in Chapter 8, Pro Tools allows you to create two types of memory locations: *markers* and *selections*. Markers identify *single points* in time (and can appear in the Markers ruler). Selections obviously identify a *range* within the timeline, such as the bridge of a song, the points where a guitar solo will be punched in/out, and so on.

Both markers and selections can be either *absolute* (a specific Minutes:Seconds reference) or *relative* (a location in bars|beats, whose absolute position depends on the current Pro Tools Tempo setting). For our hypothetical session, with a click track governed by the Pro Tools tempo, relative memory locations are most useful because your discussions with the musicians will generally refer to bars and beats (rather than minutes and seconds).

You can drop markers on the fly any time, even while recording; just press the Enter key on the numeric keypad. If you find it cumbersome or distracting to negotiate the New Memory Location dialog box while doing so, choose the Editing tab of the Preferences dialog box and enable the Auto-Name Memory Locations When Playing option. Marker 1, Marker 2, and so on will automatically be created without requiring you to open the dialog box. You can always double-click a marker to change its name or properties or drag it within the Markers ruler to change its position. (If you're in Grid mode, marker movements are snapped to the nearest grid increment.)

You can also use markers to reset where Pro Tools will start playback or to select portions of the session's timeline. To reset the Transport window's current Start position, just click on a marker in the Memory Locations window or the Markers ruler (choose View > Rulers > Markers to make the Markers ruler visible in the Edit window). If you click one marker and then Shift-click another, the Transport window's Start and End values are set to those positions. (This can be very useful for overdubs, or to perfect mix parameters while looping a specific section of the song.) For example, to select the entire second verse for playback or punch-in recording, you might click the marker Verse2 and then Shift-click Chorus2. If Link Edit and Timeline Selection is enabled (either via the Operations menu selection or by enabling the Edit window's Link Selections button), not only are both the edit and play selections set, but the contents of the current track are also selected between these markers. This will make it quick and easy to copy entire sections later (holding down the Option key—Alt key in Windows—as you drag with the Separation Grabber) when you create your slammin' extended-play remix!

Making the Most of Available Tracks

On large sessions with many source audio tracks, you may reach the limit of available playback voices in your Pro Tools system. In music projects, this can happen sooner than you think on 32-voice Pro Tools LE systems such as the Mbox 2/Mbox and Digi 002/002 Rack or M-Powered systems using M-Audio hardware. (LE/M-Powered can be expanded to 48 mono/ stereo tracks via the Music Production Toolkit option.) If you are an HD user, this will be the time to review how Pro Tools voice allocation works (as explained in Chapter 2, "Pro Tools Terms and Concepts") and see whether you can make this work to your advantage. On HD systems, if audio regions on two tracks never coincide (for example, a saxophone solo in the middle of a song and a backing vocal track at the end), they can share the same voice assignment; the effects, sends, and output assignments of one track are still completely independent of the other. Figure 13.11 shows an example of this.

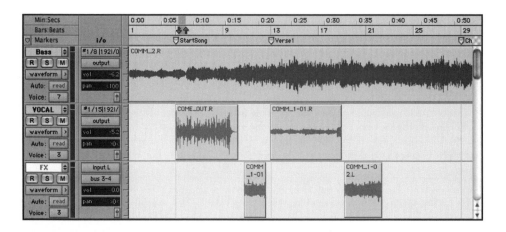

Figure 13.11 The bottom two tracks on this Pro Tools | HD system have been manually assigned to use the same voice for playback; but because their regions don't coincide, there is no conflict. Even using the same voice assignment, their volume, pan, plug-ins/inserts, and send/output destinations are completely different. (Here, the I/O assignment column is displayed in the Edit window.)

> ❄ **Tip: Thinking Ahead: Arm Yourself for Editing**
>
> When recording drums, once you have your basic levels set up, ask the drummer to give you one clean, solid hit on each drum and cymbal. Record these, and be sure to rename and keep these regions in your session. You don't have to make a big deal to the performers about possibly needing these to fix something in the mix—but you never know!

Tips for Remote Recording with Pro Tools

Recording live ensemble performances with Pro Tools is indeed a practical reality. Naturally, you will want to have as compact a setup as possible, possibly rack-mounting most of your gear for quick load in/out. Here are a few tips we've learned along the way.

❄ **Mixing board.** It can be very cost effective to use a conventional mixing board with multiple microphone inputs and individual line outs on the input channels. Obviously, the mixer's microphone preamps need to be high quality to get acceptable results. Fortunately, a number of economical small mixers out there fill the bill and might also be an ideal mixer for your Pro Tools project studio (not only providing additional microphone inputs, but also useful for monitoring multiple sources in your studio configuration). If your mixer is rack mountable, that's a benefit, too, because you can cable its channel outputs to your audio interface inputs (and the main output pair of your audio interface cabled to a mixer channel, in order to monitor the Pro Tools mix output) before you even wheel your rig into the venue.

❊ **Microphone preamplifier.** Another way to go is a dedicated, multichannel microphone preamplifier. Options range from the high end (for example, Digidesign's PRE or Focusrite's OctoPre) to more economical mid-range units for professional applications from PreSonus and others. Because these are generally rackmountable, this again can be very attractive because you can arrive at the performance with all the cable connections between the microphone preamplifier and your rackmounted audio interface already in place.

❊ **Compression/limiting.** Levels can be very unpredictable in live performance! When you're recording a live performance (or conference), you can't risk an unexpected peak in level ruining the historical document that you're being paid to capture. In the first place, be conservative with your input levels. While in a relatively controlled studio situation, you will always try to maximize input levels to improve signal/error ratio as incoming audio is digitized; it would be foolhardy to be overly aggressive about this in a live performance situation! That said, good compression/limiting on your microphone inputs can also give you peace of mind—and maybe even save your skin on occasion. Because you have compression in Pro Tools, the idea isn't to clamp down consistently on the signal, using compression to shape the sound. Instead, you want to avoid the occasional "rogue" peak from producing a horrific digital distortion sound that mars an overall good-sounding recording. You can always correct low levels in the mix afterwards, but the clipping distortion produced during recording will be there to stay.

❊ **Note: Recording Live Theater**

If you record live theater, you may find that performer levels are even more unpredictable than a rock band's club performance (which is saying a lot!). At any point, an actor is likely to step right up to your PZM microphone and scream at the top of her voice, even if her mark during rehearsal was several yards away—it's just part of the natural performance flexibility they require. But unlike a rock band, where the vocalists are inevitably close to the microphone and therefore the dynamic range has reasonable limits, in theater, each microphone is required to capture sounds anywhere from several yards to as close as a couple of feet away. So it's a great idea to have compression or limiting in place for microphones that might be subject to unexpected extreme levels (especially lead singers, lead guitar amplifiers, and front-of-stage microphones in theater).

❊ **Snake.** A snake gives you a lot of XLR connectors (and usually some 1/4-inch connectors) at one end of a single long cable. These connectors reappear at the other end as either a fan of separate cables/connectors or a stagebox with jacks. That's how you get all those microphone and line inputs from the stage back to your mixer and recording rig. (These should be balanced, by the way, to avoid transmission loss in longer cables; use a direct box and so on if required.) If you're sharing microphones and other input sources with another person mixing sound for the house system, you should use a splitter snake; double outputs at your end allow both you and the house mixer to get your input directly from the snake's channels. Figure 13.12 shows a typical live recording configuration with Pro Tools.

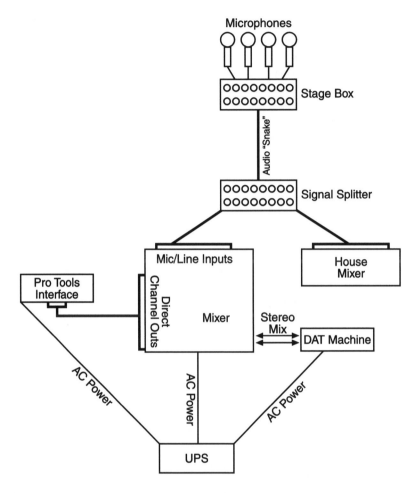

Figure 13.12 A possible setup for live recording with Pro Tools. A splitter snake provides both recording rig and house sound mixer with direct microphone (or line/direct box) feeds from the stage. We're using a clean portable mixer with multiple mic-level inputs and direct outputs from each channel to our multichannel Pro Tools audio interface. We're simultaneously feeding a rough stereo mix directly from the mixer to a DAT recorder as a precaution. Everything is on a UPS (uninterruptible power supply).

❋ **Paranoia.** Many people simultaneously record performances in stereo to a DAT recorder directly from the mixing board (rather than from the Pro Tools main L–R output). If someone kicks out your power cable or your computer hangs (it *is* a computer, after all!), at least that much of the performance will be intact as a live stereo mix on the DAT tape. A UPS (uninterruptible power supply) may also save your reputation, kicking over to battery power until you have restored the AC (and thrashed the responsible parties, if possible). Recording a DAT mix directly from the mixing board also guarantees that you'll have documented whatever portion of the performance transpires if you have no alternative but to restart your computer.

❋ **Headphones and ear plugs.** As the recordist, the usefulness of headphones for you is obvious. You will usually want a design that covers the ear fairly well to isolate outside sounds (often called *circumaural*, *closed-back*, or something similar as opposed to open or semi-open). This is not only so that you can hear what's coming through the headphones in a noisy environment, but also to protect your ears when recording extremely loud performances—that is, if you're planning to use your ears in the future! Along the same lines, a set of musician's ear plugs is highly advisable (or at the very least some cheap foam ones that you can buy in a drugstore). If the opening bands or even the house music system blows out your ears beforehand, you may miss defects or make errors while recording—not to mention incurring lasting ear damage. Don't forget to bring along an extra set for any assistants, especially if you will be sending them onstage to make adjustments during a loud performance.

❋ Tip: Monitoring Latency with Pro Tools LE and M-Powered

Any digital audio system has some small degree of delay, or *latency*, between when an analog audio signal actually enters the system, is digitized (and/or routed within the system's internal mixing environment), and then converted back to an analog audio signal on an output of your audio hardware. Even on HD systems (whose dedicated DSP cards provide mix/routing latency times so low that for practical purposes, they're usually not an issue while recording), there is still a small amount of delay required for the A/D/A (analog>digital, digital>analog) converters themselves to do their work.

But for all native (or host-based) digital audio workstations that rely on the computer's processing power for their mixing/routing tasks (as is the case with all LE and M-Powered versions of Pro Tools), monitoring latency is typically several milliseconds at the very least (and sometimes considerably more, depending on audio resolution and other factors—enough to produce a noticeable delay). You will discover that this latency can be enough to disconcert or affect the timing of your performance if you don't deal with it properly. Using a mixing board as the front end for recording microphone sources into Pro Tools and monitoring input audio directly from the board (and not via Pro Tools) is one way to bypass this problem.

Within Pro Tools LE and M-Powered software, you can also reduce latency by using the Hardware Setup dialog box to lower the Hardware Buffer Size setting to 128 (or 256) samples while recording tracks. If you have a G5, faster G4, Pentium 4, a fast Athlon XP system, or something similar, you can probably use this buffer setting all the time. However, if you're using one of the slower supported CPUs, beware: Lower buffer sizes may reduce how many simultaneous audio tracks can be recorded without system-performance problems (such as slow screen redraws or recording errors) or affect playback of sessions with complex plug-in processing and routing setups in many tracks. If that's your case, you should always set the buffer back to 512 or 1,024 samples when editing and mixing (especially when using processing-intensive plug-ins such as certain reverbs and software instruments).

The Low Latency Monitoring option in the Options menu of Pro Tools LE versions when using the Digi 002 or 002 Rack (but *not* the Mbox 2 or Mbox) provides the lowest-possible latency on outputs 1–2 of the audio hardware only. (In this case, you might have to use outputs 1–2 not only as the single cue mix send for your performers out in the studio but also for monitoring in the control room, because *Pro Tools automatically bypasses all plug-ins and sends on any tracks assigned to outputs 1–2 while Low Latency*

Monitoring mode is active. Also, remember to disable Low Latency Monitoring mode once you start mixing—otherwise, when you bounce to disk, none of the audio from any Aux Input tracks will be included in the bounced audio file! The Mbox 2 and Mbox hardware offers another interesting alternative for overcoming the latency issue. A Mix knob on the front of the interface itself allows you to fade between its direct input(s) and playback from Pro Tools. While recording, you could simply mute the track to which you're recording (so that its delayed signal doesn't interfere with the timing of your performance). However, the Mix knob adjusts how much of your (dry) signal at the input(s) goes directly into the stereo mix output from the interface (or its dedicated headphone output)—for zero-latency monitoring. However, when recording from a mono source—for example, one microphone on a guitar, voice, or wind instrument —be sure to also press the Mono button on the front panel so that this source will be heard in both left and right channels of your control room monitors or headphones.

Several of the M-Audio interfaces compatible with the M-Powered version of Pro Tools also offer a similar feature, via "direct monitoring" options where selected inputs can pass directly to other outputs on the interface itself (including headphone outputs, if available) without first being routed through the Pro Tools mixing environment.

Summary

Every musical project is different. Some classical musicians record together as an ensemble and don't require individual cue mixes or headphones—let alone a click track. Many bands don't (or won't) record with a click track. You can still edit later in musical bars and beats; that's what the Identify Beat command in Pro Tools is for! Many bands don't record all at once, of course. Instead, they layer up tracks, perhaps starting from only the most basic rhythm section in the initial recording session.

In many cases, a single cue mix is acceptable for all the simultaneous performers. If so, you could dispense with the more complex Aux In setups described here and instead use a single pre-fader send from each track to a single output pair feeding your performers' headphone mix. Even in this case, though, it's usually convenient to route these sends through a stereo bus to an Aux In, where you can apply a compressor or limiter to keep headphone levels under control.

Be sure to enable the AutoSave feature, in the Operation tab of the Preferences dialog box. And one last reminder, especially important with paying clients and any group of performers out in the studio: Save your session often as you work! Good performances are ephemeral moments. If you lose one due to a system (or human-operator) problem or power outage because you hadn't saved for many minutes, musicians may find it difficult to forgive you!

14 } Postproduction and Soundtracks

Here we explore some of the capabilities of Pro Tools for film and video soundtracks. Chapter 11, "Synchronization," provides a general background on the technical aspects of SMPTE time code and an overview of synchronization methods and peripherals for a Pro Tools configuration. We focus here on basic production strategies, tips for collaborating with users of nonlinear video-editing systems (Avid, Media 100, Apple's Final Cut Pro, Adobe's Premiere, and others), and basic postproduction methods and include a cursory overview of how you can use Pro Tools for surround mixing. The present chapter (along with Chapter 11) is merely a primer for using Pro Tools in postproduction—the particulars vary immensely according to each production facility and the immediate task at hand, and there are entire books dedicated to the subject of postproduction alone!

Synchronization Setup

As discussed in Chapter 11, there are many options for synchronizing Pro Tools to SMPTE time code. These range from simple trigger sync setups (after playback starts at the correct point, Pro Tools no longer references the time-code information to maintain speed) to external reference sync (for example, house sync or black burst, providing a common reference for both Pro Tools and the video gear) and continuous resyncing/resolving Pro Tools to the time-code master (via a Sync I/O or similar device).

Figure 14.1 shows the Sync I/O, a high-end synchronization peripheral from Digidesign interface with continuous resync/resolving capabilities for locking Pro Tools hardware with external time code or video sync. It translates SMPTE to and from VITC (video) or LTC (audio) format and can also continuously adjust the sample clock of your audio hardware to keep Pro Tools in sync with incoming time code over extended periods. It can slave to an external video reference (for example, black burst), an industry-standard word clock, or Digidesign's 256x SuperClock. Its dual Sony 9-pin serial ports can link Transport functions of Pro Tools with external video/audio devices via the MachineControl option.

Figure 14.1 Digidesign's Sync I/O is a high-end synchronization peripheral for Mac or Windows computers. (Photo courtesy Digidesign.)

If you principally deal with short-duration projects (such as 30-second spots), your requirements may not be as stringent as for creating, say, 30-minute programs or feature films, where even a small amount of drift creates real timing problems.

If your synchronization peripheral is a standard SMPTE interface (which translates incoming time-code location information from its audio or video format to MTC and then routes it into your computer, perhaps via the USB port), the Synchronization tab of the Setup > Peripherals dialog box tells Pro Tools the device type—for example, a generic MTC reader versus a Sync I/O—and which port it is connected to. (See Figures 14.2 and 14.3.)

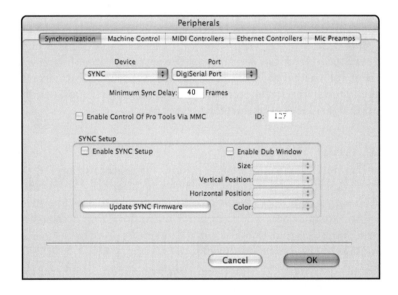

Figure 14.2 The Peripherals dialog box on a Pro Tools|HD system, using Digidesign's Sync I/O, which can add a time-code window to video signals passing through it.

MachineControl

MachineControl is an option for Pro Tools TDM systems that allows you to link the Pro Tools Transport—either as a master or a slave—with professional video decks or other compatible

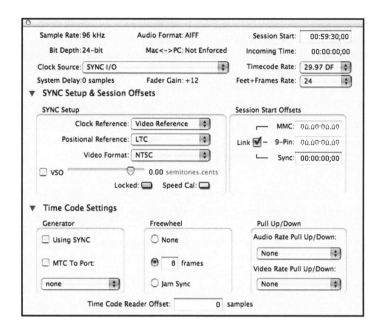

Figure 14.3 Settings in the Sync Setup section of the Session Setup window include the positional reference (the time code source) for your Digidesign synchronization peripheral.

devices via their Sony 9-pin serial ports (or V-LAN). You can also remotely arm tracks on the device for recording from within Pro Tools (using the Machine Track Arming window).

MachineControl uses a serial connection to the external devices. Digidesign's Sync I/O features Sony 9-pin serial ports. Because the HD Accel cards include the DigiSerial port, users who *don't* have a Sync I/O can also use that DigiSerial port for the MachineControl option; otherwise they would use the 9-pin serial port(s) on the synchronization peripheral itself. Both positional (SMPTE) and clock references are required for MachineControl to synchronize Pro Tools with other devices. A third option for MachineControl is to use MOTU's Digital Time-piece, connected to the USB port, for position and clock reference and the DigiSerial Port on the HD Accel card for serial MachineControl communication with other devices.

A pop-up Transport selector in the Pro Tools Transport window lets you specify the master device (Pro Tools, the MachineControl device, an ADAT with an optional interface, or a MIDI MachineControl device). When Pro Tools and an external video or audio deck are linked by MachineControl, they can be scrubbed together (meaning that you can review picture and audio in tandem).

When you select Pro Tools as the master, in Online mode, all devices connected via MachineControl respond to Transport functions from Pro Tools (while in Offline mode, they ignore the Pro Tools Transport). Naturally, if these are tape-based devices, such as video or audio decks, some time may be required for them to rewind or fast-forward to the appropriate location (with the amount of pre-roll specified in Preferences) before playback actually commences. Using Pro Tools as the master with an analog tape machine, ADAT, DA-88, or some other digital multitrack causes more wear and tear on these transports as they chase the Pro Tools Transport (and slows you down). For this reason, it is more typical to designate these machines as the master—because access to audio material is nonlinear in Pro Tools, it will instantly jump to the correct playback position once the external tape transport is ready.

When you select Machine as the master, Pro Tools follows and locks to the Machine master when in Online mode. In Offline mode, the Pro Tools Transport still controls the machine, and as you move the video master to different locations, the playback cursor in Pro Tools reflects its position.

Note that in addition to many professional video decks, several audio DATs and the Tascam DA-88 and DA-98 digital multitrack audio recorders are also compatible with the MachineControl option. The first time you enable MachineControl, it polls the serial ports to automatically detect what device types are connected. You can also configure devices manually from a pop-up menu.

AVoption|V10

Digidesign's AVoption|V10 for Windows XP systems consists of a single rackmountable interface, connected to the host computer via FireWire. This video subsystem especially supports the playback of Avid video media (including 24p/25p resolutions) within Pro Tools and provides video output for an external PAL or NTSC monitor. The rackmounted interface includes BNC connectors for analog and digital video I/O, plus FireWire connectors for DV decks and cameras. Component, composite, S-video, and SDI (Serial Digital Interface) connections are supported for input/output, as well as a Video Ref input for external black burst or house sync sources. With AVoption|V10 installed (or the Avid Mojo; see the next heading), a key difference from the standard Movie track in Pro Tools is that multiple video clips can reside in the Movie track. AVoption|V10 allows you to see Avid edits and various simultaneous clip resolutions within the Avid Movie track in Pro Tools, use a unique Scrub Movie window, and even spot video clips to new locations within the Avid Movie track. Unlike the standard Movie track in Pro Tools, the Avid Movie track includes a Record Enable button, an Offline button, and an I/O View for selecting among the available video input sources, outputs, and disk volumes for video recording. The optional Media Station|PT software also allows you to capture NTSC/PAL video from external sources directly into the Avid Movie track. This can be as simple as simply highlighting the range to capture, arming the Movie track for recording, enabling the Transport window's Online button, and then pressing Record. The included software also allows you to convert QuickTime files into Avid video format (since QuickTime files are not directly supported) and import, digitize, and render Avid sequences directly for AAF import into Pro Tools. DigiTranslator software is included as part of the AVoption|V10 package, including preconfigured "Send to Pro Tools" templates. Note that when using AVoption|V10 with HD systems, the 96i I/O cannot be the primary audio interface; it *can* be a secondary interface, however, linked to a 192 I/O or 96 I/O. Digidesign's SYNC I/O synchronization peripheral is required in order to use

AVoption|V10 and Avid Mojo (collectively known as "Avid DNA video peripherals") on Pro Tools|HD systems.

Avid Mojo

The desktop Avid Mojo video interface connects to the host computer via FireWire. It offers DV video I/O, plus analog I/O for video conversion to/from DV format and supports many of the same software features as the AVoption|V10 system. It allows HD systems to play back video via an external monitor, open video sequences created with Avid Xpress Pro and Avid Media Composer Adrenaline systems in Pro Tools, tabbing from cut to cut, and then exporting finished audio for re-integration into an original Avid sequence. Mojo supports uncompressed MXF or JFIF, DV25 and DV50, 15:1 single-frame JFIF, plus several 24P/25P progressive-scan resolutions, and supports either NTSC or PAL format. The Component Video I/O option for Avid Mojo allows you to connect component video sources to its built-in S-video and composite video jacks, breaking out to three female BNC connectors each on the input/output cables. In addition to the standard configuration, a bundle is also available that includes both the Avid Mojo and the Media Station|PT software. (DigiTranslator software must be purchased separately for Mojo systems.)

DV Toolkit (Pro Tools LE Only)

This software bundle includes DigiTranslator, which allows you to import/export projects either as an OMF (Open Media Framework) or AAF file between Pro Tools and Avid Xpress DV, FinalCut Pro, and other compliant video-editing programs. The DINR LE noise-reduction plug-in is also included (broadband noise reduction only; no hum removal). With DV Toolkit installed, the SMPTE time code (including subframes) and Feet+Frames ruler formats (which are ordinarily TDM-only) are available for Pro Tools LE systems. Pull-up and pull-down rates for audio and video are supported, as well as absolute/relative or user-defined time-code mapping when importing tracks.

> ❋ **Note: DV Toolkit**
>
> The optional DV Toolkit software bundle is only compatible with the LE version of Pro Tools (for Digi 002/002 Rack and Mbox 2, for example)—it *cannot* be used with M-Powered.

Using QuickTime Movies in Post

Chapter 11 mentioned that a QuickTime movie can be used as the video reference for post-production work, without requiring a video deck in your audio studio at all. If you are collaborating with video editors who use nonlinear systems, they can export a QuickTime movie for use as your master while posting the project in Pro Tools. (By *nonlinear* systems, we mean computer and hard disk–based editing systems—not only high-end systems using specific manufacturers' hardware, such as Avid and Media 100, but also software-only solutions such as Apple's Final Cut Pro and Adobe Premiere. These may only require a

FireWire input from a DV camera, perhaps a video accelerator card—and probably even more hard disk space than *you* require for Pro Tools!)

In either case, generally you will ask for a QuickTime video file sized down to 320×240 pixels or smaller. This minimizes the load on your system, especially if you don't dedicate a separate hard disk for video playback and/or have a video accelerator card to view the QuickTime movie on a separate computer monitor. (Both are highly recommended, especially for long durations, sessions with many tracks, complex signal processing, or high-resolution audio.) Remember that even though the frame *size* of the video should be reduced, the original frame *rate* must be maintained (usually 29.97 fps drop/non-drop in North America and 25 fps in Europe, Africa, the Middle East, and most of Asia). Likewise, if you are going to import the movie's original 48 kHz stereo audio tracks, their audio bit-depth and sample rate should be maintained. Sometimes you *won't* want to import audio from the video—for example, if an Avid editor is separately providing an OMFI file (and/or audio files) for the project, discussed later in this chapter.

The video plays in real time within the Movie window, and individual frames are displayed in the Movie track right alongside your audio waveforms, MIDI, and automation, as seen in Figure 14.4. As you jump around in the session (using the Transport buttons, memory locations, the Selector tool, and so on), the Movie window immediately reflects the new position; no waiting for rewinds, time-code lockup, and all the other encumbrances. In short, using a QuickTime file provides most of the advantages of VITC without requiring you to drag around a video tape transport while you work in Pro Tools.

❄ **Tip: Optimizing QuickTime Video Playback**

After you import audio from the QuickTime movie you've been given, if you have QuickTime Pro, it can be a good idea to make a new copy of this video file where you've deleted the soundtrack. (Use the Edit > Delete Tracks command in QuickTime Pro. Back in Pro Tools, use the File menu's Import > QuickTime Movie command and select this new copy instead.) By eliminating this now-redundant audio data within the movie, there will be less system overhead while playing back this QuickTime file in Pro Tools.

❄ **Tip: Resizing the QuickTime Video Window**

Regardless of the actual source size (in pixels) of the QuickTime movie you're using for reference within Pro Tools, there will be times when you would like the video playback window within Pro Tools to be larger or, more likely, smaller. If you've upgraded to QuickTime Pro (at $30, an absolute steal for anyone who regularly deals with QuickTime video), this is easy.

Just close your Pro Tools session and open the movie file in the QuickTime (Pro) Player. Drag the corner of the video playback window to resize according to your needs, and save. The next time you open your Pro Tools session, this QuickTime file will play back at whatever size you saved for it. No need to re-export, re-render, or anything complicated like that!

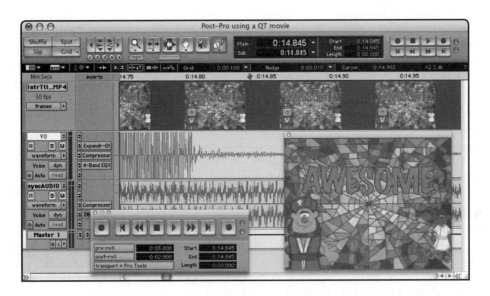

Figure 14.4 The Movie track can display thumbnails of individual frames, allowing precise placement of audio in relation to video. Use the plus (+) and minus (−) keys on the numeric keypad to jog forward and backward through the Movie track (per the current Nudge value). Hold them down to simulate Shuttle mode.

Tips for Recording Voice-Overs

First, whether you apply some compression in real time prior to the Pro Tools input or you apply it 100 percent afterward via Pro Tools plug-ins, a healthy amount of compression and/or limiting (dynamics processing, to limit the range of variation in the signal level) is essential to producing quality voice-over (VO) recordings. Especially if the narration is for a book on tape, a radio spot, or a live event, the amount of compression will be considerably higher than what is conventional for vocal recordings in a music project, for example. Appendix D, "Power Tips and Loopy Ideas," provides some additional tips, but here are several technical pointers:

✽ Be aware that large amounts of compression can sometimes darken a voice's timbre (because many of the momentary peaks may be mid/high-frequency sibilance—"s," "t," and "ch" sounds, for example). As a general rule, for the most natural-sounding results, place the EQ insert *after* the compressor in your VO channel.

✽ The Destructive Recording mode in Pro Tools is handy when recording very long narrations—for example, a 30-minute infomercial or industrial video, and *especially* books on tape that may be many hours long. Aside from using less disk space (less important as large-capacity disks continue to get more inexpensive), it can make file management and Region List management much simpler on these extremely long projects. Just be careful to check where the current insertion point is before you resume recording—it's called "destructive" for a good reason! Even if you don't use Destructive

Recording mode, it's often useful to enable Timeline Insertion Follows Playback, in Preferences > Operation (which can be toggled on and off with the letter "N," while Command Focus mode is enabled). Each time you stop, the next playback/recording will resume from the point where you left off (instead of from the same place as you started previously, which is the normal mode in Pro Tools).

* When punching in during voice-over recordings, provide a few seconds of pre-roll for the voice talent so they can match the timbre of the immediately preceding audio. For example, if you're going to pick up recording at 1:30, place the playback cursor there, and enable perhaps four seconds of pre-roll before pressing Record and Play. (Remember these keyboard shortcuts: To start recording, hold down the Command key—Ctrl key in Windows—and press the Spacebar. To stop the recording currently in progress and discard the take, press Command+period—Ctrl+period in Windows.)

* If you have a third-party multiband compressor (or limiting) plug-in, experiment with using this on your voice-over tracks (in addition to its more conventional use on the overall mix or submix). Aside from the obvious advantages for gain optimization, this offers a completely different approach for shaping vocal timbre as you alter the crossover points and dynamics settings for each frequency band.

* Pardon us for being so rudimentary, but let's just make note that a good professional-quality microphone is required (not a $100 rock 'n' roll model), along with a pop filter, to record great-sounding voice-overs! Likewise, provide a good copy stand for your voice talent (even if it's just a music stand), some pens, pencils, highlighters, a great-sounding room (not too dead, not too noisy), some decent lighting—and a glass of water!

Spotting Techniques, Sound Effects

Options for spotting sound effects and other audio events to video obviously depend on your synchronization method. If you are using an imported QuickTime movie or VITC as your timing reference (time code embedded into each frame of the video signal), then you can spot sound effects to precise locations, even when the video is stopped on a single frame. In contrast, if you're using LTC (time code location information conveyed within an audio signal) to receive SMPTE position data, the master video deck (or other device) must be in Play mode in order to send the audio signal containing this encoded SMPTE location information.

Spot Edit Mode

As explained in Chapter 6, "The Edit Window," in Spot edit mode, whenever you click on a region with the Grabber tool (or Trimmer), the Spot dialog box opens (shown in Figure 14.5). Time values entered here determine where that region's start, end, or sync point will be moved when you click OK. (See Chapter 8, "Menu Selections: Highlights," for a description of how sync points can be used to spot sound effects.) You can type in the desired start time for currently selected region(s) or click the Current Time Code field to automatically capture that value. If you're using a VITC synchronization peripheral such as Digidesign's Sync I/O or MOTU's Digital Timepiece with an external video source or MachineControl, you can simply move the master to the correct frame while stopped (using the jog/shuttle wheel on the video deck, for instance). Then, click Current Time Code (or press the =, or equals, key) to automatically enter that location into the currently selected field.

Figure 14.5 The Spot dialog box is essential for postproduction in Pro Tools. Clicking the Current Time Code field (or pressing the =, or equals, key) captures that value (if SMPTE time code is currently being sent to Pro Tools) into any currently selected field in this dialog box. Using the Trimmer tool in Spot mode also opens the Spot dialog box for adjusting a region's start or end point.

Even if you are using LTC to synchronize to your time-code master (via an audio signal containing encoded SMPTE timestamping information), you can still use this capture feature on the fly as the video master plays. Of course, if the video editor provides you with a window dub video copy with a numerical time-code window, you could crawl the tape to locate precise frame locations and enter time-code values manually. In either case, do your back a favor: Move your video deck close enough to the mouse and keyboard of your Pro Tools rig so that you don't have to stretch yourself into some grotesque posture to reach both at once! Also, note that although the Spot dialog box supports subframe precision (1/100th of a frame), time-code values can only be *captured* to the nearest whole frame.

❄ **Tip: Here, Spot!**

Whether you are in Spot edit mode or not, you can also snap regions to the current playback cursor position (if nothing is selected within the Edit window) or to the same Timeline position as the beginning of your current edit selection. With the playback stopped, just Control+click (Start+click in Windows) on that region with the Grabber tool. This is handy, for example, for forcing the beginning of an additional region to coincide with that of the currently selected region.

Here's another related trick: Make a selection in the Edit window, and then hold down the Control key (Start key in Windows) as you click and drag regions out from the Region List. The beginnings of these regions will be automatically snapped to the same Timeline position as the beginning of your current edit selection. You can use this technique to either replace the selected sound on the same track or align the new sound with it on another track.

Auto-Spotting Regions

This feature is especially useful when you're using an imported QuickTime movie, VITC, or the MachineControl option, so that time-code information is available even when the master is stopped. Enable Options > Auto-Spot Regions. When you enable Spot edit mode, clicking any region with the Grabber (or dragging it out anywhere onto a track from the Region List) automatically moves that region's beginning (or sync point, if it contains one) to the current movie, time code, or machine location.

> ### ✻ Tip: Replacing All Occurrences of a Region (HD Only)
>
> The HD version of Pro Tools makes it easy to swap all instances of a certain sound effect (or perhaps a drum sound, in musical applications) through the session. Just select the audio region you want to replace within a track, then Shift-Command-drag (Shift-Ctrl-drag in Windows) its substitute out from the Region List. The Replace Region dialog box appears. You can replace just this occurrence with the new region, all occurrences in this track, or in *all* tracks. As you can see in Figure 14.6, other options in the Replace Region dialog box let you restrict matches even further—to occurrences of the region that start and/or end at exactly the same positions in the Pro Tools Timeline. But for postproduction, the Fit To options are of special interest. Original Region Length is the most commonly used. As the new region is swapped in to replace the previous one, its length is trimmed to match if it is longer, and any excess from the old region is removed if it's shorter. Original Selection Length also trims the replacement if it is longer but doesn't remove any excess from the old region if it's shorter. The last option, Replacement Region Length, is the simplest: If shorter, the new region replaces the old one without retaining any excess length from it; if longer, the replacement region doesn't get trimmed to match the old one's length.

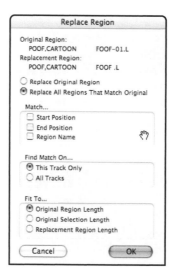

Figure 14.6 The Replace Region dialog box (Pro Tools|HD software only).

VocALign

VocALign Pro is a TDM plug-in by Synchro Arts that is useful for ADR (automatic dialog replacement), among other things. An AudioSuite version is also available, called VocALign Project (shown in Figure 14.7), which is included in the DV Toolkit bundle for LE systems (only) or can be purchased separately for either LE or M-Powered systems. There's also a standalone version of VocALign. You can use this product to automatically align the timing of one audio signal (the *dub*) to another (the *guide*). Not only are the leading edges of each detected segment within the source audio file aligned to the guide, but time compression and/or expansion are also applied. As you can imagine, this is extremely useful for doing dialog replacement while maintaining proper lip sync, as well as for quickly aligning Foley and other sound effects to original sync sound from a video shoot. Music mixers also appreciate this automated time alignment, to achieve extremely tight tracking of doubled lead or stacked-up backing vocal parts.

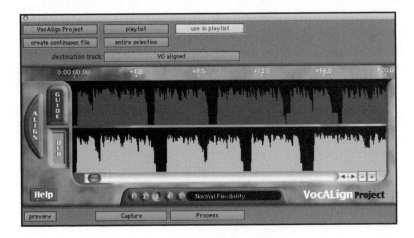

Figure 14.7   VocALign Project.

Surround Mixing

Once a multichannel audio track, Auxiliary Input track, Instrument track, or Master Fader has been created, its level meters in the Mix window display multiple channels, as does the metering within any of its plug-In windows—for example, six channels in 5.1 format. The output path of a 5.1 mix, for example, might typically be the first six outputs on your audio interface (leaving outputs 7 and 8 free for an alternate stereo mix if you wish).

※ **Note: "Point One"**

Surround format names with a ".1" indicate that there is one separate LFE (Low Frequency Effects) channel dedicated to the subwoofer. (If any surround format with two LFE channels were to become an industry standard, it would consequently have a ".2" suffix.)

The multichannel paths that you create in the I/O Setup dialog box obviously are essential to surround mixing. A 5.1 main path would consist of six mono subpaths: the five surround speakers and the LFE subwoofer feed. You can also use multichannel paths for other purposes than surround mixing, however. For example, you might create a multichannel path consisting of simultaneous stereo cue mix, monitoring, and master recorder feeds to three distinct pairs of physical outputs on your audio hardware. The I/O Setup dialog box (shown in Figure 14.8) also allows you to create multichannel paths incorporating multiple stem mixes—for example, spoken dialog, effects, or music—that are fed to separate outputs (subpaths).

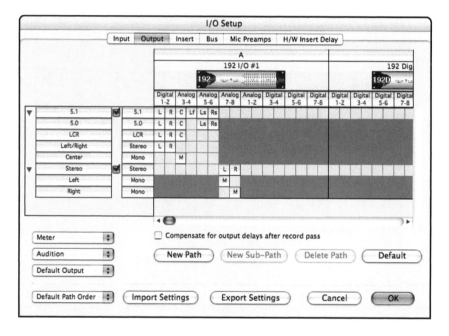

Figure 14.8 In the I/O Setup dialog box, a matrix allows you create main paths—logical groupings of inputs, outputs, inserts, or busses that consist of individual mono signal paths. The paths created in your configuration (mono or multichannel—stereo or multichannel surround) determine input and output options for audio tracks, sends, Aux In tracks, Instrument tracks, and Master Faders.

For multichannel tracks, an X/Y panner (as seen in Figure 14.9) facilitates positioning of sources within the surround field. As opposed to the standard pan sliders for stereo tracks, you move a point within a grid. An additional Divergence parameter for the X/Y panners determines how much the sound source will spread from its designated position into adjacent speakers (the lower the Divergence percentage, the wider the sound will spread into other speakers). Naturally, the Surround Mixer plug-in must be installed in your Plug-Ins folder for these features to be available (and is installed by default with Pro Tools|HD, along with the Stereo Mixer plug-in). The three Surround panner modes are X/Y, Divergence Editing, and three-knob (handy for discrete, straight-line panning between two specific speakers). The Output window for each multichannel track offers choices for alternative panning methods: X/Y panning, plus knobs for front/rear percentage, center percentage, divergence, LFE feed for the subwoofer, and other surround controls. These also appear separately when you view the panning automation data on multichannel tracks in a surround format.

Figure 14.9 X/Y panners facilitate positioning of sources within the surround field.

Surround Formats Overview

There are several surround formats in common use:

❄ **Dolby Digital.** Currently the most common format for home surround systems. It was formerly known as Dolby AC-3. Dolby Digital is used for surround-encoding most DVDs, high-definition television broadcasts, and theatrical film presentations. It's a 5.1 format (full-range channels for left, center, right, left/right surround, plus a dedicated channel for sending low frequencies to the subwoofer, known as LFE for Low Frequency Effects, from 3 to 120 Hz). Not all DVDs actually incorporate the five discrete channels (plus subwoofer channel). They may have only the Dolby Digital 2.0 soundtrack (stereo or Pro Logic compatible; this audio track is mandatory) and can additionally have Dolby Digital 1.0 (you guessed it: a mono audio track) and/or the full Dolby Digital 5.0 soundtrack, of course.

* **DTS (a.k.a. DTS Digital Surround).** A competing 5.1 format to Dolby Digital. It's also used for theatrical film presentations and sometimes as an alternate surround track option on consumer DVDs. DTS uses higher data rates for its audio stream than Dolby Digital (either 1.5 Mbps or 754 Kbps, versus 448 Kbps or 384 Kbps in Dolby Digital)—in other words, a lesser degree of "lossy" audio data compression is applied to the original audio. On consumer DVDs supporting both surround formats, the lower DTS data rates are generally used due to space considerations. Like Dolby Digital, while the majority of titles are 5.1, other channel configurations are also supported by the DTS format, including 4.1 and 4.0.

* **Dolby Surround Pro Logic.** The precursor to Dolby Digital and still the surround format used in hi-fi tracks of VHS videocassettes, LaserDiscs, and most analog television broadcasts. It's a four-channel format—left, center, right, plus a single channel for both rear surround speakers—and is backward compatible with stereo-playback systems. All four channels are matrix-encoded into a stereo audio track (and then decoded back into their individual components during playback). Therefore, Dolby Pro Logic is also known as LCRS. Dolby Pro Logic II is similar but incorporates two separate full-range audio channels for the surround speakers. In contrast, the classic Pro Logic specification uses a single band-limited channel (containing only frequencies from 100 Hz to 7 kHz) for both surround speakers.

* **THX Surround EX (a.k.a. Dolby EX).** This is an extension of Dolby Digital 5.1 and was jointly developed by Lucasfilm THX and Dolby Laboratories. In theatrical settings, the two surround speakers for Dolby Digital 5.1 are actually placed at the sides of the cinema. THX Surround EX (Dolby EX) adds two additional surround-back channels for speakers located behind the audience. For that reason, this is sometimes called a *7.1 format* (because there are seven speakers plus a subwoofer). Technically, though, in the implementation of this format for home theater, the two surround-back channels are matrix-encoded into the left and right surround channels of a 5.1 setup, so these EX formats might more correctly be called *extended 5.1*. Thanks to the use of this matrix-encoding method, EX formats are backward compatible with Dolby Digital just as Dolby Surround Pro Logic is backward compatible with stereo systems.

* **DTS-ES Discrete 6.1.** Another "extended" format. Unlike THX Surround EX (see the preceding bullet), it truly adds a discrete channel to the DTS 5.1 format for the surround-back speakers. This format is backward compatible with standard DTS decoding systems.

* **SDDS.** A 7.1 format, using seven full-range speakers plus a low-frequency effects channel: left, left-center, center, right-center, right, left surround, right surround, and LFE (subwoofer) channel.

Software and Hardware Accessories for Surround

Digidesign's Edit Pack add-on for its ProControl external control surface adds two DigiPanner motorized joystick pan controls for surround mixing (as well as other features, including an alphanumeric keyboard, a trackball, and multichannel metering).

Dolby Surround Tools 3 for TDM (shown in Figure 14.10) not only includes a surround-panning interface and supports the Pro Tools surround panner, but also complete surround encoder and decoder plug-ins matching the industry-standard SEU4/DP563 and SDU4/DP564 hardware equivalents that support sample rates up to 96 kHz. Mono/stereo and surround switching is provided, as well as a delay parameter for the surround channel. Surround Tools supports the Dolby Pro-Logic Surround format (LCRS), where information for four channels (left, center, right, plus a single channel for the two rear surround speakers) is matrix-encoded into a single stereo-compatible file—it does not support Dolby Digital 5.1 mixes.

Figure 14.10   Dolby Surround Tools is an LCRS surround encoder/decoder for Pro Tools TDM systems.

Another item to consider if you're serious about mixing in surround is the use of surround reverb plug-ins. After all, if the ostensible purpose of reverb effects is to simulate characteristics of an acoustic space, and you're mixing in 5.1 surround, how much sense can it make to use a reverb that only operates in two channels (left/right)? Digidesign's ReVibe reverb plug-in for HD systems is very impressive for this purpose, as is the TDM version of TL Space by TL Audio. Waves also offers the 360° Surround Tools plug-in bundle, including a reverb, compressor, limiter, panner, low-pass filter for the LFE channel, an encoder plug-in for quad and LCR mixes, plus other tools.

Apple's DVD Studio Pro program for Macintosh users not only supplies tools for creating DVD-Rs that can be played in any standard video DVD player (and includes MPEG-2 encoding) but also allows multiple mono WAV, AIF, or SDII file *stems* bounced out from Pro Tools to be dropped into the appropriate channel slots for encoding into a single AC-3 (Dolby Digital) surround file.

Monitoring in Surround

Here's a very economical alternative: Many current surround receivers used for home DVD viewing and Dolby Digital surround feature component audio inputs for each 5.1 surround channel. This allows you to configure six outputs from your Pro Tools audio interface as the surround output bus and connect these to your receiver in order to monitor your surround mixes in realistic conditions. (Of course, you can also switch between the surround outputs and the stereo mix.) Be aware, though, that audio inputs on consumer gear are referenced to −10 dbV, so if your audio interface is pumping out +4 dBm (which is a more common professional standard), you will be slamming its inputs! (Some Digidesign audio interfaces support switching output levels to −10 dbV reference levels.)

Various manufacturers (including Mackie, Genelec, Blue Sky, Alesis, ADAM, and JBL) offer 5.1-powered monitor packages that can be connected directly to your audio interface's outputs (or patchbay).

Naturally, when you are using multiple outputs from your Pro Tools audio interface for the surround mix, there are also many other more professional options for dedicated surround-sound monitoring. Bear in mind that you may want to opt for magnetically shielded speakers, especially if they must be located near video and computer monitors in your studio; this may particularly be an issue for the center speaker in a surround configuration.

Stereo Compatibility

Dolby Pro Logic matrix-encodes all four channels of its surround mix into a single stereo-compatible signal. You may be using the Dolby Surround plug-in (and a Pro-Logic decoder, or even a common surround-compatible receiver) to properly route the four channels of audio out to your speakers (left, center, right, plus one channel to both rear surround speakers). Before committing to a mix for Dolby Pro Logic, be sure to switch into ordinary stereo mode to make sure there are no drastically inappropriate shifts in levels or imaging when hearing the mix through only left and right speakers. (Phase problems are the most common thing to watch out for here, and the SurroundScope plug-in can be a useful tool.)

Similarly, playing a 5.1 mix back as stereo (commonly known as "downmixing") can be an important compatibility check. The Waves M360° Surround Mixdown plug-in (part of their 360° Surround Tools bundle) permits deriving mixes in stereo, mono LCR, and other formats when placed on your multichannel surround (5.1) Master Fader output. A variety of external hardware options are also available for this purpose.

❋ **Tip: SurroundScope**

SurroundScope is an optional Digidesign plug-in, provided in both TDM and RTAS formats. It provides monitoring and analysis tools to assist in the multichannel surround mixing process through visualizations of levels, phase, and surround positions of multiple channels in the surround field. SurroundScope supports common surround formats, including LCR (left-center-right), Quad, LCRS (left-center-right-surround; Dolby Surround/Dolby Pro Logic), 5.0, 5.1 (used on video DVDs), 6.0, 6.1, 7.0, and 7.1.

The plug-in's Surround display shows the surround position of the current track's signal. Input Level meters show levels for each surround channel. The Lissajous meter provides information about amplitude and phase of stereo signals to help you optimize stereo imaging. The Phase meter monitors phase coherency of the left and right channels (only) in the surround mix.

Audio Editing for Avid-Based Video Projects

It has been a few years since Digidesign merged with Avid Technology, one of the world's most important manufacturers of nonlinear (computer- and hard disk–based) video workstations. Even before that, by participating in the development of the OMF interchange format, Digidesign had positioned itself as an important audio-editing platform for video projects and for Avid in particular. Avid offers several lines of video-editing systems, including Avid Media Composer Adrenaline HD (Mac OS X/Win XP), Avid Xpress Pro (Mac OS X/Win XP Pro), Avid Xpress DV (Mac OS X/Win XP Pro), NewsCutter Adrenaline (Win XP Pro), Softimage|XSI (Win XP Pro/Linux), and Symphony Nitris (Win XP).

❋ **Tip: High-Speed Networking for Production Facilities**

If you're routinely going to transfer projects between multiple Pro Tools suites and nonlinear video-editing systems in your facility, trust us—standard Ethernet-based local area networking is not fast enough! You may want to check out some of the Fibre Channel–based networking alternatives. All these require a separately purchased networking card in your computer. Some solutions even include a high-speed file server or disk array (perhaps in a centralized machine room), which facilitates sharing files with other workstations as you collaborate on projects. We list some of these in Appendix B, "Add-Ons, Extensions, and Cool Stuff for Your Rig."

File Formats

Most commonly, nonlinear video editors can import or export AIF and WAV audio files (and SDII on some older Mac-based Avid systems) for their soundtracks. An audio-only QuickTime is essentially an AIF file as well but offers additional resources for playback by Apple's QuickTime Player. Certainly, Pro Tools can also bounce/convert your mix as a WAV file if required by a Windows-based video-editing system. (Remember that you can also bounce the mix directly into a copy of the current QuickTime movie in your Pro Tools session.) In any case, a 48 kHz sample rate is standard for most current industrial and broadcast-video applications (as opposed to the 44.1 kHz sample rate used for audio CDs), and 16-bit audio files are still more common than 24-bit. (Be sure to ask the video editor; more recent systems are moving toward 24-bit files.)

Specifically, all Avid video-editing systems understand audio files in AIF formats (AIFF-C, to be precise, even though Avid systems do *not* compress audio data within these files). In years past, Macintosh-based Avid systems supported SDII files (especially because they used Digidesign audio interfaces, and that was once the exclusive audio file format used by early Mac versions of Pro Tools). Windows-based Avid editing systems (and all Mac versions of Media Composer 8.0 and higher) also support WAV audio files or use them directly in some cases. The trend toward Broadcast WAV files as a digital audio standard (particularly for higher sample rates) continues, especially given that the AES/EBU are recommending this as a standard delivery and interchange format.

OMF, AAF, and the DigiTranslator Program

OMF and AAF are file-format standards developed between various manufacturers (especially Avid) to promote a common format for interchange of data between different computer-assisted, nonlinear editing systems for video and audio. The OMF Interchange file format (OMFI, or simply OMF—the terms are more or less synonymous even though OMF more properly refers to the entire enabling technology and a body of standards) allows all the original audio tracks from an Avid Media Composer project, for example, to be translated for a Pro Tools system. OMF stands for *Open Media Framework*. Advanced Authoring Format (AAF) is a newer standard, introduced in 2001 (and supported by versions 2.0 and higher of DigiTranslator), that encompasses both OMF and many other source formats. (Note that OMF exports are limited to 2 GB total size, which can be an issue if you export a project as a single OMF file with the source audio filed embedded within it.)

DigiTranslator is optional software that must be purchased from Digidesign (and is included in the DV Toolkit for Pro Tools LE, which is *not* compatible with M-Powered versions of Pro Tools) in order to export or import OMFI/AAF files between Pro Tools and other programs. These include video editors as well as numerous digital-audio workstations, including Digital Performer, Logic Pro, and Cubase SX. With DigiTranslator, you can import OMFI/AAF files from other video and audio workstations directly into Pro Tools via the same File > Open Session command you use to open an existing Pro Tools session. Most importantly, if necessary, DigiTranslator allows you to convert Pro Tools sessions to OMFI format for use with these other programs.

DigiTranslator (shown in Figure 14.11) converts between cuts and dissolves in the Avid environment and their counterparts in Pro Tools, regions, and fades. The Avid's audio clips are translated to Pro Tools regions. Also, volume or pan levels and automation created in

Avid are translated to Pro Tools automation on the appropriate track. Here's the basic procedure: The Avid editor exports the current project in OMFI format. (Generally, you would not export video into the OMFI file, only audio data.) The OMFI Audio Only option incorporates duplicate copies of all the Avid project's audio files into the OMFI file in AIF format; it therefore requires much more disk space. The OMFI Compositions Only option incorporates only the audio playlist into the OMFI file, and it would therefore be necessary to provide the source audio files separately for the Pro Tools system—perhaps on a shared network drive. (The Avid editor should first run the Consolidate Audio Files command. It's similar to Compact Audio in the Pro Tools Region List, except that it creates an entirely new folder to store compacted files, containing only audio clips actually used in the Avid project, rather than their entire source audio files. The editor exports the sequence with the OMFI Compositions Only option and gives you the OMFI file, plus this folder of compacted audio files created with the Consolidate command.) After that, with DigiTranslator installed on your Pro Tools rig, you can import this OMFI file directly into Pro Tools using the File > Open Session command.

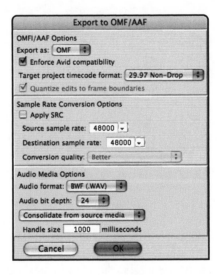

Figure 14.11 With DigiTranslator, you can transfer projects between Pro Tools and other video or audio workstations via OMF or AAF interchange format.

❊ **Note: Avid/Digi Terms**

Good communication with video editors starts with learning a few words in each other's language!

❊ **Media data.** The actual audio or video data contained in the source files. This is the largest portion within most OMF or AAF interchange files.

❊ **Metadata.** Information within the source project or session file itself that can be included in the OMF or AAF format. This includes pointers to files and information about their sample rate, bit-depth, source reel, timestamp data, and so on. Metadata also includes all the information about where parts of these files are placed in the Timeline and about automation.

* **Sequence.** Avid video-project equivalent to a Pro Tools session document.

* **Master clip.** Avid equivalent to a whole-file audio region. (In Pro Tools, audio regions that correspond to entire files *usually* appear in boldface within the Region List—but won't when the project was imported from OMF/AAF.)

* **Subclip.** Avid equivalent to an audio region within a large source audio file. A subclip represents a smaller section within a master clip, just as many audio regions represent smaller sections within whole-file audio regions.

* **Real-time audio effects.** Avid equivalent for plug-ins.

* **Automation gain (clip-based or keyframe-based).** Avid equivalent to track automation in Pro tools. For example, the Avid equivalent to volume automation in a Pro Tools track is called Avid keyframe volume.

* **Bin.** A database where master clips, subclips, effects, and sequences are organized for a project. Somewhat comparable to the Region List in a Pro Tools project. However, Avid projects can have *multiple* bins, and the feature set is understandably larger because video editors deal with more varied source media types: audio, video, animation sequences, still images, and so on.

* **Dissolve.** Strictly, a video fade to black or a mix through to another image, but video editors often use the term *dissolve* for audio fades to silence and also crossfades between two audio segments.

* **Segue.** Occasionally used as a synonym for an audio crossfade.

* **Gang.** Avid equivalent (approximately) for an Edit group. Edits performed on one track are mirrored in the others, like tracks that are grouped together in the Edit window of Pro Tools.

* **Stem.** In the film/video production industry, stems can be compared to the signal paths you define in the I/O Setup dialog box of Pro Tools (a logical grouping of inputs, outputs, or busses treated under a single name). In a film mix, source tracks might be grouped into a smaller number of stems according to type—for example, dialog, sound effects, Foley, music, and so on. Just as you might use an Auxiliary Input or Master Fader as the overall volume control for a group of tracks or output channels, in complex film mixdowns, having a large number of source tracks grouped into stems simplifies the adjustment of overall levels.

When you use OMF or AAF files to move audio from Avid to your Pro Tools system, all the original tracks and names, fades, and various other parameters are retained. (Video editors frequently use multiple tracks—for example, slugging in music cues and sound effects under the camera soundtracks, which you might refine later. They also create fades or edits on audio to correct dialog, remove extraneous noise, match video fades to/from black, and other audio operations. You get all these when the project is imported into Pro Tools.) Of course, the editor on *any* nonlinear video-editing system could also mix audio tracks to stereo and export an audio file for you or simply incorporate the full-resolution 48 kHz audio into a QuickTime movie provided as your editing reference (instead of a tape). In fact, if the editor hasn't added additional audio tracks to the original "sync" sound from the video shoot, either of these methods can frequently be just as practical as exchanging OMF or AAF files. (One drawback is that you won't have any additional audio available at region boundaries to correct clicks or artifacts at their edit points using crossfades, and so on.)

The Import Session Data dialog box provides options for how metadata from the original project will be interpreted for import into Pro Tools. For instance, you could choose to ignore rendered audio effects (this doesn't import the results of real-time EQ, etc. that have been applied in the source video project), ignore clip-based gain, or convert it to breakpoint automation. You can also choose to copy the source media files, convert to your session's audio format, and/or consolidate (compact) the source files during the import. The Consolidate Handle Length value is similar to the Padding parameter when compacting files in the Region List—it leaves a few extra milliseconds around each region boundary, so that you have the option of lengthening these for fades and so on.

> ❊ **Tip: Avid Export Templates for Pro Tools**
>
> Recent versions of Avid's Media Composer, Film Composer, Symphony, and Avid Xpress include *Export Templates* for many programs, including Pro Tools, which appear within a pop-up list in their Export dialog box. This can save you a lot of discussion (and/or confusion) when collaborating with Avid video editors. The External options leave audio files in a separate folder. The Embedded option incorporates the Avid composition and all the audio into a single large file, most practical for short-duration spots and when transferring OMFI files over a local network.

> ❊ **Caution: Render Unto Pro Tools...**
>
> Remind your collaborators on Avid video-editing systems to *render* all their AudioSuite effects before exporting OMF/AAF files of the project for use in Pro Tools! Otherwise, all these effects will be skipped when the files are imported.

Gain Optimization for Video

As a general rule, audio mixes you provide for video projects should be delivered fairly near to the maximum possible level. Perhaps the simplest approach is to use the AudioSuite menu's Normalization command on your bounced mix file (after re-importing it into the Region List). Additionally, there are supplemental audio-editing and batch-processing programs that can normalize audio files. Gain-optimization plug-ins, such as Digidesign's Maxim and several others from Waves, Ltd., are also extremely useful for this purpose because they allow you to transparently limit occasional isolated peaks within your audio program, which otherwise restrict the top limit for the normalization process.

Normalization

Normalization changes the audio level of a sound file (or a selected region within it). Typically, this process finds the peak signal level and can either automatically increase this to 100 percent (0 dB, or *full* code) or adjust it to a specified number of dB down from 0 (in which case, contrary to a common misconception, the peak audio level may actually *decrease*). The amplitude of the rest of the audio therefore changes proportionally. Most Avid systems (but not Avid Xpress) have the same AudioSuite normalization function as Pro Tools; however, you will discover that many video editors don't bother to use it. As a result, their video masters may not take advantage of the full dynamic range possible because they can only compensate audio levels empirically (and conservatively) as they lay the project back to video tape (whereas if they had mixed and normalized their soundtrack to something closer to 0 dB, they would *know* its maximum peak level).

As a general rule, we recommend that you always normalize audio mixes for video to a consistent value (−3 dB or −5 dB, for example) before sending them back to the video editor. You can do this with batch-processing programs (such as WaveConvert by Waves or Cleaner Pro by Autodesk, or with stereo audio-editing programs like Bias Peak, Steinberg WaveLab, Sony Sound Forge, and others). You can also normalize bounced mix files directly in Pro Tools using the AudioSuite function shown in Figure 14.12. Just choose the Re-import Into Session option in the Bounce to Disk dialog box, and then normalize the audio file directly in the Region List. A third option is to use gain-optimization plug-ins, such as Digidesign Maxim or the more sophisticated Waves L1, L2, or L3 on your Master Fader so that you know exactly how your maximum levels look at the main mix output before bouncing out the file.

Figure 14.12 Normalization adjusts the loudest peak in a selection to a specified level, which increases or decreases the sound's volume (depending on the settings in this dialog box) compared to its original level.

New to Pro Tools 7 is the RMS mode for the Normalization process (as opposed to the traditional Peak mode). Instead of the traditional Normalization approach where a single peak determines the maximum amount that the gain of a selection can be increased, the RMS (root-mean-square) method allows you to specify an "average" target level. Be conservative, however—depending on the dynamic range within the selected material, clipping can result.

The Gain process (another AudioSuite plug-in) also now features an RMS mode. Unlike the Normalization plug-in, it provides the useful ability to detect the current RMS (or Peak) level in the current selection. This makes it much more practical to make RMS gain adjustments (which as something more like an average level, allow you to adjust apparent loudness of the selection more accurately).

With regard to gain-optimization plug-ins, it's prudent to warn against applying these too enthusiastically to all your mixes. One's perception quickly becomes deadened to what at first seemed like a dramatic improvement in overall loudness and presence. Consequently, it's all too easy to end up squashing everything against the ceiling of your dynamic range, ultimately creating a fatiguing listening experience for your audience when sustained for any length of time.

Compression

The general practice is to compress video mixes pretty hard. This is especially true for industrial video, be it training, marketing and product videos, or video modules to be used at live events. Single-band compression (like the DigiRack compressor provided with Pro Tools and the Focusrite D3) is very effective on single audio sources—for example, the voice-over or background music in a video program. There are also many excellent single-band options for compressing entire mixes, including Digidesign's Impact and Smack! plug-ins, for example. Multiband compressors (such as Waves' C4, Drawmer Dynamics, and McDSP's MC2000 plug-ins) can often be more transparent when compressing entire mixes; they simultaneously apply differing amounts of compression in three or more frequency bands. Using multiband compression, the entire mix won't get clamped down by some momentary peak exclusively in the low-or high-frequency end of the spectrum. This often produces more natural-sounding results at higher compression ratios.

❈ **Tip: Don't Forget to Duck (A Side Order of Compression, Please)**

Side chaining is a classic dynamics-processing technique where a different audio source determines the amount of gain change to apply to a track. For example, when applying ordinary compression to a music underscore for a video project, level changes in the music itself determine the amount of gain reduction applied (per the compressor's current ratio and threshold settings). Sometimes, though, you'd like the music's level to drop whenever the voice-over is present, rising back up between phrases (a technique called *ducking*).

To duck your music underscore, create a stereo send from the VO track, routed to any unused Pro Tools bus pair. Option-click (Alt-click in Windows) the send's Level slider to set it to 0 dB. Insert a compressor plug-in on your music track (preferably before any subsequent EQ inserts in the track) and use its Key Input pop-up (called *sidechain input* in the Focusrite D3 compressor) to select the bus pair where you've sent the voice-over track's signal as the key audio source for the compression process. When you enable the external key, the voice-over's level changes control the amount of gain reduction applied to the music track. Adjust the compressor's Level and Ratio parameters for the desired amount of ducking on the music. Also, bear in mind that the Release parameter affects how quickly the music comes back up after each voice-over phrase.

Rock 'n' rollers: Small amounts of compression applied on rhythm guitars and other backing instrumental parts, which are keyed (side chained) by your lead vocal, can also be very effective. Both will seem to be in your face at the appropriate times and can give the impression that the vocal has a little more power to cut through an aggressive mix. Conversely, using the kick drum as the side chain input for an expander plug-in on a loosely played bass track can help tighten up a groove.

Digidesign's Maxim peak-limiting and gain-optimization plug-in (shown in Figure 14.13) is very effective when applied to entire mixes. Try placing Maxim on the Master Fader for your stereo mix. By flattening out isolated amplitude peaks (keeping in mind that extreme settings distort the sound), you will obtain greater overall levels afterward when you normalize the bounced mix to −.3 dB, for example. Unlike conventional hardware limiters, Maxim can read ahead so that limiting is applied with no *latency*, or reaction time, which yields more transparent results.

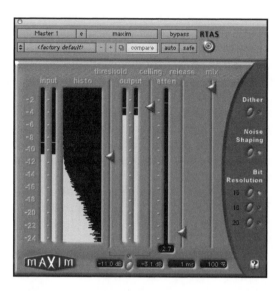

Figure 14.13 Digidesign's Maxim is a gain-optimization and peak-limiting plug-in for both RTAS and TDM architectures.

The T-Racks mastering plug-in suite from IK Multimedia also includes a 3-band limiter that is very effective on stereo mixes. You can adjust the input drive, as well as the crossover points, threshold, and output levels for each of the three frequency bands.

Several limiting plug-ins are available from Waves, including the L1, L2, and L3 Ultramaximizers. These are even more sophisticated tools for optimizing gain and bit-depth conversions in your Pro Tools projects. They offer single-band peak limiting and other functions, including Waves' proprietary IDR dithering algorithms for high-quality gain optimization and conversion to lower bit-depths. As with Maxim, you might typically insert these plug-ins on a Master Fader, although you could also use them on a vocal track, for instance. The L3 Multimaximizer (shown in Figure 14.14) is the latest and most powerful offering from Waves for gain optimization. It provides peak limiting in five separate frequency bands, with adjustable crossover points and a linear phase crossover that avoids phase distortion between bands. The brick-wall limiting in individual bands can be completely independent or progressively more linked up to the point where, at 100 percent, L3 functions like a single-band limiter. A variety of dithering options are also included and up to 12 dB of post-limiting boost or cut in each frequency band.

One last note about these gain-optimization processors: The harder you slam your mix against a limiter in order to constantly maintain maximum loudness, the less dynamic range is retained in the original material. For some applications, this may be just what you want—for example, multimedia, on-hold or background music, live events such as awards banquets, or aggressive-sounding television commercials. Keep in mind, though, that this can quickly become over-bearing and fatigue listeners (especially at louder playback levels). It's as if someone was

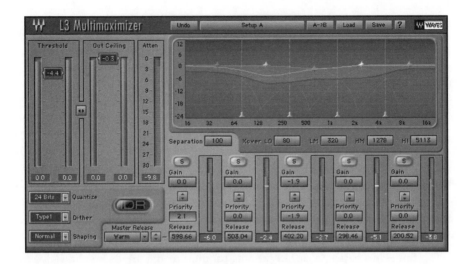

Figure 14.14 L3 Multimaximizer is a powerful gain-management and dithering plug-in for TDM.

speaking loudly all the time, shouting out each and every syllable at maximum volume—how long would you put up with *that*? As brilliant as these tools are, their excessive application—to the point of squashing all vestiges of dynamic range—is a legitimate complaint about many current movie soundtracks and *especially* CD music releases that aim to sound really "loud." Try not to lose your ear for subtlety!

Audio Editing for Linear (Tape-Based) Video Suites

In this situation, you typically play back your audio with the Pro Tools Transport in Online mode, recording from the selected outputs of your Pro Tools hardware to a master video deck. Sometimes you will perform this layback directly to the video master tape you've been using in your audio suite. In other situations, you may use tie lines to send audio directly to the video-editing suite (slaving Pro Tools to the video master as the SMPTE synchronization source), where your audio is recorded directly to the video edit master. This is preferable especially when using professional video decks with analog-only audio inputs (for example, BetaCam), because it eliminates a tape generation.

> ✻ **Note: Digital Video Decks**
>
> Professional digital video decks (like D2, D4, D1, and Digital BetaCam) generally also have digital audio inputs and outputs. (The audio tracks of a BetaCam SP deck are digitally *recorded*, but the audio I/O is strictly analog.) If your Pro Tools audio interface has AES/EBU digital I/O, this is definitely a preferable method for audio layoff and layback. Digital audio I/O on professional video gear is almost always in AES/EBU format, with XLR connectors. Manufacturers generally recommend that digital cable lengths not

exceed 30 feet, although many people successfully run greater lengths. (You should use 110-ohm digital-type cable and *not* ordinary mic/line cable, for all AES/EBU connections—especially for longer lengths!)

Audio Transfer from Tape Master

When dealing with linear (tape-based) video-editing suites, the first step in the audio post-production process is to record the existing audio on the video master into Pro Tools while synchronized to SMPTE time code. Ideally, this comes directly from the video master, even if afterward you use a tape copy of the project in your local deck as the time-code master for editing. Alternatively, audio can be transferred directly from your work tape copy; but if that's an analog copy (onto BetaCam, for instance), you're already one analog generation removed from the master's audio quality.

Here's a typical sequence for pulling the audio from a supplied video master tape into your Pro Tools session:

1. Connect the video master's stereo outputs (analog or digital, as mentioned in the Note preceding this section) to one of the input pairs on your Pro Tools audio hardware.

2. Connect the video deck's time-code output (audio if you're using LTC, video if you're using VITC) to your synchronization peripheral.

3. Create a Pro Tools session (at a 48 kHz sample rate); set the appropriate frame rate and session start time. Typically the video program itself will be preceded by color bars and tones; you should also record these so that when you lay your audio back up to the video master, you can confirm that consistent levels are maintained. Therefore, if the video program starts at 1:00:00, your actual session start time might be 0:59:00 (if your facility follows the fairly standard practice of laying down 30 seconds of tone, followed by 30 seconds before program start).

4. Create audio track(s) for recording from the video, select the appropriate input pair for the audio source, and either record-enable the track(s) or temporarily switch to Input Only Monitoring, under the Track menu.

5. Put Pro Tools in Online mode; press Play on the video master. Confirm that Pro Tools locks to time code, starting playback at the appropriate location (once it locks up to incoming time code).

6. Meanwhile, if you're recording via an analog input, adjust input levels to the Pro Tools hardware.

7. Press Record in the Pro Tools Transport and then Play *on the video master's transport.* Because Pro Tools is in Online mode, it should drop into Record/Play mode automatically. Press Stop on the video transport after the layoff is completed.

Specifications: Audio Tracks on VTRs

Digital (a.k.a. PCM) audio tracks on professional video-tape recorders use a 48 kHz sample rate. BetaCam SP is an extremely common video-tape format for industrial video (local television spots, training, product, marketing, and corporate video and video modules for playback during live events); it is also the tape format generally required by TV broadcasters throughout the world (whether they use NTSC, PAL, or SECAM video standards). BetaCam SP offers two PCM (digital audio tracks, also known as *hi-fi* on these machines) audio tracks, plus two analog/longitudinal tracks, not generally used for professional audio applications. As mentioned elsewhere in this chapter, D-2, D-5, D-1, and Digital BetaCam offer multiple digital audio tracks and feature digital I/O for audio.

DVCAM (Sony), DVCPRO (Panasonic), DV (formerly known as DVC when it was launched in 1995), and mini-DV also feature digital audio tracks (usually only two, at the 48 kHz sample rate and 16-bit resolution favored for professional work). If IEEE 1394 digital connections are used (more commonly known as *FireWire,* the original name for this specification developed by Apple, or *i.LINK,* a proprietary Sony name for its implementation of this industry-standard 1394 connector) to transfer video from cameras or decks to your hard disk–based video-editing application, the audio is also transferred digitally as part of the DV codec QuickTime file that these programs create from the DV source.

Pull-Up and Pull-Down Sample Rates

These specialty sample rates are sometimes used when film and NTSC video are used in the same project. For strictly video- or audio-only projects, they are not an issue (unless you select one of these sample rates by accident).

Film is shot and projected at 24 frames per second (fps), while NTSC color video (the American broadcast standard) uses 29.97 fps. When using Pro Tools to post audio for a film, it is convenient and cost effective to use a video copy as the image source during the editing process. Transferring each frame of a film at 24 fps to video tape at 29.97 fps presents a problem, however; the math becomes difficult. To make life easier, transfers from film to NTSC video tape use a frame rate of 30 fps (the original frame rate for black and white television).

To do a little math: 24 is divisible by 6, and so is 30. Thus, the ratio 4:5 is associated with this transfer because there are four frames of film for each five frames of video. To get around this problem, when the film is transferred to video (the Telecine process), the video records at 30 fps standard, so that 24 frames of the video can be evenly divided over the video frames. Telecine devices convert each four frames of film into five frames of video. (Each frame of video consists of two interlaced fields, while each film frame contains a complete image. The second and fourth film frames are repeated over three video fields, rather than two, producing one additional video frame for each four original film frames.)

To make the production tracks match the slower video played at 29.97 fps, the audio is recorded at standard sample rates and is then *pulled down* during playback (perhaps using Sync I/O, Nanosyncs, or TL Sync) while synchronizing to the video. During the transfer process back to film, the audio gets pulled back up.

Therefore, the 44,100 Hz sample rate can be pulled down to 44,056 Hz, and 48,000 Hz can be pulled down to 47,952 Hz. Again, unless you're working on projects involving film transfers to video for editing, you probably won't deal with these sample rates (and will generally use 48,000 Hz for most industrial and broadcast video projects).

Synchronized Layback

After you've edited the audio for a video project, you must transfer it back to the video master—in perfect synchronization, of course. Just as Pro Tools has to stay tightly in sync during the initial layoff and throughout the edit process, it naturally must maintain the correct time relationship with the image as you record your audio back to the video master. You will therefore keep Pro Tools in Online mode while the video operator enables the master video deck for audio recording (unless you're laying the audio directly back to the video tape in your own audio suite).

Sync Issues: House Sync

As explained in Chapter 11, house sync (a.k.a. *black burst*) is a stable video signal that provides a common timing reference for an entire production facility. With appropriate peripheral hardware, the audio clock of a Pro Tools hardware interface can also be resolved to this external timing reference. This eliminates drift between Pro Tools and the video master, especially important for long-duration projects, and also improves Pro Tools' lock-up time to SMPTE. Devices that can accommodate house sync for Pro Tools include the Sync I/O by Digidesign and the Digital Timepiece by Mark of the Unicorn (MOTU).

Analog versus Digital

As mentioned previously, professional digital video decks generally use AES/EBU digital I/O for audio. If your Pro Tools hardware supports it, this is a preferable way to transfer your audio back to the video master for all the obvious reasons. However, digital audio inputs on professional video gear are notoriously finicky about syncing to external digital audio source, including Pro Tools. If you experience difficulties, by all means troubleshoot the situation—but it may not turn out that you're doing anything wrong.

When a video deck is recording audio via *analog* input, you must provide reference levels for the video operator (and have the courtesy to confirm beforehand that your mix's peak levels are actually reaching maximum).

About Reference Levels

Reference levels are not an issue if you're transferring audio digitally (as long as it's not clipping at the source, right?). However, it is common practice for Volume meters on audio and especially video gear to fudge levels slightly in order to allow some extra headroom before actual clipping occurs. When you're trying to get maximum level during the layback to video (especially if you're posting one of those late-night TV commercials), trust the 0 dB tones that you put on the front end of your Pro Tools sessions (or output from the Signal Generator plug-in, discussed in the following Tip). Above all, normalize your mixes (by any of the methods described previously) to be certain that your session is actually peaking close to that level (perhaps −1 dB or more down from the maximum). Alternatively, you should experiment with compression and/or limiting inserts on the Master Fader controlling the output for the stereo mix. If your limiter is the last insert on the Master Fader and is set to a −3 dB threshold, the limiter's Reduction meter will indicate very clearly how often you're banging against the limit (if at all).

✻ **Tip: Reference Levels and Tones from Pro Tools**

For years, many Pro Tools operators have kept audio files of *tones* (100 hertz, 1 kHz, and 10 kHz) handy on their system so that they could drop them into a Pro Tools session as a level reference for external devices with analog inputs. The Signal Generator plug-in provided with Pro Tools makes this largely unnecessary, especially if you simply need a momentary reference for a video deck's analog input. Create a new, empty audio track; place the Signal Generator on it as an insert. In the Plug-In Settings window for the Signal Generator, you can specify a frequency and waveform (sine waves are preferable for this purpose), and be sure to set this plug-in's Level slider to 0 dB. If the main Volume fader for your Master Fader is also set to 0 dB, all the video operator has to do is adjust his input level until your tone registers at 0 dB, and everybody will be in agreement. Easy!

On the other hand, if you are provided tones from the video master (via either analog or digital), you should also return these same tones when you lay your audio tracks back onto the video master so that level consistency can be easily confirmed.

Summary

Postproduction professionals will note that we've only scratched the surface here. It's a huge field, and synchronization, tape formats, mix formats, and work processes vary tremendously from one facility to another. For the most part, we hope to have provided a little perspective on the process for more audio-oriented Pro Tools users. If you want to be involved in sound-track work, probably the most important thing we can say is—go out and do it! You don't have to wait for the plum assignment at a top-flight video or film house in order to start getting your act together. There are tons of independent film and video producers out there (and the advent of high-quality DV cameras with 24p resolution, plus programs like Adobe Premiere, Sony's Vegas, and Apple's FinalCut Pro have immensely increased their numbers) who would be delighted to have you collaborate on their project. Also, interactive media developers will often seek out Pro Tools collaborators for voice-over recording and postproduction of Quick-Time movies used in their applications (see the next chapter for more information about these opportunities). If the developer or editor provides a small QuickTime file for you to use, you can post video projects on any reasonably capable computer. It's a credit, it's a learning process, and it just might hit the jackpot—you never know!

15 } Sound Design for Interactive Media

Pro Tools is an excellent platform for creating music and voice-over narrations to be used within interactive applications on CD-ROM, Web pages, DVD-ROM, kiosks, and so on. It's also quite useful for creating sound effects associated with buttons and other hyperlinks (for example, while the cursor hovers over an object, and when the user clicks the button or link). You can use many different programs to create media-rich interactive content that prominently includes audio and video files at a decent resolution. The file formats and constraints for audio usage vary for each program and situation; you will need to ask the authors/programmers many questions up front before starting to design sounds for an interactive project.

The unfortunate truth is that, especially for education- and business-oriented interactive presentations (such as CD-ROMs and broadband Web pages with Flash content on the Internet or intranets within organizations), the budget for professional-quality, original audio is often dismayingly small. Among other things, this reflects the fact that many interactive authors come from graphic design backgrounds (rather than from video or audio). These authors may be less cognizant than you might expect of just how much good audio enriches the texture and quality of the interactive experience. That's why so many pieces are in circulation with noisy, poorly compressed narrations, generic button sound effects that were included with the authoring program or harvested from enthusiast Web sites, and other unfortunate audio. Indeed, you may have to *sell* these people on the benefits of using your services for professional sound design and recording; as always, the best approach is to lead by example. Bring examples of killer button sounds, background loops, clean and present-sounding voice-overs with small file sizes, and so on. Game designers, as a general rule, assign slightly more priority to sound design; there is also some interesting work to be done in the creation of Standard MIDI Files for gaming environments (using the General MIDI (GM) specification to assign sounds to MIDI channels, volume, pan, and so on).

At any rate, it's not enough to simply be the hottest Pro Tools jockey in town or an all-around studio professional (although this certainly will help). You need at least a rudimentary idea of what interactive authors actually *do* to incorporate sound files into their programs—the restrictions, the bottlenecks, and so on. If you're new to all this, probably one of the best things you can do is get together with a friend who works in a program such as Director, Flash, Visual Basic, Asymetrix ToolBook, AuthorWare, Breeze, or Icon Author. Have that person show you the exact steps that he takes to place a looping sound file as a background for a page, assign button click sounds, play sounds while the cursor is over a button, trigger graphic events or advancing frames based on audio playback location, and other operations for handling audio. Get a good look at the file import dialog boxes in that program so that you know exactly which audio file formats are supported.

As a general rule, you will need to perform the conversions down to lower sample rates or compressed audio file formats so that you can deliver all the audio files ready for plugging into the authoring environment, such as the one shown in Figure 15.1. (If you instead deliver everything at 44.1 kHz stereo, leaving it up to the interactive folks to perform audio file format conversions according to their needs, we can practically guarantee you will not be pleased with the results!) Also, be sure to ask about desired durations for sound effects (and be prepared to have to adjust these later in the process). As we mention later in this chapter, it's also extremely important to be organized and consistent about naming the audio files you deliver. If possible, try to establish these file-naming conventions with the authors in the earliest phases of the project, as you're first defining the list of required audio.

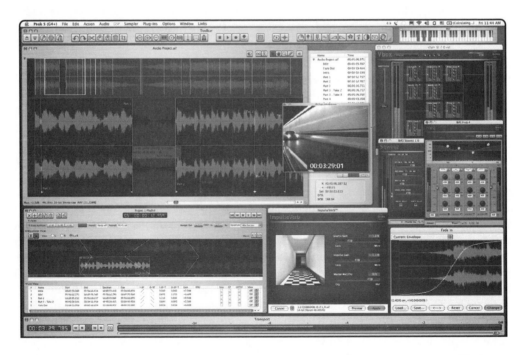

Figure 15.1   Bias Peak Pro (Mac) can be a useful companion program for Pro Tools, as can Sound Forge or WaveLab (Windows). These programs assist with supplemental file conversions and also allow creation of cue points/markers within audio files for use by interactive programs, as well as loops.

Sound Effects Libraries, Synths/Samplers, Sound Creation

General video-oriented sound effects libraries on CD can provide some useful source material for interactive sound creation as well. Bear in mind, though, that licensing agreements and intellectual property rights apply as much to an interactive CD/DVD or Web page as to a book or video program. If the sound effect library is not a *buy-out*, where the purchase price of the CD includes the right to use its contents in the creation of any other program without paying any additional royalties, you could get yourself into trouble. Read the fine print!

Obviously, when you're creating button sounds and so on, you will only be using a small portion of the generally longer sound effects provided in these libraries. And keep in mind that, unless you're deliberately creating specific stereo effects and the constraints of the project allow you to do so, button sounds are typically mono. The sound designer's craft makes use of all the tools that Pro Tools provides for sound manipulation: pitch shifting, time compression/expansion, and dynamic and filtering effects. We suggest that your mindset always be that source sound effects are only one layer in a more complex sound that you will build on multiple tracks (yes, even for a single button), rather than a solution in themselves.

We're also very fond of using synthesizers and samplers (*especially* the software-based variety for this purpose) to create interactive sound effects. Aside from the obvious benefits of a more flexible sound palette, the ability to shape sounds with filtering, and layering sounds on multiple MIDI channels to build a texture, using software instruments makes it very easy to produce *groups* of related sounds with consistent durations and dynamic levels. For example, this can be useful when creating a series of ascending tones for 5–6 similar buttons on a page. (You can also use the Pitch Shift function in the AudioSuite menu of Pro Tools on audio regions to achieve the same purpose.)

Encourage your interactive collaborators—who wouldn't dream of using clip art in professional projects—not to use "clip sounds" either! Original sound is more creative and will give their programs a much more distinctive feeling (and there's an obvious analogy to cinema here). Plus, it may also provide you more work, right?

❋ **Tip: The Envelope, Please**

The *envelope* of a sound describes the contour of its changes in amplitude, pitch, or timbral characteristics over time. When you're creating interactive button sounds from other audio files (for example, sound effects from a CD library or from other sources you've recorded), one of the common problems is that the initial *attack* of the sound may not be pronounced enough to make a satisfying impact when the user clicks the button. One solution is to add another layer (an additional sound in another Pro Tools track) with a heavier attack on the front that quickly fades out.

But first, try switching the track's data display format to Volume and simply *drawing* the loudness contour you'd like for this button sound: a full-volume spike at the beginning, ramping down to a more general level after a couple hundred milliseconds (see Figure 15.2). For simple button sounds, a similar effect could also be accomplished by using a compressor plug-in set to a high ratio, but with a very long attack.

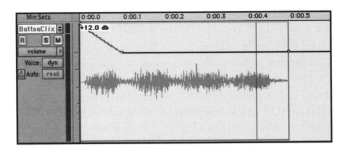

Figure 15.2 When creating button sounds for interactive media, you can use automation to create the desired volume envelope—for example, to increase the level of the sound's initial attack.

Common Multimedia File Formats

We discuss common audio file formats in Chapter 1, "About Pro Tools." Here's some additional information, specific to our context of providing audio for interactive developers:

* **WAV and AIF.** WAV was originally developed jointly by Microsoft and IBM. AIF (sometimes spelled *AIFF,* especially among Macintosh users) was originally developed by Apple Computer. This probably explains the relative abundance of these audio file formats on each platform. In other respects, the characteristics of both formats are fairly similar. Both WAV and AIF files are supported audio-recording formats for Pro Tools sessions (Mac versions can also use SDII, discussed in a moment), but WAV format is *required* for recording at sample rates higher than 48 kHz on *any* Pro Tools system. (Although technically Pro Tools uses Broadcast WAV format with the .BWV extension for recording, this is backward-compatible with WAV.) Bouncing or exporting audio to WAV format from Pro Tools may simplify the process of sharing files with many Windows audio programs (some of which do not accept AIF or especially the obsolescent SDII file format), just as AIF files are supported by almost every audio-capable Mac program. Current versions of most interactive applications on both platforms can accept *either* WAV or AIF, however.

  In interactive applications, one very common technique is to create cue points (also known as *markers*) within these audio files. A simple handler script (known as *on exitFrame* in Macromedia's programs, for example) can then tell the interactive program to wait until a specific cue point is reached in the audio file before advancing to the next frame in the sequence. By using cue points or simple time references, graphic events can be triggered as specific locations within the audio are reached during playback. This makes it possible to do things like bringing up titles and bullet points—or any other kind of graphic event—as certain words are spoken in the voice-over. Cue points must be created in separate programs, such as Bias Peak Pro, Macromedia SoundEdit 16 (now discontinued), Steinberg WaveLab, and Sony Sound Forge, usually by the authors themselves, although you may occasionally be asked to assist in this. Contrary to what you might imagine, the Marker memory locations you create in Pro Tools are *not* reflected as cue points within bounced audio files.

❀ **Sound Designer II.** Also known as SDII or SD2, Sound Designer II is a format originally developed by Digidesign for its Sound Tools stereo audio workstations. It was the native file format for early Mac versions of Pro Tools but is not directly supported by Windows versions of Pro Tools—or for any sample rates over 48 kHz on either platform. The header data in the SDII format includes information about region definitions (which, as with AIF and WAV, can also be exported into the parent SDII files from a Pro Tools session if required), loops, and so on. SDII isn't supported by any current interactive programs, and even on Mac versions of Pro Tools should *not* be used as the audio file format for sessions unless compatibility with older versions (such as Pro Tools Free 5.01 on Macintosh) is a specific concern.

❀ **MP3.** MP3, short for MPEG Audio Layer-3, is part of the MPEG compressed audio/video data standards. It uses a very effective perceptual encoding technique to greatly reduce the size of audio data. When you encode an MP3 file (MP3 encoding is an inexpensive add-on purchase for Pro Tools; a 30-day trial version is included with all versions), you choose a *bit rate* for the resulting file. The smaller the bit rate, measured in kbps (kilobits per second, also abbreviated kbit/s), the more digital *artifacts* may be noticeable in the result. As you surely know, MP3 has become extremely popular for exchanging music over the Internet because of the small file sizes it can produce (although, being a lossy compression method, there is always some proportional compromise of audio quality). MP3 is also very popular among interactive developers because it produces better-sounding audio in smaller files (compared, for example, to knocking files down to a 22,050 hertz sampling rate). Be aware, though, that MP3 is not universally supported. For example, some game-authoring programs still don't support MP3 at all. Macromedia's Director program supports MP3 files—so does AuthorWare 7 and their Breeze software for online course development (which also supports various types of streaming audio and video). Macromedia's Flash makes especially frequent use of MP3 files, given its common use in low-bandwidth Internet environments. Longer MP3 files can even be streamed as part of a Flash piece. However, for *looping* sounds (such as musical phrases and button *rollOver* sound effects) you will sometimes find that the MP3 conversion introduces a very small amount of silence at the beginning and end of the waveform that will cause your loop to hiccup in Flash. In these cases, you may be obliged to use WAV or AIF instead and allow audio compression to be applied when the final Flash project is saved out (which will not cause the looping problems).

You can also embed title, author, and copyright information into MP3 files. As with all compressed audio data formats, you will get better results if you previously apply generous amounts of audio gain compression and normalize your original audio in Pro Tools for optimal gain structure. Also, be aware that low-frequency noise, especially pops and breath noises, even at low levels, can cause problems for encoding algorithms that compress audio data (and incidentally, is *especially* problematic for time-expansion and pitch-shifting processes). Be sure to monitor your material with good speakers and listen to it at a reasonably loud volume. If necessary, try dropping a high-pass filter (using one of the DigiRack EQ plug-ins included with Pro Tools, for example) on the offending track.

❋ **AAC.** Short for *Advanced Audio Coding*, AAC, like MP3, was developed by the MPEG Group. It is used by Apple in its iTunes Music Store, the online service for purchasing and downloading music. Version 7 of Apple's QuickTime Pro can also save AAC audio files. AAC is actually part of the MPEG-4 audio spec and uses signal-processing technology from Dolby Laboratories to apply more complex compression algorithms to audio data that not only reduce the data size more efficiently than MP3 but also produce better-sounding results at any comparable data rate—*especially* for music. To put it another way, AAC encoding can obtain the same quality as an MP3 file that would be 30–35 percent bigger.

❋ **RealAudio.** This streaming, compressed audio file format, often used on the Internet, was developed by Real Networks. The RealPlayer free download also supports streaming video files (and is also notorious for invasively altering playback defaults for various media file types to make itself the default player, as well as being very difficult to completely remove from a Windows system afterward). You can reduce audio to various throughputs (with audible compression artifacts at more extreme compression levels) according to requirements. Real Networks' SureStream technology allows you to incorporate several different versions of the audio into a single file link, with the appropriate density being selected for playback according to the bandwidth available to each user when he starts playing that file over the Internet. Again, not all interactive authoring programs support RealAudio, and some require the purchase and/or licensing of a separate plug-in. RealAudio is most effective for spoken-word projects because the level of audio artifacts is rather high at typical Internet bandwidths.

❋ **AU.** Also known as mu-law or Sun/NeXT, this is the audio file equivalent of an audio data compression standard developed for telephony. 16-bit source audio is reduced to 13 bits (thereby discarding the three least significant bits and increasing quantization error) and then encoded into an 8-bit format. AU is an older standard (prior to MP3, for example) and frequently used with an 8K (8,000 Hz) sample rate. As you might imagine, from an audio engineer's perspective, this represents a pretty drastic reduction in sound quality compared to current alternatives for audio data compression. However, AU sound files are still occasionally requested by Internet developers when their methodology or authoring tools specifically require this format. Another program is required to convert your bounced mixes from Pro Tools to this format.

❋ **QuickTime.** This is principally a video format, although audio-only QuickTime files can be created. On Windows computers, QuickTime file names generally must end in the .mov extension to be recognized by QuickTime Player. One reason for using audio-only QuickTime files, for example, would be when an author creating an interactive application in Macromedia's Director wants to use the movieTime property available for all video sprites (even though the QuickTime file you provide is audio-only). This allows other events to be cued to happen at certain positions while the QuickTime file plays, or playback can be initiated from specific positions within the QuickTime file—for example, when the user clicks a button to hear a specific section.

❋ **Tip: Great-Sounding Compressed Audio in QuickTime Movies**

If you have any influence on how the audio tracks you contribute for QuickTime movies will be processed later, encourage the interactive authors you collaborate with to consider choosing the MPEG-4 codec for the soundtrack. (Figure 15.3 shows some of the export options from Apple's QuickTime Pro, which is a $30 upgrade from the free downloadable player for Windows or Mac.) There are many traditional and extreme methods (stereo to mono, reducing sample rate, the hoary old IMA compression algorithm, and others) for drastically reducing the data rate and overall file size for audio tracks in QuickTime movies. However, we think you'll agree that among the current alternatives, MPEG-4 does the least damage to your audio!

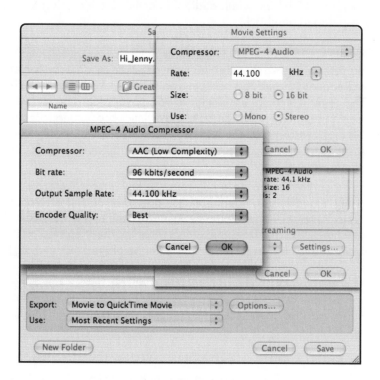

Figure 15.3 Options in the Export QuickTime Movie dialog box of QuickTime Pro include compression of the soundtrack using MPEG-4.

How Audio Is Used in Interactive Media

Terminology varies greatly from one interactive authoring program to another, but there are some common concepts for typical uses of audio. Things that can be clicked on (which may actually look like a button or simply be a linked text or graphic) should make noise when they're clicked, so the user knows that the program has responded. Often, screens within a presentation or game will play longer audio pieces or loop a smaller audio segment in order to conserve disk space and reduce competition for disk access between the graphics and audio. Of course, graphic events are frequently scripted to specific locations within a narration (that is, an audio file you've provided). Loading of graphics, animations, and other data competes with whatever audio files are playing for access to whatever disk the presentation is playing from (for example, a hard disk or CD) and for the computer's resources in general. So you need to be adept at getting good-sounding results at low file sizes. It does you no good to create luxurious, high-bandwidth audio if in actual use it's going to take forever to start playing—or skip during playback!

Voice-Overs

Voice-overs are narrations or phrases other than those spoken by an onscreen character. This is one of the most frequently requested services you will be asked to provide for interactive media projects. The general technique is similar to voice-over recording for worst-case video scenarios—you should use compression and other dynamics processing to ensure solid, consistent audio levels that overcome all the intrinsic obstacles to intelligibility during computer playback (cheap speakers or extremely tiny speakers on laptops and LCD displays, noisy computers, low playback levels, and so on).

Remember that good audio does make a difference in any interactive project. Voices need to be recorded using a quality microphone with a pop filter and in a relatively noise-free environment. In typical interactive development scenarios, the two worst noise offenders are computers with their hard disks and fans, and air conditioning/heating systems in the building. Noisy voice recordings—even for projects that will never be played on anything but computer speakers—will come back to haunt you later on. For this reason, even though it's indispensable to reality-check your audio files on cheap computer speakers before releasing to the client, make *sure* you monitor your audio work on good quality speakers and headphones; you may be surprised to discover that some users have better audio-monitoring systems on their computers than you!

Buttons/Links

There are two basic techniques for using sounds with buttons or links. First, when the user rolls his or her mouse cursor over the "hot" area, a sound file can be triggered (either a single pass or a looping sound that you create). These are called *rollOvers* in Macromedia's Director and Flash programs, Mouseovers in JavaScript, or *focus states* in some other programs. The idea is to attract the user's attention to the fact that something will happen when the screen object is clicked. Often, the rollOver incorporates a graphic effect as well—for example, a glow around the button, a color change, or an animation effect. When creating looping sounds to bounce from Pro Tools, always be sure to check them afterward in another program that can seamlessly loop audio selections. In some situations (we've particularly experienced this problem with Pro Tools Free 5.01 and occasionally with LE/M-Powered versions, and to an even greater degree in MP3 files), there is a possibility that some excess data can appear at the beginning of a bounced audio file—just enough to mess up the seamless loop you were hearing in Pro Tools.

Second, some sort of positive, auditory feedback should occur when the user clicks the button, like a click sound, a whoosh, or whatever cool audio effect you come up with. This is called a *mouseDown* event in Director and Flash (and an onClick event in JavaScript) and might also involve some graphic effect or a sound. Actually, it is more customary for the actions, sounds, and graphic effects on a button to occur on *mouseUp*—that is, when the user *releases* the mouse button—so that users can roll back off the button before releasing the mouse if they really didn't intend to click there.

Generally, we find that background and button sounds (both mouse click or mouseDown sounds and the rollOver sounds) should be lower in level than first-level content, like voice-over narrations, the contents of video files, and so on, by about 10–12 dB (a little over 30 percent of full code—remember that decibels are logarithmic, not linear). Whatever the level you set, be consistent unless there's a specific reason for making an exception. (One example would be if a particular sound still *sounds* louder, even after it has been normalized down to the same reference level as all the others. Compression or more sophisticated gain optimization plug-ins such as Digidesign's Maxim or Waves' L1, L2, and L3 can help even out levels by eliminating transients in the pre-normalization level.) It's very annoying for developers to deal with dozens of button sounds with no consistent levels between them. In short, you can't just normalize everything to full code (100 percent maximum volume) and figure you've done your job.

❄ **Tip: Squash Your Loops**

It can take a while to get the knack of creating smoothly looping musical/ambient backgrounds for interactive applications. Obviously, if you have the luxury of fading up and down from silence at the beginning and end of the loop, it's easy. But when the loop needs to repeat seamlessly (for example, a humming, glowing sound, or a funky groove), here's one trick we sometimes find useful: Apply more extreme amounts of compression (basically, limiting) on the looping selection. This increases the possibility that the end of the loop and the beginning will have similar levels, which is at least one step toward a smoother loop.

Music/Effects Backgrounds

When you create music or ambience backgrounds for scenes in an interactive CD-ROM, DVD-ROM, or Web site, be aware of what *else* will be going on while your audio is playing. If a great deal of animation and graphics interaction is occurring simultaneously, this can severely affect the throughput available for playing your audio. In this situation, if you don't reduce the size of your audio background file (for example, by reducing from stereo to mono, reducing sample rate, or using data compression), it may skip on playback—especially on slower computers, slower CD drives, or when insufficient RAM is available (which affects the program's ability to preload graphics and other content for timely playback).

Another common technique is to loop the audio backgrounds (effects or music). There are pros and cons to this technique. For one thing, it is an art to create musical loops that are both interesting enough and adequately nondescript so as not to become annoying after a couple of repetitions. There are also technical considerations. Obviously, one of the main reasons for using audio loops is to save disk space (or download time): Instead of a full 4–5 minutes of audio for the time a user may spend in each screen, perhaps only 20 seconds worth of looped audio can be equally effective. However, in Macromedia's Director, for example, looped audio files must be entirely loaded to RAM. (Normally, longer audio files stream directly from disk.) Again, depending on what else is going on and what RAM requirements the interactive authors are willing to demand of their potential audience, this may impose serious limitations on the permissible length, number of channels, and resolution for looped background audio files. (OK, here's a more specific hint for Director-based CD-ROMs: For office/consumer computers of the last 4–5 years, an extremely conservative least-common denominator might be stereo 22 kHz loops (22,050 hertz, to be precise) of up to 20–25 seconds, even when there's a healthy amount of graphics and interactivity going on at the same time. However, we certainly push it to 44.1 kHz, perhaps using MPEG-4 or MP3 data compression, when we can get away with it!)

Some programs, like the current versions of 3D GameStudio and Flash, can only loop entire audio files. Director will recognize a loop *within* an AIF file if one exists. (You must create the loop definition with another program, such as Peak, Sound Forge, or WaveLab.) As a music and sound designer, this allows you to include a header or intro that precedes the looping portion of the file. This is useful not only for music but also for looping rollOver sounds for buttons and other objects.

In Flash, interactive authors can specify how many times the audio file should loop and also create Fade In and Fade Out envelopes. If the Flash piece will be playing from a Web site, however, bear in mind that audio file sizes have to be reduced fairly drastically in order to avoid inconveniently long download times. Another pitfall to be aware of is that Flash developers often create loops lasting a certain number of frames and simply stretch your loop audio across that duration. If this is the case, find out what frame rate they're using! If it's 15 frames a second, for example, make sure your loop duration corresponds exactly to a 1/15 of a second subdivision—even if this means applying time compression/expansion afterward in Pro Tools or some other program. Do the math! Otherwise, there will be a distinct hiccup each time this Flash loop repeats.

As you can guess, you would use the Options > Loop Playback option as you perfect a selection to be bounced out for this purpose. If you are using MIDI instruments among the sound sources for a loop (that is, external devices or software synths via an Instrument or Auxiliary Input track), it is preferable to record these to an audio track before defining your looped selection and bouncing it out. (Otherwise, the decays on delay or reverb effects from the end of the looping selection may sustain across the beginning, giving a false impression of how smooth the loop really is.) Don't forget to save your bounced selection as a selection memory location before closing the session, in case you have to bounce it out again! In Chapter 6, "The Edit Window," you will find some specific hints and shortcuts for fine-tuning your selection by nudging.

❄ **Caution: Don't Assume!**

Audio selections that loop smoothly at 44 kHz within Pro Tools may not do so after they've been converted to "22K" (22,050 hertz) or converted to a compressed data format, such as MP3! Also, if subsequent normalization on the bounced loop files increases their gain, it may bring up some clicks at the loop point that were inaudible at the original volume. (One general practice that helps to avoid this is beginning and ending your loops at zero crossings.) Be sure to check your loop files (for example, in Peak, WaveLab, or Sound Forge) before turning them over to your interactive clients and collaborators! (By the way, current versions of Apple's QuickTime Player and Windows Media Player always *pause* slightly between repetitions of any audio file whose playback has been set to loop within these programs and are therefore not useful for this purpose.)

Likewise, when (non-looping) audio files you bounce out from Pro Tools don't necessarily begin or end at zero amplitude crossings, if normalization increases their gain, these non-zero values may also increase enough to produce an audible click. Be sure to *check* your normalized files, especially if their gain has been increased considerably!

❄ **Tip: For the Sake of Good Order…**

Think through the naming conventions you will use *before* starting to bounce out files for interactive projects! For the most part, multimedia authors will import your files via a standard File Open dialog box (as seen in Figure 15.4); so if you establish naming conventions to make files naturally appear in proper order, you greatly reduce the potential for confusion. For example, when you have more than 10 similarly numbered files, use leading zeroes so that file10.AIF doesn't appear between file1.AIF and file2.AIF.

If you're providing both rollOver sound and a mouseUp sound for a button (also known as focus state and click sounds, or MouseOver and OnClick in some programs), make the first part of their file names similar so they are automatically sorted together in the file list: QuitRoll.AIF, QuitClik.AIF, and so on.

If you're a Mac user, be aware that, without a file name extension, Windows programs generally don't know anything about a file's type. So unless you actually put .wav, .aif, .mov, or another appropriate extension on the files you submit to Windows developers, their programs may not even understand that they're audio files!

Sharing Well with Others: About Bandwidth

As you get into higher bit-depths and sample rates, file sizes get much larger. This creates important issues for interactive media. High-resolution audio files naturally occupy more disk space or cause longer download times from the Internet. Most importantly, when an interactive application is running, audio playback shares the computer's (and disk's) throughput

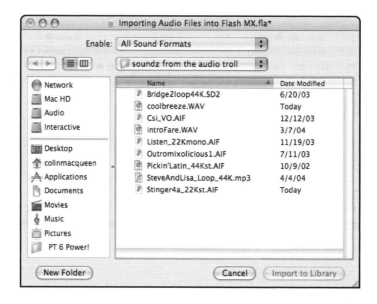

Figure 15.4   Flash, by Macromedia, can import various audio file formats. Later, audio waveforms can be viewed within its timeline while placing graphics and animation events.

capacity with the other graphic files and animation. You may get killer sound quality by maintaining your audio files at higher resolutions, but if they're going to skip during playback as the computer simultaneously reads animation and graphics from the same disk, it defeats the purpose, right? So, you need to be aware of how and when your audio files are going to be used (and especially what else is happening while they're played) and what the target system requirements are for the application. (For example, if the authors must support 12x CD-ROM playback on 266 MHz computers (or slower) with 16 MB of RAM, this imposes much more drastic limitations on audio file sizes than if they require 24x CD-ROMs, Pentium 4, or G4, or even more powerful, current computers.)

Obviously, if your source material isn't stereo, you shouldn't create stereo files for the interactive application. Believe it or not, we see people doing this all the time—for example, using stereo files for simple voice-overs! Even if your source *is* stereo—for example, music—when you find yourself obliged to make drastic reductions in audio file sizes, consider whether it's a greater loss to lose the stereo image versus losing everything above approximately 10 kHz if you drop the sample rate to 22,050 hertz (or losing all frequencies above about 5 kHz, at the even more drastic 11,025 hertz sample rate). Either option reduces the file to half of its former size. Listen to each; trust your ears!

Sample Rate

Audio file size is directly proportional to sample rate (doubling the number of samples per second doubles the file size) and to the number of channels (stereo files are twice the size of mono). As discussed in Chapter 1, under the "Digital Audio Basics" heading, higher sample rates allow the recording/playback of higher audio frequencies. For interactive applications, the two most commonly used sample rates for linear (uncompressed) audio are 22,050 samples per second and 44,100 samples per second (often shortened to "22K" or "44.1K" in digital audio parlance), although 11,025 ("11K") is also used when bandwidth available for audio is limited—for instance, when an application needs to run smoothly on much older computers or on the Internet.

Converting audio down to 22K/16-bit can actually sound OK on typical computer speakers, especially for voice-overs and button sounds (some of which can even be knocked down to 11K if high-frequency components aren't crucial). Remember that, unlike reducing bit-depth (which is discussed in the following section), reducing the sample rate to 22,050 hertz does not make your audio files any noisier; it simply eliminates high-frequency information (above about 10 kHz). One of the tricks employed by standalone file-conversion applications such as Waves Ltd.'s long-discontinued WaveConvert and Autodesk's Cleaner (Mac) or Cleaner XL (Windows) is to augment the apparent brightness of lower sample rate files by adding a slight equalization peak just below the cutoff frequency. Even if you don't have these tools at your disposal, you can approach the same effect. Just use an EQ plug-in on the Master Fader/output pair that is the source for your bounce—for example, using a high-shelf filter to add several decibels of boost from about 9.5 kHz upward before bouncing a file that you will later be converting to 22K.

Bit-Depth

Bit-depth describes the size of the digital word representing each audio sample. The number of bits (binary digits) in the number used to capture the input audio signal's voltage for each sample period determines how many discrete amplitude levels can potentially be represented. Like finer lines on graph paper, the more increments there are available (the more bits per sample), the more accurate the representation—compared to the continuous variations in the original waveform. Early computer multimedia and computer games often used 8-bit audio files (256 possible amplitude levels); the noticeable *quantization error* in 8-bit files gives them their characteristic fizzy sound quality. Incidentally, if the project really does require you to bounce out 8-bit files from Pro Tools, be sure to enable the Use Squeezer check box in the Bounce dialog box. This increases the quality of the resultant 8-bit audio somewhat, especially for voice-overs, by applying some proprietary gain processing prior to the conversion.

16-bit audio files are currently the norm for CD-ROM interactive applications. This is the same bit-depth used on standard audio CDs (which are stereo, of course, using a 44.1 kHz sample rate). 24-bit audio (with sample rates as high as 96 kHz, or even 192 kHz on Pro Tools|HD systems) is the current norm for the most demanding professional audio recordings.

Managing Audio Levels

You will generally want to make sure that the dynamic range in audio files you prepare for computer playback is consistently near the specified maximum level. For example, you will almost always use a compressor plug-in (and/or a limiting plug-in) on all your voice-over narrations to smooth out the variations in its volume. As an added benefit, this generally tends to make voice-overs more intelligible (punching through the general noise of a computer's fan and disk drives, for instance). That way, when you normalize an audio file you've bounced from Pro Tools, the peak level used by the normalization process as the benchmark for adjusting its gain will be closer to the overall levels in the rest of the file (see Figure 15.5). Another more sophisticated technique is to use gain optimization plug-ins, which apply other techniques to produce good-sounding audio at very consistent, in-your-face levels (that is, with very little variation in their dynamic range).

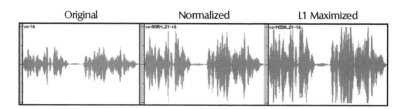

Figure 15.5 The effects of gain optimization: The first waveform was compressed during recording, prior to the Pro Tools input. The second was normalized to 100 percent (its peak level corresponds to "full code"). The third was processed with L1, by Waves. Note that its amplitude is more consistently near the maximum level.

As mentioned in the "Buttons/Links" section earlier in this chapter, normalization is a key tool for preparing audio for use in multimedia. Although any experienced Pro Tools operator keeps a careful eye on Master Fader levels in all original Pro Tools sessions, in the interactive development scenario, you frequently have to maintain extremely consistent levels throughout dozens or even hundreds of similar audio files (because the final user may be switching rapidly between them while navigating from section to section, for example). Despite the common misconception that normalizing always increases peak audio levels to 100% (and to be sure, in some very rudimentary audio programs, this *is* the only option), Pro Tools and most batch-conversion programs for audio files support normalization to any level. For example, if the main voice-over files are at nearly 100%, your entire collection of backing music loops and button effects might be normalized to −6 dB or −10 dB (50.1 or 31.6% of full code, respectively). That way, the different categories of audio files you deliver come into the authoring program "pre-mixed" instead of depending on the interactive author's skill level with audio handling and/or possibly confronting severe practical limitations for such adjustments in the authoring program itself.

For music and ambient backgrounds especially, the RMS mode of the Gain plug-in (under the AudioSuite menu) will be very useful. Adjusting the RMS gain of diverse sounds to the same level tends to more reliably make them appear to be of similar loudness. In contrast, when using the Peak mode of Normalization (or Gain) processing, isolated transients and other variations in the dynamic range of the source audio can still leave you with files that appear to be of unequal loudness, even if their peaks are all carefully adjusted to, say, −10 dB.

Audio Data Compression

Data compression reduces the size of the data representing the original audio waveforms. It is always a lossy process—some of the original information is lost. There are various methods for reducing the size of audio data; some are more effective with certain types of sounds than others (for example, for spoken word versus a music file). Of course, it's important not to confuse data compression with audio *gain* compression (which reduces the dynamic range, or volume variations, within an audio signal).

MP3 encoding (discussed earlier in this chapter) is a compression method for audio data that takes advantage of the characteristics of human hearing. We tend to hear mainly the loudest sound in each of a series of critical bands of frequency, so other sounds within the same band are converted to lower bit-depths with little noticeable deterioration of sound quality. MP3 encoding also compresses redundant data that is present in both channels. (This is, of course, a gross oversimplification of the MP3-encoding method, designed to give you a general idea.) MP3 really does provide spectacular reductions of file size before obvious digital artifacts appear. If an interactive application supports MP3 files for longer audio files (and doesn't require cue points in order to trigger events), this is a *much* more attractive option than reducing sample rate (let alone reducing bit-depth), preserving as much as possible of your original sound quality at a smaller file size. MP3 audio is especially prevalent in Flash-based Internet applications. (SWA, the Shockwave audio format associated with Flash and Director, also generally uses MP3 compression.) By all means, offer to do the MP3 audio encoding yourself rather than leaving it in the hands (and ears) of the designers. They will, however, need to provide you with guidelines for the target bit rate (audio data density, measured in kilobits per second, or kbps) according to their design requirements. Otherwise, it's all too likely that they will use some general compression preset from their host program (see Figure 15.6 for an example) that compresses audio relatively drastically in favor of retaining graphic quality.

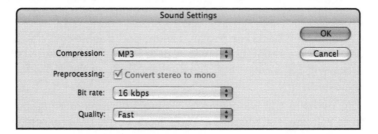

Figure 15.6 Seen here, the program's default settings for audio quality (unless changed by the user) when publishing a Flash presentation from Flash MX Professional. Ouch!

AAC and MPEG-4 audio (in some ways, two aspects of the same thing) are newer, more efficient methods of compressing audio data. By all means, if the target application supports this codec for audio, this is currently one of your best choices. For example, for a comparable quality level, MPEG-4 audio files can be as much as 30 percent smaller than MP3 (which is already far smaller than uncompressed, or linear, audio). QuickTime video files now also support MPEG-4 encoding in their audio tracks (not to be confused with MPEG-4 encoding in their video track, a different matter). In fact, if you own QuickTime Pro, you can convert the audio tracks within QT movies you've bounced from Pro Tools (see the next section) into MPEG-4 (and/or AAC when using QuickTime Pro 7). We think you'll be impressed at the sonic results, considering the huge reduction in file size.

❄ Tip: You Need Some Crappy PC Speakers!

If you create music and sound effects for the average computer, a cheap set of computer speakers is a *necessity!* Your tiny near-field studio monitors are *too* good, as are the speakers on an Apple iMac, for that matter. Always reality-check everything on the mediocre sort of mini-speakers included with the average PC (price limit $20, if you're buying them separately). Obviously, those way-low bass and percussion sounds you spent so much time on might disappear entirely (or come back in some exaggerated and unpleasant form when played on PC speaker setups with a subwoofer). The general prominence of parts within musical arrangements can change (also an issue when your files are compressed to MP3 and similar formats; beware!). Even more importantly, the perceived levels of voice-overs and dialog versus background music or sound effects will change drastically on these setups, compared to any decent studio monitors in your current configuration. Speaking from personal experience, it is not amusing when a bumpin' rave bass line becomes completely inaudible or some apparently innocuous timbre, after suffering the indignity of data compression and playback through somebody's CheezoTech computer speakers, turns into some sort of flatulent buzz.

Creating Audio for Digital Video Files

Sometimes, animations created in other programs will be converted to QuickTime, MPEG, or AVI files in order to facilitate playback within an interactive application. You can add audio from Pro Tools into new copies of existing QuickTime files via the File > Bounce to > QuickTime Movie command:

1. Select File > Import > QuickTime Movie. Locate and double-click the QuickTime file in the resultant File Open dialog box. It will appear in the Movie window of Pro Tools, and a Movie track will be created that shows thumbnails of the individual frames in the QuickTime movie.

2. If there is any audio in that QuickTime movie that you want to bring into your Pro Tools session, do so with the File > Import > Audio from Current Movie command.

3. Using the Movie window (which plays the QuickTime file in real time within Pro Tools) and the Movie track as a guide, create your soundtrack. (If you find that redrawing of the video thumbnails within the Movie track slows down the editing operation, switch it to Blocks track view.)

4. Now you are ready to bounce your audio mixdown directly back into the QuickTime movie, using the File > Bounce to > QuickTime Movie command. This will not affect the video tracks within the file; they're simply cloned into the new copy.

5. In the Bounce dialog box (shown in Figure 15.7), choose mono or stereo for the bounced audio, keeping in mind that stereo requires twice as much throughput for playback in the target program. Consult your interactive authors about data-rate guidelines for this QuickTime file. If your source Pro Tools session is 48 kHz or higher, you may also want to convert the audio to a 44.1 kHz (44,100 samples per second) sample rate. The Squeezer option appears in this dialog if you're forced to convert down to 8-bit audio within the QuickTime file. (You should be prepared to compress audio data, sacrifice stereo, and/or reduce sample rate before resorting to 8-bit audio!) Unlike Pro Tools versions prior to 6.0, you can no longer select lower sample rates of 22,050, 11,025, and so on while bouncing QuickTime movies from Pro Tools. If required, you can do the sample rate conversion in QuickTime Pro (using its File > Export command), Peak Pro, WaveLab, Sound Forge, and other audio-editing programs that support QuickTime video files. As a matter of fact, QuickTime Pro also supports a number of audio-compression codecs (including MPEG-4 and AAC) that can produce excellent-sounding small files that are compatible with most current interactive authoring environments.

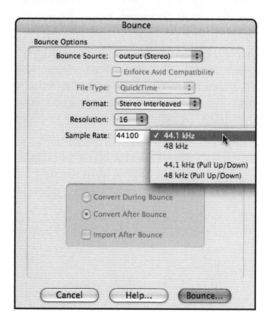

Figure 15.7 The dialog box for bouncing to a QuickTime movie. This is similar to bouncing audio files to disk but incorporates the audio output from Pro Tools as the soundtrack within a cloned copy of the QuickTime movie currently being used in the session.

Summary

How the audio you provide is used within an interactive piece varies widely between programs and from one author to the next. It's crucial to plan things out with the developers before starting to create sounds and bounce out files. Among other things, you must know what file formats and resolutions they require, the bandwidth limitations on the target computer platform (because this determines your options for sample rate or audio data compression, for example), what file-naming conventions are preferred, whether voice-overs and music underscores can be long durations or instead must be broken up scene by scene, whether the host program can loop audio smoothly, and whether Standard MIDI Files (also known as SMF; they have the .mid file name extension) are one of the preferred media types.

Pay special attention to maintaining consistent levels among all the voice-overs, button and background sound effects, videos, and music that you create for an interactive project. It is not especially convenient for interactive authors to make individual volume adjustments as they play back your sound files; in fact, it's usually a pain in the neck. So it's up to you ensure that all the sounds you create in a given category have consistent levels (normalization is an invaluable tool for this), typically with distinct levels for each category of sounds—for example, buttons, background audio, and voice-overs.

The basic concepts explored in this chapter should give you start—at least for asking the right questions when asked to produce audio for interactive projects. Although almost any current Pro Tools system is well equipped for this kind of work, the more first-hand knowledge you have about how the authors will actually use the audio you provide, the better your chances of getting the assignment.

16 Bouncing to Disk, Other File Formats

As you know, a Pro Tools project consists of a session document plus many additional audio files that are referenced by it. If you're mixing a stereo project, for example, you would listen to your audio via two outputs on your audio hardware. In fact, for those who record their mixes in real time to a video master or two-track recorder, this may be all that is required. On the other hand, you may need to create *reduction* mixes from your Pro Tools project, either as a submixing strategy for Pro Tools itself, or especially in order to create audio files for use in other programs. To cite a common example, you will frequently create stereo files from your Pro Tools mix so that you can write an audio CD (using another program) or so that a video editor or multimedia programmer can use your finished mixdown in a project. Pro Tools provides many powerful options for exporting audio files to standard formats; this chapter provides some guidelines for producing files to be used by other programs.

Bounce to Disk

The File > Bounce to > Disk command creates a new audio file containing the result of all the audio regions, automation, processing, and other MIDI/audio or mix data contained in your session (or the current selection). Exactly what you're hearing through the selected Pro Tools output pair (unmuted tracks, real-time Auxiliary Input sources and inserts, plug-in processing, automation and signal routing) will be incorporated into the bounced file. Pro Tools always bounces files to disk in real time, so external sends/returns and inserts can be used, plus any software-based instruments and effects or external sound sources connected to the audio interface (monitored through Auxiliary Inputs).

The Bounce dialog box (shown in Figure 16.1) also allows you to apply file conversion either after the file is bounced or during the bounce. For highest accuracy in the rendering of plug-in automation, Digidesign recommends converting *after* the bounce. As mentioned elsewhere, the original Mac versions of Pro Tools used Sound Designer II as the audio file format for new recordings and imported audio files. Currently, you will usually choose the more widely supported AIF or WAV file formats; in fact, Windows XP versions don't support SDII as a session recording format at all. However, regardless of the audio file type used for the original Pro Tools session, when bouncing files you can always choose some other formats.

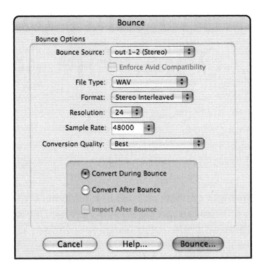

Figure 16.1 The Bounce dialog box for exporting a mix of either the entire session timeline or the currently selected range to a new file.

The Import After Bounce option brings the bounced audio file back into the Region List. It's only available, however, if you've set the bit-depth and sample rate for the bounced file to match that of the current session. Subsequently, if you are bouncing a stereo file in preparation for burning a one-off audio CD (or to provide a stereo mix file for a computer-based video editor), you will often want to normalize this re-imported audio file directly in the Region List (perhaps to 95% or less; never 100%) using the AudioSuite menu command. In this case, you would choose the Overwrite Files option in the Normalize dialog box. (Gain optimization plug-ins are also a valuable—and easily abused—tool for making sure your CDs appear to sound "loud"; see the section titled "Normalization and Gain Optimization" later in this chapter.)

Caution: Don't Get Your (Reverb) Tail Caught in the Door!

When you make a selection in order to bounce a file from Pro Tools, be aware that delay repeats and reverb decay may actually extend beyond the end of the current timeline selection. If the selection only extends to the right end of the last region, the final delay repeats or reverb decay may get abruptly cut off. If you are using these effects in the material to be bounced to disk, be sure to add enough space at the end of your selection for these to fade out naturally.

Likewise, when bouncing out audio files to be looped (for example, backgrounds for a CD-ROM or Web page), remember that as you're listening to looped playback of a selection within Pro Tools, the decay of any reverb and delay effects from the selection's end overlaps the beginning of the next repetition. You may be surprised later to hear a significant drop at the beginning of your bounced loop, because it won't include any overlapping delays from a previous repetition. To work around this problem, *duplicate* the selection to be looped and bounce out two full repetitions. Then, re-import into Pro Tools (or open in another stereo audio-editing program) and trim the new region down to only the smoothly looping second half (whose beginning *will* have the delay repeats from the previous repetition). You can then use the Export Regions as Files command in the local menu of the Region List to save the trimmed audio region out from Pro Tools as a new file for looping.

Converting to Common Audio File Formats

The Bounce dialog box allows you to select AIF files, WAV files, and Macintosh sound resource (SND), audio-only QuickTime files, MP3 files (the separately purchased MP3 Export Option is required; a 30-day trial version is included with Pro Tools), Windows Media files (Windows versions only), or MXF files (if the DigiTranslator option is installed). In Chapter 1, "About Pro Tools," you will find brief descriptions of the characteristics of each of these audio file types. Each may offer additional parameters (especially in the case of MP3) during the process of bouncing to disk from Pro Tools. You can also choose the bounced file's sample rate—for example, reducing to 44.1 kHz from your session's higher sample rate in order to burn a standard audio CD. Lastly, you can change the bit-depth of the resultant file—if your session is 24-bit, for example, you must reduce any bounced files to 16-bits in order to burn audio CDs with the more consumer-oriented programs. If you are ever forced to convert audio to 8-bit (for telephony and some interactive programs—but make sure you've considered all other options first, including data compression or lower sample rates), a check box will appear for the Squeezer option, which obtains better quality during that conversion.

For *surround* mixing, you will often need to deliver files in DTS or AC3 multichannel formats (for DTS and Dolby Digital 5.1 formats, respectively). You'll find additional information about surround mix formats in Chapter 14, "Postproduction and Soundtracks."

❋ **Note: About MXF Files**

The DigiTranslator option (software that is available singly for Pro Tools HD or LE or as part of the DV Toolkit bundle for LE systems; it is not compatible with M-Powered) enables bouncing directly to MXF file format from Pro Tools. The Material eXchange Format has been described as a "wrapper" format that facilitates interchange of audio and video material in the content creation process. The MXF file format is built upon the AAF data model and contains "clips" of "essence" (audio and MPEG/DV video, for example) plus MXF metadata informing applications about duration, required codecs, and other data that can include shot location, production company, crew or talent information, and so on. The MXF standard will become more prevalent, not only in exchange of postproduction content, but also for real-time streaming of content in broadcast networks. MXF is principally described by the SMPTE (Society of Motion Picture and Television Engineers) standard 377M. It was promoted by the Pro-MPEG forum with a coalition of manufacturers and professional organizations including SMPTE, EBU (European Broadcasting Union), and the AAF Association.

> ❋ **Note: Foreign Travel Tips for Mac Users**
>
> Macintosh files generally include a *resource fork*—a section of data within the file header that indicates the file type so that the operating system launches the appropriate program when you double-click a file from the Finder. When you burn a data CD-ROM for Windows users using Toast, choose the Mac OS and PC (Hybrid) CD option. This ensures that, as seen from the ISO (for Windows, Linux, and Unix) partition, the aliases of your audio files will have the Mac resource fork stripped out. (This is also what people mean by *flattening* a QuickTime file, or saving it as "self-contained." A data header that is specific to the Mac operating system is stripped out.) Mac-only (HFS) CDs are problematic for most Windows users—except for the more cosmopolitan ones, who have purchased a utility to read directly from HFS volumes.
>
> Also, Windows generally depends on file names having a three-letter *extension* to distinguish, say, a WAV audio file (with the extension .WAV) from a QuickTime file (with the extension .MOV). When you create files for Windows users (whether you are going to supply them on CD or over the Internet), you should *always* append the appropriate file name extension (for example, .WAV, .AIF, .MOV, .MP3, or .SD2). Indeed, this is not a bad idea even for your own purposes. We also frequently take advantage of the full 31 characters in file names (this is the maximum supported by Mac operating systems prior to 10.4) to add "22K," "stereo," "mono," or the "bounced on" date into our file names. Lastly, if you exchange Pro Tools session files with Windows users, remember that on Windows systems the Pro Tools 7 session document itself must have the .PTF extension. (Pro Tools version 6.xx and earlier use the .PTS extension.)

Bounce to QuickTime Movie

The File menu's Bounce to > QuickTime Movie command bounces the session's audio mix (or currently selected range) in real time into a new, cloned copy of the QuickTime movie file currently being used in this session. As shown in Figure 16.2, most options in the Bounce dialog box opened by this command are identical to the ones you see after selecting the File > Bounce to > Disk command. Within the new copy of the QuickTime file, your mono or stereo audio mix is added to the unchanged video track. Although you can import MPEG movies into Pro Tools, you *cannot* bounce audio back into them (or directly import the audio within them into your session—you must use some other program to extract it first). Windows XP users can use the Windows Movie Maker to add audio tracks bounced out from Pro Tools into videos that are in the WMV (Windows Media Video) format. Interactive authors will often request a lower sample rate for the audio in their QuickTime movies (like 22,050 Hz or even 11,025 Hz) in order to keep file size and throughput requirements to a minimum. If so, this can be done afterward in QuickTime Pro, Peak Pro, WaveLab, and other audio programs. When audio throughput is a concern, however, be sure to ask about using one of the current audio codecs for data compression instead, like MP3 or MPEG-4—these will sound a *lot* better than reducing the sample rate! 48 kHz is the most common sample rate for professional video applications; use this if the QuickTime movie itself is your method for returning a soundtrack to the video editor.

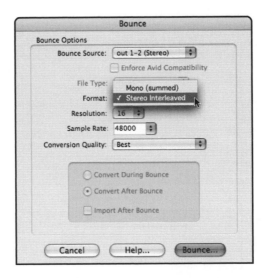

Figure 16.2 The File > Bounce to > QuickTime Movie command opens the dialog box shown here. Your audio mix will be the soundtrack within a new copy of the QuickTime movie being used in the current session.

❋ **Tip: Another Way Out**

There is another method available for exporting audio regions from Pro Tools to other file formats: the Export Regions as Files command, in the pop-up local menu of the Region List. As seen in Figure 16.3, the options here for the output file format are similar to the Bounce dialog box, with the additional option of combining split stereo regions with .L and .R suffixes into a single interleaved stereo file. This command exports selected regions as is, while the Bounce to > Disk command incorporates any real-time plug-in processing or automation applied to the current timeline selection into the bounced file. On the other hand, because the Export Regions as Files command can be used on *multiple* selected regions, it can be useful for batch exporting them out to disk.

Normalization and Gain Optimization

As explained elsewhere in this book (for example, Chapter 8, "Menu Selections: Highlights"), the normalization process locates the peak level within an audio file and, if required, increases the entire file's level to bring that peak to the level you specify (using the Level slider in the Normalize dialog box). If your original peak levels are lower than this setting, levels throughout the rest of the audio file will therefore increase proportionately (including background noise, if any) as the peak levels are increased to the specified value. This ensures that a bounced mix file (and any audio CD that you burn from this file) will peak at exactly the level you want. (We recommend normalizing to −1 dB or as much as −3 dB compared to full code—which is 0 dB—in order to leave some headroom and reduce the potential for digital "overs" occurring as this digital audio is transferred from one digital device or program to

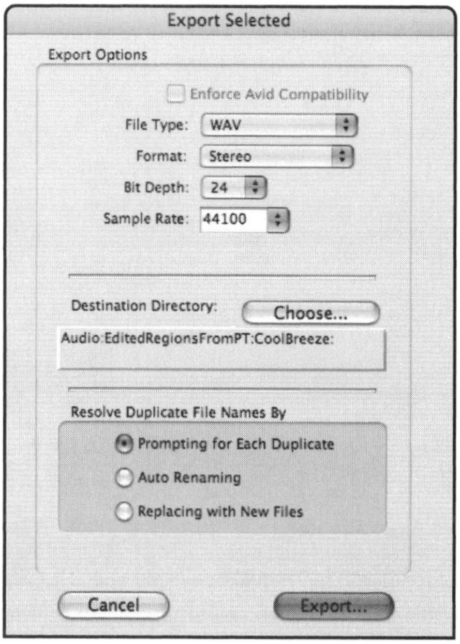

Figure 16.3 This dialog box appears when you select the Export Regions as Files command from the Region List's pop-up menu.

another.) Even more importantly, if you're recording a bounced file from a Pro Tools analog output to another device (such as a video deck), normalization helps you ensure that the reference level you provide actually represents the peak level within your audio program. On the other hand, for commercial CD and DVD mastering, unless you have the experience mastering plug-ins, have a very high-quality metering plug-in, and so on, you would be well-advised to leave this final step to the experts at a good-quality mastering house.

> ### Note: Peak/RMS Mode Selectors in Plug-ins
>
> The selection between RMS and Peak calibration modes for the Normalization function (also now available for the Gain and Signal Generator plug-ins) was introduced with Pro Tools version 7. Normalization in all previous versions worked in Peak mode only. The RMS (Root-Mean-Square) mode normalizes based on the effective *average* level of the current audio selection and is therefore most useful when normalizing to levels significantly less than 100% and especially when trying to match apparent loudness levels in multiple mixes or selections.

Contrary to what you might think, it's also very common to normalize to some *other* value than 0 dB (100 percent full code). In some cases, the normalization process might actually *reduce* the volume of files, where the peaks in the original audio exceeded the specified level for the normalization function. For example, when creating a collection of sound effects for use in multimedia, you might establish −10 dB (about 31.6 percent of full code; remember that decibels are a logarithmic scale) as the maximum level for normalizing all button sounds so that these automatically come into the interactive authoring program at relatively softer levels. Figure 16.4 shows the dialog box for the Normalize function, located under the AudioSuite menu.

Figure 16.4 The AudioSuite dialog box for the normalization function in Pro Tools. You can overwrite the original regions/files or create one/several files for the result. If multiple regions are selected, their overall peak can be the basis, or each can be individually normalized according to its own peak level.

Most importantly, when creating mix files for professional audio CDs and video projects, it can be *undesirable* to normalize to 0 dB (100 percent). There's also a great deal of discrepancy between devices from different manufacturers as to what levels appear on their meters as 0 dB. (Most have some built-in fudge factor, so that occasional peaks won't immediately produce digital distortion; but this varies from one unit to another.) The exact level where the clipping indicator will light up on these units also varies—some of them exactly at 0 dB input level, others only when this level is exceeded, or even just *before* 0 dB is reached! When bouncing out mix files to be used directly for burning one-off audio CDs, this will generally not be an issue, even when normalizing to 0 dB. However, if you're recording a normalized mix output digitally to another device (for example, to a DAT or real-time CD recorder) or especially when creating your own CD duplication master, we recommend you hedge a little on your definition of "full code." For this reason, many professionals always normalize their mixes to some lower value (−1 dB, or even −3dB), just to be on the safe side. Otherwise in certain situations, the digital audio signal you know perfectly well does not exceed 0 dB at any point will actually produce audible clipping when played back or recorded to a target digital audio device with this kind of discrepancy.

The important thing is that you should always *listen* to any audio files you bounce out or normalize! Likewise, if you record in real time to another device, listen to what was recorded, *especially* at the points within the material where you know peak levels occur. The few extra minutes spent on quality control of your output are nothing compared to the years it may take to regain a client's confidence if a problem occurs!

Normalizing Within Pro Tools

You can apply the AudioSuite > Normalize command to any audio track selection in the Edit window or directly to audio regions/files within the Region List; its dialog box is shown in Figure 16.4. Like other AudioSuite functions, you have the choice either to destructively (permanently) overwrite the contents of the currently selected file(s) or to create a new file containing the result of the processing (or several individual files, if more than one region is selected within a track). Bear in mind, of course, that many plug-ins increase the *level* of the audio passing through them—for example, when you boost one of the frequency bands in an EQ or increase the Gain parameter in a compressor. If normalizing regions in a track results in such a gain increase, be sure to check that any subsequent plug-in processing doesn't push their level into clipping. Here's a useful technique to consider: Duplicate your original track using that command in the Track menu and then apply your normalization or gain changes on that copy (without enabling the *overwrite* files option in the AudioSuite window). This makes it really easy to compare the results of your gain processing with the original without resorting to multiple undo operations, Save As techniques, and so on.

Normalizing Bounced Mixes

When you re-import your bounced mix into Pro Tools, the audio file appears in the Region List. If you wish, you can directly normalize any file or region there using the AudioSuite > Normalize command. If you imported a disparate collection of stereo mixes into Pro Tools in order to master an audio CD, for instance, one of your first steps might be to normalize them all in the Region List (always to a peak value *less* than 100 percent in order to leave yourself a little headroom for gain increases as a result of EQ, for instance) before dragging them out onto audio tracks in order to apply EQ, limiting, or whatever other processing is required.

Aside from applying normalization to files within Pro Tools, you can use a variety of other programs to apply normalization and gain optimization, including all the additional audio-editing programs mentioned later in this chapter. Other standalone programs can apply normalization as part of batch file format conversions.

Digidesign Dither Plug-ins

Especially for music applications, you should generally place dithering plug-ins, including the Digidesign Dither plug-in or their more sophisticated POW-r Dither plug-in, on the Master Fader for the output pair that you use to bounce 16-bit stereo mixes (or to record to a lower-resolution device from the digital output of your Pro Tools hardware). Dithering reduces the prominence of quantization error (noise) at low signal levels, such as the end of a long fade, when audio files are reduced to a lower bit-depth (also known as *word length* because it's the length of the binary number used to represent the amplitude value of each audio sample in the file). Dithering should always be the *last* plug-in on the Master Fader for your mix output; get in the habit of placing your dithering plug-in in its last insert slot right from the start. As shown in Figure 16.5, these dithering plug-ins have only two parameters:

> ❊ **Bit Resolution selector.** When bouncing a file, this should be set to the bit-depth of the target bounced file. When recording from digital outputs of Pro Tools, set this to the

resolution of the target device—for example, 20 bits if you're recording digitally to an ADAT XT 20. When recording out from the *analog* outputs of your Pro Tools audio hardware, set it to the maximum resolution of those analog outputs—for example, 18 bits for the original 888 or 882 I/O or the Audiomedia III card, or 20 bits for an 882 | 20 I/O or 1622 I/O. Dithering should *not* be used when recording from *analog* outputs of the 888 | 24 I/O, Mbox, Digi 001/002 (let alone the 96 I/O or 192 I/O), or any of the M-Audio interfaces for M-Powered, because their digital-to-analog converters already offer full 24-bit resolution. (When bouncing to an 8- or 16-bit file or recording digitally to a 16-bit DAT recorder from this hardware configuration, however, it would still be appropriate to insert a dithering plug-in on the Master Fader for that output pair.)

❋ **Noise shaping.** This setting applies specialized filtering to further reduce the prominence of quantization noise in the critical 4 kHz frequency band, where it is most apparent to human hearing. We generally suggest that you enable this setting. Although the older Digidesign Dither offers only on/off for noise shaping, POW-r Dither supports three different types: Type 1, Type 2, and Type 3. Which works better for each project depends on the nature of the material and your personal taste. The *DigiRack Plug-ins Guide* (a PDF included with the program) makes some general observations about this—for example, that Type 1 is flattest and perhaps best suited for solo instrument recordings or voice-overs, while Type 3 has the most pronounced noise shaping and is most suitable for material with a wide stereo image and extended frequency range. But trust your own ears on this and experiment.

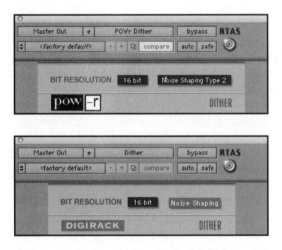

Figure 16.5 The POW-r Dither plug-in, like the older Digidesign Dither plug-in, optimizes the results when audio from ProTools is transferred digitally to a lower-resolution device or recorded analog from an audio interface with a lower maximum bit-depth than the source session. 16-bit dithering is appropriate when recording digitally to a 16-bit DAT or bouncing out a 16-bit file to disk for burning an audio CD.

Other Dithering Options

Various plug-ins for mastering and dynamics processing also include dithering. Master X³ by TC Electronics is a TDM mastering plug-in that includes 3-band dynamics processing, soft-clipping, fine gain adjustments, and dithering. The iZotope Ozone is yet another mastering plug-in, including multiband dynamics and harmonic exciter, parametric EQ, mastering reverb, stereo image control, a loudness maximizer, and dithering. The L3 Ultramaximizer from Waves (included in their Diamond and Platinum bundles) also includes dithering and noise shaping, along with its sophisticated multiband limiting.

Although this chapter is mainly concerned with dithering as an aspect of bouncing out audio files to disk, it is worth mentioning that there are also many excellent professional *hardware* devices available for real-time conversion of digital audio signals from one bit-depth or sample rate to another. These can be handy, especially when exchanging digital audio signals between multiple units in your studio (digital mixers, keyboards, effects, Pro Tools, digital multitracks, and others). For example, TC | Electronics' Finalizer provides these functions, plus other useful mastering features, including limiting, gain optimization, and multiband compression; Figure 16.6 shows the plug-in version of this justly famous piece of studio hardware (upon which the aforementioned Master X³ plug-in is based). The SRC9624 from Lucid Audio is another rackmounted device that provides real-time sample rate and bit-depth conversions. Like the Finalizer, it can also be used as a master audio clock device for the entire studio configuration. The Z-3src from Z-Systems Audio Engineering is yet another external digital audio device that provides real-time conversions for bit-depth and sample rate in a variety of formats.

Sample Rate and Bit-Depth

Regardless of whether your current Pro Tools session document is 16- or 24-bit, the Convert After Bounce dialog box allows you to choose, 24-, 16-, or 8-bit bit-depths for the bounced file. If you're going to burn a standard audio CD, for example, the source files for many CD burning programs must be 16 bits (although some, like WaveLab, Jam, and WaveBurner Pro offer their own dithering options for reducing from 24- to 16-bits during the CD-writing process). 8-bit files have a characteristic fizzy or crunchy quality, much associated with older computer applications, inexpensive video games, and toys. This is due to the high degree of quantization error—a kind of angular, digital distortion of the original waveform due to its true amplitude variations being rounded off to only 256 possible values. If you are ever required to create 8-bit files, by all means make sure that you maximize your gain first by using compression or some other dynamics processing. You should also select the Squeezer option in the Bounce dialog box to optimize conversions to 8-bit resolution, especially if your source is a voice-over file.

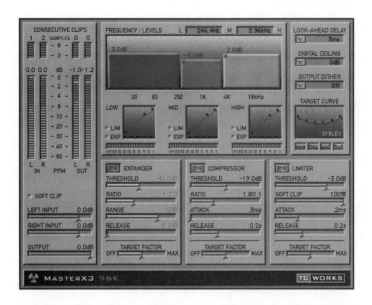

Figure 16.6 The Master X³ plug-in, from TC|Works, is a software version of the company's justly famous Finalizer. It combines several types of processing often used on stereo mixes: 3-band compression, EQ, limiting/expansion/soft clipping, gain adjustment, and dithering.

Compressed File Formats (MP3, AAC, MPEG-4, RealAudio, and So On)

Audio data compression (which should not be confused with *gain* compression of audio signals) is supported for audio tracks within QuickTime movies and is an essential part of how the above-mentioned audio file formats and MPEG (.MPG) video files are structured. QuickTime, WAV, and AIF audio files support the older Adaptive Delta Pulse Code Modulation (ADPCM) method for compressing audio data. ADPCM exists in two mutually incompatible variants:

❋ **IMA-ADPCM.** Standardized by the International Multimedia Association, it typically appears as "IMA 2:1" or "IMA 4:1" in file-conversion dialog boxes. It has been the most prevalent audio data compression format for AIF files over the years.

❋ **MS-ADPCM.** This is Microsoft's take on the format.

ADPCM uses "companding" as well as frequency-selective bit-depth reduction to reduce the size of audio data. Like the more advanced MP3 and RealAudio compression methods, discussed in a moment, this is a *lossy* process; some of the original audio information is lost. For spoken-word recordings in particular, though, you will find that ADPCM-compressed files are actually pretty decent for computer playback. Some music files and loops adapt better to this type of compression than others; it is definitely worth a few minutes of experimentation if the project requires large reductions in audio file size (bearing in mind that you must do this in a program other than Pro Tools). However, unless the authoring or telephony application for which you're bouncing out audio files doesn't support any of the more contemporary methods for audio data compression, you'll find that the sonic results of IMA and MS versions of the older ADPCM codec are decidedly inferior to MP3, MPEG-4/AAC, and other current-generation audio-compression techniques.

Although Pro Tools does support bouncing out MP3-compressed audio format (with the separately purchased MP3 option), it can only create full-linear (uncompressed) audio when you choose QuickTime, (Broadcast) WAV, SDII, and AIF formats for bouncing out audio files. However, other audio-editing and conversion programs (including Autodesk's Cleaner XL program, whose main purpose is data compression for digital video files) *can* create files incorporating ADPCM data compression for audio—a format that may still sometimes be requested for interactive media applications (and discussed in more detail in Chapter 15, "Sound Design for Interactive Media").

Tip: Better-Sounding Results with Compressed Audio Data Formats

As a general rule, the compression algorithms used for audio data don't react well to low-frequency noise. Rumble from traffic, air conditioning, and vocal pops, for example, will occasionally produce audible artifacts in compressed audio (just as they do with time-stretching and pitch-shifting processes), especially when file sizes are more drastically reduced. To avoid ugly surprises, be sure to listen to your material on a good monitoring system at reasonably high volumes before committing. Naturally, a pop-filter is a must for recording voice-overs. Also, if you need to eliminate some of this low-end garbage from recorded audio, try using the Hi-Pass filter provided by the 1-band EQ in Pro Tools; adjust its cutoff frequency as high as possible without compromising vocal timbre. Also, Apple's iTunes incorporates an option for eliminating frequencies below 10 Hz while encoding audio to MP3 format (look ahead to Figure 16.7).

MP3

MP3 is yet another file-format selection in the Bounce dialog box. (For you to be able to bounce to MP3 directly from Pro Tools, you need to purchase the MP3 Export Option after the 30-day trial version included with Pro Tools expires, but it's only about $20.) MP3, short for *MPEG Audio, Layer 3,* is a compressed audio file format that can dramatically decrease file size before severely impairing sound quality. It is, of course, a lossy process—something is lost in the compression process. You also select a bit rate for the resultant file (measured in kilobits per second, kbps), which determines the amount of compression to be applied. (Lower bit rates create smaller files, but with consequently greater deterioration of the sound quality.) When you choose the MP3 file option, a second dialog box allows you to enter title, author, genre, and copyright information. For sending approval mixes (as well as finished audio, such as voice-over recordings for corporate clients, radio spots, and so on) via the Internet, MP3 can be an excellent choice, enabling you to send a reasonably sized file as an attachment to an e-mail (perhaps choosing a bit rate of 128 kbps or less). If you are producing audio files for interactive developers (whose throughput requirements typically have be reduced in order to ensure simultaneous smooth playback alongside the interactive graphic content), be sure to ask if MP3 files are a supported format. (MP3 is the most common audio file format for Macromedia's Flash, for instance.) For your high-quality background effects and especially your music, you will be much happier with the resultant sound from MP3 compression, compared to reducing the sample rate to 22 kHz or converting the file from stereo to mono.

If you *don't* opt for the MP3 option for Pro Tools, you can always bounce out in any linear (noncompressed) audio file format and then perform the MP3 conversion afterward in another program. For example, Apple's iTunes program (included with all new Mac computers, iPods, and also downloadable for Windows, with upgrades available at http://www.apple.com) provides excellent MP3 conversions; Figure 16.7 shows some of the options iTunes provides for this in the advanced preferences for MP3 conversion options. Remember that lower bit rates reduce audio quality. You will generally find it advisable to specify the sample rate and force the number of channels to stereo if appropriate and always enable the 10 Hz high-pass filter for MP3 conversions. Joint Stereo mode is highly recommended for all data rates under 128 kbps. Other professional stereo audio-editing programs such as BIAS' Peak Pro (Mac), Sony's Sound Forge (Windows), and Steinberg's WaveLab (Windows) also provide MP3 conversion, as does Audacity, a freeware program for Mac, Windows, and Linux.

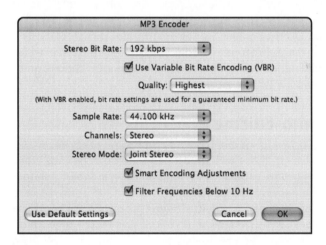

Figure 16.7 iTunes provides conversions from AIF/WAV to MP3 or AAC (a superior audio file format, related to MPEG-4). Seen here, the custom settings dialog box for MP3 conversion.

MPEG-4 and AAC

MPEG-4 is not among the audio file formats you can bounce directly from Pro Tools, but it is well worth knowing about. Ditto AAC, which stands for *Advanced Audio Coding*. These formats were developed by the MPEG Group. They're used by Apple in its online service for downloading music, the iTunes Music Store, and are supported by QuickTime Player, iTunes, and many interactive applications. In these formats, signal-processing technology from Dolby

Laboratories applies more complex compression algorithms that not only reduce data size much more efficiently than MP3 but also produce better-sounding results at any comparable data rate—*especially* for music. To put it another way, AAC encoding can obtain the same quality as an MP3 file that would be 30–35 percent bigger.

> ❄ **Note: About QuickTime Pro 7**
>
> QuickTime Pro 7, in addition to the MPEG-4 export capability already supported in version 6, added the ability to save audio files in AAC format. Other features of interest that were added in this version include real-time video capture from digital video cameras via FireWire and also support for the H.264 video codec (part of the MPEG-4 standard).

RealAudio

RealAudio is also a compressed audio format, achieving often dramatic file-size reductions, but always at some cost in audio quality. It's often used for streaming audio and video continuously over the Internet. As with exporting MP3 files, when creating RealAudio files, you enter title, author, and copyright and copy-protection information. You can select a specific Internet connection speed for your target audience (for example, 56 kilobauds, a.k.a. 56K; ISDN; cable modem; LAN) or select SureStream format, which embeds various resolutions into a RealAudio file, the appropriate stream being selected according to each user's available Internet bandwidth upon accessing the file. You can also choose an optimized codec for the resultant RealAudio file (voice, music, or both).

Additional Audio-Editing Programs

Pro Tools is a hugely powerful audio program, and some users never require anything else for audio editing. However, there will almost certainly be occasions when you will also use other audio-editing programs, especially for manipulating mono and stereo audio files. We've already alluded to the necessity of additional programs for applying certain types of audio data compression. For multimedia sound design, programs that perform batch file format conversion, sample-rate conversion, normalization, and other transformations can obviously be useful—for example, when you're saving out 39 button-click sounds and 39 associated rollOver sounds, and you want to normalize all their peaks to 10 dB down! Likewise, when creating audio files that should loop smoothly in an interactive application, you need to double-check every file in case you have to adjust loop points after conversion to 22 kHz, for instance.

Having a program handy that will edit stereo audio files directly is also very convenient for trimming start and end points of the mix files you've bounced out from Pro Tools, adding cue point markers for interactive authoring, applying effects only available in plug-in formats not available directly in Pro Tools, editing audio directly within video files, and so on. This section mentions only a few of the most common programs that can be useful for professional applications. And just to keep the record straight, Digidesign's venerable Sound Designer program (now discontinued) was the godfather of all modern audio-editing programs!

Peak Pro (Mac)

This comprehensive audio-editing program for Macintosh from BIAS supports a variety of mono, dual mono, and stereo file formats (up to 192 kHz, 32-bit floating-point resolution in the full version) and offers many file conversions (including import from audio CD and MP4/AAC and MP3 encoding from source audio files in other formats), DSP functions, looping tools, direct file transfers with various samplers, batch-file processing, and online playback of audio files while locked to external time code (MTC). Peak also supports several real-time plug-in formats, including VST and Audio Units simultaneously, in five insert slots that can be configured in series or parallel signal-routing configurations. You can also use it to insert markers (called *cue points* in some programs) into mono or stereo audio files, which are used by interactive authoring programs to cue graphic events to locations within an audio file. Peak supports video files in QuickTime, DV, and other formats, so that audio tracks within them can be edited and processed directly without rebouncing. Peak includes creation of Red Book–compliant audio CDs and POW-r Dither for reductions down to 16-bit from higher bit-depth source files. Playlists support using regions from many different source files, either for CD assembly or bouncing out a new audio file, with gain adjustments, crossfades, real-time effects, and other features.

Sound Forge (Windows)

Sound Forge, which is exclusively for Windows, is another full-featured audio-editing program now owned by Sony (originally developed by Sonic Foundry, also the developers of ACID Pro). It supports a variety of mono and stereo file formats at sample rates up to 192 kHz and 32-bit resolution and offers MP3, Windows Media, and RealAudio conversions, import from audio CD, DSP functions including sample-rate conversion, plus support for Direct X audio plug-ins with automation. Audio CDs can be burned directly from Sound Forge in track-at-once mode; it also supports file transfer with samplers, editing of audio soundtracks within video files, and non-destructive playlists of audio regions within a file. Sound Forge also supports video files (so that you can process or edit the soundtracks within them), including DV, 24p, QuickTime, AVI, MPEG, RealMedia, and WMV. Like Peak, Sound Forge supports placement of markers/cue points into files for use by interactive authoring programs and tools for creation of ACIDized loops. There's also a more economical, feature-limited version called Sound Forge Audio Studio. Sound Forge has been around for years and is overwhelmingly the most widespread program for professional editing of stereo and mono files on the Windows platform. *Sound Forge 8 Power!,* available from Thomson Course Technology, provides power tips and loads of useful theory that will help you get the most out of Sound Forge, and there is also an interactive CD-ROM, *Sound Forge CSi Starter,* by Robert Guérin. Visit http://www.courseptr.com's Music Technology section for more information.

WaveLab (Windows)

Yet another professional audio-editing program, WaveLab from Steinberg (developers of Cubase VST), is exclusively for Windows. Like the above-mentioned programs, it supports many audio file formats (including MP3, AIF, WAV, SDII, multichannel surround, and WMA Pro 5.1 and 7.1), numerous DSP effects and file/sample-rate conversions, looping and sampler tools, plus data CD-ROM and audio CD burning (including non-destructive real-time effects processing and a fully compatible implementation of the Red Book audio CD standard for duplication masters, even directly from 24-bit source files with built-in Apogee UV22 dithering), and authoring and extraction tools for DVD-Audio. Playback of audio can be synchronized to external MTC time-code sources, and the Audio-Montage feature offers non-destructive playlist editing with volume/pan automation. WaveLab also features batch processing of multiple files, including plug-in effects.

Audacity (Mac, Windows, Linux)

This is a free, open-source program for Mac OS X, Windows XP, and GNU/Linux. While it doesn't offer many of the advanced features in the aforementioned professional programs, Pro Tools users will find it surprisingly useful. It can be just the thing for trimming the start and end of bounced mix files, normalizing and making other gain adjustments, inverting polarity, changing sample rates for interactive projects, exporting MP3 or Ogg Vorbis audio files, adding end fades, or even trimming file lengths so that they loop smoothly. Audacity can also record directly to hard disk. Not too bad, for free! You can download Audacity at http:// audacity.sourceforge.net.

WaveConvert Pro, Cleaner XL, and So On

These batch file-conversion programs are immensely useful when you have to apply similar audio conversions to large numbers of files. For example, if you bounce out 12 songs for an audio CD, using a batch program to apply normalization to all 12 files at once can save you several minutes of File Open/File Save repetition. Sound designers who must convert the resolution and file format of dozens of button sounds prior to delivery (while at the same time normalizing them all to a single level) will also appreciate the ease and uniformity that is possible when using these programs. Typically, batch-conversion programs also allow you to save presets so that successive batches are converted with the same exact parameters. Because Pro Tools doesn't directly support ADPCM compression (also known as IMA) in the audio it bounces into QuickTime, WAV, or AIF files, these programs can be useful when those compressed audio formats are required (for CD-ROM playback and certain interactive applications, for instance).

WaveConvert Pro, from Waves, Ltd., is a discontinued Mac OS9 application that also works in Classic mode under OS X. It can convert audio files to and from a variety of formats (WAV, SDII, AIF, and QuickTime, including ADPCM audio data-compression formats), additionally applying normalization, gain increase to apply peak limiting, as well as Waves' own plug-ins. Although development ceased on WaveConvert Pro some time ago, it continues to be a useful tool because it supports batch processing while converting sample rates and applying normalization to a specified level, for instance.

The focus of Autodesk Cleaner (Mac) and Cleaner XL (Win) is more toward batch-processing video files (compression, cropping, frame-rate conversion, audio track conversion, and many other video-specific features). However, it also supports a variety of batch audio file–conversion processes, including normalization and file-format conversion that can be performed simultaneously. Audio and video file conversions include QuickTime (including MPEG-4 and AAC), DV, AAC, AIF, WAV, AU, Real, Windows Media video and audio (WMV/WMA) in stereo and multichannel formats, Kinoma (for Palm OS PDAs), plus MPEG 1, 2, 3, and 4. For sound designers who manage large collections of files, Cleaner can be an invaluable tool.

DVD Studio Pro (Mac)

This program from Apple allows Macintosh users to author and record DVDs. It incorporates more professional features than Apple's iDVD program, which is bundled with Macintosh models featuring Apple's SuperDrive (which can record both CD-Rs and DVD-Rs) and is part of the iLife software bundle. DVD Studio Pro encodes video into MPEG-2 for playback in any common video DVD drive and supports subtitling, multiple languages, PAL/NTSC, 4:3 or 16:9 aspect ratios, and other advanced features. As an interesting added bonus for Pro Tools users, it also includes an AC3 (Dolby Digital 5.1) encoder that allows up to eight mono AIF, SDII, WAV, or QuickTime audio file stems to be encoded into a single surround soundtrack, compatible with standard DVD players and surround receivers.

❋ **Tip: Using Pro Tools Region Definitions in Other Digital Audio Programs**

Region Synch is a Windows program developed by Rail Jon Rogut that converts in both directions between the region definitions exported to source audio files from your Pro Tools session and the region definition format used by Sony/Sonic Foundry's Sound Forge program. (In Pro Tools, region definitions are actually contained in the session document, not the source audio files it uses. Use the Export Region Definitions command in the Region List's local menu to embed pointers for regions into the source audio files themselves.) Because Sound Forge regions are also supported by Adobe Audition, n-Track Studio, Samplitude, and Steinberg's WaveLab—not to mention Sony's own Vegas and CD Architect programs—this can be immensely useful. For example, imagine you're bouncing out a long continuous file that will need CD track markers embedded into it (perhaps a live concert or an audiobook CD). Enable the Import After Bounce option, drag the bounce file onto a track, and then use the markers and events already in your session as a guide as you make selections and create a series of contiguous region definitions corresponding to each CD track. Once you export these region definitions back out into the source file and convert them to Sound Forge regions, you can use Sound Forge, CD Architect, or WaveLab to create audio CD tracks based on the region definitions within this single continuous file. You can download a demo version of this very economical Windows program at http://www.railjonrogut.com. From this same site, you can also download the immensely useful—and free—sdTwoWav program for Windows. sdTwoWav performs batch conversion of Sound Designer II files—from older Mac versions of Pro Tools, for example—to Broadcast WAV format.

Audio CD Creation

The requirements for creating one-off audio CDs for clients and promotional use are considerably more informal than when submitting a CD you've recorded as the master to a commercial CD-duplication house. If you're burning your own CDs for evaluation, for playback in standard audio and computer CD drives, or for your band to sell at local gigs, you'll generally have pretty good compatibility using almost any of the current CD-writing programs. Obviously, given the current fashion, you might want to take the time in Pro Tools to normalize your mixes and possibly apply some peak limiting and other gain optimization so that your CD slams as hard as the other discs in everyone's changer. (But don't overdo this; 100 percent full-code levels create digital overs that produce audible distortion on some systems. Relentlessly smashing every mix up against the ceiling of the dynamic range creates a fatiguing listening experience!)

On the other hand, if you plan to submit a CD-R that will directly serve as the duplication master for a commercial release, its format must conform to a set of standards called the "Red Book," which includes ISRC information and other data in the P and Q subcode channels (see the note that follows).

❄ **Note: Red Book Specification for Audio CDs**

Developed jointly by various manufacturers, particularly Sony and Philips, this specification was originally published in a book with a red cover—hence the name "Red Book." CD-DA (audio) discs permit up to 99 stereo tracks of 16-bit digital audio at a sample rate of 44.1 kHz (only!). The internal timing reference on audio CDs is grouped in hours, minutes, seconds, and frames at 75 CD frames per second (not to be confused with SMPTE frames). To be acceptable Red Book masters for commercial duplication, CDs must include all the appropriate subcode data for the P and Q channels, which only certain CD-writing programs provide, in order to create a glass master (used for stamping CD copies) directly from your CD-R. (CD masters can also be submitted on 1630 or DDP tape, which some CD-mastering programs, including Digidesign's long-discontinued MasterList CD for Mac OS9 only, can create.) If your CD-writing program cannot create the additional subcode information, you can still submit your audio on a CD-R, but expect to pay an additional setup fee.

Commercial CDs incorporate eight channels of subcode data (P, Q, R, S, T, U, V, and W), interleaved with audio data at one complete subcode frame for every 588 audio samples. However, audio CD players read only the P and Q channels. The P channel simply indicates when selections are playing. The Q channel incorporates disk and track running times, copy-prohibit and emphasis flags, a TOC (table of contents), error detection, and a UPC catalog code for the entire disk. The Q channel also includes ISRC information (International Standard Recording Code) for each track, identifying the composition's owner, country of origin, serial number, and year of production.

Programs for One-Off Copies

The following are general-purpose CD-writing programs you can use to create audio CDs as well as data CD-ROMs. Some, like Toast, allow you to adjust spacing between CD tracks. Audio CDs created by these programs will generally play just fine in most CD drives. By the way, just to clear up a common misunderstanding: These programs do create Red Book–compatible CDs. They just don't implement *all* the features of the Red Book specification (UPC, ISRC, PQ codes, and so on, as mentioned in the preceding note) that would be required for creating a master directly usable for commercial CD duplication. You might say that CDs created by these programs conform to a *subset* of the features in the Red Book specification.

Toast (Mac)

Manufactured by Roxio (formerly the software subsidiary of Adaptec, but now a division of Sonic Solutions), Toast is by far the most prevalent CD-burning program on the Macintosh platform, not least because versions of it are bundled with so many brands of CD-R drives. MP3 audio CDs, audio CDs, and enhanced audio CDs (which might include photos or videos in addition to the audio) can be created from most source audio file formats, and you can adjust the spacing between CD tracks (including zero spacing in disk-at-once mode). Although Toast doesn't implement the full Red Book standard required for direct commercial CD duplication, it is frequently bundled with Jam, which does. (Jam is discussed in more detail in a moment.) CD-Text information can be included on audio CDs created with Toast. This information (stored in the R and W subcode channels of the lead-in area on the audio CD) allows compatible players to display data such as disk title, artist name, and track titles while playing your CD. Toast supports creation of data CD-ROMs (including Mac/Win hybrid format) and data DVDs, as well as MP3 CDs, video CDs, Super Video CDs, and video DVDs. Note that Toast 7 is the current version, and Toast 6 Titanium is the minimum required version for Mac OS 10.4 ("Tiger") and higher.

iTunes (Mac)

Apple bundles this user-friendly audio CD–writing program with all Macintosh models featuring a recordable CD drive (or recordable DVD/CD drive). There is also a Windows version, which is a free download with the QuickTime player. iTunes accommodates a variety of source file formats, including AIF, WAV, and MP3. It can rip tracks from audio CDs to MP3 or AAC format (that is, it simultaneously extracts the CD audio data and applies a specified level of compression while creating one of these file types on your disk) or to AIF and WAV files with no data compression. Like Toast, the Mac version of iTunes also supports burning MP3 CDs. It includes a 10-band equalizer that can be non-destructively applied during the CD-burning process, a feature to create crossfades between CD tracks, and rudimentary tools for fine-tuning individual track levels. iTunes also provides excellent options for MP3 or AAC conversion from your source AIF and WAV mixes bounced out from Pro Tools, if you opt not to purchase the MP3 option from Digidesign (which enables direct creation of MP3-encoded files while bouncing to disk).

Easy Media Creator (Windows)

Also manufactured by Roxio, Easy Media Creator (and its predecessor, Easy CD Creator) is a prevalent CD-burning program for Windows and is included with many CD-R drives. It supports both recordable CDs and DVDs. Like Toast, it supports burning data CD-ROMs and audio CDs from a variety of different source audio file formats (including MP3) and a Sound-Stream normalizer feature to ensure consistent levels on audio tracks from multiple sources.

It supports creating Red Book–compliant ISRC codes, UPC codes, and PQ subcode channel information on audio CDs. The Platinum version allows you to adjust spacing between audio tracks.

Sound Forge (Windows)

As mentioned earlier in this chapter in the section "Additional Audio-Editing Programs," this robust, industry-standard audio-editing program from Sony (originally developed by Sonic Foundry) also includes features for *track-at-once* writing of audio CDs; support of MP3, WMA, and many other audio/video file formats; and support of source sample rates up to 192 kHz and 64-point floating point resolution. Sound Forge offers loop tuning and ACIDized loop-creation tools, automatable real-time effects including multiband compression, and DirectX plug-in support.

Programs for Creating Duplication Masters for Commercial CDs

As we've said, additional information must be incorporated into a CD master for commercial duplication. Not surprisingly, a CD-writing program included with your CD-R drive generally isn't going to support the extra features required to create a Red Book–compliant CD master. However, it *will* produce audio CDs that perform acceptably in most CD players or that a commercial CD-duplication house can use as the basis for creating a CD-duplication master after adding the appropriate data in the Q subcode channel (for a fee). The programs discussed here, however, incorporate the necessary features for professional CD duplication (from a CD-R or in some cases from a tape). As with mastering and gain optimization of your stereo mixes for release (discussed in a tip near the end of this chapter), if you aren't extremely familiar with all the requirements for assembling a duplication-ready CD master and any particular requirements of your duplication house, it is a good investment to pay an expert to do this properly. In any case, you'll need one of these programs if you need to create indexes within CD tracks or create CD track numbers *within* a single audio file (in the middle of a crossfade or applause in a live performance, for example).

Jam (Mac)

Manufactured by Roxio, the software subsidiary of Sonic Solutions (who also offer Toast and Easy Media Creator), Jam offers the necessary features to create fully Red Book–compatible audio CD masters on CD-R from a wide variety of source audio file formats, even at sample rates up to 192 kHz and with 64-bit resolution. Jam supports crossfades and non-silent pauses between tracks, up to 50 index points within each CD track, individual gain adjustment of each CD track, CD-Text, ISRC and other information in the Q subcode channel, and many other features. Like Digidesign's long-discontinued MasterList CD program, Jam allows importing regions from within audio files in the older Sound Designer II format. (Remember that the Region List menu in Pro Tools allows you to export audio region definitions into their parent sound files.) Jam offers conversion to a wide variety of audio file formats, including MP3 and AAC (MP4). Note that Roxio occasionally offers Jam bundled with Toast, its more general-purpose CD-creation program. BIAS' Peak Express audio-editing program will be offered as part of a bundle including Toast and Jam. Before purchasing any of these programs, be sure to check the Roxio and BIAS Inc. Web sites for their current offerings (http://www.roxio.com and http://www.bias-inc.com).

❊ **Note: About Digidesign's MasterList CD**

Now discontinued, this pioneering program allowed creation of Red Book–compliant audio CD masters on Macintosh computers with all the appropriate ISRC information (copyright owner, serial number, year of production) in the Q subcode channel, UPC code, and creation of 1630 and DDP tapes for CD mastering. Other supported features included crossfades and non-silent pauses between tracks, up to 50 index points within each track, individual track gain adjustment, and direct import of regions within Sound Designer II files (including Pro Tools audio regions exported into parent sound files from the Region List). Unlike some of the other programs listed, MasterList CD supported only CD-R drives attached to the Macintosh's SCSI card (not ATA, USB, or FireWire, for example) and also required a SCSI hard disk. The last version of MasterList CD released by Digidesign was 2.4, supporting only Mac OS 9.2.2 or lower— not Mac OS X, even in Classic mode! We mention it here not only because of its historical significance, but also to avoid any potential confusion, because new users will encounter many references to MasterList CD in older books and training materials.

Sony CD Architect (Windows)

This professional CD-creation program from Sony accepts source audio files at a sample rate of up to 192 kHz and 32-bit resolution, with high-quality resampling and dithering to standard CD audio. Tools for placement of CD track markers and indexes are provided, along with the requisite information for the P and Q subcode channels, UPC/EAN codes, and many other features required when creating master CDs for commercial duplication. Normalization and non-destructive gain envelopes can be applied to any audio event. More than 20 DirectX plug-ins are also included with the program and can be applied non-destructively during the CD-burning process. A variety of crossfade shapes can be created between adjacent audio regions and across CD track markers between them. CD Architect supports Sound Forge regions directly, and you can open audio events from CD Architect into Sound Forge for other types of editing.

WaveLab (Windows)

As mentioned previously, this audio-editing program from Steinberg (manufacturers of the Cubase audio/MIDI sequencer, Nuendo, and other MIDI-related software and interfaces) includes features for creating audio CDs and data CD-ROMs. Like the CD-writing programs already discussed, WaveLab can also create all the ISRC and other information in the Q subcode channel, create track numbers and indexes within a single audio file, and so on in order to produce a CD-R master for direct commercial duplication. Non-destructive, real-time VST plug-ins, multiband compression, parametric EQ, stereo expansion, and other audio processing can be applied during the CD-creation process, as well as UV22 HR dithering (the current, "high-resolution" form of Apogee's popular UV22 dithering algorithm used in many audio programs and hardware units). WaveLab also supports source audio at resolutions as high as 192 kHz, 32-bit floating point, in many different file formats. Audio-Montage playlist features include crossfades between separate files and up to 10 simultaneous real-time effects, all of which can be applied non-destructively in real time.

Nero (Windows)

This suite of software from Ahead Systems (http://www.nero.com) includes powerful tools for creating audio CDs, DVDs, CD video, and data CDs. Features for audio CD creation include crossfades, CD-Text, copyright information and UPC/EAN codes, copy-prohibit flags, index creation within CD tracks, CD track IDs within a continuous audio file, MP3 CD creation, mixed-mode and CD Extra formats, non-destructive normalization while burning CDs, and disk-at-once or track-at-once writing modes.

Tip: Leaving Mastering to the "Masters"

When we talk here about creating a CD master for duplication, we mean the physical process of organizing the data—all the IRSC and UPC/EAN codes, indexes, pre-gaps, copy-protection flags, and other data required for a commercial release. This is complicated enough; if you're not completely familiar with all this stuff, do *not* try this at home! Nowadays, most CD-duplication houses can handle this for a reasonable fee (but be sure to thoroughly check the test CD they provide, programming various track orders in your player, skipping between tracks, and other reality tests).

On the other hand, *mastering* is an entirely different process, where dynamics processing, EQ, and other processes are applied to finished stereo mixes to make them sound better, with more uniform quality. Experienced mastering engineers know how to optimize for CD, vinyl, radio, and other playback scenarios. They also occasionally work miracles, applying corrective measures for any deficiencies in your original mixes or simply making a disparate collection of tracks sound more uniform.

When submitting audio files of a mix to a mastering engineer, provide these at the maximum resolution possible, without any intrusive processing, sample rate, or bit-depth conversions on your part. Bounce the mix out at your original session's sample rate, with no dithering plug-ins, and at 24-bit resolution. Don't alter the stereo mix with dynamics processors or normalize it, either. It's better to leave this to the experts (and perhaps provide a second CD of your own squashed mixes purely as a reference if you feel this will help communicate what you're looking for), not least because they should have much more sophisticated tools (and expertise) at their disposal. If you instead supply a 16-bit audio CD, 100 percent normalized or with its dynamic range already stomped on in some other way, this severely limits a mastering engineer's flexibility. Providing such a CD as a reference only may be useful for indicating the approximate sound you're after, but provide your raw, high-resolution mixes as audio files within folders on a separate data CD-R or DVD-R.

Broadcast WAV files (files with the .WAV or .BWV extension) are becoming the preferred submission format, in part because of AES/EBU recommendations that record companies stipulate this as the delivery format for audio projects (not only mixes, but source audio tracks in the project). Nevertheless, be sure to check with your mastering engineer first, so that you bounce your Pro Tools project to the format he or she prefers.

Summary

Hopefully we've provided some context for sending your audio from Pro Tools out into the world. As always, when you're converting audio to a lower bit-depth (with an inferior signal/error ratio) or to a compressed audio data format, be sure to manage your gain structure and mix output levels to get the best-possible dynamic range and as few artifacts as possible. When collaborating with others, always ask what file format they prefer and determine all the file formats that their system or program supports; you might be able to make a useful suggestion!

Remember: Using a higher sampling rate retains higher frequencies, while higher bit-depths (24-bit samples, rather than 16-bit or 8-bit) mean less quantization error (a kind of distortion, or noise, compared to the original) in the resulting file.

17 } Pro Tools Power: The Next Step

The learning process never stops. Not only is Pro Tools constantly evolving with new software features, new audio hardware, and so on, requiring you to learn how to use them, but your own ambitions will no doubt increase as you gain more experience with audio production (and Pro Tools features)—which means you'll need to learn how to accomplish these more advanced goals!

This chapter briefly reviews typical upgrade paths for the current generation of Pro Tools hardware. (Appendix B, "Add-ons, Extensions, and Cool Stuff for Your Rig," goes into more detail about other peripheral equipment and accessories for Pro Tools systems.) In addition, we make some basic suggestions here for deepening your knowledge and enhancing your career possibilities.

Upgrade Path: For Your System

One of the things that makes a digital audio workstation like Pro Tools so attractive is that you can upgrade it as your requirements and budget dictate. You can incrementally increase the power of your production system: bigger and faster hard disks, more plug-ins, more RAM, additional or higher-resolution audio hardware, more sophisticated synchronization and MIDI connections, a faster computer.

Naturally, because Pro Tools is largely software based, the creative environment itself evolves over time. In contrast, your options for expanding and updating the system configuration are more limited with most hardware-based alternatives for editing audio and MIDI. Here are just a few features added through software-only upgrades for supported Pro Tools configurations in the last couple of years:

* The number of sends you can use increases from 5 to 10 (Pro Tools 7).
* The number of busses you can use in LE and M-Powered versions increases from 16 to 32 (Pro Tools 7).
* The maximum channels of hardware I/O available on HD systems increases to 160 (Pro Tools 7).

* Instrument tracks, similar to a MIDI track with an associated Aux In, are introduced (Pro Tools 7).

* You can use RTAS plug-ins on *any* track type except MIDI on HD systems (Pro Tools 7).

* There is now more comprehensive support of multi-CPU computers, balancing RTAS processing load across all available processors (Pro Tools 7).

* You can group regions, even on multiple, non-adjacent tracks of different types (Pro Tools 7).

* You can use region looping to create aliases for repetitions of original audio or MIDI regions (Pro Tools 7).

* When dragging multiple regions into track display area, the Drop Order feature lets you select Top to Bottom (as in previous versions) or Left to Right within a single track (Pro Tools 7).

* You can use Real-Time MIDI Properties for real-time, non-destructive quantize, transpose, duration/velocity changes, and so on with MIDI tracks (Pro Tools 7).

* You can use sample-based (tempo-independent) MIDI tracks (Pro Tools 7).

* Mirrored MIDI Editing is available—edits to a MIDI region affect all other identically named MIDI regions (Pro Tools 7).

* You can drag ACID and ReCycle (REX) files from Workspace browser into Region List, with all their time slices, and adjust them to session tempo (Pro Tools 7).

* You can drag and drop Standard MIDI Files from Workspace browser into either Region List or Track List (Pro Tools 7).

* There is now Windows XP support for dragging tracks from Red Book audio CDs in the Workspace browser (Pro Tools 7).

* The number of Marker/Selection memory locations increases from 200 to 999 (Pro Tools 7).

* The EQIII DigiRack plug-in is available (free download for versions 6.7 and higher).

* You can use Automatic Delay Compensation on Pro Tools|HD systems for adjusting time alignment of all tracks to compensate for all latencies due to virtual mixer routing or plug-in processing.

* You can use syncing delays and other plug-ins to the Pro Tools tempo via Direct MIDI subscription to Beat Clock.

* There are hierarchical plug-in menus (by category or by manufacturer).

* There are Transport buttons in the Edit window toolbar.

* You can specify color-coding for tracks and regions (as well as region groups in Pro Tools 7).

* Step-entry for MIDI is available.

* Multiple outputs from software instrument plug-ins are available.

* Support for the WMA9 audio format in Windows versions is available.

Inevitably, as your use of Pro Tools becomes more sophisticated and you tackle more ambitious projects, you make more demands on your system. The options for expanding the Pro Tools hardware itself depend on which system you're using. Some versions, such as Pro Tools|HD (as well as the older Pro Tools 24|Mix hardware and its predecessor Pro Tools III, which do not support Pro Tools 7), are modular by nature. Mbox 2/Mbox and the Digi 002/002 Rack, on the other hand, are more fixed configurations, as are the M-Audio interfaces and now-discontinued Digi 001 and ToolBox systems (although you can still enhance most of these systems via external preamps equipped with Lightpipe or S/PDIF digital outputs, as discussed in this chapter). In addition to the audio hardware itself, with the rapid advance of computer technology, there will always be more powerful platforms available for Pro Tools (but be sure to do your homework before making any upgrade; the program will *not* necessarily be compatible with brand-new motherboard chipsets, computer models, and other hardware without requiring an upgrade). Be sure to check the compatibility documents in the Support area of Digidesign's Web site before proceeding. Also, the Digidesign User Conference (DUC) is an excellent place to learn about other users' real-world experiences—you may even find parts lists and suppliers for putting together your own custom rig. In particular, with the emergence of more-sophisticated plug-ins, greater track counts, and audio resolutions, and especially software-based synthesis and sampling, you may be constantly craving more memory, storage, and processing power from your host CPU. Let's review some of the typical options (and a few potential pitfalls) for expanding your rig here.

Pro Tools Hardware Upgrades

With expandable audio hardware for Pro Tools (like Pro Tools|HD or the now-discontinued Pro Tools 24|Mix family), you have the option of expanding your audio I/O (input/output) capacity by adding a second interface. Several of the audio interfaces for Pro Tools|HD systems include vacant bays where you can install an expansion card for more analog or digital I/O, plus a Legacy Peripheral port for connecting older Digidesign audio interfaces from the 24|Mix family, such as the 888|24 I/O, 882|20 I/O, 1622 I/O, or 24-bit ADAT Bridge I/O.

You can increase the DSP capacity of these Pro Tools systems by adding extra PCI cards from Digidesign (one or more HD Accel cards on Pro Tools|HD—either within the computer itself or in a PCI expansion chassis available from Digidesign and others). Among other things, this allows you to use more simultaneous plug-ins. A larger number of simultaneous tracks, sends, inserts, and so on may also be supported, if your previous DSP capacity was limiting this in larger sessions.

Each additional HD Accel card on a Pro Tools|HD system also increases the number of hardware I/O channels your system can support by connecting more audio interfaces.

Pro Tools|HD systems already support daisy-chaining two 96 I/O, 96i I/O, 192 Digital I/O, or 192 I/O interfaces on the HD Core card (the only PCI card in core HD|1 configurations). Each HD Accel card you add supports 32 more potential channels of I/O (the Pro Tools HD|2 configuration has one HD Accel card; the HD|3 has two). Therefore, even on the entry-level Pro Tools HD | 1 system, adding a second audio interface to increase your physical I/O for audio from 16 to 32 channels doesn't require any additional cards.

The fact that HD systems support a greater number of interfaces and audio I/O channels on each PCI card than the older 24 | Mix hardware is especially important, because expanded configurations with previous generations of TDM hardware could quickly exceed the available number of card slots in most computers. For example, current Macintosh G5 and G4 models (like the G3 and predecessors in the PowerMac series) have only three or four PCI slots. On a Pro Tools 24 | Mix system, with one Mix Core card, a SCSI card (very specific models were recommended for most TDM configurations, especially at higher resolutions and track counts), and a single Mix Farm card, three PCI slots were already filled. On a three-slot computer, not only were you prevented from installing a second Mix Farm card (and you can never have too much DSP power!), but more importantly, you had nowhere to put a second graphics card if required for running two monitors (which is always *highly* recommended for serious Pro Tools work).

For expanded configurations with many audio cards, you can add an external PCI expansion chassis to the computer (connected via a single PCI card in one of its internal slots), such as the rackmountable seven-slot, 64-bit Expansion Chassis from Digidesign (not compatible with PCIe cards; see the Caution following this paragraph). (Be sure to carefully check the Compatibility section of the Digidesign Web site; only a very limited number of expansion chassis are certified for use with Pro Tools, and some of these cannot be used with certain computer models!) With Pro Tools | HD and a powerful computer, however, the greater processing power of each Pro Tools card (compared to previous 24 | Mix hardware) means that greater track counts and higher audio resolutions are supported even when only the available PCI slots within the computer are used.

> ❄ **Caution: PCI versus PCI Express**
>
> Macintosh G5 computers introduced at the end of 2005 feature a new card slot specification known as PCI Express, or PCIe (which will also available on forthcoming Windows computers). Because the existing PCI cards for Pro Tools | HD are incompatible with this newer expansion slot format, Digidesign has introduced PCIe-compatible Pro Tools | HD configurations. (The conventional PCI/PCI-X configurations will continue to be available for users of other computers, since the PCIe cards are not backwardly compatible.) Digidesign is also offering the Expansion | HD chassis, a six-slot external PCI expansion chassis, connected via a separately purchased PCIe or conventional PCI/PCI-X card, installed in the appropriate slot in the host computer (Mac, and eventually Windows). This allows you to use existing PCI/PCI-X cards for Pro Tools | HD with a host computer that only offers PCIe expansion slots.

Computer Hardware and Operating System Upgrades

The biggest item here is a second monitor. If you're working long hours, especially with larger Pro Tools sessions, this makes a huge difference in your productivity. You can view the Mix and Edit windows on separate monitors, and you can keep more Plug-in and Output windows anchored and visible, which really speeds up work. Many currently available graphics cards supporting dual monitors provide excellent results with Pro Tools. On most G5 and G4 Macintosh models, only an Apple DVI-to-ADC adapter is generally required to connect a second monitor.

Adding more RAM to your computer can also improve the operation of Pro Tools. For most current systems, 640 MB should be considered the rock-bottom minimum for any practical purposes, with more than 1 GB recommended in most cases (and in fact required on most PC motherboards, where matching pairs of RAM modules are the norm and you would accordingly jump directly to 1 GB anyway).

Certainly, the faster your disks, the more channels of audio can play back reliably. (7,200 RPM is recommended for all but the smallest configurations; 10,000 RPM is also worth a look.) If you ever approach 90 percent disk capacity, you're asking for trouble! Mbox 2, Mbox, and Digi 002 users (as well as those who use the older Digi 001 and Pro Tools Free 5.01) will eventually want to expand beyond the internal drive supplied with their computer, especially to support higher track counts and/or higher sample rates or bit-depths. Aside from installing an additional ATA drive internally, faster FireWire and SATA drives (as well as SCSI, of course) are a better option for these users because of their superior performance with Pro Tools in particular—as long as you confirm that any drive you buy meets the requirements posted on Digidesign's Web site. Many don't, and aside from general performance issues can actually cause error messages in the program!

Before laying out your hard-earned cash to upgrade to any new operating-system release for your computer, make absolutely *sure* it is compatible with your current Pro Tools software. The same applies for new motherboard chipsets and computer models. Digidesign maintains current Compatibility documents in the Support area of their Web site (http://www.digidesign.com).

Audio production is a demanding real-time application, and you will find that Digidesign is fairly conservative about certifying new operating systems and hardware. If the contacts at your Digidesign dealer are technically qualified regarding computer hardware and operating system issues, seek their advice. Otherwise, contact Digidesign Sales and Support via e-mail. You will also find the latest skinny in the Digidesign User Conference at http://duc.digidesign.com (keep in mind that, as with all online forums, posts here can range from helpful and technically impeccable to histrionic). In short, if your Pro Tools system is currently working, don't be stampeded into the latest operating system upgrade until you've done adequate research. Otherwise, if you must experiment on yourself, don't beat up on Digidesign if you experience unpleasant side effects!

Pro Tools Software Upgrades

Digidesign regularly releases new versions of the Pro Tools software. As a registered user, you are entitled to these upgrades (at a reduced fee for major version upgrades, and usually free for downloadable minor ones). Be sure to verify that each software upgrade is appropriate for your hardware, though. Sometimes an incremental version exists simply to support new hardware and may not be required by—or even compatible with—your current configuration!

As is common with other software manufacturers, Digidesign offers a series of maintenance upgrades between major upgrades of the Pro Tools software. Again, some of these exist merely to support new hardware options. Be sure to check out all the Read Me information on Digidesign's site (and the Compatibility documents, of course) before downloading and installing any upgrade. And *be sure to register your Pro Tools system* so that you are informed of important upgrades and new products; likewise, let them know if you change your address (you can do this on the Digidesign Web site). From our experience, Digidesign has been very good about not selling user lists to junk mailers. At most, you'll occasionally receive announcements directly from Digi, along with the sporadic invitation to a road show or product presentation in your area.

❄ **Tip: Second-Hand Pro Tools Systems**

If you've purchased a second-hand Pro Tools system, you can still register with Digidesign, which entitles you to service and future upgrades. (The PDF document for the Transfer of Ownership form is available in the Customer Service section of Digidesign's Web site, and must be printed and signed by both you *and* the seller! Also, for your own records, make sure to get the original sales receipt for any used Pro Tools system you purchase, if possible.

Pro Tools Peripherals

Upgrading from a simple MIDI interface to a multiport model or adding sophisticated SMPTE synchronization (with reference sync, if your hardware supports it) are typical upgrade paths for many users. An external control surface is another (see Appendix B for information about these). Rackmountable high-performance hard drives from Avid, Glyph, and others are also an attractive option; unlike most hard drives, their performance level specifically with Pro Tools is guaranteed, and they're also designed to be relatively *quiet*. This brings up another common Pro Tools peripheral: an acoustical housing of some sort to isolate the fan noise from the computer and hard drives from your critical control room listening environment. (USB and VGA extenders are an attractive option, allowing you to move the computer and drives out of the control room altogether; see Appendix B.) If working in a home-project studio, a well-ventilated closet may be a good solution.

Audio Hardware

Certainly, there are a lot of great microphones and microphone preamps that you can add to your system—the sky's the limit! As mentioned various times in this book, Digidesign's PRE, an eight-channel mic preamp, is attractive not only because its microphone preamps sound great, but also because you can control its settings directly from the Pro Tools session via MIDI and the I/O Setup dialog box on HD systems. Each time you reopen a session document, all previous settings on the PRE are restored. This is a huge help for maintaining consistency in your levels and overall sound throughout multiple songs, recording dates, and overdub sessions.

Combining a multichannel Pro Tools system with external reverbs, compressors, and other effects is simple using sends or hardware I/O inserts (routed through the inputs/outputs of your audio interface). As a Pro Tools user, though, you're more likely to build up the majority of your arsenal for effects processing via plug-ins, rather than stacking up boxes in your studio racks. As you can guess by this point in the book, that's exactly what we would suggest!

If there are multiple digital audio devices in your studio, you might also investigate the master audio clock (also known as *word clock* or *word sync*) generators that are available. If all your Pro Tools audio hardware, multitrack digital recorders, DAT recorders, digital effects and patchbays, and so on are slaved to a single sample clock source, this can make life much simpler, facilitating digital transfers and phase-accurate playback. Just as when using a synchronization peripheral to slave your audio hardware to a house sync (black burst) video signal, having the playback speed of all your playback and recording devices precisely slaved together at the hardware level reduces lock-up times and facilitates maintaining sync over extended periods of time. Extremely high-quality clock sources can also audibly improve sonic quality—especially on older Mix|24 or Digi 001 systems, as well as most of the current hardware options for Pro Tools LE and M-Powered versions.

Digidesign also periodically offers hardware upgrades at a reduced price for existing users, especially when introducing new hardware. The Hardware Exchanges section of the Digidesign Web site lists offers currently in effect. Your decision will depend mainly on many factors, including money, money, and money. Other issues include whether you mostly require more inputs and outputs, a superior recording resolution, or a different *type* of I/O (multitrack digital formats such as Lightpipe or TDIF, for example). Also, be sure to consider what *other* equipment upgrades may be occasioned by your Pro Tools upgrade. (For example, your existing hard disk setup for an older Pro Tools 24|Mix configuration with a single eight-channel interface may be entirely inadequate for 16 simultaneous channels of 24-bit, 96 kHz audio with an HD or Digi 002 system.)

If the most pressing need is for a greater number of simultaneous audio inputs and outputs in Pro Tools, you might consider acquiring an additional audio interface. (Bear in mind the simple fact that doubling your number of simultaneous audio sources for recording proportionately increases the load on your system and disk space/performance requirements.) Hardware expansion options depend on which base configuration of Pro Tools you're using. Figure 17.1 shows some options for an expanded Pro Tools|HD configuration.

Pro Tools|HD Systems

The 192 I/O, 192 Digital I/O, 96i I/O, and 96 I/O audio interfaces have an expansion port where you can directly connect a second HD audio interface via DigiLink cable. The HD Core card itself, included with all Pro Tools|HD systems, supports up to 32 channels of I/O (for example, two of these audio interfaces). Additional audio interfaces can also be connected to each HD Accel card (or to the older HD Process card) in your system. Among current preconfigured HD Accel configurations, one HD Accel card is included with Pro Tools|HD 2 Accel, and two are included with Pro Tools|HD 3 Accel.

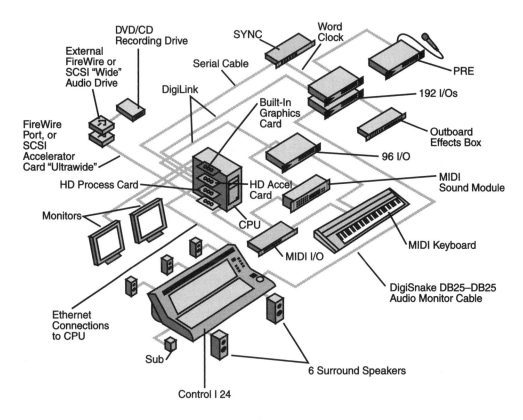

Figure 17.1 An expanded Pro Tools | HD configuration.

Alternatively, these HD audio interfaces (except the 96i I/O) also include a Legacy Peripheral port, where you can attach some older audio interfaces from the Pro Tools 24 | Mix hardware family (888|24, 882|20, 1622, or 24-bit ADAT Bridge I/O). The Legacy Peripheral port supports either a single 16-channel interface or two 8-channel interfaces (using Digidesign's 16-channel cable adapter). These interfaces are, of course, limited to their original sample rate of 44.1 or 48 kHz. The Expansion and Legacy Peripheral ports cannot be used simultaneously (because they both use Group B, input/output channels 17–32 on the host HD card).

The 96 I/O provides 16 simultaneous channels of I/O (from the 20 available I/O connections), although for each channel pair, you can select among eight analog ins/outs, ADAT Lightpipe I/O, AES/EBU digital I/O (XLR connectors), and S/PDIF digital I/O (coaxial or optical). This audio interface supports sample rates of 96, 88.2, 48, and 44.1 kHz.

The 96i I/O provides 16 analog inputs and two analog outputs (all with 1/4-inch TRS jacks) and S/PDIF digital I/O with RCA jacks only (no AES/EBU or ADAT Lightpipe). Unlike the 96 I/O, this interface has no Legacy Peripheral or Expansion ports. The gain on inputs 1–4 can be continuously varied via software (Hardware Setup) between −12.0 dBV and +4 dBu, while inputs 5–16 can be switched via software between −8 dBV and +4 dBu.

The 192 I/O also supports a maximum of 16 channels of simultaneous I/O, and up to a 192 kHz sample rate (including all the sample rates supported by the 96 I/O, plus 176.4 and 192 kHz). It features an I/O card bay, where you can install eight additional analog inputs, analog outputs, or digital I/O (via the 192 AD, 192 DA, or 192 Digital cards). This allows up to 16 analog, ADAT, or TDIF inputs or outputs simultaneously. The basic interface includes eight channels of analog I/O DB-25 connectors that require DigiSnake breakout cables with conventional XLR or TRS audio connectors (although you can also wire compatible cables yourself or order these from other sources). There are up to 16 channels of 48 kHz ADAT Lightpipe digital I/O (two sets of eight, the second of which can be configured for optical S/PDIF at even higher sample rates), eight channels of Tascam TDIF I/O, eight channels of AES/EBU digital I/O (accessed via a second 25-pin D connector, identical to that used for TDIF), plus two additional channels of standard S/PDIF or AES/EBU digital I/O. The 192 I/O is also the only Digidesign interface to offer real-time sample rate conversion on incoming digital signals and includes a soft-clip limiting feature. Again, any 16 of these ports can be active simultaneously. If you have both the 192 I/O and a 96 I/O on your system, the 192 I/O should always be the first interface connected to the Pro Tools|HD card. A DigiLink cable is connected from the Expansion port on the first interface to the Primary port of the second interface.

The 192 Digital I/O is similar to the 192 I/O, without the eight-channel analog input and output sections and with a second digital section. The base unit has two sets of ADAT Lightpipe inputs/outputs (16 channels), plus two TDIF connectors (another 16 channels), plus two additional channels of standard S/PDIF or AES/EBU digital I/O. It additionally provides 16 channels of single-wire AES/EBU I/O (or up to eight channels of dual-wire AES/EBU I/O at a 192 kHz sample rate) via two 25-pin D connectors. Digidesign sells a 12-foot snake cable that breaks out each set of AES/EBU channels from the DB25 connector on these interfaces (that is, a D-shaped 25-pin connector) to the standard XLR connectors (four male and four female) commonly used for AES/EBU digital connections to and from other gear.

> ❄ **Note: Slave Clock Connections on Your Audio Interfaces**
>
> In Digidesign's external audio interfaces prior to Pro Tools|HD, a short cable with BNC connectors was used to connect the Slave Clock Out of the primary interface (the first interface connected to the core Pro Tools card) to the Slave Clock In of the next interface, and so on through the last interface on the system (even if these interfaces were connected to different Digidesign cards in the host computer or expansion chassis). This ensured that the audio sample clocks in all the interfaces were slaved together for sample-accurate synchronization between them at the hardware level. Pro Tools|HD audio interfaces use Loop Sync ports for a similar purpose. The Loop Sync output of the primary interface is connected to the Loop Sync input of the secondary interface and so on through any other interfaces on the system. Finally, if *all* the interfaces are HD hardware (192 I/O or 96 I/O families), the Loop Sync output of the last HD audio interface is connected back to the first interface's Loop Sync *input*. (On the other hand, if your last interface is a legacy peripheral such as the 888|24 I/O, its Slave Clock Out should *not* be connected back to the primary interface's Loop Sync input!)

Alternatively, as mentioned previously, you could also slave Pro Tools audio interfaces—and all the other digital audio gear in your studio—to a centralized clock source in a star configuration. Ideally, this would be a standalone unit (such as the highly accurate clock generators available from Lucid Audio and others), although an extra-stable sample clock output from certain high-end devices (or an add-in card on certain digital mixers) might also serve this purpose.

One last note about Pro Tools|HD hardware: In addition to the 12-foot DigiLink cable supplied with the HD Core card and the 18-inch DigiLink cable supplied with each HD audio interface, you can also order these cables in 25-, 50-, or even 100-foot lengths. This would allow you to move one or all of your audio interfaces into the studio or soundstage, eliminating many meters of analog cabling (and its associated potential for noise, hum, and RF interference) from the input path to the analog-digital converters on your HD audio interface. (The maximum length for 192 kHz operation is 50 feet, while at 96 KHz operation, 100-foot DigiLink cable length is supported.)

Note: Plug-ins for Pro Tools|HD

One of the most attractive features of Pro Tools is that it offers you the ability to expand its functionality through additional plug-ins and other auxiliary software. This chapter and Appendix B focus mainly on hardware-expansion possibilities, however. Scores of developers are constantly introducing new software, plug-ins, and upgrades for their Pro Tools–compatible products, and any comprehensive listing here of the latest cool stuff and its capabilities would become outdated very quickly. Your best starting point for the latest information about plug-ins is always the Plug-in Finder on Digidesign's Web site, usually accessed from the product page for your particular system.

Nevertheless, since the introduction of Pro Tools|HD, an entire generation of TDM plug-ins has emerged that specifically require the TDM II processing architecture and the more powerful 321 DSP chips on the HD cards (versus the previous implementation of TDM technology on Mix|24 cards. Not surprisingly, the sonic results of these more processing-intensive plug-ins can be quite impressive. Here are some notable examples:

* **ReVibe (Digidesign).** A room modeling reverb, supporting sample rates up to 96 kHz and 5.x surround formats, with independent reverb, early reflection, and level controls for the rear channels.

* **Impact (Digidesign).** This compressor plug-in supports sample rates up to 192 kHz and surround formats up to 7.1. It's mainly designed for use on the mix bus (that is, on the Master Fader track for the mix outputs and the source for bouncing your mixdown to disk), although it also supports side chaining and has many other applications. Impact's sound and the simulated ballistic characteristics of its on-screen gain-reduction meters emulate classic compressors used on mixing consoles.

* **Smack! (Digidesign).** Although also available in an RTAS version for all Pro Tools systems, the TDM version of this compressor/limiter plug-in requires HD hardware. It supports sample rates up to 192 kHz and multichannel formats, offering controllable harmonic distortion and side chaining, with many tonal coloration possibilities that are especially useful for music applications.

* **MDW Hi-Res Parametric EQ (Massenburg Design Works).** An EQ plug-in that offers five fully adjustable bands, each of which can function as a boost/dip, low-pass/high-pass, or low-shelf/ high-shelf filter. In addition to the 6 dB/octave slopes available for the low- and high-pass filter mode on all bands, band 5 also supports 18 or 24 dB/octave slopes. Frequency selections are available from 10 Hz to

41 kHz. This EQ plug-in operates at 48-bit resolution and high sample rates (at 88.2 or 96 kHz, for example, even in sessions that are 44.1 or 48 kHz) and can be used on mono, stereo, or multichannel tracks. It emulates the constant-shape reciprocal filter curves of Massenburg's own GML 8200 parametric filter (a high-end stereo hardware unit). Many parametric EQ plug-ins are available for Pro Tools, but when the *inventor* of the parametric EQ (not to mention award-winning producer, engineer, and sound designer) puts one out, it's worth a listen!

❀ **Forte Suite (Focusrite).** Also available in an RTAS version, the TDM version of this plug-in requires HD hardware. It emulates a channel strip on Focusrite's high-end Forte recording console from the mid-80s, using physical modeling to simulate the vintage ISA 110 EQ, plus the expander, gate, de-esser, and surround compressor from the 130 series (with side chaining capability) for multiple effects in a single plug-in instance.

❀ **TL Space (TL Labs).** Among other things, this convolution reverb simulates reverberant spaces, as well as well-known digital, spring, and plate reverbs. It can use up to eight DSP chips to accomplish its extremely processing-intensive tasks without latency, including multichannel surround configurations. Based on an "impulse response" (derived from a recording of the ambient space or similar device), TL Space convolves the incoming signal, imposing that space's characteristics upon it. Of particular interest is their online library of impulse responses, to simulate new spaces.

❀ **Amp Farm 3 (Line 6).** While previous versions of Amp Farm supported older TDM hardware, the current version requires Pro Tools|HD and supports sample rates up to 192 kHz and the Digidesign VENUE console. This is a modeling plug-in for guitar amplifiers and cabinets that includes various microphone models and placements.

❀ **SOLID (Sound Fuel).** This software instrument plug-in models analog subtractive and FM synthesis (via either two waveform oscillators in subtractive mode or two sets of dual FM operators in FM mode). ADSR envelopes are provided for the amplifiers and filters, plus 2 LFOs (low-frequency oscillators) that you can sync to the MIDI Beat Clock. You can control virtually all of its parameters by MIDI (and consequently by any MIDI-capable control surface), and extremely low latency is one of its salient features. Through Dynamic Groups, velocity, aftertouch, and so on can control frequency modulation, oscillator mix, envelope times, and LFO amount/frequency. Each instance of SOLID supports 8-channel multitimbral operation, and up to 32-voice polyphony (16 voices on non-Accel HD systems). Internal effects are provided, including Chorus, Flanger, Distortion, and Delay, and can be used independently on the eight multitimbral patches.

❀ **Octavox (Eventide).** This is a flexible, eight-voice diatonic harmonizer plug-in. Individual control over tuning, volume, panning, and delay with feedback is provided for each voice. Using its unique Notation Grid interface, you can create complex sequences and textures by spreading the harmonized voices (in up to an eight-octave range) across bars and beats, in sync to the current Pro Tool tempo.

❀ **Eventide Reverb (Eventide).** Includes reverb algorithms from Eventide's DSP4000, Eclipse, and Orville hardware units. 3-band parametric EQ is provided both before and after the reverb. A dual delay is provided, as well as a compressor that can be placed either before or after the reverb stage. A Glide Rate setting for the Room Size parameter can be automated for some interesting pitch change effects in the ambience. Up to 32 snapshots of this plug-in's parameters can be stored and then recalled manually, via MIDI program changes or automation.

❀ **Sonic NoNOISE (Sonic Solutions).** This extremely powerful tool for audio restoration (removal of broadband noise, peak distortion, clicks, crackling, hum, and buzz) is also available as an AudioSuite process, but requires Pro Tools|HD hardware for non-destructive, real-time operation as a TDM plug-in.

Pro Tools 24|Mix Systems (Discontinued)

24|Mix systems do not support the current Pro Tools 7 software (or any other version higher than 6.4.1). The Mix Core card supports either a single audio interface or two using Digidesign's optional 16-channel cable adapter. (The Slave Clock Out of each primary interface is connected to the Slave Clock In of the secondary interface and so on through the rest of the interfaces, so that their sample clocks are in sync.) Each Mix Farm or Mix I/O card added to your configuration supports up to 16 channels of additional I/O. This can be either two 8-channel audio interfaces or a single 16-channel interface, such as the 1622 I/O or ADAT Bridge. (In addition to I/O, each Mix Farm card also increases your DSP capacity for plug-ins and higher track counts.) Among the options for upgrading sound quality on Mix| 24 systems, perhaps the two most significant are adding an extremely stable, high-quality digital word clock source (options from Apogee, Lucid, and other companies are listed in Appendix B) and/or adding very high-quality, outboard A/D converters that you can then connect to one of the digital inputs on the Digidesign audio interface.

Digi 002/002 Rack Systems

This hardware offers inputs for recording up to 18 channels simultaneously (eight analog, eight ADAT Lightpipe, and two S/PDIF digital); see Figure 17.2. For musical applications, however, having only eight analog inputs can be a little tight.

Figure 17.2   Analog and digital audio connectors on the Digi 002/002 Rack.

You can also use standalone mic preamps with digital outputs to expand your analog input capacity (budget permitting), through either the S/PDIF or Lightpipe input section on your Digi 002 or Digi 001 interface. Mono, stereo, and eight-channel models are available according to your requirements and budget. Here are just a few examples:

* **ART Digital MPA.** Dual channels, with hardware inserts, S/PDIF, AES/EBU, and Lightpipe output.

* **dbx ProVocal.** Mono, with compression, gate, de-esser, chorus/flanger, reverb and delay effects, and S/PDIF output supporting sample rates up to 48 kHz.

* **dbx 3.** High-end. One mic pre channel with a tube preamp section, 3-band EQ, compressor, de-esser, S/PDIF, and AES/EBU outputs, supporting sample rates up to 96 kHz.

* **dbx 786.** High-end. Dual mic pre, with S/PDIF or AES/EBU output at sample rates up to 96 kHz via optional 704X card (which also includes word clock input/output).

❋ **Joemeek TwinQ/OneQ.** Dual or single channel, with 4-band EQ, enhancer, de-esser, compression, and digital output in AES/EBU or coaxial/optical S/PDIF format, supporting sample rates up to 96 kHz. A word clock input is also provided.

❋ **Aphex 1788A.** High-end. Eight-channel microphone preamp with optional digital output card for ADAT Lightpipe, TDIF, and AES/EBU supporting sample rates up to 96 kHz (although 48 kHz is the highest sample rate supported for Lightpipe). A word clock input is also provided. Includes a built-in limiter for the microphone inputs. Can be remote-controlled via MIDI from Windows software or optional hardware controller in order to keep analog cable runs from microphones as short as possible.

❋ **PreSonus DigiMax LT or DigiMax 96k.** Mid or high-end. Eight channels, with Lightpipe output, hardware inserts, and BNC connector for word clock sync. The LT model supports sample rates up to 48 kHz (which is the highest sample rate supported by standard Lightpipe connections in any case), while the 96K version supports 96 kHz. The 96K version additionally provides four separate S/PDIF or AES/EBU outputs, depending on the optional breakout cable you select. It also includes a limiter on each input channel.

❋ **PreSonus DigiTUBE.** Economical, single-channel unit with 3-band EQ and S/PDIF digital out supporting sample rates up to 48 kHz. Also includes word clock input with a BNC connector.

❋ **Focusrite ISA 220 (mono) or ISA 430mkII (dual) with optional digital output board.** High-end, with parametric/shelving EQ, compressor, de-esser and optional digital output card supporting S/PDIF (optical or coaxial), AES/EBU, word clock and Digidesign SuperClock output, and supporting sample rates up to 96 kHz.

❋ **Focusrite OctoPre/OctoPre LE.** The OctoPre is another high-end unit. Eight channels with compression/limiting and word clock input/output, plus S/PDIF, AES/EBU, via an digital output card (plus Lightpipe digital outputs with a more sophisticated version of the digital output card), and supporting sample rates up to 96 kHz. The OctoPre LE is a more economical version, although it does support sample rates up to 192 kHz.

❋ **Focusrite Liquid Channel.** Physical modeling unit for various mic preamps and compressors, with AES/EBU digital output and BNC connection for word clock sync, controllable via included software over USB connection. Supports sample rates up to 192 kHz.

You can use Digidesign's Command|8 control surface with the Digi 002 Rack system (in order to have physical faders; transport controls; and knobs/sliders for controlling pan, send levels, plug-in parameters, and so on within the Pro Tools software). Focusrite developed it for Digidesign. When combined with the Digi 002 system, the Command|8 acts as an expander to the built-in control surface on that interface, providing 16 faders for mixing and automation. It also provides a monitoring section for external sources and dedicated outputs for the control room and headphones.

Some users will also add an extremely stable, high-quality digital word clock source to their 002 systems (options from Apogee, Lucid, and other companies are listed in Appendix B).

Digi 001 Systems (Discontinued)

Most of the audio hardware expansion options for the Digi 002/002 Rack listed in the previous section also apply to the Digi 001. In particular, since its internal microphone preamps, A/D converters, and sample clock have some significant quality limitations (reflecting the available technology and economics of the time), upgrades to these can make a big difference in sound quality on these legacy systems.

Mbox 2 Systems

The Mbox 2 offers up to four simultaneous inputs and outputs, if you use both the analog and digital connections simultaneously. As you can see in Figure 17.3, the microphone preamps provided for channels 1 and 2 (in addition to their separate line and instrument level jacks) are designed by Digidesign and are a step up from those included in the original Mbox. The S/PDIF digital output always mirrors analog outputs 1–2. Obviously, one of the attractive options for the S/PDIF digital input might be a mega-dollar, high-end mic preamp with digital output (and perhaps including some internal effects, if you prefer to apply some moderate amount of compression or limiting prior to the record input). Incidentally, if that high-end digital recording source itself also happens to provide an extremely stable (low-jitter) clock reference, this can also contribute to your recording quality. As with many other audio interfaces, adding a high-quality digital word clock source (which, in the absence of a dedicated BNC connector for this purpose, would be connected via the S/PDIF input) can also improve the sonic quality of your recordings. Like other audio interfaces, while recording or monitoring a digital input, an Mbox 2 can slave its internal sample clock to that source. (When you switch to the S/PDIF input source in the Hardware Setup dialog box, the Clock Source selector automatically preselects S/PDIF instead of internal sync.) Some MIDI modules and guitar/bass preamps also offer S/PDIF digital outputs. Using digital audio connections wherever possible can reduce accumulated background noise in your projects—especially after you layer up many tracks—and makes managing input levels much simpler.

Figure 17.3 You can use the analog and digital connections on the Mbox 2 independently for 4×4 operation.

Mbox Systems

Unlike the current Mbox 2, the original Mbox is always limited to two simultaneous inputs and two simultaneous outputs—either the 1/4-inch phone jacks for Mic, Line, or Instrument levels, or S/PDIF connectors (RCA) for stereo digital I/O, as shown in Figure 17.4. (Digital outputs 1–2 always mirror analog outputs 1–2.) The Focusrite-designed microphone preamps in this interface sound offer acceptable quality for a unit at this price. As with the Mbox 2, if you're a lone wolf and don't require more than two simultaneous inputs (for example, you're a composer with a project studio, or you're a voice-over artist), by adding a high-quality mic preamp with digital output and a stable sample clock, good microphones, and a quiet room, your recording quality can sound very professional.

Figure 17.4   The coaxial S/PDIF digital connections on the back of the original Mbox use RCA jacks.

The analog inserts in its input signal path are another unique feature of the original Mbox. (The Mbox 2 does not include analog inserts.) A special insert cable (the same kind used for inserts on small Mackie and Soundcraft boards) breaks this 1/4-inch TRS (tip/ring/sleeve) connection out into two 1/4-inch TS (tip/sleeve) plugs; each of the Mbox's two mono analog inputs has an insert jack where this type of cable can be connected. The cable's two TS plugs are connected to the input and output on any external device you want to patch in prior to the input of the A/D (analog-to-digital) conversion stage within this interface while recording or monitoring an external source. For instance, if you wanted to use a killer-sounding analog compressor or limiter to permanently color the sound incorporated into the recorded track, you could insert it here in the record input signal chain.

M-Powered Systems

Many of the M-Audio interfaces that are compatible with Pro Tools M-Powered include S/PDIF digital inputs (with the exception of the Delta 44, Mobile Pre USB, Fast Track USB, Black Box, and Ozone, for example). For these, the comments already made in this chapter about the advantages of high-quality mic preamps with digital outputs also apply. The ProjectMix I/O and FireWire 1814 also offer ADAT Lightpipe inputs (as well as outputs), so the previously listed multichannel mic preamps with this type of digital output would also be an excellent complement to these units. (In fact, using the ADAT Lightpipe input is necessary in order to fully exploit their full I/O potential.) Figure 17.5 shows the analog and optical inputs on the rear of the FireWire 1814 interface.

Figure 17.5   Analog and optical I/O (usable as either ADAT Lightpipe or optical S/PDIF) on the rear of the FireWire 1814 interface by M-Audio. A separate breakout cable provides connections for coaxial S/PDIF.

In addition to the ability to slave the interface's sample clock for audio recording and playback to a selected digital input (shared by all M-Audio interfaces that have an S/PDIF and/or ADAT Lightpipe input), the ProjectMix I/O also includes BNC connectors exclusively dedicated to word clock input and output.

Upgrade Path: For Your Mind

In Appendix A, "Further Study and Resources on the Web," you'll find a few suggestions for further study, including Web sites, CD-ROM training (see the next section), magazines, and books. Regardless of what further study you undertake, the most important thing is to try to make some time in your schedule to get crazy with Pro Tools. Experiment with dopey mixing effects and other offbeat ideas to build up your arsenal of techniques—even though yes, it *is* hard to find time for this in a working production facility! Also, take advantage of opportunities to undertake projects with your Pro Tools system that are completely outside your daily routine. If your audio-engineering work with Pro Tools mainly involves video post, take on a CD-mastering project for a local band. If you're mainly a music mixer, record a spoken-word piece, be it a narration for a training piece, a local poet reciting her work, a family history, a radio spot, or what have you. The left-field requests these clients make can take you into areas of Pro Tools—not to mention into effects applications and signal-routing techniques—that you may not have explored before. You're guaranteed to learn something along the way that will prove useful in your regular work.

Cool School Interactus

Hey, have we mentioned the *CSi* (*Cool School Interactus*) CD-ROM series more than a few dozen times? These interactive CD-ROMs for Mac and Windows walk you through basic digital audio concepts and specific Pro Tools examples. Several volumes deal with Pro Tools specifically; one is an overview of digital audio workstations and digital audio in general (with modules about synchronization and MIDI). Others cover Logic Audio, Digital Performer, Nuendo, and a variety of other audio programs. There's also *Cubase SX CSi Master*, as well as the more entry-level *Cubase SX3 CSi Starter*. In the *Starter* series, you will find volumes about Pro Tools, Reason, GarageBand, ACID, Logic, Digital Performer, Sound Forge, and SONAR. Of particular interest in the *Master* series is a volume by Steve Thomas dedicated to intermediate and advanced concepts, *Pro Tools 7 CSi Master*; several of the movie tutorial examples on the CD in the back of this book are drawn from that disc. Other *CSi Master* volumes cover Nuendo, Ableton Live, Cubase SX3, Digital Performer, and audio plug-ins in general, as well as one about Waves plug-ins specifically. In comparison to, say, reading this book, the CD-ROM learning experience is more nonlinear, using well-thought-out movie tutorials to show real-world applications of the Pro Tools software. (Pardon the self-promotion here; but honestly, these contain huge amounts of information and loads of movie tutorials to walk you through program operations step by step.)

Career Options

Pro Tools is used in music-production studios, video-production houses, film studios, radio- and television-broadcast stations, film and historical archives, record companies, multimedia-development houses, and audiobook-publishing houses. If you are trying to establish yourself as a Pro Tools operator, don't wait around for your perfect vision of a job to materialize. Get out there and visit the production houses in your community; ask to see their installations and how they operate. Remember that *any* job that keeps you working in Pro Tools on a daily basis will help you hone your skills with the program. Even if your ambition is music production, remember that many of the Pro Tools techniques you master while posting industrial videos or recording the spoken-word bits for Web and CD-ROM projects will carry over into subsequent phases of your career.

If you are a musician using Pro Tools in a home-project studio, consider working for some other local clients. Take an ad out in the local paper; offer to record singer/songwriter demos at a fixed rate for a fixed number of hours, including a CD copy at the end of the session. Of course, you will have to fix the parameters of the services you offer according to your system's capabilities; if you've got only one or two microphones, you can't have a whole steel drum band trooping into the basement or spare bedroom! Be aggressive in your initial pricing. If you do a good job, a fair percentage of these people will book additional hours and subsequent sessions. Even with a single microphone, any Pro Tools system is perfectly equipped to record oral histories or any other spoken-word piece, such as an author or poet reading her work, or for corporate-training or motivational presentations.

With many of the more portable systems (for instance, an Mbox 2/Mbox, Digi 002, or several of the M-Audio interfaces with a recent iMac or appropriately powerful Mac/Windows laptop), you can go on-site to record, making your service even more attractive. You might prepare an offer of *x* dollars for *x* hours, including two CD-R copies, or something along these lines. Again, you're guaranteed to learn something along the way, thereby improving your Pro Tools chops. For that matter, if you have a good-quality matched pair of microphones, you can even record local music and theater performances on location with your luggable Pro Tools rig. (Just make sure nobody pours a drink into your computer!) If you have a high-quality DAT recorder, you could instead take that out on location and then transfer the recording to Pro Tools for editing and for mastering of the CD. And of course, you can write off your audio-equipment purchases, mileage, and so on against any declared income!

If you have a friend who needs a voice-over demo, offer to record it for him or her—for *free*, if necessary! Interactive media developers are increasingly contracting voice talent directly—if with your collaboration this friend can deliver finished voice-over files in immediately usable formats (see Chapter 15, "Sound Design for Interactive Media," for more information), you can both make some money!

Maintaining a Learning Attitude and Finding Additional Resources

This book has pursued two objectives: First, to provide a quick start for novice Pro Tools users, condensing the most essential features and techniques (and crucial technical concepts) in order to be productive with Pro Tools in the shortest time possible. Secondly, we've tried to make some specific, useful suggestions for people already using the program, including insights that will be useful even for experienced Pro Tools operators.

However, this is just a start. If you've spent some time with the excellent manuals and PDF documentation Digidesign provides with Pro Tools, you've probably noticed many additional keyboard shortcuts, tool modes, parameters, dialog-box selections, and other application-specific information that we don't discuss. This is not only for space considerations (and the obvious fact that *this book isn't intended as a substitute for the manual*), but also because we've deliberately sought to narrow this book's focus somewhat. Building on the essential facts, this book aims to walk you through typical situations for applying Pro Tools features rather than taking the one-size-fits-all, purely descriptive approach that a technical manual must follow.

In short, then, we urge you to *read the Digidesign documentation!* Take a printout of the *Pro Tools Reference Guide* home or out to lunch with you (after you've finished *this* book, of course). Print out the *Keyboard Shortcuts* document, make notes to yourself about shortcuts and features you want to remember, and post them around your keyboard and monitor.

> **Tip: Give Your (or Your Employer's) Printer a Break**
>
> In the DigiStore section of Digidesign's Web site, you can purchase printed manual sets that include the *Pro Tools Reference Guide*, the *DigiRack Plug-ins Guide*, and the *DigiBase Guide*, containing the same text as the PDF versions included with the program in a spiral-bound book. Other products available in the DigiStore include keyboard stickers for Mac and Windows versions of Pro Tools, a padded carrying case for the Digi 002/002 Rack, Digidesign cables, plug-ins, and software upgrades—plus the usual shirts, caps, and pens with the manufacturer's logo, of course!

Make time to experiment with features and techniques; try something excessive! Seek out other Pro Tools users and spend time with them as they work; you can always pick up something, even from users who, in theory, are less technically grounded in Pro Tools than you are. Especially if your Pro Tools work is routinely in a single field (like audio for video, for example), pick up some great ideas by collaborating with other Pro Tools operators who use the program for something completely different (like music production, or multimedia).

There are many learning resources out there. A few suggestions are collected in Appendix A. Digidesign's Web site includes the Digidesign User Conference online forum, plus an excellent technical document library with downloadable reference guides for their software and hardware add-ons for Pro Tools. The Digidesign site also offers QuickTime tutorials about Pro Tools, QuickTips, and an online DigiZine. Other learning options for Pro Tools users include the *CSi* (*Cool School Interactus*) series of instructional CD-ROMs (see http://www.courseptr.com and the CD in the back of this book for movie tutorial examples from this series). In Appendix A, you will also find suggestions for further study.

Summary

As a Pro Tools user, you're involved with one of the most popular and powerful audio tools available. Once again, if you're just breaking into the business, make some calls to local production facilities—not only to network, but also to learn how they work with Pro Tools. We can tell you, after collaborating with so many Pro Tools users over the years, that there's rarely one best way to do things. Every time you sit next to another Pro Tools user as she works (at any level), you have a chance to learn something. Don't stop there, though; Find an opportunity to teach someone *else* how to use Pro Tools. Not only is this a swell thing to do, but as anyone who has ever taught will tell you, in the process of clarifying your ideas for someone else's benefit, you will attain a higher level of knowledge yourself.

The following Appendices provide additional technical information, tips (be sure to check out Appendix D, "Power Tips and Loopy Ideas," if you're already an experienced Pro Tools user!), resources for further study, plus information about archive and backup.

Thanks for reading. Enjoy!

Appendix A

Further Study and Resources on the Web

You may wish to dig deeper into digital audio, sound recording in general, or MIDI, depending on your interests and immediate requirements. We've been at this for years and certainly never run out of interesting things to study! What follows here is very brief—a few pointers for learning more about subjects related to Pro Tools.

Books About Audio

* *Pro Tools 6 Power!* by Colin MacQueen and Steve Albanese. Published in 2004 by Thomson Course Technology. A predecessor to this book, covering 6.xx versions of Pro Tools. If you are using a Digi 001 or 24|Mix system (which are limited to versions 6.4.1 and lower of the Pro Tools software), this may be the best book for you.

- *Pro Tools Power!* by Colin MacQueen and Steve Albanese. Published in 2001 by Muska & Lipman Publishing, a division of Course Technology. Another predecessor to this book, covering 5.xx versions of Pro Tools.

- *Digital Audio Dictionary* by Colin MacQueen and Steve Albanese. Published in 1999 by Howard W. Sams & Co. Yes, us again—a large glossary in book form.

- *Digital Audio Explained: For the Audio Engineer* by Nika Aldrich. Published in 2004 by Sweetwater Press. One of the best sources for practical information about digital audio. The author provides in-depth, clearly written explanations about sample rate, bit-depth, digital filters, ADC/DAC design, sample clocking, dithering, and other key concepts. If the rudimentary digital audio concepts in Chapters 1 and 2 were all news to you, this is a great place to start. Our favorite chapter, and required reading for all you experienced digital audio workstation cosmonauts, is "The Myths of Digital Audio."

- *Principles of Digital Audio, Fifth Edition* by Ken C. Pohlmann. Published in 2005 by McGraw-Hill. First published in the 1980s, and still a top source for a very technical, theoretical grounding in digital audio.

- *Sound Recording Handbook* by John Woram. Published in 1989 by Howard W. Sams. Provides in-depth information about recording in general—analog *and* digital audio—at a rewardingly technical level.

- *Audio Production Techniques for Video* by David Miles Huber. Published in 1987 and again in 1992 by Butterworth-Heinemann. In-depth postproduction information, including all the "old school" techniques.

- *Modern Recording Techniques, Sixth Edition* by David Miles Huber and Robert E. Runstein. Published in 2005 by Focal Press. Excellent reference for audio recording in general, and for digital audio. This book is used in many schools and universities.

- *Handbook of Recording Engineering, Fourth Edition* by John Eargle. Published in 2002 by Springer. Comprehensive reference work about general audio recording.

- *Handbook for Sound Engineers,* edited by Glen Ballou. Published in 2005 by Focal Press. Current version of the series, descended from the Audio Cyclopedia. Massive and authoritative reference resource; deep, detailed technical information on a wide range of general audio topics, circuit diagrams, formulas, graphs—the works!

- *The Art of Mixing, Second Edition* by David Gibson and George Petersen. Published in 2005 by Artistpro. A thought-provoking book about mixing from a visual perspective, applicable to any analog/digital mixing environment.

- *Mastering Audio: The Art and the Science* by Bob Katz. Published in 2002 by Focal Press. Excellent discussion of both analog and digital audio principles, dithering, jitter, bit-depth and sample-rate issues, noise reduction, equalization, metering, and other good stuff.

- *Pro Tools for Video, Film, and Multimedia* by Ashley Shepherd. Published in 2003 by Course Technology PTR. Coverage of mixing/sync and delivery formats, plus description of Pro Tools editing and mixing techniques in general.

Magazines

- ❋ *Electronic Musician*
- ❋ *Keyboard*
- ❋ *Mix Magazine*
- ❋ *Recording*
- ❋ *EQ*
- ❋ *Sound on Sound*
- ❋ *Tape Op*

CD-ROM Training

Okay, modesty aside (since the authors of this book are involved in their development), the *Cool School Interactus* CD-ROM series is one of the best interactive learning tools out there for digital audio workstation training. Several volumes in the *CSi* series focus specifically on Pro Tools, from basic digital audio concepts to MIDI, synchronization concepts, signal routing, and plug-in architecture and automation. Narrated movie tutorials walk you through techniques in Pro Tools as you watch and hear program operations, with specific recommendations—and slammin' soundtracks! Be sure to check out the movie tutorial examples from *Pro Tools 7 CSi Starter* and *Pro Tools 7 CSi Master* on the *CSi LE* CD-ROM in the back of this book. Also, see this publisher's Web site, http://www.courseptr.com, for further information. Additional titles in either the *Master* or *Starter* lines in the *CSi* series cover Waves plug-ins, plug-ins in general, Reason, Ableton Live, Logic, Cubase SX, Digital Performer, SONAR, ACID, Sound Forge, and GarageBand.

www.digidesign.com

Be sure to thoroughly investigate the Support section on Digidesign's Web site, where you will find a FAQ, compatibility documents, and software downloads. Digi also posts a majority of the manuals and Read Me files for their hardware and software products in the Technical Documents Library. This is an extremely useful resource when you're trying to figure out if an expansion option or upgrade is suitable for your own needs. Information is also provided about technical support and customer service, as well as hardware exchange offerings for users upgrading to more powerful or recent systems. The interactive Answerbase is also a great resource, especially for newbie questions. Digidesign's monthly online magazine, *DigiZine*, is of interest for Pro Tools users at *all* levels. In the DiSK (Digidesign Sound Knowledge) section of the site, *DiSK Flix* tutorials (in streaming QuickTime or Windows Media format) are educational, and definitely are recommended for all new Pro Tools users.

If you click International Sites at the top of the page, you can choose from among various languages for the Digidesign Web site (with a significant quantity of translated technical documents and product information), including Spanish, French, Italian, German, Japanese, Chinese, and Korean.

> ❋ **Tip: DAE Errors**
>
> If you ever get an error message from Pro Tools citing a DAE Error number, you can research this problem on Digidesign's Web site. Go to the Support area and choose the Answerbase. Type the error number (it's not necessary to enter the words "DAE Error") into the Text Search field to see possible causes and remedies for your problem.

Other Useful Web Sites

duc.digidesign.com

The Digidesign User Conference is a free forum hosted by Digidesign, with sections for Pro Tools TDM, LE, and M-Powered versions on Windows or Macintosh, DigiDelivery, Pro Tools Free 5.01, Digidesign's external control surfaces, and other products, as well as forums specific to Post and Surround users. Especially if you are a new user, you should lurk here for a while—it's unquestionably the best forum for Pro Tools users at any level. Aside from the occasional user rants and squabbles found on any online forum, there are some pretty smart folks involved here, offering productive advice and opinions to the brave souls who post dumb questions you may be too embarrassed to ask! It's also very active during nights and weekends; the advice you obtain from other users might get you out of a jam sometime. Just be sure to include your actual question or topic in the subject line of your post (as opposed to, say, "Help!"), and specify exactly which version of the Pro Tools software and hardware you're using, so that people can help you. Even veteran Pro Tools users will find some fairly high-fiber content here. *Highly* recommended!

www.whatis.com

This site is oriented toward information technology (IT) in general, but over the years has been an invaluable resource for sorting out acronym clutter and manufacturer jargon. When the alphabet soup and cryptic computer talk has you stymied, this may be a good place to start!

www.harmony-central.com

Topics here range from the gear-related, the technical, the music business, to the just plain silly (not that there's anything wrong with that!). Of particular interest to Pro Tools users: the Recording forum, Phil O'Keefe's In the Studio Trenches forum, Craig Anderton's Sound, Studio & Stage forum, and Nuestro Foro (en español).

www.musicplayer.com

Like www.harmony-central.com, this site's forums run the gamut with regard to music and audio. Of particular interest to Pro Tools users: David Frangioni's Studio Tech forum, Ethan Winer's Acoustics forum, the Project Studio forum, and the Keyboard Corner.

www.synthzone.com

This exhaustive, well-organized site has a little bit of everything: links to manufacturers and pages dedicated to MIDI instruments, dealers, MIDI software, alternate tunings, information about soundcards and audio hardware, and digital audio workstation software (including Pro Tools, of course). It's really a useful resource. Kudos to Nigel Spencer, who maintains, designs, and owns it!

www.digitalprosound.com/

As advertised, this site features a collection of information about products and techniques related to professional digital audio. The Techniques section is of the most interest, with article titles like "Soldering 101 for Recording Studios," "Avoiding Clicks with Crossfading," "Voiceover 101," "The Art of Noise Reduction," "Mixing and Mastering Tips," "Noise Free Computing," and "Introduction to Interactive Game Audio," to name just a few.

www.recording.org

This is another general audio Web site that includes a section of forums about digital audio workstations and other topics. Within the DAW area, you may find occasional posts about Pro Tools, Digidesign hardware, and related topics, but again, you will more frequently find experienced users and reliable information about Pro Tools–specific issues on the Digidesign User Conference. Nevertheless, because even Pro Tools–based studios contain audio devices from many other manufacturers, some of the forums here can be a valuable resource. As with all online forums, though, bear in mind that the experience and maturity level of members here runs the full gamut. If you decide to register in any of the forums we mention here and participate in a thread yourself, please be respectful and tolerant—and *helpful*!

www.gearslutz.com

In these online forums, you will find both project studio folks and industry heavy-hitters, with threads about studio gear, digital audio, musical instruments, and discussions about many computer-based audio/MIDI programs, including Pro Tools.

www.tapeop.com

This is the companion Web site for a bi-monthly magazine (available by free online subscription) about music recording, with tips and gear reviews, plus excellent interviews with engineers, producers, and artists. Tape Op maintains a refreshingly practical focus, placing more emphasis on how-to's and how-they-did-it than on glamour profiles of the latest electronic gizmos. Online forums can also be found on this site.

www.apple.com/pro/

Mac users of Pro Tools should explore this part of Apple's Web site for an excellent section regarding music and audio solutions using their products. This is a great place to get heads-up information about new Apple models and operating systems, product releases from numerous audio and MIDI manufacturers supporting the Mac platform, and some very good articles about specific artists and solutions. Also, if you're using a qualified Mac, be sure to check out Apple's "music toolkit" program, GarageBand. As we discovered while creating the *CSi Starter* volume about GarageBand, this program is a blast even for experienced pros, and of course, individual tracks or submixes can be exported from GarageBand as AIF files for further mayhem in Pro Tools.

www.aes.org

This is the Audio Engineering Society's Web site. Although you must be a member to access the online journal and some other areas, the technical articles in PDF format are available to anyone visiting the site, as are most of the standards documents (including their *Recommended Practices* documents). For digging deeper into technical aspects of audio production, this is one of the most reliable sources available. Pro Tools audio professionals especially should read the 2003 document *AESTD1002.1.03-10*, "Recommendation for Delivery of Recorded Music Projects." Among other things, this document suggests Broadcast WAV format (BWF) as the standard delivery format for digital audio files, lists recommended sample rates, provides printable forms for recording, mixing, and duplication notes, and provides track sheets, delivery labels for analog and digital media, and an excellent (albeit brief) technical glossary.

www.midi.org

This official Web site of the MIDI Manufacturers Association provides the technical dope on the *MIDI Specification* itself, plus proposed and forthcoming standards, many of which are available in downloadable form. A comprehensive About MIDI section includes educational articles about the MIDI basics, General MIDI, Standard MIDI Files, and XMF (eXtensible Music Format) files, at both beginning and more advanced technical depths. If you're new to MIDI and want to explore beyond the very basic MIDI concepts laid out in Chapters 2, "Pro Tools Terms and Concepts," and 10, "MIDI," this should be your first online stop.

Schools

Pro Schools (facilities offering intensive, standalone training by Digidesign-certified instructors), certified training locations, and sponsored colleges offer Pro Tools certification courses. These three-day courses include Pro Tools 101 and 201, 210M and 310M (music), and 210P and 310P (postproduction). Go to the Training area of Digidesign's Web site for more information about certification courses and training centers. There, you'll also find some offerings for online courses, and some free online quizzes to test your knowledge (*Pro Tools 101 Basic Quiz* and *Pro Tools 101 Exam*).

Appendix B

Add-ons, Extensions, and Cool Stuff for Your Rig

There are tons of options—both hardware- and software-based—for expanding a Pro Tools configuration. Given the huge number of software plug-ins available for Pro Tools and how quickly they are updated, you should always start by referring to Digidesign's Web site for information about them, and then confirm the absolute-latest versions on each plug-in developer's own Web site. Accordingly, this appendix concentrates on *hardware* enhancements for the various Pro Tools system configurations. Digidesign offers multiple audio interfaces, additional cards and I/O, the MachineControl option, rackmounted high-performance hard drives, and so on. This was discussed in Chapters 3, "Your System Configuration," and 17, "Pro Tools Power: The Next Step." Here are a few other ideas you may find useful.

External Control Surfaces

Using nothing more than a mouse or trackball to control all the functions in Pro Tools is a perfectly practical method. Indeed, this is how the vast majority of Pro Tools users operate. (We recommend that all Mac users currently using a no-button factory model mouse switch to a two-button wheeled mouse (or trackball) for use with Pro Tools—if nothing else, for the ability to scroll vertically and horizontally in the Edit window without moving the cursor from the track display area!) Nevertheless, it can sometimes be convenient to use a more sophisticated physical peripheral in a fast-paced professional studio environment, with dedicated buttons, faders, and so on that you can operate with two hands—and without looking down. For one thing, multiple physical faders allow you to automate mixes on the fly, moving several faders simultaneously and independently. (With a mouse or trackball, of course, you can only drag one slider at a time. Despite the advantages of grouping tracks in the Mix or Edit windows to gang their faders together, you could never, say, move one fader up while moving a second one down.) External control surfaces (also known as *virtual control surfaces*) are nice, too, because they can be larger and can be placed out in the control room for access from various positions by various people if necessary. Having large, tactile transport buttons and illuminated buttons for record-enabling and muting tracks facilitates a more heads-up relationship between the Pro Tools operator and performers or other collaborators. The more upscale virtual controllers for Pro Tools have large, illuminated level meters and illuminated parameter displays for track names, levels, pan, and many other features similar to standalone digital mixers, plus dedicated controls for functions that are specific to Pro Tools. In short, they facilitate rapid, two-fisted operation of Pro Tools, which can really increase productivity—especially when you have a roomful of clients or performers.

ICON Integrated Console Environments

The ICON family of integrated console solutions currently centers around two console/control surfaces that can be used with Pro Tools: the large-format D-Control (see Figure B.1) and the medium-format D-Command. Both of these offer motorized faders, buttons, rotary encoders, transport control, and signal routing options. They also both use the rackmounted XMON monitoring/cue mix module, and are purchased as part of various bundled configurations for surround, music, or postproduction that include Pro Tools|HD hardware and various Digidesign peripherals. (All of the current Surround, Music, or Post bundles include a Pro Tools|HD 3 Accel Core system, one or more 192 I/Os, a Sync I/O, a DigiDelivery Serv|LT unit, and an HDpack plug-in bundle. Other peripherals and plug-ins vary according to the configuration.)

D-Control

The core D-Control *tactile worksurface* consists of a Main Unit, plus a single 16-channel Fader Module that can be mounted on either side of it. You can add up to four more optional Fader Modules to this basic configuration, for a maximum of 80 channel strips/faders. There are dedicated LED displays for the Main/Sub time indicators, and for the Start, End, and Length fields of the Pro Tools software on the Main Unit. Dedicated buttons are provided for switching between windows in the Pro Tools software, such as Mix, Edit, Transport, Memory Locations, MIDI Operations, Beat Detective, and others. Additional dedicated buttons for Pro Tools functions include the four edit modes, track height up/down, and Edit menu commands such as Undo, Redo, Cut, Copy, Paste, and Repeat. You can use a Focus channel strip in the center Master Module for editing any selected channel's parameters without leaving the center of the console. In addition, the D-Control has dedicated EQ and Dynamics panels on the Master

Module that you can switch to control any channel on the fly. The D-Control has a built-in alphanumeric keyboard, a two-button trackball, and a shelf for an optional computer monitor or swinging arm for mounting a flat-panel display. A built-in talkback microphone and switch are also included, with a dedicated monitoring section for internal/external talkback, listen-back, input source selectors for the control room, separate level controls for main and near field monitors, Dim and Mute buttons, input selection, and separate controls for three cue mixes, as well as level controls for headphone outputs and a feed to loudspeakers out in the studio room. The D-Control connects to the Pro Tools|HD Accel system's host computer via Ethernet (10BaseT, with RJ45 connectors).

In addition to touch-sensitive, motorized Penny & Giles faders, each channel strip on the Fader Module has six multifunction rotary encoders with LED rings around them to indicate current parameter values or metering. LED meters are provided for each channel strip, plus eight channels of metering for the master section. 29 illuminated pushbuttons per channel strip are provided for switching channel modes, attributes, and so on. LED displays indicate channel names or the currently selected editing parameter for each channel strip.

There is an optional Surround Panner module available for D-Control that includes a color LCD touchscreen, two touch-sensitive joysticks with Punch buttons, two touch-sensitive rotary encoders with LED rings, and six mode buttons for each panner. Among other methods, you can move sources in the surround field by dragging onscreen icons within the LCD display. An AutoGlide function allows programming smooth transitions from one setting to the next. Other interesting creative options are available when various plug-in parameters are custom-assigned to the XY axes of the Surround Panel module—for example, filter frequencies, feedback amounts on delays, modulation depths for LFOs, and so on.

In addition to supporting surround mixing, the rackmounted XMON Monitor System, which is included in D-Control configurations (as well as the D-Command), provides dedicated out-puts used for three separate stereo cue mixes, talkback, listenback, studio monitors, and headphones. It is connected to the D-Control via a single 15-pin cable.

D-Command

The D-Command has been described by Digidesign as a "mid-format" console. The Main Unit features a central control section with monitoring and communications controls and eight touch-sensitive, motorized 100mm channel faders. The D-Command communicates with the host Pro Tools computer system via Ethernet, using RJ-45 connections and a separate Ethernet hub (not included) to which both are connected. Each channel strip has two rotary encoders, with LED rings to show either the current parameter setting or metering. It is expandable up to 24 faders via a single 16-channel Fader Module, which would be connected to an additional port on the same Ethernet hub as the computer and the Main Unit of the D-Command. On each channel strip, one 6-channel LCD beneath the rotary encoder displays information about the current parameter, while another serves as a scribble strip (displaying channel name, or plug-in parameters if the channel mode is flipped). Each of these channels can function independently, in a separate mode from the others. There are illuminated pushbuttons and bar-graph meters on each channel, plus eight more bar-graph meters in the Master section.

The center section has dedicated control panels for editing EQ (with 12 rotary controls) and dynamics plug-ins (with six rotary controls and dedicated output, gain reduction meters). The transport panel includes a jog/shuttle wheel (which you can also use to scrub and then trim region boundaries to that point), and dedicated buttons for Loop Playback, TrackPunch, QuickPunch, MachineControl, and other functions. The D-Command includes the same XMON remote, rackmounted analog I/O audio monitor and communications system as the D-Control. The monitoring section on the D-Command itself provides control for up to two 5.1 surround inputs, three stereo inputs, and two cue sends. Like the D-Control, the D-Command (shown in Figure B.2) is for HD systems only and does not support M-Powered or any LE version of Pro Tools.

Figure B.1 The basic D-Control tactile worksurface consists of a Master Module plus a 16-channel Fader Module. It can be expanded up to 80 channels/faders. (Photo courtesy of Digidesign.)

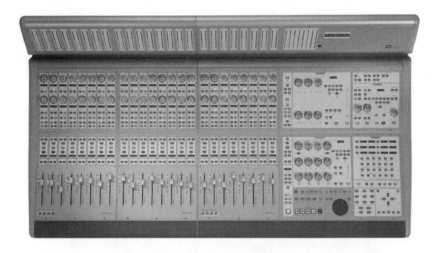

Figure B.2 The D-Command tactile worksurface consists of a Main Unit with eight channel strips, which you can expand via a 16-channel Fader Module. (Photo courtesy of Digidesign.)

ProControl (Discontinued)

This dedicated control surface from Digidesign for TDM/HD versions of Pro Tools offers eight motorized 100mm faders and dedicated Transport controls (with scrub/shuttle wheel); see Figure B.3. Although it is no longer being manufactured, the ProControl is fully supported in current versions of Pro Tools. You can add up to five optional Fader Expansion Packs to this system, each providing eight additional channel strips. The optional Edit Pack expansion unit is essential for surround mixing with ProControl, as it features two joystick panners. The Edit Pack module also incorporates a color-coded computer keyboard for Pro Tools, a numeric keypad, and a built-in trackpad similar to those used on laptop computers.

The Analog Monitor section on the base ProControl unit supplies analog audio I/O in the form of DB-25 connectors that use DigiSnake cable kits to either break out to XLR connectors or connect directly to a corresponding DB-25 connector on a Digidesign audio interface. (Alternatively, you can order compatible cable harness kits from third parties. You can also build your own if you prefer Mogami, Belkin, or some other brand of cable, or require a custom snake configuration to connect the gear in your studio.) Dedicated inputs are provided for a talkback and listenback microphone (as well as the built-in talkback microphone), and you can use either of these for recording slates (via a dedicated Slate audio output on the ProControl, which you would connect to an input on your Pro Tools audio interface). A control room monitoring section allows you to select between four sources, two sets of speakers, and headphone outputs. It also offers Dim, Mute, and Mono switches. You can also flip control of plug-in parameters to the main faders for convenience while recording automation for plug-ins. Unlike the Control|24, the ProControl does not feature any mic-level inputs.

Like the other external control surfaces from Digidesign, ProControl offers dedicated controls for many functions in the Pro Tools software, including buttons for Transport functions, selection of editing tools and edit modes, a scrub/shuttle wheel, and Save, Undo, and Redo buttons, to name a few. You can use the two dedicated footswitch inputs to punch in/out of recording, play/stop, or enable talkback.

ProControl connects to your Pro Tools host computer via Ethernet (10BaseT, using RJ-45 connectors; a hub is required if you use any optional expansion modules, because these incorporate their own Ethernet connectors). For Mac versions of Pro Tools, you select the ProControl via Setup > Peripherals; in Windows, you use the Network Control Panel to change the binding for this peripheral. ProControl also features In and Out connectors for MIDI.

Figure B.3   ProControl, by Digidesign, communicates with Pro Tools via your host computer's Ethernet connection (10baseT, with RJ-45 connectors). (Photo courtesy of Digidesign.)

Control|24

The Control|24 combines a virtual control surface for either TDM/HD or LE versions of Pro Tools (but *not* M-Powered) with 16 phantom-powered Class A mic/line preamps engineered by Focusrite; see Figure B.4. The first two channels also include an instrument-level direct box setting. The Control|24 features a surround monitoring section and a built-in talkback microphone for communicating with performers out in the studio (or onstage). It also includes a dedicated 8×2 analog line mixer, which can be useful for submixing multiple keyboards, live feeds from a mixing board, or other outboard devices. 24 touch-sensitive moving faders are provided, as well as dedicated EQ and dynamics switches on each channel; illuminated switching for Mute, Solo, Record Enable, Channel Select, and Automation buttons for each channel, and dedicated Transport keys with a scrub/shuttle wheel. There are dedicated buttons for Loop Play, Loop Record, QuickPunch, Online, and Pre-/Post-Roll enable functions in the Pro Tools software. Modifier keys are provided, which you can use while enabling buttons or changing parameters, like the Command, Option, Control (Ctrl, Alt, and Start on Windows), and Shift keys.

The back panel of the Control|24 has numerous analog connectors, including 16 line/microphone inputs with phantom power, slate and dual aux inputs and outputs, plus two DB-25 connectors for connection to Pro Tools audio interfaces via DigiSnake cables (eight output channels each). A third DB-25 connector provides eight outputs for speakers (via a DigiSnake breakout cable). Like Digidesign's ProControl, the Control|24 communicates with the Pro Tools program via a 10BaseT Ethernet connection (RJ45 connectors).

Figure B.4 Control|24, by Digidesign. (Photo courtesy of Digidesign.)

Command|8

The Command|8 connects to the host computer via USB (Universal Serial Bus); see Figure B.5. Transport controls, eight motorized faders, and eight rotary encoders with LED rings around them indicate current parameter values or metering. The unit has a backlit LCD display (two rows of 55 characters) for track information and parameter values. Each channel strip has Solo, Mute, and Channel Select buttons. Dedicated buttons are provided for Transport controls, Mix, Edit and Plug-in windows, Loop Play/Record, Undo, and creating Memory Locations. You can use a Zoom button and arrow keys in the navigation section to zoom in or out. Flip buttons on each channel strip allow you to reassign their main faders to send levels or plug-in parameters on that track. The Command|8 incorporates a one-in, two-out MIDI interface and a footswitch jack for hands-free punch in/out of recording.

The monitoring section of the Command | 8 was designed by Focusrite; the back panel includes two stereo input pairs for the audio sources to be monitored through the Command | 8. Typically, you would connect outputs 1–2 of your Pro Tools audio interface to the Main input, and use the External Source input for a CD player or video, for example. A "Speakers" output is also provided for monitoring your main stereo output from the Command | 8—like the two audio inputs, you can switch it between −10 dBV and +4 dBu level. Via the Control Room section on the front panel of the unit, you can switch this output between the Main and External Source inputs, and this output features Mute and Mono buttons. Finally, there is a headphone jack on the front panel with its own level control.

The Command | 8 can be used with TDM/HD, LE or M-Powered versions of Pro Tools (and also Avid Media Composer). You can combine it with other tactile control surfaces from Digidesign, such as the Pro Control, Control | 24, or the Digi 002 itself. You can also use this unit as a control surface for the rackmounted Digi 002 Rack, while combining the Command | 8 as a fader expansion unit with the Digi 002 yields a total of 16 faders. It can also operate in a standalone MIDI controller mode for use with other MIDI applications.

Figure B.5 Digidesign's Command | 8 control surface communicates with the host computer via USB, incorporates a MIDI interface, and also offers control room monitoring features. (Photo courtesy of Digidesign.)

CM Labs MotorMix

Each MotorMix control surface module provides eight motorized faders; see Figure B.6. You can add additional modules to your system as your requirements (and budget) increase. MotorMix communicates bidirectionally with the Pro Tools program via MIDI; fader changes and other parameter adjustments in one are immediately reflected in the other. The MotorMix also includes an 80-character backlit LCD display and LED illuminated switches. You can use the eight nonmotorized rotary pots to alter values of many different controls in Pro Tools (for example, send levels, pan controls, or plug-in parameters). A Rotary selector determines which of up to seven different target parameters on target tracks the rotary pots control, while in Plug-In mode, all eight of them control various parameters within the currently active Plug-in window. There are dedicated Pro Tools Transport controls, plus dedicated buttons for Pro Tools window and Mix/Edit group selection. In Locate mode, dedicated controls enable QuickPunch, Loop Record, memory locations, and so on.

Once you add MotorMix as a controller in your MIDI setup, you select it as your external controller for Pro Tools from a pop-up selector in the MIDI Controllers tab of the Setup > Peripherals dialog box.

Figure B.6 MotorMix, by CM Labs.

CM Labs Dashboard

The Dashboard is another virtual control surface for Pro Tools; see Figure B. 7. It offers dedicated Transport keys, a jog/shuttle wheel, Locator, Navigator, and Zoom control sections, an eight-character time-code display, an 80-character backlit LCD panel (for track names and display of control parameters), a numeric keypad (for data entry or recalling memory locations in Pro Tools), and a talkback microphone. The Dashboard has eight controls that you can assign to various Pro Tools functions (send or plug-in levels, pan, and so on). Mute and Solo keys are provided on each channel strip, as well as Burn switches for enabling recording and automation in Pro Tools tracks. Dedicated keys are available for Cut, Copy, Paste, Delete, Save, and Undo commands in the Pro Tools Edit menu. A Monitor Interface Module (also known as the *MIM*, an external breakout box) is included, with analog audio inputs where you can connect mix outputs from Pro Tools in order to feed audio to your control-room speakers, studio speakers, headphone amps, and so on. You can use the Dashboard as an edit section in combination with the MotorMix.

Figure B.7 Dashboard, by CM Labs.

Mackie HUI

Although now discontinued, the HUI, short for *Human User Interface*, is still being used daily in many production facilities; see Figure B.8. This control surface by Mackie Designs communicates bidirectionally with Pro Tools via MIDI. It provides eight motorized faders, plus illuminated virtual rotary potentiometers (*V- pots*), for controlling pan, send levels, and so on. There are two microphone preamps with analog insert points. The HUI features dedicated Transport controls for Pro Tools (also including buttons for Online mode, Loop Record, and QuickPunch, and a scrub/shuttle wheel), plus dedicated switches for Edit/Mix/Transport window selection and enabling Mix/Edit groups. A numeric keypad facilitates data entry and recall of memory locations in Pro Tools. The HUI has dedicated Save and Undo buttons for Pro Tools, as well as Zoom and Cursor Control buttons, and buttons that toggle between edit modes and editing tools. Dedicated buttons are also provided for the Edit menu commands Capture/Separate Region, Cut, Copy, Paste, and Delete. You can flip send levels to the main faders for convenience while writing automation, for example. The HUI offers mic preamps and a dedicated Control Room monitoring section (with three-source selection, plus Mute and Mono buttons), and a talkback microphone and button. You can use a footswitch input for the talkback function, and you can monitor channel levels via eight stereo, 12-segment LED meters on the HUI.

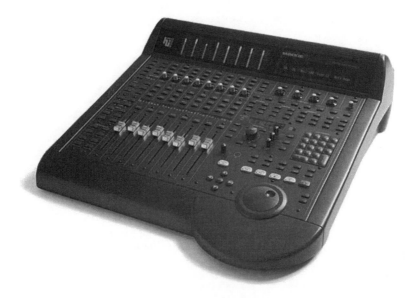

Figure B.8 HUI, by Mackie.

Mackie Control Universal

This is a more recent control surface by Mackie Designs that communicates with Pro Tools via MIDI using the HUI protocol; see Figure B.9. It also directly supports a number of other DAW programs, including Logic Pro, Cubase SX, Nuendo, SONAR, Digital Performer, and others. Overlays are included for the Master section of the unit, showing the program functions for Pro Tools, Cubase SX, Nuendo, SONAR, Digital Performer, and Cool Edit Pro. You can order other program overlays for a small fee from Mackie's Web site.

The Mackie Control Universal includes motorized, touch-sensitive 100mm Penny & Giles faders (eight channel faders plus a master fader), V-pot rotary encoders (multifunction, assignable knobs that you can use for send levels, pan or plug-in parameters, and many other purposes), and dedicated Record, Solo, Mute, and Select buttons on every channel. There are also dedicated Transport buttons, a jog/shuttle wheel for the Transport or scrubbing audio within tracks, a backlit LCD display showing metering and track names, plus a dedicated seven-digit display for time code. When used with Pro Tools (and as printed on that overlay for the unit), the Mackie Control Universal has dedicated zoom controls; and buttons that directly open the Mix, Edit, Transport, and Memory Location windows, as well as others for Enter (OK) and Cancel, Undo, and other functions. A Plug-in button switches the LCD display to that view, and V-pots 1–4 control values of plug-in parameters in the currently active Plug-in window. The Pan button assigns V-pot knobs to that function on all channels. You can also select Pro Tools automation writing modes from dedicated buttons. You can add additional Mackie Control Extender fader expansion packs (eight channel strips each) to the base unit.

Figure B.9 Mackie Control Universal.

J.L. Cooper CS-10^2

The relatively inexpensive CS-10^2 also communicates with Pro Tools via MIDI; see Figure B.10. It provides eight nonmotorized faders, plus dedicated Transport keys and a scrub/shuttle wheel. Above the faders, there is a strip of eight buttons that you can switch to various functions: solo, mute, memory location, track selection, record enable, and target channel strip (selects which track will be affected by the single rotary pan and five send level controls; alternatively, you can map these rotary controls to control parameters in the currently active plug-in window). A Master Status button is used to cycle through these button modes. You can add eight-fader CS-10^x expander units, for a maximum of 32 physical faders usable with Pro Tools (three CS-10^x units; a larger number of faders is supported with some other programs).

Function keys 1–9 are also provided on the CS-10^2. For example (in reverse order), F9 toggles Online mode on/off; F8 cycles through the Edit window tools; F7, F6, and F5 work like the Command, Control, and Option modifier keys (Ctrl, Start, and Alt in Windows). F4 and F3 correspond to the Edit > Separate Region > At Selection and Region > Capture commands used for creating new region definitions, and F2 and F1 are used to set the selection end and start points.

Figure B.10   CS-10, by J.L. Cooper.

J.L. Cooper CS-32 MiniDesk

This unit is not only relatively inexpensive, but also very small—about 9×9 inches; see Figure B.11. It features 32 20mm faders (organized in upper and lower rows of 16 faders each) with buttons usable for mute, solo, and record-enable functions on each of these channel strips. To be completely frank, it should be pointed out that on 20mm faders, a very small movement on this controller produces a *big* movement of the Pro Tools fader—some users may find this to be a problem. Dedicated Transport buttons, cursor keys, and a weighted jog/scrub wheel are also included. You can use its Quick Function keys to select most commonly used editing functions, and use the six rotary encoder controls on the top panel for panning or adjusting plug-in parameters. The CS-32 MiniDesk is compatible with many MIDI/audio programs, including Digital Performer, Reason, and Pro Tools (which treats it as an expanded CS-10^2 with 32 faders), and is available in MIDI and USB versions.

Figure B.11   CS-32 MiniDesk, by J.L. Cooper.

Frontier Designs TranzPort

The TranzPort is a wireless remote control unit for Pro Tools and other digital audio workstations; see Figure B.12. A small RF receiver (the Tranzceiver, which communicates with the remote at 2.4 GHz) is connected to a USB port on your Mac or Windows computer, and the remote itself runs on four AA batteries. You can locate it as far as 30 feet (10 meters) away from the receiver without requiring line of sight. It weighs about one pound and is 7×5.5 inches in size, supports mounting on a mic stand, and also accommodates a footswitch for punching in/out of recording mode. There are 18 buttons for functions including transport control, Rec/Solo/Mute for the currently selected track, and a dedicated Undo button (as well as others relating to markers, Loop, and QuickPunch modes). You can use its data wheel to scroll or scrub in the Pro Tools timeline. Communication is two-way, so that time code, current track name, volume/pan values, and so on can be displayed on the TranzPort's 2×20 character LCD display. To use this unit with Pro Tools, you use its own control panel to put the TranzPort in HUI emulation mode, and then open Pro Tools and add a HUI controller in the Peripherals dialog—choosing Frontier Designs TranzPort as the Receive From and Send To assignment. With this gizmo, you can easily control monitoring levels and basic recording functions from the sound booth or across the studio, away from noisy computers. It's just the thing for project studios and people who have to perform while running the recording rig.

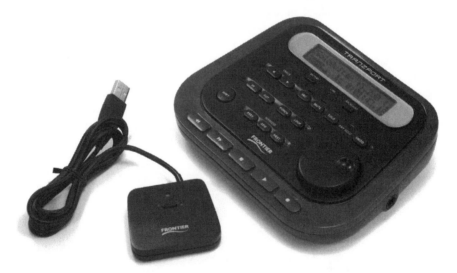

Figure B.12   TranzPort, by Frontier Designs (shown here with the USB receiver that attaches to the host computer).

Synchronization Peripherals

As explained in Chapter 11, "Synchronization," if you need to synchronize playback and recording of Pro Tools to an external SMPTE time code source, you must add an external synchronization peripheral to your core Pro Tools configuration. Digidesign itself offers two devices (with features to resolve audio playback speed over extended periods of time to either a clock or a video reference, or to the incoming time code itself). There are also many third parties offering excellent synchronization peripherals (often doubling as a MIDI interface) at a variety of performance levels and price points. Just a few are mentioned in this section, and new models continually appear, of course. In addition to starting playback or recording at the appropriate time according to *location* information received from SMPTE (or MIDI) time code, all the options listed here offer the additional ability to *slave* (resolve) the internal sample clock of Pro Tools hardware to an external source.

Digidesign Sync I/O

Digidesign's Sync I/O is a high-end synchronization peripheral that connects to Mac or Window computers via USB; see Figure B.13. It translates SMPTE time code to and from VITC (video) or LTC (audio) format, and can also resolve (continuously adjust) the sample clock of your audio hardware to keep Pro Tools in sync with incoming time code over extended periods. Alternatively, the Sync I/O can resolve the sample clock of the Pro Tools hardware to an external video reference (black burst/house sync), industry-standard word clock (1x the audio sample rate), or Digidesign's SuperClock (a timing reference for audio hardware operating at 256x the sample rate). The Sync I/O can *burn* a time code window into video signals passing through it. Dual Sony 9-pin serial ports can be used to link Transport functions of Pro Tools with external video/audio devices, if the optional MachineControl software is installed in Pro Tools.

Figure B.13 Sync I/O. (Photo courtesy of Digidesign.)

MOTU MIDI Timepiece AV (USB)

The MIDI Timepiece AV connects to the host computer (Mac or Windows) via its USB port; see Figure B.14. This rackmountable interface (one-unit high) features eight independent MIDI Ins/Outs for 128 total MIDI channels, all of which are individually accessible from within

Pro Tools (via the Audio MIDI Setup on Mac, or via the supplied MOTU drivers for Windows). This unit includes hardware synchronization outputs (9-pin ADAT Sync and word clock) on the MTP AV, plus a Video Sync input. (The Video Sync input and the word clock output have BNC connectors.) You can switch the word clock output between 1x and 256x the sample rate used to slave your Pro Tools hardware to the MTP AV, which in turn you can *genlock* (slave to match frame rates) to the black burst/house sync video signal at its Video Sync input. The MTP AV also supports LTC (audio, via a 1/4-inch phone input) time code at any SMPTE frame rate, and can convert this to hardware sync (ADAT or Pro Tools SuperClock) for resolving your audio hardware's sample rate to this time-code reference. The MTP AV is also a full-featured MIDI patchbay, merger, and processor. You can access all of its features from the front panel during live performance, or—more importantly for Pro Tools users—via the included software. The MIDI Express XT and the Micro Express are simpler MIDI/SMPTE interfaces in MOTU's product line.

Figure B.14 MIDI Timepiece AV, a multiport MIDI interface from MOTU, which also offers LTC synchronization.

MOTU Digital Timepiece

This unit supports SMPTE synchronization in LTC, VITC, and MTC formats; see Figure B.15. It also features a number of hardware sync options, including video sync (for house sync/black burst), ADAT sync, DA-88 sync, MIDI MachineControl, Sony 9-pin, S/PDIF, 1x word clock, and 256x SuperClock for resolving Pro Tools audio interfaces to the DTP (and thereby to whatever synchronization master is currently selected for the Digital Timepiece—for example, internal, video, or ADAT). It supports phase-locked synchronization between Pro Tools (or other digital audio workstations) and digital multitrack recorders such as Alesis ADAT, Tascam DA-88, DA-98, and so on, at sample rates of 44.1 kHz or 48 kHz. The Digital Timepiece can also generate LTC (audio-based *linear* time code), and/or burn a time-code window into video signals passing though it. It has a Sony 9-pin serial port for machine control of compatible video decks and DATs, and also supports MIDI MachineControl (and MIDI Time Code) via its two MIDI In/Out connectors. However, it is *not* a MIDI interface for connecting your keyboards, controllers, and modules to the computer via MIDI; a separate device is required for that.

Figure B.15 Digital Timepiece, by MOTU, is a synchronization peripheral, not only for SMPTE (LTC, VITC, and MTC), but also for many different varieties of hardware sync, including 256x SuperClock for Digidesign hardware and black burst video sync.

Digital Patchbays and Routers

Users with many digital audio devices in their studios will definitely want to look into *digital patchbays*. Reaching around to the rear panels of rackmounted devices every time you want to switch digital inputs and outputs between multiple devices is inconvenient and will inevitably damage cables over the long run (or even worse, the connectors on the gear itself). Digital patchbays and routers provide a convenient way to move digital audio signals around between Pro Tools, multitrack digital recorders, effects, DAT recorders, and so on, without having to bend over and show your rear end to clients as you swap digital cables on the back of these devices. Many of these units also translate between different digital formats—so you could route ADAT channels into Pro Tools via S/PDIF, quickly switch the S/PDIF or AES/EBU inputs/outputs on your Pro Tools audio interface between several other devices in the studio, and so on.

Z Systems OptiPatch and z-8.8a Digital Detanglers

The OptiPatch is an ADAT Lightpipe patchbay (eight-in, eight-out) and distribution amplifier with real-time sample-rate conversion. Stereo optical S/PDIF signals are also supported on the same Toslink connectors used for Lightpipe. It also supplies bidirectional conversions between Lightpipe and S/PDIF optical stereo formats (with sample-rate conversions, if required, between the 96 kHz maximum on S/PDIF and the 48 kHz maximum supported by Lightpipe). You can order the z8.8 Digital Detangler in various 8-way configurations; for example, four AES/EBU, two S/PDIF coaxial plus two S/PDIF optical, or all AES/EBU. Of particular interest is the x8.8a unit, another automated ADAT Lightpipe patchbay and distribution amplifier that can perform real-time, bidirectional conversions between Lightpipe, AES/EBU, and S/PDIF. Z Systems offers many other Detangler units for routing multiple AES/EBU and Lightpipe connections, some of which you can order in custom configurations.

Z Systems z-128.128r Digital Detangler Pro

The z-128.128r is an automated patchbay, router, and distribution amplifier for digital audio signals in AES/EBU or S/PDIF formats at sample rates up to 192 kHz, housed in a five-unit high rackmountable chassis; see Figure B.16. Router-control software (via an RS-422 serial connection) is provided for both Mac and Windows. From the basic 16×16 configuration, you can add 16-channel expansions for up to 128 input/input channels. (There is also a z-256.256r model, with—you guessed it!—double the maximum number of inputs/outputs.) Breakout cables are required to break its DB-25 connectors out to eight standard XLR or RCA connectors (for AES/EBU or S/PDIF, respectively), and Z systems also offers an adapter cable for interfacing this unit with the DB-25 connectors used for AES/EBU digital audio on Digidesign's 192 I/O and 96 I/O audio interfaces for Pro Tools|HD.

Figure B.16   Back panel of the z-128.128r Digital Detangler Pro, by Z systems.

Word Clock and Sync Generators

As mentioned elsewhere in this book, in studios with multiple digital audio devices, it can be very useful to synchronize the audio sample clocks of all these devices to a single, central source (similar to the way house sync is used in video studios to synchronize frame rates). Obviously, this source's clock must be extremely stable. For some situations—such as recording from a digital source or playing Pro Tools back in sync with a digital multitrack—it may be sufficient to simply lock them together via word-clock connections on the audio interfaces or use the Clock Source option in the Hardware Setup dialog to synchronize Pro Tools to the digital input. Some devices generate a stable clock reference as part of their standard features (like the Finalizer, from TC Electronics, not to mention Digidesign's own Sync I/O). Some digital mixers offer an optional card (such the Apogee Electronics Clock I/O card for the Mackie Digital 8-bus) that can provide a stable clock reference to Pro Tools and other digital audio devices. Nevertheless, for larger configurations and especially for demanding, high-resolution audio, professional users will opt for a higher-quality standalone word clock/ sync generator to effectively eliminate jitter (sonic artifacts caused by minute variations in the sample clock) that can degrade the sonic image. Here are just a few examples.

Lucid Audio GENx-6, GENx6-96, and SSG192

All three of these devices from Lucid Audio act as extremely stable master clock sources for digital audio configurations. The GENx-6 supports word clock at sample rates of 44.1 kHz or 48 kHz. The GENx6-96 not only adds support for 88.2 kHz and 96 kHz sample rates supported by Pro Tools|HD systems, but also directly supports Digidesign's 256x SuperClock format—used for the 888, 882, and 1622 audio interfaces on 24|Mix systems. The SSG192 is Lucid Audio's current high-end product, adding 192 kHz sample rate support; the capability to generate or synchronize to black burst/house sync, AES-3, AES-11, and other sources; and four clock outputs whose format you can set independently. See Figure B.17.

Figure B.17   The SSG192, by Lucid Audio.

Aardvark Audio AardSync II

The AardSync II supports 1x word clock, Digidesign 256x SuperClock, AES/EBU sync, and video black burst/house sync in NTSC/PAL formats, at sample rates up to 96 kHz (including pull-up and pull-down sample rates). See Figure B.18.

Figure B.18   Front and back panels of the Aardsync II, by Aardvark Audio.

HHB/Rosendahl Nanosyncs

The Nanosyncs supports 1x word clock, Digidesign 256x SuperClock, AES/EBU sync, and video black burst/house sync, at sample rates up to 96 kHz; see Figure B.19. It incorporates four video outputs (supporting both NTSC and PAL), ASES/EBU and S/PDIF sync outputs, plus six separately configurable word-clock outputs with BNC connectors.

Figure B.19   Front and back panels of the Nanosyncs, by HHB/Rosendahl.

Session Control TL-Sync

The TL-Sync supports 1x word clock, Digidesign 256x SuperClock, AES/EBU sync, and video black burst/house sync, at sample rates up to 96 kHz , and four video outputs (including PAL video format); see Figure B.20. It includes two low-jitter, isochronous digital clock rate generators. It also supports the Pro Tools MachineControl option in virtual 9-pin mode or via MIDI MachineControl. It converts incoming LTC (SMPTE time code) or video sync to word clock or SuperClock format for Pro Tools. Originally developed by Timeline Vista, the TL-Sync is now manufactured by Session Control, who also offers the RC-Sync remote control for this unit.

Figure B.20   The TL-Sync, by Session Control.

Apogee Big Ben

This high-end, extremely low-jitter digital clock source from Apogee Electronics supports sample rates up to 192 kHz; see Figure B.21. Inputs/outputs include two AES/EBU digital with XLR connectors, S/PDIF on both coaxial and optical connectors, ADAT Lightpipe, S/MUX II or IV, and six BNC connectors for word clock (1x only for highest sample rates, up to 2x at 96 kHz or 88.1 kHz, or up to 256x at 48 kHz and 44.1 kHz). The SureLock feature maintains steady clock adjustment if there is any interruption (and subsequent reestablishment) of an incoming clock source. With the optional X-Video card, incoming video sync (black burst) or video sync generation is also supported in PAL or NTSC, with pull-up and pull-down sample rates. An optional X-FireWire card supports clocking and format conversions with other FireWire devices. The Big Ben also includes a front-panel LCD display for the exact sample rate.

When using the Big Ben on HD systems with multiple audio interfaces, attach each one directly to the Big Ben via its Ext In word clock input (with BNC connector), rather than connecting these interfaces together via their LoopSync ports in the usual fashion. You then go into the Session Setup window of Pro Tools and select Word Clock as the clock source for each of your HD interfaces.

Figure B.21   Big Ben, by Apogee Electronics.

Ergonomics, Rackmounting, Extenders

Let's face it, you spend long hours working at your Pro Tools rig. Whatever helps you to hunch, stretch, strain, hunt, or squint a little less will improve your quality of life! Standard office furniture—and for that matter, typical computer workstation furniture—doesn't always provide the most ergonomic setup for the way you work in Pro Tools. Just how many times a day are you willing to stand up, bend over, or take 2.5 steps across the room to adjust a mic preamp or effect, arm a DAT for recording, and so on, before it's worth investing a little time and money in improving the *efficiency* of your working style? After all, the less wear and tear the work itself makes on your patience and sustained concentration, the more creative you can be, right? Besides, it just looks and feels better to have all your gear neatly racked, your system components readily accessible at convenient angles—and your cables organized!

Digidesign Pro Tools Custom USB Keyboard (Macintosh)

This USB keyboard for Macintosh computers has color-coded sections; see Figure B.22. Text for standard Pro Tools key commands is printed in each key, as well as the standard QWERTY characters. Because this represents an additional expense (and costs more than conventional Mac replacement keyboards), many, including yours truly, have been skeptical about the value of this option. However, after watching several new users adapt to Pro Tools on systems equipped with this keyboard, it's clear that it really does shorten the learning curve in many cases. An added benefit is that these users adapt more quickly to using keyboard shortcuts instead of onscreen controls and menu commands.

Figure B.22   Digidesign's Pro Tools Custom USB keyboard for Macintosh. (Photo courtesy of Digidesign.)

Rackmounting, Workstation Furniture

You can certainly build your own studio furniture (in some rooms this is a necessity), or perhaps adapt some existing computer workstation furniture for your project studio. Alternatively, various manufacturers provide worksurfaces and rackmounting systems that are specifically tailored to the needs of digital audio workstation users.

Omnirax
Omnirax offers various lines of workstation furniture, including the Force 12 and Force 24 workstation desks (with rackmount systems) for Pro Tools; see Figure B.23. Omnirax was the

first company to address the special needs of digital audio workstation users, especially with the ProStation and ProStation Jr. The Synergy S6C24 XL is designed to house Digidesign's Control|24; see Figure B.24. The Coda workstation has a space for a small virtual control surface like the Mackie HUI, the Coda D8 holds a Mackie Digital 8-bus, and Coda EX is designed for Digidesign's ProControl. This is a solid company that has supported Pro Tools since the earliest days, and it really stands behind its products. Features specifically aimed toward digital audio workstation users include bridges for mounting computer monitors and near-field audio monitors, various configurations of rackmounting both above and below the work surface, cable channels, heavy-duty casters, and a sliding shelf for easy access to the computer.

Figure B.23   The Force 24 is a workstation desk for a Pro Tools system.

Figure B.24   The Synergy S6C24 XL is custom-designed to house Digidesign's Control|24; it's flanked by 12-space rack bays.

Argosy Console

Argosy's studio furniture includes slanted bays for computer monitors, plus rackmounting and worksurfaces for computer keyboards, trackballs or mouse pads, and so on. The company's 90 and 70 series consoles include a variety of models that are custom-fitted for Digidesign's ProControl or Control|24 (as well as models for many popular mixers). Also of interest is their Mirage DC-24, specifically designed for the D-Command; see Figure B.25. It includes a padded armrest, a pull-out tray for a computer keyboard and mouse, plus two 19-inch rack spaces, each six units high.

Figure B.25   Argosy's Mirage DC-24 is designed for Digidesign's D-Command.

Noren Products

This company's AcoustiLock acoustic isolation enclosures for your computer, hard drives, and rackmounted gear (various sizes are available) allow your Pro Tools system to remain in the control room without creating a noise problem. Of particular interest to Pro Tools users is their Quietly Cool vCab model, with 13 units of rackmounting, plus three more units on top that slide to the rear for access to cabling patchbays and other frequently accessed devices. Their sealed enclosures feature "heat pipe" convection cooling and require no fans, while providing noise reduction factors greater than 99 percent.

Sound Construction and Supply

This company manufactures Isobox Studio and Isobox Post acoustic isolation enclosures for your computer, hard drives, and rackmounted gear (various sizes are available), so that your Pro Tools system can remain in the control room. The Isobox line includes thermostatically controlled fans with digital intake/exhaust temperature displays, thermal alarms, efficient sound traps, and intake HEPA filters for the fans. Sound Construction and Supply also offers custom workstation furniture, including consoles specifically for the D-Command, ProControl, and Control|24.

Marathon Computer

Marathon offers systems for rackmounting Macintosh G5 and G4 computers vertically. They also offer slide-out rail options, rackmounts for flat-panel displays and monitors, and slide-out rack trays specifically for computer keyboards. These racks can be fitted into standard 19-inch rackmount enclosures, and because you don't have to open the case to attach the rackmounting adapters, the computer's warranty is not voided. Marathon also offers kits for refitting the guts of certain G4, G3, and iMac models into a rack space enclosure.

Marathon's Deskmount is a mounting system that you attach to the underside of a desk or work surface, allowing you to get your G5 Macintosh CPU off the floor by sliding its upper handles into the custom-fitted rails of the Deskmount. (On G4/G3 versions, you replace the upper handles of the CPU with an aluminum backbone that slides into the Deskmount's mounting bracket.) Marathon also makes some excellent switching systems, for using a single USB keyboard and mouse with several computers.

If you're considering some sort of mounting product for a Macintosh computer, a visit to Marathon's Web site (http://www.marathoncomputer.com) is definitely worth the trip. You'll find some clever ideas, and get a load of their wise-guy attitude. Consider, for example, the company's instructions about suitable surfaces for attaching the Deskmount:

> "Particle board, fiberboard, Masonite, MDF, OSB, hardwood, plywood, steel, Plexiglas, neutronium, or just about any element from the Periodic Table that is a solid at room temperature and doesn't spontaneously react exothermically with gases normally found in air. Liquids would not be a good bet; don't try to attach your DeskMount to water, especially moving water. Or live animals. Most anything else is fair game, though."

Extenders

When things don't quite reach in your studio configuration, you may be able to solve the problem with a simple trip to your local audio or computer store. Slightly longer cables for balanced audio connections, MIDI, monitors, FireWire devices, and so on are readily available. (Caution: If you're using an original Mbox, do not replace or extend the USB cable that comes with this unit! Otherwise, no matter how much you spend on premium USB extender cables or ferrite chokes, you'll hear a very annoying high-pitched modulating noise on the Mbox's analog outputs.) Digidesign's DigiLink cabling system supports very long runs of cable—up to 100 feet, or 50 feet at 192 kHz sample rates—which conceivably allows you to put your audio interfaces and Digidesign PRE microphone preamps out in the studio or even on stage, minimizing the length of analog cabling in your setup. Sometimes, however, you need to separate things in a different way—for instance, when your CPU and peripherals need to be in an equipment room or closet, far from your monitor and keyboard. Without the proper equipment, this separation can be impractical or can degrade the display quality, which certainly won't make it any easier to work for extended periods of time.

Gefen

This company offers some interesting products for removing noisy computers from the control room entirely. Gefen's CAT5 • 1000 system (one sender, one receiver) permits the separation of a standard VGA monitor (analog video at resolutions up to 1920×1200) and USB keyboard/mouse from a Mac/Windows computer by up to 330 feet, using a single Category-5 (CAT-5) cable (a four twisted-pair cable type, also used for 100 Mbps and gigabit Ethernet networks). See Figure B.26. The CAT5 • 1000 also features a mini 1/8-inch stereo audio connection, so that the computer's built-in sound I/O can be brought out to the remote location as well. The CAT5-1500 version offers design refinements for video quality at longer cable lengths, while the CAT5-1000HD version supports DVI or HDMI computer video sources. The CAT5 • 5000 system offers similar features, but uses two CAT-5 cables to support two monitors connected to independent video outputs from the computer, and is ideal for dual-screen Pro Tools users. The remote monitors, keyboard, and mouse can be separated by up to 330 feet of cable from the computer's CPU (while simultaneously maintaining local monitors, keyboard, and mouse at the CPU's location). Gefen also offers a variety of USB-only extenders, FireWire repeaters and extenders (including one that supports fiber-optic cable runs for FireWire of up to 1640 feet), audio distribution amps using CAT-5 cable to support cable lengths up to 1,000 feet, monitor converters, and other extremely clever accessories for physically extending a computer or video configuration.

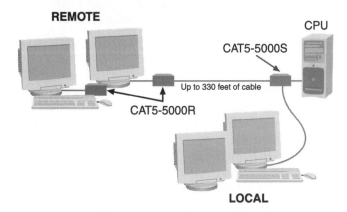

Figure B.26   The CAT5 • 5000 system, by Gefen.

Monitoring Control

With enough mic preamp channels, and with one of these sophisticated units for input/output selection in the control room and communication with performers out in the studio, conventional mixing boards could be eliminated entirely from many control rooms! Look for additional alternatives to arrive in the marketplace from upscale manufacturers.

Mackie Big Knob

This tabletop unit combines talkback functions (with an internal microphone for communicating with performers out in the studio), selection between up to three sets of studio monitors, selection between up to four stereo input sources (for example, line inputs for the Pro Tools mix, and playback from DATs, CDs, or videos in your studio; the fourth input is phono level for turntables), and a line level selector and trim knobs on the rear panel. It includes two headphone outputs and a studio output (to the performers' room) with level controls, plus dedicated Mono, Mute, and Dim (attenuate) buttons and a footswitch input for the talkback function. Oh yes, and of course, there's a big knob for controlling playback volume! See Figure B.27.

Figure B.27 The Big Knob, by Mackie.

Presonus Central Station

A rackmountable unit (with optional remote control), the Central Station offers talkback functions with an internal or external microphone, selection between up to three outputs (TRS balanced stereo pairs—Speakers, Main, and Cue) and two stereo Headphone outputs with individual level controls. See Figure B.28. You can select up to five inputs (two TRS balanced stereo pairs, Aux Input with RCA connectors, and S/PDIF digital switchable between coaxial and optical Toslink inputs). The front panel has dedicated Mono, Mute, and Dim (attenuate) buttons, and a large 30-segment input LED with peak/hold. The CSR-1 remote control is cabled to the rackmounted unit via a DB-9 connector, allowing tabletop control of the talkback, master monitoring volume, input/output switching, and mono, dim (attenuation), and mute functions. It features its own internal talkback microphone.

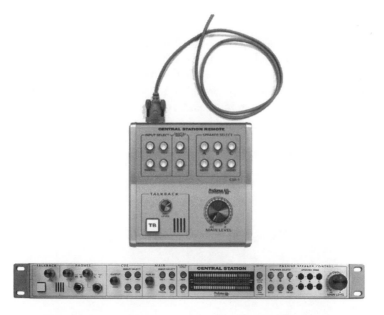

Figure B.28 Central Station, by Presonus, with the CSR-1 remote.

Samson C-control

Samson calls this unit a "control room matrix," and it certainly offers a lot of flexibility for a very economical price (about $100); see Figure B.29. The C-control allows switching between four pairs of stereo line outputs, three sets of line outputs for studio monitors, and three sets of stereo line outputs for output to other devices (a DAT or a CD burner, for example). There's a main Volume knob for the control room, and a second Volume control for matching the volume of speaker sets one and two when switched. A headphone amplifier with level control is provided, as well as a talkback section with a built-in condenser microphone that you can route to either the stereo outputs or the cue output for headphones. The C-control also has Mono, Dim, and Mute switches.

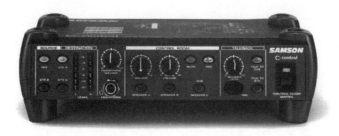

Figure B.29 C-control, by Samson.

Cranesong Avocet

This is a stereo controller for selecting between three digital stereo inputs and three analog stereo inputs whose input gain can be trimmed within a range of 8 dB each; see Figure B.30. Balanced line-level outputs are provided for up to three sets of speakers, while the headphone output can be fed either from the selected program source or from the third analog input. The Avocet includes Mono, Mute, and Dim buttons. You can connect an external talkback microphone, but no phantom power is provided by the Avocet.

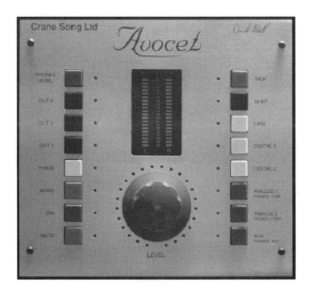

Figure B.30   Front panel of the remote control for the Avocet, by Glyph.

Storage, Digital Audio Networking

There are many alternatives for disk and tape subsystems that you can use with Pro Tools, and everyone's requirements are different. Here we simply mention a few items that may be of special interest to Pro Tools operators working in larger studios or production houses.

Glyph Technologies

Glyph offers a variety of rackmountable disk and tape subsystems for Pro Tools. These include the Trip series of rackmountable enclosures, customizable with a selection of FireWire and SCSI hard drives, plus a series of AIT tape drives for backup/archival, in 35, 50, 100, and 200 GB capacities. Glyph's GT series is a line of hot-swappable FireWire drive enclosures for Pro Tools and other digital audio workstations, many accommodating multiple cartridges ranging from 80 GB to 400 GB. See Figure B.31. There are cheaper drive options out there, but you get what you pay for. Glyph is a company that specifically understands the particular requirements of Pro Tools users (for example, *quiet*), and is there to back you up if problems ever occur. Also, unlike most drive manufacturers, Glyph doesn't make mechanism and firmware changes to its drives without guaranteeing that they will continue to support current versions of Pro Tools—which is worth a *lot*!

Figure B.31 The GT308 hot-swappable FireWire drive enclosure, by Glyph, has bays for eight hot-swappable FireWire drives, plus tape drives for backup/archival.

Studio Network Solutions

Their globalSAN X-4 is specifically designed for installations with multiple Pro Tools systems, and as with other globalSAN products, the end-user workstations communicate with the server via gigabit Ethernet. This unit uses the iSCSI protocol and provides 1.4 terabytes of storage (four 400 GB SATA drives, in a RAID configuration) within a 1U rackmounted enclosure. (Impressed? They also make a 9.6 terabyte system for Avid and Final Cut users!) The throughput offered by the globalSAN X-4 supports two Mac or Windows workstations simultaneously playing back 96 tracks each of 48 kHz, 24-bit audio. This is serious stuff for high-resolution, high-capacity facilities—a perusal of the users and quotes listed on SNS site makes it clear that this is one of the solutions that many of the "big kids" use. This company also specializes in Fibre Channel–based storage area networks (SANs) for sharing hard drives between Pro Tools workstations. (Each computer requires a Fibre Channel card.) Current offerings include the sanMP (multiplatform, Fibre Channel–based, and using the iSCSI protocol), globalSAN (similar features, but IP-based and operating over gigabit Ethernet cabling; this product line includes the aforementioned globalSAN X-4), and A/V SAN PRO (shared network storage, with disk arrays attached to a fibre switch controller). Studio Network Solutions also offers the Fibredrive for Mac and Windows, available in 73 and 146 GB capacities; see Figure B.32. The Fibredrive connects via Fibre Channel to a PCI card in the host computer, and supports much greater sustained throughput for real-time audio and video data than FireWire drives (Pro Tools playback on a dual-processor G5 of 192 simultaneous tracks of 48 kHz, 24-bit audio from a single drive, according to the manufacturer). To increase capacity, you can daisy-chain multiple accessory drives after the main unit.

Figure B.32   The Fibredrive, by Studio Network Solutions.

DigiDelivery

DigiDelivery allows Pro Tools users to collaborate in sessions, or to simply deliver finished spots and other media over the Internet. (It's the successor to Digidesign's DigiStudio service.) It consists of administrator and client software utilities, plus a dedicated DigiDelivery server—a rackmounted unit known as a "network appliance," which is purchased from Digidesign (although any user with Web access can receive a DigiDelivery). The feature set is developing rapidly, so your best source for updated information (as always) is the Digidesign Web site. Nevertheless, here's a quick overview of what DigiDelivery is all about.

You can deliver files of almost any type (including source Pro Tools sessions) to up to 100 recipients simultaneously. Administrators of a DigiDelivery server can manage server settings and accounts via a Web browser. A client application (available for both Mac OS X and Windows XP) must be installed on both the sending and receiving computers; it's a free download from Digidesign's Web site at http://www.digidesign.com/digidelivery/clients/. An account on a DigiDelivery server is required; this account could belong to the sender or the recipient (at no cost), or you can rent one from some third party for a monthly fee and then access it via the Internet. When sending Pro Tools sessions from Mac to Windows computers, it should be noted that SDII (Sound Designer II) format is not supported for the source session's audio files. (This is always the case when transferring to Windows disk volumes.) In this case, you should first use the File > Save Copy In command, creating a new copy of the Pro Tools Mac session with all the source audio files converted to Broadcast WAV (or AIFF) format.

Digidesign offers two options for medium or large production facilities that wish to own their own DigiDelivery server: the Serv|LT and Serv|GT (respectively supporting a limit of 20 or 80 pending deliveries on their internal 80 or 500 GB internal drives). In fact, a Serv|LT unit forms part of the Surround, Music, and Post bundles for D-Control. Reporting and billing functions are included so that you can bill clients for usage. With the Server-to-Server Relay feature, you can make project deliveries to the recipient's server (overnight, for example) without requiring the client to initiate the download.

The enabling technology for DigiDelivery is RocketDeliver and RocketServer. When you upload a Pro Tools session (which you can do directly from the File menu in current versions of Pro Tools), its associated media files are automatically gathered and uploaded, regardless of their present location on your system's audio disks. As soon as you post a delivery, an e-mail notification is sent to the recipients that, if you choose, contains that user's unique encryption key for opening the delivered files. At the time of this writing, while there is no limit on the size of deliveries, no individual file can be over 16 gigabytes. Obviously, when you are uploading multiple full-resolution audio files, a high-speed Internet connection (such as T1, T3, cable modem, or DSL) is essential. More detailed information about the DigiDelivery service is available on Digidesign's Web site. See Figure B.33.

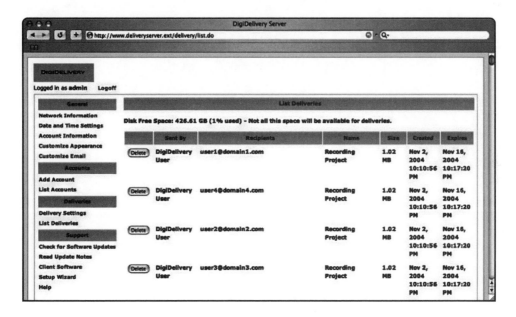

Figure B.33 The Web-based interface for managing a DigiDelivery server.

Appendix C}

Archive and Backup

Digital audio data occupies *large* amounts of disk space. As seen in Table 3.1 in Chapter 3, "Your System Configuration," even at 16-bit resolution and a 44.1 kHz sample rate (like an audio CD), each stereo minute of audio consumes 10 MB of disk space. If you're using Pro Tools | HD and recording 24-bit audio at 192 kHz, each minute on each stereo track occupies 68.8 MB!

The large size of Pro Tools projects means that some of the more common methods of backing up and archiving data can become inconvenient. A graphic designer, for example, might make daily backups to Zip (or Jaz) disks, and copy completed projects to recordable CDs or DVDs (CD-R or DVD-R) for long-term storage. But if your Pro Tools projects incorporate multiple takes on multiple tracks (let alone higher sample rates), they already may exceed the capacity of these disk formats. An extra level of complexity is introduced when multiple disks are used for audio recording, both for space considerations and to spread the recording/playback load for better performance—especially when using higher resolutions on Pro Tools | HD systems. In order to effectively back up or archive your projects, you need to understand exactly how Pro Tools handles the audio files referenced in a session.

Where Pro Tools Stores Session Data

As you know, the principal document of Pro Tools is the session document. This file contains all the track and region names, pointers to the parent audio files (and video files, if applicable), the automation and mixing/signal routing, and all MIDI data. Session documents contain no audio data, so they are relatively small (generally well under a megabyte, even including a fair amount of MIDI data). As explained in Chapter 8, "Menu Selections: Highlights," the File > Save As command allows you to create successive iterations of your session document, which will all continue to reference the same Audio Files and Fade Files folders, also using these for any new audio recordings. If you instead create a copy of the current Pro Tools session using the File > Save Copy In command, that session document will use its *own* Audio Files and Fade Files folders to create any subsequent files. This Save dialog box provides the option to copy all audio files currently being used in the source session to the new session document's Audio Files folder. If you *don't* copy all the audio files, the new session copy still looks to the current session's Audio Files folder for the currently used audio files—and to make a backup or archive copy of that new session, you would need to copy *both* Audio Files folders in order to include all its source audio files.

The current session's Audio Files folder contains all audio recordings made within this session. In addition, audio files created as a result of processing functions in the AudioSuite menu (such as Pitch Shift, Time Compression/Expansion, or Normalization) are also stored here. Lastly, when you copy source audio files in the Import Audio dialog box (rather than simply adding them as a reference to their original location, if they're already compatible with your session's selected audio file format), copies are also placed within this session's Audio Files folder. (Stereo source files are also copied to dual mono files when imported, and are placed in the Audio Files folder.)

The DigiBase browser windows help keep track of which files are being used in the current session document and where they reside. The Workspace browser shows all disk volumes on your system, which folders and media files they contain, which drives are designated for audio recording and/or playback, and most importantly, how much free space is currently available. When preparing for backup or archive, though, you will find the Project Browser window (shown in Figure C.1) especially useful. Among other helpful information about the audio files used in the current session, the Path column allows you to quickly confirm the disk and folder locations where these files reside.

As you create fades and crossfades in your audio tracks, fade files are automatically generated by Pro Tools. Each time you adjust the duration of a fade, a new fade file is created for it (and played back at the appropriate moment within the track). Each of these fade files is an audio file at your session's specified bit-depth and sample rate, and not surprisingly, they are stored in the Fade Files folder. However, be aware that you don't necessarily have to back up the Fade Files folder. When you open an existing session, if any fade files are not found, a dialog box will appear with a check box to re-create any missing fades (which might take a minute or so in very complex sessions). Fade files that are no longer in use will not be re-created.

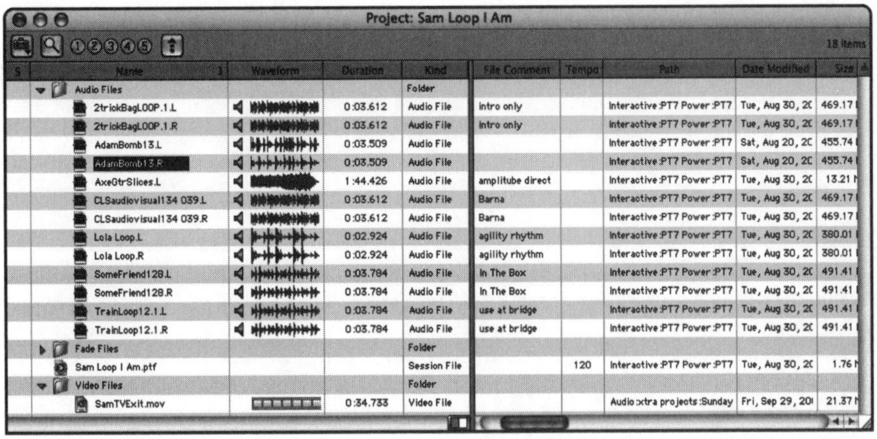

Figure C.1   The Project Browser window helps keep track of audio file formats and disk locations.

Using *multiple disks* for audio recording, however, makes the backup and archive scenario a little more complicated. In Setup > Disk Allocation, you can select a specific disk for recording from each audio track. Alternatively, using round-robin allocation, Pro Tools will cycle to the next eligible audio drive for storing audio files with each new audio track you create. (In either case, only disks that have been designated as Record volumes—as opposed to Playback or Transfer only—in the Workspace browser window are eligible.) Whenever additional disks are used for recording audio (other than the one on which the session file itself resides), a folder with the same name as your session folder is automatically created on the other disk(s), containing Audio Files and Fade Files folders used for tracks allocated to that record drive. So, if you're using multiple disks for audio recording and playback in your Pro Tools projects—which is extremely likely with Pro Tools|HD at higher sample rates—you also need to back up these additional folders on the other disks (in addition to the source session folder) to make sure you've included all the session's source files.

Lastly, bear in mind that not all the audio files used in a Pro Tools session necessarily reside in the Audio Files folder. When an audio file imported into your Pro Tools session from another location doesn't require any conversion, that file remains in its original location—unless you intentionally use the Copy button instead of the Add button in the Import Audio dialog box so that it will be copied into the current session's Audio Files folder (see the following tip, however). For instance, you might keep a folder of standard sound effects for use in multiple projects, or use mixes bounced from other programs or Pro Tools sessions. These could be used in Pro Tools directly from their original location. (In the Import Audio dialog box, Pro Tools would inform you that the file can be added directly to the current session because the file's audio file format and resolution already match the current session, and you would therefore use the Add button instead of the Copy button.) In this case, you may opt to archive these along with each session where they are used (to ensure a complete, self-contained archive), or to archive these commonly accessed files separately.

> ❈ **Tip: Preferences for Importing Audio**
>
> In the Operation tab of the Preferences dialog box, you can enable the Automatically Copy Files on Import option. Using this feature, audio files imported into Pro Tools are always copied into the Audio Files folder of the current session, even if their audio format would have permitted them to be used from their original location. Although this increases your usage of disk space, it has several advantages. First, when making your nightly backups or archiving the finished project, you know for sure that all its source audio files are inside its Audio Files folder (or several Audio Files folders, if you're using multiple disks for audio recording in this session). Second, it can be less dangerous! The Region List's Compact Selected command, as well as its Clear Selected command using the Delete button, permanently alter or delete the original audio files. So does any processing applied with AudioSuite menu options when their Overwrite Files mode is enabled. If you use audio files in multiple sessions (and especially if several people use the same Pro Tools system), a careless moment can have catastrophic consequences for some other Pro Tools session document. Having each session make new copies of all imported audio files reduces the risk of this occurring. You still must be careful about this, however, when using the File > Save As command to save successive iterations of a session document; remember that all these session copies continue to use the same Audio Files and Fade Files folders!

In a professional studio setting, it can be a good idea to keep track sheets and project logs for your Pro Tools sessions, indicating which audio files are used and their disk locations. This will make archiving and retrieving multiple sessions easier. The Project Browser window and (on TDM systems) the File > Export > Session as Text command make this much easier. You could save these text files, print them, or include them in word-processing documents. Alternatively, you could build a simple database (in FileMaker Pro, for example) with a text field in the database record for each archived session, where you can paste this text data exported from Pro Tools. (While you're at it, create additional fields for the project name, client, session sample rate, and bit-depth, microphones used, account rep, or whatever other information about the session you think could be useful to recall in the future.)

Why and When Should You Save Your Data?

Backup and archiving are performed for different reasons, as explained later in this appendix. In either case, though, as a Pro Tools user, you are dealing with very large amounts of data. Zip disks, for example, have been popular for office and graphics users, but are much too small for most Pro Tools situations. Also, remember these commands in the Region List's submenu: Select Unused, Clear, and Compact. By eliminating unused takes and compacting longer audio files in which you've used only a few small segments, you can free up considerable disk space and also make your backup/archive smaller. Just be sure you take the time to think through what you're doing; don't get ahead of yourself eliminating unused regions if you will be compositing a track from multiple takes afterward, for example!

Backup

Backup is a precaution; you must regularly make safety copies of all your important data (like, say, your client's projects) so that if some disaster (disk malfunction, smoke damage, virus damage, or operator error) causes it to be lost from your computer, you can go back to these safety copies instead of losing the entire project. It's kind of like what your dentist says about your teeth: You don't have to take care of all of them, just the ones you don't want to lose! Ideally, you should make backup copies every work day if you have a fast, convenient means of doing so. Also, you really should store your backup copies in a different room—or, ideally, in a different building. After all, what good will it do you to back up your work if your CD/DVD backup copies are sitting in a box next to the computer and there's ever a fire in the studio? At the very least, you should perform a fairly thorough backup of all your important data once a week—assuming that you don't mind potentially losing an entire week's worth of work, or you think you can explain to your clients how you've lost several days worth of recordings!

You should also periodically back up your entire computer. The bottom line? The more convenient it is to back up the huge amounts of data you generate in Pro Tools, and the faster it is, the more often you will do it! And while we're on the subject of data security, consider investing in a small fireproof box. Keep all your original disks from Pro Tools (including authorization disks, if any, and all other related programs) organized in this single location. With the insurance money, you can purchase new computers and audio hardware, but all the installation materials will be a real hassle to get again. (Not as bad as losing the actual *work* you've done in Pro Tools if you aren't backing up your project data on a regular basis, and possibly your client—but you get the idea!)

Archive

Archiving is more long-term storage and should be performed on finished projects or seldom-used files that you don't wish to keep on your system for space considerations or other reasons. As with backing up, when archiving, take a moment to carefully eliminate any unused audio regions and compact the remaining audio files in your Pro Tools session (being extra careful to confirm they aren't also being used in other sessions) before archiving this session folder and its related files (for example, bounced mixes) off your system. Even so, for most Pro Tools users, recordable CDs are simply too small and inconvenient for anything but very small projects; recordable DVDs are much more practical, even for mid-sized and project studios.

> ❋ **Tip: Create and Maintain a Database of Your Archived Work!**
>
> Once you've been at this for a while, you'll likely have a very large number of archived disks. Locating and retrieving a specific session or project can become unwieldy if you don't get yourself organized. There are many solutions for this, but here is a method that has worked for us: Number each archive disk, of course. Then, build a simple database (we use FileMaker Pro, by Claris, although Microsoft Access would also serve this purpose). While archiving off each disk, enter all the information about the project files it contains into this database, plus the date of archive, the disk number, who performed the archive operation, and so on. This makes it really easy to find a project among the hundreds of archive discs you may have accumulated. If you prefer to purchase a solution for this, have a look at Studio Suite, by AlterMedia (http://www.studiosuite.com). This studio management application for Mac and Windows includes an archive database. It also prints labels (with bar codes) for media, does time tracking for booking and billing your studio rooms, equipment, and people, generates invoices, organizes equipment inventory and barcoding, keeps maintenance logs, and creates patchbay labels. Studio Suite also features a contact manager, to-do lists, a calendar, templates for purchase orders, and a petty-cash tracker!

CD-R, DVD-R

A standard data CD-ROM holds nearly 700 MB of data. This seems like a lot to most users, but for backing up or archiving audio (and even worse, video) data, 700 MB suddenly isn't so spacious after all. Let's say you record 16 channels continuously for four minutes, at a bare-minimum 16-bit, 44.1 kHz resolution (higher bit-depths and/or sampling rates of course creating larger files). Your Audio Files folder will already be over 364 MB, and you haven't even started creating fade files, new files/regions with AudioSuite functions, or bouncing out mix files yet—let alone recording multiple takes of the same song or recording overdubs!

If you *have* to archive or back up such a project to CD-R, you can use a program like Retrospect to automatically split it to multiple discs. However, using this method, it's not so easy afterward to retrieve just one or two files from this session without reloading the entire project to your system. Alternatively, you could take the time to split up your project files into a series of folders that are smaller than 700 MB each, and then burn each of these to a separate CD, which is burdensome and takes a surprising amount of time. In short, unless you exclusively do short-duration sessions with a small number of tracks, it's *highly* desirable to have a DVD recording drive on your Pro Tools computer; at today's prices, it can be considered a must!

A 4.7 GB recordable DVD (either DVD+R or the somewhat less popular DVD-R format) actually holds about 4.3 GB of data. If your Macintosh computer has a recordable DVD drive (SuperDrive), you can use Roxio's Toast Titanium program or the Finder itself to record data to DVDs and CDs, while Nero, Easy Media Creator, and other programs are practical choices for this on Windows systems. Due to their larger capacity, recordable DVDs are an excellent choice for archiving Pro Tools projects (especially with smaller numbers of tracks and shorter durations), because many of them *will* fit into 4 GB or so—and if not, can perhaps be split between two discs rather than, say, nine or 10 CDs!

The capacity of each DVD can still be rather small for Pro Tools users with a large number of high-resolution audio tracks in their sessions, however. As with CD-Rs, splitting large sessions onto multiple DVDs can be unwieldy and time-consuming. More recent double-layer DVD formats offer capacities up to 8.5 GB on a single-sided disc (DVD+R9 media). When using current double-layer (also known as dual-layer) models to write to conventional DVD-R and DVD+R media, 8× and 16× write speeds are supported. For users who record at higher sample rates, longer durations, or higher track counts, a double-layer drive for backing up data to DVD can be a good option.

Blu-ray Disc

Blu-ray is yet another optical format that is quickly gaining support. The name derives from the fact that disk drives for Blu-ray use a blue-violet laser to read and write data at higher densities, rather than the longer-wavelength red laser in current DVD drives and recorders. While a 36.5 Mbps transfer rate is the current 1.0 specification (useful for recording and playback of HDTV at full quality, among other things), the Blu-ray Disc Association (BDA) is currently working on a 2.0 specification that will double this transfer rate, with further speed increases predicted over the coming years. A single-layer Blu-ray disc offers 25 GB capacity, while dual-layer versions reach 50 GB. In addition to the BD-ROM format that will be used for pre-recorded content and the BD-RE format for HDTV recording, of special interest to users of media workstations are the BD-R (recordable) and BD-RW (rewritable) Blu-ray disc formats. The BDA includes Apple, Dell, Hitachi, HP, JVC, LG, Mitsubishi, Panasonic, Pioneer, Philips, Samsung, Sharp, Sony, TDK, Thomson, 20th Century Fox, and the Walt Disney Company. Obviously, as this format becomes more ubiquitous, it will be of great interest to those of us who manage large quantities of media data!

Note: Apple's SuperDrive

The SuperDrive included in many Macintosh computers reads audio CDs, CD-ROMs, and data or video DVDs. It can also record data or audio onto write-once CDs (CD-R), rewritable CDs (CD-RW), and data or video onto write-once DVDs (DVD-R), but *not* DVD-RW.

What About Rewritable Media?

Users often ask about rewritable media for backup and archive (CD-RW, CD+RW, DVD-RW, DVD+RW, and the older DVD-RAM format). Rewritable media undoubtedly has a place in the backup/archive strategy for any Pro Tools system, but always in conjunction with write-once media. First, keep in mind that some older consumer audio CD players (and older computer CD drives) won't play rewritable CDs at all, so these are a potentially problematic option for burning audio mixes to CD. At any rate, given how inexpensive recordable CD media has become, there's really no reason not to use write-once CD media for trial audio mixes anyway. Even for backup and archive, there's a cost issue to consider. You can buy a pretty large number of write-once disks for the price of a single rewritable disc, so for long-term archival, write-once disks (CD-R, DVD-R) are generally the way to go. Given how inexpensive they have become, write-once CD-Rs can even be a practical choice for daily/weekly backup of smaller sessions—not to mention all the other non-audio files that are essential to running a studio (billing, archived databases, and correspondence, for example). The price disparity is especially dramatic for recordable CDs (CD-R). Sold in spindles of 50–100, they're currently well under 30 cents each, versus up to eight or ten times more for a single CD-RW. The price differential for DVD-R versus DVD-RW is similar (again, prices for DVD drives and media have dropped so much over the past few years that CD backup isn't really the solution we recommend for most Pro Tools users anyway). So you could potentially save ten incremental archive/backups as your project progresses for the same price as a single backup on a rewritable disc. (Some of the more rudimentary CD/DVD writing programs don't support creating multisession discs on rewritable media, so each previous backup on the recordable disc must be erased in order to write a new session.) Furthermore, if your projects are important (and your clients just might think so), you really should have more than one generation of backup. Otherwise, what happens if the last version you backed up was already damaged without you knowing it?

All this being said, many Pro Tools users will find rewritable discs to be a very practical part of their backup routine. For example, at the end of each day, you could back up your session onto a rewritable DVD (or several, if necessary), rotating through two or three different daily discs as a safety precaution. When the project was finished, it would then be archived off the system onto conventional write-once DVDs or a tape backup system. As long as the CD players you will be using for this purpose support rewritable CDs, these can also be a good option for burning trial mixes for listening on home stereos, boom boxes, automobile stereos, and so on.

Rewritable DVD Formats

DVD+RW is a rewritable DVD format; its discs can be read by most standard DVD drives (either in computers or in standard video DVD players). DVD+RW uses 4.7 GB media. This is currently the most common rewritable DVD format among computer users. The DVD-RW format developed by Pioneer is similar, but lacks the built-in media defect management features of the DVD+RW format, which was developed by a coalition of large manufacturers. If you're buying a DVD recording drive, you can cover your bets if necessary by choosing a model that supports both "plus" and "dash" rewritable formats for DVDs. By all means, get the fastest drive you can afford—given their larger capacity, the difference between a 16× DVD burner and a 2× model represents a lot fewer minutes waiting for the process to be completed.

Now largely obsolete, DVD-RAM drives allowed recording up to 2.6 GB or 4.7 GB (single- or dual-sided media). DVD-RAM drives could also read standard DVDs, CD-ROMs, and audio CDs. DVD-RAM cartridges were encased in a caddy and couldn't be used in standard video DVD players; partially for that reason, most users opted for the DVD+RW and DVD-RW formats instead. On the plus side, a DVD-RAM cartridge could ostensibly be rewritten up to 100,000 times (versus 1,000 for DVD+RW, for example). In the past, Apple offered DVD-RAM drive options for certain G4 Macintosh computers (although the CD/DVD-R SuperDrive is more common). This format is mentioned here for the sake of completeness; recorders supporting the DVD+RW and/or DVD-RW formats are a more practical choice (drives that support *both* formats obviously offer more flexibility).

❋ **Note: Toast Titanium (Mac)**

This disc-burning program from Roxio (now a division of Sonic Solutions) supports writing a variety of disc formats, including CD-R, CD-RW, DVD-R, DVD+RW, and DVD-RAM. For manual backup, it can often be sufficient (as long as you know where all the files used in your Pro Tools sessions reside). Among the CD formats Toast supports: audio CD (CD-DA), CD-ROM in Mac (HFS), Windows (ISO), or hybrid Mac/Win formats, Video CD; CD-I, MP3 CD, and Enhanced Music CD. Toast Titanium versions 6 and higher support writing multiple sessions to DVD+RW discs (in other words, the previous day's backup wouldn't have to be erased from the recordable DVD before backing up today's data). Although a basic version of Toast is often bundled with third-party CD or DVD-recording drives for Macs, you must purchase the Titanium upgrade to take advantage of all these features. The Toast Titanium 6 bundle also includes Déjà Vu backup software for Macintosh.

Toast 7 supports data spanning when creating archive CDs or DVDs. Large data sets are automatically split across multiple disks as they are burned, and restoring from these multi-disk archives (either the entire set or a single file) is equally easy. Also of note is Toast 7's ability to convert audio files to OOF, FLAC, and AAC formats, as well as the creation of audio DVDs that are compatible with standard DVD players, with onscreen video menus and up to 50 hours of audio.

Removable Disk Options for Data Backup

If your smaller Pro Tools projects fit their capacity, you may find that removable disk drives are acceptable for daily backups, such as Iomega's REV removable drive systems (35 GB), or their once-popular Jaz (1 or 2 GB; now discontinued). It's generally faster to copy data to these drives than to burn a CD/DVD copy, and once you make the initial investment in the drive itself plus a few disk cartridges (which you should also rotate through a couple of backup generations), it can be easy and economical to make your daily backups in this manner. Zip disks (100, 250, or 750 MB), are generally too small and slow for Pro Tools users, except perhaps multimedia sound designers who deal with relatively short audio durations and a smaller number of tracks, or perhaps as a transfer medium for mixes and voice-overs when collaborating with video editors. Remember that these are all magnetic storage devices; this is *not* the way to archive projects for years!

As the price per gigabyte of hard-disk storage continues to plummet each year, many Pro Tools users have found external or removable hard drives to be an excellent option for daily back-ups. Given that compact external FireWire drives are available in 160 GB capacities for under $150, they can be the ideal "removable media" for backing up large sessions on a daily basis. And because these are full-performance hard drives, the transfer rates are also faster than DVD, tape, or most of the removable disk drive systems just mentioned. Before walking out of your studio at the end of the session, you just drag your session folders (and supplementary Audio Files/Fade Files folders, if the session spans multiple disks) onto the FireWire drive. You then unhook that drive, drop it into your briefcase or backpack, and take it home with you for safekeeping. For that matter, you can spend a little more for an external FireWire drive that meets the performance requirements for Pro Tools; that way, if a disaster occurs in your own studio, you can simply open this session directly from the FireWire disk attached to some other Pro Tools system.

Additionally, inexpensive FireWire caddies (enclosures into which you can swap a drive mechanism) are widely available. This can be another way not only to access the contents of a disk from another system, but also to swap various disks into a single enclosure as projects come and go.

More sophisticated removable hard drive systems are also available for Pro Tools. For example, Glyph offers the rackmountable GT 103 unit with bays for up to three hot-swappable "GT Key" FireWire hard drive cartridges, with capacities up to 400 GB each (7,200 rpm mechanisms using the Oxford 911 chipset). Not only does this facilitate using hard drives as a backup medium, but it also allows the same Pro Tools system to be used simultaneously for many large sessions (because each one could use a completely separate set of removable hard disks, if necessary).

Yet another backup strategy is the use of disk imaging or mirroring systems, such as Norton's Ghost, or features for this included in the Mezzo or Nero Ultra software suites, which are discussed in the "Backup Software" section at the end of this appendix. Having a mirror image of an audio drive is obviously a useful function; these programs, however, can also image the disk where the operating system and all your program files reside. Should these ever become corrupted or lost due to media defects, a virus, operator error, or loss of the computer itself, having this snapshot of the previous system state to go back to will be hugely important, saving downtime and possibly avoiding the loss of a client.

Of course, once the project is complete and you want to permanently *archive* the session, you will want to look at one of the other more cost-effective data-storage formats discussed here (DVD or tape archive, for example).

❄ **Tip: Respect for the Older Generation (Of Backup!)**

If your projects are mission critical (in other words, it could mean losing a client—or your job—if you were to lose an entire project due to a system malfunction, virus, or human error), then you should take a serious attitude toward backup. Consider this scenario: You faithfully back up your Pro Tools session at the end of the day (or night!), turn out the lights, and go home. In the dead of the night, a fire breaks out, your nitwit partner or intern throws your session in the trash, a virus trashes your entire system in spectacular fashion, your computer kicks the bucket of natural causes, or the Morlocks creep in and drag your computer (not to mention your priceless time machine) off to their underground lair. Okay, possibly after calling the insurance company and making necessary repairs/replacements, you're ready to reload your session and audio files from the backup copy. (You've also cleverly stored your backups in a different room or building to prevent them from being damaged by the very same smoke or fire as the computer itself, right?) Much to your dismay, though, you discover that your session file or audio files were already damaged (or "corrupted") when you backed them up.

To avoid anguish, embarrassment, and everlasting torment, you should work through two or three different generations of backup. For example, if you are using rewritable media (CD-RW, DVD-RW, 35 GB REV disks, tape, and so on), you should rotate through two or three disks (writing backup dates in pencil as you go). That way, if yesterday's file copies were already damaged when backed up, you can always go back to the day before yesterday, or the day before that.

Tape Backup Options

Back when the largest removable disk solutions were 1 GB or less, tape drives were the only practical way to back up or archive large media projects. Currently, common tape formats include (data) DAT/DDS, DLT, Exabyte, LTO-2 (Ultrium), OnStream ADR, AIT (Sony), and others. Many of these are supported by the Retrospect and Mezzo backup programs (see the next section), and you will find them in numerous production facilities. To be brutally frank, though, tape backup/restore has traditionally been much slower and not especially more reliable than disk-based alternatives. However, some of the current high-capacity tape drives, including the AIT and Exabyte Mammoth types, offer excellent data-transfer rates (higher than recordable DVDs, for example), and are an excellent choice for professional facilities, especially when large projects need to be archived on a regular basis.

For daily backups (as opposed to long-term archiving of data), here's how the general trend goes in media production (as opposed to, say, banking, where capacity requirements increase at a more modest rate): People buy tape subsystems for backup because the daily capacity they require exceeds that of currently available (or economical) removable disk storage. Then time marches on, and widely available disk formats overtake the capacity of yesterday's tape drives. Meanwhile, media applications relentlessly push toward higher resolutions (like you Pro Tools|HD types recording at 24-bit, 192 kHz—hey, Flipper says to tweak the high end on the banjo track at about 75 kHz!), and consequently require the latest-generation, even-higher capacity tape storage systems. Whatever model you choose, within a couple of years it will be superseded by another unit with higher transfer rates or larger capacity.

Currently, LTO drives are available from various manufacturers in capacities per cartridge of 100, 200, or 400 (compressed) GB, and up to 16 cartridge slots, allowing up to 6.4 TB (terabytes) to be archived in a single operation. AIT systems offer uncompressed capacities of 25, 50, or 100 GB per tape (AIT-1, AIT-2, AIT-3, AIT-4). Some DLT tapes reach 40 GB (while SDLT starts at 110 GB), Exabyte VXA tapes reach 33GB, and Exabyte Mammoth tapes reach 60 GB, uncompressed. In most of these cases, multi-tape "jukebox" or "library" configurations are also available, with greatly superior capacities. Not too long ago, 2 GB on a DAT (DDS) tape or 5 GB on an 8-millimeter Exabyte tape was considered impressive! Expensive as these tape cartridges are (especially because you will be rotating through several generations of backup tapes, if you're serious), if your facility is archiving off a very large number of copies during the course of a year (that is, multiple projects, multiple suites, daily incremental backups, and weekly full backups), it will eventually work out to be cheaper to use tape rather than large-capacity disks for backup and data storage. The economics of your own situation will determine the best solution. If you generally work with mid-sized or small Pro Tools sessions at 48 kHz sample rates or less, and only 12–32 channels of I/O, then some combination of recordable-rewritable DVDs, large-capacity removable disk systems, or external FireWire drives may be more than sufficient for your backup and archive requirements.

As mentioned in the "Backup Software" section near the end of this appendix, dedicated backup software always includes the capability for incremental backups; only files that have actually changed since the previous backup are copied off to tape. This not only greatly decreases the storage capacity required for nightly backups, but also makes the operation much quicker (because unchanged files aren't being copied to tape). For large facilities with multiple users and projects, this is the most reliable solution.

One last observation about removable data storage, either on tape or disk: These systems often have a limited commercial existence. It is entirely possible that, in perhaps seven or eight years, a given data-storage format that everybody is using right now may be a) no longer manufactured, b) hard to find removable media for, or c) incompatible with current computers and operating systems. We encourage you to be conservative; take a good hard look at who manufactures the drive and how widespread it is beyond the media-production industry. Even so, consider what you would do today if someone handed you a 44 MB SyQuest cartridge (the de facto standard about 15 years ago for transporting what were considered "large" quantities of data between computer systems) containing a Sound Designer file to be remastered. Because of this rapid cycle of obsolescence for data-storage media, commercial production facilities often must take the time and expense to periodically transfer their vaults to more current storage formats, or otherwise maintain older computer systems and antique storage peripherals for the sole purpose of retrieving these archived projects when necessary.

> ❋ **Caution: Ya Gotta Keep 'Em Separated!**
>
> Storing all your backups and archived projects right next to your computer only increases the chances that both will be simultaneously destroyed by the same smoke, heat, fire, beer party, flood, or Texas twister! Of course, you only need to worry about this for important data—if it will be okay to irretrievably lose your client's archived projects, feel free to put all your eggs in one basket. Otherwise, you should ideally store backups/archives in a second building (even better, *two* copies, in separate locations), or at the very least, store them in a different room—in a fireproof box! Even without such disaster and offsite storage scenarios, given how inexpensive recordable DVD media is, you should consider making *two* archive copies for important projects—just in case one of them turns out to be damaged or has a write error that you didn't detect at the time.

Backup Software

As previously mentioned in the preceding "Tape Backup Options" section, one of the essential techniques for tape backup is the ability to perform daily incremental backups. In this method, the software looks at modification dates for every file on the disk volumes selected for backup, and copies only those files that have been modified since the date and time of the last full or incremental backup to tape. This saves time and avoids wasting tape space on redundant copies of files that haven't changed. Many excellent backup programs are available. Only three will be mentioned here—two because they're ubiquitous and also perform admirably, and a third because it understands the project structure of Pro Tools sessions (and many other media programs), which makes the backup and archival process more efficient.

* ❋ Retrospect Backup, by EMC Dantz, is a widespread and highly reliable backup program for Windows and Macintosh. Retrospect can perform incremental and full backups from multiple disk locations (including other networked computers), which can be stored and repeated later and programmed to occur at specific dates and times. It supports various disk types and tape drives (LTO, DAT/DDS, DLT, VXA, Exabyte Mammoth, and Exabyte, among others). This program can also back up to CD-R discs (and can span several CD-Rs for a single backup—since 650 MB per CD is so small!). Retrospect doesn't have any intrinsic understanding of how Pro Tools projects are structured, however. It is your responsibility to understand that a Pro Tools session may use files and folders on multiple disks, and to make sure these are all included in the selected data for backup.

* ❋ Nero Ultra, by Ahead Systems, includes the NeroBackItUp utility for programmed backup operations (either full or incremental). The Nero Ultra suite of software also provides excellent tools for creating data CDs and DVDs, an audio editor that supports DirectX plug-ins, a driveimaging utility, and, among other things, robust capabilities for creating audio CDs.

* ❋ Mezzo, by Grey Matter Response, is an interesting alternative for Macintosh systems, especially for users who manage multiple large projects or for facilities where the person responsible for backups may not be the main Pro Tools operator. Like Retrospect, Mezzo supports numerous tape formats (OnStream ADR, AIT-1, AIT-2 and AIT3 up to 100 GB, DLT, LTO, Exabyte, Exabyte Mammoth, and DDS-1/DDS-2 data DAT, to name a few)

and disk types including recordable DVDs. Mezzo allows for incremental and full backups to be programmed for repeated use at specific dates and times—even from a central point over a network. However, the great strength of Mezzo is that it understands the data structure of Pro Tools (not to mention Digital Performer, Adobe Premiere, Avid Media Composer and Film Composer, Avid Xpress, Apple FinalCut Pro, and Media 100). When you schedule a Pro Tools session for backup, Mezzo examines your session file to determine which audio files and folders are referenced by this Pro Tools session, no matter where they reside on your computer's disks. This ensures that the entire project is backed up, and doesn't require the operator to know where the audio files used in Pro Tools may be stored. When you later restore a Pro Tools project, the files and folders are copied back to their multiple disk locations. Furthermore, Mezzo tracks changes in the audio files and session document as you continue working on a project, enabling you to make nightly, incremental backups of only those files that have been changed. The program can also restore, verify, or back up Pro Tools sessions in the background while you continue working in Pro Tools; it understands idle time and manages not to interfere with audio recording and playback. Current versions of Mezzo also support drive mirroring, so that exact copies of multiple drives will always be available in the event of a malfunction (again, taking advantage of idle time for this feature, in order not to interfere with the performance of Pro Tools).

Appendix D

Power Tips and Loopy Ideas

Pro Tools is a huge program, and Digidesign has really done a remarkable job making it adaptable to so many different environments (music, spoken word, postproduction, and interactive authoring, to name just a few). Necessarily, there are many features that even expert users may overlook.

We've had the privilege of working with Pro Tools since the very first versions, and have also been fortunate enough to learn from many creative professional Pro Tools users among our friends and clients. What follows is a potpourri of cool tricks and clever workarounds we've picked up along the way. Hopefully, you will find some of these inspiring! Also, for good measure, we threw in a few good keyboard shortcuts that too many users seem to overlook (even though these shortcuts are listed in the great *Keyboard Shortcuts* PDF document provided by Digidesign—which you've already printed out, of course).

Mixing and Processing Tips

Invert Polarity

Many Pro Tools users seem to miss the fact that many plug-in windows (including the DigiRack EQs, dynamics processors, and delays) have a Phase Invert button (usually to the right of the plug-in's main Input, Gain, or Threshold slider). When this button is enabled, the polarity of any signal passing through the plug-in is reversed. This is a good one to remember, for example, if you ever place microphones on both the front and back of a combo guitar amplifier, or the top and bottom of a snare drum. If one of these paired tracks is pulling air while the other one is pushing, you're not going to be happy with the sound.

Waaaah! I Can't Turn the Tape Around to Create Backward Reverb!

Okay, stop your analog sniveling—creating *preverb* is easy. For the sake of argument, let's say you're creating this effect for the lead vocal track. Here's what to do:

1. In the Edit window, select the entire vocal track, starting from the beginning of the session's timeline and extending a few seconds past the end of the last region in the track (to be sure you can record the entire reverb decay *after* the end of the reversed selection).

2. Duplicate the vocal track's current playlist (using the pop-up selector just to the right of the track's name in the Edit window), and name this new version Reverse.

3. Apply the AudioSuite menu's Reverse function to the vocal selection (creating one continuous file for the reversed result of the entire selection).

4. Create an Aux In with a reverb plug-in, and select a Pro Tools bus as this Aux In's input source.

5. Create a send from the vocal track, routed to the reverb Aux In's selected input bus, and adjust the reverb parameters to suit your taste.

6. Assign the reverb Aux In's output to yet another Pro Tools bus.

7. Create a *new* audio track, and choose *that* bus as its input source.

8. Record-enable this new audio track.

9. With the reversed vocal region still selected, press Record to record the reverb Aux In's output into this new audio track.

10. Select the new audio region you've just created by recording, and reverse it (again using the AudioSuite menu function).

11. Use the vocal track's Playlist selector to switch back to its original, forward version. You should now hear the backward reverb ramping up before each peak in the vocal track. (If you also want to hear normal reverb following the forward vocal, assign the output of your reverb Aux In back to the main stereo mix instead of the bus to which it's currently assigned.)

12. If you want to get fancy (especially because backward reverb often sounds sloppy *within* vocal phrases), insert a compressor on the backward reverb track and side chain it with an external key whose source is the bus you're using for the reverb send from the vocal track itself. (Set the ratio of the compressor very high, and its threshold low.) Whenever the vocal track is present, it will duck down the backward reverb.

Squeaky-Clean Acoustic Guitar and Electric Bass

To reduce string squeak on acoustic guitars and especially electric bass (caused by fingers sliding along the strings as they shift positions), you can sometimes get results with a de-esser plug-in. Just slide the frequency down more into the range of 4–5 kHz or lower. Activate the Key Listen feature as you slide around the de-esser's Frequency parameter (which defines the center of the narrow band where compression will be applied) to focus on the offending squeaks. Then, adjust the Threshold setting as far down as you can get away with before noticeably altering the instrument's timbre. (There's more latitude on an electric bass; because its fundamental frequencies are lower, harmonics up in the squeak zone are spaced farther apart.)

Adjusting Individual Volume Levels in Grouped Tracks

Ordinarily, after you create a Mix group, adjusting the volume level of any of its track faders will move all the faders up or down, maintaining their relative positions. This can be very convenient, for example, for seven or eight drum tracks, several backing vocal tracks, and so on. But what if you want to individually adjust the volume of one track in a group? Obviously, you could use the Mix Groups List (in the lower-left area of the Mix window) to temporarily disable the group, adjust the track's volume fader, and then reenable the group. (Groups in this list are active only when they're highlighted.) But there's a quicker way: While holding down the Control key (Start key in Windows), you can individually adjust any fader in an active group.

Delay Compensation, with Time Adjuster Plug-in

Generally speaking, each plug-in introduces a small amount of delay in a track's signal path. For example, in Pro Tools HD, this delay is about four samples for a majority of DigiRack plug-ins, while it can be significantly greater for some third-party plug-ins that perform more complex processing. Let's say you're recording a drum set, with multiple microphones and tracks, at a 44.1 kHz sample rate, or 44,100 samples per second. If you inserted three plug-ins on your snare track (for example, a gate, a compressor, and an EQ), you've delayed the snare track by about 12 samples. At this sample rate, that's 0.3174 milliseconds. Assuming that the hi-hat and snare microphones bleed into each other, this could be enough to cause some smearing in the higher frequencies. (As may be obvious, at higher sample rates, this 4-sample delay represents a shorter time interval.)

The Time Adjuster plug-in provides up to 8195 samples of delay compensation adjustment. It also provides positive or negative gain adjustment, and a Phase (Polarity) Inversion function. You do not have to get crazy trying to adjust for plug-in delays on every single mono track. But in cases like the one outlined here, where the same signal is present in two different tracks, this is an important issue that can improve the overall sound of your mix—if you're willing to do the math.

On Pro Tools | HD systems, Automatic Delay Compensation automatically takes care of plug-in processing delay adjustments for you. Manual adjustments with the Time Adjuster plug-in are generally not necessary. Nice!

You can also use one of the Long Delay plug-ins (with its Mix value set to 100%) to compensate when track delays are instead caused by microphone placement. While you can also use the Time Adjuster plug-in for this purpose, its maximum delay amount may be insufficient for some applications (especially in live situations), and it's frequently more convenient to work in milliseconds rather than samples. (If you already know the distances involved in the microphone placement that cause the time alignment problems in the first place, you can use the well-known and simple formulas for calculating the corresponding delay times.)

Setting Tempo-Related Delays by Ear

Pro Tools allows you to set the timing of delay repeats to note values (in relation to the current session tempo) in all the DigiRack delay plug-ins except for Short and Slap delay. Chapter 12, "The Pro Tools Groove," discusses a manual method for setting delays to 1/8 note, 1/4 note, or other musical values with certain third- party delay plug-ins. Here's yet another way to do it, which doesn't even require calculating a tempo map for the session:

1. Assuming you have a snare backbeat (or perhaps a reasonably steady kick figure) in the song, create a send from this track to the delay.
2. Set your Feedback parameter to several repeats—perhaps about 25 percent or so.
3. Solo the snare/kick track and the Aux In track where this delay plug-in is instantiated.
4. While listening to playback, adjust the delay time until the repeats are in time with the 1/4 notes. This setting gives you the length of each 1/4 note, which then becomes your timing reference for calculating 1/8 and 1/16 note delays (1/2 or 1/4 the delay time), 1/4 triplet delays (2/3 the delay time), and so on.

Groovy Pre-Delays

One of the typical novice mistakes heard in cluttered-sounding Pro Tools mixes are multiple delays, with sloppy timings that clatter around in a nonmusical fashion. We find that setting delay times to specific musical note values, relative to the song's tempo, usually helps create more natural and open-sounding mixes. Hey, it can be hard enough to get the musicians to play in good time in the first place, without introducing even more random timing factors into the total! Remember that most *reverb* plug-ins also feature pre-delay times; adjusting these to tempo-related 1/8 note or 1/16 note values can also help create a better-sounding mix.

EQ: The Zero-Sum Game

Beginning engineers always seem to attack every equalization problem by *boosting* frequencies. Bass guitar or kick drum doesn't have enough edge? Crank it up! Not enough buzz-saw aggression on the crunch guitar part? Lash on some 2,500 Hz! The problem is, maximum level (*full-code*, or 0 dB) for the mix never changes. Consequently, because EQ is a *gain* change in a specific frequency range, boosting one instrument's level (or range within that instrument's frequency spectrum) can have more or less the same effect as *reducing* the gain of all others proportionately.

With this idea of a fixed ceiling in mind, experienced mixers often apply the technique of carving out frequency bands for instrumental parts, using gain reductions in specific, relatively narrow frequency ranges on other instrumental parts so that they compete less for those ranges of frequencies. On many great mixes, for example, if you were to solo perhaps the bass guitar part, you (or the bass player) might think it could really use a lot more clack in the low midrange. But by slightly notching out these frequencies in the bass part, the engineer has created a space for the corresponding clack of the beater striking the kick drum, which consequently comes forward in the mix—exactly what the song *as a whole* required.

Here's another example: For competing keyboard and guitar parts, instead of radically boosting that frequency range somewhere around 2–2.5 kHz, giving edge to crunchy rock guitar parts, try notching this same range downward in the keyboard part. You may find that the guitar really didn't need much more level or EQ at all—once it's no longer getting shouted down in this important frequency band.

It can be very misleading if you make all your EQ adjustments on individual tracks while they are soloed (especially if a performer is standing at your shoulder at the time, obsessing about his sound). Instead, when adjusting EQs, try to think in terms of the entire mix and the important places where each part needs to fit into the overall frequency spectrum in order to complement vocals and other instrumental parts. As far as overall volume adjustments are concerned, remember that the maximum level for the mix is always the same, so to put it simplistically, *boosting* one instrument's level (or one frequency range) is like turning *down* all the others!

EQ and Stereo/Surround Panning

Where you pan a sound in a stereo or surround mix will also affect your decisions about EQ. Among other factors, two sounds might not conflict as badly in a given frequency range if they are panned to widely separated positions. Furthermore, on a simple perception level, the timbre of a sound can seem to change according to position. However, as with delays, reverb, and other time parameters, relying on the inherent separation in your stereo or multichannel surround mix can come back to bite you later. Even if you aren't using stereo delays, chorus effects, and so on, it's very important to listen to your stereo mix in mono (or your surround mix in stereo, and so on) before making any final decisions about EQ. You may often be surprised at the logjam of conflicting frequencies present in your mix that weren't apparent in your controlled monitoring environment. To optimize their mixes for unpredictable real-world playback situations, you will see experienced engineers frequently switching between stereo and mono (and/or surround) as they make decisions about levels and EQ. You should, too!

Path Meter View in Output Windows

A surprising number of experienced Pro Tools users overlook this feature. Right next to the Close button at the top of Output windows (either for tracks or sends) is another button for the Path Meter view. Click this button to open up an additional right panel in the Output window, where a Level meter for the track or send's assigned path appears.

One great use for this feature is when many sends are assigned to the same bus (for example, the source for an Auxiliary Input track with a reverb or delay plug-in). Just as you can produce clipping and distortion on audio tracks, Aux In tracks, Instrument tracks, and Master

Faders, the summed signals from multiple sends can distort a bus on its way to the destination effect. After opening the Output window for any of the sends assigned to this bus, just click the Path Meter View button to see what kinds of levels are going on in the bus that is this send's destination. Like other Level meters in Pro Tools, the Path meter in an Output window has red clipping indicators in its top segment; you can clear these indicators by clicking them with the mouse or by using the Track > Clear All Clip Indicators command.

Gimme More in the Cans, Man!

This tip reviews yet another way of setting up a cue (headphone) mix in Pro Tools, using a multichannel audio interface. The headphone mix provided to performers is a crucial aspect of any recording session, especially when multiple performers are physically isolated from each other and depend on the headphone mix to hear each other. Here's what to do:

1. In the Mix window, set up your basic mix in Pro Tools (because your main volume and fader settings have no effect on recording levels, right?) as the performers run through the song. We're going to base the initial headphone mix on the mix you are monitoring in the control room.

2. Create a stereo send (send "A," for example) for the headphone mix so you can adjust its balance separately from the control room mix. Hold down the Option key (Alt key in Windows) as you create this send on any audio track (using the pop-up selector) so that the same send is simultaneously created on *all* audio tracks.

3. You could simply designate a stereo output pair on the audio interface as the destination for this send, but instead, let's choose an internal bus pair in Pro Tools (for example, bus 3–4) as the destination.

4. Use the Track > New command to create a stereo Auxiliary Input. Choose bus 3–4 (the destination of all the send A's we've created) as the input for the Aux In. This Aux In not only provides you with a single Volume fader for the headphone mix (which you could have also accomplished with a Master Fader for whatever stereo output is feeding the performers' headphone mix), but gives you the flexibility to apply compression, reverb, and so on to the musicians' cue mix without affecting what you hear in the control room through outputs 1–2.

5. Set the output assignment of this Aux In (and change this track name to Cue Mix while you're at it) to the output pair on your audio interface that will be connected to the performers' headphone amplifier—for example, outputs 3–4.

6. Open View > Sends A–E, and select send A, which you just created in step 2. You now see mini faders in each track; these control the level of send A.

7. Hold down the Option key (Alt key in Windows) and click on the P button in any of these sends to switch them all to pre-fader (so their level and mute status will be unaffected by that of the track itself, allowing you to make these changes in the control room during recording without affecting the headphone mix).

8. If you are using Pro Tools LE or M-Powered, you must set each send level separately (remember that as a starting point, you can Option-click (Alt-click in Windows) each

send's level slider to set it to 0 dB). If you are using Pro Tools HD, however, you can copy the current main mix to all these sends. Select all tracks by holding down the Option key (Alt key in Windows) and clicking on any track's name. Select Edit > Copy to Send. In the dialog box, copy the current values of the Volume and Pan settings to send A as the destination, and then click OK.

Once you've established this cue mix setup, here's one easy way to switch to monitoring the headphone mix in the control room in order to make adjustments (we're assuming that outputs 1–2 on the interface are the source of the control room monitoring mix):

1. Option-click (Alt-click in Windows) on any audio track's Mute button to mute them all. (Your pre-fader sends will be unaffected by this.)

2. Create a stereo send from the Cue Mix Aux In to outputs 1–2. Don't forget to Option-click (Alt-click in Windows) this send's level slider to set it to 0 dB!

3. When you're finished making adjustments, mute this send, and then Option-Click (Alt-click in Windows) as before to unmute your source audio tracks again.

By setting your cue mix as just described, you could even automate this mix going out to the performers' headphones, or use additional sends to route reverb and effect outputs to its bus, providing a near-finished product mix for the talent, which will be especially appreciated during last-minute overdubs. All this takes much less time than manually dialing in a headphone mix on an analog mixing console—leaving you more time for creative aspects of the production.

Creating a Tape-Flange Effect on the Entire Mix

In the old days, flanger effects were created by running a stereo mix through a second tape machine, and then manually applying pressure on the flange of that tape reel to vary its playback speed. When the output from this second machine was combined with the direct mix, the interaction between the original and pitch/time-shifted versions of the waveform created a distinctive whooshing sound, once especially popular as a psychedelic (and shagalicious!) drop-in effect for song transitions.

Although there are plug-ins available with great flanger effects based on modulated delays, there's a simple technique for creating this effect "organically" in any version of Pro Tools without requiring any plug-in processing at all. Our technique focuses on creating this effect on an entire stereo mix for a song section, but it's equally applicable to submixes or individual tracks:

1. Create a stereo Pro Tools track and place your stereo mix into it.

2. In order to experiment with just a short section, use the Edit > Separate Region > At Selection command to define a new region for a verse, chorus, or drum fill that you think is a good candidate for this effect. (And if you do so, copy this separated region to some later point in the track, after the end of the entire mix.)

3. Create another stereo audio track (or another grouped pair of mono tracks, in pre-5.1 versions), and Option-drag (Alt-drag in Windows) to copy your original mix/region into this new stereo track.

4. With the copied region(s) still selected in your new track, use the AudioSuite menu's Pitch Shift function to lower their pitch by a small amount, about 2 or 3 *cents* (hundredths of a semitone), making sure to disable (clear) the Time Correction check box. You want the Pitch Shift function to create new audio regions/files for the result (in other words, *don't* select the Overwrite Files option). The new, pitch-shifted region(s) will be slightly *longer* than the original. If you press Play now, you will hear that the two versions already flange against each other.

5. In Slip edit mode, select the original region, and set your Nudge Value to one-millisecond increments.

6. Use the + (plus) key to nudge the start point of the original region later in time than the pitch-shifted version. (In our example, you'll probably get best results somewhere between about 3 and 18 milliseconds.) Each time you press Play to hear the results of nudging the original region, notice that the most dramatic part of the flange sweep comes a number of seconds after the beginning of the selection. Therefore, to get best results, experimentation may lead you to start your effect a few seconds earlier—your ears will guide you!

7. When you have a sound you like, you can bounce the result to disk (re-importing it into the session), and then drop this flanged section into your original stereo mix. If you used the Edit > Separate Region > At Selection command, as described previously, it's easy to identify where your flanged drop-in belongs.

For the ultimate curl, invert the polarity of the pitch-shifted region when creating this effect. You can do this destructively via the AudioSuite menu, or in real-time by dropping in any of the Digi plug-ins with a Phase (Polarity) Invert button—it looks like a crossed-out zero.

Fatten Up Your Horns

If you have a real-time pitch-shifting plug-in available on your system (such as Digidesign's free DPP-1 (Digital Pitch Processor) for TDM, Auto-Tune, Pitch 'n Time, Pitch Doctor, Pure Pitch, or Octavox), this can be handy for beefing up your horn parts by adding additional octaves on certain instruments. For example, say your horn section consists of two trumpets, an alto sax, and a trombone, all recorded on separate mono tracks. Here's what you do:

1. Place EQ and compressor plug-ins on each source track.

2. Set your compression to a fairly high ratio, say 4:1, and adjust the EQ according to your taste.

3. Insert a pitch shifter on each trumpet track, and also on the trombone track.

4. Set both trumpets to +12 semitones—in other words, one octave upward.

5. Set the pitch shift on the trombone track to −12 semitones (one octave down).

6. Set the Mix % wet parameter to 50 percent (even amounts of the wet and dry signals), but experiment with lower percentages (that is, a lesser proportion of processed signal) for a subtler effect, especially on the suboctave you're adding to the trombone track.

7. Create a reverb send from all these tracks to a stereo bus pair, corresponding to the input selection of an Aux In where you've placed a reverb plug-in specifically for the horns.

8. Assign the outputs of all the audio tracks and the output of the horn reverb Aux In to another stereo bus pair.

9. Create a new Aux In track, set its input to monitor that bus, and place a stereo compressor on this Aux In. Not only is the entire horn mix being gain-controlled by single compressor, but so is the reverb on that horn mix.

A Change of Venue

This is really more of a general tip for novice mixers. If you only listen to your mix in one room, and always on the same playback system, upon subsequent listening elsewhere, you will almost certainly discover that there is much room for improvement. Before you bless any mix, burn a quick CD and play it on a few home stereos, boom boxes, and of course, the infallible gold standard for critical listening: your car! The prominence of vocals, delays, and reverbs, and especially the character of the low end, really does change radically according to the playback situation. We guarantee that performing this reality check early in the mix process will make you happier with the final results.

Editing Tips

New Track Shortcuts

Okay, everybody learns the Shift+Command+N shortcut (Shift+Ctrl+N in Windows) for opening the New Track dialog box fairly early in their experiences with Pro Tools. However, because too many experienced users never memorize the keyboard shortcuts within this dialog box—even though they're clearly indicated in Digidesign's PDF documentation—let's recap them here:

❊ While holding down the Command key (Ctrl key in Windows), the left/right arrows switch between mono and stereo (not applicable to MIDI tracks, of course), and the up/down arrows cycle through the possible track types—audio, Auxiliary Input, Instrument, Master Fader, or MIDI.

❊ While holding down the Command+Option keys (Ctrl+Alt keys in Windows), the up/down arrows switch between the Track Timebase options for the current track entry field—Samples (absolute) or Ticks (relative).

❊ You can create multiple track types simultaneously without leaving this dialog box by clicking the + sign at the end of each row. Alternatively, Command+plus/minus (+/−) on the numeric keypad (Ctrl+plus/minus in Windows) adds or deletes new rows of track entry fields.

Yes, I Know! No, Really!

Pro Tools is really good about warning you when an operation will be irrevocable, destructively modifying (or eliminating) audio data. This is a wonderful thing, and it has saved many inexperienced (and veteran) users from making a mistake. Sometimes, though, you are perfectly sure about what you're doing, and don't want to click through a second alert box to confirm it (like when you're clearing unusable audio tracks and deleting them from disk—gone forever). In these cases, hold down the Option key (Alt key in Windows) as you click the first OK button; you can bypass the confirmation dialog boxes. But please, *think* before you click!

Able Was I 'Ere I Saw Elba—Audio Palindromes

If you're looping background ambient effects (very short loops in the dynamo hum, unearthly glimmer category, for instance, that you might use a mouse rollOver sound in an interactive program), here's a technique that has occasionally helped us loop the unloopable:

1. Create a loop that plays the selection forward, then backward, so that its beginning and end points are identical.

2. Make a duplicate of the selection to be looped (via the Edit > Duplicate command). Select the second copy, and then apply the AudioSuite > Reverse command.

So far so good, but when you select both the forward and backward versions of the region for looped playback, we can almost guarantee the loop will not be smooth because you have one repeated sample at both region boundaries, and that's going to produce an audible glitch. Think about it: If the material in your original region is 12345, and you append a reversed copy to this, the result is a loop that goes 12345|54321|12345|54321, and so on, when what you want is a loop that goes 12345432|12345432|12345432. Get it? To fix this problem, switch to Shuffle mode, and trim exactly one sample off the beginning and end of the reverse copy—no more, no less. (This is easier if you change the time units of the Main location indicator to Samples.) If your single forward loop was already pretty close, you might now have a smoother loop, which as a bonus is also twice as long. Remember: Selections that begin and end at zero crossings generally have a greater chance of looping smoothly.

Export Region Definitions for Use in Other Sessions

This isn't so much a cool tip as a friendly reminder: Unless you're in Destructive Recording mode, each time you record on a Pro Tools audio track, a new audio file is created. A single region appears in the Region List that represents the entire audio file for that take. As you edit the audio in your tracks, additional region definitions are created automatically by Pro Tools, and of course the commands in the Edit menu's Separate Region submenu also create new region definitions. However, by default, these region definitions are contained only in the originating Pro Tools session document, not in the audio files themselves. If you try to import regions from one of these audio files into another Pro Tools session, only the whole-file region appears in the Import Audio dialog box (and not all the other region definitions within it that you created in the first session).

There are times when you *will* want to use region definitions from a session in other Pro Tools sessions, other audio programs, or even in a sampler program or plug-in. For example, if you create multiple regions within a drum track in order to build up new grooves, you might want to use these bits and pieces in other sessions. The Export Region Definitions command in the Region List's local menu does this for you. Region definitions from the current Pro Tools session are exported into their parent sound files, and are subsequently visible in the Import Audio dialog box from any other Pro Tools session.

Cycling Through the Edit Modes (Edit Window)

Pressing the single open quote (`) key (the unshifted equivalent to the tilde (ñ) key on US English keyboard layouts, although it may be elsewhere in other languages) enables you to cycle between the four Edit modes (Shuffle, Slip, Spot, and Grid).

Cycling Through the Edit Tools (Edit Window)

Pressing the Esc key (Mac) or the center mouse button, if you have one (in Windows), enables you to cycle between the Edit tools (Zoomer, Trimmer, Selector, Grabber, Smart tool, Scrubber, and Pencil).

Making Selections with the Timebase Ruler (Edit Window)

To make selections with the timebase ruler in the Edit window, do the following:

1. Double-click anywhere in any of the timebase rulers to select the entire session (from the beginning of the session timeline, including all regions—and/or automation breakpoints—in all tracks).

2. Option-click and drag (Alt-click and drag in Windows) within any timebase ruler to make an edit selection on all tracks simultaneously.

3. You can also use the Markers ruler to make selections. First, position the edit cursor and/or make a track selection, either by clicking an existing marker or by using one of the edit tools within a track. Then, shift-click on the previous or next marker to extend your current selection up to that point.

Extending the Current Selection with the Tab Key (Edit Window)

You can use the Tab key to extend the current selection in the Edit window. Here are your options:

✳ **Shift+Tab.** Extends the selection to the next region boundary (end of the current region, or to the beginning of the next region).

✳ **Option+Shift+Tab (Control+Shift+Tab in Windows).** Extends the selection to the previous region boundary (beginning of the current region, or to the end of the previous region).

✳ **Control+Shift+Tab (Start+Shift+Tab in Windows).** Extends the selection to include the entire next region.

✳ **Option+Control+Shift+Tab (Control+Start+Shift+Tab in Windows).** Extends the selection to include the entire previous region.

More Tab Key Tricks (Edit Window)

Here are yet more Tab key shortcuts in the Edit window:

* **Tab.** Each time you press the Tab key, the playback/edit cursor jumps forward in the current track to the next region boundary (beginning or end), sync point (if any region contains one), or fade beginning/end.

* **Option+Tab (Control+Tab in Windows).** Same as above, except the cursor location moves backward.

* **Control+Tab (Start+Tab in Windows).** Selects the next region or fade in the current track.

* **Option+Control+Tab (Control+Start+Tab in Windows).** Selects the previous region or fade in the current track.

Power Scrubber (Edit Window)

Many users underestimate the usefulness of the Scrubber tool for editing. Here are a few tricks you should know:

* While using the Selector tool, you can hold down the Control key (or hold down the right mouse button, and then click and drag in either Mac or Windows) to temporarily switch to the Scrubber tool.

* If you also hold down the Shift key as you scrub, the current edit selection is extended to the point where you stop scrubbing; this makes it really easy to locate audio events by ear! (This Shift key selection technique also works when the Scrubber tool itself is selected.)

* To drag at extra-slow speed, for finer precision, hold down the Command key (Ctrl key in Windows)—try using this in combination with the previous two modifier keys!

* For extra-*fast* scrubbing (Shuttle mode), hold down the Option key (Alt key in Windows). Shuttle mode is also available when temporarily switched to scrub mode while using the Selector tool, and you can also use it with the Shift key to make edit selections.

* Remember that unlike some other programs, Pro Tools only scrubs *audio*, not MIDI events.

The Three-Button Quickstep for Switching Windows

If you are using a mouse or trackball with three buttons, consider assigning a macro to the third button—for example, the Command+Equal shortcut (Control+Equal in Windows) that switches between the Mix and Edit windows.

Nudging and Grid Mode

You don't always have to open these pop-up selectors to change between their preset values! Here are a couple of shortcuts that will save you some mouse travel, plus some very useful nudging techniques.

* To toggle through the preset Grid Values for the time units currently in use (for example, to select between whole bars and various note values when in Bars:Beats mode), hold

- down Control+Option (Start+Alt in Windows) as you use the +/– (plus/minus) keys on the numeric keypad.

❋ To toggle through the preset Nudge Values for the time units currently in use, hold down Command+Option (Ctrl+Alt in Windows) as you use the +/– (plus/minus) keys on the numeric keypad.

❋ To nudge selected regions, MIDI notes, or automation breakpoints left or right, use the +/ (plus/minus) keys on the numeric keypad.

❋ To extend or shorten the *left* edge of the current selection by the current Nudge Value, press Shift+Option (Shift+Alt in Windows) as you nudge. To extend or shorten the selection's *right* edge, hold down Shift+Command (Shift+Ctrl in Windows) instead.

❋ To nudge the *contents* of a region without affecting the left-right boundaries of the region itself, hold down the Control key (Start key in Windows) as you nudge.

Commands Focus Mode

A dismaying number of Pro Tools users never explore the utility of that little a…z button in the Edit window's toolbar. Shame on you! This book has reminded you many times about printing out the entire Keyboard Shortcuts PDF document included with Pro Tools. But if nothing else, definitely print out the pages about Commands Focus Mode. Many single-keystroke shortcuts here can really speed up your editing Pro Tools. To name just a few, you can execute commands like cut, copy, paste, and undo with only single letters (no need to hold down a Command modifier key on Mac, or Ctrl on Windows). The A and S keys trim the Start/End of the current region to the insertion point, 1–5 on the alphanumeric keyboard select the five zoom preset buttons, F creates a default fade type without having to open the Fades dialog box, and Shift+P moves the edit selection upward one track while Shift+";" (semi-colon) extends it downward. (Incidentally, Pro Tools provides two other keyboard focus modes for one-keystroke operations—each of them even more underused than Commands Focus! The Region List and Track List both have their own a…z button. When the Region List Focus is enabled, you can select regions just by typing the first few letters of their names on your computer keyboard. With Groups List Focus enabled, mix and edit groups can be enabled or disabled simply by typing the Group ID letter.)

General Tips

Digidesign CoreAudio (Mac)

If you choose this option when installing Pro Tools, the Macintosh operating system can redirect all Mac sound input and/or output through your Digidesign hardware. (This is configured under System Preferences > Sound.) The Digidesign CoreAudio Manager application lets you change the Buffer Size, monitor which client audio applications are using CoreAudio, and even open up the Hardware Setup dialog box for your Digidesign hardware.

Digidesign WaveDriver (Windows)

If you choose this option when installing Pro Tools, third-party audio programs can direct sound input/output through channels 1–2 of your Digidesign hardware (Digi 002, Mbox 2, Mbox, Digi 001, or Audiomedia III— Pro Tools|HD and other TDM hardware is not supported). WaveDriver can also be installed for the supported Digidesign hardware even if the Pro Tools software is not installed on that computer, and it supports resolutions up to 24-bit, 96 kHz on the Digi 002. It can either be configured as the default Windows sound playback device (for Windows Media Player, for example) or supported directly by programs such as Sound Forge. Digi MME Helper is a free utility from Rail Jon Rogut Software for configuring additional programs in the Registry for WaveDriver.

Calculators for Tempos and Note Values to Milliseconds

Several Web sites offer calculators for tempos and note values:

* **http://www.macmusic.org/softs.** Check out the freeware application called Music Math (for either Mac OSX or OS9), written by Laurent Colson. It converts between beats per minute (BPM) and equivalent millisecond settings for your delay (or LFO modulation rate on a flanger, hmmm?). It also converts between sample durations and tempos, MIDI notes and frequencies, as well as transposition and time-stretching values. Note that you can view this site in French or English (click on the flag icon to select a language).

* **http://www.analogx.com/contents/download/audio/delay.htm.** For Windows users, AnalogX also offers a free downloadable Delay Calculator.

* **http://deepsound.net/calculs.html.** You can directly perform all kinds of useful calculations related to music production on this Web page, including BPM/delay time calculations and conversions to tempo-related LFO modulation frequencies. You can calculate, for example, the equivalent BPM for a selection of x bars, with a duration of x samples, at a given sample rate; plus there are handy "time stretch" calculations. You can convert frequencies to their nearest musical pitches (and MIDI note numbers) here, and vice versa. Created by Deep Sound (JC Lemay, a Paris-based musician, composer, and remixer), this page is available in both French and English.

Widgets for Mac OS X "Tiger"

Among the myriad utilities you can add to the Dashboard (sticky notes, weather, gas prices, travel, webcams, voice notes, and so on), there are several that specifically pertain to audio and studio applications. Some of our current favorites available via the Apple website include: Audio Calculator (by Lensco.be; for conversions between BPM and milliseconds), Oblique (by Guy D2; a widget version of the Oblique Strategies creative unblocking tool made famous by Brian Eno, Peter Schmidt, and Peter Norton), and Bean Counter (by Seven; enter your hourly wage, and this widget calculates your earnings in real time—just the thing to keep your attitude adjusted while clients argue and/or rehearse on the clock!).

Things That Make Pro Tools Get Cranky

Everyone's system has its own set of peccadilloes, but here's a short list of things that can be problematic on almost any Pro Tools system:

* ❋ Energy-management, power-saver, and energy-saver features of the operating system (usually enabled via control panels on Windows, or System Preferences on Mac)
* ❋ Screen savers (also enabled in control panels or System Preferences)
* ❋ Background disk optimizers, system-monitoring software, and the like
* ❋ Network/Web activities (like serving up MP3 files; duh!)
* ❋ Fragmented hard drives (Speed Disk or Disk Warrior to the rescue!)
* ❋ Extremely full hard drives (over 90 percent is always a problem)
* ❋ Missing or incorrect SCSI termination
* ❋ Hard drives without DMA enabled in Properties (Windows)
* ❋ Not repairing disk permissions from time to time with the Disk Utility—especially after installing any updates to Pro Tools or its plug-ins (Mac)
* ❋ Norton's File Saver

You Don't Have to Archive Your Fade Files Folder!

Pro Tools creates separate audio files for every fade you create inside the Fade Files folder. In large or complex sessions, fades can occupy quite a lot of disk space, which increases storage requirements and time required for archiving projects off your Pro Tools system if you simply copy the entire session folder. If you're struggling to make projects fit onto a DVD-R, and you need to free up only a small additional amount of space, remember that it *isn't* necessary to copy the contents of the Fade Files folder! In this case, go ahead and throw this folder's entire contents into the Trash/Recycle Bin before you archive off the session folder and its contents. The next time you open the Pro Tools session, a dialog box will ask you "Where is Fade x?" Click the Skip all Fades button, and Pro Tools will recreate all fade files required by the session. On sessions with many long fades, this may take a minute—but that's much better than needlessly adding 5, 10, or more megabytes to the size of every archived project!

More Tips for Recording Voice-Overs

Here are a few tidbits we've picked up along the way with regard to recording the spoken word:

* ❋ Lip smack and cottonmouth—the bane of your existence, right? And the more you compress that voice-over to squash it right up to a consistent level, the worse it gets. (There you are, maniacally editing out these extraneous noises for hours on end!) Here's an old trick that might still be new to you. If you're hearing clicks and snaps each time the narrator breathes or opens his or her mouth, offer your talent a few bites of a nice, crispy apple! (We enjoy a nice Fuji or Granny Smith, but anything fairly tart will do the

trick.) If you don't have any apples handy (or you're afraid your voice talent will think you're a nut job), bring apple juice instead. This works!

❋ Here's another dumb trick we've used in recent years that makes it *much* faster to edit all those retakes, false starts, and so on in a long voice recording. Buy one of those cricket-type clickers at your local five-and-dime store. (They're also widely available at pet stores, because they're used for obedience training—which wouldn't hurt with some voice talent we've known, either, come to think of it!) Each time your voice talent is ready to restart a take or resume after studio chatter, have him or her click a couple of times in the general vicinity of the microphone. Afterward, you'll have instantly recognizable markers in the audio waveform for making your selections, cuts, and other editing operations. This technique is *especially* useful if you record many of your own voice-overs, where it's not convenient to mark locations of retakes during the actual recording process.

❋ When editing voice-overs recorded in noisy environments (for example, from on-location interviews, around office or industrial ventilation systems, or anywhere near a computer), after chopping them up into keeper segments, you may find that the background noise popping in and out with each audio region is bothersome. Use the Batch Fades dialog box to create fade-ins and fade-outs on individual regions so that these transitions will at least be a little smoother. (This technique can be equally useful for guitar fills played through a noisy amplifier, vocal lines, drum hits that you've split into individual regions using the Split Silence feature with a healthy amount of start and end pad, or just about anything that's intermittent within a track.) Select all regions in the track, and then press Command+F (Ctrl+F on Windows). In the Batch Fades dialog box, select the fade-in/out shapes you want (Standard is a good place to start). In the Length field underneath the Create new fade ins and outs check box, try an initial setting of 50 milliseconds or so. If you've already trimmed the beginning of each VO region too tightly and the attacks on initial words are overly softened by the fade, repeat the operation using a fade-in shape with a steeper slope.

❋ Professionals who do character voice work may cringe at this heretical suggestion (and to be sure, Mel Blanc and Daws Butler didn't need no stinkin' Pro Tools tricks)… When using the same voice talent for many different characters (as in cartoons, or simulation scenarios for training videos), a very small amount of pitch shift up or down can be surprisingly effective. The idea is not necessarily to apply some extreme amount as a special effect (not that there's anything *wrong* with that!), but instead to work in ranges of perhaps a semitone or two at most that listeners won't identify as pitch-shifted. The reason this works so well is that no matter how adept actors may be at pitching their voices, the characteristic resonances or formants of each individual's vocal tract remain more or less constant. Pitch shifting also shifts these formants, and a very small amount can help sell the idea that it's a different person. (Be sure to notice that the Pitch Shift dialog box has a Fine slider for adjusting pitch shift in increments of 1/100th of a semitone, called *cents*. A few tenths of a semitone can make all the difference between the pitch-shifted audio sounding processed or natural.)

Transferring Sequences from MIDI Workstations into Pro Tools

Suppose you or your clients have songs already recorded into a standalone MIDI sequencer, drum machine, or standalone MIDI workstation (a keyboard synthesizer that includes an internal sequencer for MIDI recording). You'd like to bring this MIDI data into Pro Tools in order to start adding vocals and other audio tracks. Unfortunately for you, the device in question can't save a Type 1 Standard MIDI File (SMF) to diskette; otherwise, you would simply use the File > Import > MIDI to Track command, which creates MIDI tracks as necessary for each MIDI channel within the source file that contains data.

Your alternative is to record the device's MIDI output in real time. But you have a challenge: The only MIDI source that Pro Tools can synchronize to is MIDI Time Code (MTC—a variant of SMPTE time code, which is an *absolute* time reference), while the MIDI sequencer can only generate or synchronize to MIDI Beat Clock (also known as MIDI Sync—a *relative*, tempo-derived time reference, based on 24 clocks per 1/4 note). Don't despair; it can easily be done!

1. Use the Setup > MIDI > MIDI Beat Clock command to enable generation of this data on the appropriate MIDI output for your external MIDI sequencer.

2. Go into the setup of the external MIDI sequencer and change its synchronization mode so that it slaves to an external MIDI Beat Clock rather to than its own internal tempo setting. (For example, on a Roland keyboard workstation, change the sequencer's Sync Mode from Internal to Slave.) Your external sequencer should now start/stop playback as you press Play/Stop in Pro Tools.

3. Set an appropriate tempo in Pro Tools, because its MIDI Beat Clock output now controls the playback tempo of the external MIDI sequencer. (Of course, if the *audio* output from the external MIDI device is connected to your Pro Tools hardware, you will have to create an Aux In to monitor it within Pro Tools, right?)

4. Create 16 MIDI tracks in Pro Tools (or fewer, if you already know exactly which of the sequencer's tracks/channels contain MIDI data). Set their input selectors to channels 1–16 on the appropriate MIDI input/device.

5. Arm all these MIDI tracks for recording by holding down the Option key (Alt key in Windows) as you enable the Record button on any one of them.

6. Press Record and Play in the Pro Tools Transport to record the multichannel MIDI output of your external sequencer into Pro Tools.

7. Afterward, remember to assign appropriate device/channel *output* destinations for each of the MIDI tracks, and also to take your external sequencer out of slave sync mode (and/or disable MIDI Beat Clock output from Pro Tools)!

Mixing ADAT Projects with Your Two-Channel Pro Tools System

Let's say you have an Mbox 2 or original Mbox, or one of the M-Audio interfaces that doesn't offer an ADAT Lightpipe optical input. A musical group asks if you could do a killer Pro Tools mix from their ADAT master tape. You know that at least eight channels of audio need to be transferred (even more, if the project spans two or three ADAT tapes), but again, your system doesn't have ADAT Lightpipe. Furthermore, your Pro Tools hardware can only record two channels simultaneously. So you think it over—and say "Yes, I *can* do it!" (Beware: This technique involves recording onto your client's master tape. If you are unfamiliar with ADAT recording and transport functions, get someone to help you out.)

You're going to simultaneously record two or three seconds of identical audio (a single click, or a low-frequency square wave) onto *all* tracks of the ADAT master tape, a safe distance prior to the beginning of the song you want to transfer (for example, at least 30 seconds earlier, if that much blank space is available). This allows you to record the ADAT tracks two at a time into Pro Tools, and then visually align them later (by connecting each pair of ADAT analog outputs to the analog inputs of Pro Tools). Having either an identical single percussive click or a brief, very low-frequency square waveform on every track of the ADAT master will make the precise attack in each track distinctly visible when you zoom into sample level on these tracks in Pro Tools. You then drag the regions around in Pro Tools until these clicks or initial waveforms line up precisely, *to the same exact sample number.*

Here's another handy idea: Other than an electrical click, or something similar, another potential source for your alignment reference might be the Signal Generator plug-in in Pro Tools itself. Choose a square waveform, and the lowest 20 Hz frequency. (Incidentally, using the 2-input recording mode available on all ADAT models—except the original model with the black front panel—allows you to record onto all eight tape tracks simultaneously from ADAT inputs 1 and 2, where you would connect the analog stereo output from Pro Tools or another reference sound source.) First, enable the Signal Generator plug-in's Bypass button. Start recording on the ADAT, disable the plug-in's Bypass button again (so that the Signal Generator's output is audible again), record for two seconds, and then press Stop on the ADAT transport. (Be careful not to record right over the beginning of their song, OK? We've warned you!) The leading, square edge of the first square waveform provides an excellent reference for properly realigning all the ADAT track pairs once they've been transferred into Pro Tools.

Granted, it would be nice to transfer all eight tracks digitally into Pro Tools via a Lightpipe input. But believe us, if you're using kHz and 24-bit depth, and you manage your input levels for analog recording from the ADAT, most people won't hear the difference—and we won't tell on you! Nonetheless, if any two ADAT tracks *are* definitely a stereo pair (for example, drums overheads or piano microphones), record these two simultaneously into Pro Tools to absolutely ensure precise alignment between them.

Appendix E }

Signal Flow in Pro Tools

Audio Tracks

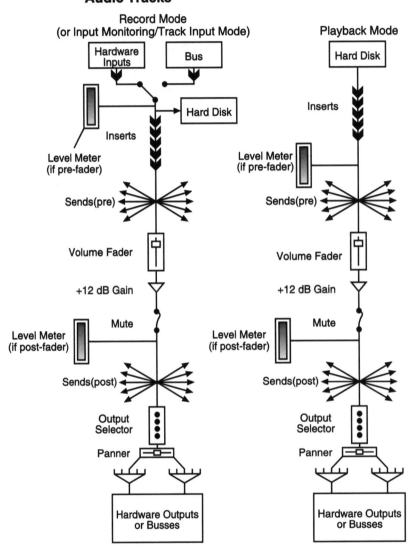

Figure E.1   Signal flow for an audio track during recording (as well as when Input Only Monitoring is enabled, or with the TrackInput button enabled on HD systems), and during playback. Notice that the main volume fader is located just before the output stage (and any post-fader sends), and therefore has no effect on input recording levels!

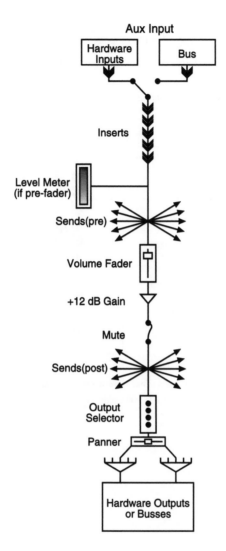

Figure E.2 Signal flow for an Auxiliary Input track. Its input source can be either a physical input on the audio hardware or one of the internal mixing busses in Pro Tools. Notwithstanding their associated MIDI track in the Edit window, from a signal flow perspective Instrument tracks are identical to Aux Ins (and could actually be used as such). In practice, on either type of track, the actual signal source may originate from a plug-in on one of its insert points—a software instrument or the Click and Signal Generator plug-ins, for example.

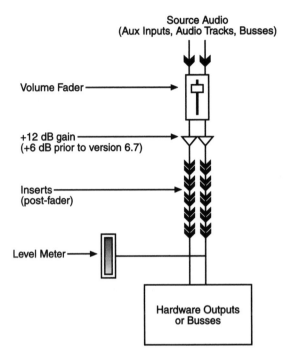

Figure E.3 Signal flow for a Master Fader track. There are no sends on a Master Fader, and unlike audio tracks, Aux In tracks, and Instrument tracks, the Insert section on a Master Fader is always post-fader.

Index

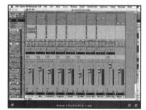  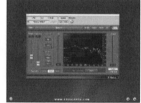